Limits of Constraint

Limits of Constraint

THE ORIGINALIST JURISPRUDENCE OF HUGO BLACK, ANTONIN SCALIA, AND CLARENCE THOMAS

James B. Staab

University Press of Kansas

Published by the University Press of Kansas (Lawrence, Kansas 66045), which was organized by the Kansas Board of Regents and is operated and funded by Emporia State University, Fort Hays State University, Kansas State University, Pittsburg State University, the University of Kansas, and Wichita State University.

Library of Congress Cataloging-in-Publication Data

Names: Staab, James Brian, author.
Title: Limits of constraint : the originalist jurisprudence of Hugo Black, Antonin Scalia, and Clarence Thomas / James B. Staab.
Description: Lawrence, Kansas : University Press of Kansas, 2022. | Includes bibliographical references and index.
Identifiers: LCCN 2021050553
ISBN 9780700633302 (cloth)
ISBN 9780700633319 (ebook)
Subjects: LCSH: Constitutional law—United States. | Black, Hugo LaFayette, 1886–1971. | Scalia, Antonin, 1936–2016. | Thomas, Clarence, 1948–
Classification: LCC KF4550 .S725 2022 | DDC 342.73—dc23/eng/20220331
LC record available at https://lccn.loc.gov/2021050553.

Printed in the United States of America

10 9 8 7 6 5 4 3 2 1

The paper used in this publication is recycled and meets the minimum requirements of the American National Standard for Permanence of Paper for Printed Library Materials Z39.48-1992.

To my wife, Renée, and our three children:
Ashley, Oliver, and Nicholas

Contents

Acknowledgments

I am pleased to have the opportunity to thank the many people who either inspired me or provided assistance during the writing of this book. Henry J. Abraham and David M. O'Brien, my two mentors from the University of Virginia, passed on their love of the Supreme Court to me. Henry's *Justices, Presidents, and Senators* remains a classic in the discipline, and David impressed on me the important connection between law and politics. John Dinan, a friend and colleague, read the entire manuscript and provided sage advice on how to reduce its length and clearly articulate its goals. I would also like to thank Lee Epstein for providing statistics from the Supreme Court database, including the voting agreement between Justices Scalia and Thomas in nonunanimous cases.

Over the course of this project, I conducted research in the Manuscript Division of the Library of Congress, where I examined the papers of Hugo Black, William Brennan, Thurgood Marshall, and Harry Blackmun. The staff there is unparalleled. Jeff Flannery, now retired, sent me several documents when I was unable to travel to Washington, DC. I also conducted research at the George H. W. Bush Presidential Library and Museum in College Station, Texas, where I had the privilege of reading Clarence Thomas's pre–Supreme Court speeches, many of which have never been published. Cody McMillian and Buffie Hollis provided invaluable assistance during my visit there. I would also like to thank Vanesa Chappell, Interlibrary Loan assistant at the University of Central Missouri, who located many hard-to-find items, even when it did not seem possible. I am grateful to my chair and the deans who supported sabbaticals, research trips, and travel to conferences, including Gregory Streich, Gersham Nelson, and Mike Sawyer. Caleb Ross, one of our outstanding students, put together the index for this book, which was funded by the Center for Teaching and Learning.

I am pleased that this book is being published by the University Press of Kansas. I have long admired the quality of the books published by UPK, and it was my first choice. As this project matured over an extended period, I had the pleasure of corresponding with Fred Woodward and Chuck Myers, both of whom provided wise counsel and encouragement. Editor David Congdon was terrific to work with. He provided keen insight regarding the book's organization and main arguments and made the necessary editorial recommendations to improve its quality. Linda Lotz did a masterful job copyediting this book. Her attention to detail is truly impressive and appreciated.

Last, I would like to thank my family. Over the years, I have brought my laptop along on numerous family trips, but they never complained. In their own way, they provided indispensable encouragement, and this book is dedicated to them.

Introduction

As is well known, the late Supreme Court justice Antonin Scalia was an originalist. In his view, the chief object of constitutional interpretation was to discern the original meaning of the relevant provision at the time of its adoption. During his tenure on the Supreme Court (1986–2016), Scalia wrote extensively on the subject and gave countless speeches defending an originalist approach.[1] In fact, one of Scalia's lasting legacies will be the extent to which he popularized originalism within the legal community and in American society generally. Scalia was a sharp critic of the philosophy of a "living" Constitution, which maintains that judges have the authority to update the Constitution's broad principles based on changes in society. As Scalia saw it, a living Constitution gives judges too much discretion and is inconsistent with a democratic system based on consent of the governed. Instead, Scalia claimed that the Constitution's original meaning was fixed and unalterable, unless changes were made by the formal amendment process prescribed under Article V.

Not as well known (or perhaps forgotten) is that Hugo Black—that great champion of New Deal liberalism—was an originalist. Black, a towering figure on the Supreme Court from 1937 to 1971, was a legal positivist who (like Scalia) placed primacy on text and history in interpreting the Constitution.[2] Black's criticism of his colleagues' use of balancing tests, such as "shocks the conscience" and "fundamental fairness," found considerable support in Justice Scalia's opinions and extrajudicial writings. Scalia also agreed with Justice Black that when judges impose their own values on the Constitution, they usurp the role of the elected branches of government and act as roving constitutional conventions. Consequently, both justices were strenuous critics of judicial reliance on natural law, especially under the due process clause. "I like my privacy as well as the next one," Black famously wrote in *Griswold v. Connecticut* (1965), "but I am nevertheless compelled to admit that government has a right to invade it unless prohibited by some specific constitutional provision."[3]

Clarence Thomas, appointed to the Supreme Court in 1991, is also an originalist. Justice Thomas has defended an originalist approach to constitutional interpretation as the best way to reduce discretion and to satisfy the ideal of "impartiality" in judging.[4] Although he has not authored as many books or articles on the subject as Scalia and Black have, Thomas's originalist approach is abundantly clear in his judicial opinions. Across a whole host of constitutional areas, Thomas has sought to discern the original meaning of provisions. For example, in *U.S. Term Limits Inc. v. Thornton* (1995), Thomas wrote an eighty-one-page dissent in which he argued that the states, as an original matter, had the authority to impose term limits on members of Congress.[5] In several cases, Thomas has urged his colleagues to reexamine the "substantial effects" test used in commerce clause cases.[6] Thomas has also argued that the establishment clause is a federalism provision that "resists" application to the states;[7] he has challenged the "intelligible principle" used in nondelegation cases;[8] and he has distinguished himself among his colleagues by calling for a reexamination of the original meaning of the privileges or immunities clause.[9] As Ralph Rossum observes, Thomas (more so than Scalia) has been willing "to scrape . . . to the bare wood" to restore the original meaning of the Constitution, even if it means overturning numerous precedents to do so.[10] In fact, Scalia's "faint-hearted" originalism, which made him less willing to overrule Supreme Court precedents, received extensive criticism from libertarian conservatives. In a 2006 article, professor Randy Barnett concluded that "Scalia is simply not an originalist."[11]

This book examines the originalist philosophies of Hugo Black, Antonin Scalia, and Clarence Thomas. Originalism is often discussed as if its adherents have the same views on constitutional issues, but that is not the case. Just as the framers of the Constitution had different perspectives on various constitutional issues such as separation of powers, judicial review, the scope of executive power, federalism, and the importance of a bill of rights, so do these three originalists. Despite some important areas of common ground in the originalist philosophies of Black, Scalia, and Thomas, they reached different conclusions on numerous issues involving constitutional law. Rather than rehash theoretical debates about the merits of originalism, this book examines originalism in operation by focusing on the judicial opinions of these three prominent Supreme Court originalists.[12]

If the conclusion of this book is correct—that is, the results reached by Black, Scalia, and Thomas diverge across a wide array of constitutional issues—then originalism promises more than it can deliver. A fundamental claim made by originalists is that their theory of constitutional interpretation limits judicial discretion. In this view, constitutional text and original meaning provide guideposts for interpretation that are separate and apart from a judge's subjective views. However, if these three devout originalists reached contrary results in numerous areas of constitutional law (and sometimes quite dramatically so), then originalism's "restraint" value does not hold up in practice. At the end of the day, constitutional text and history are more malleable than the proponents of originalism are willing to admit, and the philosophical and policy views of these three originalists have had a substantial impact on how they decided particular cases.

Another major objective of this book is to resurrect Justice Black as a defender of an originalist approach. Even though Justice Scalia is regarded as one of the chief architects of modern originalism, Black's tenure on the Supreme Court (1937–1971) preceded Scalia's (1986–2016) and Thomas's (1991–present) by several decades. Ironically, Black is not even recognized as a comrade in arms among modern conservative originalists. If anything, his jurisprudence is regarded as historically inaccurate[13] or unprincipled.[14] However, Black was probably the court's first full-throated originalist, which raises interesting questions about why his large body of judicial work is not even cited in the recommended readings of modern conservative originalists.[15] I maintain that Black's Jeffersonian persuasion is simply not congenial to modern conservative originalists. For example, he was skeptical of executive power, which would have made him a sharp critic of president George W. Bush's policies during the war on terror—most of which were supported by Scalia and Thomas. Black's absolutist reading of the First Amendment also differs from that of modern-day conservative originalists, who tend to be pro national security. Black constitutionalized Jefferson's "high wall" theory of the establishment clause—an interpretative approach to the First Amendment that has been roundly denounced by modern conservative originalists, including Scalia and Thomas. Moreover, Black's "total" incorporation theory of the Bill of Rights has not found support in the opinions of Scalia and Thomas—although for different reasons.

A final objective of this book is to point out the important jurisprudential differences between Scalia and Thomas. Even though these two justices frequently voted together (90.9 percent of all cases), there were important fault lines in their originalist philosophies.[16] In addition to Thomas's greater propensity to reexamine Supreme Court precedents, these two originalists came to different conclusions in numerous areas of constitutional law. For example, Scalia never joined one of Thomas's opinions in which he called for the court to reexamine the "substantial effects" test. Scalia believed that

Congress's authority to regulate commerce should not be strictly construed, and he did not regard the Tenth Amendment as an affirmative limit on national power. The two justices also interpreted the judicial tests used in administrative law cases differently. For example, Scalia did not join Thomas's request for the court to more closely examine its nondelegation doctrine. For Scalia, the nondelegation doctrine was "preeminently *not* a doctrine of technicalities," and he maintained that most excessive delegation claims presented nonjusticiable political questions.[17] Nor did Scalia join Thomas's broad-scale attack on *Chevron* deference. From his first days on the Supreme Court, Scalia regarded *Chevron* as "a watershed decision," and in 2001 he wrote a solo dissent in which he sharply criticized his colleagues for not applying *Chevron* deference to informal agency decisions.[18] Although Scalia did change his mind about one particular aspect of *Chevron* deference,[19] he never questioned the need for broad delegations of power when it came to the modern administrative state.[20] Thomas, by contrast, has called for a reexamination of *Chevron* itself. In his view, the court's deferential approach to agencies' interpretation of statutes conflicts with the principle of separation of powers and has accelerated the growth of the administrative state. These significant differences (as well as others) are examined in this book.

Chapter 1 provides biographical sketches of the three originalists. One basic assumption of this book is that personal backgrounds and philosophies matter in terms of how judges interpret laws. For example, Justice Black's unflinching support of the New Deal can be traced back to his childhood in Clay County, Alabama. The Great Depression, which coincided with Black's tenure in the US Senate, had a severe impact on his home state, and he was convinced (along with other New Dealers) that the states could not manage the complexities of the problem. On the Supreme Court, Black was an early and avid supporter of a broad construction of Congress's commerce power.

Meanwhile, Justice Scalia's favorable disposition toward presidential power was honed when he served in various executive posts in the 1970s. One of his first assignments as assistant attorney general during the Ford administration was to determine whether President Nixon's papers and tapes were his personal property. Scalia concluded that they were—an opinion that had considerable support at the time[21]—but it resulted in the immediate passage of the Presidential Recordings and Materials Preservation Act of 1974. During a time of deep distrust between Congress and the presidency, Scalia served as the point man for the Ford administration and boldly defended presidential power before a hostile Congress. On one occasion, Scalia gave such an expansive interpretation of executive privilege that senator Edmund Muskie (D-ME), chair of the Subcommittee on Intergovernmental Relations, felt compelled to interrupt him:

> The whole thrust of the issue is that we get information from the executive branch, in your view, only as a matter of grace. The notion that the Congress has as a matter of constitutional right the power to inquire into anything that happens in the executive branch is challenged by your logic. . . . I will listen to the rest of your statement, but I have listened for 10 pages here to this logic that is the most incredible exposition of this point of view that I have been exposed to in all the time I have been in the Senate. . . . With that why don't you proceed and give your argument whatever credibility you can.[22]

Clarence Thomas's libertarian views were instilled during his childhood in segregated Georgia. Myers Anderson, Thomas's maternal grandfather and self-described hero, taught his two grandsons the value of hard work, independent thinking, and self-reliance. Prominently displayed in Thomas's Supreme Court chambers is a bust of his grandfather with the inscription: "Old Man Can't is dead. I helped bury him."[23] That was Anderson's usual response when Clarence and his brother suggested they could not accomplish a particular task. Thomas's can-do attitude is combined with a strong distaste for elites. If the Man could fathom a legal justification for segregation, how can African Americans trust other forms of social engineering by elites? When busing was being used to integrate public schools in Boston, Thomas called it a "harebrained social experiment" and swore that he would never let his son, Jamal, "go to a public school, even if [he] had to starve to death to pay his tuition."[24] Justice Thomas has criticized social engineering in other areas of the law, including voting rights, affirmative action, economic development, crime, and abortion. Citing Frederick Douglass, Thomas insists that what blacks want from their fellow Americans "is not benevolence, not pity, not sympathy, but simply *justice*."[25]

The next three chapters provide comprehensive overviews of the jurisprudence of each originalist. Chapter 2 examines Justice Black's jurisprudence, a major theme of which was Thomas Jefferson's influence on his judicial philosophy. Of all the Founding Fathers, Jefferson placed the most faith in popular democracy. True republicanism, he believed, was measured by the extent to which the people actually governed and made decisions for themselves. "I own I am not a friend to a very energetic government," Jefferson wrote. "It is always oppressive."[26] For this reason, Jefferson deeply distrusted executive power and was an early and steadfast proponent of a bill of rights. "A bill of rights," he wrote to James Madison, "is what the people are entitled to against every government on earth, and what no just government should refuse or rest on inference."[27]

As a young man, Black was an avid admirer of "the Sage from Monticello" and read "nearly everything by and about Jefferson."[28] Black's Jeffersonian persuasion was particularly noticeable during his ten-year tenure in the US Senate, where he referenced Jefferson in speeches on numerous topics, including secrecy in government, corporations ("not an unmixed blessing"), regulation of obscenity, freedom of the press, economic opportunity, executive power, and FDR's controversial court-packing plan. As his son, Hugo Black Jr., once remarked, Jefferson was his father's "number 1, number 2, and number 3 hero."[29] Most importantly, Black's judicial opinions reflected a Jeffersonian philosophy, especially in the areas of freedom of speech, separation of church and state, religious freedom, and the scope of executive power. One could also make a good case that Black's total incorporation theory; his broad interpretation of the Fifth and Sixth Amendments; his deferential approach to social and economic regulation; his strenuous advocacy of one person, one vote; and his principled stance against the separate but equal doctrine all represent modern interpretations of Jefferson's political philosophy.

Chapter 3 examines Justice Scalia's originalist philosophy. In contrast to Black, Scalia's jurisprudence was influenced by Jefferson's chief political nemesis: Alexander Hamilton. Hamilton was the founding generation's strongest defender of a natural aristocracy. He distrusted popular democracy because people were motivated primarily by their passions and self-interest.[30] To put the US Constitution on a solid foundation, Hamilton argued that it should "go as far in order to attain stability and permanency, as republic principles will admit."[31] Hamilton thus became the founding generation's strongest defender of the least popular branches of government: the executive and the judiciary. If these two institutions were given "a permanent share in the government," he argued, they could be counted on to "check the unsteadiness" of the mass of the people.[32]

Justice Scalia revealed his Hamiltonian disposition in several speeches from the 1980s. At a conference on federalism, then-professor Scalia invoked

Hamilton (not Jefferson or even Madison) for his perspective on the subject.[33] "If a resurrected and updated Alexander Hamilton had been invited to this conference," Scalia told his mostly conservative audience, "the subjects he would have expected to hear addressed are quite different from—and the tenor of his own remarks would have been quite the opposite of—what we have heard over the past few days."[34] Moreover, even though Scalia was a sharp critic of the living Constitution, he was *not* a populist. Scalia defended an expansive interpretation of executive power under Article II and the standard of "good behavior" for federal judges.[35] He also criticized the Seventeenth Amendment as "a burst of progressivism" that substantially impaired states' rights.[36] Moreover, Scalia's view that the government cannot regulate money in politics, as well as his criticism of *New York Times v. Sullivan* (1964)[37]—in which the court required public officials to prove "actual malice" to win their libel suits—substantially supported Hamilton's elite theory of who governs.

Chapter 4 discusses Justice Thomas's originalist jurisprudence. In contrast to Black and Scalia, Thomas's interpretative approach to the Constitution was not influenced by a single Founding Father. In fact, in pre–Supreme Court speeches Thomas praised both Jefferson and Hamilton for their unique contributions to the American republic.[38] Thomas is also a great admirer of Abraham Lincoln and supports the Lincolnian conception of the Constitution.[39] However, the one person who had the most profound influence on Thomas's originalist jurisprudence was his grandfather, Myers Anderson. "What I am [today] is what he made me," Thomas wrote in his revealing autobiography. Although he did not recognize it earlier, Thomas now believes that his grandfather was "the greatest man" he has ever known.[40] Anderson preached the value of hard work and taught his grandsons that to be truly free, "a man had a right and an obligation to produce. And the right to keep what he produced." Hard work not only provided a sense of economic freedom otherwise denied in the segregated South but also fostered important character traits such as "self-discipline, self-respect, [and] true generosity."[41] One of Thomas's favorite memories of his grandfather is watching him survey his cornfield. "The sight of a tall stand of corn must have been more nourishing to his spirit than the corn itself was to his body," Thomas recalled.[42]

To call Justice Thomas simply a "libertarian," however, is not wholly accurate.[43] Although he was evasive during his confirmation hearings, Thomas's originalist jurisprudence is fundamentally rooted in natural law.[44] Prior to his appointment, Thomas gave several speeches in which he argued that "important parts of the Constitution were inexplicable" without resort to the Declaration of Independence.[45] As a judge, Thomas has pieced together a unique combination of libertarianism and natural law. In terms of the former, Thomas is a strong defender of corporate speech, commercial speech, school vouchers, parental rights, property rights, and gun rights. Thomas has also sought to limit the scope of federal power under the commerce clause and the administrative state. Thomas's natural law instincts are evident in affirmative action cases in which he has argued that any form of racial classification violates the Declaration of Independence. Interestingly, Thomas's natural law views (especially as they relate to the rule of law, separation of powers, and judicial function) circumscribe some of his libertarian instincts.[46] For example, unlike some libertarian scholars, Thomas has rejected a general right of privacy[47] and a more activist judiciary in the defense of economic rights under the due process clause.[48]

The next two chapters examine the major fault lines in the originalist philosophies of the three justices. Chapter 5 examines the differences between Hugo Black, on the one hand, and Antonin Scalia and Clarence Thomas, on the other. There are fundamental differences between them across many constitutional areas. For example, Black was a small *d* democrat who supported a deferential approach to legal standing, whereas Scalia and Thomas have defended a rigid interpretation of legal standing and have been critical of "citizen" lawsuits. In interbranch disputes, Black was a strong defender of the prerogatives of Congress and interpreted the powers of the presidency narrowly. By contrast, Scalia and Thomas have been strong defenders of an "energetic" executive and have supported Alexander Hamilton's broad definition of executive power under Article II.

The three originalists also have profoundly different interpretations of federalism. Black regarded Congress's authority to regulate commerce as plenary and did not believe it stopped at state boundaries. Early on, Scalia appeared to embrace a Hamiltonian "political process" approach to federalism, but over time he gravitated toward a Madisonian "middle ground" approach.[49] For his part, Thomas is a principled defender of states' rights who believes the Tenth Amendment limits the exercise of federal power. There are also important differences in other constitutional areas, including whether the government can regulate libel, how the establishment clause should be interpreted, whether the Second Amendment protects an individual's right to bear arms, the rights of the accused (particularly the Fifth and Sixth Amendments), property rights, and the principle of one person, one vote. Most important, the different methodological approaches of the three originalists would have resulted in contrasting opinions in *Brown v. Board of Education of Topeka* (1954).[50] Justice Black joined that unanimous opinion, which struck down segregation in public schools. In pre–Supreme Court speeches, Justice Thomas called *Brown* a "landmark" case, but he also criticized the court's reliance on psychological studies, which likely would have resulted in a concurring opinion.[51] Meanwhile, Justice Scalia's originalist approach (based on text and tradition) would have put him on the losing side of *Brown*.

Chapter 6 examines the contrasting originalist philosophies of Scalia and Thomas. In addition to their different interpretations of the tests used in administrative law cases, these two justices differed on important questions of constitutional law, including whether US citizens classified as "enemy combatants" have the right of habeas corpus,[52] whether Congress can regulate the use of homegrown marijuana for medicinal purposes,[53] and whether Congress can require the State Department to designate "Israel" on the passports of US citizens born in Jerusalem.[54] For most of his judicial tenure, Thomas did not challenge Scalia's opinion in *Employment Division, Department of Human Resources of Oregon v. Smith* (1990),[55] which held that the free exercise clause is not violated when neutral, generally applicable laws only incidentally impact religion. However, in a 2021 decision Thomas joined two opinions that called for *Smith* to be overturned.[56]

Despite their agreement that the Fourth Amendment does not require a warrant in all cases, Scalia and Thomas reached different outcomes in important search-and-seizure cases. The two justices also had different interpretations of anonymous speech, the rights of minors, the court's "obstacle" preemption jurisprudence, and the modern relevance of the privileges or immunities clause. Finally, these two originalists maintained very different perspectives on whether judges can rely on natural law in making decisions. Scalia was a legal positivist who argued that judges cannot rely on *any* extralegal sources, including the Declaration of Independence, whereas Thomas believes the Constitution is incomprehensible without resort to natural law and, in particular, the Declaration of Independence. These different perspectives were most apparent in affirmative action cases, but they surfaced in others as well.

The conclusion offers final thoughts on originalism as a method of interpreting the Constitution. The chief value of originalism is that it reminds judges of the importance of the Constitution's text and history. Justice Scalia was most persuasive when he criticized his colleagues for ignoring the *clear* language of the Constitution in death penalty cases. Because the words of the Constitution clearly contemplate capital punishment,[57] Scalia's argument that judges should not outlaw the practice has persuasive appeal. However, much of the language of the Constitution lacks the precision to support a literal or fixed method of interpretation. Although some constitutional language is precise (e.g., the minimum age to run for the presidency), other constitutional language is not so clear and contains what justice Robert Jackson aptly described as "majestic generalities."[58] For example, what constitutes "freedom of speech," "unreasonable searches and seizures," "cruel and unusual punishments," "due process of law," and "equal protection of the laws"? For that matter, what constitutes "Cases or Controversies," the authority "to regulate Commerce . . . among the several States," or "executive power"? Most people would not regard these phrases as either plain or fixed. The central argument of this book is that if Hugo Black had sat on the Supreme Court with Antonin Scalia and Clarence Thomas, they would have been on opposite sides of many constitutional controversies. As judge J. Harvie Wilkinson III has pointed out, originalism does not constrain judicial behavior; rather, it is another "cosmic" constitutional theory that, in practice, has not limited judicial policymaking.[59]

1. Biographical Sketches

In 1881 Oliver Wendell Holmes Jr. presciently observed, "The life of the law has not been logic: it has been experience."[1] As much as we may want judges to be neutral and disinterested decision makers—or what chief justice John Roberts has called "umpires"—the reality is that personal backgrounds and values do shape the law, particularly when it comes to the broad principles of the US Constitution. "We may try to see things as objectively as we please," Benjamin Cardozo candidly remarked. "None the less, we can never see them with eyes except our own."[2] The biographical sketches of Hugo Black, Antonin Scalia, and Clarence Thomas presented in this chapter shed light on how their childhood experiences, education, and professional work influenced how they interpreted the Constitution.

HUGO BLACK

Hugo LaFayette Black was born on February 27, 1886, to William LaFayette "Fayette" Black and Martha "Della" Toland Black in the family farmhouse in Clay County, Alabama. Hugo was the last of eight children and was named after Victor Hugo, as his sister was reading a novel by that author at the time.[3] Hugo's father was a farmer and store owner who was actively involved in local Democratic politics. His mother, whom Hugo adored, inspired his lifelong interest in books. When Hugo was three, the family moved to Ashland, the county seat, so the children could receive a better education. Black attended Ashland Academy, a private school that offered both elementary and high school courses. Even though Black was a superior student, he dropped out at age sixteen due to an altercation with the school's coprincipal, whom Hugo believed had unfairly punished his sister for whispering at her desk.[4]

Law School and Private Practice

Following in the footsteps of his older brother Orlando, Black attended Birmingham Medical College for one year but soon found that the medical profession was not for him.[5] In 1904 he enrolled at the University of Alabama

Law School in Tuscaloosa. At the time, the law school consisted of two faculty members and forty-five students. The two professors, William S. Thorington and Ormond Somerville, used a lecture style of instruction rather than the case method. Soon after the Supreme Court's decision in *Lochner v. New York* (1905),[6] striking down a maximum hour law for bakers, Professor Somerville advised his students "that legislators, not judges, should make the laws."[7] Black graduated from law school in the top third of his class and earned the distinction of Phi Beta Kappa.

Black began practicing law in his hometown, but he struggled to attract clients because Ashland already had enough attorneys. Making matters worse, a huge fire consumed a large section of the downtown square, destroying his law office and a large collection of law books he had recently purchased with an inheritance.[8] With only $50 to his name, Black set out for Birmingham, one of the fastest growing industrial cities in the South. Initially, business was slow, but Black and his law partner, Barney Whatley, managed to pay their bills by doing collection work. To drum up business, Black joined various civic organizations, including the Elks, Masons, Odd Fellows, Woodmen of the World, and Knights of Pythias.[9]

Police Court Judge

Black's early legal practice consisted mostly of worker compensation claims against Birmingham's coal and steel industries. Many of his clients were African Americans who had been arrested for petty crimes (gambling or vagrancy) and placed in the notorious convict lease system.[10] Black's performance as a trial attorney made such a favorable impression on A. O. Lane, the local circuit court judge, that he asked Black to serve as the new police court judge—a position that reportedly combined the workloads of three full-time judges and paid an annual salary of $1,500.[11] Black reluctantly accepted the position, on the condition that he could continue to build his private practice. Displaying his usual boundless energy, Judge Black heard cases each workday from 8:30 a.m. to 12:00 p.m. and occasionally on Saturdays. On April 12, 1911, his first day on the job, Black disposed of fifty-five cases and later set a record by hearing 150 cases in one morning session.[12]

Birmingham was one of the most crime-ridden cities in America and had a long history of racial injustice. Judge Black's docket was filled with minor criminal offenses such as disorderly conduct, assault and battery, vagrancy, loitering, and prostitution. Black was known for administering justice even-handedly, regardless of race or class. In one case, Charles H. Mandy, the daily reporter for the *Birmingham Age-Herald*, criticized Black for releasing eleven African Americans charged with disorderly conduct at a dance. The judge sided with the defendants because the white police officer had failed to establish the crime beyond a reasonable doubt. "With all due respect," Mandy reminded Judge Black, "a negro's testimony does not go very far against that of a white man, especially if it happens to be a [police] officer."[13]

In another case, a black furnace worker was charged with severely beating a white man who was employed as a collector for a secondhand furniture store. The defendant was unable to make installment payments on the furniture he had purchased because his wife was sick and they faced substantial medical expenses. When the collector came to reclaim the merchandise, the man pleaded with him, stating that his wife could not be moved from her bed. Paying no attention, the collector started to enter the door, at which point the defendant beat him severely. Judge Black asked to see the defendant's hands and noticed that they bore calluses like shoe soles. He also learned that the defendant had paid $94 for furniture that was worth only $50. "You go back to your sick wife," Black told the defendant, "and if I hear of you paying any more on that furniture, I'm going to put you in jail—not for beating this man, but for—well, contempt of court." He then told the collector, "You'd better go back to the furniture store and your doctor; and if I hear of you bothering this Negro again I'm going to put you in jail for—well, a long, long time."[14]

During his eighteen months as police court judge, Judge Black was exposed to some of the seamiest aspects of urban life. Upon his resignation, he observed that his responsibilities had been "an invaluable experience" that provided him with "a broad insight into human nature."[15] In the fall of 1912 Black resumed his law practice full time and quickly established himself as a formidable trial attorney. He was particularly gifted at convincing white juries to exercise equal justice. In one case, Sam Bradford, a black miner, had been injured when a roof caved in on him. Black convinced an all-white jury to rule in Bradford's favor. On appeal, the Alabama Supreme Court reversed that decision because the trial judge had not instructed the jury that Bradford was partially responsible for working in a dangerous area.[16] This was one of many occasions when Black was frustrated by an appellate court's reversal of a jury award.[17] Nonetheless, Black's success as a trial attorney was apparent. In 1913 the largest corporate law firm in Alabama offered him a full partnership, but

Black respectfully declined.[18] He was considering a run for county solicitor and did not want to become known as a "defendant's lawyer."[19]

Jefferson County Solicitor

In early 1914 Black ran for the position of solicitor in Jefferson County. The upstart Black—a Birmingham resident for only seven years—ran against three better known candidates, including the fifteen-year incumbent Harrington P. Heflin.[20] Undeterred, Black ran a tireless grassroots campaign and asked people what they wanted in a county prosecutor. Instead of publishing lengthy columns about himself in newspapers, Black preferred to post flyers and run catchy newspaper ads.[21] One highly effective technique was to distribute pasteboard strips the size of theater tickets. Printed on both sides was this question: "Black or Heflin: Which?"[22] Black won convincingly, receiving 2,271 more votes than the second-place finisher Heflin.[23]

As the county's chief prosecutor, one of the first things Black had to tackle was an enormous backlog, which stood at a staggering 3,268 cases.[24] The convict fee system was partly responsible because the salaries of various law enforcement officials (sheriffs, deputies, justices of the peace, clerks) were based on the number of people "in" the criminal justice system.[25] After taking office, Black discovered that many of the individuals locked up in the city's jails should not be there. One of his first decisions was to dismiss five hundred cases from the previous administration's docket, which raised some eyebrows and even led to calls for his impeachment.[26] Instead, Black concentrated on the most serious crimes, ninety-two of which were capital cases.[27] During his tenure, ten men were sentenced to death (two for armed robbery), and Black received convictions in thirty-nine cases of first-degree murder and fifty-three cases of second-degree murder.[28]

Black continued to earn a reputation for evenhanded justice. In one case, he charged Louis Walton, a wealthy businessman, with murdering his junior partner, Moses Barton, on whom Walton had taken out a $30,000 life insurance policy. Despite Walton's alibi, Black called him "a calculating, cold-blooded murderer who killed for money."[29] Members of the Birmingham business community found it hard to believe that one of their own could be guilty of murder.[30] The jury deadlocked, and Black promised a retrial. But before the second trial began, Walton killed himself after taking out an insurance policy on his own life.[31]

When Alabama became a dry state in 1915, Birmingham forbade liquor advertisements in newspapers. In one case, Black, an ardent prohibitionist,[32] sought an injunction against a local newsstand that continued to sell periodicals containing advertisements for alcoholic beverages.[33] Black took the position that if alcohol was illegal, advertisements for liquor could also be banned. He lost the case at trial but won his appeal to the Alabama Supreme Court.[34] Even though Justice Black would become an absolutist in free speech cases, he did not extend that same protection to commercial speech.[35]

Black's strident and effective prosecutorial skills did not go unnoticed by the state attorney general's office. Attorney general William Logan Martin asked Black to serve as special assistant attorney general in the investigation of a major whiskey ring in the small town of Girard, just across the Chattahoochee River from Columbus, Georgia. State officials, acting on a tip, had discovered thousands of gallons of illegal liquor behind trap doors and false walls in various buildings in Girard. Barrels of liquor were also found in the waters of the Chattahoochee, tied to the shore with ropes.[36] Many individuals were charged with bootlegging, including a few local officials, but some of the defendants went into hiding. When six of the ringleaders failed to show up for trial, Black introduced a motion calling for the immediate destruction of the confiscated liquor. As Black saw it, the defendants were fugitives, so they had no standing to contest the destruction of the alcohol.[37] Opposing counsel objected, but by the time he was able to get a court-ordered injunction, a substantial amount of the liquor had already been disposed of.[38] It was also discovered that some of the contraband had been found in locations not specifically mentioned in the warrant. On this issue, the Alabama Supreme Court ruled in favor of state officials on the grounds that the confiscated liquor was illegal.[39] Ironically, Black's former law professor Ormond Somerville cast the lone dissent. The tactics Black employed to uncover the whiskey ring provide early evidence of his narrow interpretation of the Fourth Amendment.[40]

As the county prosecutor, Black also led the investigation into police brutality in Bessemer, Alabama, a small mining and steel town southwest of Birmingham. After hearing reports that police officers used physical abuse to obtain confessions, Black convened a special grand jury to examine conditions in the town's prison. Black interrogated several police officers himself, including A. D. Maddox, who admitted to slapping black defendants in the face to get them to confess. In one case, Maddox defended his brutal tactics by saying, "He never did ask us *not* to hit him."[41] The final grand jury report, authored by Black, detailed the brutal "third-degree" methods used by several named police officers. It mentioned repeated instances of prisoners being taken out of their cells in the middle of the night and beaten "until they were red with their own blood."[42] The report concluded that the police officers' actions were "dishonorable, tyrannical, and despotic" and a clear violation of both the Alabama and US Constitutions. Fundamental rights should "not be surrendered to any officer or set of officers," Black wrote, "so long as human life is held sacred and human liberty and human safety of paramount importance."[43] Given this unfortunate experience, Black adopted a policy of never prosecuting a case based on a confession alone,[44] and it undoubtedly influenced his expansive interpretation of the self-incrimination clause as a Supreme Court justice.

Due to the enactment of a bizarre state law that prevented the county prosecutor from appointing his own staff attorneys, Black resigned his position on July 12, 1917.[45] He later described his thirty months as Jefferson County prosecutor as the "most demanding" work of his career, including his ten years as a US senator and thirty-four years as a Supreme Court justice. Black's office had an enormous caseload and a remarkable success rate. As Steve Suitts points out, Black was "responsible for one-third of all criminal cases throughout Alabama," and "his office tried almost thirty-five hundred serious criminal defendants, a third of whom were convicted." Based on his decision to focus on serious crimes, Black "dismissed almost four thousand cases, one third for charges relating to prohibition and about nine hundred relating to charges of 'gaming' or shooting craps." "Virtually all dismissals," Suitts notes, "involved African American defendants."[46]

World War I and Postwar Practice

Shortly before he resigned as county prosecutor, Black enlisted in the military. Always a skeptic when it came to war, he did not initially support US involvement in the European conflict, but after the United States declared war in 1917, he signed up to serve his country.[47] After completing basic training at Fort Oglethorpe, Black was commissioned as a captain with the Eighty-First Field Artillery. He was later reassigned to another brigade at Fort Sill, Oklahoma, which meant that he never deployed to France.[48]

After the war, Black returned to his law practice in Birmingham and essentially had to start over financially.[49] He and his new law partner, Colonel Crampton Harris, had a general practice. They represented unions during several postwar strikes, as well as prisoners and employees injured in workplace accidents.[50] Black's forte was personal injury cases. He was an adept cross-examiner and preferred jury trials to bench trials. His notoriety as a trial attorney resulted in more clients and referrals from other attorneys, and he became the first attorney in Birmingham to establish a lucrative personal injury practice.[51]

Even though Black had a reputation for fairness, honesty, and evenhandedness, he was not above appealing to local prejudices to win a case. One such case involved Mary Miniard, a white woman, who was traveling by train with her husband and eight-month-old baby from Chicago to Birmingham in April 1919. Mrs. Miniard claimed that for the first eight hours of the trip, she was harassed by a mentally disturbed black woman who called her "vile names."[52] During the trial, Black referred to the black passenger as "crazy" and a "nigger." Insinuating that the railroad company had done nothing to ensure Miniard's safety, Black challenged the conductor: "You knew *this lady* was in there," and "you knew there was a lot of nigger men and women, and you knew this woman was crazy?"[53] Even though no physician corroborated Mrs. Miniard's emotional distress, she received a sizable $2,999 award from an all-white male jury.[54]

Another case involved Edwin R. Stephenson, a Methodist preacher, who was charged with murdering Father James Coyle, a Catholic priest. Stephenson was upset with Coyle for marrying his daughter, Ruth, to Pedro Gussman, a Catholic man of Puerto Rican descent. Ruth testified before the grand jury that her father "hated" Catholics and believed "that Catholicism was rotten."[55] During the trial, Black called Gussman a "negro, dago, or a Puerto Rican" and "adjusted the courtroom shades to deflect any direct sun light 'so that Gussman's complexion would be accentuated.'"[56] The defense claimed that Stephenson had acted in self-defense, despite two eyewitness accounts stating that he had shot Coyle without provocation. The all-white jury, which, according to the press, "was packed with Klansmen," acquitted Stephenson.[57]

US Senator

In 1926 senator Oscar W. Underwood, a thirty-year member of Congress and two-time presidential candidate, decided not to run for reelection. Even before Underwood's official announcement, Black had decided to run for the seat. This time, Black ran against four more prominent Democratic candidates: Thomas Kilby, a former governor; John H. Bankhead Jr., son of a longtime member of Congress and brother of a current House member; Lycurgus Breckenridge "Breck" Musgrove, a wealthy coal mine operator and past senatorial candidate; and James J. Mayfield, a former state supreme court justice. Unfazed, Black ran another tireless grassroots campaign. He drove his Model T Ford to every county in Alabama. During campaign stops he played checkers with the village champions, took copious notes about all the people he met, and then wrote follow-up letters urging their support.[58]

During the speech that launched his campaign, Black identified the key issues as strict enforcement of Prohibition, low tariffs, better roads, development of rivers and harbors, anti-immigration policies,[59] veterans' benefits, campaign expenditure limits, and cheap fertilizer for farmers from Muscle Shoals.[60] He emphasized his populist roots, expressed regret that politicians no longer represented "the rights of the common people," and portrayed his opponents as either scions of family dynasties or connected to powerful corporate interests. Does the Constitution require that "the Son of a Senator shall be a Senator, but the son of a farmer must always have to be a farmer?" Black asked.[61] Black won the Democratic nomination by carrying forty-two of Alabama's sixty-seven counties and getting 32 percent of the overall vote.[62] Alabama was essentially a one-party state, so Black easily defeated the Republican candidate, Edmund H. Dryer, with 81 percent of the vote.[63] At age forty, Black became the junior senator from Alabama.

The Seventieth Congress, to which Black was elected, did not convene until December 1927—a full thirteen months after the election. Black took full advantage of this long hiatus by boning up on ancient and modern history, particularly the American founding. Black's senior colleagues were impressed by his command of historical events and figures. One early issue that Senator Black had to deal with was the future purpose and management of Muscle Shoals. During World War I, the federal government had built two plants near Muscle Shoals to manufacture nitrates for explosives, but the plants' postwar use remained uncertain. The Coolidge and Hoover administrations envisioned Muscle Shoals as a producer of electricity and fertilizer for the region but insisted that it be privately run—a position Black initially supported.[64] However, senator George W. Norris (R-NE) wanted the government to run the power plants, keeping control out of the hands of powerful corporate interests. Ultimately, Black and Norris reached a compromise. Black supported public ownership of Muscle Shoals, and Norris included a provision in the bill that required the plant to produce fertilizer for farmers—an issue Black felt passionate about.[65] "It still is not the measure I should like to see written," Black told his Senate colleagues, "but I realize that legislation is a matter of compromise."[66]

One of Black's most controversial early votes was the one he cast against the La Follette–Costigan bill, which would have created the Emergency Relief Board and allocated $375 million for needy Americans. Black supported the aims of the law but strongly opposed the creation of another federal bureau in Washington, DC. "Too much power is dangerous," Black observed, "whether it be vested in a government or a group of specially privileged plutocrats." "The real liberal," he said, "who has come down through the ages holding aloft the torch of liberty, has not stood for concentration of power in a centralized government or in the hands of a particular group."[67]

Black was reelected to the Senate in 1932 during a realigning election that put Franklin Roosevelt in the White House and gave Democrats control of both houses of Congress. Even though FDR and Black became fast friends and allies, they had to overcome a significant difference of opinion in the early months of the administration. On December 21, 1932—more than three months before Roosevelt assumed office—Black introduced a bill that would have mandated a thirty-hour workweek. He believed that limiting the maximum number of hours employees could work would open up job opportunities for the unemployed.[68] Remarkably, Black wrote the bill in pencil at his desk on the Senate floor.[69] However, FDR viewed Black's bill as too rigid, describing it as having "the rhythm of the cow."[70] In particular, the president believed the bill would curtail productivity and did not adequately account for different agricultural and business practices. As a result, FDR offered a different version of the bill that would eventually become the National Industrial Recovery Act (NIRA). Although Black supported the goals of the NIRA, he did not like the idea of trade and industrial associations creating codes of fair competition.[71] "This bill, if it shall pass and become a law," Black protested, "will transfer the law-making power of this Nation, insofar as the control of industry is concerned, from Congress to the trade associations."[72] Black felt vindicated when the Supreme Court struck down major portions of the NIRA as a violation of the nondelegation doctrine.[73]

On most other legislative matters, Black and FDR were on the same page. Black proposed or supported bills establishing The Fair Labor Standards Act, the Social Security program, the National Labor Relations Board, unemployment compensation, universal health insurance, federal aid to education, and the regulation of lobbyists. He also supported FDR's proposal that the United States join the World Court—which failed to get the approval of the Senate. During a time of ardent isolationism, Black justified his vote on the grounds that it could lead to peace. In a letter to a concerned constituent, Black explained, "I am opposed to war whenever it can possibly be avoided. I am of the opinion that those who clamor for war are prompted by propagandists who, in turn, are prompted by incentives given them by those who desire to get rich from war."[74]

During his time in the Senate, Black was a tireless and fierce investigator of government waste and corruption. In 1934 he chaired a committee investigating the shipping and air-mail industries. The five-person committee—known as the Black Committee—discovered that only a few major companies profited from the government subsidies supporting the delivery of mail. In response, FDR hastily called for the US Air Force to deliver the mail, but the military was ill equipped to undertake such a large task, and twelve air force personnel were killed. Congress responded with the Air Mail Act of 1934, which substantially restricted government subsidies to mail carriers.[75]

The following year, Black led the investigation into the extensive lobbying tactics used by public utility companies to defeat the Wheeler-Rayburn bill. The bill contained a so-called death-sentence provision that would terminate large holding companies regarded as incompatible with the public interest. During the investigation, the Black Committee discovered that negative telegrams about the bill sent to members of Congress were fraudulent, that the utility companies had drafted speeches for members of Congress who opposed the bill, and that the companies had advertised extensively in newspapers in an attempt to influence public opinion. The total amount spent by the utility companies was estimated to be $1 million, although Black thought it might be five times that amount.[76] The Black Committee turned the tide. After an initial defeat, the bill was passed in August 1935 as the Public Utilities Holding Company Act.

Being called before the Black Committee was an intimidating experience. Black was always polite, but he was a tenacious questioner of witnesses. In fact, some of his tactics were described as "dictatorial." For example, in early 1936 the Black Committee broadened its investigation into the lobbying practices of organizations such as the Liberty League, Farmers Independence Council of America, Southern Committee to Defend the Constitution, and Sentinels for the Republic. Because all these organizations were opposed to the New

Deal, the Black Committee was accused of blatant partisanship. When several of these groups' representatives withheld information from the committee, Black defended a broad use of Congress's subpoena power to obtain the original telegrams from Western Union, which ultimately resulted in a lawsuit.[77] When a judge upheld the organizations' request for an injunction, Black was furious. He believed that Congress's investigatory authority was plenary and that the courts did not have the authority to enjoin the practices of a coordinate branch of government. The Fourth Amendment, Black observed, represented "the crystallized sentiment of people who had felt oppression and who wanted to protect themselves in every manner from it." By contrast, the lobbyists in this case, he argued, were invoking the Constitution

> not in the cause of human liberty, but to trample upon human rights; not to elevate and raise the multitudes of the world from the oppression of the powerful and the great, but to continue the unearned and unjustifiable power and prestige of those who sit in high places and pour out their wealth in order to corrupt the pure streams of public thought and to utilize the press or the radio or whatever organization they may control for the purpose of misleading and deceiving the people of America.[78]

Nomination to the Supreme Court

In May 1937 Willis Van Devanter announced his retirement, giving FDR his first opportunity to appoint a Supreme Court justice. Van Devanter was one of the "Four Horsemen" who opposed virtually every aspect of the New Deal. Joseph T. Robinson (D-AR), the Senate majority leader, was the front-runner for the position, but he died of a heart attack in July. The White House reportedly had a list of sixty to seventy-five names that was eventually winnowed down to seven. On that short list were four federal judges, solicitor general Stanley Reed, senator Sherman Minton (D-IN), and Black.[79] Not wanting any leaks by the press, President Roosevelt kept his decision close to the vest. To the surprise of many, he nominated Black on August 12.

Black's nomination met with mixed reactions. Some claimed he was not qualified to be a Supreme Court justice because he had not attended an elite law school and had little judicial experience. Others claimed that this was a "spoils" appointment because Black was such a steadfast and vocal supporter of the president's court-packing plan. Still others viewed FDR's choice as shrewd politics. FDR calculated that the Senate could not reject one of its own. More broadly, the president wanted to nominate a person who would support his social and economic programs. As Roger Newman points out, being a "liberal" from the South made Black "an absolute anomaly."[80] On August 16 the Senate Judiciary Committee approved Black's nomination by a vote of 13–4, and the next day the entire Senate confirmed his nomination by a vote of 63–16.

Black's Supreme Court appointment received renewed scrutiny when it was revealed that he had been a member of the Ku Klux Klan (KKK) prior to his election to the Senate. One month after his confirmation, Ray Sprigle, a reporter for the *Pittsburgh Post-Gazette*, published a six-part syndicated story that detailed Black's association with the Klan and suggested that he was still a member.[81] These dramatic revelations sent a shock wave across the country and caught many by surprise. FDR professed that he had no prior knowledge of Black's membership in the Klan, but that is highly unlikely.[82]

Black and his wife, Josephine, were on vacation in Europe and had to cut their trip short and return home to deal with the controversy. Black's much-anticipated national radio address, which took place on October 1, 1937, attracted "the second largest radio audience of the decade."[83] During the address, which lasted only eleven minutes, Black admitted to being a member of the KKK prior to his tenure as a senator. "I did join the Klan," Black candidly told the audience. "I later resigned. I never re-joined." Black also admitted to receiving a "Grand Passport" membership card from the Klan in September 1926, when he won the Democratic nomination for the US Senate. Black explained that the card was "unsolicited" and that he "never used it" and "did not even keep it." At the conclusion of his remarks, Black vowed never to speak about the subject again.[84]

On the rare occasion when he broke that vow, Black justified his decision to join the Klan primarily as a matter of political expediency. He maintained that if a person wanted to run successfully for statewide office in Alabama in the 1920s, he had to join the Klan.[85] Interestingly, in a 1967 interview Black cited another reason for joining: because most corporate lawyers and jurors were members of the Klan, Black reasoned that he would be at disadvantage (in terms of winning cases) if he did not join. "I figured I'd better be even up," Black told the *New York Times*.[86] At the time, the Birmingham chapter of the Klan apparently did not have an extensive record of violence, but it is more than a little ironic that Hugo Black, that great champion of civil rights on the Supreme Court, joined an organization whose violent acts (and white supremacist tenets) did so much to harm race relations in the United States.[87] In fact, after his vote in *Brown v. Board of Education* (1954),[88] in which the Supreme Court struck down segregation in the public schools, Black was regarded as a traitor in Alabama, and he did not officially return to his beloved home state for sixteen years.[89]

ANTONIN SCALIA

In contrast to Hugo Black, Antonin Scalia hailed from the North. Born on March 11, 1936, in Trenton, New Jersey, "Nino" was the only child of Salvatore "Eugene" Scalia and the former Catherine Panaro. Eugene's family immigrated to the United States from Sicily when he was seventeen, and Catherine was a first-generation Italian American.[90] Following Sicilian tradition, Nino was named after his paternal grandfather, Antonino, a laborer who worked in the sulfur mines of Sicily.[91] Nino attended kindergarten at Grant Elementary School in Trenton, where his aunt Eva A. Panaro taught and played piano for the weekly songfest.

When Nino was six his family moved to Elmhurst, New York, where Eugene began a thirty-year teaching career at Brooklyn College. Years later, Scalia described his father as "stern," but he had tremendous respect for him. In fact, Scalia often said his father was more of an intellectual than he was.[92] He also quoted his father of the subject of character: "Brains are like muscles," Eugene told his son. "You can hire them by the hour. . . . The only thing that's not for sale is character."[93] Catherine, described by her son as "doting," was a grammar school teacher and his primary caretaker.[94] Scalia credited his mother with keeping him out of trouble. "She made it her job to know who I was hanging out with," he said in a 2008 interview. "We had them over to my house and she was den mother for the Cub Scouts, things of that sort."[95]

The elder Scalias stressed the importance of hard work and individual responsibility. Proudly displayed in Scalia's Supreme Court chambers was a small framed quotation: "Nothing is easy." Scalia demanded a lot of himself as well as others. "He'd catch a mistake that we had made," observed former law clerk Paul Cassell, and say, "Well, it's hard to get it right."[96] Scalia was known for his painstaking work on both the substance and the style of his judicial opinions. When an opinion was near completion, he would call his law clerk into the office, and they would review the opinion line by line—a process known as "booking." Library carts containing all the sources cited in the opinion were available so the justice and his law clerk could check each one for accuracy.[97]

As the only child of two well-respected and demanding teachers, Scalia grew up in an intellectually stimulating household. His father, an authority on Dante, taught three Romance languages at Brooklyn College: Italian, French, and Spanish. As George Kannar points out, Scalia's literal (or textualist) approach to interpreting the law was influenced by his father, who translated Italian authors such as Giosuè Carducci, a nineteenth-century Italian poet and recipient of the Nobel Prize for literature.[98] Eugene defended a "literal" translation of Carducci's work, calling it "one of the chief merits of a translation." Taking a humble view of the translator's craft, the elder Scalia wrote: "The most that a translation can hope to do . . . is to stimulate an interest" in the work being translated. "It is only by direct communion with [the poet's] page that people can come to fully appreciate" what is unique about the work.[99] One of Justice Scalia's most enduring contributions to originalism was his argument that the text of the Constitution should take precedence over the framers' intentions, which he undoubtedly learned from his father.[100]

Scalia's love of law and politics came from his mother's side of the family. One of his uncles, Vincent R. Panaro, was the first Democrat elected mayor of Ewing Township, a small community just outside of Trenton. Eugene regarded Vincent as an important role model for his son.[101] Uncertain what he wanted to do after graduating from college, Scalia visited his uncle's law office in downtown Trenton. "I had an Uncle Vince," Scalia told an honors class in 2008. "Okay, most Italians have an Uncle Vince," he joked. "Vince was a lawyer and I used to visit his law offices in downtown Trenton now and then. He seemed to have a good life, so I said give it a shot. And, as it turned out, it was what I love."[102]

School Days

For elementary school and junior high, Nino attended public school in Elmhurst. P.S. 13 was a polyglot of many ethnicities, including Greek, Irish, German, Jewish, and Italian. Scalia later described it as "the face of New York City." Scalia's parents likely wanted their son to assimilate into American culture, but they also wanted him to have some Catholic training.[103] On

Wednesday afternoons, he was one of the students who participated in New York's released-time program, leaving school early to receive religious instruction at a local church or synagogue. In speeches, Scalia often mentioned this program as a positive example of government accommodation of religion in the United States.[104] Scalia, a self-described "greasy grind," worked tirelessly on his academics and received all As.

For high school Nino attended St. Francis Xavier in Manhattan, a prestigious Catholic military prep school for boys. The curriculum at Xavier was "rooted in and quieted by religious principles," and each school day started with a morning prayer.[105] The high school was also renowned for preparing its students for modern warfare. The cadets wore military-style uniforms and were required to participate in the junior ROTC program. For Scalia, the program's most important lesson was "discipline, and duty, and sacrifice," and he rose to the rank of lieutenant colonel. He later lamented that Xavier no longer required ROTC participation due to the antiwar protests of the 1960s.[106]

Xavier's curriculum was in the classical tradition and included three years of Greek and four years of Latin. As usual, Scalia committed endless hours to his studies. During his four years at Xavier, he never got a grade below 90 percent and received numerous honors.[107] Scalia did manage to find time to take part in extracurricular activities too. He was president of the drama society and played the lead role in *Macbeth* in his senior year. Years later, Scalia told a group of high school students that it was "probably the most significant thing" he had ever done. "You know how many lines there are in *Macbeth*," Scalia jokingly told the students.[108] Music was always a major part of Scalia's life, and while at Xavier he played the French horn and, as a member of the marching band, participated in parades in New York City. Scalia was also on Xavier's junior varsity rifle team. He later enjoyed telling audiences how he carried his .22 carbine target rifle on the subway to and from school. "Can you imagine doing that today? In New York? 'Look out—there's a man with a gun.'"[109]

Scalia's political views also started to take shape at Xavier. Although his family had strong ties to the Democratic Party, Nino was a staunch conservative.[110] When Dwight Eisenhower ran for president in 1952, Nino took issue with Ike's comment that he was a conservative in economic matters but a liberal in humans affairs. Even as a high school student, Scalia saw this as a false distinction and contended that economic rights were intimately connected to civil rights.[111] "Few of us," Scalia later remarked at a conference on economic rights, "would have much difficulty choosing between the right to own property and the right to receive a *Miranda* warning."[112] William Stern, a classmate of Scalia's who later served as campaign manager for Mario Cuomo's 1982 New York gubernatorial race, described Scalia as "an archconservative Catholic." "He could have been a member of the Curia," Stern said. "He was a top student in the class. He was brilliant, way above everybody else."[113] To no one's surprise, Scalia was class valedictorian.

It was also during his teenage years that Scalia's interest in hunting developed. He hunted rabbits with his paternal grandfather on weekend trips to Long Island, sparking a lifelong passion for the sport. In his Supreme Court chambers, Scalia proudly displayed "Leroy," the head of a nine hundred–pound Rocky Mountain elk he shot in Colorado.[114] Scalia's avid interest in hunting undoubtedly influenced his interpretation of the Second Amendment. "The hunting culture begins," Scalia said in a 2006 speech, "with a broader culture that is not hostile toward firearms." "That attitude of associating guns with nothing but crime is what has to be changed," he added. "It's not necessarily a matter of getting your friends into hunting. If you can't get them into hunting, get them into skeet shooting, or anything that shows that guns are not things that are used only by bad people."[115]

College and Law School

After graduating from Xavier, Scalia attended Georgetown University—another distinguished Jesuit school—located in the nation's capital. At Georgetown, he studied history, both ancient and modern, and took courses on "American constitutional history and American foreign policy."[116] He also participated in school plays and was president of the Mask and Bauble theater club. As Bruce Murphy points out, Scalia also became an accomplished debater and was a member of the Philodemic Society, the oldest debate program in the country. He and his partners were two-time winners of the Hall of Fame Tournament at New York University. In fact, during Scalia's senior year, his debate team was ranked "the best collegiate debating team in the nation."[117] The skills he honed as a national debater undoubtedly influenced Scalia's approach to oral argument. Prior to his appointment to the Supreme Court, the justices rarely questioned counsel during these important public sessions. Almost single-handedly, Scalia changed that tradition. From his first days on the court, Scalia asked sharp and incisive questions in an effort to get to the case's underlying issue and steer the argument in a certain direction. As his colleague Samuel Alito aptly put it, Scalia transformed oral argument from a dull affair into a "contact sport."[118] Scalia graduated from Georgetown in 1957 with a bachelor's degree in history and was again class valedictorian. In his commencement speech, Scalia referred to his classmates as "the chosen few" and encouraged them to continue to seek the truth and not forsake their Catholic faith as they pursued their careers. "If we will not be the leaders of a real, a true, a Catholic intellectual life," he told his classmates, "no one will!"[119]

Following in the footsteps of his uncle Vince, Scalia started law school at Harvard University in the fall of 1957. His distinguished professors at Harvard included Lon Fuller, Paul Freund, Louis Jaffe, and Albert Sacks.[120] One of the courses he took, The Legal Process, is credited with launching a new school of jurisprudence in the United States.[121] The course was usually team-taught by Henry Hart and Albert Sacks, but Sacks taught it solo when Scalia was enrolled. Scalia's jurisprudence is sometimes associated with the legal process school, but there is little evidence of this.[122] In response to the atrocities committed in Nazi Germany during World War II, legal process theorists wanted to bring more objectivity (or morality) to the legal enterprise and emphasized a judicial decision-making process called "reasoned elaboration." According to this concept, judges should base their decisions on reasons or principles that transcend the particular case in order to avoid being seen as "naked power organs."[123] Scalia agreed with the legal process school's focus on neutral principles, but he insisted that those principles must be derived from the text and original understanding of the Constitution.[124] In fact, during his time on the Supreme Court, Scalia was an acerbic critic of the reasoned elaboration approach to decision making.[125] In judicial decisions and extrajudicial speeches, Scalia drew a sharp distinction between law and morality. "There are times," he wrote, "when even a bad rule is better than no rule at all." He also admitted that he had "never been able to isolate obligations of justice, except by defining them as those obligations that the law imposes."[126]

Marriage, Catholicism, and Law Practice

While at Harvard, Scalia met Maureen McCarthy on a blind date. A high school valedictorian and the daughter of a Massachusetts physician, Maureen was a senior at Radcliffe College, pursuing a degree in English. After a seven-month courtship, they married on September 10, 1960. According to close friend and former solicitor general Rex E. Lee, the couple's parents considered the marriage a mixed union: Italian Catholic and Irish Catholic.[127] During their fifty-five-year marriage, Nino and Maureen had nine children—five sons and four daughters—and thirty-six grandchildren. In a 2008 interview, Scalia admitted that he and Maureen did not set out to have nine children. "We're just old-fashioned Catholics, you know. Playing what used to be known as Vatican Roulette."[128] By all accounts, they had a loving and mutually supportive relationship.[129] During his Supreme Court swearing-in ceremony, Scalia gave special thanks to Maureen, whom he described as "an extraordinary woman, and without whom I wouldn't be here or if I were here, it wouldn't have been as much fun along the way."[130]

Nino and Maureen's relationship was enriched by their deep Catholic faith. Nino preferred a traditional Latin Mass and was known to leave churches if the religious teachings and practices were too liberal. One interesting example of his rejection of modern church doctrine involved capital punishment. In his 1995 encyclical letter, Pope John Paul II contended that the death penalty was inconsistent with the sanctity of human life and therefore could not be imposed by the state "except in cases of absolute necessity: in other words, when it would not be possible to otherwise defend society."[131] At a 2002 conference, Scalia took strong exception with this "new" catechism on capital punishment. He contended that it contradicted Christian teaching dating back to St. Paul, which held that the state, as "the minister of God," could "execute wrath upon him that doeth evil." Scalia also regarded the pope's encyclical letter as "disastrous" for Catholics who wanted to pursue public office, and he argued that any federal judge who could not impose the death penalty should resign from the bench.[132]

Scalia graduated magna cum laude from Harvard with an LLB in 1960 and began his legal career as an associate at Jones, Day, Cockley, and Reavis in Cleveland, Ohio. At the time, the firm had only about seventy-five lawyers, but it now ranks as one of the largest law firms in the world. Colleagues recalled Scalia as a "brash, instantly likable guy who lit up the firm with his legal abilities and eager conservatism."[133] Scalia's boldness was on display during his recruitment party, where he debated eight of the firm's partners until three in the morning over whether Sunday blue laws were constitutional. Scalia contended that they were, while his future employers argued the opposite. Coworkers at Jones Day fondly remembered Scalia as the "life-of-the-party," playing the piano and belting out show tunes during social events.[134] Scalia was well liked at the firm, even by those who differed with him politically. Richard

W. Pogue, a managing partner, recalled that Scalia always liked to debate. "But even when you disagreed with him," Pogue observed, "you couldn't help but like him."[135] Scalia dabbled in a bit of everything at Jones Day, including "real estate, corporate financings, labor, and antitrust discovery." Because the firm had other, more experienced trial attorneys, Scalia had limited exposure to the courtroom, which was one of the reasons the American Bar Association rated him only "qualified" when he was nominated to the DC Court of Appeals. James Lynn, who was instrumental in Scalia's hiring, was not surprised when he decided to pursue an academic career. Scalia's only weakness at the firm, Lynn later observed, was that "perhaps he wanted to spend more time on a problem than you might like in a practice. But that's part of what drove him to teach and later drove him to be a judge."[136] Although Scalia left Jones Day before becoming a partner, the senior partners unanimously agreed that he had been on track to earn that distinction during his six years with the firm.

The University of Virginia and Government Service

In 1967 Scalia left his lucrative law practice at Jones Day to become a law professor at the University of Virginia (UVA). During his time at UVA, Scalia published several articles and taught courses on contracts, conflict of laws, comparative law, and commercial transactions. Although his time as a full-time professor at UVA was short—just four years—he continued to teach at the university long after he accepted various government positions. From 1983 to 1986, for example, he was the John A. Ewald Jr. Distinguished Visiting Professor of Law and occasionally taught a course titled Regulated Industries.

In 1971 Scalia was appointed as the first general counsel for the Office of Telecommunications Policy (OTP) in the Nixon administration. In that position, Scalia was credited with brokering an important compromise among the television networks, the cable industry, and the motion picture industry over retransmission rights of copyrighted programs on cable.[137] As OTP general counsel, Scalia also criticized the fairness doctrine, which required broadcasters to present contrasting views on controversial subjects. In a 1972 speech before the Federal Communications Bar Association, Scalia argued that although the fairness doctrine had good intentions, the cost was too high in terms of First Amendment values.[138] Interestingly, Scalia later joined a DC Court of Appeals decision authored by judge Robert Bork holding that the fairness doctrine was *not* statutorily required, thereby opening the door for the Federal Communications Commission to abandon the doctrine on both constitutional and policy grounds.[139]

In September 1972 President Nixon appointed thirty-six-year-old Scalia as the third chair of the Administrative Conference of the United States—an independent federal agency staffed by cabinet members, agency heads, and administrative law experts. The purpose of the Administrative Conference was to conduct studies and make recommendations to administrative agencies and the three branches of government about the efficiency, adequacy, and fairness of administrative procedure. During Scalia's tenure as chair of the conference, it held seminars on administrative procedure; conducted comprehensive statistical analyses of how the different agencies were operating, including the commencement of an exhaustive study of the Internal Revenue Service; and published the first manual for administrative law judges. As head of the conference, Scalia also served as its mouthpiece and testified before Congress on several topics. In April 1973, for example, he testified on the creation of a new Consumer Protection Agency, about which he had mixed opinions.[140] During his tenure, Scalia was heartened by increased funding for the Administrative Conference. In the foreword to the conference's 1973–1974 report, Scalia observed: "While the capacity of the Conference is increasing, the need for its efforts is increasing as well. Improvement of administrative procedure in the past was sometimes impeded by the fact that the subject did not attract enough attention; there was insufficient awareness of its importance to sound government."[141]

In August 1974 Scalia formally resigned his law professorship at the University of Virginia to become assistant attorney general for the Office of Legal Counsel in the Justice Department. It was during this time that Scalia honed his appreciation for executive power. On numerous occasions, Scalia testified before Congress on subjects related to interbranch disputes, including the scope of executive privilege and the president's ability to enter into executive agreements. During his time in the Justice Department, Scalia also actively campaigned against the legislative veto, which allowed Congress to overrule decisions made by administrative agencies by a one-house or two-house veto.[142] At various forums and in his writings, Scalia argued that the legislative veto was an impractical and unconstitutional device for monitoring the actions of the federal bureaucracy.[143] Scalia also testified against a national "newsmen's privilege"—the right to withhold information or the identity of sources from state and federal investigators when subpoenaed to appear before a grand jury or a court. Although Scalia conceded that such a privilege did not violate the letter of the Constitution, he testified that it conflicted with "the spirit of federalism" because Congress would be intruding on the criminal law practices of the fifty states.[144] A common theme throughout Scalia's congressional testimony was that Congress should have more confidence in the executive branch. As he explained at a 1976 conference on congressional oversight:

> While I question neither the legitimacy nor the desirability of the congressional oversight function, both in its purpose and in its importance, it should, in my view, be subordinate to the function of legislating. You might ask yourselves when you read the daily newspapers how many of the congressional activities which are reported pertain to the difficult and politically risky process of hammering out specific and detailed legislative proposals, and how many consist of much more scintillating inquiries into alleged executive malfeasance or inefficiency, with no particular legislative purpose in mind.
>
> As I say, I believe the latter function is necessary and useful, but in this role the Congress is merely backstopping the President, who has the primary responsibility for, in the words of the Constitution, "taking care that the laws be faithfully executed."[145]

The American Enterprise Institute and the University of Chicago

After Jimmy Carter defeated Gerald Ford in the 1976 presidential election, Scalia temporarily left public office and accepted a position as a scholar-in-residence at the American Enterprise Institute (AEI). In that capacity, Scalia participated in "brown-bag" lunches with several leading conservatives of the time, including Robert Bork, Laurence Silberman, James Miller III, Jeane J. Kirkpatrick, Rudolph Penner, Irving Kristol, Jude Wanniski, and Herbert Stein. They engaged in free-flowing and lively discussions about important issues of the day, including supply-side economics. During these open forums, Scalia often discussed his views about the separation of powers and, in particular, his opposition to the legislative veto.

Scalia left AEI in the summer of 1977, and that fall he joined the law faculty at the University of Chicago, where he taught courses on contracts, administrative law, and constitutional law. While at Chicago, Scalia became the first faculty adviser for the law school's chapter of the Federalist Society (discussed more extensively in the conclusion). Scalia continued his association with AEI, and in 1978 he participated in an AEI roundtable on "An Imperial Judiciary: Fact or Myth?" during which he criticized the Supreme Court's decisions on abortion rights and school busing.[146] He also served as the editor of *Regulation*, a bimonthly magazine published by AEI that was devoted to analyzing the implications of US government regulatory policy. In that capacity, Scalia expressed strong support for President Reagan's plan to implement "central clearance" of all government regulations, believing that "big brother" clearance by the Office of Management and Budget (OMB) would prevent individual agencies from imposing excessive costs on private industry and allow for a more uniform and comprehensive regulatory program. He also criticized the 1974 amendments to the Freedom of Information Act as "the Taj Mahal of the Doctrine of Unanticipated Consequences, the Sistine Chapel of Cost/Benefit Analysis Ignored."[147]

From 1981 to 1982 Scalia served as chair of the Administrative Law Section of the American Bar Association. In one of his chairman's messages, Scalia challenged the progressive view of public administration, which assumes that expert "neutral technocrats" can make rules based on a commonly understood public interest. In contrast to this "enlightened" conception of administrative law, Scalia defended a theory of public administration based on "political discretion," where there are no discernible right or wrong answers to regulatory problems. More needed to be done, Scalia argued, to bring "the political, accommodationist, value-judgment aspect of rulemaking out of the closet." "What an agency wishes to do and not to do," he added, "within a broad range of alternatives available under its charter—is up to the agency itself. It is a large and important area of political discretion."[148] Scalia's belief that agency decisions often involve political choices shaped his view that courts should give considerable deference to administrative agencies—a point of view the Supreme Court embraced two years later in *Chevron U.S.A., Inc. v. Natural Resources Defense Council, Inc.*[149]

DC Court of Appeals

In 1982 Ronald Reagan appointed Scalia to the US Court of Appeals for the District of Columbia, considered the second most influential court in the country. During his four-year tenure on that court, Scalia authored 135 published opinions: 105 majority opinions (77.8 percent), 5 concurring opinions

(3.7 percent), 7 concurring in part and dissenting in part opinions (5.2 percent), and 18 dissenting opinions (13.3 percent). His jurisprudence was marked by a formalistic interpretation of separation of powers;[150] a strict interpretation of legal standing;[151] a deferential view of executive power, particularly in foreign affairs;[152] broad immunity for executive branch officials;[153] an expansive interpretation of the "state secrets" privilege;[154] and judicial deference to administrative agency action.[155] In one of Scalia's most important opinions, *Synar v. United States* (1986),[156] he held for a three-judge panel that the removal provision of the Balanced Budget and Emergency Deficit Control Act violated separation-of-powers principles. Based on his strident pro-executivist views, Scalia's colleagues jokingly referred to him as "new monarchist."[157] Abner Mikva, one of Scalia's liberal colleagues, aptly observed that Scalia was a conservative, but he was not "antigovernment."[158]

Nomination to the Supreme Court

In May 1986 chief justice Warren E. Burger unexpectedly retired from the Supreme Court, which gave President Reagan the opportunity to appoint the nation's sixteenth chief justice. For only the third time in the country's history, the president nominated a sitting justice as chief justice: William H. Rehnquist. This meant that there was still a vacancy to be filled. The two leading contenders were Scalia and Robert Bork, both of whom were serving on the DC Court of Appeals. The Reagan administration chose Scalia for several reasons. At fifty years old, he was nine years younger than Bork. In addition, Scalia did not have the controversial "paper trail" that would later plague Bork during his own confirmation battle. Finally, Scalia's ethnicity was a major consideration. No Italian American had ever been appointed to the Supreme Court, and this was reportedly *the* decisive factor for Reagan. Having appointed Sandra Day O'Connor as the first female Supreme Court justice, Reagan liked the idea of firsts.[159] In light of the controversy that surrounded him during his judicial tenure, Scalia's confirmation hearings were surprisingly uneventful. He was confirmed unanimously on September 17, 1986, by a vote of 98–0. During the swearing-in ceremony, President Reagan lauded both Rehnquist and Scalia as practitioners of "judicial restraint."[160]

CLARENCE THOMAS

Clarence Thomas was born on June 23, 1948, in Pin Point, Georgia, a small town located eleven miles southeast of Savannah. Clarence was the second of three children born to Leola Williams and M. C. Thomas. Unfortunately, M. C. abandoned the family when Clarence was just two years old, and he had little contact with his biological father. His mother (nicknamed Pigeon) struggled to earn enough money to support her children. Initially, they lived at the home of Leola's aunt Annie Green. Even though Thomas described the house as a "shanty," it provided the family with a sense of security and home-cooked meals.[161] However, Clarence's younger brother, Myers, and a cousin accidentally burned down the house, leaving the family homeless. Leola sent her daughter, Emma Mae, to live with relatives, and she moved to Savannah with her two sons.

Thomas described life in Savannah as hell. "Overnight," he recalled, they "moved from the comparative safety and cleanliness of rural poverty to the foulest kind of urban squalor." The family lived in a one-room tenement with a common kitchen and a barely usable outhouse. Thomas still remembers "the sickening stench of the raw sewage that seeped and sometimes poured from the broken sewer line."[162] The apartment lacked electricity, had inadequate heating, and was limited in space. Leola and Myers shared the one bed, and Clarence slept in a chair. Living in Savannah was Clarence's first experience with chronic hunger. The boys never knew when (or if) they would get their next meal. For breakfast they often ate cornflakes with water and evaporated milk.[163]

On her meager salary of $10 a week, Leola could no longer support her two growing boys. With few other options, she asked her father, Myers Anderson, and her stepmother, Christine "Tina" Hargrove Anderson, to take the boys, aged seven and five. Although Clarence was extremely hurt by this decision at the time, he later regarded it as the most consequential of his life. Myers Anderson (Clarence called him Daddy) was a strict disciplinarian who ran his house with an "iron will." When the boys arrived at their grandparents' home, Anderson told them, "The damn vacation is over."[164] A fiercely independent man, Anderson had started a wood-delivery business, which he later expanded to coal, ice, and ultimately fuel oil. For additional income, he restored and leased old houses. For the first time in their lives, Clarence and his brother shared a real bedroom, used an indoor bathroom, and enjoyed the convenience of major appliances.

During the school year, Clarence and Myers helped their grandparents with the family business and did chores around the house. During the summer months, they worked on the family farm in nearby Liberty County, and in fact, the boys helped build the summer farmhouse on the property owned by the Anderson family since the 1870s. On Christmas Day 1957, Anderson drove the two boys out to the site and mapped out the location for the farmhouse. Later that spring, he and his two grandsons completed "a simple four-room" cinder-block house and then added "garages, a barn, and other facilities" over the summer. From then on, the two boys planted and harvested corn, vegetables, and sugarcane each summer. They also learned how to clean fish; skin deer, raccoons, and squirrels; pluck chickens; and slaughter hogs. The work was arduous and often had to be performed in ninety-degree Georgia heat, but the boys rarely complained. Although he did not realize it at the time, Clarence came to regard his grandfather as his hero.[165]

Catholic School Days

Thomas attended segregated Catholic schools in Savannah, first St. Benedict the Moor Grammar School and then St. Pious X High School. His teachers were Irish Franciscan nuns who taught a Christian theology grounded in the innate equality of human beings. Unlike the prejudice seen elsewhere in Georgia, the sisters believed that God had created all persons equal, irrespective of race. The nuns backed up their religious convictions by sitting with their black pupils in the "colored" section of Savannah's buses, earning them the nickname "Nigger Sisters."[166] The curriculum at St. Benedict's included "English, mathematics, history, geography, spelling, and handwriting."[167] The sisters emphasized hard work and self-discipline, and Thomas credits the nuns for pushing him to do his best and giving him the confidence to think independently and survive in a competitive world. "Although a solid education does not guarantee success," Thomas later observed in a moving tribute to the nuns, "failure is guaranteed *without* it."[168] Thomas gets emotional when he recalls the moral lessons he learned from the sisters. At one point he called Sister Mary Virgilius Reidy, his eighth-grade teacher and principal, and asked: "Why was it that you sisters could do for us black kids what nobody else could do or did do?"[169]

Inspired by the Franciscan nuns and his deeply religious grandparents, Thomas decided to pursue the priesthood. He first attended St. John Vianney, a pre-seminary high school close to his home. The curriculum at St. John's consisted of "religion, Latin, English, music, and physical education," as well as courses in "geometry, algebra, physics, art, German, and chemistry."[170] Thomas's teachers remembered him as "a young man of few words," but they were impressed by his work ethic and determination. In addition to spending countless hours studying, Thomas was a standout athlete who competed in football, basketball, baseball, and track.[171] He also wrote articles for the *Pioneer*, the school newspaper, and became one of its coeditors.

Thomas described his years at St. John's as "difficult and lonely." After his freshman year, he was the only black student enrolled at the school, and he had his first experience with racial bigotry.[172] One night after the lights had been turned off in the dormitory, a fellow student yelled out, "Smile, Clarence, so we can see you." Even more upsetting to Thomas was the fact that no one said anything in response.[173] On another occasion, a fellow seminarian wrote in Thomas's yearbook, "Keep on trying Clarence, one day you will be as good as us."[174] Thomas's response to these racial insults was to work even harder. At the age of sixteen he learned that "it was better to be respected than liked."[175] Thomas had the last laugh: in his three years at the school, he maintained an A (92 percent) average in all his courses.[176]

Seminary, Holy Cross, and Yale

Despite incidents of discrimination, Thomas continued to pursue the priesthood. He enrolled at Immaculate Conception Seminary, a Benedictine college in northwestern Missouri. Even though he was one of only three black students in the freshman class of sixty-two, Thomas made fast friends. He excelled in academics and was regarded as the best athlete at the school.[177] He also enjoyed the formality of wearing "a cassock and Roman collar to morning and evening prayers, as well as to Mass."[178] However, Thomas could not escape racism, including an appalling comment made by a fellow seminarian when Dr. Martin Luther King Jr. had been shot. "That's good," the student remarked. "I hope the son of a bitch dies."[179] More generally, Thomas was frustrated that the Catholic Church failed to take an aggressive stance against racial discrimination in the United States. At the end of his freshman year, he withdrew and returned home to Savannah.

Dropping out of seminary did not sit well with Daddy, whose immediate reaction was to kick his grandson out of the family home. Clarence moved in with his mother and found a proofreading job at Union Camp Corporation, a paper company in Savannah. However, the work environment was unbearable. Racially derogatory remarks were written on the bathroom walls, and Clarence's white coworkers treated him with disrespect.[180] The job at Union Camp coincided with the volatile summer of 1968, which witnessed the assassination of Robert Kennedy. Thomas recalled that he was filled with anger and resentment and felt like his life was spiraling out of control. Fortunately, Sister Mary Carmine, his chemistry teacher from St. John's, had urged him to apply to Holy Cross College earlier that spring. Not seeing many alternatives, Thomas boarded a train for Worcester, Massachusetts, in September 1968.

Founded in 1843, Holy Cross is the oldest Catholic college in New England, and at the time, the private Jesuit school was all male. By 1968, Holy Cross had eliminated some of its original core curriculum. Latin was no longer mandatory, and students were not required to take one-third of their coursework in religion or philosophy. In contrast to Immaculate Conception, attendance at daily Mass was not compulsory, and students did not have to wear coats and ties to classes. This suited Thomas just fine. He no longer attended Catholic church and, in an act of defiance, wore "surplus Army clothes and footwear" to class.[181]

Holy Cross gave Thomas his first taste of political activism. He was secretary of the new Black Student Union (BSU) and helped draft its constitution. Most BSU members held Marxist beliefs and were sympathetic to the radical politics of black nationalism. Thomas did not share their collectivist attitudes, but he was attracted to the black empowerment movement.[182] In fact, one of the few adornments in his dorm room was a poster of Malcolm X.[183] In December 1969 Thomas participated in a walkout precipitated by the belief that black students had been disproportionately punished for an earlier protest on campus. Thomas was one of sixty BSU members who packed up their bags and walked off campus.[184] Due to the negative publicity surrounding the event, the administration quickly backed down and granted amnesty to all the students involved in the earlier protest.[185]

Thomas was also an outspoken critic of the Vietnam War. Like many black Americans, he believed that the war in Southeast Asia was a "white man's war." At protests in Worcester, Thomas wore a button reading, "No Vietnamese ever called me nigger."[186] In the spring of 1970, members of the BSU took a station wagon to Harvard Square and participated in a massive antiwar protest. The crowd chanted, "Ho, Ho, Ho Chi Minh" and demanded the release of political prisoners in the United States.[187] Before long, the rally turned into a full-scale riot, and police shot tear gas into the crowd. After returning to campus, Thomas was horrified that he had been involved in such an unruly protest and immediately asked God for forgiveness. In one sense, Thomas's politics at Holy Cross were the most radical of his life, but the black nationalists' emphasis on self-empowerment was well aligned with the unspoken political philosophy of his grandfather.

Thomas's future independent streak was also detectable at Holy Cross. During his second semester, the BSU voted 24–1 to have a separate black corridor on the fourth floor of Healy Hall. Thomas was the only dissenter.[188] He viewed this form of self-segregation as not much different from Jim Crow. "I felt that if blacks wanted to be by themselves socially, they could go to Howard University," he told the alumni magazine.[189] After some soul-searching, Thomas decided to live on the segregated floor, but only after BSU members agreed to let his white roommate, John Siraco, live with him.

Thomas's views of affirmative action were also taking shape at Holy Cross. Worcester was an ethnically diverse community, but it was not racially diverse.[190] Thomas was one of twenty blacks who enrolled at Holy Cross in the fall of 1968.[191] To attract more black students, Holy Cross began an aggressive recruitment campaign that resulted in the admission of forty more black students in the fall of 1969. After noticing that some of his fellow black students were struggling or even failing, Thomas began to wonder about the benefits of affirmative action. "Why," he asked, "were these gifted young people being sacrificed on the altar of an abstract theory of social justice—and who profited from their failure?"[192] He also began to see affirmative action as class based. The beneficiaries of affirmative action, he argued, were not economically disadvantaged blacks but middle- and upper-class blacks who did not need financial assistance. Instead of stereotyping the black community as a monolith, Thomas contended that opportunities should be based on socioeconomic status.

Although politics (and, in particular, racial politics) played a prominent role in Thomas's life at Holy Cross, he did not lose sight of his ultimate goal: a college education. Thomas graduated from Holy Cross with high honors and a degree in English literature.[193] One day later he married Kathy Ambush, a student at Anna Maria College, whom he had met during his second year at Holy Cross.[194]

With the priesthood no longer an option, Thomas decided to pursue a law degree. He was accepted at several top-notch universities, including Harvard, Yale, and the University of Pennsylvania, but he chose Yale because he thought Harvard was too conservative. Thomas's time at Yale was not satisfying, however. As a new husband, he did not have much time for a social life. He also became deeply concerned about finances, particularly after the birth of the couple's son, Jamal, during Thomas's second year at Yale. Thomas had to take out several student loans to cover his tuition, which he did not completely pay off until after he began his tenure on the Supreme Court. But there were other things about Yale that upset Thomas. He deeply resented what he called the "herd mentality" of his classmates, particularly on issues of race and welfare.[195] As a beneficiary of Yale's affirmative action program, Thomas felt that his professors and white classmates treated him as inferior. Every day he had to prove to them that he belonged there. "The professors and students resented your very presence," Thomas later remarked.[196]

During his senior year, Thomas had his heart set on a job with a law firm in Atlanta, but he did not get the offer. That rejection, as well as others, led Thomas to believe that race was the primary reason why he was not hired. "I'd learned the hard way that a law degree from Yale meant one thing for white graduates and another for blacks, no matter how much anyone denied it." He dramatically claimed that he had "made a mistake" by attending Yale Law School and regarded his law degree from Yale as worthless.[197]

Missouri Attorney General's Office

Thomas ultimately found employment in the Midwest. Jack Danforth, a Yale alumnus and young Republican attorney general from Missouri, had come to Yale to recruit staff attorneys for his office. Thomas liked Danforth from the start and thought he was honest and sincere. The salary was low ($10,800 per year), but the position provided abundant litigation experience.[198] In fact, only a few days after he was sworn in to the Missouri bar, Thomas argued his first case before the Missouri Supreme Court.

Initially, Thomas handled criminal appeals, which impacted his view of race and the criminal justice system. Prior to accepting the position in Missouri, Thomas had thought that institutional racism was the primary reason so many blacks were incarcerated. That perception changed during his time in the attorney general's office. One case in particular influenced his attitude. Vernon Torrence, a black man, had been convicted of raping and sodomizing a black woman two times. On appeal, the defendant argued that the victim should not be able to testify about the sexual acts that took place at the second location because they were separate crimes. Thomas successfully argued before the Missouri Court of Appeals that the testimony about the second sexual assault was admissible because the entire series of events was part of a single criminal transaction.[199] Rather than attribute the defendant's actions to family background or societal forces, Thomas placed the responsibility directly on Torrence himself and called him a "vicious thug."[200]

After handling criminal appeals for a year, Thomas was assigned to the civil division, where he supervised tax cases—an area of the law he much preferred. After initial doubts that he would enjoy his job in Jefferson City, Thomas later described his work in the Missouri attorney general's office as "the best job I've ever had."[201] When Jack Danforth decided to run for the Senate in 1976, Thomas accepted a private-sector position with Monsanto, a multinational agrochemical corporation based in St. Louis. Monsanto's in-house attorneys were earning more money than other lawyers employed at major firms in St. Louis, so Thomas took the job to ease his family's financial struggles. He did not like it, however. There was not enough work to go around, and he found the work uninteresting. In 1979 he received a phone call from Senator Danforth's office, asking him to consider serving as a legislative aide in Washington, DC. Although the compensation package did not match Monsanto's, the Thomases decided to move to the nation's capital. Thomas's one request was that he not be assigned civil rights matters. Senator Danforth honored that request and gave him responsibilities in the areas of energy, the environment, and public works.

Washington, DC

Although money was tight, Thomas enjoyed working in the nation's capital. He became close friends with Jay Parker, the black conservative editor of the *Lincoln Review*. He also met and became friends with Thomas Sowell and Walter Williams, two prominent black conservative economists. In November 1980 Thomas did something he had never done before: he voted for a Republican—Ronald Reagan. One month later he attended a Black Alternatives Conference in San Francisco. During a wide-ranging interview with the *Washington Post*'s Juan Williams, Thomas criticized minimum wages, rent control, busing, and affirmative action as harmful to the dignity of black Americans.

He also explained why he supported school vouchers and sent his own son to private school at a cost of $1,400 per semester: "The public schools don't educate people," Thomas said. "They teach them they can get by without working." Thomas also criticized the views of major leaders of the civil rights movement. "I'm tired of blacks being thought of only as poor people, people on welfare, people who are unemployed," he remarked. "That's the only way the Jesse Jacksons and the other black leaders talk about black people. To them we're all a monolith." Finally, Thomas criticized the welfare system, using his own sister, Emma Mae, as an example: "She gets mad when the mailman is late with her welfare check. That is how dependent she is. What's worse is that now her kids feel entitled to the check too. They have no motivation for doing better or getting out of that situation."[202]

In March 1981 the Reagan administration offered Thomas the position of assistant secretary for civil rights in the Department of Education. Initially, he was reluctant to accept the job. Like Reagan, he questioned whether a Department of Education was even necessary, and he did not want to be seen as an affirmative action hire. His friend Jay Parker convinced Thomas to take the position. "Aren't you tired of just *talking* about problems?" Parker asked. "Wouldn't you like to try doing something about them for a change?"[203] During his time at the Department of Education, Thomas expressed concern about the future of traditional black colleges in the United States. After *Brown v. Board of Education*, civil rights groups pushed for integration of formerly segregated schools, but Thomas argued that this threatened historically black schools. "How will desegregation policies which ultimately eliminate black colleges help black people?" Thomas asked students at Clark College. "I don't have the slightest idea."[204] For Thomas, traditional black colleges performed an invaluable function during the difficult period of segregation.

Thomas appreciated the Reagan administration's smaller government philosophy, but he took issue with the administration's position on civil rights. When the Voting Rights Act came up for renewal, the administration balked at the "central clearance" requirement for southern states. Thomas did not disagree with this concern, but he thought the administration should have come out more forcefully in favor of voting rights.[205] However, the position that concerned Thomas the most—and made him consider resigning—was the Justice Department's handling of *Bob Jones University v. United States* (1983).[206] Bob Jones, a private religious university, had been granted tax-exempt status by the Internal Revenue Service (IRS), even though it discriminated on the basis of race. In 1970 the IRS informed Bob Jones that it would no longer receive favorable tax treatment because of its discriminatory practices. President Reagan did not believe the IRS had the authority to revoke Bob Jones's tax-exempt status, so he asked the Justice Department not to oppose the university's lawsuit. Thomas understood the legal argument, but he believed the administration's litigation strategy was deeply flawed and made it look hostile to civil rights.[207] As Thomas saw it, *Bob Jones* was another blown opportunity by the Republican Party to attract more black voters.[208]

In 1982 President Reagan selected Thomas to chair the Equal Employment Opportunity Commission (EEOC)—a position he had previously stated he would never accept.[209] When Thomas arrived, the EEOC was in a state of disarray. He is credited with establishing a mission statement, renovating the building, creating new personnel policies, and instituting a computerized accounting system.[210] He also tackled the enormous backlog of cases. Thomas's predecessor, Eleanor Holmes Norton, had used a "rapid charge" system to deal with the large volume of employment discrimination claims she had inherited. According to this strategy, racial imbalances in the workplace could be corrected through large class actions and quick settlements, which often required employers to establish hiring goals and timetables. Soon after his arrival Thomas discontinued that practice, which he regarded as inconsistent the EEOC's mandate to investigate *individual* claims of discrimination under Title VII of the Civil Rights Act of 1964. During Thomas's leadership, the EEOC moved to a "full investigation" approach, which required more time and resources but was more consistent with Thomas's view of the agency as a law enforcement body.[211]

Thomas's tenure at the EEOC was politically challenging. He received criticism from both sides of the political aisle. On the left, he was called an Uncle Tom for backtracking on established civil rights policies and methods because it was not always easy to prove individual cases of discrimination. On the right, Thomas occasionally battled with Justice Department officials who wanted to dismantle all forms of affirmative action, particularly during his early years at the EEOC. For example, in a case involving the New Orleans police department, the Justice Department filed a brief opposing goals and timetables as part of the consent agreement.[212] Thomas felt blindsided by the Justice Department's litigation strategy and threatened to file a brief of his own if the department did not back down.[213]

It was also during this time that Thomas engaged in an intensive self-education program. He hired two special assistants, Ken Masugi and John Marini, as personal advisers and speechwriters. Both men had received graduate degrees at Claremont McKenna College and had been mentored by Harry Jaffa, a professor of American political philosophy and history. Masugi was an expert on American political thought, and Marini was a specialist on Congress and the separation of powers. The two men assigned Thomas readings in European and American history (including John Locke's *Second Treatise of Government, The Federalist Papers*, and *Democracy in America*), as well as scholarly works on Congress. During lunches and long walks, the three men would talk about these texts, and Thomas occasionally turned his staff meetings into graduate school seminars. Thomas felt liberated by their discussions. In contrast to his mundane responsibilities at the EEOC, these sessions gave Thomas an opportunity to think deeply about important issues: race, freedom, democracy, constitutionalism, natural law. As Ken Foskett points out, "Thomas's speeches suddenly were filled with references to great philosophers and esoteric musings about freedom and democracy."[214] More specifically, Thomas gravitated toward Jaffa's natural law philosophy, particularly his writings on Lincoln and how the Great Emancipator connected the abolition of slavery to the Declaration of Independence.

In spring 1986 Thomas met Virginia "Ginni" Lamp at a conference on affirmative action. (His marriage to Kathy Ambush had ended in divorce in 1984.) A native of Omaha, Nebraska, Ginni was serving as a lobbyist for the Chamber of Commerce. Thomas was reluctant to get involved in another relationship (especially a mixed-race one), but the couple soon became inseparable.[215] After a one-year courtship, they married on May 30, 1987, and Thomas still refers to Ginni as his "best friend" and "bride." They share the same political views, especially as they relate to the role of government and individual freedom.[216] Over the course of their marriage, Thomas became a diehard University of Nebraska fan, especially the women's volleyball team. The couple also enjoys long summer trips in their forty-foot motor home.[217]

DC Court of Appeals

On October 20, 1989, president George H. W. Bush nominated Thomas to serve on the DC Court of Appeals.[218] Even though Thomas's tenure on that court was short (fifteen months), he managed to participate in 145 cases, and his law-and-order views were apparent in his opinions. In two cases he wrote the majority opinion rejecting a challenge to a drug conviction.[219] In another case he authored the opinion holding that exigent circumstances justified police entry of a hotel room that was not listed on a warrant.[220] Perhaps reflecting the court's docket, Thomas gave a speech on administrative law in which he questioned the amount of deference federal judges give to administrative agencies under the *Chevron* doctrine.[221] Thomas also forecast how he would handle affirmative action cases. In a decision handed down after he was nominated to the Supreme Court, Thomas wrote the 2–1 decision striking down a federal affirmative action program that gave women preference in broadcast licensing. Applying intermediate scrutiny—the standard at the time[222]—Thomas found that there was insufficient evidence that increasing the number of female owners of radio and television stations would lead to more "diversity" of opinion or programming.[223]

Nomination to the Supreme Court

At the end of the Supreme Court's 1990–1991 term, Thurgood Marshall, the first African American justice, announced his retirement. After considering a few other candidates, George H. W. Bush nominated Clarence Thomas to replace Marshall. At the formal announcement in Kennebunkport, Maine, the president referred to Thomas as "the best qualified" person at the time.[224] The fact that Thomas, a conservative, would be replacing Marshall, one of the court's legendary liberal justices, meant that his confirmation would be a fierce battle.

Although Thomas's nomination was announced on July 1, the confirmation hearings did not begin until September 10, which allowed interest groups to weigh in on the nominee. Many (but not all) civil rights and women's rights groups came out against Thomas.[225] Using its rating system of "well-qualified," "qualified," and "not qualified," the American Bar Association rated Thomas 0–12–2, with one member abstaining. Thomas testified before the Senate Judiciary Committee on September 10–16 for approximately twenty-five hours. Among the more interesting aspects of his testimony were Thomas's claims that he had never discussed (privately or publicly) the merits of *Roe v. Wade* and that his interest in natural law was "purely from a political theory standpoint" and would not impact the way he decided cases.[226] On September 27 the Senate Judiciary Committee split 7–7 on whether to approve Thomas's nomination, but it sent the nomination to the full Senate for consideration.

However, the confirmation hearings took a dramatic twist when an FBI report was leaked to the press regarding a sexual harassment claim by Anita Hill. Hill, a law professor at the University of Oklahoma, had worked for Thomas in the early 1980s as a special assistant at both the Department of Education and the EEOC. The FBI had interviewed Hill and Thomas, but after the allegation was made public, the Senate Judiciary Committee decided to reconvene its hearings and asked both individuals to testify. On the morning of October 12 Thomas firmly denied the allegations. He testified that he could not fathom what he might have said or done to Professor Hill that would cause her to allege that his interest in her was anything other than professional. Hill then testified for six to seven hours. She claimed that Thomas had asked her out socially on several occasions, and when she repeatedly said no, he "pressed" her about why she would not go out with him. She also testified about being uncomfortable when Thomas talked about sex at work, particularly his description of sex scenes in pornographic films and claims about his own sexual prowess.[227] Hill claimed that by late 1982, the work environment at the EEOC had become so bad that she became ill and was concerned that Thomas would give her less important assignments or dismiss her entirely. Hill testified that, on her last day at the EEOC, Thomas had told her "it would ruin his career" if she "ever told anyone [about] his behavior."[228]

Later that evening, a tired and visibly angry Thomas refuted Hill's allegations. Even though he admitted that he had not watched her testimony, Thomas "unequivocally, uncategorically [*sic*]" denied "each and every allegation" made by Hill. More broadly, Thomas accused the Senate Judiciary Committee of participating in "a high-tech lynching for uppity-blacks who in any way deign to think for themselves."[229] At one point, Thomas suggested that he might withdraw his nomination, but he quickly clarified that he wanted to clear his name.[230] Thomas testified again the entire next day. The ideological differences between Marshall and Thomas would have made the Senate vote close, even without Professor Hill's testimony. On October 15 Thomas was confirmed by a vote of 52–48—the closest margin of victory for a Supreme Court nominee in more than a hundred years.[231]

2. Hugo Black's Originalism: Jeffersonian

I suppose that [Thomas] Jefferson, like so many men in public life, made so many and such varied statements at different times under different circumstances that it would be possible for a number of people to feel that they followed Jefferson, even though their courses were very different.

—*Hugo Black*[1]

One cannot adequately appreciate justice Hugo Black's originalist philosophy without a clear understanding of the extent to which it was influenced by the political philosophy of Thomas Jefferson. Black did not openly describe himself as a Jeffersonian (particularly after he became a Supreme Court justice), but he did not exactly hide his commitment to Jeffersonian principles either.[2] The origins of Black's Jeffersonian faith can be traced to his boyhood in Clay County, Alabama. Most of the people who lived in Clay County were farmers, whom Jefferson described as the "chosen people of God."[3] As a young man, Black often cited Jefferson in conversations with family and friends. Virginia Durr, Black's sister-in-law, recalled that the future Supreme Court justice quoted Jefferson to her "all the time."[4] When he ran for the Senate, Black campaigned as a populist candidate and proclaimed his opposition to the consolidation of "gigantic [banks] such as our forefathers never dreamed would be."[5]

Black's Jeffersonian persuasion was most apparent during his time in the Senate. Before the start of the Seventieth Congress, he embarked on a rigorous self-education program during which he "read or reread almost all writings by Thomas Jefferson."[6] One of Senator Black's most treasured books was an original four-volume collection of Jefferson's writings published by his grandson in 1829.[7] Black referenced that collection in many Senate speeches. "None of my books do I prize more highly," Black told his Senate colleagues, "and none have been read by me with more interest and sympathy than those which contain every word that was ever uttered by that great American."[8] "In practically everything . . . [Jefferson] said," Black claimed in another speech, "I agree with him."[9] During his first years in Congress, Black argued that the Senate should end its custom of voting on presidential nominations in closed session.

"I agree with Mr. Jefferson," he told his fellow senators, "in his criticism as to holding the Constitutional Convention in secret."[10]

Black's absolutist views of the First Amendment were also foreshadowed during his time in the Senate. Responding to a bill that would have banned obscene materials from entering the country, Black questioned why lawmakers would fear the distribution of literature regarded as injurious to the morals of the people when the churches were open. He noted that, following "the philosophy of Thomas Jefferson," it was much more dangerous to allow a bureau of government to serve as a censor of the people's reading materials:

> How can those of us who claim to believe in the doctrine of American liberty, those glorious principles in which this Republic was conceived, in which it was born, through which it has come on down the years of its glorious career, say that the very books that formed the basic philosophy on which Jefferson and his friends acted shall be barred to-day at the port of entry because they dare to assert the irrevocable right of the people to their own liberty and to assert the right to that liberty whenever tyranny and oppression lay their unholy hands upon them.[11]

In a 1936 Senate speech Black expressed sympathy for Jefferson's understanding of freedom of the press. "This country believes in the principle of a free press," Black said, "and most of its people probably agree with Thomas Jefferson in the statement he made, that if he had to choose between a free government and a free press he would choose a free press, because a free press would bring about a free government."[12] In his legislative speeches, Black made effective use of populist rhetoric and described the economic crisis plaguing the country as a class struggle. "The greatest purpose of my life," Senator Black stated, and the reason he had run for the Senate, was "to bring about a nearer approach to social and economic justice."[13] In one speech, Black quoted from the partisan works of Claude G. Bowers, the author of a book on Jefferson and Alexander Hamilton.[14] Like Bowers, Black described Hamilton as the defender of the plutocrats, who believed people were "beasts" and could not be trusted. Meanwhile, Jefferson was portrayed as the defender of the common man and a supporter of popular democracy and a broad scope of liberty consistent with constitutional government. "I am opposed to any such [Hamiltonian] political philosophy," Black told his Senate colleagues. "I stand squarely upon the Jeffersonian principle that the people of the Nation are worthy to be trusted" and that "the foundation principle of this Government is that the people are fit to rule and ought to rule."[15]

In disputes over the separation of powers, Black also aligned himself with Jefferson. Revealing a Jeffersonian distrust of executive power, Black often associated executive power with greed, corruption, and corporate interests. In a debate over a reapportionment bill, Black objected that the executive branch would be tasked with generating the calculations to determine the membership in Congress. "The followers of Hamilton, the followers of that man who believed in a rule not by the people but in a rule by the privileged classes are in the saddle, booted and spurred, riding roughshod over the privileges of the people as they whittle and whittle away from their representatives and place [power] in the hands of one man."[16] Black also opposed the creation of the Federal Emergency Relief Board not because he disagreed with the aims of the law but because it empowered the executive branch to make decisions on behalf of the people. "Power! Hamiltonianism!" Black thundered from the Senate floor. "No province of Rome in the days of its greatest glory was ever made any more subject to the imperial purple in that city than the States of this Republic will be subject to bureaucratic control if this bill should become a law in its present form."[17]

Black's "aggressive" support of FDR's controversial court-packing plan also relied extensively on Jeffersonian principles. After his landslide reelection in 1936, FDR wanted to reorganize the federal judiciary by appointing one Supreme Court justice for every judge over the age of seventy. In his radio address defending the plan, FDR explained that one of the bill's purposes was to appoint judges who have "a present-day sense of the Constitution" and "who have had personal experience and contact with modern facts and circumstances."[18] In defending the reorganization plan, Senator Black drew parallels between FDR's legislative proposal and President Jefferson's support of a bill to repeal a Federalist effort to pack the courts. "Those in 1802 who opposed Mr. Jefferson's judiciary bill as being unconstitutional insisted upon delay," Black stated in one speech. "They insisted that the change should come by an amendment to the Constitution, if at all. They beg to wait until the people should again speak, although their voice had been heard in thunder tones as they repudiated the philosophy of Federalism and adopted the magnificent liberalism of Thomas Jefferson."[19] In a national radio address, Black noted that the "prevailing dominant five-judge economic and social philosophy is becoming a part of our Constitution—not by amendments approved by our people but by the decisions of lifetime judges." Citing Jefferson on three separate occasions, Black observed that an "all-powerful and omnipotent" Supreme Court was inconsistent with government by the people, and he contended that the founders "were not willing to trust lifetime judges with omnipotent powers over governmental policies."[20]

Black also relied on Jeffersonian principles in speeches delivered after his appointment to the Supreme Court. In a remarkable speech before the Southern Conference on Human Welfare, Black praised Jefferson as "a great Southerner, a great humanitarian and a great American, who always contended that just governments must organize and exercise their powers so as to secure the inalienable rights of all people to life, liberty and happiness." He then asked members of the conference to analyze current problems—including freedom of speech, property rights, education, religious freedom, and human welfare—from a Jeffersonian perspective.[21] During the height of the Red Scare, Black delivered the commencement address at Swarthmore College, where his daughter Jo-Jo was graduating. "We desperately need today a new Jefferson," Black told the graduates, "and a new baptism in his sane and sound faith in complete freedom to think, speak, and write."[22]

Most importantly, Justice Black relied on Jeffersonian principles in his judicial opinions, especially in the area of freedom of speech. One of Black's favorite quotes from Jefferson came from his first inaugural address: "If there be any among us who would wish to dissolve this Union or to change its republican form, let them stand undisturbed as monuments of the safety with which error of opinion may be tolerated where reason is left free to combat it."[23] Black's admiration for Jefferson was not limited to free speech issues, however. His opinions on freedom of the press, church-state matters, and religious freedom were also influenced by the Sage from Monticello. In addition, his opinions in cases involving the separation of powers revealed a Jeffersonian distrust of executive power. Finally, Black's interpretations of the incorporation doctrine, the rights of the accused (particularly the Fifth and Sixth Amendments), property rights, civil rights ("all men are created equal"), and reapportionment ("one person, one vote") can all be regarded as consistent with a Jeffersonian philosophy. In correspondence with Joseph Wershba, who wrote an op-ed piece commemorating Justice Black's twenty-fifth anniversary on the Supreme Court, Black responded: "You were . . . right in indicating my admiration for Thomas Jefferson and his philosophy which came into my life long before I became an Associate Justice and even long before I was a

Senator."[24] As his former law clerk Daniel Meador pointed out, "Few persons, if any, in the twentieth century have been more devoted to Jefferson's credo than Black. To him, Jefferson's views on freedom of speech and religion had a powerful appeal. So completely did he embrace these and other ideas of Jefferson that at the age of 84 he was called 'an unreconstructed Jeffersonian.'"[25] This chapter examines Black's originalist philosophy in the areas of the First Amendment, separation of powers, federalism, rights of the accused, property rights, due process, and equal protection.

FIRST AMENDMENT

One area in which Justice Black consistently cited Thomas Jefferson was the First Amendment. Even though some have questioned Jefferson's own commitment to freedom of speech and the press,[26] Black was an absolutist in interpreting the First Amendment and often credited his views to Jefferson.[27] In his Carpentier lectures at Columbia University, Black described his absolutist position with typical dramatic flair:

> My view is, without deviation, without exception, without any ifs, buts, or whereases, that freedom of speech means that government shall not do anything to people, or, in the words of the Magna Carta, move against people, either for the views they have or the views they express or the words they speak or write. Some people would have you believe that this is a very radical position, and maybe it is. But all I am doing is following what to me is the clear wording of the First Amendment that "Congress shall make no law . . . abridging the freedom of speech or of the press."[28]

Like Jefferson, Black believed that the First Amendment was "the foundation" of the US Constitution and an essential bulwark to democracy.[29] During his long tenure on the Supreme Court, Black consistently argued that the government could not outlaw any political organization or idea simply because it was regarded as unpopular, offensive, or revolutionary. If ideas turned into action, then (and only then!) could government take action to regulate the behavior. "I believe with Jefferson," Black stated in a 1962 interview, "that it is time enough for government to step in to regulate people when they *do* something, not when they *say* something, and I do not believe myself that there is *any* halfway ground if you enforce the protections of the First Amendment."[30]

During the Red Scare, the federal government criminalized advocacy of communism as well as membership in the Communist Party. It also required loyalty oaths by government employees and investigated communist associations, both inside and outside of government. Black consistently dissented in all these cases.[31] Borrowing from Justice Holmes's "marketplace of ideas" conception of the First Amendment, Black maintained that the guarantees of the First Amendment "must be accorded to the ideas we hate or sooner or later they will be denied to the ideas we cherish."[32] Like Holmes, Black acknowledged that if communism is able to command majority support in the United States, it has a right to prevail.[33] However, Justice Black was confident that would not happen. "I would . . . leave the Communists free to advocate their beliefs in proletarian dictatorship publicly and openly among the people of this country with full confidence that the people will remain loyal to any democratic Government truly dedicated to freedom and justice—the kind of Government which some of us still think of as being 'the last best hope of earth.'"[34]

Obscenity

Justice Black's absolutist interpretation of the First Amendment did not allow any exception for obscenity. In the late 1960s and early 1970s the justices occasionally watched movies at the Supreme Court building to determine whether they were "obscene." In one famous memo, Black informed his colleagues that he would "not be attending the showings of 'I, a Woman' and 'I Am Curious (Yellow).'"[35] Black explained that viewing the films would not change his opinion that barring the showing of those movies would violate the First Amendment. "Sex is a fact of life," Black wrote in one case:

> Its pervasive influence is felt throughout the world and it cannot be ignored. Like all other facts of life it can lead to difficulty and trouble and sorrow and pain. But while it may lead to abuses, and has in many instances, no words need be spoken in order for people to know that the subject is one pleasantly interwoven in all human activities and involves the very substance of the creation of life itself.[36]

Black also raised concerns about the judicial role in defining obscenity. "There are grave doubts in my mind," he wrote in a 1959 case, "as to the desirability or constitutionality of this Court's becoming a Supreme Board of Censors—reading books and viewing television performances to determine whether, if permitted, they might adversely affect the morals of the people throughout the many diversified local communities in this vast country." "Censorship," he added, "is a deadly enemy of freedom and progress. The plain language of the Constitution forbids it. I protest against the Judiciary giving it a foothold here."[37]

Freedom of the Press

Like Jefferson, Black was a staunch proponent of freedom of the press. The press performs essential functions in a republican form of government. It educates the citizenry on important issues of the day and serves as a check on elected officials.[38] One of Justice Black's early opinions on this issue came in *Bridges v. California* (1941).[39] In two consolidated cases, a newspaper and a labor leader were convicted of and fined for contempt of court because they had criticized judges' handling of pending cases. The Supreme Court was so divided on these cases that they had to be reargued. Justice Black eventually wrote the opinion and rejected the common-law doctrine that allowed a person to be punished for commenting on a pending case *outside* the courtroom. In contrast to Justice Frankfurter, who argued that the First Amendment (like all other guarantees of the Bill of Rights) was an inheritance from England, Black maintained that "the First Amendment was something very new and distinctly American."[40] Even though Black relied on the clear and present danger test, his future absolutist position was noticeable in *Bridges.* "The only conclusion supported by history," wrote Black, "is that the unqualified prohibitions laid down by the framers were intended to give to liberty of the press, as to other liberties, the broadest scope that could be countenanced in an orderly society."[41]

Another one of Black's significant free press opinions came in the Pentagon Papers Case—fittingly, his last as a Supreme Court justice. In *New York Times v. United States* (1971),[42] the Nixon administration requested federal court injunctions to prevent the *New York Times* and *Washington Post* from publishing excerpts of a forty-seven-volume "classified" study of the Vietnam War. The administration contended that publication of the documents would jeopardize national security and violated the Espionage Act of 1917. The *New York Times* appealed a temporary injunction by the Second Circuit, and the government appealed a decision by the DC Court of Appeals rejecting a similar request for an injunction. However, that court granted a stay of its order pending appeal.

Acting on an expedited basis, the Supreme Court granted certiorari on June 25, 1971, heard oral arguments the next day (a Saturday), and delivered its opinion four days later on June 30. In a 6–3 per curiam opinion, the Supreme Court held that the government's request for injunctions constituted a prior restraint in violation of the First Amendment. Justice Black wrote a concurring opinion in which he took issue with some of his colleagues who were "willing to hold that the publication of news may sometimes be enjoined." "The history and language of the First Amendment," wrote Black, "support the view that the press must be left free to publish news, whatever the source, without censorship, injunctions, or prior restraints."[43] Underscoring what he regarded as *the* essential function of the First Amendment, Black maintained that "the press was to serve the governed, not the governors." "Only a free and unrestrained press," he added, "can effectively expose deception in government. And paramount among the responsibilities of a free press is the duty to prevent any part of the government from deceiving the people and sending them off to distant lands to die of foreign fevers and foreign shot and shell."[44] After the decision was announced, Black's wife, Elizabeth, remarked: "Honey, if this is your swan song it's a good one."[45]

Libel

Justice Black's absolutist approach to the First Amendment also led him to conclude that citizens and the institutional press are completely immune from libel actions if they write about matters of public concern. For support of this view, he relied on Thomas Jefferson, who argued in the Kentucky Resolutions (1798) that the purpose of the First Amendment is to protect "in the same sentence, and under the same words, the freedom of religion, of speech, and of the press: insomuch, that whatever violates either, throws down the sanctuary which covers the others, and that libels, falsehood, and defamation, equally with heresy and false religion, are withheld from the cognizance of federal tribunals."[46] On this basis, Black was a sharp critic of criminal libel and regarded the Alien and Sedition Act of 1798 as one of the worst violations of freedom of speech in US history.[47] He also believed that neither individual citizens nor the press could be civilly punished for criticizing their elected officials. In *New*

York Times v. Sullivan (1964),[48] the Supreme Court required public officials to show "actual malice" before they could win awards for civil damages. Justice Black concurred in *Sullivan*, but he did not believe the court went far enough. The "actual malice" test, Black wrote, is "an elusive, abstract concept, hard to prove and hard to disprove." In contrast to the majority, Black said that "the *Times* and individual defendants had an absolute, unconditional constitutional right to publish in the *Times* advertisement their criticisms of the Montgomery agencies and officials."[49] In subsequent cases, Black continued to criticize *Sullivan* and argued that it should be abandoned altogether. "These cases illustrate," Black wrote in two consolidated cases handed down in 1967, "the accuracy of my prior predictions that the *New York Times* constitutional rule concerning libel is wholly inadequate to save the press from being destroyed by libel judgments."[50] In another case, Black argued that absolute immunity should extend to suits brought by private individuals if the subject is a matter of public concern.[51]

Church-State

In interpreting the establishment clause, Justice Black embraced Jefferson's "high wall" theory of church-state relations. In his famous letter to the Danbury Baptist Association, then-president Jefferson wrote:

> Believing with you that religion is a matter which lies solely between Man & his God, that he owes account to none other for his faith or his worship, that the legitimate powers of government reach actions only, & not opinions, I contemplate with sovereign reverence that act of the whole American people which declared that *their* legislature should "make no law respecting an establishment of religion, or prohibiting the free exercise thereof," thus building a wall of separation between Church & State.[52]

In *Everson v. Board of Education of the Township of Ewing* (1947),[53] the Supreme Court constitutionalized Jefferson's interpretation of the First Amendment. "In the words of Jefferson," Black wrote for the court, the establishment clause "was intended to erect 'a wall of separation between church and State.'"[54] Ironically, Black supported the bus-fare reimbursement program at issue in *Everson*,[55] but he defended a strict neutralist perspective during the remainder of his tenure. The establishment clause, Black reasoned, "requires the state to be neutral in its relations with groups of religious believers and non-believers."[56] "Neither a state nor the Federal Government can set up a church," he wrote. "Neither can pass laws which aid one religion, aid all religions, or prefer one religion over another."[57]

Black also wrote the Supreme Court's decision in *Engel v. Vitale* (1962),[58] which struck down state-sponsored, nondenominational prayers in public schools. Reflecting his strict separationist views, Black wrote that "the constitutional prohibition against laws respecting an establishment of religion must at the least mean that in this country it is no part of the business of government to compose official prayers for any group of the American people to recite as a part of a religious program carried on by government."[59] One year later, Black joined the Supreme Court's decision banning the reading of ten Bible verses in public schools.[60] Black then subsequently joined the court's decision in *Lemon v. Kurtzman* (1971),[61] which established the three-pronged test used to determine whether the establishment clause has been violated.[62]

Religious Freedom

In terms of the free exercise clause, Justice Black (like Jefferson) believed religious freedom was a personal choice and he opposed any form of government compulsion on the subject.[63] No government, Black wrote in *Everson*, "can force nor influence a person to go to or to remain away from church against his will or force him to profess a belief or disbelief in any religion."[64] For this reason, Black's vote in *Minersville School District v. Gobitis* (1940) must be regarded as an anomaly.[65] In that case, the Supreme Court upheld compulsory flag salutes in public schools, which were being challenged by two Jehovah's Witnesses who had been expelled from school for not participating in the daily practice. Somewhat surprisingly, Justice Black joined the 8–1 decision but soon expressed regrets. In *Jones v. City of Opelika* (1942),[66] decided just two years later, Black explained why he thought *Gobitis* had been "wrongly decided." "The First Amendment," he wrote, "does not put the right freely to exercise religion in a subordinate position. We fear, however, that the opinions in these and in the *Gobitis* case do exactly that."[67] Then, in *West Virginia State Board of Education v. Barnette* (1943),[68] Black joined the court's decision overturning *Gobitis*. In an opinion written by Justice Jackson, the court based its decision on freedom of speech (or, in this case, the freedom not to speak). Justice Black, by contrast, rested his concurrence on religious freedom. "Neither our domestic tranquility in peace nor our martial effort in war," wrote Black, "depend on compelling little children to participate in a ceremony which ends in nothing for them but fear of spiritual condemnation."[69]

During his tenure, Justice Black joined the Supreme Court's opinion applying the free exercise clause to the states.[70] He wrote the opinion overturning Maryland's religious oath test for public office.[71] Black also joined the court's decision in *Sherbert v. Verner* (1963),[72] where it applied strict scrutiny (for the first time) in a case involving a Seventh-Day Adventist who had been denied unemployment compensation because she refused to work on her Sabbath. In other cases, Black was exceedingly deferential when it came to the question of what constitutes "religion." For example, in *United States v. Ballard* (1944),[73] Black joined the court's decision that the truth of religious doctrines or beliefs cannot be submitted to a jury. That case involved criminal charges against representatives of the "I Am" movement who had been charged with procuring money through the mail by claiming supernatural powers to cure illnesses. Black also wrote the majority decision in *Welsh v. United States* (1970),[74] which provided a broad interpretation of the "conscientious objector" exemption under the Universal Military Training and Service Act. Even though Congress explicitly excluded "essentially political, sociological, or philosophical views" and "merely personal codes" from the exemption, Black's reading of the statute covered "all those whose consciences, spurred by deeply held moral, ethical, or religious beliefs, would give them no rest or peace if they allowed themselves to become a part of an instrument of war."[75]

SEPARATION OF POWERS

In traditional disputes over the separation of powers, Justice Black was a strong defender of the prerogatives of Congress. During his time in the Senate, Black told his colleagues that the framers "attempted to place checks" on the president and "make the legislative branch of Government the dominant, superior power because it was filled by representatives fresh from the masses of the people of the country."[76] He also worried that public sentiment was moving in the direction of "the Hamiltonian pathway of concentration until it seems that the old idea of the fathers of this country has been completely abandoned."[77]

As the author of the controversial decision in *Korematsu v. United States* (1944),[78] which upheld President Roosevelt's executive order authorizing the use of internment camps for Japanese Americans during World War II, Black could be mistaken as a proponent of executive power, but that was not the case. *Korematsu* was the exception to the rule. In interpreting Article II, Justice Black narrowly construed the powers of the executive branch and did not regard the president as having any sort of implied or inherent powers. Black's opinion in *Youngstown Sheet & Tube Co. v. Sawyer* (1952)[79]—known as the Steel Seizure Case—is more representative of his interpretation of the powers of the executive branch. In that case, the Supreme Court rejected President Truman's claim of inherent authority to seize the steel industries during a national emergency. Black narrowly construed the president's lawmaking authority to that of "recommending . . . laws he thinks wise and the vetoing of laws he thinks bad."[80] He also rejected the executive branch's claims of inherent authority under the vesting clause, the take-care clause, or the commander in chief provision of Article II. Interestingly, Justice Black thought Congress had the authority to seize the steel industries if it wanted to, but he did not believe the executive branch did. "This is a job of the Nation's lawmakers," Black wrote, "not for its military authorities."[81]

Consistent with his opinion in *Youngstown*, Black embraced a narrow construction of executive power in other cases. For example, in *Duncan v. Kahanamoku* (1946),[82] he wrote the decision restricting the use of military tribunals for civilians during martial law in Hawaii. As discussed in chapter 5, Black also dissented in a case in which the Supreme Court denied habeas corpus relief to foreign enemy combatants tried by military tribunals during World War II.[83] In *Zemel v. Rusk* (1965),[84] the Supreme Court upheld the authority granted to the secretary of state under the Passport Act of 1926 to deny passports to those traveling to Cuba. Chief Justice Warren held for the 6–3 court that the State Department had previously restricted travel to specified areas of the world for national security reasons, and it now regarded travel to Cuba as a security threat because "Cuba is the only area in the Western Hemisphere controlled by a Communist government."[85] Justice Black filed a vigorous dissent. He acknowledged that Congress had ample power to enact legislation regulating the issuance and use of passports for travel abroad.[86] However, he argued that the president is "completely devoid" of such lawmaking authority and "has no more power to make laws by labelling them regulations than to do so by calling them laws."[87] Black also rejected the government's argument that the president has "inherent" power to make regulations governing the issuance and use of passports. Drawing on his opinion from *Youngstown*, Black argued that "regulation of passports, just like regulation of steel companies, is lawmaking—not an executive, law-enforcing—function."[88]

FEDERALISM

One of the challenges in making the case that Hugo Black was a consistent follower of Jefferson's political philosophy comes in the area of federalism. Although there are important exceptions,[89] Black's jurisprudence was not generally known as supportive of states' rights.[90] In addition to his total incorporation theory of the Bill of Rights (discussed in the next section), Black interpreted Congress's commerce authority as "a police power,"[91] which, interestingly, he defended on both Hamiltonian *and* Jeffersonian grounds.[92] In lockstep with the liberal progressives of his time, Black did not believe the states were capable of resolving the economic calamity caused by the Great Depression, and he supported Hamiltonian means to accomplish Jeffersonian purposes.[93] Black's broad interpretation of the commerce clause was demonstrated throughout his long public career. As a US senator, he supported his thirty-hour workweek bill by arguing that the nation's unemployment rate (25 percent) had a substantial effect on the economy. "Who can say," Black asked his Senate colleagues, "with 12,000,000 men unemployed in America, with commerce between the States practically stopped, that the lack of purchasing power on the part of those people is wholly disconnected with interstate commerce?" "It would certainly be strange and unusual," he added, "to say that the Congress of the United States can protect the people from a conspiracy to fix the prices of goods, but at the same time cannot protect them from conditions which are bringing death, starvation, misery, and destruction, all over the land."[94]

Appointed to the Supreme Court shortly after the so-called constitutional revolution of 1937, Black joined his colleagues in granting more deference to Congress over social and economic matters. In *United States v. Darby Lumber Co.* (1941),[95] a unanimous Supreme Court upheld the Fair Labor Standards Act of 1938, which established minimum wages and maximum hours in the workplace. According to Justice Stone, author of the court's opinion, the Tenth Amendment does not limit federal power because it "states but a truism that all is retained which has not been surrendered."[96] In *Wickard v. Filburn* (1942),[97] the court unanimously sustained a national quota on wheat production under the Agricultural Adjustment Act of 1938.

Two years later, Justice Black authored the decision in *United States v. South-Eastern Underwriters Association* (1944),[98] which extended the scope of the Sherman Act to cover the insurance industry. "Our basic responsibility in interpreting the Commerce Clause," wrote Black, "is to make certain that the power to govern intercourse among the states remains where the Constitution placed it." "That power," he added, "as held by this Court from the beginning, is vested in the Congress, available to be exercised for the national welfare as Congress shall deem necessary."[99] Finally, Justice Black joined the two consolidated decisions handed down in 1964 that upheld Title II of the Civil Rights Act of 1964 based on a broad construction of the commerce clause.[100]

INCORPORATION

One of Justice Black's most important legacies was the position he took regarding the incorporation doctrine. After conducting extensive research on the debates of the Thirty-Ninth Congress, Black concluded that *all* the guarantees of the Bill of Rights, without exception, were intended to apply against state power. He first made this argument in a dissenting opinion in *Adamson v. California* (1947).[101] In that case, Admiral Adamson had been sentenced to death for murdering an elderly woman, but the prosecutor had commented on his failure to take the stand. The majority, taking a selective incorporation approach, declined to apply the self-incrimination clause to the states. Justice Black filed a vigorous dissent. "One of the chief objects," Black wrote, "that the provisions of the [Fourteenth] Amendment's first section, separately, and as a whole, were intended to accomplish was to make the Bill of Rights, applicable to the states."[102] Black relied on representative John Bingham (R-OH), whom he called the "[James] Madison of the first section of the Fourteenth Amendment."[103] He also included an appendix to his opinion, which contained several excerpts from the debates of the Thirty-Ninth Congress. Black said he could support the selective incorporation process as a second-best option, but he thought it gave judges too much discretion in deciding which rights are fundamental and which are not. For him, judges lacked such broad authority to either limit or expand rights protected by the Constitution. Even though the Supreme Court has never accepted Black's total incorporation theory, it has moved substantially in that direction over time.[104]

FOURTH AMENDMENT

Justice Black's interpretation of the Fourth Amendment was not particularly robust, primarily because he did not believe it contained the same absolutist language as other provisions of the Bill of Rights.[105] In general, Black did not believe the Fourth Amendment required that every search be made pursuant to a warrant.[106] "The majority rejects the test of reasonableness provided by the Fourth Amendment," Black wrote in *Coolidge v. New Hampshire* (1971), "and substitutes a *per se* rule—if the police could have obtained a warrant and did not, the seizure, no matter how reasonable, is void."[107] Black regarded this as an inaccurate interpretation of the Fourth Amendment, which speaks of "unreasonable searches and seizures." "The relevant test," he argued, "is not the reasonableness of the opportunity to procure a warrant, but the reasonableness of the seizure under all the circumstances."[108]

During his time on the Supreme Court, Black was exceedingly deferential to law enforcement in Fourth Amendment cases. For example, in *Chimel v. California* (1969),[109] the court heard a case examining the scope of the "search incident to arrest" exception to the Fourth Amendment. Ted Chimel was arrested at his home for burglary of a coin shop, and although the three police officers had an arrest warrant, they did not have a search warrant.[110] Without Chimel's consent, the officers searched "the entire three-bedroom house, including the attic, the garage, and a small workshop."[111] In a 6–2 decision, the Supreme Court ruled that the full-blown search of Chimel's house violated his Fourth Amendment rights because the search was not confined to the area "within the immediate control" of the defendant. Justice Black joined Justice White's dissent, which relied on earlier cases holding that a warrantless search "incident to a lawful arrest" may extend to those areas under the "possession" or "control" of the defendant where unlawful evidence could be found. Because the officers had probable cause to believe that there was evidence of the crime in Chimel's home, White reasoned that the court should "follow past cases and permit such a search to be carried out without a warrant, since the fact of arrest supplies an exigent circumstance justifying police action before the evidence can be removed."[112] Black's vote in *Chimel* was consistent with earlier decisions he had supported (now overturned by *Chimel*) that permitted broad searches of apartments and businesses based on the search-incident-to-arrest exception.[113]

Another illustration of Black's deferential approach in Fourth Amendment cases was his dissenting opinion in *Coolidge v. New Hampshire.*[114] In that case, the defendant was sentenced to life in prison for the murder of a fourteen-year-old girl. When he was arrested, the police seized his 1951 Pontiac, which was parked outside in the driveway. Two days later, the police searched and vacuumed the vehicle, which revealed particles of gunpowder. The Supreme Court ruled that the warrant to search the car was defective because it had been signed by the state's attorney general, rather than by a neutral and detached magistrate. The court also considered whether one of the exceptions to the Fourth Amendment should apply. In an opinion by Justice Stewart, the court held that neither the "search incident to arrest" exception, the "automobile" exception, nor the "plain view" doctrine justified a search of the vehicle two days after the defendant's arrest. Justice Black disagreed. He argued that the search warrant was not defective merely because it had been signed by the attorney general, given that the police had provided sufficient evidence to demonstrate probable cause to issue the warrant. Black also argued that the car could be seized as a search incident to arrest, under either the automobile exception or the plain-view doctrine, because "there was probable cause to believe that the car had been used in the commission of the murder and that it contained evidence of the crime."[115]

Justice Black also had a fairly loose interpretation of what constituted "probable cause." In *Terry v. Ohio* (1968),[116] the Supreme Court ruled that a "stop-and-frisk" based only on "reasonable suspicion" was permissible under the Fourth Amendment. In that case, a police officer stopped and frisked three individuals he believed were casing a store for a future robbery. In his initial draft of the decision, Chief Justice Warren reasoned that probable cause was necessary to conduct a stop, but his analysis changed substantially after receiving an extensive memo from Justice Brennan.[117] In his final opinion, Warren disclaimed reliance on the warrant clause and instead relied on the reasonableness clause, presumably because most of the justices ultimately concluded that probable cause was lacking in the case. "When an officer is justified in believing that the individual whose suspicious behavior he is investigating at close range is armed and presently dangerous to the officer or to others," wrote Warren, "it would appear to be clearly unreasonable to deny the officer the power to take necessary measures to determine whether the person is in fact carrying a weapon and to neutralize the threat of physical harm."[118]

In stark contrast to his colleagues, Justice Black never wavered from his initial view that probable cause *was* present in the *Terry* case. In his draft concurrence, which he later withdrew, Black agreed "with the Court that under the circumstances here the policeman had probable cause to believe that the men were armed, and that [Officer McFadden] did not violate the Fourth Amendment by making the limited search of the men." "I heartily agree," he wrote, "with the Court's refusal . . . to substitute the words 'reasonable suspicion' for the words 'probable cause' or to add the words 'reasonable suspicion' to the words the Framers used." "There is," he added, "no reason to use the 'reasonable suspicion' term unless it means something more or something less than probable cause; if it does it would change the meaning the Framers wrote into the Amendment, thereby making a constitutional change courts are not vested with power to make."[119]

Even though Black withdrew his draft concurrence and joined Warren's majority opinion, there is additional evidence that he continued to believe that probable cause was present in *Terry*. On the same day the court decided *Terry*, the justices handed down two companion "stop and frisk" cases from the state of New York. In *Peters v. New York* (1968),[120] the justices unanimously agreed that probable cause was present, so the court affirmed the conviction of the lower court. There was disagreement among the justices, however, in *Sibron v. New York* (1968).[121] On March 9, 1965, a New York police officer watched Sibron from 4:00 p.m. to midnight, during which time he had conversations with multiple known drug addicts. Suspecting that Sibron was in possession of drugs, the officer approached him. When Sibron mumbled something and reached inside his left jacket pocket, the officer simultaneously reached into the same pocket and pulled out heroin. The Supreme Court (8–1) overturned Sibron's conviction on the grounds that although the police officer had reasonable suspicion to stop Sibron, it was unreasonable for the officer to reach into his jacket. In contrast to *Terry*, the court concluded that the same level of danger was lacking here.

Justice Black disagreed. He was the only justice to affirm the conviction based on the grounds that probable cause existed. Even though the court clearly relied on reasonable suspicion in *Terry*, Black characterized that decision in the following manner:

> The Court had decided today in *Terry v. Ohio* and in No. 74 *Peters v. New York*, that a policeman does not violate the Fourth Amendment when he makes a limited search for weapons on the person of a man who the policeman has *probable cause* to believe has a dangerous weapon on him with which he might

> injure the policeman or others or both, unless he is searched and the weapon is taken away from him.[122]

Black then went on to explain why he thought probable cause was present in *Sibron.* "I think there was probable cause for the policeman to believe that when Sibron reached his hand to his coat pocket, Sibron had a dangerous weapon which he might use if it were not taken away from him."[123] Underscoring his deferential approach in Fourth Amendment cases, Black concluded his solo dissent by writing, "It is not only wise but imperative that where findings of facts of reasonableness and probable cause are involved in such state cases, we should not overturn state court findings unless in the most extravagant and egregious errors. It seems fantastic to me even to suggest that this is such a case."[124]

Electronic Eavesdropping

Justice Black also embraced a literal interpretation of what objects are protected by the Fourth Amendment. In several cases Black dissented when the Supreme Court held that electronic eavesdropping is covered by the Fourth Amendment.[125] In *Katz v. United States* (1967),[126] the court ruled that a wiretap placed on a public telephone booth violated a reasonable expectation of privacy under the Fourth Amendment. Black dissented alone. He argued that because the Fourth Amendment protects only material things—"persons, houses, papers, and effects"—electronic eavesdropping falls outside its scope. "A conversation overheard by eavesdropping," wrote Black, "whether by plain snooping or wiretapping, is not tangible, and under the normally accepted meaning of the words, can neither be searched nor seized."[127] Accordingly, Black would not support what he regarded as "language stretching" by the court. If the framers wanted to ban eavesdropping, he maintained, they could have done so. "I will not distort the words of the Amendment in order to 'keep the Constitution up to date' or 'to bring it into harmony with the times,'" he reasoned. "It was never meant that this Court have such power, which in effect would make us a continuously functioning constitutional convention."[128]

Exclusionary Rule

The exclusionary rule was another area of Fourth Amendment law that Justice Black struggled with. The exclusionary rule prohibits the use of unlawfully obtained evidence during the prosecution's case-in-chief. In *Wolf v. Colorado* (1949),[129] the Supreme Court declined to apply the exclusionary rule to state prosecutions because it was regarded as "a matter of judicial implication." Justice Black concurred. He argued that "the federal exclusionary rule is not a command of the Fourth Amendment but is a judicially created rule of evidence which Congress might negate."[130] Black later changed his mind. In *Mapp v. Ohio* (1961),[131] the Supreme Court ruled that the exclusionary rule must be followed in all state prosecutions. Black wrote separately to explain why he now believed the exclusionary rule was required under the Constitution. The Fourth Amendment alone, he argued, did not support the exclusionary rule, but, "considered together with the Fifth Amendment's ban against compelled self-incrimination, a constitutional basis emerges which not only justifies but actually requires the exclusionary rule."[132]

Nevertheless, Black's skepticism about the exclusionary rule continued. In *Bumper v. North Carolina* (1968),[133] the Supreme Court reversed a conviction, finding that a search was illegal because the police had falsely claimed they had a search warrant. "When a law enforcement officer claims authority to search a home under a warrant," Justice Stewart wrote for the court, "he announces in effect that the occupant has no right to resist the search."[134] Black dissented. Describing the brutal nature of the crime (two counts of rape and two counts of attempted murder), Black wrote: "I think it is a fair assumption that refusal to reverse a conviction of a defendant, because of the admission of illegally seized evidence, where other evidence conclusively demonstrates his guilt, is not going to lessen police sensitivity to the exclusionary rule, thereby reducing its deterrent effect."[135] Moreover, in *Coolidge*, decided three years later, Black repeated his view that the language of the Fourth Amendment by itself does not support the exclusionary rule. Instead, Black claimed that the Fifth Amendment contains its own exclusionary rule and that, because there was no act of compulsion in this case, the exclusionary rule should not apply.[136]

FIFTH AMENDMENT

With the possible exception of William O. Douglas, no one in Supreme Court history has defended a broader interpretation of the self-incrimination clause than Hugo Black. Since his days as a prosecutor for Jefferson County, Black was a skeptic of "voluntary" confessions. The grand jury investigation he conducted of police brutality in the small town of Bessemer revealed that law enforcement regularly used torture to garner confessions from prisoners. As a Supreme Court justice, Black wrote several important opinions involving coerced confessions, which laid the groundwork for the court's decision in *Miranda v. Arizona* (1966).[137] In *Chambers v. Florida* (1940),[138] he authored the opinion finding that the interrogation of four black teenagers violated the due process clause of the Fourteenth Amendment. In that case, Robert Darsey, an elderly white man, had been robbed and murdered in Pompano, Florida. The police rounded up forty African American men without arrest warrants and interrogated them over the course of six days. On the seventh day, the officers concentrated on Chambers and three other defendants, and each of them confessed after an all-night session of interrogation, earning the name "sunrise confessions." "Tyrannical governments," Black wrote for the Supreme Court, "had immemorially utilized dictatorial criminal procedure and punishment to make scapegoats of the weak, or of helpless political, religious, or racial minorities and those who differed, who would not conform and who resisted tyranny."[139] *Chambers* marked the first time the court found that a compelled confession was based on duress rather than physical torture.

Four years later, Black wrote the court's decision in *Ashcraft v. Tennessee* (1944).[140] In that case, the defendant was charged with hiring a man to kill his wife, and his confession came after thirty-six continuous hours of interrogation under high-powered lights at the Shelby County jail. For a 6–3 court, Black held that the confession was not voluntary. "It is inconceivable that any court of justice in the land," wrote Black, "conducted as our courts are, open to the public, would permit prosecutors serving in relays to keep a defendant witness under continuous cross-examination for thirty-six hours without rest or sleep in an effort to extract a 'voluntary' confession."[141]

Two decades later, Black joined the Warren Court's decision in *Escobedo v. Illinois* (1964),[142] which held that denying the right to counsel during an interrogation violated the Sixth Amendment. He then joined the court's 1966 decision in *Miranda*, which held that police officers must provide specific warnings to suspects when they are in custody and being interrogated. Black also wrote the decision three years later that expanded the *Miranda* ruling to in-home interrogations.[143] Black's expansive interpretation of the Fifth Amendment did not always garner the support of a majority of his colleagues. In one dissenting opinion, Black maintained that the Fifth Amendment should apply to the forced extraction of physical evidence, such as fingerprints or blood samples.[144] Black also joined a dissenting opinion by Justice Douglas that argued the government could not grant immunity to obtain confessions.[145]

SIXTH AMENDMENT

Reflecting his long-held desire to help the "little guy," Justice Black also wrote many significant right-to-counsel decisions. During his first term on the Supreme Court, Black wrote the 6–2 decision in *Johnson v. Zerbst* (1938),[146] which held that an attorney must be provided in *all* federal criminal cases, not just capital cases. "The purpose of the constitutional guaranty of a right to counsel," Black wrote, "is to protect an accused from conviction resulting from his own ignorance of his legal and constitutional rights, and the guaranty would be nullified by a determination that an accused's ignorant failure to claim his rights removes the protection of the Constitution."[147] However, four years later, in *Betts v. Brady* (1942),[148] the court ruled that the Sixth Amendment's right-to-counsel provision was not fundamental and that the states had to provide an attorney only in "special circumstances." Black filed a vigorous dissent. The majority's decision, wrote Black, could not "be reconciled with 'common and fundamental ideas of fairness and right,'" and it "subjects innocent men to increased dangers of conviction merely because of their poverty."[149] Black's view that counsel must be provided to the poor in state criminal prosecutions ultimately prevailed. In *Gideon v. Wainwright* (1963),[150] the court ruled that the right to counsel was indeed a fundamental right, and that an attorney had to be provided to those who could not afford one in state prosecutions. "Reason and reflection," Black wrote for the court, "require us to recognize that in our adversary system of criminal justice, any person hauled into court, who is too poor to hire a lawyer, cannot be assured a fair trial unless counsel is provided for him."[151] On the same day, Justice Black joined Justice Douglas's decision holding that counsel must be provided to a defendant on a first appeal as a matter of right.[152]

Remarkably, Justice Black's sense of equal justice under the law led him to conclude that individuals must have the assistance of counsel in all *civil* cases if they could not afford it. After initially dissenting in *Boddie v. Connecticut* (1971),[153] in which the court ruled that the state had to pay the filing costs in divorce proceedings for the poor, Black argued in a subsequent case that both court filing fees *and* attorney expenses must be borne by the state in all civil cases. The Supreme Court denied certiorari in *Meltzer v. C. Buck LeCraw & Co.* (1971),[154] which challenged court fees in various types of civil cases based on the equal protection clause. Justice Black filed a passionate dissent from denial of certiorari. "In my view," he wrote, "the decision in *Boddie v. Connecticut* can safely rest on only one crucial foundation—that the civil courts of the United States and each of the States belong to the people of this country and that no person can be denied access to those courts, either for a trial or an appeal, because he cannot pay a fee, finance a bond, risk a penalty, or afford to hire an attorney." He added:

> Some may sincerely believe that the decision in *Boddie* was far more limited in scope—that is, applies only to divorce cases. Other people might recognize that this constitutional decision will eventually extend to all civil cases but believe that it can only be enforced slowly step by step, so that the country will have time to absorb its full import. But in my judgment *Boddie* cannot and should not be limited to either its facts or its language, and I believe there can be no doubt that this country can afford to provide court costs and lawyers to Americans who are now barred by their poverty from resort to the law for resolution of their disputes.[155]

EIGHTH AMENDMENT

Not unlike his view of the Fourth Amendment, Justice Black thought the Eighth Amendment was lacking in precision. Thus, he was willing to leave the question of what constitutes "cruel and unusual punishments" largely to the democratic process. Nor did he question the constitutionality of the death penalty. When he was the prosecutor for Jefferson County, Black obtained death sentences on ten separate occasions, two of them for armed robbery.[156] He also consistently supported the death penalty as a Supreme Court justice. In *Boykin v. Alabama* (1969),[157] the defendant pleaded guilty to five indictments charging common-law robbery, which, at the time, was punishable by death in Alabama. After a brief trial, a jury sentenced him to death on all five counts. On appeal, Boykin challenged the constitutionality of his punishment on two grounds: (1) the death penalty should not be allowed for common-law robbery, and (2) jurors had too much discretion in imposing death sentences. The Supreme Court, however, reversed his sentence on different grounds. In an opinion by Justice Douglas, the court overturned the lower court because the arraigning judge did not establish an "adequate record" to substantiate that Boykin's guilty plea was voluntary.

Justice Harlan, joined by Justice Black, dissented. Harlan wrote that he could not "subscribe to so bizarre a result" because the defendant himself never claimed that his guilty plea was involuntary. Justice Black wanted to go further. In a memo to Harlan written five days before the case was handed down, Black requested that the following paragraph be added to his colleague's dissent: "Mr. Justice Black concurs in this dissent except for what is said in Note 3. As for the contentions that imposition of the death penalty for common-law robbery is cruel and unusual punishment in violation of the Fourteenth Amendment and that to permit a jury to inflict the death penalty without any standards denies due process, he would reject them on the ground that they are frivolous."[158] Harlan was able to convince Black not to include that paragraph in the final draft of his dissent.

During the 1970–1971 term—which was Justice Black's last—he had an opportunity to write an opinion on whether the death penalty violated the Eighth Amendment. The Supreme Court was considering two state statutes that allowed sentencing juries unlimited discretion in determining the appropriateness of the death penalty. In *McGautha v. California* (1971),[159] the court ruled that such discretion did not run afoul of the Fourteenth Amendment's due process clause—a decision that would be reversed one year later in *Furman v. Georgia* (1972).[160] Black filed a concurring opinion and, unlike his colleagues, considered the Eighth Amendment issue. The "cruel and unusual" provision of the Eighth Amendment, Black reasoned, "cannot be read to outlaw capital punishment because that penalty was in common use and authorized by law here and in the countries from which our ancestors came at the time the Amendment was adopted." "It is inconceivable to me," he added, "that the framers intended to end capital punishment by the Amendment."[161]

PROPERTY RIGHTS

Justice Black's progressive leanings were apparent when it came to economic and property rights. As a US senator, he voiced support for what is sometimes called a constitutional "double standard"—that is, the idea that courts should give greater protection to civil rights than to economic or property rights.

There was a "growing hostility," Black told his Senate colleagues shortly after FDR's election, "to permitting a blind and extravagant worship of property rights to smother, submerge, and take away fundamental and inherent human rights."[162] Early in his judicial tenure, Black continued to support the idea that human rights are preferred over property rights. "The power of the States to regulate property must be distinguished from constitutional procedural rights protecting life and liberty," Black wrote in the initial draft of a 1939 decision. At the suggestion of Chief Justice Hughes, Black removed that contentious sentence from the final opinion, but he never completely abandoned the distinction between property rights and civil rights.[163]

Contracts Clause

For the most part, Justice Black's interpretation of specific constitutional provisions dealing with property and economic rights was deferential and nonabsolutist. During his first term, the Supreme Court ruled that a state had violated the contracts clause by statutorily withdrawing tenure from a public school teacher.[164] Black filed a solo dissent in which he argued that an earlier statute did not create a binding contract between the state and its teachers; therefore, Indiana was free to modify its educational policies as it saw fit. Reflecting his Jeffersonian instincts, Black emphasized that one of the historical purposes of the state is to educate its citizens. "Indiana, in harmony with our national traditions," he wrote, "seeks to work out a school system, offering education to all, as 'essential to the preservation of free government.'" "That great function of an advancing society," he added, "has heretofore been exercised by the states." Moreover, Black defended a limited role for the courts in interpreting the contracts clause. "I believe the people of Indiana, if they prefer, have the right under the Federal Constitution to entrust this important public policy to their elective representatives rather than to the courts." "Democracy permits the people to rule," he added. "I cannot agree that the constitutional prohibition against impairment of contracts was intended to—or does—transfer in part the determination of the educational policy of Indiana from the legislature of that State to this Court."[165]

Wood v. Lovett (1941)

Three years later, Black filed another dissent in a contracts clause case. In the early 1930s, 25 percent of real estate in the state of Arkansas was tax delinquent.

To offset these revenue losses, the Arkansas legislature passed a law in 1935 allowing it to reclaim tax-delinquent property and resell it. To immunize potential purchasers from claims by those who had lost their property, the law provided that any irregularities in the proceedings prior to the state's acquisition of the property were *not* grounds for voiding the sale. In 1937 the Arkansas legislature repealed the 1935 law. In 1939 Lovett sued to cancel the state tax deeds issued to Wood in 1936 and to quiet title. Lovett claimed that the property had been owned by his predecessors for nearly a century before being lost to the state in 1933 for nonpayment of taxes. Lovett also alleged numerous irregularities in the sale of the property to the state back in 1933, including insufficient description of the property. In *Wood v. Lovett*,[166] the Supreme Court ruled against Lovett. The opinion by justice Owen Roberts stated that the purpose of the 1935 law "was to assure one willing to purchase from the State a title immune from attack on the grounds theretofore available."[167] The 1937 repeal of the law, Roberts reasoned, modified this basic understanding and therefore constituted an impairment of contracts under Article I, section 10 of the Constitution.

Justice Black filed a vigorous dissent. In contrast to the majority, he focused on the financial challenges caused by the Great Depression. Arkansas was not the only place suffering from tax delinquency; in fact, "at the depth of the depression, over 20% of all real property in the United States was tax delinquent."[168] For Black, the repeal legislation was an effort to resolve this problem. After initially believing that land sales would solve the problem, Arkansas legislators "became convinced that the law had worked directly contrary to the state's policy of obtaining benefits believed to flow from continuity of possession by home owners and farmers."[169] Black did not believe the repeal law violated the contracts clause either. There was "no express obligation on the part of Arkansas," Black reasoned, "that its general laws concerning forfeiture of property and sale of land should remain static. Nor do I believe that any such obligation can properly be implied."[170] In reaching this conclusion, Black cited language from Chief Justice Hughes's opinion in *Home Building & Loan Association v. Blaisdell* (1934) that "the [contracts clause] prohibition is not an absolute one and is not to be read with literal exactness like a mathematical formula."[171] "The *Blaisdell* decision," Black concluded, "represented a realistic appreciation of the fact that ours is an evolving society and that the general words of the contract clause were not intended to reduce the legislative branch of government to helpless impotency."[172]

City of El Paso v. Simmons (1965)

Twenty-four years later, however, Black defended a more literal (indeed, absolutist!) view of the contracts clause. Since 1876, Texas had sold public property to its citizens and used the proceeds to support its public schools. Purchasers were required to make annual payments of one-fortieth of the principal and interest at 3 percent. If purchasers were unable to pay the annual interest on the property, it was forfeited to the state; however, they could regain title to their property if they paid the full amount of interest due to the state treasury. When the lands owned by Greenbury Simmons were originally purchased, there was no time restriction on the right to repurchase property after forfeiture. In 1941, however, Texas imposed a five-year limit. Simmons attempted to reclaim lands he had forfeited to the state, but his application arrived two days after the five-year period. The state subsequently sold the property to the City of El Paso. Simmons claimed that the 1941 law violated the contracts clause.

When the case made it to the Supreme Court, the justices ruled that the 1941 law did *not* impair the obligation of contracts. In *City of El Paso v. Simmons*,[173] the court held (8–1) that not every modification of the remedies or substance of a contract violates Article I, section 10. Justice Black filed the solo dissent, contending that Texas had reneged on its contractual obligation. As Black saw it, in the early part of the twentieth century, the state attempted to attract residents to its borders by offering inexpensive property, but once oil and minerals were discovered and property values soared, "the State decided it had made a bad deal and wanted out."[174] In terms of constitutional analysis, Black claimed that Texas had violated the literal command of the contracts clause: "No State shall . . . pass any . . . Law impairing Obligation of Contracts."[175] Black noted that the framers' purpose in enacting the contracts clause was to ensure "that men should not have to act at their peril, fearing always that the State might change its mind and alter the legal consequences of their past acts so as to take away their lives, their liberty or their property."[176] Black was especially upset with the court's use of a "balancing" test. Under such an approach, the court admitted that an obligation of the contract had been impaired, but because the modification was not too severe, the state was not prevented from imposing a time limit on property reinstatements. Citing several of his absolutist dissents from First Amendment cases, Black reasoned that he could not countenance such an approach because it leads to a diminution of individual rights.

Analysis

How does one reconcile Justice Black's opinions in *Lovett* and *Simmons*? There are probably several explanations. The fact that the state was a party to the contract in *Simmons* was an important distinction, which Black emphasized. He cited the court's early decision in *Fletcher v. Peck* (1810),[177] where the Georgia legislature tried to repeal a corrupt land sale made under an earlier state law. *Fletcher*, Black argued, "much like the present case," was "an attempt by a State to relieve itself of the duty of honoring land grants which it regretted having made."[178] Another explanation of Black's seemingly different interpretations of the contracts clause is that he appeared to be more supportive of property rights in the 1960s. In a 1960 speech, Black said that all the guarantees of the Bill of Rights were absolutes and he included all of the individual-rights provisions in the original Constitution.[179] In a major sit-in case decided in 1964, Black argued in dissent that twelve African American protesters challenging a segregated restaurant in Baltimore could be convicted for trespassing on private property.[180] Then in *Amalgamated Food Employees Union Local 590 v. Logan Valley Plaza* (1968),[181] he argued in dissent that union organizers do not have a right to picket in front of a supermarket in a private mall.[182]

A final explanation for Justice Black's different interpretations of the contracts clause in *Lovett* and *Simmons* lies in how he might have perceived the economic justice issues in the two cases. In *Lovett*, a landowner was seeking to reclaim property forfeited to the state during the Great Depression, whereas in *Simmons*, a landowner was seeking to reclaim property under laws existing at the time of the purchase but was prevented from doing so by a subsequent law imposing a time limit on reinstatements. In fact, in *Simmons*, Black criticized Texas for repudiating its contract, whereby it "undoubtedly gained millions of dollars," while purchasers "lost those millions." "It is commonplace," he added, "that land values steadily rise when population increases and rise sharply when valuable minerals are discovered, and that many sellers would be much richer and happier if when lands go up in values they were able to welch on their sales." "No plethora of words," he concluded, "about state school funds can conceal the fact that to get money easily without having to tax the whole public Texas took the easy way out and violated the Contract Clause of the Constitution as written and as applied up to now."[183]

Takings Clause

Black also took a deferential approach to the takings clause, which states that "private property" shall not "be taken for public use, without just compensation." In *United States v. Causby* (1946),[184] the Supreme Court ruled that low-flying airplanes over a family farm constituted a taking of property. In that case, the Causbys owned a 2.8-acre chicken farm located a third of a mile from an airport in Greensboro, North Carolina. In 1942 the federal government obtained the right to use the airport for military aircraft. Before that time, activity at the airport had caused some noise at the Causby farm, but the larger military planes made the property uninhabitable and destroyed the family's chicken farm.[185] In an opinion by Justice Douglas, the court ruled that the Causbys must be compensated for the loss of their chicken farm.

Justice Black dissented. Reflecting his deferential view of Congress's commerce power, Black criticized the majority for imposing "relatively absolute constitutional barriers" on Congress's ability to regulate the growth of air transportation. "Old concepts of private ownership of land should not be introduced into the field of air regulation," Black wrote. "I have no doubt that Congress will, if not handicapped by judicial interpretations of the Constitution, preserve the freedom of the air, and at the same time, satisfy the just claims of aggrieved persons." Black also questioned the judicial role in cases involving the takings clause. "The solution of the problems precipitated by these technological advances and new ways of living cannot come about through the application of rigid constitutional restraints formulated and enforced by the courts," he wrote.[186] Eight years later, Justice Black joined the court's unanimous decision in *Berman v. Parker* (1954),[187] which broadly interpreted the "public use" requirement of the takings clause to cover redevelopment of "blighted areas" in Washington, DC.

DUE PROCESS

The due process clauses of the Fifth and Fourteenth Amendments prohibit both the federal and state governments from depriving a person of "life, liberty, or property, without due process of law." The concept of due process originated with the Magna Carta of 1215, and Justice Black interpreted it as guaranteeing certain procedural rights based on the extant "law of the land."[188]

Beginning in the late 1800s, however, the Supreme Court began to recognize certain unenumerated (or "substantive") rights under the "liberty" provision that were applied against state and federal power—a doctrinal development called "substantive due process." During the *Lochner* era (1897–1937),[189] conservative courts struck down laws dealing with minimum wages, maximum hours, and child labor on the grounds that they violated the "liberty of contract" under the due process clause. No person was a fiercer critic of the liberty of contract doctrine than Hugo Black. He opposed the doctrine on both philosophical and judicial grounds. During his time in the Senate, Black argued that the economic theory underlying the doctrine led to "social and political disintegration." "It brought starvation wages; health-breaking long hours of work; child labor in mills; business to bankruptcy; and farmers to crushing mortgages."[190] On judicial grounds, Black argued that substantive due process gave five judges of the Supreme Court omnipotent power over the rights of the people. "The Constitution . . . never gave to the majority of the Judges of the Supreme Court," Black observed in one speech, "power to declare that the sovereign State of New York, with its millions of people, could not pass laws to abolish the sweatshop by providing minimum wages or by prohibiting unduly long hours of work in industry."[191]

During his thirty-four years on the Supreme Court, Black was a steadfast opponent of the liberty of contract doctrine. He wrote the court's decision in *Lincoln Federal Labor Union v. Northwestern Iron Metal Company* (1949),[192] which upheld two state laws prohibiting employers from denying employment to nonunion members. Black traced the sordid history of "yellow-dog" contracts in US history and concluded that, since "the due process clause erects no obstacle to block legislative protection of union members, we now hold that legislative protection can be afforded non-union members."[193] Black also wrote the court's unanimous opinion in *Ferguson v. Skrupa* (1963).[194] In that case, Kansas made it unlawful for any person to engage in the business of "debt adjusting." A three-judge district court panel struck down the law as an unreasonable regulation of a lawful business practice under the due process clause of the Fourteenth Amendment, but the Supreme Court reversed that ruling. Black maintained that it was not the courts' place to decide whether debt adjustment was a moral or immoral business practice. "Legislative bodies," he wrote, "have broad scope to experiment with economic problems, and this Court does not sit to 'subject the State to an intolerable supervision hostile to the basic principles of our Government and wholly beyond the protection which the general clause of the Fourteenth Amendment was intended to secure.'" "Whether the legislature," Black added, "takes for its textbook Adam Smith, Herbert Spencer, Lord Keynes or some other is no concern of ours."[195]

Right of Privacy

Justice Black's rejection of substantive due process included a general right of privacy. In *Griswold v. Connecticut* (1965),[196] the Supreme Court struck down a state law banning the advocacy and use of contraceptives among married and unmarried couples. Expressing the views of five members of the court, Justice Douglas ruled that the law violated the right of privacy found in the penumbras of the First, Third, Fourth, Fifth, and Ninth Amendments. Justice Black filed a vigorous dissent. Although he found the Connecticut law "every bit as offensive" as his colleagues did, he could not find a right of privacy in the text of the Constitution. Black was particularly troubled by the concurring opinions that relied on the Fourteenth Amendment's due process clause and the Ninth Amendment.[197] "I discuss the due process and Ninth Amendment arguments together," Black wrote, "because on analysis they turn out to be the same thing—merely using different words to claim for this Court and the federal judiciary power to invalidate any legislative act which the judges find irrational, unreasonable or offensive."[198] Black also took the opportunity to criticize the idea of a living Constitution. "I realize that many good and able men have eloquently spoken and written, sometimes in rhapsodical strains, about the duty of this Court to keep the Constitution in tune with the times," he wrote. "The idea is that the Constitution must be changed from time to time and that this Court is charged with a duty to make those changes," but "for myself, I must with all deference reject that philosophy." "The Constitution makers knew the need for change and provided for it." The amendment process specified in Article V "was good for our Fathers," Black concluded, "and being somewhat old-fashioned I must add it is good enough for me."[199]

Abortion

During his last term on the Supreme Court, Justice Black rejected a constitutional right for a woman to obtain an abortion. In *United States v. Vuitch* (1971),[200] he authored the court's decision holding that a Washington, DC, law criminalizing abortions, with the exception of those "necessary for the preservation of the mother's life or health," was constitutional. Black reasoned that the word "health" in the statute was not vague and that the lower court had erred in dismissing a lawsuit against Dr. Milan Vuitch for performing abortions in the nation's capital. Although the Supreme Court did not reach the constitutional argument, Black made it clear during the conference in the case that he did not support a woman's right to an abortion. "[I] can't go [along] with [a] woman's claim of constitutional right to use her body as she pleases," Black remarked.[201] "This country," he added, was "founded by Puritans."[202]

Procedural Due Process

Justice Black also rejected *procedural* due process claims that he believed approximated natural law or substantive due process arguments. In *Sniadach v. Family Finance Corp.* (1969),[203] for example, the Supreme Court held that individuals have a right to notice and an opportunity to be heard before their wages are frozen in prejudgment garnishment proceedings. In an opinion by Justice Douglas, the court viewed wage garnishment in advance of judgment as "a most inhuman doctrine," imposing tremendous hardships on wage earners. In solo dissent, Black accused his colleagues of "judicial usurpation of state legislative power to decide what the State's laws shall be."[204]

Similarly, Justice Black dissented in *Goldberg v. Kelly* (1970),[205] in which the court ruled that welfare recipients must have procedural due process protections before their benefits can be terminated. "I regret very much," Black wrote in dissent, "to be compelled to say that the Court today makes a drastic and dangerous departure from a Constitution written to control and limit the government and the judges and moves toward a constitution designed to be no more and no less than what the judges of a particular social and economic philosophy declare on the one hand to be fair or on the other hand to be shocking and unconscionable."[206] Eight days later, Justice Black filed yet another dissent in a case in which the court ruled that proof beyond a reasonable doubt is constitutionally required in criminal cases involving juveniles.[207] Black observed that there are many express rights that protect criminal defendants, but one of them is not the standard of proof in criminal cases. When the court interprets due process to include whether the legislation comports with fundamental fairness, Black maintained, it takes away "the most fundamental individual liberty of our people—the right of each man to participate in the self-government of his society."[208]

EQUAL PROTECTION AND STATE ACTION

The equal protection clause was another area of the Constitution that Justice Black regarded as inexact. If discriminatory conduct could in any way be attributed to the state, he regarded it as presumptively suspect. Early in his tenure, Black wrote or joined several important opinions broadening the scope of the state action doctrine. In *Smith v. Allwright* (1944),[209] the Supreme Court struck down Texas's "white primary" on the grounds that, although political parties are private organizations, they perform essential public functions and therefore cannot restrict the right to vote to only white citizens. In *Marsh v. Alabama* (1946),[210] a decision authored by Justice Black, the court ruled that a company town cannot forbid the distribution of religious pamphlets by a Jehovah's Witness. "Ownership does not always mean absolute dominion," Black reasoned. "The more an owner, for his advantage, opens up his property for use by the public in general, the more do his rights become circumscribed by the statutory and constitutional rights of those who use it."[211] Two years later, in *Shelley v. Kraemer* (1948),[212] Black joined Chief Justice Vinson's unanimous opinion striking down restrictive covenants when they are enforced by the courts.[213]

On the one hand, Black believed that if the government was not clearly involved in discrimination, the federal courts could not intervene to provide a remedy under the equal protection clause. As noted earlier, Black dissented in several important sit-in cases in the mid-1960s. He also dissented in a case in which the Supreme Court ruled that a public park, which had been designated under a charitable trust to be used exclusively by white people, must remain in the public domain after its trustees objected that the city was allowing blacks to use it.[214] Justice Black then wrote a follow-up decision in *Evans v. Abney* (1970),[215] which allowed that same public park to revert back to the testator's heirs based on a Georgia court determination that the testator's intention could no longer be fulfilled.[216]

On the other hand, if a state legislature or Congress wanted to ban discrimination in places of public accommodation, Black was exceedingly deferential. For example, in the same year the Supreme Court handed down *Bell v. Maryland* (1964)[217]—one of the major sit-in cases—it also upheld Title II of the Civil Rights Act of 1964, which banned discrimination in places of public accommodation. In a separate concurring opinion, Black regarded the petitioners' property rights argument as "highly ironical," in that "it would use the guarantee of due process—a guarantee which plays so important a part in the Fourteenth Amendment, an amendment adopted with the predominant aim of protecting Negroes from discrimination—in order to strip Congress of power to protect Negroes from discrimination."[218] Likewise, Justice Black did not believe the Thirteenth Amendment imposed the same state action concerns as the Fourteenth Amendment. In *Jones v. Alfred H. Mayer Co.* (1968),[219] he joined the court's holding that Congress had the authority to regulate the sale or rental of private property under the Civil Rights Act of 1866, based on its power to regulate the badges and incidents of slavery under the Thirteenth Amendment.

Revealing his small *d* Jeffersonian sympathies, Justice Black deferred to the democratic process in other types of equal protection disputes, even when there was arguably a racial motivation behind the laws or actions in question. In the late 1960s the Supreme Court heard several fair housing cases in which Black sided with citizen initiatives and referenda that prevented African Americans from renting or buying homes. In Akron, Ohio, the city charter was amended by the initiative process to require that any ordinance involving the sale of housing be approved by a majority of the voters before taking effect. The result of the amendment was to stay the operation of the city's fair housing ordinance. Nellie Hunter, a black resident, was told by a real estate agent that she could not show her any houses because "all of the owners had specified they did not wish their houses shown to Negroes." In *Hunter v. Erickson* (1969),[220] the Supreme Court ruled that the charter amendment violated the equal protection clause because the law placed special burdens on racial minorities within the governmental process. Black dissented. He claimed that there was no constitutional bar to the city amending its charter, and he accused the majority of depriving the people of the authority to govern themselves.[221]

On a related issue, Justice Black also dissented in *Harper v. Virginia Board of Elections* (1966),[222] in which the Supreme Court struck down a state poll tax (not to exceed $1.50 a year) to participate in elections. In an opinion by Justice Douglas, the court ruled (6–3) that "a State violates the Equal Protection Clause of the Fourteenth Amendment whenever it makes the affluence of the voter or payment of any fee an electoral standard."[223] In dissent, Black argued that the court's interpretation of the equal protection clause went against its original meaning because "property qualifications existed in the Colonies and were continued by many States after the Constitution was adopted." Black agreed with the court "in disliking the policy of the poll tax," but he maintained that his views were not "a justifiable reason for holding this poll tax law unconstitutional." "Such a holding," he argued, would "be an exercise of power which the Constitution does not confer upon me."[224]

Desegregation

As a Supreme Court justice, Hugo Black took the principled stance that segregation is a per se violation of the Constitution.[225] He joined the early decisions in cases brought by the NAACP that challenged the "separate but equal doctrine" in graduate and professional schools. During the justices' conference in *McLaurin v. Oklahoma State Regents* (1950), Black told his colleagues: "It is not *equal* to isolate. . . . I can't say that the Fourteenth Amendment was not intended and designed to prevent a caste system—and that is what this is. It is a hangover from the days when the Negro was a slave, and the racial humiliation of sitting together."[226] Black took the same position in *Brown v. Board of Education of Topeka* (1954),[227] in which the court struck down segregation in elementary and secondary schools. Even though Black warned his colleagues there would be "trouble" in the South, he believed segregation was a clear violation of the equal protection clause. Drawing on his own experience growing up in the Deep South, Black explained that segregation was based on "the belief that Negroes are inferior." He noted that "the Civil War Amendments have as their basic purpose the abolition of such castes, and to protect the Negro against discrimination on account of color."[228]

In addition, Justice Black either wrote or joined several post-*Brown* opinions dealing with remedies for historically segregated school districts—although he was never satisfied with the "all deliberate speed" language from *Brown II* (1955).[229] Black joined the court's unanimous decision in *Cooper v. Aaron* (1958),[230] which denied a school board's request to delay desegregation efforts for two and a half years after governor Orval Faubus attempted to prevent nine black schoolchildren (the "Little Rock Nine") from attending high school in Arkansas.[231] In *Griffin v. County School Board of Prince Edward County* (1964),[232] Black wrote the court's decision holding that the closing of public schools in Prince Edward County, Virginia, violated the equal protection clause. The county closed its public schools and then offered publicly funded grants for children to attend private nonsectarian schools, none of which admitted black children. Writing for the court, Black said there was only one reason for the actions taken by the county: "to ensure . . . that white and colored children in Prince Edward County would not, under any circumstances, go to the same school." "Whatever nonracial grounds," he added, "might support a State's allowing a county to abandon public schools, the object must be a constitutional one, and grounds of race and opposition to desegregation do not qualify as constitutional."[233] Justice Black also joined the court's decision in *Green v. County School Board of New Kent County* (1968),[234] which required that school boards take affirmative steps to integrate their schools, given that "freedom-of-choice" plans had not proven to be a sufficient remedy in historically segregated communities.

Prior to his retirement, Justice Black also joined the unanimous decision in *Swann v. Charlotte-Mecklenburg Board of Education* (1971),[235] in which the court, relying on its equitable powers, approved mandatory busing in school districts with a history of de jure (legally mandated) segregation. Writing for the court, Chief Justice Burger accepted the district court's conclusion that "assignment of children to the school nearest their home serving their grade would not produce an effective dismantling of the dual system."[236] It should be noted, however, that Black had reservations about busing in the North, where segregation was not clearly state sponsored. In a memo related to *Keyes v. School District Number One*, a decision the court postponed until one year after Black's retirement, he observed: "The Fourteenth Amendment simply does not grant federal courts power to remedy educational inequality when inequality does not stem from state action."[237]

One Person, One Vote

Justice Black was the undisputed champion of the "one person, one vote" principle in reapportionment cases. In *Colegrove v. Green* (1946),[238] the Supreme Court examined the congressional map of Illinois, where the population in the largest district was 914,053 and the population in the smallest district was 112,116. In a badly divided decision (3–1–3), Justice Frankfurter, writing for two other justices,[239] concluded that reapportionment was "a political thicket" for which the federal judiciary could not provide a remedy. Justice Rutledge disagreed with Frankfurter on that point, but he voted to dismiss the case for want of equity. Justice Black, with whom Justices Douglas and Murphy joined, filed a vigorous dissent, arguing that reapportionment was a justiciable controversy and that the federal courts should exercise their equitable powers in resolving malapportioned congressional districts. If a law gives "certain citizens a half-vote and others a full vote," Black wrote, it violates the equal protection clause. "Such discriminatory legislation," he added, "seems to me exactly the kind that the equal protection clause was intended to prohibit."[240] Although Black cited both Article I, section 2 of the Constitution and the equal protection clause, he concluded that the right to vote was fundamental and that half a vote was not the same as a full vote.

Black continued to defend his position by filing several dissents from denial of certiorari throughout the 1940s and 1950s.[241] By the early 1960s the Supreme Court's membership had changed, and Black's position became the prevailing view. In the landmark case *Baker v. Carr* (1962),[242] the court reversed *Colegrove* and ruled that reapportionment was judicially cognizable under the equal protection clause. Two years later, the Supreme Court handed down two major decisions providing a remedy. Black authored the decision in *Wesberry v. Sanders* (1964),[243] which required the "one person, one vote" principle for congressional districts. Interestingly, Black based the decision on Article I, section 2 of the Constitution, not the equal protection clause.[244] Four months later, Black joined the 8–1 decision in *Reynolds v. Sims* (1964),[245] which applied the same principle to both houses of state legislatures, based on the equal protection clause. In a 1970 interview with professor Tinsley Yarbrough, Black explained his objection to malapportionment in Jeffersonian terms. "'In our system,' Black remarked, 'the people are sovereign,' and any apportionment scheme which gives some voters greater weight than others interferes with the ideal of popular sovereignty." "In such a system," he added, "any substantial deviation from equally weighted voting was . . . inherently 'irrational.'"[246]

This chapter attempted to provide a comprehensive account of Justice Black's jurisprudence. Although he is not often recognized as such, Hugo Black was the Supreme Court's *first* systematic and all-encompassing originalist.[247] The Constitution, in his hands, was truly a "legal bible," and he always carried a pocket-sized copy with him.[248] Justice Black relied on both text and history in interpreting the First Amendment. For Black, the First Amendment was a "bold effort" by the framers "to establish a country with no legal restrictions of any kind upon the subjects people could investigate, discuss and deny." They knew, "better perhaps than we do today, the risks they were taking. They knew that free speech might be the friend of change and revolution. But they also knew that it is always the deadliest enemy of tyranny."[249] On this basis, Black argued that the government cannot punish individuals for their ideas or political associations, no matter how revolutionary they might seem. Only when ideas turn into action (e.g., unlawful conduct, marches, picketing, sit-ins) does the government have the authority to regulate behavior.

Like Jefferson, Black viewed the institutional press as an essential bulwark to constitutional democracy. The press not only supplies the information necessary for people to make informed decisions but also serves as an important check on elected officials. In the Pentagon Papers Case, Black did not even want to hear oral arguments until the temporary injunctions against the newspapers had been lifted. "Every moment's continuance of the injunctions against these newspapers," Black wrote, "amounts to a flagrant, indefensible, and continuing violation of the First Amendment."[250]

Justice Black's views of the religion clauses were also consistent with Thomas Jefferson's political philosophy. In interpreting the establishment clause, Black called for a "high wall" between church and state. Despite the outcome in *Everson*, Black consistently applied a strict neutralist perspective during his remaining years on the Supreme Court. He wrote the court's decision in *Engel v. Vitale*, striking down nondenominational prayers in public schools, and, as discussed in chapter 5, he defended a strict neutralist perspective in other cases. Black shared Jefferson's view that religion is a personal choice with which the government should not interfere. After initially supporting the court's decision in *Gobitis*, Black joined the 6–3 decision in *Barnette.* More so than his colleagues, Black rested his concurring opinion on religious freedom. Justice Black also supported strict scrutiny in religious freedom cases and a broad interpretation of military exemptions for conscientious objectors under federal statutes.

In interbranch disputes, Black (like Jefferson) defended a narrow interpretation of executive power. In the Steel Seizure Case, Black strictly construed the express powers granted to the president under Article II and rejected all claims of implied and inherent powers. Black applied that same narrow interpretation of executive power in other cases, including whether the president has the authority to regulate passports for those traveling to Cuba and whether foreign enemy combatants have the right of habeas corpus. Justice Black's total incorporation theory can also be interpreted as Jeffersonian. One of Jefferson's two major objections to the Constitution was the absence of a bill of rights, and he insisted that "the people are entitled to [a bill of rights] against every government on earth, general or particular, & what no just government should refuse, or rest on inference."[251]

In the area of criminal procedure, Justice Black supported a narrow interpretation of the Fourth Amendment. His basic position was that searches and seizures have to be "reasonable," which does not always require a warrant supported by probable cause. His interpretation of "probable cause" was also deferential. He rejected application of the Fourth Amendment to electronic surveillance and argued that the Fourth Amendment, by itself, does not support the exclusionary rule—although he believed that the rule is supported by a combination of the Fourth and Fifth Amendments.

In contrast to the Fourth Amendment, Justice Black's interpretations of the Fifth and Sixth Amendments were more expansive. Based on his days as a prosecutor in Birmingham, Black was distrustful of "voluntary" confessions. On the Supreme Court, he provided a robust interpretation of the self-incrimination clause and wrote many of the decisions laying the groundwork for *Miranda v. Arizona.* Similarly, Justice Black's concern for equal justice under the law resulted in a robust interpretation of the right-to-counsel provision of the Sixth Amendment. He wrote the court's decisions in *Johnson v. Zerbst,* which required attorneys in all federal cases, and in *Gideon v. Wainwright,* which required state governments to provide attorneys to the poor. During his last term on the court, Justice Black argued that the states must provide attorneys in all civil cases.

As a former prosecutor, Justice Black was unfazed by the death penalty.[252] He supported capital punishment in many Supreme Court decisions, including cases involving robbery and rape.[253] At the same time, he insisted on fair procedures in death penalty cases (explored in more detail in chapter 5).

In the area of property and economic rights, Justice Black supported the constitutional double standard, particularly during his early years on the court. When it came to the contracts clause, he articulated a nonabsolutist position and supported the court's decision in *Blaisdell.* Although he defended a more robust interpretation of the contracts clause in *City of El Paso v. Simmons,* that opinion can also be explained on economic justice grounds. In interpreting the takings clause, Justice Black took a deferential approach. In *United States v. Causby,* he argued in dissent that courts should not hamstring congressional efforts to regulate air transportation. He also did not support a narrow interpretation of what constitutes "public use" under the takings clause.

No Supreme Court justice was a stronger critic of substantive due process than Hugo Black. He rejected the doctrine "root, branch, and entirely," including the *Lochner* era decisions, a general right of privacy, and a woman's right to choose.[254] Justice Black believed that substantive due process gave judges too much discretion and opened the door to natural law arguments. He also disagreed with procedural due process claims that were akin to natural law reasoning. When it came to the equal protection clause, Justice Black either joined or wrote decisions expansively interpreting the state action doctrine. At the same time, his Jeffersonian instincts led Black to support the democratic process even when race might have been a motivating factor behind a law. On the subject of racial segregation, Justice Black was a forceful critic and based his opposition on originalist grounds. As he explained in a post-*Brown* case, "I did not vote to hold segregation in public schools unconstitutional on . . . [the] theory [that the equal protection clause can be used to keep the Constitution up to date]." He continued, "I thought when *Brown* was written, and I think now, that Mr. Justice Harlan was correct in 1896 when he dissented from *Plessy v. Ferguson*."[255] Justice Black also wrote or joined several decisions calling for affirmative steps to end segregation in the United States, including *Griffin*, *Green*, and *Swann*.

One of Justice Black's other important judicial legacies was the one person, one vote principle in reapportionment cases. He dissented in *Colegrove v. Green* but pressed his colleagues to reexamine the issue. After the court's composition changed in the 1960s, he joined the 6–2 decision in *Baker v. Carr*, which recognized that reapportionment is a justiciable issue. He then wrote *Wesberry v. Sanders*, which applied the one person, one vote principle to congressional districts, and he joined the court's decision in *Reynolds v. Sims*, which applied the same principle to both houses of state legislatures.

Justice Black often said he was willing to give a "liberal" construction to the guarantees *expressly* mentioned in the Bill of Rights.[256] He broadly interpreted the First Amendment to make no exception for obscenity or libel. Except for the Fourth Amendment, Black liberally interpreted the rights of the accused. Only Justice Douglas rivaled Black in his expansive interpretation of both the self-incrimination and the right-to-counsel provisions. At the same time, Black did not view the due process and equal protection clauses as providing "a blank check" for judges to impose their own conceptions of justice on the people.[257] "A judge untethered by a text," Black believed, "is a dangerous instrument."[258] For Black, the Constitution itself is "a living document" because it contains the mechanism by which it can be changed by the people under Article V.[259] As we saw in this chapter, he rejected the idea of a living Constitution in many areas of constitutional law, including whether the Fourth Amendment covers electronic surveillance, the permissibility of the death penalty, the right of privacy, a woman's right to obtain an abortion, and the constitutionality of poll taxes.

3. Antonin Scalia's Originalism: Hamiltonian

The views of Alexander Hamilton (a draftsman) bear [no] more authority than the views of Thomas Jefferson (not a draftsman) with regard to the meaning of the Constitution.

—*Antonin Scalia*[1]

Whereas Hugo Black's originalist philosophy was deeply shaped by the political philosophy of Thomas Jefferson, Antonin Scalia's originalist jurisprudence was fundamentally influenced by Alexander Hamilton. Of all the Founding Fathers, Hamilton was the least optimistic about popular democracy. Human nature is at its worst, Hamilton believed, in popular assemblies, where "regard to reputation has a less active influence" on the actions of men and where there is a tendency toward mob rule.[2] Hamilton's generally dark understanding of human nature made one important exception: he believed that "a few choice spirits" could rise above their own self-interest and make decisions on behalf of the people.[3] Harking back to a classical view of honor, Hamilton regarded the "love of fame" as "the ruling passion of the noblest minds" and that which provides the greatest stimulus for "arduous enterprises for the public benefit."[4] More than any other founder, he wanted to build a republican government on a solid foundation. In a speech delivered at the New York ratifying convention, Hamilton observed, "When you have divided and nicely balanced the departments of government; when you have strongly connected the virtue of your rulers with their interest; when, in short, you have rendered your system as perfect as human forms can be; you must place confidence; you must give power."[5]

At various times during his lengthy public career, Antonin Scalia identified himself as a Hamiltonian. At a 1982 conference on federalism, Scalia invoked Hamilton for his guidance on the subject. Since most conservatives were defenders of a free-market system, he suggested passing federal legislation that would prohibit (or at least limit) state regulation in such areas as the cable, construction, and housing industries. Why not limit, Scalia asked, state court tort theories of "enterprise liability" or "design defect," which subject interstate businesses to greatly increased damages? Or, what about "antitrust" and "antiescape" laws that excessively penalize businesses? Scalia lamented that not a single federal statute simply said, "the states shall not regulate." Scalia urged the members of the conference, "as Hamilton would have urged you—to keep in mind that the federal government is not bad but good. The trick is to use it wisely."[6]

Antonin Scalia revealed a Hamiltonian predisposition in other pre–Supreme Court speeches. Just a few days before his nomination to the Supreme Court, Scalia gave a speech at the Justice Department where he criticized the earliest iteration of modern conservative originalism: original intent. In several high-profile speeches, attorney general Edwin Meese had argued that "the policy of [the Reagan] administration [would be] to press for a Jurisprudence of Original Intention."[7] Even though Scalia agreed with Meese's basic objective—that is, the Constitution should *not* be interpreted based on a "living Constitution"—he disagreed that the focus should be on the framers' *intent.* In fact, Scalia maintained that if the framers themselves were asked whether the Constitution should be interpreted based on their own intentions, they would answer with a resounding "no." For evidence of this, Scalia cited explicit statements by prominent Founding Fathers, including Hamilton's remarks in his opinion on the national bank: "Whatever may have been the intention of the framers of a constitution, or of a law, that intention is to be sought for in the instrument itself."[8] Instead of the subjective intentions of the framers, Scalia defended a method of constitutional interpretation based on "original meaning," which he defined as "the most plausible meaning of the words of the Constitution to the society that adopted it—regardless of what the Framers might secretly have intended." However, in stark contrast to his rejection of the use of legislative history in interpreting statutes,[9] Scalia claimed that the views of "the most knowledgeable people of the time" were not "irrelevant" in understanding what the words of the Constitution originally meant. Scalia then committed what might be considered a Freudian slip. Instead of citing James Madison (the so-called father of the Constitution) as the intellectual force behind the Constitution, Scalia gave that distinction to Hamilton: "It is not that 'the Constitution must mean this because Alexander Hamilton thought it meant this, and he wrote it'; but rather that 'the Constitution must mean this because Alexander Hamilton, who for Pete's sake must have understood the thing, thought it meant this.'"[10]

Justice Scalia also invoked Hamilton in a public exchange over constitutional interpretation. During a 2008 program titled "A Conversation on the

Constitution: Judicial Interpretation," justice Stephen Breyer defended an evolutionary approach to constitutional interpretation, whereby certain "unchanging values" of the Constitution must be applied to new circumstances. He then claimed that both Hamilton and Madison supported the concept of unelected judges protecting minority rights against the tyranny of the majority. In response, a clearly disgruntled Scalia scoffed, "Hamilton would jump out of his skin if he thought that the Constitution he supported allowed for nine elected judges to change the meaning of [the] document from year to year."[11]

As a judge, Antonin Scalia's originalist approach to constitutional interpretation reflected the two main pillars of Hamilton's political philosophy: a strong distrust of popular democracy and an elite theory of who should govern. Notwithstanding Scalia's strenuous criticism of the "living" Constitution, he was no fan of direct democracy. In one case involving the separation of powers, Scalia wrote the majority opinion striking down a federal law for attempting to reopen civil actions previously determined by the court to be time barred. To support that ruling, Scalia recounted the history of why the founders had supported judicial review in the first place. "The vigorous, indeed often radical, populism of the revolutionary legislatures and assemblies," wrote Scalia, "increased the frequency of legislative correction of [judicial] judgments." "'The period 1780–1787,'" he continued, "was a period of 'constitutional reaction' to these developments, 'which . . . leaped suddenly to its climax in the Philadelphia Convention.'"[12]

In *Williams-Yulee v. State Bar of Florida* (2015),[13] the Supreme Court upheld a state regulation banning the direct solicitation of campaign donations by judicial candidates. In dissent, Scalia speculated that the reason more states were electing judges was "the people's realization that their judges can become their rulers—and (it must be said) from just a deep-down feeling that members of the Third Branch will profit from a hearty helping of humble pie, and from a severe reduction of their great remove from the (ugh!) People." In parentheses, Scalia then observed, "It should not be thought that I myself harbor such irreverent and revolutionary feelings; but I think it likely—and year by year more likely—that those who favor the election of judges do so."[14]

Justice Scalia was also acutely aware of the antidemocratic role performed by federal judges. He relished telling audiences that his "most important job as a judge was to say 'no' to the people."[15] In one speech he expanded on this theme. The reason judges have life tenure, he explained, is so they "can tell the people to go take a walk. The most important thing I do in my job is to tell the majority that it can't do what it wants to do, because the Constitution forbids it. I stand between you and the majority, with the Constitution in my hand. And essentially, I tell the people, you know, 'people be damned, you cannot do this. The Constitution forbids you.'"[16]

Like Hamilton, Scalia defended an elite governing class. Scalia's advocacy of a formalistic interpretation of the separation of powers, his broad interpretation of executive power, and his defense of the standard of good behavior for federal judges all reflected an elite theory of who should govern. In a 2010 interview, Calvin Massey asked Scalia if he supported term limits for federal judges. Scalia could not fathom why anyone would want to impose term limits, calling it "a solution in search of a problem." In constitutional cases, he said, the standard of good behavior is essential. "The current society expresses its wishes through the legislature," observed Scalia. "But if you do believe that a Constitution places some limits on the current society in light of society over time, it seems to me you would prefer a Court that represents the society over time."[17]

In a 1987 address to the American Bar Association, Scalia implored the nation's lawyers to take steps to preserve the prestige and reputation of federal judgeships. When he graduated from law school, he recalled, the federal judiciary had a reputation for the "big case." Scalia lamented that, with the tremendous increase in the federal courts' docket, judges are spending more time on "cases of overwhelming triviality." He warned that if this problem persists, "the stature of the job, and the quality of the people it attracts, will decline." "Elitism has never been popular in democratic society," Scalia remarked, "though the Founding Fathers, if one can believe the *Federalist Papers*, thought that the life-tenured judges they were creating would constitute a 'natural aristocracy' (of ability rather than wealth). But if it is desirable, then I think the time is well past due to consider the means of preserving it."[18]

Justice Scalia's jurisprudence in specific areas of constitutional law could also be said to support an elite ruling class. As a federal judge, Scalia strictly interpreted the three-part test to determine legal standing, which had the effect of limiting the number of citizen lawsuits brought in federal court.[19] He also wrote important opinions limiting the availability of class-action suits and other forms of liability under federal statutes.[20] Scalia was a sharp critic of the regulation of money in politics, which supported a Hamiltonian conception of who should govern.[21] At the time of the founding, Hamilton maintained that the "rich and well born" ought to have a permanent share in the government, since "they will check the unsteadiness of the [mass of the people], and as they cannot receive any advantage by a change, they therefore will ever maintain good government."[22] Scalia's criticism of the landmark decision in *New York Times v. Sullivan* (1964)[23] also reflected an elite view of American democracy. In *Sullivan*, the Supreme Court required proof of actual malice before a public official could win a libel suit. In judicial opinions, Scalia took strong exception to the "public bumping" and heavy burden placed on public officials as a result of *Sullivan*.[24]

Justice Scalia's elite conception of the federal government was also apparent in his criticism of the Seventeenth Amendment, which allowed the direct election of US senators. In a 2010 debate with Justice Breyer, Scalia described the Seventeenth Amendment as "a burst of progressivism" that resulted in a decline of states' rights.[25] Based on these remarks, Scalia was described as jumping on the anti–Seventeenth Amendment bandwagon,[26] but Scalia's negative view of that amendment dated back to the late 1980s. In a 1988 speech at American University, Scalia remarked that the Seventeenth Amendment signaled "the beginning of the end for the states." Under the original Constitution, US senators were chosen by state legislatures and thus could be held accountable by those legislatures for their decisions. That all changed, Scalia explained, with the adoption of the Seventeenth Amendment. Senators are now elected by popular vote and are less beholden to the interests of the states. Scalia lamented this development but said there is little the courts can do. Federalism "is a losing battle and has been a losing battle since the adoption of the Seventeenth Amendment," he observed.[27]

This chapter examines Justice Scalia's originalist philosophy across a wide array of constitutional areas, including separation of powers, executive power, federalism, freedom of speech, separation of church and state, religious freedom, the Second Amendment, rights of the accused, property rights, due process, and equal protection. Because Hamilton's political philosophy was an important influence in how Scalia interpreted the Constitution—a fact he himself acknowledged[28]— those areas in which that influence was most apparent are highlighted.

SEPARATION OF POWERS

It would not be an exaggeration to say that separation of powers was Justice Scalia's strongest doctrinal commitment. He once referred to that doctrine as "the cornerstone of our Constitution and the North Star of our founding fathers' constellation."[29] Like James Madison and Alexander Hamilton, Scalia defended separation of powers as the chief bulwark of individual liberty in the US political system. He also shared their fundamental distrust of congressional power.[30] In a 2013 interview, Scalia said it was laughable that the presidency could ever be described as "imperial" when, under the Constitution, the "900-pound gorilla" in Washington is Congress. "If Congress can get its act together," Scalia said, "it can roll over the president."[31] Scalia's concern about congressional usurpation of executive power led him to be the Supreme Court's staunchest defender of a formalistic interpretation of separation of powers—a position that was first defended by Alexander Hamilton.[32] Accordingly, with the exception of a few instances in which a sharing of powers is contemplated under the Constitution, Scalia maintained that the three departments of government should be kept strictly separate.

Justice Scalia's formalistic interpretation of separation of powers was most conspicuously displayed in classic interbranch disputes between Congress and the president. As a court of appeals judge, Scalia wrote the opinion for a three-judge panel of the DC District Court striking down the removal provision of the Balanced Budget and Emergency Deficit Control Act of 1985.[33] In a lengthy opinion touching on many subjects, Scalia contended that Congress's power to remove the comptroller general would have devastating effects on the separation of powers and impede the president's ability to control public officials who perform executive functions. "Once an officer is appointed," Scalia wrote, "it is only the authority that can remove him, and not the authority that appointed him, that he must fear and, in the performance of his functions, obey."[34]

Another example of Scalia's formalistic interpretation of separation of powers came in *Mistretta v. United States* (1989).[35] At issue in that case was the creation of the US Sentencing Commission, which had been established by Congress under the Sentencing Reform Act of 1984. The commission consisted of seven members, three of whom had to be federal judges, and it was placed in the judicial branch. All seven members of the commission were appointed by the president, by and with the advice and consent of the Senate, and they could be removed by the president only for "good cause." The Supreme Court rejected the petitioner's arguments that the act conferred excessive rule-making authority on the commission in violation of the nondelegation doctrine, and that the commission's establishment in the judicial branch violated the doctrine of separation of powers by vesting the judges appointed to the commission with rule-making (or legislative) authority. Scalia filed a solo dissent. For the only time in his long judicial career, Scalia argued that a federal law violated the nondelegation doctrine. What made this delegation of rule-making authority different from other lawful delegations of power, Scalia maintained, was that Congress had conferred rule-making authority on the US Sentencing Commission without making it subject to executive or judicial control.[36] "The power to make law at issue here," he wrote, "is not ancillary but quite naked." "The situation is no different in principle," he added, "from what would exist if Congress gave the same power of writing sentencing laws to a congressional agency such as the General Accounting Office, or to members of its staff."[37]

Justice Scalia's most important separation-of-powers opinion came in *Morrison v. Olson* (1988),[38] which was handed down during his second term on the Supreme Court. *Morrison* involved a challenge to Title VI of the Ethics in Government Act of 1978, which allowed for the appointment of independent counsels to investigate alleged federal crimes by high-ranking officials in the executive branch. In an opinion authored by Chief Justice Rehnquist, the court (7–1) upheld the law. The majority concluded that the independent counsel was an "inferior" officer of the United States who, pursuant to the appointments clause, could be appointed by a court of law.[39] The majority also rejected the Reagan administration's various arguments based on separation of powers, one of which concerned restricting the president's ability to remove independent counsels.[40] According to Rehnquist, even though the act reduced the attorney general's control over the investigation and prosecution of certain alleged crimes, the limitations were not so severe as to impede the president's ability to perform his constitutional duties.

Matching the length of the court's decision, Scalia's solo dissent comprised thirty-seven pages, major portions of which he read from the bench. In contrast to the majority, Scalia argued that the independent counsel was a "principal" officer of the United States who must be nominated by the president and confirmed by the Senate to comply with the appointments clause. Rather than spending a lot of time on this relatively "technical" point, Scalia devoted most of his opinion to explaining how the act violated "the absolutely central guarantee of just Government": separation of powers. Scalia portrayed this case as being about power. Usually, separation-of-powers questions come to the Supreme Court "clad, so to speak, in sheep's clothing," wrote Scalia, but here, "this wolf comes as a wolf."[41] Scalia described the criminal investigation of assistant attorney general Olson as a "bitter power dispute between the President and the Legislative Branch." He also viewed Congress's authority to review the attorney general's decision *not* to seek the appointment of an independent counsel as "acrid with the smell of threatened impeachment."[42] The act's fatal defect, according to Scalia, was the "good cause" restriction on the president's ability to remove an independent counsel. In his view, this violated the framers' design of a unitary executive and "enfeebled" the president's authority in several ways. "How frightening it must be," wrote Scalia, "to have your own independent counsel and staff appointed, with nothing else to do but investigate you until investigation is no longer worthwhile—with whether it is worthwhile not depending upon what such judgments usually hinge on, competing responsibilities." "By its shortsighted action today," Scalia warned, "I fear the Court has permanently encumbered the Republic with an institution that will do it great harm."[43]

EXECUTIVE POWER

Justice Scalia's views on executive power most clearly identified him as a Hamiltonian. In his article defending originalism as a method of interpreting the Constitution, Scalia defined "executive power" as including all those "traditional powers of English Kings," except those "expressly reassigned" under the Constitution or "inherently incompatible with republican government."[44] Based on such a broad construction of executive power, Scalia defended various implied and inherent powers belonging to the president, including the removal power, the president's authority to enter into executive agreements, executive privilege, presidential immunity from court-ordered injunctive and declaratory relief, and civil immunity from lawsuits.[45]

"Sole Organ" Theory

Consistent with his broad construction of executive power, Scalia defended the "sole organ" theory of the presidency in conducting foreign affairs—another concept that can be traced back to Hamilton.[46] As the nation's assistant attorney general, Scalia told members of Congress, "Authorities since Alexander Hamilton have found within [the vesting clause] the power to conduct foreign relations."[47] In a case handed down when he was on the DC Court of Appeals, Scalia filed a sharp dissent when the court ruled that a challenge to the

Reagan administration's establishment of a regional military training center in Honduras did not constitute a nonjusticiable political question.[48] Judge Scalia criticized his colleagues for getting involved in a political controversy about which "judges know little." He also argued that the court had no jurisdiction in the case and that a court injunction would "undermine Honduran confidence in the ability of the United States to speak and act with a single voice in the region."[49]

Judge Scalia wrote another significant US foreign policy opinion as a member of the DC Court of Appeals, this one involving Nicaragua. In the 1980s the Reagan administration gave financial and military support to the so-called Contra rebels who were attempting to overthrow the communist Sandinista regime. This support was later challenged in *Sanchez-Espinoza v. Reagan* (1985),[50] when twelve Nicaraguan citizens claimed that they or their families had been tortured by the Contras, resulting in "summary execution, murder, abduction, torture, rape, wounding, and the destruction of private property and public facilities."[51] In an opinion by Judge Scalia, the DC Court of Appeals dismissed the petitioners' suit. Scalia could find no statute that specifically authorized compensatory damages against government officials in suits brought by citizens of foreign countries. Moreover, in terms of the request for injunctive relief by the Nicaraguan petitioners, Scalia determined that such relief would not be appropriate because the case involved foreign policy, a matter committed to another branch of government.

War on Terror

Following the September 11, 2001, terrorist attacks against the United States, Scalia was a strong defender of the Bush administration's decision to deny habeas corpus relief to foreign "enemy combatants" held at Guantanamo Bay, Cuba. In *Rasul v. Bush* (2004),[52] the Supreme Court ruled that these detainees could seek judicial relief under the federal habeas corpus statute, but Scalia filed an impassioned dissent accusing the majority of "judicial adventurism of the worst sort." For Scalia, the plain meaning of the federal statute denied jurisdiction to federal district courts. In response to *Rasul*, Congress passed the Detention Treatment Act of 2005 (DTA), which deprived federal courts of the authority to hear habeas corpus claims by Guantanamo Bay detainees. In *Hamdan v. Rumsfeld* (2006),[53] the Supreme Court ruled that the DTA cannot be applied retroactively to pending cases, and Scalia filed another vigorous dissent. He argued that the statute makes no distinction between pending and future cases and therefore should be read to apply to cases pending on the date of the statute's enactment. He also claimed that the district court's order prohibiting ongoing military commission proceedings "brings the Judicial Branch into direct conflict with the Executive in an area where the Executive's competence is maximal and ours is virtually nonexistent."[54]

Finally, in *Boumediene v. Bush* (2008),[55] the Supreme Court struck down the "jurisdiction-stripping" provision of the Military Commissions Act of 2006, which explicitly denied habeas corpus relief to Guantanamo Bay detainees in pending cases. For the majority, Justice Kennedy held that the detainees have a constitutional right to habeas corpus because, "in every practical sense Guantanamo is not abroad; it is within the constant jurisdiction of the United States."[56] In dissent, Scalia argued that foreign enemy combatants are not entitled to the constitutional privilege of habeas corpus and that the court's decision was an "arrogant" violation of separation of powers. "The game of bait-and-switch," wrote Scalia, "that today's opinion plays upon the Nation's Commander in Chief will make the war harder on us. It will almost certainly cause more Americans to be killed."[57]

FEDERALISM

Justice Scalia's views of federal-state relations evolved over time and reflected a "split personality."[58] During his confirmation hearings, Scalia defended the "political process" approach to federalism—a perspective that was first defended by Alexander Hamilton.[59] When asked to provide his "general philosophy" about the role of the federal judiciary relative to federalism, Scalia stated:

> The fact is, it seems to me, that the primary defender of the constitutional balance . . . is the Congress. It is a principle of the Constitution that there are certain responsibilities that belong to the State and some that belong to the Federal Government, but it is essentially the function of Congress—the Congress, which takes the same oath to uphold and defend the Constitution that I do as a judge, to have that constitutional prescription in mind when it enacts the laws.[60]

However, Scalia's views changed over time. In his opinion for the Supreme Court in *Printz v. United States* (1997),[61] Scalia took the unusual step of explaining why he thought James Madison's views prevailed over Hamilton's on the subject of federal-state relations. According to Scalia, although Hamilton's and Madison's views were similar on many subjects, that was not the case when it came to federalism. He argued that "it was Madison's—not Hamilton's—[views of federalism] that prevailed, not only at the Constitutional Convention and in popular sentiment . . . but in the subsequent struggle to fix the meaning of the Constitution by early congressional practice."[62] Scalia's pivot toward a more moderate Madisonian approach to federal-state relations was arguably a strategic move.[63] Based on his newly discovered Madisonian perspective, Scalia joined his colleagues in the so-called federalism revolution of the 1990s. During that period, the Supreme Court placed some restrictions on Congress's authority to regulate interstate commerce,[64] as well as its ability to allow individuals to bring federal lawsuits against their own state governments under the Eleventh Amendment.[65]

Justice Scalia's switch to a Madisonian perspective was not complete, however. During his time on the Supreme Court, Scalia was a strenuous defender of federal preemption, particularly when a federal statute could be read to nullify expansive state theories of liability under the common law.[66] Moreover, Scalia never deviated from his view that the Tenth Amendment does not constitute a substantive limit on federal power. During a 2008 lecture at the University of Central Missouri, Scalia was asked what he thought of the Tenth Amendment. "I don't think of it very much," Scalia comically remarked. "As I think our opinion holds, so what else is new? It's just a repetition of the understood fact that the federal Constitution is a Constitution of enumerated powers; that the only powers the federal government has are those given to it by the Constitution and that all the other ones remain with the states."[67] On several notable occasions, Scalia also sided with national power in a federalism dispute.[68] For example, in *Gonzales v. Raich* (2005),[69] Scalia joined the court's decision upholding the federal government's authority to regulate homegrown marijuana used for medicinal purposes. In a separate concurring opinion, Scalia argued that "Congress may regulate even those intrastate activities that do not themselves substantially affect interstate commerce," if they are "an essential part of a larger regulation of economic activity, in which the regulatory scheme could be undercut unless the intrastate activity were regulated."[70] Scalia also placed some reliance on *Wickard v. Filburn* (1942),[71] which is widely regarded as one of the most far-reaching interpretations of the commerce clause in Supreme Court history.[72]

At the same time, in *National Federation of Independent Business v. Sebelius* (2012),[73] Scalia joined a coauthored dissent that argued that the Patient Protection and Affordable Care Act of 2010 is unconstitutional because the provision requiring individuals to purchase insurance is not a regulation of economic activity. "The health care 'market' that is the object of the Individual Mandate," the joint dissent maintained, "not only includes but principally consists of goods and services that the young people primarily affected by the Mandate *do not purchase.*" "They are," it continued, "quite simply not participants in that market, and cannot be made so (and thereby subjected to regulation) by the simple device of defining participants to include all those who will, later in their lifetime, probably purchase the goods or services covered by the mandated insurance."[74]

Even though Scalia rejected a strict constructionist interpretation of federal power, he found other ways to protect the interests of the states. He was a vigorous critic of the Supreme Court's "negative" commerce clause jurisprudence, which allows courts to strike down state laws that substantially burden or discriminate against interstate commerce, even in the absence of congressional legislation on the subject.[75] He wrote the court's decision striking down the interim provisions of the Brady bill on the grounds that Congress cannot conscript local officials into carrying out a federal program.[76] He also voted to overturn *Missouri v. Holland* (1920),[77] which held that treaties can expand the authority of the federal government to regulate the activities of the states.[78]

FIRST AMENDMENT

As an originalist, Justice Scalia maintained that the First Amendment, adopted in 1791, secured only "the then extant speech rights of Englishmen."[79] In this view, the First Amendment protects against the common-law doctrine of no prior restraints. But Scalia supplemented his original understanding of the First Amendment with judicial precedent. "Originalism, like any other theory of interpretation," Scalia wrote, "must accommodate the doctrine of stare decisis; it cannot remake the world anew."[80] For example, he relied on and arguably expanded the court's use of strict scrutiny in political speech cases by defending a wide variety of contentious speech. Even though he personally disagreed with flag burning as a form of protest, Scalia cast the deciding vote in *Texas v. Johnson* (1989),[81] which struck down a state flag-desecration law.

Scalia later explained that the "bedrock principle" of the First Amendment is that "government may not prohibit the expression of an idea simply because society finds the idea itself offensive or disagreeable."[82]

Scalia also wrote the opinion for the Supreme Court in *R.A.V. v. City of St. Paul* (1992),[83] which struck down a city's hate-speech ordinance. Instead of relying on the court's traditional overbreadth analysis, Scalia held that the ordinance amounted to viewpoint discrimination. Traditional types of unprotected speech (e.g., libel, obscenity, fighting words) are not "entirely invisible to the Constitution," Scalia argued. "Those who wish to use 'fighting words,'" he maintained, "in connection with other ideas—to express hostility, for example, on the basis of political affiliation, union membership, or homosexuality—are not covered by the statute."[84] Scalia also wrote the court's opinion striking down a state ban on violent video games for children;[85] he joined the court's decision striking down a federal ban on the sale or possession of videos depicting animal cruelty;[86] and he joined the decision in *Snyder v. Phelps* (2011),[87] in which the court ruled that the Westboro Baptist Church had the right to protest at military funerals.

Along the same lines, Justice Scalia was a forceful defender of free speech at abortion clinics. In *Hill v. Colorado* (2000),[88] the court upheld an eight-foot speech-free buffer zone around abortion clinics as a reasonable time, place, and manner restriction. Scalia filed a vigorous dissent, arguing that the regulation was content based and therefore had to satisfy the court's strict scrutiny analysis. Scalia also defended a very robust view of the First Amendment in the area of campaign finance regulation. One of Scalia's early opinions on the subject came in *Austin v. Michigan Chamber of Commerce* (1990),[89] where the court upheld a state law banning the use of corporate funds for independent expenditures in support of, or in opposition to, any candidate for state office. The majority found that because corporations receive special advantages under state law that allow them to amass large treasuries that could unduly influence the political process, the state has a compelling interest to restrict corporate speech.[90] Scalia filed a blistering dissent, calling the decision "Orwellian," "illiberal," and "incompatible with the absolutely central truth of the First Amendment: that government cannot be trusted to assure, through censorship, the 'fairness' of political debate."[91]

Scalia continued to criticize restrictions on electioneering advertisements by corporations. In *McConnell v. FEC* (2003),[92] the Supreme Court upheld the electioneering communications provision of the Bipartisan Campaign

Reform Act, which prohibited express advocacy by corporations and unions for or against any candidate in federal elections within thirty days of a primary or sixty days of a general election. "This is a sad day for the freedom of speech," Scalia wrote in his dissenting opinion.[93] Scalia challenged the primary rationale behind the provision: corruption or the appearance of corruption. Unless there was an outright bribe (i.e., a quid pro quo type of arrangement), he maintained that the government had no business regulating the amount of influence in elections. Four years later, Scalia called for *McConnell* to be overturned because, in his view, it created an "unworkable" legal regime.[94] Ultimately, Scalia's plea was heeded by his colleagues. In *Citizens United v. FEC* (2010),[95] the Roberts Court overruled *Austin* and *McConnell* (in part) and held that government restrictions on independent expenditures by corporations during elections constitute viewpoint discrimination.

However, Scalia never claimed to be an absolutist in interpreting the First Amendment. "Even the prohibition against content discrimination that we assert the First Amendment requires is not absolute," Scalia wrote in one case.[96] Thus, he was willing to find a number of exceptions to the First Amendment. As noted earlier, Scalia did not believe the First Amendment protects against libel suits, and he maintained that the court's decision in *New York Times v. Sullivan* was inconsistent with the original meaning of the First Amendment.[97] Moreover, during his first term on the court, Scalia called into question the *Miller* test, which is used to determine whether a publication is obscene.[98] "In my view," wrote Scalia, "it is quite impossible to come to an objective assessment of (at least) literary or artistic value, there being many accomplished people who have found literature in Dada, and art in the replication of a soup can."[99] Scalia called for a "reexamination" of *Miller*—although he never vigorously pursued the idea. Instead, during his time on the court, Scalia voted consistently to allow states and localities to determine what is obscene or immoral.[100]

Justice Scalia also took the position that the government can place conditions on speech that it supports financially. He joined the majority decision in *Rust v. Sullivan* (1991),[101] which banned the use of federal money to counsel abortion as a method of family planning. He voted in favor of congressionally imposed decency standards for funding of the arts.[102] Scalia joined the majority decision in *Rumsfeld v. Forum for Academic and Institutional Rights* (2006),[103] which upheld a federal ban on funding to universities that refused to give military recruiters access to school resources because of the military's

"Don't Ask, Don't Tell" policy. In *Agency for International Development v. Alliance for Open Society International* (2013),[104] Scalia dissented from the court's holding that requiring nongovernmental organizations to *adopt* a policy "explicitly opposing prostitution and sex trafficking" to obtain federal funding violates the First Amendment. "The First Amendment does not mandate a viewpoint-neutral government," Scalia argued in dissent.[105] As long as unfunded organizations remained free to engage in free speech, he saw no constitutional problem.

In other First Amendment areas, Scalia placed tradition above free speech rights. In *Rutan v. Republican Party of Illinois* (1990),[106] for example, Scalia argued in dissent that the hiring and firing of government employees can be based on political patronage. "When a practice not expressly prohibited by the text of the Bill of Rights bears the endorsement of a long tradition of open, widespread, and unchallenged use that dates back to the beginning of the Republic, we have no proper basis for striking it down," Scalia wrote.[107] In two subsequent cases, he applied the same logic to independent contractors.[108] Along these same lines, Scalia argued that public employees have diminished free speech rights. In *Rankin v. McPherson* (1987),[109] he dissented when the court overturned the dismissal of a public employee for remarking after the assassination attempt on President Reagan: "If they go after him again, I hope they get him." Scalia argued in dissent that the comment was not a matter of public concern, and even if it was, the public employer's interest in maintaining a public image consistent with law enforcement outweighs the employee's free speech rights.[110]

Church-State

Justice Scalia often said that the "most disreputable" aspect of the Supreme Court's jurisprudence involved the religion clauses.[111] One of his pet peeves was the idea that government must be neutral between religion and nonreligion. Scalia claimed that the strict neutralist perspective was simply not true and had its origins in Napoleon's France. As he observed in one speech, the principle of *laïcité*, or secularism, prohibits public officials from invoking the deity.[112] But in America, Scalia claimed, US presidents have always invoked God in public addresses. In one case, Scalia went so far as to argue that when presidents invoke God, it is "*inescapably* the God of monotheism." "With respect to public acknowledgment of religious belief," Scalia wrote, "it is entirely clear from our Nation's historical practices that the Establishment Clause permits this disregard of polytheists and believers in unconcerned deities, just as it permits the disregard of devout atheists."[113]

Scalia believed that because the establishment clause does not place many (if any) limits on government accommodation of religion, the Supreme Court should defer to long-standing American traditions.[114] As he put it in one speech, if the "formulaic" tests the court uses conflict with "long-standing tradition that contradicts them, it is the abstraction and not the tradition that must cease."[115] On this basis, Scalia supported a wide variety of governmental accommodations of religion, including school vouchers;[116] equal access to school facilities;[117] student fee allocations for religious groups and their publications;[118] prayers at graduation ceremonies;[119] student-led prayers at football games;[120] the Pledge of Allegiance in public schools;[121] the teaching of creation science on an equal footing with evolution theory;[122] religious displays on government property,[123] including the Ten Commandments;[124] and sectarian prayers at city council meetings.[125]

Scalia's reliance on tradition in interpreting the establishment clause made him a vociferous critic of the different tests the Supreme Court uses in church-state cases. For example, he scathingly criticized the three-pronged *Lemon* test.[126] In one case, Scalia comically referred to *Lemon* as "some ghoul in a late-night horror movie that repeatedly sits up in its grave and shuffles abroad, after being repeatedly killed and buried."[127] In another case, he called for its internment.[128] Scalia was also a sharp critic of justice Anthony Kennedy's "coercion" test. In *Lee v. Weisman* (1992),[129] the court struck down sectarian prayers at graduation ceremonies. Scalia filed a vigorous dissent in which he criticized Kennedy's analysis as "psychology practiced by amateurs" and referred to the coercion test as "the bulldozer of [the court's] social engineering."[130]

Free Exercise Clause

In the area of religious freedom, Justice Scalia began his tenure by articulating a very narrow construction of the free exercise clause. In *Employment Division, Department of Human Resources of Oregon v. Smith* (1990),[131] Scalia wrote the majority decision denying a religious exemption to a state's criminal law. Alfred Smith and Galen Black, two Native Americans, had been fired from their jobs because they ingested peyote for sacramental purposes at their church. For the court, Scalia held that neutral, generally applicable laws that only incidentally impact religion do not have to be supported by a "compelling state interest."[132] Both liberals and conservatives derided Scalia's opinion and his suggestion that religious freedom was no longer a fundamental right. In response, Congress passed the Religious Freedom Restoration Act of 1993 (RFRA), which restored strict scrutiny analysis when a law substantially burdens religion, irrespective of whether it is neutral or discriminates against religion.[133]

Scalia's view that *Smith* was decided correctly never wavered. In *City of Boerne v. Flores* (1997),[134] he defended his opinion when the court limited the application of RFRA to federal laws. In a separate concurrence, Scalia argued that "the historical evidence put forward by the dissent does nothing to undermine the conclusion we reached in *Smith*."[135] Likewise, Scalia never abandoned his criticism of *Sherbert v. Verner* (1963),[136] in which the court required strict scrutiny in religious freedom cases.[137] During the oral argument in *Holt v. Hobbs* (heard in 2014), Scalia remarked, "Bear in mind I would not have enacted [the Religious Land Use and Institutionalized Persons Act], but there it is. It says there has to be a compelling state interest" when a government (state or federal) imposes a substantial burden on religious exercise in prisons.[138]

At the same time, when Congress restored strict scrutiny in certain areas of the law, Scalia heeded its wishes. He joined the court's decision in *Cutter v. Wilkinson* (2005),[139] which rejected a facial challenge to the Religious Land Use and Institutionalized Persons Act. Then, in *Holt v. Hobbs* (2015),[140] he joined a decision that rejected a state prison's policy of preventing an inmate from growing a short beard. Scalia also joined a 2006 decision granting a religious exemption for the União do Vegetal, an American branch of a Brazilian sect, to use *hoasca*, a hallucinogenic tea, during communion.[141] And in *Burwell v. Hobby Lobby Stores* (2014),[142] Scalia joined the 5–4 decision holding that the implementation provisions of the Patient Protection and Affordable Care Act, which required certain for-profit businesses to carry all contraceptive devices approved by the Food and Drug Administration, violated RFRA. In another case involving religious freedom, Scalia joined Justice Alito's dissent when the court held that a Christian student organization at a public university cannot deny membership based on religious belief or sexual orientation.[143] Finally, in *Locke v. Davey* (2004),[144] the court upheld a state law denying Promise Scholarships to students pursuing theology degrees. Scalia filed a heated dissent, arguing that the law discriminated on the basis of religion.

SECOND AMENDMENT

Justice Scalia's most important opinion for the Supreme Court—albeit a controversial one—was *District of Columbia v. Heller* (2008).[145] The District of Columbia had one of the most restrictive gun laws in the country. It was a crime for DC residents to possess handguns in their homes, and it required that any lawfully owned firearms, such as registered long guns, be kept unloaded and disassembled or bound by a trigger lock or similar device. Dick Heller, a special police officer at the Federal Judicial Center, applied for permission to own a handgun and keep it in his home but was denied. Heller argued that the restrictive regulation violated the Second Amendment. In a 5–4 decision, the court ruled in his favor.

Scalia began his original meaning analysis of the Second Amendment with its text: "A well-regulated Militia, being necessary to the security of a free state, the right of the people to keep and bear Arms, shall not be infringed." Instead of beginning with the prefatory clause, Scalia started with the operative clause: "the right of the people to keep and bear Arms, shall not be infringed." Scalia argued that the phrase "the right of the people" referred to an individual right, not a collective right, and he cited three other provisions of the Bill of Rights using similar language.[146] He also examined founding-era dictionaries and state constitutions to conclude that the publicly understood meanings of the phrases "to keep" and "bear Arms" were not limited to gun possession for martial purposes. Then, turning to the prefatory clause, Scalia acknowledged that the primary purpose of the Second Amendment was to address the Anti-Federalist concern that the federal government could disarm the militia.[147] However, Scalia argued that the central purpose was not a limitation on the broader right of the people to own guns for self-defense. "The prefatory clause," Scalia wrote, "does not suggest that preserving the militia was the only reason Americans valued the ancient right; most undoubtedly thought it even more important for self-defense and hunting."[148]

In reaching this result, Scalia acknowledged that the Second Amendment was not absolute. He maintained that regulations regarding concealed weapons and the possession of guns in sensitive areas (such as schools and government buildings) were still permissible. He also insisted that restrictions on gun sales to the mentally ill or felons would not run afoul of the Second Amendment. However, he concluded that DC's complete ban on operable handguns in the home was a violation of the Second Amendment. "What is not debatable," Scalia wrote, "is that it is not the role of this Court to pronounce the Second Amendment extinct."[149]

Heller was a groundbreaking decision because no federal court prior to 2001 had held that the Second Amendment conferred an individual right to bear arms disconnected from the state militia.[150] Even though Scalia recognized that there were limits to the types of guns American citizens could lawfully possess, he later joined a dissent from a denial of certiorari by Justice Thomas, which argued that a city's categorical ban on semiautomatic weapons likely violated the Second Amendment.[151] In a 2013 interview, Scalia called *Heller* his "legacy opinion" because it was "the most complete originalist opinion that I've ever written."[152]

RIGHTS OF THE ACCUSED

Justice Scalia generally defended a crabbed view of the rights of the accused—although there were some notable exceptions.[153] In some cases, Scalia made technical distinctions that favored criminal defendants. In *Arizona v. Hicks* (1987), for example, he wrote the majority opinion finding that a "cursory inspection" of stereo equipment constituted a search. "It matters not that the search uncovered nothing of any great personal value to respondent," wrote Scalia. "A search is a search, even if it happens to disclose nothing but the bottom of a turntable."[154] In another case, Scalia dissented when the court ruled that suspicionless testing of customs agents did not violate Fourth Amendment rights.[155] He also dissented when the court found that it was permissible to detain individuals without a warrant for up to forty-eight hours before a probable-cause hearing.[156]

Ironically, Scalia's support of the common-law trespass doctrine favored the accused in several important Fourth Amendment cases. Scalia wrote the Supreme Court's opinion in *Kyllo v. United States* (2001),[157] which held that use of a thermal imaging device to detect heat emanating from a home constituted a search. He also wrote the decision in *Florida v. Jardines* (2013),[158] ruling that the use of a narcotics-detecting dog around a homeowner's front porch violated the Fourth Amendment. And he wrote the court's decision in *United States v. Jones* (2012),[159] where the justices unanimously ruled (albeit on different grounds) that placement of a global positioning system (GPS) device on a jeep beyond the time allowed on the warrant violated the Fourth Amendment.

Confrontation Clause

Another constitutional provision that Scalia defended in a principled manner was the Sixth Amendment's confrontation clause. In cases involving in-court testimony, Scalia interpreted that provision literally to require face-to-face confrontation. For example, in *Coy v. Iowa* (1988),[160] he wrote the majority opinion striking down the use of screens to protect child sexual assault victims from their alleged assailants. And he dissented in *Maryland v. Craig* (1990),[161] in which the court upheld the use of a one-way closed-circuit television to present testimony by an alleged child sexual abuse victim. "Seldom has this Court failed so conspicuously to sustain a categorical guarantee of the Constitution against the tide of prevailing current opinion," wrote Scalia.[162]

Scalia won a major victory in a case examining the confrontation clause's application to out-of-court testimonial statements. In *Crawford v. Washington* (2004),[163] the defendant had been convicted of assault and attempted murder for stabbing a person who, he believed, had tried to rape his wife, Sylvia. The prosecution admitted into evidence Sylvia's tape-recorded statements to police officers to show that the stabbing was not self-defense. However, she was not available to testify at trial because of the state's marital privilege law. For the majority, Scalia overruled a prior decision of the court,[164] which had allowed out-of-court statements by an unavailable witness "if they bore adequate indicia of reliability"—that is, if they fell within a firmly rooted hearsay exception or they bore particularized guarantees of trustworthiness. Relying on English common law, Scalia concluded that "the Framers would not have allowed admission of testimonial statements of a witness who did not appear at trial unless he was unavailable to testify, and the defendant had had a prior opportunity for cross-examination."[165] "Where testimonial statements are at issue," wrote Scalia, "the only indicium of reliability sufficient to satisfy constitutional demands is the one the Constitution actually prescribes: confrontation."[166]

Following *Crawford*, Scalia wrote the Supreme Court's decision in *Davis v. Washington* (2006),[167] which established the "primary purpose" test for distinguishing between testimonial and nontestimonial statements. He also wrote the decision in *Giles v. California* (2008),[168] which rejected application of the "forfeiture by wrongdoing" exception to the facts of that case. According to Scalia, that exception to the confrontation clause applies only if the defendant engaged in conduct designed to prevent the witness from testifying. Scalia then wrote the court's decision in *Melendez-Diaz v. Massachusetts* (2009),[169] ruling that affidavits reporting the results of forensic evidence are "testimonial" and therefore subject to the requirements of *Crawford.*

Toward the end of his judicial career, however, Scalia felt that his colleagues were backtracking from a principled defense of *Crawford.* In *Michigan v. Bryant* (2011),[170] the Supreme Court ruled that a dying man's identification and description of his alleged shooter were nontestimonial because the primary purpose of the evidence was to enable the police to assist in an ongoing emergency. Scalia filed an impassioned dissent, claiming that the court's "opinion distorts our Confrontation Clause jurisprudence and leaves it in a shambles." "Today's tale—a story of five officers conducting successive examinations of a dying man with the primary purpose, not of obtaining and preserving his testimony regarding his killer, but of protecting him, them, and others from a murderer somewhere on the loose—is so transparently false that professing to believe it demeans this institution," wrote Scalia.[171] In an unusual concurrence in *Ohio v. Clark* (2015),[172] Scalia accused the author of the court's decision, Samuel Alito, of wanting to overturn *Crawford.* "The author unabashedly displays his hostility to *Crawford* and its progeny," wrote Scalia, "perhaps aggravated by [an] inability to muster the votes to overrule them." "But snide detractions," he continued, "do no harm; they are just indications of motive."[173] Interestingly, prior to his authorship of the court's decision in *Heller*, Scalia often cited *Crawford* as his most important opinion.[174]

Right to a Jury Trial

Another guarantee that Justice Scalia robustly defended was the Sixth Amendment's right to a jury trial in criminal cases.[175] Federal and state sentencing laws allowed judges to increase penalties in certain circumstances based on a preponderance of the evidence. Beginning with two dissents in 1998, Scalia argued that such judicial discretion violated the defendant's right to have a jury decide all facts that could enhance punishment—a viewpoint that ultimately garnered majority support.[176] In *Blakely v. Washington* (2004),[177] for example, Scalia wrote the court's decision applying the so-called *Apprendi* rule to state sentencing guidelines. *Apprendi v. New Jersey* (2000) required that "any fact that increases the penalty for a crime beyond the prescribed statutory maximum must be submitted to a jury, and proved beyond a reasonable doubt."[178] The right to a jury trial, Scalia wrote in *Blakely*, "is no mere procedural formality, but a fundamental reservation of power in our constitutional structure." "Just as suffrage ensures the people's ultimate control in the legislative and executive branches," Scalia observed, "jury trial is meant to ensure their control in the judiciary."[179] Then, in another case, Scalia joined the court's decision applying *Apprendi* to federal sentencing guidelines—although he dissented to the part of the decision that allowed federal judges discretionary (as opposed to mandatory) authority to alter sentences.[180]

Fourth Amendment

Despite Justice Scalia's principled opinions in the aforementioned areas, he was not the "pin-up" of the criminal defense bar he sometimes portrayed himself to be.[181] Statistically, Scalia sided with the government in 72 percent of criminal cases, which placed him seventh among the thirty-six justices who served on the Supreme Court from 1946 to 2016.[182] Accordingly, the "liberal" results he reached in certain areas of criminal law must be balanced with his interpretation of other constitutional guarantees protecting the rights of the accused. In Fourth Amendment cases, Justice Scalia took the position that a warrant was not required for a search or an arrest to be considered constitutional. "What [the Fourth Amendment] explicitly states regarding warrants," Scalia explained in a 1991 case, "is by way of limitation upon their issuance rather than a requirement of their use."[183] In a 2015 case, Scalia elaborated on his reading of the Fourth Amendment. The two clauses of the amendment (the reasonableness clause and the warrant clause), he observed, "seem to be independent—and directed at entirely different actors." "The former," he explained, "tells the executive what it must do when it conducts a search, and the latter tells the judiciary what it must do when it issues a search warrant." The warrant clause, Scalia concluded, is "a guidepost" in determining whether a search is reasonable, but "the only constitutional *requirement* is that a search be reasonable."[184]

Justice Scalia also supported a number of exceptions to the warrant requirement. For example, he supported the "stop and frisk" based on reasonable suspicion, even though he was not certain that pat-downs complied with the Fourth Amendment. "I frankly doubt," Scalia wrote in one case, "whether the fiercely proud men who adopted our Fourth Amendment would have allowed themselves to be subjected, on mere suspicion of being armed and dangerous, to such indignity. . . . I adhere to the original meaning, however. And though I do not favor the mode of analysis in *Terry* [*v. Ohio*], I cannot say its result was wrong."[185] Scalia also was very deferential toward searches based on exigent circumstances and consent.[186] He deferred to school administrators and local officials to conduct administrative searches based on "special needs." For example, he wrote the majority opinion holding that suspicionless drug testing of student athletes is permissible,[187] he joined the opinion allowing suspicionless drug testing of students who participate in competitive extracurricular activities,[188] and he filed a vigorous dissent when the court overturned a local policy of conducting involuntary drug tests on pregnant women suspected of using drugs.[189] In *City of Los Angeles v. Patel* (2015), Scalia dissented from a ruling nullifying a municipal ordinance that required hotel operators to make their registries available to the police on demand.[190] Moreover, Scalia voted to allow strip searches of individuals charged with minor offenses when they were admitted into the general jail population.[191]

Justice Scalia also authored a couple of interesting decisions involving the "seizure" of persons under the Fourth Amendment. In *California v. Hodari D.* (1991), he wrote that it was improper to suppress a small rock of crack cocaine thrown to the ground during a chase when there was no "application of physical force" or submission to an officer's "show of authority."[192] Scalia also wrote the decision in *Scott v. Harris* (2007),[193] which held that it was reasonable to use a "precision intervention technique" (applying the push bumper of a police car to the rear of a vehicle) during a high-speed chase when the suspect posed a substantial and immediate risk of serious physical injury to others.

Once again, however, Scalia drew some important lines. He voted with the majority in holding that a strip search of a minor in a public school violated the Fourth Amendment.[194] In a 2009 decision, Scalia argued in a concurring opinion that *New York v. Belton* (1981)[195] should be overturned—a ruling that allowed police officers to search the compartment of an automobile even when a suspect has been arrested and placed in the backseat of a police car.[196] In a 2013 case, Scalia dissented when the Supreme Court allowed DNA testing of individuals charged with violent crimes as part of the routine booking process. In contrast to the majority, Scalia argued that DNA swab tests are different from fingerprinting because the primary motive is not the identification of suspects but the investigation of crimes.[197] That same year, he joined the court's decision finding that per se warrantless, nonconsensual blood tests of suspected drunk drivers violate the Fourth Amendment.[198]

Electronic Surveillance

Reminiscent of Justice Black, Scalia advocated a literal interpretation of those objects protected by the Fourth Amendment: "persons, houses, papers, and effects." In *Minnesota v. Carter* (1998),[199] he filed a concurring opinion in which he criticized the "fuzzy" standard established in *Katz v. United States* (1967),[200] which recognized a reasonable expectation of privacy against warrantless electronic eavesdropping. Scalia argued that this "notoriously unhelpful" test has allowed judges to substitute their own expectations of privacy for those of the American people. "When that self-indulgent test is employed (as the dissent would employ it here) to determine whether a 'search or seizure' within the meaning of the Constitution has *occurred* (as opposed to whether that 'search or seizure' is an 'unreasonable' one), it has no plausible foundation in the text of the Fourth Amendment," wrote Scalia.[201] In response to her colleague's analysis, Justice Ginsburg wrote that Scalia's "lively" opinion gave her "a strong sense of déjà vu" that "vividly recalls the opinion of Justice Black *in dissent* in *Katz*."[202]

Exclusionary Rule

Justice Scalia did not believe the exclusionary rule was constitutionally required—although he stopped short of calling for it to be overturned.[203] Instead of trying to overturn *Mapp v. Ohio* (1961),[204] the case that nationalized the exclusionary rule, Scalia wrote or joined opinions limiting its reach. He wrote the 5–4 decision in *Hudson v. Michigan* (2006),[205] which found that the exclusionary rule does not apply in "knock and announce" cases. "The costs here are considerable," wrote Scalia. "In addition to the grave adverse consequences that exclusion of relevant incriminating evidence always entails (viz., the risk of releasing dangerous criminals into society), imposing that massive remedy for a knock-and-announce violation would generate a constant flood of alleged failures to observe the rule."[206] He also joined the court's decisions in *Arizona v. Evans* (1995)[207] and *Herring v. United States* (2009).[208] In the former case, the Supreme Court ruled that the exclusionary rule does not apply to an arresting officer's good-faith belief that a warrant is still outstanding due to an error committed by an employee in the clerk's office. In the latter case, the court refused to apply the exclusionary rule when a similar error was committed by an employee in the sheriff's office.

Fifth Amendment

In Fifth Amendment cases, Justice Scalia defended a *very* narrow interpretation of the self-incrimination clause. He was a sharp critic of *Miranda v. Arizona* (1966),[209] where the Supreme Court required that criminal suspects be warned of their right to remain silent and to have an attorney present during questioning by police.[210] Remarkably, only two years after *Miranda*, Congress enacted the Omnibus Crime Control and Safe Streets Act, which applied the pre-*Miranda* standard of "the totality of circumstances" in federal courts, not whether a defendant had been given the *Miranda* warning. In *Dickerson v. United States* (2000),[211] the court struck down that law. "Whether or not we would agree with *Miranda*'s reasoning and its resulting rule were we addressing the issue in the first instance," Chief Justice Rehnquist wrote for the court, "the principles of *stare decisis* weigh heavily against overruling it now." "*Miranda*," he added, "has become embedded in routine police practice to the point where the warnings have become part of our national culture."[212]

Justice Scalia filed a sharply worded dissent that was joined only by Justice Thomas. Scalia maintained that *Miranda*'s prophylactic rules were not constitutionally required. "There is . . . simply no basis in reason," he wrote, "for concluding that a response to the very first question asked, by a suspect who already *knows* all of the rights described in the *Miranda* warning, is anything other than a volitional act." He thus called for *Miranda* to be overruled. "Far from believing that *stare decisis* compels this result," Scalia claimed, "I believe we cannot allow to remain on the books even a celebrated decision—*especially* a celebrated decision—that has come to stand for the proposition that the Supreme Court has power to impose extraconstitutional constraints upon Congress and the States."[213] In other cases, Scalia either wrote or joined opinions limiting the scope of *Miranda*.[214]

Sixth Amendment

Justice Scalia also defended a narrow construction of the Sixth Amendment's right-to-counsel provision. In *Padilla v. Kentucky* (2010),[215] the Supreme Court held that the defendant's Sixth Amendment rights had been violated when his attorney misadvised him about the possibility of being deported if he entered a guilty plea for drug distribution. Scalia began his dissent by observing that the Sixth Amendment, as an original matter, "meant only that a defendant had a right to employ counsel, or to use volunteered services of counsel."[216] Scalia acknowledged that the court had rejected such a narrow interpretation of the Sixth Amendment by requiring the government to provide counsel for the poor and by mandating that the appointed attorney be "effective."[217] Nonetheless, he claimed that because the Sixth Amendment's right to counsel was limited to criminal prosecutions, Padilla's claim that he had received bad advice from his attorney was not a Sixth Amendment issue. "The Constitution," Scalia wrote, "is not an all-purpose tool for judicial construction of a perfect world; and when we ignore its text in order to make it that, we often find ourselves swinging a sledge where a tack hammer is needed."[218]

In other right-to-counsel cases, Scalia voted to limit its scope. He wrote vigorous dissents in two consolidated cases in which the Supreme Court applied the Sixth Amendment to the plea-bargaining stage of criminal cases.[219] "Criminal justice today," Justice Kennedy wrote for the court, "is for the most part a system of pleas, not a system of trials." He noted that 97 percent of federal convictions and 94 percent of state convictions are the result of guilty pleas.[220] Nonetheless, Justice Scalia drew a distinction between a plea bargain and the actual trial. The plea-bargaining process, he reasoned, is not "covered by the Sixth Amendment, which is concerned not with the fairness of bargaining but with the fairness of conviction."[221] Scalia also dissented when the court held that the Sixth Amendment applies to civil contempt proceedings.[222] He then dissented when the court held that states can insist on representation by counsel for those who are mentally competent to stand trial. "Until today," Scalia wrote in dissent, "the right of self-representation has been accorded the same respect as other constitutional guarantees." "The only circumstance," Scalia contended, "in which we have permitted the State to deprive a defendant of this trial right is the one under which we have allowed the State to deny *other* such rights: when it is necessary to enable the trial to proceed in an orderly fashion."[223] Finally, Scalia had an extremely low bar for how effective counsel must be. For example, he wrote a dissenting opinion in a death penalty case and argued that a procedural error (untimely filing of an appeal) should *not* be excused when counsel "abandoned" the defendant.[224]

Eighth Amendment

In interpreting the Eighth Amendment, Justice Scalia was very deferential to state legislatures in determining what constitutes "cruel and unusual punishments." He detested "the evolving standards of decency" test established by the Supreme Court in *Trop v. Dulles* (1958), where the Warren Court ruled that the Eighth Amendment "must draw its meaning from the evolving standards of decency that mark the progress of a maturing society."[225] Scalia ridiculed that test as a natural law concept that gave judges too much discretion. In judicial opinions and speeches, Scalia also rejected the use of foreign law in determining what constitutes cruel and unusual punishment in the United States.[226] Instead, Scalia based his reading of the Eighth Amendment on tradition. "When judges test their individual notions of fairness against an American tradition that is deep and broad and continuing, it is not the tradition that is on trial, but the judges."[227]

In an early noncapital case, Scalia wrote the decision upholding a mandatory life-without-parole sentence for the possession of more than 650 grams of cocaine. Scalia examined the historical understanding of the "cruel and unusual punishments" provision and concluded that it did not require proportional sentencing—an interpretation that was supported by only one other justice at the time.[228] Scalia subsequently joined the court's decision upholding a "three-strikes" law from the state of California, and he dissented in a case disallowing life sentences without parole for juveniles convicted of nonhomicidal offenses.[229] In one of Scalia's last opinions,[230] he filed a vigorous dissent in a case in which the court gave retroactive effect to its decision in *Miller v. Alabama* (2012).[231] That case held that mandatory life-without-parole sentences for juveniles who commit homicidal offenses violate the Eighth Amendment.

As for the death penalty itself, Justice Scalia believed that it is constitutionally permissible, and he could be quite sharp with colleagues who disagreed with him.[232] He argued that the Eighth Amendment does not prohibit mandatory death penalty statutes, nor does it prevent states from placing limits on mitigating circumstances.[233] Scalia also was not sympathetic to procedural challenges to imposition of a death sentence. He joined the court's decision in *McCleskey v. Zant* (1991),[234] which placed limits on the so-called abuse of writ process in capital cases. Scalia saw no constitutional obstacle to the use of victim impact statements during the sentencing phase of capital cases.[235] In *McCleskey v. Kemp* (1987),[236] he joined the 5–4 decision rejecting a challenge to a death sentence based on statistical evidence of racial discrimination in the use and imposition of the death penalty. In a remarkable memo to his colleagues, Scalia explained that, since "the unconscious operation of irrational sympathies and antipathies, including racial, upon jury decisions and (hence) prosecutorial decisions is real, acknowledged in the decisions of this court, and ineradicable, I cannot honestly say that all I need is more proof."[237] In a 2009 case Scalia argued that an "actual innocence" claim is an insufficient reason to retry a person who has been sentenced to death.[238]

Justice Scalia also took the position that the Supreme Court should not get involved in determining who is eligible for the death penalty. For example, Scalia authored vigorous dissents in cases striking down the death penalty for the intellectually disabled[239] and minors.[240] In *Roper v. Simmons* (2005), the decision disallowing the death penalty for sixteen- and seventeen-year-olds, Scalia wrote:

> The Court thus proclaims itself sole arbiter of our Nation's moral standards—and in the course of discharging that awesome responsibility purports to take guidance from the views of foreign courts and legislatures. Because I do not believe that the meaning of our Eighth Amendment, any more than the meaning of other provisions of our Constitution, should be determined by the subjective views of five Members of this Court and like-minded foreigners, I dissent.[241]

Scalia also dissented in a decision that negated the death penalty for the crime of raping a child.[242] Taking a literal view of the words "cruel and unusual punishments," Scalia did not believe the provision applies to prison beatings and conditions.[243] In *Brown v. Plata* (2011),[244] the Supreme Court upheld a three-judge district court order requiring the state of California to reduce populations in overcrowded prisons because the "toxic" environment violated the medical and mental health needs of inmates under the Eighth Amendment. In dissent, Scalia described the lower court's order as "perhaps the most radical injunction issued by a court in our Nation's history."[245]

PROPERTY RIGHTS

Like Justice Black, Scalia rejected a return to the *Lochner* era—although he did so for different reasons. In response to calls for the Supreme Court to take a more activist approach in defending economic rights under the due process clauses of the Fifth and Fourteenth Amendments,[246] Scalia called this "the moment of truth" for conservatives. "Every era raises its own peculiar threat to constitutional democracy," Scalia wrote in 1985, "and [judicial activism] represents the distinctive threat of our times."[247] Scalia worried that such an activist approach would open the door to claims of other rights under the due process clause, including the right to have an abortion, the right to die, and the right of sexual preference. On this basis, he dissented in decisions that recognized a corporation's right to be protected against excessive awards of punitive damages under the due process clause.[248] "Since the Constitution does not make [excessive punitive damages] any of our business," Scalia reasoned, "the Court's activities in this area are an unjustified incursion into the province of state governments."[249]

When it came to specific constitutional provisions dealing with property rights, such as the takings clause, Justice Scalia provided an expansive interpretation. In *Nollan v. California Coastal Commission* (1987),[250] he wrote the court's opinion holding that property owners must be compensated when they are required to provide a public easement in front of their beachfront property as a condition of receiving a building permit. After closely examining the zoning regulation, Scalia rejected the commission's stated purpose (visual access to the ocean from the road) as illegitimate and referred to the building restriction as "an out-and-out plan of extortion." The next year, Scalia wrote a dissenting opinion in which he argued that a city's "rent control" ordinance constituted a taking because it establishes "a welfare program privately funded by those landlords who happen to have 'hardship' tenants."[251]

Scalia authored the Supreme Court's decision in *Lucas v. South Carolina Coastal Council* (1992).[252] In 1986 David Lucas purchased two vacant lots on a South Carolina barrier island, where he planned to build single-family homes. Two years later, the state legislature enacted the Beachfront Management Act, which prevented Lucas from erecting any permanent habitable structures on his two parcels. Scalia held for the 6–3 court that the deprivation of all economic use of property constitutes a taking. "When the owner of real property has been called upon to sacrifice all economically beneficial uses in the name of the common good, that is, to leave his property economically idle, he has suffered a taking," wrote Scalia.[253] Interestingly, Scalia conceded that the takings clause, as an original matter, applies only to physical appropriations of land, but he reasoned that the text of the Fifth Amendment is not so limited.[254]

Justice Scalia joined the Supreme Court's decision in *Dolan v. City of Tigard* (1994),[255] which required local governments to satisfy a "rough proportionality" test—more stringent than the rational basis test—before they can compel property owners to make public improvements as a condition for the development of commercial property. Scalia joined Justice O'Connor's dissent in *Kelo v. City of New London* (2005),[256] in which the court broadly construed "public use" under the takings clause to include "economic development." Scalia also wrote the court's decision in *Stop the Beach Renourishment v. Florida Department of Environmental Protection* (2010),[257] which rejected property owners' argument that their beachfront property rights had been taken as a result of state efforts to restore eroded beaches. For a plurality, however, Scalia argued that a taking can be accomplished by decisions of the state judiciary. In 2015 Scalia joined the court's holding that the takings clause applies to both real and personal property.[258]

SUBSTANTIVE DUE PROCESS

Along with Hugo Black, Justice Scalia was one of the most strenuous critics of substantive due process in Supreme Court history. He maintained that *substantive* due process is an oxymoron and allows "freewheeling lawmaking" by judges.[259] As he understood it, due process requires fair procedures, but it does not allow judges to create substantive rights based on evolving societal values or natural law. As Scalia explained in one case, "there is no right to 'liberty' under the Due Process Clause. . . . The Fourteenth Amendment *expressly allows* States to deprive their citizens of 'liberty,' *so long as 'due process of law' is provided.*"[260]

Privacy and Abortion

Based on this interpretation, Scalia rejected a general right of privacy under the Constitution. Unlike Justice Black, however, Scalia was much less sympathetic to the underlying right in question.[261] "The right to be left alone," Scalia remarked in a 2008 speech, "good God, this is anarchy."[262] Scalia acknowledged that American citizens have privacy rights, but he limited those rights to areas specifically mentioned in the Bill of Rights, such as the Fourth Amendment. For this reason, Scalia did not believe the Constitution protects a woman's right to obtain an abortion, and in his third term on the Supreme Court, he called for the overturning of *Roe v. Wade* (1973).[263] "It thus appears," Scalia lamented in a concurring opinion, "that the mansion of constitutionalized abortion law, constructed overnight in *Roe v. Wade*, must be disassembled doorjamb by doorjamb, and never entirely brought down, no matter how wrong it may be."[264] In *Planned Parenthood of Southeastern Pennsylvania v. Casey* (1992),[265] in which the court upheld the essential holding of *Roe*, Scalia filed an acerbic dissent. "The Imperial Judiciary lives," he proclaimed, and dramatically compared the court's decision to *Dred Scott v. Sandford* (1857). "We should get out of this area," Scalia concluded, "where we have no right to be, and where we do neither ourselves nor the country any good by remaining."[266]

Right to Die

Justice Scalia did not believe the due process clause covered end-of-life decisions either. In *Cruzan v. Director, Missouri Department of Health* (1990),[267] the Supreme Court recognized a qualified right to turn off life support. In a concurring opinion, Scalia argued that because the Constitution does not address the subject of suicide, "federal courts have no business" making rules about the termination of life support, "including suicide by refusing to take appropriate measures necessary to preserve one's life."[268] Under the common law, Scalia maintained, there is no difference between "starving oneself to death" and "putting a gun to one's temple."[269] "The point at which life becomes 'worthless,'" he reasoned, "and the point at which the means necessary to preserve it become 'extraordinary' or 'inappropriate,' are neither set forth in the Constitution nor known to the nine Justices of this Court any better than they are known to nine people picked at random from the Kansas City telephone directory."[270]

Right of Sexual Preference

In another area of substantive due process, Scalia rejected a right of sexual preference. In *Lawrence v. Texas* (2003),[271] the court struck down a state law banning only same-sex sodomy. In dissent, Scalia argued that a right of sexual preference is not a fundamental right based on American traditions, and therefore the states can regulate it. Scalia analogized bans on homosexual sodomy to state laws prohibiting "bigamy, same-sex marriage, adult incest, prostitution, masturbation, adultery, fornication, bestiality, and obscenity." He also accused the majority of imposing its "homosexual agenda" on the American people. "Many Americans do not want persons who openly engage in homosexual conduct as partners in their business, as scoutmasters for their children, as teachers in their children's school, or as boarders in their home," wrote Scalia. "They view this as protecting themselves and their families from a lifestyle that they believe to be immoral and destructive."[272]

Other Substantive Due Process Claims

Justice Scalia rejected other substantive due process claims as well. In *Michael H. v. Gerald D.* (1989),[273] Scalia wrote the majority opinion dismissing a paternity suit by the putative father of a child conceived during an adulterous relationship. In the 5–4 decision, the court upheld the presumption under state law that a child born to a married woman living with her husband is the child of the marriage. In a footnote, Scalia argued that fundamental rights under the due process clause should be defined at the most specific level, and as applied to this case, the fundamental right at issue was the preservation of the marital family, not the liberty interest a biological father might have in maintaining a legal relationship with his daughter.

In another case, Scalia dissented when the Supreme Court recognized parents' substantive due process right to direct the upbringing of their children.[274] He acknowledged that parental rights are among the "unalienable Rights" contemplated by the Declaration of Independence, but he did not believe federal judges were authorized to enforce such rights. He wrote:

> While I would think it entirely compatible with the commitment to representative democracy set forth in the founding documents to argue, in legislative chambers or in electoral campaigns, that the state has *no power* to interfere with parents' authority over the rearing of their children, I do not believe that the power which the Constitution confers upon me *as a judge* entitles me to deny legal effect to laws that (in my view) infringe upon what is (in my view) that unenumerated right.[275]

Scalia voted against several claims that the government had to take affirmative steps to protect children from harm under the due process clause. For example, he joined the 6–3 decision holding that social services employees were not constitutionally responsible for failing to remove a child from his custodial father, even though the agency had received several complaints that the father was abusing the child.[276] Scalia also wrote the court's opinion in *Town of Castle Rock v. Gonzales* (2005),[277] which rejected a claim that police officers could be held responsible for not protecting three children murdered by their father, even though there was probable cause to believe a restraining order had been violated.

Finally, in *NASA v. Nelson* (2011), Scalia rejected a right of "informational privacy" and stated, "That counsel invoked the infinitely plastic concept of 'substantive' due process does not make this constitutional theory any less invented."[278] The one major exception to Scalia's consistent rejection of substantive due process was his "acquiescence" in the court's doctrine of selective incorporation. Scalia provided the pivotal fifth vote in *McDonald v. City of Chicago* (2010),[279] where the court incorporated the Second Amendment to apply against state power—even though he had previously stated that the Second Amendment does not apply to the states.[280]

EQUAL PROTECTION

Justice Scalia also defended a very narrow construction of the equal protection clause, the fundamental purpose of which, in his view, was to outlaw racial discrimination. During his tenure, Scalia did not support the Supreme Court's post-*Brown* decisions that required affirmative steps to dismantle segregated public schools. In *Green v. County School Board of New Kent County* (1968),[281] the court ruled that "freedom of choice" plans were not always an adequate remedy to effectuate a unitary school system. Instead, the court required that lower courts consider all aspects of school operations, including student assignments, faculty, staff, transportation, extracurricular activities, and facilities. In a separate concurrence in *Freeman v. Pitts* (1992),[282] Scalia argued that *Green* put an unjustifiable burden on school districts, requiring them to prove a "negative." According to Scalia, they had to show "that the [racial] imbalance [in their school districts] is not attributable to their past discrimination."[283] Scalia believed that school districts should be required to rectify racial imbalances in their schools only if they continue to have discriminatory policies. In fact, Scalia criticized the majority for not going far enough to counteract the effects of *Green.* "While it is perfectly appropriate for the Court to decide this case on [a] narrow basis, we must resolve—if not today, then soon—what is to be done in the vast majority of other districts, where, though our cases continue to profess that judicial oversight of school operations is a temporary expedient, democratic processes remain suspended, with no prospect of restoration, 38 years after *Brown*."[284] Later that same term, Scalia wrote a separate opinion contending that *Green* should not apply at universities.[285] He also joined the 2007 Roberts Court decision that struck down two *voluntary* desegregation plans as a violation of the Fourteenth Amendment's equal protection clause.[286]

Gender Discrimination

Based on his narrow construction of the equal protection clause, Scalia did not believe it applied to gender discrimination. In a 2010 interview with law professor Calvin Massey, Scalia called the application of the equal protection clause to sex discrimination "a modern invention."[287] He also took the opportunity to criticize the levels of scrutiny used by the Supreme Court in such cases. "I've never been a fan" of the tiered analytical approach, he observed, because it puts "a thumb on the scale." Scalia's response to those who thought the equal protection clause should cover gender discrimination was that they should amend the Constitution. "If you think it's a good idea [to guarantee women equal protection of the law]," Scalia said in 2012 interview, "amend the Constitution! Which is what they did to give women the vote."[288]

Scalia's most important gender discrimination opinion came in *United States v. Virginia* (1996).[289] In that case, the Supreme Court was faced with a challenge to the all-male admissions policy of the Virginia Military Institute (VMI). Founded in 1839, VMI had the distinctive mission of producing "citizen soldiers," and it employed a unique form of physical and mental training (the "adversative method") that instilled a strong moral code in its cadets. For the court, Justice Ginsburg held that Virginia had not provided an "exceedingly persuasive justification" for its single-sex admissions policy and therefore could no longer deny admission to qualified women. "However 'liberally' this plan serves the State's sons," Ginsburg wrote, "it makes no provision whatever for her daughters. That is not *equal* protection."[290] In solo dissent, Scalia lamented that the court's decision was "shut[ting] down an institution that has served the Commonwealth of Virginia with pride and distinction for over a century and a half." He praised the institution's commitment to "manly honor," called the court's decision "illiberal," and described its analysis as "not law, but politics-smuggled-into-the-law."[291]

Gay and Lesbian Rights

Justice Scalia did not believe the equal protection clause covered discrimination on the basis of sexual orientation either.[292] In *Romer v. Evans* (1996),[293] the court struck down a Colorado constitutional amendment that removed gays, lesbians, and bisexuals from the protection of antidiscrimination laws. According to Justice Kennedy, author of the court's opinion, the amendment lacked a legitimate purpose and seemed "inexplicable by anything but animus toward the class it affects."[294] In dissent, Scalia accused the majority of "mistak[ing] a Kulturkampf for a fit of spite."[295] He characterized the amendment as "a modest attempt by seemingly tolerant Coloradans to preserve traditional sexual mores against the efforts of a politically powerful minority to revise those mores through use of the laws."[296]

In *Obergefell v. Hodges* (2015),[297] decided during Scalia's last full term, the Supreme Court struck down state laws banning same-sex marriage under both the due process and equal protection clauses. Justice Kennedy, writing for the majority, held that such laws deprive gays and lesbians of the fundamental right to marry and the material benefits and legal rights associated with such a union. "Under the Constitution," he wrote, "same-sex couples seek in marriage the same legal treatment as opposite-sex couples, and it would disparage their choices and diminish their personhood to deny them this right."[298] In dissent, Justice Scalia wrote one of the most sarcastic opinions in Supreme Court history.[299] Claiming that he was not taking a position on the merits of gay marriage, Scalia wanted "to call attention to this Court's threat to American democracy." "Today's decree says that my Ruler, and the Ruler of 320 million Americans coast-to-coast, is a majority of the nine lawyers on the Supreme Court," wrote Scalia. "This practice of constitutional revision by an unelected committee of nine," he added, "always accompanied (as it is today) by extravagant praise of liberty, robs the People of the most important liberty they asserted in the Declaration of Independence and won in the Revolution of 1776: the freedom to govern themselves."[300]

Affirmative Action

Justice Scalia was also a sharp critic of affirmative action. At a 1979 conference, he played the role of "antihero" on a panel discussing the merits of affirmative action. Scalia found fault with affirmative action both in principle and in practice.[301] In principle, he argued that any sort of "restorative justice" based on historical racial discrimination was a violation of the equal protection clause. "I owe no man anything, nor he me, because of the blood that flows in our veins," wrote Scalia.[302] He questioned the practicality of affirmative action and argued that it perpetuates racial stereotypes and the idea of the inherent inferiority of blacks. "And it is obvious to the public that (to the extent these schools flunk *anyone* out) the same factor that produced special admissions will also tend to produce special retention and, ultimately, special graduation. Thus, insofar as 'public image' is concerned, the immediate and predictable effect of affirmative action is to establish a second-class, 'minority' degree, which is a less certain certificate of quality."[303]

In Supreme Court cases, Scalia questioned whether affirmative action actually helps minorities if they are unsuccessful at the educational institutions to which they are admitted. In his final year on the court, Scalia participated in the early stages of *Fisher II* (2016).[304] During the oral argument, he expressed support for the so-called mismatch theory. When attorney Gregory G. Garre, the university's counsel, raised a concern that the number of minorities at the University of Texas would drastically decline if the court struck down its affirmative action program, Scalia responded:

> There are those who contend that it does not benefit African-Americans to get them into the University of Texas where they do not do well, as opposed to having them go to a less-advanced school, a slower-track school where they do well. One of the briefs pointed out that most of the black scientists in this country don't come from schools like the University of Texas. They come from lesser schools where they do not feel that they're being pushed ahead in classes that are too fast for them. I'm just not impressed by the fact that the University of Texas may have fewer [African American students]. Maybe it ought to have fewer. . . . I don't think it stands to reason that it's a good thing for the University of Texas to admit as many blacks as possible.[305]

During his time on the Supreme Court, Justice Scalia rejected affirmative action at every turn. In *City of Richmond v. J. A. Croson Co.* (1989),[306] the court struck down a municipal ordinance requiring prime contractors to award 30 percent of all subcontracting to minority-owned businesses. Scalia filed a concurring opinion in which he agreed with the court's use of strict scrutiny but disagreed with the majority's suggestion that state and local governments can *occasionally* consider race to ameliorate the effects of past discrimination. "In my view," wrote Scalia, "there is only one circumstance in which the States may act by race to 'undo the effects of past discrimination': where that is necessary to eliminate their own maintenance of a system of unlawful racial classification."[307] In *Adarand Constructors, Inc. v. Pena* (1995),[308] the court used strict scrutiny to strike down a federal affirmative action program. In a short concurring opinion, Scalia observed, "under our Constitution there can be no such thing as either a creditor or debtor race. . . . In the eyes of government, we are just one race here. It is American."[309]

Justice Scalia dissented in *Grutter v. Bollinger* (2003),[310] in which the Supreme Court upheld the affirmative action program of the University of Michigan Law School, which considered race a "plus" in admissions decisions. Scalia criticized the educational benefits of "cross-racial understanding" as something that cannot be taught or graded. "For it is a lesson of life rather than law," Scalia wrote, "essentially the same lesson taught to (or rather learned by, for it cannot be 'taught' in the usual sense) people three feet shorter and twenty years younger than the full-grown adults at the University of Michigan Law School, in institutions ranging from the Boy Scout troops to public-school kindergartens."[311] For Scalia, "the Constitution proscribes government discrimination on the basis of race, and state-provided education is no exception."[312]

Justice Scalia also contended that affirmative action aimed at overcoming historical discrimination against women was unlawful. In 1978 the Santa Clara County Transportation Agency voluntarily adopted an affirmative action program to increase the number of female employees in certain job categories. At the time, none of the 238 skilled craft worker positions were held by women. In a 6–3 decision, the Supreme Court rejected a challenge to the program under Title VII of the Civil Rights Act because the program was voluntary and no applicant had been excluded from consideration.[313] Scalia filed a blistering dissent, arguing that the court's opinion conflicted with the plain language of the Civil Rights Act. "A statute designed to establish a color-blind and gender-blind workplace," wrote Scalia, "has thus been converted into a powerful engine of racism and sexism, not merely *permitting* intentional race- and sex-based discrimination, but often making it, through operation of the legal system, practically compelled."[314]

This chapter examined the major themes of Justice Scalia's originalist jurisprudence. Reminiscent of Alexander Hamilton, Scalia believed the most important part of the Constitution is the separation of powers. In a 1992 speech, Scalia described the Bill of Rights as "technically an afterthought" and "the fruit, not the root, of the constitutional tree." Scalia remarked that if he had to choose between living in the former Soviet Union, which had a respectable but ineffectual bill of rights, and living in England or Australia—"two of the holdouts in the modern rush toward these Bills of Rights"—he would choose one of the latter countries.[315] Like Hamilton, Scalia believed that the protection of individual freedom should be a carefully designed structure of government.[316]

For Scalia, the primary institutional threat to the US constitutional system was Congress. Based on this understanding, he attempted to fortify the less dangerous branches of government. As described in this chapter, Scalia was a strong defender of executive power. In *Morrison v. Olson*, he argued that the "for cause" limitation on the president's authority to remove independent counsels violated the separation of powers.[317] Scalia also supported the sole organ theory and numerous implied and inherent powers belonging to the executive branch. Despite Scalia's criticism of the "living" Constitution, he was a strong defender of an independent judiciary. During his confirmation hearings, then-judge Scalia dismissed the idea of electing federal judges or making the process of impeachment easier. "All of those things were considered and rejected" by the framers, Scalia testified, "in favor of an extraordinarily strong—extraordinarily, more so than most of the states now—an extraordinarily strong and independent Federal judiciary." "I think it was a conscious decision by the framers," he added, "and I happen to think that it was a good one."[318]

In the area of federalism, Scalia initially defended a Hamiltonian political process approach to national-state relations, where the states' primary protection is found in the structure of government and the electoral process. Scalia later gravitated toward a Madisonian approach and cast the pivotal fifth vote in the so-called federalism revolution of the 1990s. Strategically, this allowed Scalia to be a major player in the federalism disputes decided during his time on the Supreme Court. In those cases in which he supported the national policy objective, such as the regulation of medicinal marijuana, he supported the authority of the federal government. In those cases in which he did not, such as national health care, he sided with the states or the individual.

When it came to the First Amendment, Scalia defended a robust interpretation of political speech. He took a principled approach in *Texas v. Johnson*, which held that flag burning is protected symbolic speech; he wrote the decision in *R.A.V. v. City of St. Paul*, where the court ruled that a city's hate-speech ordinance was underinclusive; and he wrote or joined several other opinions that protected a considerable amount of contentious speech. Justice Scalia was also the court's leader in pushing for greater protection of corporate speech. He filed a vigorous dissent in *Austin v. Michigan Chamber of Commerce*, where he argued that a state ban on the use of corporate funds to pay for electioneering ads constituted viewpoint discrimination. After a few initial defeats, Scalia's point of view would prevail in *Citizens United*.

At the same time, Justice Scalia never claimed to be a free speech absolutist. Based on his interpretation of the definite article "the" in the free speech clause, Scalia contended that the First Amendment does not cover obscenity nor libel.[319] He believed that government employees can be hired or fired based on their political views and that they have reduced free speech rights in the workplace. Scalia also argued that the government can impose conditions on the money it allocates based on the viewpoints it supports.

Justice Scalia defended a narrow construction of the establishment clause. He was a sharp critic of the strict neutralist perspective and supported a wide variety of government-sponsored accommodationist practices, including school vouchers, prayers at graduation ceremonies, balanced treatment in the teaching of evolution and creation science, religious displays on government property, and sectarian prayers at town hall meetings. Similarly, Scalia defended a narrow interpretation of the free exercise clause. He wrote the Supreme Court's decision in *Employment Division, Department of Human Resources of Oregon v. Smith*, which held that neutral, generally applicable laws do not have to survive strict scrutiny. After Congress passed the Religious Freedom Restoration Act and the Religious Land Use and Institutionalized Persons Act, Scalia applied strict scrutiny in religious freedom cases. For example, he joined the court's decision in *Burwell v. Hobby Lobby Stores* and wrote a vigorous dissent in *Locke v. Davey*.

Scalia's most important Supreme Court opinion was *District of Columbia v. Heller*, which held that the Second Amendment protects an individual right to own guns for self-defense. Utilizing an original public meaning approach, Scalia concluded that the prefatory clause of the Second Amendment cannot be read to limit the broader individual right contemplated by the operative clause. He also determined that the words "to keep" and "bear Arms" are not limited to martial purposes. As discussed in this book's conclusion, Scalia's opinion in *Heller* is contestable on originalist grounds. Ironically, his individual-rights interpretation of the Second Amendment was not supported by the Federalists—although it did have some support among Anti-Federalists. Neither Alexander Hamilton nor James Madison supported an individual right to bear arms.[320]

Justice Scalia's penchant for bright-line rules saw him reach "liberal" results in certain areas of criminal procedure. His common-law approach to the Fourth Amendment protected homeowners from modern technological advances. He also defended robust interpretations of the confrontation clause and the right to a jury trial under the Sixth Amendment. Other than these "liberal" results, Scalia maintained a very restrictive view of the rights of the accused. He did not believe that electronic surveillance is covered by the Fourth Amendment; he was a critic of the exclusionary rule; he voted to overturn *Miranda*; and he narrowly interpreted the right to counsel under the Sixth Amendment. When it came to the Eighth Amendment, Scalia argued that the phrase "cruel and unusual punishments" did not contemplate a proportionality principle. In capital cases, he was a strong and vocal proponent of the death penalty. He wrote vigorous dissents in cases prohibiting the death penalty for the intellectually disabled and minors. And in Scalia's view, the Eighth Amendment does not apply to prison beatings and conditions.

Although he rejected a return to the *Lochner* era, Justice Scalia wrote several opinions that expanded the scope of the takings clause, including *Nollan v. California Coastal Commission* and *Lucas v. South Carolina Coastal Council*. Like Justice Black, Scalia was a fervent critic of substantive due process, believing that it allowed "freewheeling lawmaking" by judges. On this basis, he rejected a general right of privacy, right to abortion, right to die, right of sexual preference, and various other substantive due process claims. Scalia also defended a very narrow conception of the equal protection clause, which, in his view, did not apply to gender discrimination cases nor to discrimination on the basis of sexual orientation. "When the Fourteenth Amendment was ratified in 1868," Scalia wrote in *Obergefell*, "every State limited marriage to one man and one woman, and no one doubted the constitutionality of doing so." "That resolves these cases," he concluded.[321] Finally, Scalia was a strong critic of affirmative action, which, in his view, violated the individual rights premise of the equal protection clause.

4. Clarence Thomas's Originalism: Natural Law Libertarian

I have come here today not in anger or to anger, though my mere presence has been sufficient, obviously, to anger some. Nor have I come to defend my views, but rather to assert my right to think for myself, to refuse to have my ideas assigned to me as though I was an intellectual slave because I'm black.

—*Clarence Thomas*[1]

The person who had the most significant impact on Clarence Thomas's libertarian jurisprudence was his maternal grandfather, Myers Anderson. Rising between 2:00 and 4:00 a.m. each day, Anderson preached that hard work could overcome any major challenge. "Where there is a will, there is a way," he told his two grandsons.[2] Idleness was "the devil's workshop," and the boys were required to do chores around the house and work long hours at the family farm during the summer. If "you did not work, you did not eat." A fiercely proud and independent man, Anderson refused to work for anyone else. When Clarence asked his grandfather why he worked so hard for a family business that did not generate much income, his response was: "It's mine."[3] Thomas is convinced that his grandfather's work ethic and independence gave him a sense of freedom (economic) largely denied to the black community in the segregated South.

Thomas Sowell, the black conservative economist and syndicated columnist, also had a major impact on Thomas's libertarian philosophy. In his memoir, Thomas recounts how Sowell's *Race and Economics* (1975) captured his emerging views on race in the United States. At a time when Thomas was uncertain about his own political views, Sowell emboldened him to reject that "all-us-black-folks-think-alike nonsense." He also appreciated Sowell's forthright opposition to "school busing, racial quotas, and increasing the minimum wage," which he saw as harmful to blacks and their sense of pride.[4] Rather than supporting quick fixes to resolve racial inequality, Sowell preached "self-reliance, work skills, education, [and] business experience."[5] After reading *Race and Economics*, Thomas was an instant convert—although, in reality, Sowell only put into words what Thomas had already been thinking. In a 1987 interview Thomas described *Race and Economics* as "manna from heaven," and he praised Sowell as not only his "intellectual mentor" but also his "salvation" in terms of shaping his political views.[6]

The works of Ayn Rand, the renowned libertarian political philosopher, also had a substantial impact on Thomas's worldview. Thomas regularly invites his law clerks to his home to watch the movie version of *The Fountainhead*, which recounts the story of Howard Roark, an idealistic architect who challenged the norms of his profession. As David Savage points out, Thomas can relate to Roark's unwillingness to compromise and his nonconformist attitudes. "If you think you are right, there is nothing wrong with being the only one," Thomas explained. "I have no problem being the only one."[7]

Justice Thomas combines a distinctive libertarian philosophy with a deep and abiding faith in natural law. Myers Anderson taught Clarence that "all of our rights as human beings came from God, not man," and that segregation violates God's law.[8] This concept of inherent equality was reinforced by the Franciscan nuns who taught Clarence in the segregated Catholic schools of Savannah.[9] During his chairmanship of the Equal Employment Opportunity Commission, Thomas's affinity for natural law gained a philosophical foundation when he was introduced to the works of Harry Jaffa, a Straussian political philosopher and admirer of Abraham Lincoln. In *Crisis of the House Divided* (1959), Jaffa countered the revisionist narrative that there was no major philosophical difference between Lincoln and Stephen Douglas on the issue of slavery. One hundred years after the famous Lincoln-Douglas debates, Jaffa referred to the substance of those debates as "the intellectual and moral contest of the highest order."[10] In contrast to Douglas's popular sovereignty thesis, Lincoln claimed that slavery is morally wrong and fundamentally at odds with the Declaration of Independence.

After reading *Crisis of the House Divided*, Thomas began quoting Jaffa in lectures and publications.[11] He also started to defend what is known as the Lincolnian interpretation of the American founding, which posits that the Constitution cannot be understood without resort to the Declaration of Independence and its central moral tenet: "all men are created equal." Interestingly, Thomas's natural law beliefs initially put him at odds with several Justice Department officials in the Reagan administration, including Edwin Meese, William Bradford Reynolds, and Charles Cooper, whose original intent approach to the Constitution drew a sharp distinction between law and morality. "The standard of 'original intention,'" Thomas said in a 1988 speech, "could provide no guidance, since it tried to understand the Constitution apart from its underlying principles."[12] Thomas's disagreement with his fellow conservatives did not prevent him from becoming an originalist himself, but it was an originalism based on natural law. Thomas pays homage to the Great Emancipator each year by taking his law clerks to Gettysburg.

This chapter examines Justice Thomas's originalist philosophy, which represents an interesting blend of libertarianism and natural law, by taking a closer look at his opinions in the areas of federalism, executive power, free speech, religion, rights of the accused, property rights, substantive due process, the privileges or immunities clause, incorporation, and equal protection.

FEDERALISM

One constitutional area in which Justice Thomas has clearly distinguished himself among his colleagues is federalism. Thomas has embraced a traditional Jeffersonian states' rights perspective. Thomas Jefferson was a strict constructionist regarding the powers of the national government. He believed that the words of the Constitution had been "specially drawn" and had a specific and definite meaning. For example, in defining the word "commerce," Jefferson contended that there is a sharp distinction between the production (or manufacture) of an object of commerce, on the one hand, and its distribution into the streams of commerce, on the other.[13] He also argued, anticipating the Supreme Court's decision in *Hammer v. Dagenhart* (1918),[14] that the authority to regulate commerce is limited to interstate matters and cannot reasonably be interpreted to reach the completely internal commerce of a state. Jefferson buttressed his strict constructionist interpretation of federal power with a robust view of the Tenth Amendment, which he called "the foundation of the Constitution."[15]

Justice Thomas has clearly aligned himself with Jefferson on the scope of national power. In *United States v. Lopez* (1995),[16] the Supreme Court struck down the Gun Free Zones Act of 1990, which banned the possession of a gun within one thousand feet of a private or public school. Chief Justice Rehnquist, writing for the 5–4 court, relied on the "substantial effects" test, which requires Congress to provide a rational basis to support its claim that a particular economic activity has a substantial effect on interstate commerce. Applying that test in *Lopez*, the court found that there was no rational basis for concluding that possessing a firearm in and around schools has a substantial effect on interstate commerce.

In a concurring opinion, Justice Thomas argued that his colleagues did not go far enough. The substantial effects test, in his view, was a modern invention and was inconsistent with the original meaning of the commerce clause. Thomas contended that the Constitution "uses the word 'commerce' in a narrower sense" and "does not support the proposition that Congress has authority over all activities that 'substantially affect' interstate commerce."[17] "Taken to its logical extreme," Thomas observed, the substantial effects test "would give Congress a 'police power' over all aspects of American life."[18] Thomas cautioned that a reexamination of the substantial effects test would not "necessarily require a wholesale abandonment of our more recent opinions," but he thought it was imperative to take another look at the limits of the commerce power to avoid giving Congress "a blank check."[19]

In subsequent cases, Thomas continued to criticize the substantial effects test. In *United States v. Morrison* (2000),[20] the Supreme Court struck down a provision of the Violence against Women Act of 1994 because it exceeded Congress's commerce authority. "By continuing to apply this rootless and malleable standard [the substantial effects test]," Thomas wrote in a short concurring opinion, "the Court has encouraged the Federal Government to persist in its view that the Commerce Clause has virtually no limits." "Until this Court replaces the existing Commerce Clause jurisprudence with a standard more consistent with the original understanding," he added, "we will continue to see Congress appropriating state police powers under the guise of regulating commerce."[21]

In two other cases, Thomas applied his strict interpretation of the commerce clause in a losing effort. In *Gonzales v. Raich* (2005),[22] he dissented when the court upheld Congress's authority to prosecute cultivators of homegrown marijuana for medicinal purposes under the Controlled Substances Act. "Our federalist system," Thomas wrote in his dissent, "allows California and a growing number of other States to decide for themselves how to safeguard the health and welfare of our citizens."[23] And in *National Federation of Independent Business v. Sebelius* (2012),[24] Thomas joined a coauthored dissent arguing that the Patient Protection and Affordable Care Act is unconstitutional in its entirety. In a short separate dissent, Thomas revisited his argument that the substantial effects test provides "virtually no limits" to Congress's commerce power. "The Government's unprecedented claim in this suit," he wrote, "that it may regulate not only economic activity but also *inactivity* that substantially affects interstate commerce is a case in point."[25]

In addition to applying a strict constructionist interpretation to the commerce clause, Justice Thomas has applied it to other enumerated powers belonging to Congress, including the general welfare clause,[26] the necessary and proper clause,[27] and the Indian commerce clause.[28] He has also been a sharp critic of the Supreme Court's negative commerce clause jurisprudence. In *Camps Newfound/Owatonna v. Town of Harrison* (1997),[29] he rejected the usual justifications for the dormant commerce clause—that is, Congress has exclusive authority over interstate commerce or, by its silence, Congress has implicitly preempted state laws. Thomas could find no support for either justification under the original meaning of the Constitution and therefore called for the court to abandon the doctrine altogether.[30] Justice Thomas also joined court decisions limiting the federal government's power to abrogate state sovereign immunity under the Eleventh Amendment,[31] and he has called for the abandonment of the court's "obstacle" preemption jurisprudence.[32]

Tenth Amendment

In addition to his narrow construction of Congress's enumerated powers, Justice Thomas has defended a robust view of the Tenth Amendment as an important source of reserved powers for the states. This was particularly evident in his dissenting opinion in *U.S. Term Limits, Inc. v. Thornton* (1995),[33] where the Supreme Court (5–4) ruled that the states do not have the reserved authority to impose term limits on members of Congress. Justice Stevens, the author of the court's opinion, held that the qualifications clauses (age, residency, and citizenship) are exclusive and do not permit the states to impose additional qualifications on members of Congress. Stevens also argued that even if it could be assumed that the states possess, as part of their original powers, some control over congressional qualifications, there is abundant evidence that the Constitution deprives them of any such authority.

Justice Thomas could not have disagreed more. In a long, extensively researched dissent, he strongly objected to the majority's "original powers" thesis, which "fundamentally misunderstands the notion of 'reserved powers'" under the Tenth Amendment.[34] According to Thomas, the people of the individual states are "the ultimate source of the Constitution's authority," not any "undifferentiated people of the Nation as a whole."[35] In fact, Thomas maintained that there is no such thing as the popular sovereignty of a collective people in the United States because the Constitution does not contemplate that the collective "people will either exercise power or delegate it," nor does it "recognize any mechanism for action by the undifferentiated people of the Nation."[36] For Thomas, the fact that ultimate sovereignty resides with the people of the several states is "enshrined" by the Tenth Amendment, which declares that "the powers not delegated to the United States by the Constitution, nor prohibited by it to the states, are reserved to the States respectively, or to the people." Because the people of the several states are the only "true source of power" recognized by the Constitution, Thomas argued that they do not need any affirmative constitutional grant of power to supplement the qualifications of their representatives in Congress. On the question of state-imposed term limits, Thomas observed, "the Constitution is simply silent. . . . And where the Constitution is silent, it raises no bar to action by the States or the people."[37]

Faithless Electors

Justice Thomas renewed his reservation-of-powers argument a quarter century later in a case in which the Supreme Court upheld the states' authority to penalize electors for not voting for the presidential candidate they had pledged to support. In *Chiafalo v. Washington* (2020),[38] authored by Justice Kagan, the court unanimously held that Article II, section 1, clause 2 gives the states broad authority to appoint electors and to impose conditions on their appointment.[39] Because the Constitution does not preclude states from placing restrictions on the discretion of electors, Kagan concluded that the state of Washington could impose a $1,000 fine on three electors who did not adhere to their pledges in the 2016 presidential election.[40]

Justice Thomas agreed with the majority's conclusion, but he argued that its interpretation of Article II, section 1, clause 2 was "highly questionable." Citing his own opinion from *Thornton*, Thomas argued that the clause in question provides the method of selecting electors, but it says nothing at all about how electors are supposed to behave once they are appointed. The "fundamental principle" of the Constitution, wrote Thomas, is that "when the Constitution is silent, authority resides with the States or the people." "Rather than contort the language of both Article II and the state statute," Thomas argued, "I would acknowledge that the Constitution simply says nothing about the States' power in this regard."[41]

EXECUTIVE POWER

Despite being a libertarian conservative, Justice Thomas has proven to be a strong defender of executive power, particularly in the areas of national security and foreign affairs. Thomas has favorably quoted Alexander Hamilton's theory of an energetic executive from Federalist No. 70 and, in particular, his emphasis on "unity."[42] On this basis, Thomas, like Scalia, has been a strenuous critic of *Humphrey's Executor v. United States* (1935),[43] which placed limits on the president's authority to remove the heads of independent regulatory agencies. In a 2020 case, Thomas called for *Humphrey's Executor* to be overturned. That decision, Thomas wrote, "poses a direct threat to our constitutional structure, and, as a result, the liberty of the American people."[44]

During the war on terror, Thomas was the only justice to side with the Bush administration in every case. In *Rasul v. Bush* (2004),[45] he joined Justice Scalia's dissent, which argued that foreign "enemy combatants" held at Guantanamo Bay do not have *statutory* authority for their habeas corpus petitions to be heard in federal courts. In *Hamdi v. Rumsfeld* (2004),[46] handed down the same day, Thomas filed a solo dissent, arguing that a US citizen could be detained indefinitely during the war on terror. In Thomas's view, the executive branch's determination that Hamdi was an enemy combatant should receive substantial (if not complete) deference from the courts. For support of his opinion, Thomas relied on the Authorization for the Use of Military Force (AUMF), passed shortly after the 9/11 attacks, but he also strongly suggested that the president's "inherent" powers under Article II supported the administration's detention policies.

In *Hamdan v. Rumsfeld* (2006),[47] Thomas argued, again in dissent, that the AUMF allows for the use of military commissions. He stated that, as the "sole organ" of the country in foreign affairs, the executive branch's determination to use military commissions to try enemy combatants should be respected by the judiciary. "The Court," he wrote, "without acknowledging its duty to defer to the President, adopts its own, admittedly plausible, reading of Common Article 3." However, when there are "two plausible, and reasonable, interpretations" of a treaty provision, Thomas argued, "our precedents require us to defer to the Executive's interpretation."[48] Two years later, Thomas dissented when the Supreme Court struck down section 7 of the Military Commissions Act of 2006 as an unconstitutional suspension of the habeas corpus clause.[49]

Inherent Powers

Justice Thomas has also found broad inherent power belonging to the president in other cases. In *Zivotofsky v. Kerry* (2015),[50] Thomas argued in a concurring opinion that the president has the exclusive authority to issue passports under Article II's vesting clause.[51] On this basis, he voted to strike down a federal law that required the secretary of state to record "Israel" as the country of birth for a US citizen born in Jerusalem. During the Trump administration, the Supreme Court upheld the revised travel restrictions on immigrants entering the country from eight countries, most of which had Muslim-majority populations.[52] In an opinion by Chief Justice Roberts, the court placed primary reliance on the broad delegation of power granted to the president under the Immigration and Nationality Act.[53] In a concurring opinion, Thomas took the position (not joined by any other justice) that the president has the "*inherent* authority to exclude aliens from the country" and that the travel restriction did not require statutory authorization. He also argued that the evidence of "anti-Muslim discrimination [was] unpersuasive."[54] As discussed in chapter 6, Justice Thomas has *not* defended broad powers of the presidency in domestic affairs. He has called for a reexamination of the nondelegation doctrine and *Chevron* deference, which would limit the growth of the administrative state.

Deferred Action for Childhood Arrivals

In a 2020 case Justice Thomas argued that the Trump administration's rescission of the Deferred Action for Childhood Arrivals (DACA) program was lawful. In the summer of 2012 the Obama administration created the program allowing children of undocumented aliens to apply for a two-year forbearance of removal from the country. Some 700,000 individuals availed themselves of this opportunity, which also included work authorization and eligibility for various federal benefits, including Social Security and Medicare. In September 2017 the Trump administration began to wind down the program. Elaine C. Duke, acting secretary of the Department of Homeland Security (DHS), issued a memorandum stating that DACA should be terminated and setting forth how the program would be phased out. That memorandum was challenged by beneficiaries of DACA, as well as other impacted parties, on the grounds that it was arbitrary and capricious under the Administrative Procedure Act (APA).

In *Department of Homeland Security v. Regents of the University California* (2020),[55] the Supreme Court (5–4) ruled that the Trump administration's rescission order was unlawful. Chief Justice Roberts held that the memorandum concentrated on the unlawfulness of extending work authorization and benefits, but it did not address DACA's primary concern: forbearance of removal. The chief justice also faulted the rescission order for not considering the reliance interests of DACA recipients in the wind-down process. Justice Thomas dissented. He argued that because Congress had not authorized the Obama administration to alter the legal status of a class of aliens under the Immigration and Nationality Act, the program "was unlawful from its inception." He also argued that the program's establishment did not comply with the notice and comment requirements of the APA. On this basis, he did not believe the Trump administration's DHS had to provide additional policy justifications or considerations for its rescission order. "DHS," Thomas wrote, "had no authority here to create DACA, and the unlawfulness of that program is a sufficient justification for its rescission."[56]

Executive Immunity

In 2020 the Supreme Court handed down two major decisions involving subpoena requests for former president Trump's financial records and personal papers, both of which raised questions of first impression. The first case involved a criminal subpoena issued by Cyrus Vance Jr., the district attorney for Manhattan, which requested nearly ten years of Trump's financial records to uncover possible violations of state law. Trump sued Vance in federal district court, arguing that he was absolutely immune from the state's criminal process, citing both Article II and the supremacy clause. In a 7–2 decision, the Supreme Court held that a president has no categorical absolute immunity from a state criminal subpoena.[57] As a historical matter, Chief Justice Roberts observed that all presidents have complied with criminal subpoena requests. Roberts placed particular reliance on chief justice John Marshall's circuit court opinion in *United States v. Burr* (1807),[58] which required President Jefferson to turn over correspondence in Aaron Burr's treason trial. In terms of Trump's specific arguments, Roberts rejected the idea that compliance with a subpoena request would necessarily divert a president's time, undermine his leadership both at home and abroad, or make the president a target of harassing lawsuits. Roberts pointed out that courts have the necessary tools to protect the president from frivolous or malicious prosecutions, and he cited a common-law maxim: "the public has a right to every man's evidence," including the president's.[59]

Justice Thomas dissented. Although he agreed that presidents are not absolutely immune from state criminal subpoenas (the justices were unanimous on that point), he criticized the majority for not considering the president's request for an injunction in this case. Thomas raised concerns about the "troublingly broad" subpoena request by Vance. He also emphasized presidents' extraordinary constitutional responsibilities in both foreign and domestic affairs and observed that courts have limited understanding of why presidents might be unable to comply with a subpoena request. Based on these considerations, Thomas argued that if the president claims he cannot abide by a subpoena request, courts should defer to that judgment. "When the President asserts that matters of foreign affairs or national defense preclude his compliance with a subpoena," Thomas wrote, "the Judiciary will rarely have a basis for rejecting that assertion."[60]

Congressional Subpoenas

In *Trump v. Mazars USA, LLP* (2020),[61] handed down the same day as *Trump v. Vance*, the Supreme Court reversed lower court judgments granting four broad subpoena requests, issued by three different House committees, seeking information about President Trump's finances. Each of the committees cited a different legislative purpose for the subpoenas. The Permanent Select Committee on Intelligence, for example, sought financial information from the president, his family members, and business entities as part of an investigation into foreign efforts to undermine the US political process. The president, in his personal capacity, filed two suits in federal court, arguing that the subpoenas lacked a legitimate legislative purpose and violated the separation of powers; he did not claim, however, that the documents were protected by executive privilege.

In a 7–2 decision, again authored by Chief Justice Roberts, the court ruled that the House subpoena requests did not adequately consider the burdens imposed on the presidency. The court acknowledged that the subpoena power is an adjunct of Congress's authority to legislate, and it rejected President Trump's argument that there must be a "demonstrated, specific need" for the requested financial information. Nonetheless, the court faulted Congress for ignoring the fact that the president "is the only person who alone composes a branch of government." Additionally, in contrast to subpoenas sought by a prosecutor or a private party, subpoenas from Congress raise distinct separation of power concerns because Congress is a rival institution. "Without limits on its subpoena powers," Roberts wrote, "Congress could 'exert an imperious controul' over the Executive Branch and aggrandize itself at the President's expense, just as the Framers feared."[62]

Justice Thomas again dissented. He was the only justice to argue that a subpoena of "the President's private, nonofficial documents" is not a valid exercise of Congress's legislative powers. As an original matter, Thomas argued that no enumerated power under Article I, section 8 supports Congress's authority to issue subpoenas for personal papers, and such subpoenas are not "a necessary implication of Congress' legislative powers." Thomas also criticized the Supreme Court's decision in *McGrain v. Daugherty* (1927)[63]—which reached the opposite conclusion—as inconsistent with the original meaning of the Constitution. "The opinion in *McGrain*," Thomas wrote, "lacks any foundation in text or history with respect to subpoenas for private, nonofficial documents. It fails to recognize that Congress, unlike Parliament, is not supreme."[64] Although Thomas conceded that Congress could potentially get such documents pursuant to an impeachment investigation, "Congress' legislative powers," he reasoned, "do not authorize it to engage in a nationwide inquisition with whatever resources it chooses to appropriate for itself."[65]

FIRST AMENDMENT

Justice Thomas is a fairly strong defender of political speech, but there are a number of important exceptions. Since his days as a student at Yale Law School, Thomas has been a strong critic of what he calls the "herd mentality" and the idea that all blacks have to think alike. In a 1993 speech, Thomas called this conformist attitude the "New Intolerance" and reflected back to when some of his intellectual black friends (Clarence Pendleton, Walter Williams, and Jay Parker) faced "character assassination" for their unorthodox views. "Instead of seeing signs on public doors saying, 'No Coloreds Allowed,'" Thomas observed, "the signs I saw were 'No Nonconforming Ideas Allowed.'"[66]

For this reason, Justice Thomas has been willing to strike down broadly written hate-speech laws that are suggestive of political correctness. For example, he joined Justice Scalia's decision in *R.A.V. v. City of St. Paul* (1992),[67] which held that a bias-motivated crime ordinance constituted viewpoint discrimination under the First Amendment. He joined the Supreme Court's decision in *United States v. Stevens* (2010),[68] which struck down a federal ban on the commercial sale of videos depicting cruelty to animals, and he joined the court's decision in *Snyder v. Phelps* (2011),[69] which overturned a civil damages award against the Westboro Baptist Church for protesting at military funerals. And, like Justice Scalia, Thomas has argued that "buffer zones" around abortion clinics constitute viewpoint discrimination.[70]

At the same time, Justice Thomas has been reluctant to side with free speech rights if the speech in question can be considered "intimidating." In *Virginia v. Black* (2003),[71] for example, the Supreme Court struck down a 1952 Virginia law that made it unlawful for any person to burn a cross on public or private property with the intention to intimidate. At issue in the case was a provision that treated cross burning as "prima facie evidence" of an intent to intimidate a person or group of persons. Justice O'Connor, for a plurality, determined that the prima facie evidence provision made the statute unconstitutional because not all cross burnings are done with the intention to intimidate.[72] O'Connor observed that "cross burning originated in the 14th century as a means for Scottish tribes to signal each other." And although cross burnings have been used by the Ku Klux Klan as distinct and powerful messages of intimidation and violence, they have also "remained potent symbols of shared group identity and ideology" used during rallies, initiations, and marriages.[73]

Justice Thomas filed a solo dissent. Recounting the unique and violent history of cross burnings in the United States, Thomas challenged the idea that such an act could ever be done *without* an intention to intimidate. "In our culture," Thomas wrote, "cross burning has almost invariably meant lawlessness and understandably instills in its victims well-grounded fear of physical violence."[74] For this reason, he argued that cross burnings constitute conduct rather than speech and therefore are not protected by the First Amendment. During the oral argument in this case, Thomas, who at the time rarely asked questions, challenged deputy solicitor general Michael Dreeben's understating of the virulent effects of cross burnings in America. "Now, it's my understanding," Thomas told Dreeben, "that we had almost 100 years of lynching and activity in the South by the Knights of Camellia and—the Ku Klux Klan, and this was a reign of terror and the cross was a symbol of that reign of terror."[75]

Threats over the Internet

Justice Thomas also dissented in a 2015 case involving threats over the internet. True threats, the Supreme Court has held, are unprotected by the First Amendment. Anthony Douglas Elonis posted violent rap lyrics on Facebook using a pseudonym. The messages were directed at his ex-wife, coworkers, local law enforcement, a kindergarten class, and an FBI agent. In one post about his former wife, Elonis wrote: "If I only knew then what I know now . . . I would have smothered your ass with a pillow, dumped your body in the back seat, dropped you off in Toad Creek, and made it look like a rape and murder."[76] Elonis claimed he did not intend these communications to be actual threats; instead, they were therapeutic attempts to relieve stress. Under a 1939 federal law, he was found guilty on four counts of transmitting threats in interstate commerce and sentenced to forty-four months' imprisonment.[77]

In *Elonis v. United States* (2015),[78] the Supreme Court (8–1) reversed his conviction. In an opinion by Chief Justice Roberts, the court ruled that for the defendant to be punished criminally, the jury must find that he subjectively intended his statements to be understood as threats. Justice Thomas filed the solo dissent. He maintained that the federal statute required only "general intent"—that is, the defendant knew his communication would be construed as a threat by a reasonable observer. Thomas placed particular reliance on an 1896 obscenity case in which the court found that the defendant did not have to know the materials he sent in the mail were obscene for him to be convicted under federal law.[79] "Had Elonis mailed obscene materials to his wife and a kindergarten class," Thomas reasoned, "he could have been prosecuted irrespective of whether he intended to offend those recipients or recklessly disregarded that possibility." "Yet," he continued, "when he threatened to kill his wife and a kindergarten class, his intent to terrify those recipients (or reckless disregard of that risk) suddenly becomes highly relevant. That need not—and should not—be the case."[80]

Commercial Speech

Justice Thomas's libertarian views are apparent in cases involving commercial speech. Commercial speech was not protected by the First Amendment because advertisements were considered a lesser form of speech that could be misleading or deceptive.[81] In the 1970s, however, the Supreme Court began to extend First Amendment protection to commercial speech. The modern four-part test was adopted in *Central Hudson Gas & Electric Corp. v. Public Service Commission of New York* (1980),[82] and it requires the court first to determine whether the expression concerns lawful activity and is not misleading. If so, the other three parts of the *Central Hudson* test come into play: (1) whether the government interest is substantial, (2) whether the expression directly advances the government's interests, and (3) whether the regulation is no more extensive than necessary to serve the government's interests. In comparison to other levels of scrutiny, *Central Hudson* is often regarded as a form of intermediate scrutiny.

Justice Thomas does not support the *Central Hudson* test and has argued that strict scrutiny should be applied in commercial speech cases. He has argued that there is no meaningful distinction between lawful commercial speech and political speech. He first made this argument in a separate concurrence in *44 Liquormart v. Rhode Island* (1996).[83] In that case, the Supreme Court struck down two state laws that broadly banned the advertisement of liquor prices by vendors and the news media, except at the point of sale. In an opinion by Justice Stevens, the court held that, under the *Central Hudson* test, the state laws did not directly advance the state's interest in temperance because Rhode Island ranked in the upper 30 percent of states in the per capita consumption of alcoholic beverages.

Justice Thomas filed a concurring opinion. He was the only justice to argue that the *Central Hudson* test should not be used because "the government's asserted interest is to keep legal users of a product or service ignorant in order to manipulate their choices in the marketplace." Such an interest, Thomas maintained, was "*per se* illegitimate" and "can no more justify regulation of 'commercial' speech than it can justify regulation of 'noncommercial' speech."[84] In a decision handed down five years later, Thomas made explicit what he perhaps left implicit in *44 Liquormart*. "I continue to believe," Thomas wrote, "that when the government seeks to restrict truthful speech in order to suppress the ideas it conveys, strict scrutiny should be applied, whether or not the speech in question may be characterized as 'commercial.'"[85]

Campaign Contributions

Justice Thomas has also been a forceful critic of campaign finance regulations. The Federal Election Campaign Act of 1971 (FECA), as amended in 1974, imposed limits on expenditures and contributions in federal elections. In *Buckley v. Valeo* (1976),[86] the Supreme Court struck down restrictions on how much money individual candidates can spend on their own elections, but it sustained contribution limits. With respect to the latter, the court regarded the regulation of contributions as a less direct form of speech and the government's interest in preventing corruption (actual or perceived) as a substantial state interest.

Beginning in 1996, Justice Thomas criticized what he called the "speech-by-proxy" analysis of *Buckley*.[87] According to Thomas, there is no meaningful distinction between expenditures and contributions under the First Amendment; therefore, any law that restricts the amount of money a person can contribute to a campaign should be subject to strict scrutiny. "The decision of individuals to speak through contributions rather than through independent expenditures is entirely reasonable," Thomas observed in one case. "Political campaigns are largely candidate focused and candidate driven. Citizens recognize that the best advocate for a candidate (and the policy positions he supports) tends to be the candidate himself."[88]

Other Areas of First Amendment Law

As discussed in chapter 6, Justice Thomas has written important opinions arguing that anonymous speech is protected under the First Amendment,[89] and that the Supreme Court should apply strict scrutiny to disclaimer and disclosure requirements under campaign finance laws.[90] In contrast, he has supported a very limited view of free speech rights in other areas. Perhaps reflecting his own childhood experience,[91] Thomas has defended a narrow interpretation of the free speech rights of minors.[92] In the area of obscenity, Thomas has relied on the three-part *Miller* test,[93] and he joined one of Justice Scalia's opinions finding that nude dancing is not protected by the First Amendment.[94] Thomas has also supported Scalia's position that the government can place conditions on the speech it subsidizes.[95] He voted in favor of regulating public employees' speech,[96] and he joined Scalia's dissenting opinion that independent contractors who work on behalf of the government are not immune from termination because of their political views.[97] As examined in chapter 5, Thomas also believes that libel is one area of First Amendment law that the states can completely regulate. In a 2019 opinion, he argued that the "actual malice" test established in *New York Times v. Sullivan* (1964)[98] is inconsistent with the original meaning of the First Amendment.[99] Justice Thomas also dissented in a 2012 case in which the court struck down the Stolen Valor Act, which made it a crime to make false claims about receiving the Congressional Medal of Honor.[100]

Establishment Clause

Justice Thomas's interpretation of the establishment clause is distinctive—although it does have some historical support.[101] Since 1947, when the Supreme Court first incorporated the establishment clause to apply against the states, Thomas has been the only justice to seriously contend that the establishment clause "resists" incorporation.[102] Based on his research of the founding generation, Thomas has maintained that the establishment clause was "a federalism provision" designed to prevent the establishment of a national church. For support of this interpretation, Thomas cites the fact that "at least six States had established churches in 1789."[103] It is ironic, Thomas remarked in one case, that incorporation of the establishment clause "would prohibit precisely what [it] was intended to protect—*state* establishments of the religion."[104]

Thomas has argued that the only religious practices that can be proscribed at the state level are those that employ "actual legal coercion" to force an individual to participate. He cites as examples a requirement that a citizen attend an established church or pay taxes to generate church revenue.[105] Interestingly, Thomas's "actual legal coercion" test is derived not from the establishment clause—which, according to Thomas, was not intended to apply against the states—but from the free exercise clause, which protects an individual's ability to choose whether to participate in religious exercises. In contrast to the establishment clause, Thomas believes the free exercise clause *was* intended to apply to state power under the Fourteenth Amendment.[106]

Based on his "no incorporation" theory of the establishment clause, Justice Thomas's interpretative approach would essentially allow the establishment of churches at the state level. Because his colleagues have been unwilling to go that far, Thomas has supported a wide array of accommodationist practices. In *Zelman v. Simmons-Harris* (2002),[107] the court rejected an establishment clause challenge to Ohio's school voucher program, which provided tuition assistance for students to attend public or private schools in Cleveland. In an impassioned concurring opinion, Thomas observed that "public school education has failed poor inner-city blacks." School vouchers, he argued, do not force students to go to religious schools; they simply give them more choices to pursue a better education. "There would be a tragic irony," wrote Thomas, "in converting the Fourteenth Amendment's guarantee of individual liberty into a prohibition on the exercise of educational choice." Quoting Frederick Douglass, Thomas proclaimed that "education . . . means emancipation. It means light and liberty. It means uplifting of the soul of man into the glorious light of truth, the light by which men can only be made free."[108]

Thomas has supported an accommodationist approach to the establishment clause in other cases. He has supported the use of student activity fees to help finance religious publications at public universities.[109] He wrote the court's decision in *Mitchell v. Helms* (2000),[110] which rejected a challenge to a federal program that gave educational materials and equipment, including computers, to religious elementary and secondary schools. He joined the court's opinion that a monument of the Ten Commandments located on the grounds of the Texas state capitol did not have to be removed,[111] and he dissented when the court ruled that placing large copies of the Ten Commandments in two courthouses in Kentucky violated the establishment clause.[112] Thomas also wrote a separate concurring opinion in a case in which the court upheld sectarian prayers at town council meetings.[113]

Like Justice Scalia, Thomas maintains that government does not have to be neutral between religion and irreligion.[114] On this basis, he has been a strong critic of the various tests the Supreme Court uses to determine whether there has been a violation of the establishment clause. Throughout his judicial tenure, Thomas has called for the *Lemon* test to be overturned.[115] In a 2019 case he argued that *Lemon* has no support based on the original meaning of the establishment clause, and has been "manipulated to fit whatever result the Court aimed to achieve," causing confusion in the states and lower courts. Since "the *Lemon* test is not good law," Thomas concluded, "I would take the logical next step and overrule the *Lemon* test in all contexts."[116]

The court's other tests have not fared any better in Thomas's opinions. In 2011 he wrote a solo twenty-page opinion contending that the court's "endorsement" test lacked a "sound analytical framework for evaluating governmental use of religious symbols."[117] Thomas also criticized Justice Kennedy's "coercion" test, which was used to strike down sectarian prayers at graduation ceremonies.[118] In one case, Thomas reasoned that if Kennedy's coercion test were applied to the Pledge of Allegiance in public schools, the court would have to strike down the practice because a daily pledge is more coercive than a one-time prayer at a graduation ceremony. Thomas, however, rejected Kennedy's coercion test, writing, "Peer pressure, unpleasant as it may be, is not coercion." He concluded, "The kind of coercion implicated by the Religion Clauses is that accomplished '*by force of law and threat of penalty.*'"[119]

Religious Freedom

During his confirmation hearings, Judge Thomas expressed skepticism about the Supreme Court's decision in *Employment Division, Department of Human Resources of Oregon v. Smith* (1990),[120] which held that neutral, generally applicable laws that only incidentally burden religious practices do not have to be supported by a compelling state interest.[121] For much of his judicial tenure, however, Thomas did not challenge Scalia's reasoning in that case. In fact, Thomas joined the court's decision in *City of Boerne v. Flores* (1997),[122] which ruled that Congress cannot modify the court's ruling in *Smith* for state and local practices under section 5 of the Fourteenth Amendment.[123] However, in a 2021 case, Thomas joined two opinions that called for *Smith* to be overturned.[124] In the principal dissent, Justice Alito argued that the "severe holding" in *Smith* was not consistent with the text of the free exercise clause. He also claimed that it "swept aside decades of established precedent" and "has been undermined by subsequent scholarship on the original meaning of the Free Exercise Clause."[125] In place of *Smith*, Alito (along with Thomas) argued that all laws that substantially burden religion should be examined with the highest level of scrutiny: strict scrutiny.

During his tenure, Justice Thomas has supported religious freedom claims in many cases. In *Church of the Lukumi Babalu Aye v. City of Hialeah* (1993),[126] he joined the court's decision that local ordinances that targeted the religious practice of animal sacrifice violate the free exercise clause. In *Gonzales v. O Centro Espirita Beneficente União do Vegetal* (2006),[127] he joined the court's holding that applying the Controlled Substances Act to *hoasca*, a hallucinogenic tea used by a União do Vegetal church, violates the Religious Freedom Restoration Act of 1993 (RFRA). In two separate decisions, Thomas sided with the religious freedom claims of prisoners under the Religious Land Use and Institutionalized Persons Act of 2000 (RLUIPA).[128] In *Cutter v. Wilkinson* (2005),[129] the court unanimously rejected a facial challenge to the RLUIPA, finding that the legislation represents a reasonable accommodation for religious practices in the prison setting.[130] Thomas concurred. Because the case challenged a federal law, Thomas had to determine to what extent the establishment clause limits the federal government. For Thomas, the primary purpose of the establishment clause was to protect state establishments from federal interference, but it did not prohibit "Congress from enacting legislation 'respecting religion' or 'taking cognizance of religion.'" In other words, the federal government did not have to be neutral when it came to religion. Interestingly, Thomas noted that the RLUIPA could potentially be challenged under Congress's commerce and spending powers, but since those issues were not raised by the parties to the case, he declined to pass judgment on them. However, Thomas's respect for states' rights was reflected in his decision for the court in *Sossamon v. Texas* (2011).[131] He wrote the 6–2 decision finding that state sovereign immunity trumps a prisoner's right to obtain monetary relief against a state under the RLUIPA.

In an area in which the Supreme Court has stated there is "play in the joints" between the establishment clause and the free exercise clause, Justice Thomas has joined or written several important opinions. In a 2020 case Thomas argued in a concurring opinion that the court's strict neutralist interpretation of the establishment clause has had the effect of discriminating against religion. "Until we correct course on that interpretation," Thomas wrote, "individuals will continue to face needless obstacles in their attempt to vindicate their religious freedom."[132] Earlier, Thomas joined Justice Scalia's dissent in *Locke v. Davey* (2004),[133] where the court held that a Promise Scholarship Program, paid out of a state's general fund, cannot be used to support degrees in devotional theology. The court based its ruling on the long-held view that the government cannot fund the training of clergy. In a 2017 case Thomas called for the court to reconsider its ruling in *Locke*. "This Court's endorsement in *Locke* of even a 'mil[d] kind' of discrimination against religion remains troubling," wrote Thomas.[134]

Then, in *Espinoza v. Montana Department of Revenue* (2020),[135] the Supreme Court held that a state regulation that prohibited students from using a tax-supported scholarship program to attend religious schools violated the free exercise clause. In an opinion by Chief Justice Roberts, the court applied strict scrutiny and held that the Montana Supreme Court had erred in holding that the program violated the "no-aid" provision of the Montana Constitution. Thomas filed a concurring opinion in which he stated again, "*Locke* incorrectly interpreted the Establishment Clause," and although "returning the Establishment Clause to its proper scope will not completely rectify the Court's disparate treatment of constitutional rights, . . . it will go a long way toward allowing free exercise of religion to flourish as the Framers intended."[136]

Ministerial Exception

Justice Thomas has staked out a unique perspective regarding the "ministerial exception" under the free exercise clause. Under this doctrine, religious organizations are immune from charges of employment discrimination because judicial review of their governance decisions, including employment disputes, would impair their independence and religious mission. In *Hosanna-Tabor Evangelical Lutheran Church and School v. Equal Employment Opportunity Commission* (2012),[137] the Supreme Court unanimously ruled that the exception applied to a "commissioned minister" who claimed she had been unlawfully fired by her employer, a Lutheran church and school, because of her disability. Justice Thomas filed a solo concurrence in which he argued that "the Religion Clauses require civil courts to apply the ministerial exception and to defer to a religious organization's good-faith understanding of who qualifies as its minister."[138] Then, in *Our Lady of Guadalupe School v. Morrissey-Berru* (2020),[139] the court expanded the ministerial exception to teachers who were hired to carry out the mission of religious schools but were not "ministers" and lacked extensive religious training. Justice Thomas, joined by Justice Gorsuch, argued in a concurring opinion that courts should not inject themselves into the determination of what constitutes a minister. "What qualifies as 'ministerial,'" wrote Thomas, "is an inherently theological question, and thus one that cannot be resolved by civil courts through legal analysis."[140]

Religious Discrimination

Justice Thomas has supported religious claims when the policies of an organization or business are alleged to be discriminatory. For example, he dissented when the court upheld a law school's decision to deny student activity funds to a Christian organization that excluded homosexuals and anyone who held different religious convictions.[141] And in *Masterpiece Cakeshop v. Colorado Civil Rights Commission* (2018),[142] Thomas joined the court's decision that requiring the owner of a bakery, Jack Phillips, to make wedding cakes for gay couples violated the free exercise clause. In a concurring opinion, Thomas argued that Phillips's free speech rights had also been violated. According to Thomas, the baking of a wedding cake is creative artistic expression, which requires the court to apply its highest level of scrutiny. Finally, in *Fulton v. City of Philadelphia* (2021),[143] Thomas joined the court's ruling that a city's refusal to renew a contract with Catholic Social Services unless it agreed to certify same-sex couples as foster parents violated the free exercise clause.

Contraceptive Mandate
Justice Thomas has participated in several cases challenging the contraceptive mandate under the Patient Protection and Affordable Care Act (ACA). The ACA itself did not require employers to provide contraceptive coverage to their female employees, but 2011 guidelines issued by the Health Resources and Services Administration (HRSA) did. The HRSA interpreted one provision of the ACA ("preventative care and screenings" without "any cost sharing requirements") to include all contraceptive methods and sterilization procedures approved by the Food and Drug Administration. After concerns were raised that such a requirement would impinge on religious freedom, the HRSA initially exempted religious employers (the so-called church exemption) but then expanded the exemption to include eligible religious nonprofits, which were required to self-certify their eligibility for the exemption ("the self-certification accommodation").

Justice Thomas joined the court's ruling in *Burwell v. Hobby Lobby* (2014),[144] which granted closely held corporations an exemption from the contraceptive mandate based on the Religious Freedom Restoration Act (RFRA). He also participated in the court's 4–4 decision in *Zubik v. Burwell* (2016),[145] which did not reach the issue of whether the self-certification process imposed a substantial burden under the RFRA.[146] Thomas then wrote the court's decision in *Little Sisters of the Poor Saints Peter & Paul Home v. Pennsylvania* (2020),[147] which upheld the Trump administration's expanded exemptions for employers to opt out of contraceptive coverage for "religious" and "moral" reasons. Because the ACA did not require contraceptive coverage, Thomas held for the 7–2 court that the HRSA was vested with "virtually unbridled" discretion to decide what constitutes preventative care and screenings, and it could identify and create exemptions from its own guidelines. Thomas also rejected arguments that the administration did not follow notice and comment requirements under the Administrative Procedure Act before promulgating the new rules.

RIGHTS OF THE ACCUSED

By and large, Justice Thomas has provided a narrow interpretation of the rights of the accused—although, as with Scalia, there are notable exceptions. Myers Anderson impressed on his grandsons the importance of taking individual responsibility and not making excuses for one's behavior. He told them, "If you go to jail, I will not bail you out, and I will not visit you."[148] Thomas's cardinal rule in criminal cases is personal responsibility. The reason we have a criminal justice system, he maintains, is to hold people accountable for their actions. In fact, Thomas believes strict punishments can teach important moral lessons, and he blames the lack of responsibility in today's society on what he calls a "culture of victims" and the "rights revolution" of the 1960s, when lawyers and courts began to accept societal explanations for criminal behavior, resulting in a "Get Out of Jail Free" mentality. "Punishing people," Thomas insists, "is an expression of society's resolve that certain behavior will not be tolerated either because it hurts others, is counterproductive, or is offensive to the sensibilities of our culture."[149] During his confirmation hearings, Thomas recalled that when he was a judge on the DC Court of Appeals, he would look out his office window and see the "converted buses that [brought] in the criminal defendants to our criminal justice system, busload after busload." He thought at the time, "But for the Grace of God there go I."[150] Thomas's strict law-and-order values are borne out statistically. Since the 1930s, he ranks as the fourth most conservative justice in the area of criminal procedure.[151] In several cases, Thomas has gone to great lengths to describe the impact of crime on victims and their families.[152]

Like Justice Scalia, Thomas has defended a broad interpretation of certain guarantees protecting the rights of the accused. He has drawn a sharp line in Fourth Amendment cases if the search violates the common-law trespass doctrine. He has joined opinions banning the warrantless use of thermal imaging devices to detect heat radiating off a person's home,[153] the warrantless use of global positioning system (GPS) devices on cars,[154] and the warrantless use of dogs to sniff the front porch of a person's home.[155]

During his first term on the Supreme Court, Thomas wrote a concurring opinion, joined only by Scalia, contending that the court's decision in *Ohio v. Roberts* (1980)[156] was inconsistent with the original meaning of the confrontation clause.[157] Subsequently, Thomas joined Scalia's opinion in *Crawford v. Washington* (2004),[158] which overturned *Roberts* and now bars the use of testimonial statements at trial without the opportunity for cross-examination.

Based on a broad interpretation of the Sixth Amendment's right to a jury trial, Thomas has supported the so-called *Apprendi* rule, which requires that any fact, other than a prior conviction, that increases the penalty for a crime beyond the statutory maximum must be proved to a jury beyond a reasonable doubt.[159] Thomas joined the court's decisions holding that *Apprendi* applies to both state and federal sentencing guidelines, whereas previously, judges had been allowed to increase sentences based on a preponderance of the evidence.[160] Moreover, he voted to overturn the remedial part of the court's opinion in *United States v. Booker* (2005)—the case that applied *Apprendi* to the US sentencing guidelines—on the grounds that the court still permitted federal judges to use discretion to increase sentences based on a reasonableness standard.[161] Thomas wrote the 5–4 decision in *Alleyne v. United States* (2013),[162] which held that any facts that increase mandatory *minimum* sentences must also be proved to a jury beyond a reasonable doubt.

Fourth Amendment

Justice Thomas has defended a more restrictive interpretation of the rights of the accused in other cases. Except for the common-law trespass doctrine, Thomas has exhibited a *very* deferential attitude toward law enforcement in Fourth Amendment cases. In a 2004 case the court held that the search of a residence based on a defective warrant violated the Fourth Amendment.[163] Thomas dissented. Like Justices Black and Scalia, he argued that the Fourth Amendment does not explicitly require a warrant. The general purpose of the Fourth Amendment, according to Thomas, is to prohibit general writs of assistance. Thomas observed that the court's jurisprudence "has vacillated between imposing a categorical warrant requirement and applying a general reasonableness standard."[164] Even in those cases involving presumptively unreasonable searches—that is, those conducted without a warrant—Thomas observed that the court has carved out a number of exceptions. Rather than continuing this confusing state of affairs, he urged his colleagues to "turn to first principles" and assess the actual relationship between the reasonableness clause and the warrant clause of the Fourth Amendment. In the case at hand, he simply asked whether the search was reasonable and decided that it was.[165]

Exceptions

Based on his original understanding of the Fourth Amendment, Thomas has joined opinions extending the authority of police officers to conduct "stop and frisks" based on reasonable suspicion.[166] For example, he wrote the court's decision in *Navarette v. California* (2014),[167] which held that a police officer who pulled a car over based on an anonymous tip had reasonable suspicion to do so. He also wrote the 2020 decision holding that it was reasonable for a police officer to assume that the driver of a car was the person with a revoked license unless there was evidence to the contrary.[168] Justice Thomas has also supported the "consent" exception to the Fourth Amendment. In *Georgia v. Randolph* (2006),[169] he dissented when the court ruled that a wife's consent to search a residence was invalid when the husband was physically present and refused to give his consent. Thomas viewed the court's decision as "unduly formalistic." "When a citizen leads police officers into a home shared with her spouse to show them evidence relevant to their investigation into a crime," wrote Thomas, "that citizen is not acting as an agent of the police, and thus no Fourth Amendment search has occurred."[170]

Justice Thomas has also been supportive of law enforcement when searches are conducted based on "exigent circumstances." He joined the majority opinion in *Kentucky v. King* (2011),[171] which held that the warrantless entry of an apartment based on exigent circumstances was reasonable, even though the police created the exigency. Thomas has been the only justice to support routine nonconsensual blood tests to determine the blood alcohol concentration (BAC) of suspected drunk drivers. In *Missouri v. McNeely* (2013),[172] the defendant was stopped by a police officer for speeding and crossing the center line. When he refused a Breathalyzer test to measure his BAC, he was arrested and then taken to a nearby hospital for a blood test, which revealed that his BAC was well above the legal limit. McNeely moved to suppress the blood test result, arguing that taking his blood without his consent or a warrant violated his Fourth Amendment rights. In an 8–1 decision, the Supreme Court agreed and rejected the state's per se rule that exigent circumstances always exist when an officer has probable cause to believe a person has been driving under the influence of alcohol.

In a solo dissent, Thomas argued that "the Court should not adopt a rule that requires police to guess whether they will be able to obtain a warrant before 'too much' evidence is destroyed." "Even a slight delay," Thomas maintained, "may significantly affect probative value in borderline cases of suspects who are moderately intoxicated or suspects whose BAC is near a statutory threshold that triggers a more serious offense."[173] Thomas reaffirmed his *McNeely* dissent in *Birchfield v. North Dakota* (2016),[174] where the court held that the search-incident-to-arrest doctrine allows warrantless Breathalyzer tests based on suspicion of drunk driving. For the court, Justice Alito distinguished the privacy interests between Breathalyzer tests and blood alcohol tests. Thomas agreed with the court's judgment but argued that the same reasoning should apply to warrantless blood tests. "The compromise the Court reaches today is not a good one," wrote Thomas. "By deciding that some (but not all) warrantless tests revealing the blood alcohol concentration . . . of an arrested driver are constitutional, the Court contorts the search-incident-to-arrest exception to the Fourth Amendment's warrant requirement." "The far simpler answer to the question presented," he maintained, "is the one rejected in *Missouri v. McNeely*."[175]

Administrative Searches

In judicial opinions, Thomas has been exceedingly deferential in administrative search cases. He wrote the 2002 decision allowing drug testing of all public school students who participate in competitive extracurricular activities.[176] He was the only justice to argue that a strip search of a middle school student did not violate the Fourth Amendment. In that case, thirteen-year-old Savana Redding was strip-searched based on the suspicion that she was distributing prescription and over-the-counter drugs in school. In a twenty-one-page solo dissent, Thomas argued that the strip search was reasonable and that the court should not supervise the administration of schools.[177] Thomas also joined the decision in *Maryland v. King* (2013),[178] where the court allowed DNA testing of individuals charged with violent crimes as part of the routine booking procedure. And in a 2015 case Thomas joined a dissenting opinion by Justice Scalia, which argued that a municipal ordinance requiring hotel operators to make their registries available to the police on demand did not violate the Fourth Amendment.[179]

Katz *and the Exclusionary Rule*

Like Justices Black and Scalia, Thomas does not believe the Fourth Amendment covers electronic surveillance. In a 2018 case he argued that the two-part *Katz* test "has no basis in the text or history of the Fourth Amendment," and he called on the court to reconsider it.[180] Likewise, Justice Thomas does not believe the exclusionary rule has a basis in the Constitution. For most of his judicial career, Thomas has either joined or authored opinions limiting the reach of the exclusionary rule,[181] and he joined several important opinions that expanded the scope of the "good faith" exception to the exclusionary rule.[182] In one of Thomas's most noteworthy opinions on the subject, he wrote the majority opinion expanding the "attenuation doctrine," which is used to determine whether the discovery of incriminating evidence is so remote from an unlawful stop that the deterrent benefit of exclusion is less than its costs.

In *Utah v. Strieff* (2016),[183] the defendant was stopped by a police officer after leaving a residence where "narcotics activity" was believed to be taking place. After receiving an anonymous tip and intermittently surveilling the house for a week, Officer Fackrell detained Edward Strieff as he left the house and walked toward a convenience store. During the stop, Fackrell asked for identification and discovered that Strieff had an outstanding warrant for a traffic violation. After conducting a search incident to arrest, Fackrell discovered that Strieff possessed "a baggie of methamphetamine and drug paraphernalia." The Supreme Court assumed that there had been no "reasonable suspicion" to detain Strieff, so the question turned on whether the discovery of the illegal drugs was so attenuated from the unlawful stop as to allow the admission of the evidence against him. In the 5–3 decision, Justice Thomas held for the court that the officer's discovery of the arrest warrant attenuated the connection between the unlawful stop and the evidence seized incident to arrest. Thomas noted that although the search took place in close proximity to the time of the unlawful stop, the discovery of the outstanding arrest warrant was a crucial intervening circumstance that was wholly independent from the illegal stop. The fact that Officer Fackrell did not act maliciously was a major factor in the court's decision. At most, Thomas observed, Fackrell had been negligent in making the stop.

In a 2018 case Thomas questioned the constitutionality of the exclusionary rule altogether. In *Collins v. Virginia* (2018),[184] the court held that a warrantless search of a motorcycle that was partially covered by a white tarp and parked in the defendant's driveway violated the Fourth Amendment. In a solo concurring opinion, Thomas agreed with the court's result but raised fundamental questions about the court's authority to impose the exclusionary rule on the states. Under the common law, Thomas maintained, "the only remedies for unconstitutional searches and seizures were 'tort suits' and 'self-help.'" "The exclusionary rule," he wrote, "appears nowhere in the Constitution, postdates the founding by more than a century, and contradicts several longstanding principles of common law."[185] Thomas thus concluded that the court should revisit its decision in *Mapp v. Ohio* (1961),[186] which nationalized the exclusionary rule to apply to the states.

Fifth Amendment

Justice Thomas has defended a narrow interpretation of the Fifth Amendment's self-incrimination clause, which provides that "no person . . . shall be compelled in any criminal cases to be a witness against himself." Thomas joined Scalia's dissent in *Dickerson v. United States* (2000),[187] which held that *Miranda* warnings must be provided in federal cases. He has also written decisions limiting the scope of *Miranda.* For example, he wrote the Supreme Court's decision in *United States v. Patane* (2004),[188] which held that failing to give *Miranda* warnings did not prevent use of the physical fruits of the suspect's unwarned but voluntary statements. Most significantly, Thomas has argued that the Fifth Amendment does not prohibit a prosecutor or judge from commenting on a defendant's failure to testify. "At the time of the founding," Thomas wrote in one case, "English and American courts strongly encouraged defendants to give unsworn statements and drew adverse inferences when they failed to do so." "A defendant is not 'compelled . . . to be a witness against himself,'" he added, "simply because a jury has been told that it may draw an inference from his silence."[189]

Thomas has joined opinions limiting the scope of *Miranda.* In a 2004 case he joined a dissenting opinion that stated a two-step interrogation technique (interrogate first and then Mirandize) did not violate the Fifth Amendment.[190] In a 2011 case he joined a dissenting opinion that maintained the suspect's age (in this case, thirteen) is not material in determining whether a person believes he or she is in custody.[191] Finally, he joined court opinions holding that the accused must "unambiguously" invoke the right to remain silent[192] and that obtaining an un-Mirandized confession in a conference room at a prison did not constitute "custody" under the Fifth Amendment.[193]

Sixth Amendment

Justice Thomas has also defended a crabbed view of the Sixth Amendment's right to counsel. In *Garza v. Idaho* (2019),[194] the court held that the defendant was denied the effective assistance of counsel when he signed two plea agreements waiving his right to appeal. In dissent, Justice Thomas argued that the fundamental purpose of the Sixth Amendment was to discard the common-law rule denying the accused the right to retain the services of counsel. He thus took issue with the Supreme Court's decisions in *Johnson v. Zerbst*

(1938)[195] and *Gideon v. Wainwright* (1963),[196] which required the government to pay for counsel in federal and state cases, respectively, if the defendant could not afford an attorney. "Neither one of these opinions," Thomas contended, "attempted to square the expansive rights they recognized with the original meaning of the 'right . . . to have the Assistance of Counsel.'" "The guarantees of the Sixth Amendment, he observed, "certainly seek to promote reliable criminal proceedings, but there is no substantive right to a particular level of reliability."[197]

During his tenure on the Supreme Court, Thomas has authored or joined opinions narrowing the scope of the Sixth Amendment. In one case he argued in dissent that the right to counsel does not apply to civil contempt proceedings.[198] In 2012 he joined two dissents authored by Justice Scalia contending that the Sixth Amendment does not apply to plea bargains.[199] He joined another Scalia dissent authored that same year maintaining that the Sixth Amendment was not violated when two attorneys "abandoned" their client in a death penalty case.[200] In a 2018 case Thomas dissented when the court held that an attorney's admission of his client's guilt (against his wishes) violated the Sixth Amendment.[201]

Eighth Amendment

Justice Thomas has interpreted the Eighth Amendment's ban against "cruel and unusual punishments" very narrowly. In *Ewing v. California* (2003),[202] Thomas joined the majority decision holding that California's "three-strikes" law did not violate the Eighth Amendment and maintained in a short concurring opinion that "the Cruel and Unusual Punishments Clause . . . contains no proportionality principle." In *Graham v. Florida* (2010),[203] the Supreme Court ruled that it was cruel and unusual to impose life sentences without the possibility of parole on minors for nonhomicidal offenses. Thomas dissented. "The ultimate question in this case," Thomas wrote, "is not whether a life-without-parole sentence 'fits' the crime at issue here or the crimes of juvenile nonhomicide offenders more generally, but to whom the Constitution assigns that decision."[204]

Thomas has also been deferential to state laws dealing with eligibility for the death penalty. He dissented in two cases in which the Supreme Court ruled that it was no longer permissible to impose the death penalty on the intellectually disabled and minors.[205] He also dissented when the court disallowed the death penalty for the offense of raping a child.[206] Additionally, Justice Thomas has not supported various procedural obstacles to the death penalty. In a 2009 case he rejected an "actual innocence" claim made by a death row inmate.[207] In *Baze v. Rees* (2008),[208] Thomas wrote a concurring opinion when the court upheld the "three-drug protocol" used to administer lethal injections. He argued that the provision banning "cruel and unusual" punishments was meant to outlaw "tortuous" punishments, and he cited some of the grisly methods used in England and in the colonies before the adoption of the Eighth Amendment.[209] Next to those punishments, Thomas argued, lethal injection could not possibly be considered cruel and unusual because it was not "deliberately designed to inflict pain."[210] In a 2015 opinion Justice Thomas argued that he had "not seen a capital crime that could not be considered sufficiently 'blameworthy' to merit a death sentence."[211]

Justice Thomas has also been a strong critic of *Batson* challenges, many of which have been filed in capital cases. In *Batson v. Kentucky* (1986),[212] the Supreme Court ruled that prosecutors cannot use their peremptory challenges to remove jurors for racially discriminatory reasons. Thomas has always questioned the constitutionality of *Batson*. During his first term, Thomas complained that the court has "exalted the right of citizens to sit on juries over the rights of the criminal defendant, even though it is the defendant, not the jurors, who faces imprisonment or even death."[213] In a 2016 case he filed a solo dissent when the court found evidence of purposeful discrimination by a prosecutor who removed all four black prospective jurors in a capital case.[214] Thomas also filed a dissent, joined by Justice Gorsuch, in *Flowers v. Mississippi* (2019),[215] where there was evidence of a pattern of racial discrimination in the use of peremptory challenges in six capital trials. In all, forty-one of forty-two black prospective jurors had been struck during those trials, including five out of six in the sixth trial.

Finally, Justice Thomas has literally interpreted the word "punishments" in the cruel and unusual punishments clause. In several opinions he has argued that the Eighth Amendment does not apply to the treatment of prisoners. One of Thomas's most significant Eighth Amendment opinions dates back to his first term on the Supreme Court. Keith Hudson, a prisoner in the Louisiana state penitentiary, claimed that he had been beaten by two prison guards while in handcuffs and shackles, causing "minor bruises and swelling to his face, mouth, and lip." The beating "also loosened Hudson's teeth and cracked his partial dental plate, rendering it unusable for several months."

During the beating, the supervisor on duty told the security officers "not to have too much fun."[216] In *Hudson v. McMillian* (1992),[217] the court ruled (7–2) that the use of excessive force can constitute cruel and unusual punishment under the Eighth Amendment, even if it does not result in serious injury.

Justice Thomas wrote the dissent (joined by Scalia), which questioned whether the Eighth Amendment applies in cases involving the treatment of prisoners. The "use of force that causes only insignificant harm to a prisoner may be immoral," Thomas wrote, "it may be tortious, it may be criminal, and it may even be remediable under other provisions of the Federal Constitution, but it is not cruel and unusual punishment."[218] In a subsequent case, Thomas noted that the Eighth Amendment was not applied to prison conditions until the court's decision in *Estelle v. Gamble* (1976),[219] which, he claimed, is inconsistent with the original meaning of the Constitution.[220] "Today's expansion of the Cruel and Unusual Punishments Clause," Thomas wrote in *Hudson*, "is, I suspect, yet another manifestation of the pervasive view that the Federal Constitution must address all ills in our society." "The Eighth Amendment," he added, "is not, and should not be turned into, a National Code of Prison Regulation."[221] In other cases, Thomas applied the same reasoning to unreasonable health risks (a prison cellmate who smoked five packs of cigarettes per day) and rape.[222] In a 2011 decision Thomas joined a dissent authored by Justice Scalia, which argued that the Eighth Amendment does not apply to overcrowded prisons.[223]

ECONOMIC FREEDOM

In pre–Supreme Court speeches, Clarence Thomas defined economic freedom as the notion that "a man had a right and obligation to produce. And, the attendant right to keep what he produced."[224] On a daily basis, Thomas's grandfather reminded him that "hard work produced the house we lived in, the clothes we wore and the food we ate."[225] Economic rights were not considered "venal" or "dirty"; rather, they instilled in the worker certain moral qualities, "such as self-discipline, self-respect, true generosity, not to mention health and comradeship."[226] Thomas argued that "utopian schemes" of wealth redistribution are really "an attack on people like my grandfather." The push for greater economic security, he maintained, meant that his grandfather "would have to work hard not only for himself but also for a host of others." "Isn't this the very definition of slavery?" Thomas asked.[227]

Lochner *Era*

In light of Thomas's strong belief in economic freedom, one might expect him to support a return to the *Lochner* era, but that has not been the case. Prior to his appointment, Thomas resisted pleas for the federal judiciary to defend economic and property rights more aggressively under the due process clauses. Even though he supported the philosophical aims of these libertarian thinkers, Thomas (like Scalia) raised concerns about the judicial role. "I find attractive the arguments of scholars such as Stephen Macedo," Thomas said in a 1987 speech, "who defend an activist Supreme Court, which would strike down laws restricting property rights." "But the libertarian argument," he added, "overlooks the place of the Supreme Court in a scheme of separation of powers. One does not strengthen self-government and the rule of law by having the non-democratic branch of government make policy."[228] Since his appointment to the Supreme Court, Thomas has written or joined several opinions repudiating the "liberty of contract" doctrine.[229] "In *Lochner*," he wrote in one case, "the Court located a 'right of free contract' in a constitutional provision that says nothing of the sort."[230] Consistent with this view, Thomas has rejected a substantive due process right of corporations to be immune from awards of excessive punitive damages.[231]

Takings Clause

At the same time, Justice Thomas has supported a more active judicial role in cases involving the takings clause. In his first term on the Supreme Court, Thomas joined the decision in *Lucas v. South Carolina Coastal Council* (1992),[232] which held that a land-use regulation that deprived a property owner of the total economic use of two parcels of land constituted a per se taking. In a 1994 case Thomas joined the court's ruling requiring a "rough proportionality" test to determine whether conditions placed on commercial property development are legitimate.[233] One year later, Thomas argued that the rough proportionality test should also apply to legislatures, not just local zoning commissions or state agencies.[234] And in *Tahoe-Sierra Preservation Council v. Tahoe Regional Planning Agency* (2002),[235] Thomas argued in dissent that temporary regulations prohibiting all productive uses of property must be subject to *Lucas*'s per se rule.

In a 1998 decision Thomas joined an opinion authored by Justice O'Connor holding that a federal law (the Coal Act) that required retroactive payments of medical benefits to former coal miners constituted a taking.[236] In a solo concurring opinion, Thomas argued that the law also likely violated the ex post facto clause, which historically has been interpreted as applying only to criminal penalties.[237] In a 2015 decision Thomas joined a 5–4 ruling that the takings clause applies to personal property, not just real estate.[238] Interestingly, two years later, Thomas argued in a dissenting opinion that the Supreme Court has never attempted to ground its opinions on regulatory takings in the original meaning of the Constitution. Observing that "it was generally thought that the Takings Clause reached only 'direct appropriation' of property . . . or the functional equivalent of a 'practical ouster of the [owner's] possession,'" Thomas argued that the court should reexamine its regulatory takings jurisprudence to determine "whether it can be grounded in the original public meaning of the Takings Clause of the Fifth Amendment or the Privileges or Immunities Clause of the Fourteenth Amendment."[239] In a 2021 decision Thomas joined the court's holding that a California regulation granting labor organizations a right of access to an employer's property constituted a per se physical taking of property.[240]

Thomas also authored a dissenting opinion in a case involving a local government's use of eminent domain to promote "economic development." In *Kelo v. City of New London* (2005),[241] a municipality approved a comprehensive development plan to reinvigorate the community's economic vitality. Suffering from economic distress (high unemployment and a reduced population), the city of New London received state approval to coordinate a variety of commercial, residential, and recreational uses of land in the hope of creating new jobs and increasing tax revenue. The city council authorized the New London Development Corporation, a nonprofit entity, to purchase or acquire property through eminent domain proceedings. Susette Kelo, along with eight other petitioners whose property was located in the development area, argued that the plan did not constitute a "public use" as required by the takings clause.

In an opinion by Justice Stevens, the court held that eminent domain for economic development qualifies as a public purpose. Even though the properties in question were not blighted or otherwise in poor condition, the court reasoned that the city had "carefully formulated an economic development plan that it believes will provide appreciable benefits to the community."[242] Justice Thomas dissented. He argued that the court's precedents have strayed too from the takings clause's original meaning and should be reconsidered. In his view, "public use" requires that "the government may take property only if it actually uses or gives the public a legal right to use the property."[243] By making this argument, Thomas called into question two precedents: *Berman v. Parker* (1954),[244] which allowed the redevelopment of "slum" or "blighted" areas in Washington, DC; and *Hawaii Housing Authority v. Midkiff* (1984),[245] which upheld Hawaii's Land Reform Act, authorizing the transfer of fee titles from lessors to lessees to reduce the concentration of landownership under the state's feudal land-tenure system. Thomas emphasized that the "urban renewal" planning upheld in *Berman* had a disproportionately negative impact on black communities.[246] "Public works projects in the 1950's and 1960's," Thomas wrote, "destroyed predominantly minority communities in St. Paul, Minnesota, and Baltimore, Maryland." And in 1981 "urban planners in Detroit, Michigan, uprooted the largely 'lower-income and elderly' Poletown neighborhood for the benefit of the General Motors Corporation." For this reason, Thomas argued, "urban renewal projects have long been associated with the displacement of blacks." "In cities across the country," he wrote, "urban renewal came to be known as 'Negro removal.'"[247]

SUBSTANTIVE DUE PROCESS

In addition to being critical of the jurisprudence exhibited during the *Lochner* era, Thomas has not been supportive of other substantive due process claims. In his first term on the Supreme Court, he rejected a challenge to a Louisiana state law that allowed criminally insane acquittees to be retained in psychiatric hospitals if they were regarded as "dangerous" but were no longer "insane."[248] In dissent, Thomas argued that there is no fundamental right to "freedom from bodily restraint" nor a right to be "freed from indefinite detention."[249]

In a 1999 case Thomas filed a vigorous dissent when the court struck down Chicago's gang congregation ordinance. The majority ruled that the ordinance was vague and thus gave the police too much discretion in dispersing groups of people for loitering. Although the majority did not find a violation of substantive due process, Thomas denied that any such right existed under the Constitution. Citing the "human costs" of gang violence, as well as the long history of antiloitering statutes, Thomas criticized the court for placing more importance on gang members' freedom of movement. "The people who will have to live with the consequences of today's opinion," Thomas wrote, "do not live in our neighborhoods." Quite the contrary, he argued, "the people who will suffer from our lofty pronouncements are people like Ms. Susan Mary Jackson; people who have seen their neighborhoods literally destroyed by gangs and violence and drugs."[250]

Right of Privacy

During his confirmation hearings, Thomas expressed agreement with justice John Marshall Harlan's concurring opinion in *Griswold v. Connecticut* (1965),[251] which recognized married couples' right to use contraceptives under the Fourteenth Amendment's due process clause.[252] However, in *Lawrence v. Texas* (2003),[253] Thomas rejected that interpretation of the due process clause. Texas police officers, responding to a report of a weapons-related disturbance in a private residence, witnessed two men engaging in private consensual sex. The men were arrested and convicted under a Texas law that criminalized deviate sexual intercourse with a member of the same sex. The Supreme Court overturned the state law as a violation of the "liberty" provision of the due process clause. In dissent, Thomas observed that the Texas law was "uncommonly silly" and that law enforcement had more "worthy" things to do, but he rejected a general right of privacy under the Fourteenth Amendment, including a right of sexual preference.[254]

ABORTION

Despite testifying during his confirmation hearings that he had never discussed the merits of *Roe v. Wade* (1973),[255] Justice Thomas voted to overturn that decision during his first term on the Supreme Court.[256] Eight years later, in *Stenberg v. Carhart* (2000),[257] the court struck down a state law outlawing partial-birth (or late-term) abortions because it did not contain a health exception. In dissent, Thomas penned his first lengthy opinion on the subject. He contended that *Roe* was "grievously wrong" and that the Constitution does not deprive "the people of this country of the right to determine whether the consequences of abortion to the fetus and to society outweigh the burden of an unwanted pregnancy on the mother." "Although a State *may* permit abortion," Thomas contended, "nothing in the Constitution dictates that a State *must* do so."[258]

In *Gonzales v. Carhart* (2007),[259] the court essentially overturned *Stenberg* by upholding the federal Partial-Birth Abortion Ban Act of 2003. Thomas wrote a short concurrence in which he argued "that the Court's abortion jurisprudence, including [*Planned Parenthood of Southeastern Pennsylvania v.*] *Casey* and *Roe v. Wade* . . . has no basis in the Constitution."[260] Then, in a 2016 case, Thomas dissented from the court's decision striking down Texas's requirement that physicians performing abortions have admitting privileges at a hospital no more than thirty miles away. In dissent, Thomas wrote that he remained "fundamentally opposed to the Court's abortion jurisprudence"[261]—a position he reaffirmed four years later when the court struck down a nearly identical Louisiana law. "Our abortion precedents are grievously wrong," Thomas wrote in that case, "and should be overruled."[262]

Justice Thomas wrote a separate opinion in *Box v. Planned Parenthood of Ind. & Ky., Inc.* (2019),[263] where the court upheld one provision of a state's abortion law prescribing how to dispose of fetal remains. Unlike his colleagues, Thomas alone proceeded to address another provision of the law on which the court had denied certiorari. That provision made it illegal to perform an abortion if the provider knew the mother was seeking the abortion solely because of the child's race, sex, diagnosis of Down syndrome, or related characteristics. In a long concurring opinion, Thomas expressed support for the state regulation because, in his view, the state had a compelling interest in "preventing abortion from becoming a tool of modern-day eugenics." "With today's prenatal screening tests and other technologies," Thomas wrote, "abortion can easily be used to eliminate children with unwanted characteristics." "The individualized nature of abortion," he added, "gives it even more eugenic potential than birth control, which simply reduces the chance of conceiving *any* child."[264]

Right to Die

Justice Thomas has rejected a substantive due process "right to die." In *Washington v. Glucksberg* (1997),[265] he joined the court's decision upholding a state law criminalizing physician-assisted suicide. In *Gonzales v. Oregon* (2006),[266] the court ruled that former attorney general John Ashcroft had exceeded his authority when he prohibited doctors from prescribing regulated drugs under the Controlled Substances Act (CSA) for use in physician-assisted suicide. In a separate dissent, Thomas criticized the majority for retreating from its decision one year earlier in *Gonzales v. Raich* (2005),[267] where the court broadly construed the CSA to cover the medicinal use of marijuana. Although Thomas still expressed unease about the scope of the CSA, he concluded that it was now "water over the dam" and that the CSA could, as a matter of statutory interpretation, be applied to the states' police powers to regulate the health, safety, and welfare of the people.[268]

Gay Marriage

Justice Thomas also rejected a substantive due process right to marry for same-sex couples. In *Obergefell v. Hodges* (2015),[269] the Supreme Court struck down state laws that either denied marriage licenses to people of the same sex or did not recognize same-sex marriage licenses from other states. Justice Thomas dissented. After conducting a historical examination of the meaning of "due process" from the Magna Carta to the Fourteenth Amendment, Thomas concluded that "liberty" under the due process clause means "freedom from physical restraint." Unlike antimiscegenation laws that allowed the criminal punishment of interracial couples who married,[270] Thomas argued that the petitioners in this case "have [not] been imprisoned or physically restrained by the States for participating in same-sex relationships." In fact, gay and lesbian couples "have been able to hold civil marriage ceremonies in States that recognize same-sex marriages and private religious ceremonies in all States."[271] What gay and lesbian couples really wanted, Thomas contended, were the government benefits associated with marriage, including tax benefits, inheritance and property rights, and the right to health insurance, workers' compensation, death certificates, and survivor benefits. According to his interpretation of liberty, Thomas argued that the petitioners were not entitled to these benefits. "Our Constitution," he wrote, "like the Declaration of Independence before it . . . was predicated on a simple truth: One's liberty, not to mention one's dignity, was something to be shielded from—not provided by—the State."[272]

PRIVILEGES OR IMMUNITIES

At the same time, Justice Thomas has sought to resuscitate the Fourteenth Amendment's privileges or immunities clause as a source of fundamental rights. In *Troxel v. Granville* (2000),[273] the Supreme Court overturned a state law that allowed visitation rights "at any time" and whenever "visitation may serve the best interest of the child." Jenifer and Gary Troxel petitioned a state court for the right to increase their visitation privileges with their two grandchildren, Isabelle and Natalie. Tommie Granville, the children's mother, opposed the expansion of visitation rights.[274] The Supreme Court struck down the state's broad visitation law as a violation of a parent's right to raise her children as she sees fit under the due process clause. Thomas concurred, observing that although he had misgivings about the court's substantive due process jurisprudence, the parties in this case did not challenge it. Based on the court's earlier decision in *Pierce v. Society of Sisters* (1925),[275] which recognized parents' fundamental right "to rear their children, including the right to determine who shall educate and socialize them," Thomas agreed with the majority that such a right exists under the Constitution.[276] However, he strongly suggested in a footnote that the right was better lodged under the Fourteenth Amendment's privileges or immunities clause.[277] He also took issue with his colleagues in the majority for not clearly articulating the level of scrutiny that should be applied in such cases. For Thomas, parents' right to rear their children was fundamental; therefore, strict scrutiny should be applied. "The state of Washington," he wrote, "lacks even a legitimate governmental interest—to say nothing of a compelling one—in second-guessing a fit parent's decision regarding visitation with third parties."[278]

In other cases, Thomas has more explicitly relied on the Fourteenth Amendment's privileges or immunities clause. In *Saentz v. Roe* (1999),[279] the court struck down California's dual-track welfare program, which limited welfare benefits for newly arrived residents (less than one year) to the amount of benefits they would have received from their previous state of residence. In an opinion by Justice Stevens, the court ruled that the one-year residency restriction was a violation of the right to travel under the Fourteenth Amendment's privileges or immunities clause. Justice Thomas dissented. While he acknowledged that the privileges or immunities clause is a source of fundamental rights, he did not believe welfare benefits constituted such a right. Relying on justice Bushrod Washington's "landmark opinion" in *Corfield v. Coryell*

(1825),[280] which provided an early interpretation of Article IV's privileges and immunities clause, Thomas concluded that, "at the time the Fourteenth Amendment was adopted, people understood that 'privileges or immunities of citizens' were fundamental rights," not "every public benefit established by positive law."[281] Thomas "would be open to reevaluating [the privileges or immunities clause's] meaning in an appropriate case," but he cautioned that it should be based on what the members of the Thirty-Ninth Congress meant by the Fourteenth Amendment. "We should also consider," he maintained, "whether the Clause should displace, rather than augment, portions of our equal protection and substantive due process jurisprudence." "The majority's failure to consider these important questions," Thomas added, "raises the specter that the Privileges or Immunities Clause will become yet another convenient tool for inventing new rights, limited solely by the 'predilections of those who happen at the time to be Members of this Court.'"[282]

The opportunity for Justice Thomas to reevaluate the original meaning of the privileges or immunities clause came eleven years later in *McDonald v. City of Chicago* (2010).[283] Two municipalities had effectively banned the possession of handguns by private citizens. Several of the Chicago petitioners, including Otis McDonald, wanted to keep handguns in their homes for self-defense. Having ruled two years earlier that the Second Amendment conferred an individual right to bear arms,[284] the legal question presented in *McDonald* was whether the Second Amendment was fundamental and should apply to the states. Relying on the court's traditional incorporation analysis, Justice Alito, for a *plurality* of justices, held that the Second Amendment was fundamental under the Fourteenth Amendment's due process clause because it was "deeply rooted in this Nation's history and tradition" and "necessary to our system of ordered liberty."[285]

Justice Thomas supplied the crucial fifth vote to apply the Second Amendment to the states, but he strongly disagreed with the court's analysis. Thomas began his opinion by observing that it was incomprehensible how a substantive right, such as the right to keep and bear arms, could be "enforceable against the States" through the due process clause, which speaks only of "process."[286] After conducting a careful historical examination of the original meaning of the Fourteenth Amendment, Thomas determined that the more appropriate vehicle for incorporating the Second Amendment was the privileges or immunities clause. Thomas pointed out that the chief sponsors of the Fourteenth Amendment—representative John Bingham (R-OH) and senator

Jacob Howard (R-MI)—had argued in various widely circulated speeches that one of the primary purposes of the privileges or immunities clause was to nationalize all the guarantees of the Bill of Rights.

In arriving at that conclusion, Thomas had to contend with an 1873 decision that narrowly interpreted the privileges or immunities clause. In the *Slaughter-House Cases* (1873),[287] the Supreme Court held that the state of Louisiana did not violate the privileges or immunities clause by granting a monopoly of livestock butchering to one company in New Orleans. It held that the privileges or immunities clause was not intended "as a protection to the citizen of a State against the legislative power of his own State" but instead protected only rights as a US citizen.[288] Justice Thomas rejected the *Slaughter-House* interpretation of the privileges or immunities clause because, in his view, it sapped the provision of any substantive meaning by defining "the two sets of rights [state and federal] as mutually exclusive." For Thomas, state and federal citizenship rights "overlap," and the privileges or immunities clause "establishes a minimum baseline of rights for all American citizens."[289]

Thomas also rejected three separate Supreme Court decisions holding that the privileges or immunities clause did not incorporate the Second Amendment.[290] Importantly, Thomas limited his analysis to the precise question involved: whether the Second Amendment should apply to the states. Whether other guarantees of the Bill of Rights should apply to the states under the privileges or immunities clause was left for another day. Thomas also chose not to resolve the question of whether other unenumerated rights can be considered privileges or immunities of state and national citizenship—although he strongly suggested that they could be.[291] Since *McDonald*, Thomas has joined opinions that incorporated the Eighth Amendment's excessive fines clause and the Sixth Amendment's right to a unanimous jury in criminal cases. In each case, he argued that those rights should apply to the states under the privileges or immunities clause.[292]

EQUAL PROTECTION

The central moral (and legal) principle that guides Justice Thomas's equal protection analysis is the inherent equality of man, which lies at the core of the Declaration of Independence. As he explained in a 1988 book chapter, "Black Americans had always based their claim for freedom and dignity on the Constitution and the higher law tradition that formed it." "The Declaration of Independence," he added, "said that 'all men are created equal,' and they knew that this final, self-evident truth had to apply to them—or it applied to no one at all."[293] On this basis, Thomas has been a forceful critic of the Supreme Court's decision in *Dred Scott v. Sandford* (1857),[294] which sanctioned slavery in the United States. He has also sharply criticized the court's decision in *Plessy v. Ferguson* (1896),[295] which established the "separate but equal" doctrine. Both these decisions, Thomas has argued, conflicted with the higher law background of the US Constitution.[296]

Justice Thomas has also described *Brown v. Board of Education* (1954)[297] as a landmark decision. "Although it overturned the *Plessy v. Ferguson* doctrine of 'separate but equal' in the area of education only," Thomas said in a 1984 speech, "it also marked the beginning of an era of at least overt consensus that segregation and racial injustice were illegal and morally wrong—a consensus that opened the floodgates to the era of reform considered by many to be the second reconstruction."[298] At the same time, Thomas has criticized the *Brown* court's reliance on psychological studies attempting to demonstrate that segregation in public schools "generates a feeling of inferiority [in black schoolchildren] that may affect their hearts and minds in a way unlikely ever to be undone."[299] In a 1987 interview, Thomas recalled his own experience attending segregated schools. "You can really learn how to read off those books, even if white folks aren't there."[300]

Integration

Justice Thomas has been sharply critical of integration efforts post *Brown.* He has argued that racial imbalances in public schools do not violate the Constitution. "It never ceases to amaze me," Thomas wrote in a 1995 concurrence, "that the courts are so willing to assume that anything that is predominantly black must be inferior."[301] In two consolidated desegregation cases in 2007, Thomas disputed the social science research claiming that integrated schools provide a better education. "In reality," he wrote, "it is far from apparent that coerced racial mixing has any educational benefits, much less that integration is necessary to black achievement."[302] Thomas also disagreed with the three compelling state interests cited by Justice Breyer in dissent to support voluntary integration efforts.[303] None of them, he argued, survive the court's strict scrutiny analysis when it comes to racial classifications. Finally, Thomas cautioned about reliance on "current societal practice and expectations," "deference to local officials," and "practical consequences," because these things were cited by the opponents of *Brown* as reasons to retain segregated schools. "If our history has taught us anything," Thomas wrote, "it has taught us to beware of elites bearing racial theories."[304]

Affirmative Action

Justice Thomas has also been a strenuous critic of affirmative action. In *Adarand Constructors, Inc. v. Pena* (1995),[305] the Supreme Court applied strict scrutiny to a federal affirmative action program for the first time.[306] In a separate concurring opinion, Thomas took issue with his dissenting colleagues' belief that "benign" discrimination is not as pernicious as laws mandating segregation and slavery. "There is a 'moral [and] constitutional equivalence,'" Thomas wrote, "between laws designed to subjugate a race with those that distribute benefits on the basis of race in order to foster some current notion of equality." "Government cannot make us equal," Thomas contended, "it can only recognize, respect, and protect us as equal before the law."[307]

Justice Thomas has authored important opinions in cases involving affirmative action in higher education. In *Grutter v. Bollinger* (2003),[308] the Supreme Court upheld an affirmative action program at the University of Michigan Law School, which considered race a "plus" in admissions decisions. The court accepted the university's argument that "diversity" in the classroom is a compelling state interest that benefits all students. In dissent, Thomas criticized the court for deferring so readily to the university's diversity argument. Thomas argued that the only justification for racial classifications under the equal protection clause is a "pressing public necessity," which he defined as an action "the State must take to provide a bulwark against anarchy, or to prevent violence."[309] By this measure, Thomas concluded that the educational benefits of having a diverse student body are not compelling.

Justice Thomas also challenged the sincerity of the university's diversity argument. If Michigan really cared about having a diverse student body, Thomas maintained, it could have pursued several race-neutral measures, such as eliminating the Law School Admissions Test (LSAT), on which blacks statistically receive lower scores, as a criterion for acceptance. He also disputed whether diversity improves education. "The Court never acknowledges," Thomas wrote, "the growing evidence that racial (and other sorts) of heterogeneity actually impairs learning among black students."[310] Moreover, Thomas argued that the university's affirmative action program did not help "the truly underprivileged"; instead, it was an attempt by the university to retain its "elite" status and the "aesthetic" of a diverse student body. Finally, Thomas raised concerns about those minority students who were admitted to the law school and did not succeed. "Nowhere in any of the filings in the Court," Thomas wrote, "is any evidence that the purported 'beneficiaries' of this racial discrimination prove themselves by performing at (or even near) the same level as those students who receive no preferences."[311] This not only stamps those affirmative action students with a "badge of inferiority" but also places a stigma on those minorities who were admitted to the institution without the benefit of affirmative action.

Justice Thomas participated in two cases involving an affirmative action program at the University of Texas. To achieve a more diverse student body, the University of Texas combined the state's "10 percent" law with a holistic approach that allowed race to be a consideration for admission. In 2008 Abigail Fisher, a white female, was denied admission to the university and claimed reverse discrimination. When the Supreme Court first heard the case (*Fisher I*), it remanded the case to the Fifth Circuit to reconsider its judgment using strict scrutiny.[312] Justice Thomas filed a passionate concurring opinion and argued that *Grutter* was "a radical departure" from the court's use of strict scrutiny and should be overturned. Thomas also questioned the "benign" nature of affirmative action and said there was no evidence that blacks and Hispanics could close the educational gap after being admitted to the University of Texas.

When the case went back to the Supreme Court in 2016 (*Fisher II*), the justices upheld the program using strict scrutiny.[313] Thomas filed a short dissent. "The Constitution abhors classifications based on race," he observed, "because every time the government places citizens on racial registers and makes race relevant to the provision of burdens or benefits, it demeans us all."[314] He once again called for *Grutter* to be overturned on the grounds that "a State's use of race in higher education admissions decisions is categorically prohibited by the Equal Protection Clause."[315]

This chapter has examined Justice Thomas's originalist jurisprudence across a whole host of constitutional areas. When it comes to federalism, Justice

Thomas is a principled defender of states' rights and has called for a reexamination of the "substantial effects" test. In several different cases, Thomas has made the argument that the states have considerable residual authority under the Tenth Amendment. Based on these two related interpretations, Thomas clearly believes the Tenth Amendment is an affirmative limit on federal power. If Congress cannot support its legislation based on one of its enumerated powers (which he strictly construes), then the power must reside with the states.

Justice Thomas has defended an expansive interpretation of executive power under Article II, particularly in the areas of foreign affairs and national security. As a libertarian, Thomas does not support government "entitlement" programs,[316] but he has supported Hamilton's "unified" executive, the "sole organ" theory of the presidency, and ample implied and inherent powers under Article II. During the Trump administration, Thomas stood out in defending broad claims of executive immunity in the face of both a criminal subpoena and a congressional investigation. As discussed in chapter 6, Thomas's view of the presidency is not as robust in domestic matters, as he has called for a reexamination of the Supreme Court's "intelligible principle" (nondelegation cases) and *Chevron* deference (agency discretion).

In interpreting the First Amendment, Justice Thomas has not supported broadly written "offensive" speech laws, but he has taken the position that cross burnings are not protected political speech. Thomas also cast the sole dissent in *Elonis v. United States*, where the Supreme Court ruled that subjective intent (*mens rea*) is required before a person can be criminally punished for sending threatening messages over the internet. Thomas has called for strict scrutiny in several cases involving commercial speech and campaign contribution limits. As discussed in chapter 6, he believes that anonymous speech is protected under the First Amendment and that strict scrutiny should apply to disclaimer and disclosure requirements under campaign finance laws. In other areas of First Amendment law, Thomas has not supported a robust view of free speech. He has defended a very limited view of the free speech rights of minors; he has supported the regulation of obscenity; and he believes that the government can place conditions on the speech it subsidizes and that public employees have reduced free speech rights. Thomas also believes that the states have broad (perhaps plenary) authority to regulate libel.

When it comes to the establishment clause, Thomas has argued that it "resists" incorporation, which means that the states can establish religions if they want to do so. He has also supported a wide variety of state programs that accommodate religion, including school vouchers, public assistance to religious schools, prayers at graduation ceremonies, religious displays on public grounds, and sectarian prayers at city council meetings. In fact, he has argued that individuals cannot successfully challenge the government's accommodation of religion unless they are "legally coerced" to participate. In the interplay between the establishment clause and the free exercise clause, Thomas has argued that a broad interpretation of the former leads to discrimination on the basis of the latter. In a 2021 case Thomas voted to overturn the Supreme Court's decision in *Smith.*

In the area of criminal procedure, Thomas's voting record belies a robust interpretation of the rights of the accused—although there are important exceptions. Like Justice Scalia, his support of the common-law trespass doctrine has led to some "liberal" results in Fourth Amendment cases, and he has broadly interpreted the confrontation clause and right to a jury trial under the Sixth Amendment. At the same time, Thomas has been very deferential toward law enforcement in Fourth Amendment cases. He believes the touchstone of the amendment is "reasonableness," and he has supported several important exceptions to the warrant requirement. Thomas has also argued that electronic surveillance is not covered by the Fourth Amendment and that the Supreme Court's decision in *Mapp v. Ohio* should be reexamined.

Justice Thomas has defended a narrow interpretation of the self-incrimination clause. In a 2000 case he voted to overturn *Miranda*, and he has authored opinions that would allow the prosecutor or judge to comment on a defendant's failure to take the stand. In Sixth Amendment cases Thomas has questioned court decisions requiring state and federal governments to furnish counsel for those who cannot afford one. He has also defended a very low bar for what constitutes effective assistance of counsel. In interpreting the Eighth Amendment, Thomas has argued that there is no requirement of "proportionality" in noncapital cases; he has supported substantial deference to the states over the use of, eligibility for, and methods of carrying out the death penalty. Justice Thomas has also defended a narrow interpretation of the Eighth Amendment, arguing that the provision does not apply to prison beatings, unhealthy conditions, and sexual assaults.

In the area of economic and property rights, Justice Thomas has rejected a return to the *Lochner* era, but he has broadly interpreted the takings clause. He has authored or joined several opinions in which the court used a higher level of scrutiny to assess land-use restrictions. In *Kelo v. City of New London,* he argued in solo dissent that the government cannot take property unless it "actually uses or gives the public a legal right to use the property." In so doing, he called for the overturning of two Supreme Court precedents.

Justice Thomas has rejected *all* substantive due process claims, including a general right of privacy, a right of sexual preference, a woman's right to obtain an abortion, and a right to die. In *Obergefell v. Hodges*, Thomas dissented on the grounds that gay and lesbian couples were not being criminally punished in states that did not recognize same-sex marriage. As he saw it, they were merely being denied the economic benefits associated with marriage, which the government has no obligation to provide. In contrast, Thomas has contended that the privileges or immunities clause is an important source of fundamental rights, suggesting that parental rights and regulatory takings should fall under that provision but not welfare benefits. In several incorporation cases, Justice Thomas has argued that the privileges or immunities clause is the only legitimate way to apply the Bill of Rights to the states.

It is apparent that Justice Thomas's foremost principle in interpreting the equal protection clause is the Declaration of Independence's famous phrase: "all men are created equal." "That's natural law in a nutshell," Thomas wrote in his autobiography. "If all men are created equal, then no man can own another man, and we can only be governed by our consent."[317] On this basis, Thomas has been a strong critic of *Dred Scott* and *Plessy*. He applies that same moral principle to integration efforts and affirmative action, believing that "there is a 'moral [and] constitutional equivalence' between laws designed to subjugate a race with those that distribute benefits on the basis of race in order to foster some current notion of equality."[318] Thomas has voted to strike down two voluntary desegregation efforts and has rejected affirmative action in employment and higher education. As discussed in chapter 5, he is also a strong critic of racial gerrymandering.

5. Black v. Scalia and Thomas

This chapter begins the analysis of the major fault lines in the originalist philosophies of Hugo Black, Antonin Scalia, and Clarence Thomas. It explores the differences between Justice Black, on the one hand, and Justices Scalia and Thomas, on the other. As already pointed out, there were also important areas of agreement among the three originalists. Each of them rejected substantive due process across the board, including a liberty of contract, a right of privacy, and a woman's right to obtain an abortion. They also sharply criticized the Supreme Court's negative (or dormant) commerce clause jurisprudence. In *Southern Pacific v. Arizona ex. rel. Sullivan* (1945), Justice Black argued in a dissenting opinion that the court was acting like a "super-legislature" in striking down a state law on the grounds that it interfered with interstate commerce.[1] All three justices have argued that the "touchstone" of the Fourth Amendment is reasonableness.[2] In their view, a warrant is not necessary to determine whether a search or an arrest is lawful. In other Fourth Amendment cases, the three originalists have supported several important exceptions, including "stop and frisks" based on reasonable suspicion;[3] they have agreed that the objects of the Fourth Amendment ("persons, houses, papers, and effects") do not include electronic surveillance; they have expressed serious doubts about the constitutionality of the exclusionary rule; and they have not approved of *Bivens* claims.[4]

In other areas of constitutional interpretation, all three originalists have sharply criticized restrictions on the use of peremptory strikes during the voir dire process in jury trials.[5] They have also argued that the Eighth Amendment does not prohibit the death penalty—although, as discussed later, Justice Black would have been more scrupulous than Justices Scalia and Thomas in ensuring that constitutional protections are afforded in such cases. In interpreting the equal protection clause, the three originalists have rejected what is known as the "political process" doctrine.[6] For this reason, a strong case can be made that the three justices would have been on the same page in *Harper v. Virginia Board of Elections* (1966),[7] where the Supreme Court struck down state-imposed poll taxes.[8]

Despite these important areas of agreement, there are fundamental differences in how Black, Scalia, and Thomas interpreted specific constitutional provisions. This chapter examines these differences in the areas of legal standing, separation of powers, federalism, incorporation, freedom of speech, church-state, religious freedom, the Second Amendment, rights of the accused, property rights, and equal protection.

LEGAL STANDING

Legal standing is a judicial doctrine that asks whether the parties to a case have a sufficient stake in the controversy to adjudicate it in federal court. During his tenure on the Supreme Court, Justice Black supported a deferential approach to legal standing. His interpretation of Article III's "case or controversy" requirement was not as lenient as that of his judicial ally, Justice Douglas, but it was not very stringent either.[9] By contrast, Justices Scalia and Thomas have defended a rigid interpretation of legal standing. In a 1983 law review article, Scalia argued that legal standing is "a crucial and inseparable element" of separation of powers, which, if interpreted correctly, prevents "an overjudicialization of the processes of self-governance."[10] Scalia also contended that strict enforcement of legal standing relegates courts to their traditional function of protecting individual rights and not the more undemocratic function of protecting majoritarian rights. Lurking beneath Scalia's rigid defense of legal standing was a desire to protect the executive branch's authority to faithfully execute the laws. Scalia ridiculed the charge that "important legislative purposes, heralded in the halls of Congress, [can be] lost or misdirected in the vast hallways of the federal bureaucracy." That is a good thing, he observed. "Yesterday's herald is today's bore."[11]

Citizen Lawsuits

Justice Black retired from the bench before the environmental revolution took off, but there is substantial evidence that he would have supported standing in such cases. During his last term on the Supreme Court, Black wanted to hear a case filed by a conservation group that objected to the construction of a federal highway that would run through two sections of a public park in San Antonio, Texas. "This case disturbs me greatly," Black began his dissent from denial of certiorari. Describing the park as "a lovely place for people to retreat from the frantic pace of bustling urban life to enjoy the simple pleasures of open space, quiet solitude, and clean air," Black lamented that now "the people of San

Antonio and the birds and animals that make their home in the park will share their quiet retreat with an ugly, smelly stream of traffic pouring down a super six-lane 'North Expressway.'"[12]

Justice Black also expressed support for citizen lawsuits. "In the last several years," he observed, "Congress has enacted coordinated legislation designed to protect our Nation's environment from destruction by water pollution, air pollution, and noise pollution." "This legislation," he pointed out, "has come about in response to aroused citizens who have awakened to the importance of a decent environment for our Nation's well-being and our very survival." Black expressed frustration that "the efforts of our citizens and the Congress to save our parklands and to preserve our environment" did not get "a more hospitable reception . . . in the Executive Branch or, thus far, in the courts."[13] In a companion case, Black criticized the secretary of transportation for failing to comply with the intentions of Congress, which he called "the highest law-making body of this Nation." "I regret that I am compelled to conclude for myself that, except for some too-late formulations, apparently coming from the Solicitor General's office, this record contains not one word to indicate that the Secretary raised even a finger to comply with the command of Congress." "It is our duty," he added, "to remand this whole matter back to the Secretary of Transportation for him to give this matter the hearing it deserves in full good-faith obedience to the Act of Congress."[14]

In stark contrast, Justices Scalia and Thomas called for restrictions on "citizen lawsuits." Scalia claimed that Article III's "case or controversy" provision strictly limits Congress's ability to extend standing to those individuals who do not satisfy its "core" requirements. Congress, in his view, cannot convert a generalized grievance into a legal right. In *Lujan v. Defenders of Wildlife* (1992),[15] Scalia wrote the court's decision denying standing to a wildlife conservation group that challenged a revised joint ruling by the secretaries of the interior and commerce that the "consultation" requirement of the Endangered Species Act of 1973 (ESA) no longer applies to government activities outside the United States. Scalia concluded that the plaintiffs did not satisfy the "injury in fact" requirement because they failed to show how injury to the animals would "imminently" injure them. The plaintiffs' intentions to "some day" return to places they had previously visited, Scalia observed, does not "support a finding of the 'actual or imminent' injury" required by prior case law.[16] Scalia then chastised Congress for including a "citizen suit" provision in the federal law. "To permit Congress to convert the undifferentiated public interest in executive officers' compliance with the law into an 'individual right' vindicable in the courts is to permit Congress to transfer from the President to the courts the Chief Executive's most important constitutional duty, to 'take Care that the Laws be faithfully executed.'"[17] Justice Thomas joined Scalia's opinion in *Lujan*.

Taxpayer Lawsuits

The three originalists also viewed taxpayer lawsuits differently. In *Flast v. Cohen* (1968),[18] a decision that Justice Black joined, the court allowed taxpayers to challenge federal funding under the Elementary and Secondary Education Act of 1965. The petitioners claimed that federal money was being used for instruction, textbooks, and other educational materials in religious and sectarian schools. In reaching its decision, the court established a two-part test to determine whether a taxpayer has legal standing. First, there has to be a connection between the party's status as a taxpayer and an exercise of congressional power under the tax and spending clauses of Article I, section 8. Second, there has to be a nexus between the taxpayer's status and a specific constitutional limitation imposed on Congress's tax and spending authority.

Justices Scalia and Thomas have been sharp critics of *Flast*. In *Hein v. Freedom from Religion Foundation* (2007),[19] the Supreme Court upheld president George W. Bush's faith-based and community initiatives program. Justice Alito, writing for the court, ruled that *Flast* did not apply because the money that supported the program came from general appropriations granted to the executive branch, not from a specific congressional enactment pursuant to Congress's tax and spending authority. In a concurring opinion, Justice Scalia (joined by Justice Thomas) saw this as a distinction without a difference. "If this Court is to decide cases by rule of law rather than show of hands," wrote Scalia, "we must surrender to logic and choose sides." He added:

> Either *Flast v. Cohen* should be applied to (at a minimum) *all* challenges to the government expenditure of general tax revenues in a manner alleged to violate a constitutional provision specifically limiting the tax and spending power, or *Flast* should be repudiated. For me, the choice is easy. *Flast* is wholly irreconcilable with the Article III restrictions on federal-court jurisdiction that this Court has repeatedly confirmed are embodied in the doctrine of standing.[20]

In subsequent cases, Scalia (joined by Thomas) continued to criticize *Flast*.[21]

INTERBRANCH DISPUTES

The three originalists differed in their interpretations of classic interbranch disputes. Based on his Jeffersonian philosophy, as well as his ten-year stint in the US Senate, Hugo Black was a strong defender of the prerogatives of Congress. He regarded Congress as the predominant institution in the US governmental system and viewed the executive branch (and its departments) as distinctly subordinate. During his time in the Senate, Black voiced concerns that Congress has "yielded inch by inch" and "surrendered step by step" its legislative powers to the executive branch "to the point of impotency." He blamed this development on "the successors to the Hamiltonian idea" who desire government by one man and who follow "the sentiment that the President alone can be trusted." Separation of powers, Senator Black told his colleagues, is "part of an age-old conflict between the believers in a government of, for, and by the people and those who believe in control of the people by one or a few." He contended that "there is nothing in the simple act of electing a man to the Presidency that makes him a creature of infallibility." "His election does not endow him with superhuman traits; it does not relieve him from the common frailties of mankind," he stated. "Those who wrought when this Constitution was made realizing the fact that it would never be possible to secure a man who would rise above the common frailties of all mankind, or of the grasping avarice for power, attempted to place checks on him."[22]

Justices Scalia and Thomas, by contrast, have been strong executivists. Scalia made concerted efforts during his time in the executive branch to defend the powers of the presidency. Like Black, Scalia thought Congress was the predominant branch of government, but for him, that meant fortifying the less dangerous branches (the presidency and the judiciary) against encroachments from the legislature.[23] As President Ford's assistant attorney general, Scalia told members of Congress that interbranch conflicts often come down to trust. "Senator, I think what it comes back to in some degree is the requirement of trust. . . . I think what you are saying is quite true if you have a President who is not trustworthy. But that is certainly a rare occurrence—and when it does happen it does not last for long, it appears."[24]

Justice Thomas has also proven to be a strong defender of executive power, especially in the areas of foreign policy and national security. As head of the Equal Employment Opportunity Commission (EEOC), Thomas dreaded testifying before Congress. He viewed such requests as an unnecessary waste of taxpayer money and as politically motivated.[25] For Thomas, congressional oversight of the executive branch was an unfortunate example of Congress losing its way as a deliberative institution. "When Congress shuns its legislative role," he said in a pre–Supreme Court speech, "many decisions are left, by necessity, to be decided by the bureaucracy and courts." "However wise or just such decisions might be," he added, "they can never substitute for the kind of broad-based consensus provided when a majority of people's representatives have made a decision."[26]

In an effort to fortify the executive branch from attacks by Congress, both Scalia and Thomas supported Alexander Hamilton's unitary executive. As pointed out in previous chapters, they supported the "sole organ" theory in foreign affairs.[27] Both justices were also strong critics of *Humphrey's Executor v. United States* (1935),[28] in which the court limited the president's authority to remove the heads of independent agencies. "It has . . . always been difficult," Scalia wrote in *Synar v. United States* (1986), "to reconcile *Humphrey's Executor*'s 'headless fourth branch' with a constitutional text and tradition establishing three branches of government."[29] In a 2020 case Justice Thomas rejected the "nature of functions" test adopted in *Humphrey's Executor*, which restricted the president's removal authority if the agency performs "quasi-legislative" or "quasi-judicial" functions. Such a distinction, Thomas argued, is not constitutionally supportable because Congress cannot delegate its legislative authority to an administrative agency, nor can it "authorize the use of judicial power by officers acting outside of the bounds of Article III." Therefore, Thomas called for *Humphrey's Executor* to be overturned. "Continued reliance on *Humphrey's Executor* to justify the existence of independent agencies creates a serious, ongoing threat to our Government's design," wrote Thomas.[30] In stark contrast, Justice Black joined the unanimous decision in *Wiener v. United States* (1958),[31] which restricted the president's authority to remove members of the War Claims Commission based on the reasoning of *Humphrey's Executor.*

SCOPE OF EXECUTIVE POWER

In a famous debate with James Madison, Alexander Hamilton defended an expansive interpretation of presidential powers under Article II. Writing under the pseudonym "Pacificus," he justified the Washington administration's

"Proclamation of Neutrality" in the war between France and Great Britain based on two different constitutional provisions. First, Hamilton relied on the vesting clause of Article II, which provides that "the executive Power shall be vested in a President." For Hamilton, that provision conferred a broad grant of authority on the executive branch, "subject only to the *exceptions* and *qualifications*... expressed in the instrument" and "principles of free government."[32] Hamilton also cited the "take care" clause, which states that the president has the duty to "take Care that the Laws be faithfully executed." Hamilton interpreted that provision as giving the president broad discretionary authority to decide how to execute the laws.

Justice Black flatly rejected Hamilton's broad interpretation of Article II. "It is my intention to do the best I can to uphold the rights of the representatives of the people in the legislative body," Senator Black told his colleagues. "They are the ones who are given the power to make laws. They are given the power to coin money. They can declare war. They are given the power to regulate commerce. They are given all of the great powers of government, and executive power is given in one line. That power is 'to execute the law.'"[33] As a Supreme Court justice, Black also defended a restrictive view of executive power. In *Youngstown Sheet & Tube Co. v. Sawyer* (1952),[34] the court struck down President Truman's executive order attempting to seize the steel industries during the Korean War. For the court, Black observed that no congressional statute authorized the president's actions, and he emphatically rejected the government's argument that the seizure order could "be implied from the aggregate of his powers under the Constitution"—that is, the vesting clause, the take care clause, and the commander in chief provision. "In the framework of our Constitution," Black noted, "the President's power to see that the laws are faithfully executed refutes the idea that he is to be a lawmaker."[35]

In contrast, Justices Scalia and Thomas have endorsed Hamilton's broad definition of executive power under Article II. Scalia once defined "executive power" as including everything that is not expressly forbidden by the Constitution nor patently incompatible with republican principles.[36] Justice Thomas has also defended a broad interpretation of presidential powers, particularly in the international arena. In a separate opinion in *Zivotofsky v. Kerry* (2015), Thomas argued that "executive power" includes all those foreign affairs powers that are not otherwise allocated under the Constitution. For support of this view, Thomas relied on the language differences between Article I's vesting clause ("all legislative Powers herein granted") and Article II's vesting clause ("the executive Power shall be vested in a President of the United States"). Because the vesting clause of Article II does not contain the same qualifier "herein granted," Thomas argued that the president's authority in foreign affairs is not limited to the enumerated powers listed under Article II.[37]

Foreign Enemy Combatants

The three justices' varying perspectives on executive power are illustrated by their different interpretations of the habeas corpus rights of foreign enemy combatants. In *Johnson v. Eisentrager* (1950),[38] the Supreme Court (6–3) ruled that alien enemy combatants tried extraterritorially by military commissions do not have a constitutional right to habeas corpus. In that case, twenty-one German nationals were tried and punished by a US military commission in China for aiding the Japanese after Germany's unconditional surrender. They were then incarcerated at the Landsberg prison in Germany. Justice Robert Jackson found "no instance where a court, in this or any other country where the writ [of habeas corpus] is known, has issued it on behalf of an alien enemy who, at no relevant time and in no stage of his captivity, has been within its territorial jurisdiction."[39] To hold otherwise, Jackson reasoned, would jeopardize the war effort because it would require the trial participants to be transported to the United States. In addition, it "would diminish the prestige of our military commanders" by requiring them to appear before civilian courts and account for their actions, thereby diverting their "efforts and attention from the military offensive abroad to the legal defensive at home."[40]

Justice Black dissented. He disputed the idea that foreign enemy combatants captured overseas have no habeas corpus rights. "Does the prisoner's right to test [the] legality of a sentence then depend on where the Government chooses to imprison him?" Black asked.[41] In Black's view, any person, including an enemy alien, deprived of his liberty by the US government falls within its legal jurisdiction. Although he did not go so far as to say that alien combatants captured overseas possess all the constitutional rights of American citizens, he thought that, at a minimum, they had a right to habeas corpus. Revealing a skepticism about executive power, Black described the majority's analysis as dangerous because it would allow the executive branch too much discretion in choosing where to try and imprison noncitizen enemy combatants. "The Court is fashioning wholly indefensible doctrine," wrote Black, "if it permits the executive branch, by deciding where its prisoners will be tried and imprisoned, to deprive all federal courts of their power to protect against a federal executive's illegal incarcerations."[42]

Following the September 11, 2001, terrorist attacks, the George W. Bush administration imprisoned foreign enemy combatants at Guantanamo Bay, Cuba. Relying on the Authorization for the Use of Military Force (AUMF), as well as the Supreme Court's decision in *Eisentrager*, the Bush administration maintained that it could detain the captured combatants indefinitely because federal courts have no jurisdiction over alien enemy combatants captured and held outside of the territorial jurisdiction of the United States. In *Rasul v. Bush* (2004),[43] the Supreme Court ruled that the federal habeas corpus statute *does* provide federal district courts with jurisdiction to hear alien detainees' claims. Justice Scalia, joined by Thomas, dissented. "From this point forward," Scalia wrote, "federal courts will entertain petitions from these prisoners, and others like them around the world, challenging actions and events far away, and forcing the courts to oversee one aspect of the Executive's conduct of a foreign war."[44]

Then, in *Boumediene v. Bush* (2008),[45] the Supreme Court (5–4) struck down the "jurisdiction-stripping" provision of the Military Commissions Act of 2006, finding that it violated Article I, section 9 of the Constitution. Justice Kennedy held that since the United States had complete jurisdiction and control over the prison at Guantanamo Bay, the alien enemy combatants must be afforded the constitutional right of habeas corpus. Scalia filed a sharply worded dissent, joined by Thomas, in which he claimed that the court had "blatantly misdescribe[d] important precedents, most conspicuously Justice Jackson's opinion for the Court in *Johnson v. Eisentrager*." "What drives today's decision," wrote Scalia, "is neither the meaning of the Suspension Clause, nor the principles of our precedents, but rather an inflated notion of judicial supremacy." The court's decision, he predicted, will harm the country because some of the released detainees have already gone back to the battlefield. "The Nation will live to regret what the Court has done today," he concluded.[46]

Special Prosecutors

Another illustration of the three originalists' different interpretations of executive power can be found in the Supreme Court's decision in *Morrison v. Olson* (1988).[47] In that case, the court upheld Title VI of the Ethics in Government Act, which authorized the appointment of independent counsels to investigate criminal activity by high-ranking government officials. Under the law, independent counsels were appointed by a special division of judges and could be removed by the attorney general only for "good cause."[48] Applying a functionalist approach to the separation of powers, Chief Justice Rehnquist held that the act did not unduly impede the president's ability to perform his constitutional duties. "It is undeniable," Rehnquist acknowledged, "that the Act reduces the amount of control that the Attorney General and, through him, the President exercise over the investigation and prosecution of a certain class of alleged criminal activity," but the limitations were not so severe as to interfere with his constitutional responsibilities.[49] The principle of separation of powers, Rehnquist concluded, does not require that "the three Branches of Government 'operate with absolute independence.'"[50]

Justice Scalia filed a scathing dissent. Utilizing a formalistic interpretation of separation of powers, Scalia observed that Article II provides that "the executive Power shall be vested in the President of the United States," which "does not mean some of the executive power, but all of the executive power."[51] If the prosecution of crime is a purely executive power, reasoned Scalia, and if the act deprives the president of exclusive control over the exercise of that power, then it must be struck down. In his view, those two questions could only be answered in the affirmative. The investigation and prosecution of crime, he wrote, are "quintessentially" executive functions and "the virtual embodiment of the power to 'take care that the laws be faithfully executed.'" "A system of separate and coordinate powers," Scalia acknowledged, "necessarily involves an acceptance of exclusive power that can theoretically be abused."[52] However, he regarded this theoretical possibility as a necessary by-product of a carefully calibrated system of separation of powers, which protects individual liberty by not allowing any one branch of government too much power.

Justice Black would not have agreed with Scalia's analysis in *Morrison.* The majority did not dispute that the investigation and prosecution of crime are executive functions, but the important question was whether all aspects of those functions had to fall under the immediate influence of the president. The Ethics in Government Act had been enacted in response to the Nixon administration's abuses of power, including the so-called Saturday Night Massacre, when President Nixon ordered his attorney general to fire special prosecutor Archibald Cox. Based on his distrust of executive power, Justice Black would have supported legislative efforts to avoid tampering with independent investigations of the executive branch. It should also be recalled that the law allowed a special prosecutor to be removed for "good cause," and unlike other removal cases, Congress did not reserve the removal power to itself.[53]

Like the majority in *Morrison*, Justice Black would have viewed the Ethics in Government Act as a functional way of checking abuses of power without unduly intruding on the president's ability to carry out his constitutional duties. Given Justice Black's Jeffersonian instincts, he likely would have seen Scalia's dissent as pro-monarchy or Hamiltonian. Justice Thomas did not participate in *Morrison*, but in a pre–Supreme Court speech he lauded Scalia's dissent as the most important opinion written since *Brown v. Board of Education* (1954).[54]

Executive Privilege

Over the years, Alexander Hamilton's broad construction of Article II has formed the basis of various claims of implied or inherent presidential authority, including executive privilege.[55] Justice Black was opposed to all forms of secrecy in government.[56] During Black's time in Congress, the Hoover administration signed the London Naval Treaty, which was intended to reduce naval armaments among the United States, Great Britain, and Japan. The administration, however, declined a request by the Senate Foreign Relations Committee, on which Black served, to turn over certain documents and communications related to the formation of the treaty. Secretary of state Henry Stimson justified that decision on the grounds that turning over the material would not be "compatible with the public interest." Senator Black drafted a resolution requiring the administration to turn over the documents before the Senate would ratify the treaty. Black did not oppose the treaty's aims, but he contended that a vote should be postponed until "the rights of the Senate . . . have been recognized and respected by a subordinate department of the Government created by the Congress."[57] "Personally," Black said, "I have always been and am still opposed to secret diplomacy. I believe in publicity in foreign as well as domestic affairs." As a result, he argued that "the Senate is entitled to all the information there is to be had in order that it may pass intelligently on treaties which can only become effective through Senate action."[58] Senator Black saw the State Department's refusal as yet another "attempt to whittle off on the part of the Executive one more legislative function." "It is a step," he argued, "toward that which Alexander Hamilton sought in the

Constitutional Convention and which all lovers of despotic government have always sought—a one-man power."[59]

Meanwhile, Justices Scalia and Thomas have been strong defenders of executive privilege. During his time as the nation's assistant attorney general, Scalia testified before Congress on several occasions and defended a broad interpretation of executive privilege. Testifying only a few years after the scandals of the Nixon administration, Scalia recognized "that anyone saying a few kind words about executive privilege . . . is in a position somewhat akin to the man preaching the virtues of water after the Johnstown flood, or the utility of fire after the burning of Chicago." "But," he added, "fire and water are . . . essential elements of human existence. And executive privilege is indispensable to the functioning of our system of checks and balances and separation of powers." "I hope," Scalia said, "you will not seek to eliminate a vital element of our system merely because it may sometimes have been abused."[60]

Justice Thomas has also defended a robust view of executive privilege. In *Cheney v. United States District Court* (2004),[61] the George W. Bush administration challenged a broad discovery order by a federal district court involving the proceedings of the National Energy Policy Development Group (NEPDG). Bush created the NEPDG to advise and make recommendations about national energy policy, and he appointed vice president Dick Cheney as its chair. All the official members of the group were federal government employees, but two public interest groups (Sierra Club and Judicial Watch) contended that private individuals and lobbyists participated in the group's proceedings as well.[62] The district court ordered that all nonprivileged documents related to the group's work be produced, but it deferred ruling on the government's claim that such a discovery request would encroach on the president's constitutional powers. The court of appeals affirmed.

In an opinion by Justice Kennedy, the Supreme Court remanded the case back to the court of appeals to determine whether the district court's broad discovery ruling violated the principle of separation of powers. The Supreme Court distinguished *United States v. Nixon* (1974),[63] which required President Nixon to turn over tape recordings of Oval Office meetings, because that case involved a subpoena in a criminal case, where the search for truth is essential to justice. Moreover, Kennedy distinguished *Nixon* because the discovery order in this case requested "everything under the sky." In a concurring opinion that was joined by Scalia,[64] Justice Thomas contended that the federal law requiring that records related to an advisory committee be made public raised both constitutional and statutory issues.[65] The constitutional issue, in his view, related to the president's ability to receive confidential advice from his advisers, and the statutory issue related to whether the respondents would get the relief they requested if the discovery order was allowed.[66] Rather than let the court of appeals decide whether the district court had abused its discretion, Thomas concluded that the lower court should be instructed to grant the government's writ of mandamus, which essentially meant that no discovery would be permitted, the vice president would be dropped from the case, and there would be a summary judgment based on the bare-bones administrative record. It is safe to say that Justice Black would not have joined that opinion.

FEDERALISM

The three originalists had dramatically different interpretations of federalism. As Roger Newman points out, Justice Black was "a New Dealer before there was a New Deal."[67] During his time in the Senate, Black supported a thirty-hour workweek, unemployment compensation, Social Security, national health care, federal money for public education, and the regulation of lobbyists. Black defended these legislative programs based on a broad interpretation of Congress's powers under Article I. Interestingly, Black based his originalist interpretation of the commerce clause on Chief Justice Marshall's opinion in *Gibbons v. Ogden* (1824),[68] telling his colleagues that Congress's authority to regulate interstate commerce, "like all others vested in Congress, is complete in itself, may be exercised to its utmost extent, and acknowledges no limitations, other than are prescribed in the Constitution." For Senator Black, this meant "that the Federal Government, with reference to the regulation of interstate commerce, had vested in it full and complete power, the same as though there had been no State lines."[69]

Justice Scalia began his judicial career by defending a political process approach to federal-state relations. In contrast to his more ardent states' rights colleagues, Scalia expressed support for the Supreme Court's decision in *Garcia v. San Antonio Metropolitan Transit Authority* (1985),[70] which held that the states' chief protection lies in the structure of the federal system and the political process itself. "It is very hard to find a distinct justiciable line between those matters that are appropriate for the states and those that are appropriate for the Federal Government," Scalia testified during his confirmation hearings.

"Finding that line," he added, "is much easier for a legislator than for a court, and by and large the courts have not interfered."[71] As pointed out in chapter 3, Scalia's thinking shifted in this area, and he moved toward a Madisonian perspective in federal-state relations.[72]

Of the three originalists, Justice Thomas is the most principled defender of states' rights. Rather than viewing the Tenth Amendment as a constitutional redundancy, Thomas (like Thomas Jefferson) believes it "is the foundation of the Constitution" and represents an affirmative limit on federal power. In *U.S. Term Limits, Inc. v. Thornton* (1995),[73] Thomas supported his argument that the states can impose term limits on members of Congress by claiming that the people in each state are "the ultimate source of the Constitution's authority." In fact, he argued, there is no such thing as "the consent of the undifferentiated people of the Nation as a whole." Since "nothing in the Constitution deprives the people of each State of the power to prescribe eligibility requirements for the candidates who seek to represent them in Congress," Thomas concluded that they have the authority to do so.[74] Justice Black would not have agreed with Thomas's dissent in *Thornton*.[75]

Commerce Clause

Justice Thomas has supported a strict constructionist interpretation of the commerce clause. In a concurring opinion in *United States v. Lopez* (1995),[76] he claimed that the definition of "commerce" had a much narrower scope to the founding generation. It "consisted of selling, buying, and bartering, as well as transporting for these purposes," he maintained. Thomas also drew a sharp distinction between the production of goods and their movement in the streams of commerce. "Agriculture and manufacturing involve the production of goods," he argued. "Commerce encompasses traffic in such articles."[77]

By contrast, Justice Black was a sharp critic of a strict constructionist interpretation of the commerce clause. During his time in the Senate, Black derided the Supreme Court's decision in *Hammer v. Dagenhart* (1918),[78] which struck down the nation's first child labor law. In that 5–4 decision, the justices made a formalistic distinction between production and commerce. The federal law "does not regulate transportation among the States," Justice Day wrote for the court, "but aims to standardize the ages at which children may be employed in mining and manufacturing within the States." Since there was nothing inherently wrong with the goods produced at a textile mill, he reasoned, "the mere fact that they were intended for interstate commerce transportation does not make their production subject to federal control under the commerce power."[79] Senator Black referred to the court's decision in *Hammer* as "a complete departure from the proper construction which was originally given to the Constitution."[80] By contrast, Justice Thomas's strict constructionist interpretation of Congress's commerce power supports the court's decision in *Hammer*. Meanwhile, a good case can be made that Justice Scalia would not have supported *Hammer* as an original matter.[81]

In several cases, Justice Black also supported the "substantial effects" test in interpreting Congress's commerce power—a test that Justice Thomas has strongly criticized. Black joined the court's decision in *United States v. Darby Lumber Co.* (1941),[82] which overturned *Hammer* and upheld the Fair Labor Standards Act of 1938. He also joined the court's unanimous opinion in *Wickard v. Filburn* (1942),[83] which sustained a national quota on wheat production under the Agricultural Adjustment Act of 1938. In fact, John Frank, one of Black's former law clerks, said his boss "was keen for the result" in *Wickard*.[84] Justice Scalia occasionally criticized *Wickard*'s expansive interpretation of the commerce clause, but he also relied on it in one case.[85] Moreover, in a 2013 interview, Scalia claimed that the court's broad construction of the commerce clause (including *Wickard*) was "liked . . . at the time" and has "been widely accepted by the society." "So it's water over the dam," he added, and "I don't fight that one, even though I think it was wrong."[86] Meanwhile, given Justice Thomas's rejection of the substantial effects test, he would have dissented in *Darby* and *Wickard*.

The three originalists also would have taken different sides in *Perez v. United States* (1971).[87] In that case, the Supreme Court (joined by Black) upheld a federal law that criminalized loan sharking. "Extortionate credit transactions, though purely intrastate," Justice Douglas wrote for the court, "may in the judgment of Congress affect interstate commerce."[88] By contrast, Justices Scalia and Thomas described *Perez* as "a close second" to *Wickard* in providing "the most expansive assertion of commerce power in [US] history."[89]

National Health Care

The three originalists viewed congressional authority to regulate health care very differently. During his time in Congress, Black pushed for a national health insurance system. On January 7, 1935, he submitted a resolution calling for a study to be conducted on a system of national medical insurance, but because the American Medical Association (AMA) opposed the resolution, it never made it out of committee. However, Senator Black refused to give up. During his last year in Congress, Black sensed that the AMA no longer opposed the study, so he resubmitted his resolution, which provided:

> That the Committee on Education and Labor is hereby directed and instructed, either acting through the full committee or through a duly appointed subcommittee, as soon as practicable, to make a full and complete investigation in order to determine the best and most effective kind of Federal legislation to provide a national public-health policy throughout this entire United States and to report to the Senate as early as practicable the recommendations outlining the kind of legislation it is believed will most effectively accomplish this goal.[90]

Senator Black regarded health care as a basic human right, but he was uncertain whether there should be "a system of national hospitals" or "a system of state or national health and accident insurance." Nonetheless, Black insisted, "humanity and social justice demand that it must be studied."[91]

Justices Scalia and Thomas dissented in a major case challenging the Patient Protection and Affordable Care Act of 2010 (ACA). In an effort to reduce the cost of health insurance, the law required that most individuals purchase health insurance—the so-called individual mandate. Failure to do so would result in a penalty payable to the federal government when taxpayers filed their tax returns. In *National Federation of Independent Business v. Sebelius* (2012),[92] the Supreme Court upheld the individual mandate. In an opinion by Chief Justice Roberts, the court rejected the argument that the mandate could be supported by Congress's commerce power, but it held that the individual mandate was supported by Congress's taxing power.

Justices Scalia and Thomas (along with Justices Kennedy and Alito) wrote a joint dissent in *Sebelius*. The dissenters agreed with Roberts that the individual mandate lay outside the scope of Congress's commerce authority. If Congress could require people to purchase health insurance, the dissenters argued, it would "make mere breathing in and out the basis for federal prescription and to extend federal power to virtually all human activity."[93] However, they also argued that the individual mandate was not constitutionally supported by Congress's taxing power. Accordingly, they voted to overturn the ACA entirely. Justice Black would not have agreed with the joint dissent in *Sebelius.* In contrast to Roberts, however, he would have agreed with Justice Ginsburg's concurring opinion, which argued that the ACA was fully supportable by a broad construction of Congress's commerce authority.

INCORPORATION

Justice Black defended total incorporation of the Bill of Rights to the states. In his view, the history of the Fourteenth Amendment demonstrated that the first section, "taken as a whole, was thought by most of those responsible for its submission to the people, and by most of those who opposed its submission, sufficiently explicit to guarantee that thereafter no state could deprive its citizens of the privileges and protections of the Bill of Rights."[94] Justice Scalia took the polar opposite view. He argued that *no* theory of incorporation was supportable by the text of the Fourteenth Amendment—although he "acquiesced" in the selective approach under the due process clause.[95] Justice Thomas, meanwhile, has defended a selective approach to incorporation, but only under the Fourteenth Amendment's privileges or immunities clause. He has also suggested that the provision could be used to incorporate the entire Bill of Rights to the states and certain fundamental rights not mentioned in the Bill of Rights.[96] Neither Black nor Scalia would have supported the latter view.

These different perspectives can be seen in operation by examining one of the few guarantees of the Bill of Rights that has not been incorporated to the states. The Seventh Amendment provides: "In Suits at common law, where the value in controversy shall exceed twenty dollars, the right of trial by jury shall be preserved, and no fact tried by a jury, shall be otherwise re-examined in any Court of the United States, than according to the rules of the common law." Justice Black believed the Seventh Amendment "was every bit as important as any other part of the Bill of Rights."[97] When he was a trial attorney in Birmingham, Black's personal injury awards were often overturned on appeal—a fact that upset him greatly.[98] As a Supreme Court justice, he filed several dissents in cases in which his colleagues upheld reversals of jury awards in personal injury and wrongful death cases.[99] Black interpreted the Seventh Amendment to mean that "questions of the sufficiency of the evidence are for the jury—not the trial judge or the appellate court—to decide, and that where a jury has found sufficient evidence to support a verdict, that determination should not be set aside on appeal unless there is no evidence to support the verdict."[100] Although Justices Scalia and Thomas have opposed a substantive due process right protecting corporations from awards of excessive punitive damages,[101] neither has ever suggested that the Seventh Amendment should be incorporated to apply against state power.

FIRST AMENDMENT

All three originalists defended robust interpretations of political speech,[102] but there were differences in how they interpreted the free speech and free press clauses. Justice Black regarded those two clauses as the "heart" of the Constitution, and he could be quite eloquent in describing their importance to a constitutional democracy. "Freedom to speak and write about public questions," Black wrote in a 1941 case, "is as important to the life [of] our government as is the heart to the human body." "In fact," he added, "this privilege is the heart of our government," because "if that heart be weakened, the result is debilitation; if it be stilled, the result is death."[103] Justice Black approvingly quoted Thomas Jefferson on the importance of a free press. "Were it left to me to decide," Jefferson wrote in a 1787 letter, "whether we should have a government without newspapers, or newspapers without government, I should not hesitate a moment to prefer the latter."[104]

It is hard to imagine either Justice Scalia or Justice Thomas speaking of freedom of speech or of the press in such a manner. In fact, prior to his appointment to the Supreme Court, Scalia was regarded as "the worst enemy of free speech in America today."[105] In a 1982 article, Scalia criticized the amendments to the Freedom of Information of Act for lacking the necessary balance between the need for public information and other competing interests, including national security. "The defects of the Freedom of Information Act," Scalia wrote, "cannot be cured as long as we are dominated by the obsession that gave them birth—that the first line of defense against an arbitrary executive is do it yourself oversight by the public and its surrogate, the press."[106]

During his confirmation hearings, Justice Thomas was stung by the negative coverage he received from the press. "The mob I now faced carried no ropes or guns," Thomas wrote in his memoir. "Its weapons were smooth-tongued lies spoken into microphones and printed on the front pages of America's newspapers." "It no longer sought to break the bodies of its victims," he added.

"Instead it devastated their reputations and drained away their hope."[107] Scalia's and Thomas's deferential approach to executive power in the areas of foreign policy and national security strongly suggests that they would have been on the opposite side of Justice Black's dissents in the Red Scare cases handed down in the 1950s and 1960s.[108] It is also highly unlikely that they would have signed onto the court's opinion in *New York Times v. United States* (1971)[109]—the Pentagon Papers Case—where Black argued that "every moment's continuance of the injunctions against these newspapers amounts to a flagrant, indefensible, and continuing violation of the First Amendment."[110]

Holder v. Humanitarian Law Project

One case that illustrates the three justices' different perspectives was handed down by the Roberts Court. In *Holder v. Humanitarian Law Project* (2010),[111] the Supreme Court was faced with an as-applied challenge to a federal ban on providing "material support" to designated foreign terrorist groups.[112] In addition to monetary support, the law banned supplying "service," "training," "expert advice or assistance," and "personnel" to such groups. The petitioners, two US citizens and six domestic organizations, wanted to "train" members of the Kurdistan Workers' Party (PKK) of Turkey to use humanitarian and international law to resolve their disputes peacefully; "teach" members of the PKK how to petition various representative bodies, such as the United Nations, for relief; and "engage in political advocacy" on behalf of both the PKK and the Tamils of Sri Lanka. However, they feared being prosecuted because the State Department had designated the two groups foreign terrorist organizations.[113] The petitioners argued that the ban on providing "material support" to terrorist groups was impermissibly vague and violated free speech and free association rights, since the government did not have to prove that they specifically intended to further the unlawful purposes of these organizations.

In an opinion by Chief Justice Roberts, which was joined by Justices Scalia and Thomas, the court upheld the ban. Even though the government argued that the case should be governed by the *O'Brien* test (a form of intermediate scrutiny), the court used strict scrutiny because the regulation was content based.[114] Nonetheless, the justices (6–3) held that the government's interest in combating terrorism "is an urgent objective of the highest order." Roberts observed that the "material support" provided to these terrorist organizations could be used to facilitate their unlawful activities because "money is fungible" and "foreign terrorist organizations do not maintain legitimate *financial* firewalls between those funds raised for civil, nonviolent activities, and those ultimately used to support violent, terrorist operations."[115] The court did not say the judiciary had no role to play in national security and foreign policy matters, but it determined that, in this instance, "Congress and the Executive are uniquely positioned to make principled distinctions between activities that will further terrorist conduct and undermine United States policy, and those that will not." The ban on material support, Roberts reasoned, was "a preventative measure." "It criminalizes not terrorist attacks themselves, but aid that makes the attacks more likely to occur." He added that, "when seeking to prevent imminent harms in the context of international affairs and national security," the government "is not required to conclusively link all the pieces of the puzzle before we grant weight to its empirical conclusions."[116]

It is safe to say that Justice Black would not have agreed with the court's decision in *Humanitarian Law Project* (*HLP*). Black was an absolutist when it came to political speech, and the petitioners in *HLP* wanted to use their expertise to teach and train members of these organizations to resolve disputes peacefully and to petition the United Nations for relief—all of which are lawful activities and quintessential examples of political speech. In *Brandenburg v. Ohio* (1969),[117] a decision that Justice Black joined,[118] the court held that a state cannot forbid advocacy of *illegal* action unless there is incitement of imminent lawless action. As David Cole has pointed out, the federal law in *HLP* criminalized "speech advocating only nonviolent, lawful ends on the ground that such speech might unintentionally assist a third party in criminal wrongdoing."[119] Justice Breyer, who dissented in *HLP*, questioned the court's analysis of the fungible nature of material support, since the petitioners were not providing financial support but were offering their expertise (teaching, training, and advocacy) so the organizations could pursue lawful, peaceful actions. Breyer argued that the federal statute should be read to contain a *mens rea* requirement—that is, the government must show that persons charged under the ban "provided support that they knew was significantly likely to help the organization pursue its unlawful terrorist aims"—a sentiment Justice Black would have shared.[120] Finally, although the court applied strict scrutiny in *HLP*, it was exceedingly deferential to the government and did not consider any less restrictive means.[121]

Public Employees

The three originalists also had different interpretations of the free speech rights of government employees. In *United Public Workers of America v. Mitchell* (1947),[122] Black dissented from a ruling that upheld the Hatch Act, which prohibits federal employees from active involvement in political campaigns. The court deferred to Congress's judgment that political activities by government employees can "interfere with the efficiency of the public service."[123] Black argued that the legislation "muzzles" millions of Americans simply because they work for the federal government. The First Amendment, he wrote, "includes a command that the Government must, in order to promote its own interest, leave the people at liberty to speak their own thoughts about government, advocate their own favored governmental causes, and work for their own political candidates and parties." "Our political system," he added, "different from many others, rests on the foundation of a belief in rule by the people—not some, but all the people."[124]

Justice Scalia authored several opinions that would have severely limited the free speech rights of public employees. In *Rutan v. Republican Party of Illinois* (1990),[125] the Supreme Court struck down a state policy that based the hiring, promotion, and transfer of public employees on political patronage. Justice Brennan applied strict scrutiny and cited two earlier decisions that struck down the practice of firing public employees for their political views.[126] "The question in the patronage context," Brennan wrote, "is not which penalty is more acute [being fired or refused a job] but whether the government, without sufficient justification, is pressuring employees to discontinue the free exercise of their First Amendment rights."[127]

Justice Scalia filed a blistering dissent. He argued not only that hiring decisions can be based on political patronage but also that public employees can be fired for their political beliefs.[128] Scalia pointed out that political patronage has a "venerable and accepted tradition" in the United States, which has fostered a strong two-party system and reduced political fragmentation and influence by interest groups. He also objected to the court's use of strict scrutiny in such cases and argued that a balancing test was more appropriate. "Today the Court makes its constitutional civil service reform absolute," wrote Scalia, "extending to all decisions regarding government employment." In two subsequent cases, in which he was joined by Thomas, Scalia applied the same logic to independent contractors who perform services for the government.[129]

Unconstitutional Conditions

Congress has broad authority to regulate the speech it subsidizes, but the Supreme Court has held that it cannot place a condition on the receipt of a subsidy that infringes on constitutionally protected rights, even though the government has no obligation to offer the benefit in the first place. In a long line of cases, Justice Scalia broadly supported the government's authority to condition the speech it subsidizes.[130] As he put it in one speech, "when the government decides not to pay for your speech, it is not 'abridging' the freedom of speech within the meaning of the First Amendment."[131] The unconstitutional conditions doctrine postdated Justice Black's tenure on the court, but he would have strongly disagreed with Scalia's position.

One case that illustrates these different perspectives is *Agency for International Development v. Alliance for Open Society International* (2013).[132] In that case, the Roberts Court struck down a federal law that required nongovernmental organizations (NGOs) to *adopt* a particular policy position supported by the government. Under the Leadership Act,[133] NGOs were required to embrace a policy "explicitly opposing prostitution and sex trafficking" as a condition of receiving federal funds to fight the spread of HIV/AIDs. The NGOs opposed the policy requirement because it could alienate certain host governments and diminish their effectiveness in working with prostitutes. In an opinion by Chief Justice Roberts, the court (6–2) held that the requirement is an unconstitutional condition under the First Amendment because it effectively requires the NGOs "to pledge allegiance to the Government's policy of eradicating prostitution."[134] For support, Roberts cited famous language from Justice Jackson's opinion in *West Virginia Board of Education v. Barnette* (1943): "If there is any fixed star in our constitutional constellation, it is that no official, high or petty, can prescribe what shall be orthodox in politics, nationalism, religion, or other matters of opinion or force citizens to confess by word or act their faith therein."[135]

Justice Scalia filed a sharply worded dissent that was joined by Justice Thomas. "The First Amendment does not mandate a viewpoint-neutral government," Scalia argued. As he saw it, the government conveys messages in various ways all the time and is thus entitled to "enlist the assistance of those who believe in its ideas to carry them to fruition." The Constitution, he said, "does not prohibit government spending that discriminates against, and injures, points of view to which the government is opposed."[136] As long as unfunded organizations remain free to engage in free speech activities, Scalia saw no constitutional problem. Those organizations simply had to rely on their own resources. Scalia also took issue with the court's view that the organizations in this case were being coerced. If an organization objects to a condition placed on the receipt of federal funding, he reasoned, its recourse is to decline the funds. More fundamentally, Scalia argued that the policy requirement was necessitated by the Constitution itself. "Americans need not support the Constitution," he wrote. "They may be Communists or anarchists." But he pointed out that all public officials at both the national and state levels of government are "bound by Oath or Affirmation, to support [the] Constitution." "The Framers saw the wisdom of imposing affirmative ideological commitments prerequisite to assisting in the government's work. And so should we."[137]

Justice Black would have strongly disagreed with Scalia's analysis in this case. Based on this reasoning, Scalia arguably would have supported loyalty oaths for public employees and teachers back in the 1950s and 1960s. In fact, in a subsequent case, Justice Thomas (echoing Scalia's analysis) wrote that the Constitution "excludes viewpoints such as communism and anarchism" because "those engaged in government work must swear an oath to support our Constitution's republican form of government."[138] Justice Black, in contrast, staunchly opposed loyalty oaths for government employees. "I am certain," Black wrote in one case, "that loyalty to the United States can never be secured by the endless proliferation of 'loyalty' oaths." "Loyalty," he added, "must arise spontaneously from the hearts of people who love their country and respect their government."[139] "These laws," Black wrote in another case, "rest on the belief that government should supervise and limit the flow of ideas into the minds of men," the result of which would be to "mould people into a common intellectual pattern." "Quite a different governmental policy," he concluded, "rests on the belief that government should leave the mind and spirit of man absolutely free."[140]

Obscenity

The three originalists had contrasting views on the scope of the First Amendment. Black extended his absolutist interpretation of the First Amendment to cover obscenity. The question of what is "obscene," Black said in a 1968 interview, is too subjective. "I understand that pornography sounds bad. But

I never have seen anybody who'd say what it is. Nobody."[141] In judicial opinions, Black maintained that the Supreme Court was "about the most inappropriate Supreme Board of Censors that could be found." "So far as I know," he wrote in a 1959 case, "judges possess no special expertise providing exceptional competency to set standards and to supervise the private morals of the Nation."[142] For this reason, he argued that the court should abandon the project altogether. "I can imagine no more distasteful, useless, and time-consuming task for the members of this Court," Black wrote during his last term, "than perusing [books, magazines, and movies] to determine whether [they have] 'redeeming social value.'"[143]

Justices Scalia and Thomas have both supported restrictions on obscenity. In fact, in a 2012 lecture, Scalia argued that Hugo Black misinterpreted the First Amendment. The First Amendment, Scalia observed, "says that government shall not abridge 'THE freedom of speech'—that is, the freedom of speech which was the understood right of Englishmen."[144] For Scalia, this meant that the First Amendment does not cover all forms of speech, including obscenity. Ironically, Scalia would have agreed with Justice Black that the Supreme Court is the most unlikely "Board of Censors," but he interpreted that to mean that states and localities can regulate morality without restriction. "Our society prohibits," Scalia wrote in one case, "and all human societies have prohibited, certain activities not because they harm others but because they are considered, in the traditional phrase, '*contra bonos mores*,' *i.e.*, immoral," including "sadomasochism, cockfighting, bestiality, suicide, drug use, prostitution, and sodomy."[145] Justice Thomas has also supported limitations on obscenity—although, as discussed in the next chapter, he has been less restrictive than Scalia.

Libel

Justices Black, Scalia, and Thomas have interpreted the government's authority to regulate libel in disparate ways. Justice Black believed that commentary on matters of public concern (even if false) is absolutely protected by the First Amendment. He joined the Supreme Court's decision in *New York Times v. Sullivan* (1964),[146] which required public officials to demonstrate "actual malice" to win their libel suits; however, in a concurrence he expressed regret that the majority did not go far enough in protecting freedom of the press. In a subsequent case, Black lamented, "What a short and inadequate step this Court took in the *New York Times* case to guard free press and free speech against the grave dangers to the press and the public created by libel actions."[147] "Extravagant, reckless statements and even claims that may not be true," Black wrote in a 1970 case, "seem to me an inevitable and perhaps essential part of the process by which the voting public informs itself of the qualities of a man who would be President."[148]

Meanwhile, Justices Scalia and Thomas have argued that defamation is not protected at all by the First Amendment. As a court of appeals judge, Scalia took strong exception to the Supreme Court's decision in *New York Times v. Sullivan.* In *Ollman v. Evans* (1984),[149] he filed a sharp dissent in which he characterized an article written by syndicated columnists Rowland Evans and Robert Novak as "a classic and cooly crafted libel." He also ridiculed the attack-dog journalism represented by the "Media Age" and speculated whether those persons

> are right who discern a distressing tendency for our political commentary to descend from discussion of public issues to destruction of private reputations; who believe that, by putting some brake upon that tendency, defamation liability under existing standards not only does not impair but fosters the type of discussion the first amendment is most concerned to protect; and who view high libel judgments as no more than an accurate reflection of the vastly expanded damage that can be caused by media that are capable of holding individuals up to public obloquy from coast to coast and that reap financial rewards commensurate with that power.[150]

Similarly, Justice Thomas has argued that *Sullivan* is inconsistent with the original meaning of the First Amendment. In *McKee v. Cosby* (2019),[151] the Supreme Court denied certiorari in a case brought by Kathrine McKee, an alleged rape victim of actor Bill Cosby. McKee claimed that she had been defamed by a widely circulated letter written by Cosby's lawyer. In a concurring opinion, Thomas agreed with his colleagues that McKee was a "limited-purpose" public figure who had to prove actual malice to win her libel case. However, Thomas argued that *Sullivan* and its progeny are not supported by the original meaning of the First Amendment. Libel laws at the time of the founding, Thomas observed, were exclusively the province of the states, and the First Amendment did not abrogate English common law. He noted that prior to *Sullivan*, public officials and public figures were able to bring civil defamation suits without the need to show actual malice. In fact, he contended that under the common law, libelous statements against public officials were regarded as more injurious than defamation against private individuals. "Libel of a public official," wrote Thomas, "was deemed an offense 'most dangerous to the people, and deserv[ing of] punishment, because the people may be deceived and reject the best citizens to their great injury.'"[152] With *Sullivan*, Thomas argued, the court federalized libel law throughout the United States. "We did not begin meddling in this area until 1964," he maintained, "nearly 175 years after the First Amendment was ratified." "We should reconsider our jurisprudence in this area."[153]

Libertarianism

Interestingly, in certain areas of First Amendment law, Justices Scalia and Thomas can be considered more libertarian than Justice Black. Black consistently drew a sharp distinction between speech and conduct.[154] Accordingly, among the speech-plus-conduct cases in which he participated, Black did not support an individual right to burn the American flag.[155] By contrast, Justice Scalia cast the critical fifth vote in *Texas v. Johnson* (1989),[156] which struck down a state law banning the desecration of the American flag. Justice Black joined the court's decision in *Valentine v. Chrestensen* (1942),[157] which held that commercial speech is not protected under the First Amendment, while Justices Scalia and Thomas have argued that commercial speech *is* protected by the First Amendment. As the next chapter shows, Justice Scalia accepted the court's use of intermediate scrutiny (the *Central Hudson* test) in such cases,[158] while Thomas has argued for the use of strict scrutiny.[159]

Corporate Speech

Justices Scalia and Thomas have placed a premium on corporate speech. Beginning with *Austin v. Michigan Chamber of Commerce* (1990),[160] Scalia argued in dissent that bans on electioneering ads by corporations amount to viewpoint discrimination. In *McConnell v. Federal Election Commission* (2003),[161] both he and Thomas argued that the Bipartisan Campaign Reform Act's time restrictions on electioneering ads by corporations violate the First Amendment—although in a losing effort. However, in *Citizens United v. Federal Election Commission* (2010),[162] the Supreme Court reversed course and overturned

Austin and part of *McConnell*, with Justices Scalia and Thomas joining the 5–4 decision.

What Justice Black would have done in a case like *Citizens United* is a most intriguing question. During his time in the Senate, Black expressed skepticism about the growth of large corporations and what he described as the emerging "plutocracy" in the United States. In one speech, Black stated that corporations "have not been an unmixed blessing" and wondered whether the country "did not open a Pandora's box when [it] created the idea of the original corporation." "I somewhat agree," he told his Senate colleagues, "with Thomas Jefferson . . . and the ideas of others who foresaw the dangers of corporations."[163] Moreover, only four months into his first term on the Supreme Court, Black filed a solo dissent arguing that the Fourteenth Amendment cannot be read to apply to corporations. The word "person" in the due process clause, Black contended, was a reference to natural born persons.[164] Eleven years later, he joined a dissent by Justice Douglas, arguing that the Fourteenth Amendment's equal protection clause does not apply to corporations.[165]

At the same time, Justice Black seemed to move away from this point of view, particularly as it related to the First Amendment. For example, he participated in two cases in which the court reviewed a federal ban on independent "expenditures" by unions and corporations in federal elections. In the first case, the Congress of Industrial Organizations and its president were indicted for publishing and distributing an article in the *CIO News* that supported a particular candidate for Congress. The defendants were charged under the Labor Management Relations Act of 1947 (LMRA), which banned "expenditures" by labor unions in connection with any federal election. They won their motion to dismiss at the district court level, but the government appealed. In *United States v. Congress of Industrial Organizations* (1948),[166] the Supreme Court avoided the constitutional issue by simply holding that the LMRA did not apply to the publication at issue.

However, a concurring opinion written by Justice Rutledge and joined by Justice Black argued that the publication did, in fact, fall within the "sweepingly comprehensive" federal ban imposed by the LMRA. Unlike the majority, Rutledge also addressed the constitutional issue. "A statute," he wrote, "which, in the claimed interest of free and honest elections curtails the very freedoms that make possible exercise of the franchise by an informed and thinking electorate, and does this by indiscriminate blanketing of every expenditure made in connection with an election, serving as a prior restraint upon expression not in fact forbidden as well as upon what is, cannot be squared with the First Amendment."[167]

Nine years later, the Supreme Court was faced with another challenge to LMRA's ban on independent expenditures by unions. In *United States v. International Union United Automobile, Aircraft and Agricultural Implement Workers of America (UAW-CIO)* (1957),[168] the defendant was charged with using union treasury funds to pay for television commercials that supported certain candidates in the 1954 congressional elections. Justice Frankfurter, writing for the court, allowed the cases to proceed because, unlike the earlier case, the television ads had a broader audience and were an attempt to influence the election. Justice Douglas, joined by Black, wrote a vigorous dissent, arguing that the LMRA, "as construed and applied, is a broadside assault on the freedom of political expression guaranteed by the First Amendment."[169]

Justice Black's votes in these two cases provide substantial evidence that he would have joined the court's decision in *Citizens United.* The LMRA, unlike the Bipartisan Campaign Reform Act (BCRA), imposed a blanket ban on independent expenditures, but that probably would not have made a constitutional difference to Justice Black. In fact, he wrote the decision in *Mills v. Alabama* (1966),[170] where the court overturned the criminal conviction of a newspaper editor who wrote an op-ed about a ballot issue on the day of the election. Justice Black's votes in the LMRA cases involved electioneering ads by unions, but the law covered both unions and corporations, and Justice Douglas's dissent in *UAW-CIO* did not distinguish between the two. "Some may think," Douglas wrote in that case, "that one group or another should not express its views in an election because it is too powerful, because it advocates unpopular ideas, or because it has a record of lawless action. But these are not justifications for withholding First Amendment rights from any group—labor or corporate."[171]

Hard-Money Limits

Even though Justice Black likely would have supported the court's ruling in *Citizens United,* he would not have opposed hard-money limits in state and federal elections. In *Buckley v. Valeo* (1976), the Supreme Court sustained campaign contribution limits under the Federal Election Campaign Act (FECA) on the grounds that they impose "only a marginal restriction upon the contributor's ability to engage in free communication."[172] In contrast to limits on expenditures by the political candidates themselves, the court reasoned that contribution limits encroached less on free speech rights. "At most," the court held in *Buckley*, "the size of the contribution provides a very rough index of the intensity of the contributor's support for the candidate."[173] The court also accepted the government's argument that the prevention of corruption (real or perceived) is a substantial state interest, and it upheld FECA's reporting and disclosure requirements. *Buckley* was handed down five years after Hugo Black retired from the Supreme Court, but there is considerable evidence that he would have supported the court's decision on those issues. In fact, a good argument can be made that he would have supported FECA's expenditure limits.

When Black ran for the Senate, he ran as the "poor man's" candidate.[174] In his opening campaign speech he told the hometown crowd, "I am not now, and have never been a railroad, power company, or corporation lawyer. They have never shaped my ideals, fashioned my political creed, nor helped me in my aspirations for public office." Black pledged to stay within the $10,000 spending limit established by state and federal law, but he accused several of his running mates of exceeding that limit.[175] He also promised not to accept indirect support from any interest groups. "You will, therefore, neither receive multitudinous literature nor see numerous advertisements in my behalf paid for by imaginary clubs," Black remarked. "I do not believe the people want a United States Senator who is willing to buy the help of political parasites and machine politicians."[176] Additional evidence of Black's support for contribution limits can be found in the second LMRA case in which he participated. Justice Douglas appended the following footnote in his dissent: "If Congress is of the opinion that large contributions by labor unions to candidates for office and to political parties have had an undue influence upon the conduct of elections, it can prohibit such contributions. And, in expressing their views on the issues and candidates, labor unions can be required to acknowledge their authorship and support of those expressions."[177]

In stark contrast, Justices Scalia and Thomas have argued that *Buckley*'s rationale for limiting contributions in federal campaigns is deeply flawed and should be overruled. In several cases, Justice Thomas (joined by Justice Scalia) has argued that there is no constitutional distinction between expenditures and contributions.[178] "When an individual donates money to a candidate or to a partisan organization," Thomas wrote in a 1996 case, "he enhances the donee's ability to communicate a message and thereby adds to the political debate, just as when that individual communicates the message himself." "Indeed," he added, "the individual may add more to political discourse by giving rather than spending, if the donee is able to put the funds to more productive use than can the individual."[179] Thomas also rejected *Buckley*'s analysis that contributions are a less direct form of speech, or what he called the "speech by proxy" rationale. According to Thomas, even direct expenditures must go through certain intermediaries, such as an advertising agency or a television station. "The only possible difference," he noted, "is that contributions involve an extra step in the proxy chain."[180] For this reason, Thomas (joined by Scalia) would have subjected state and federal contribution limits to strict scrutiny.

Fairness Doctrine

Based on the foregoing analysis, it is likely that the three originalists would have been on opposite sides of other fair election issues. Justice Black joined the Supreme Court's decision in *Red Lion Broadcasting v. Federal Election Commission* (1969),[181] which upheld the personal-attack and political-editorial rules of the fairness doctrine. "There is nothing in the First Amendment," Justice White wrote for a unanimous court, "which prevents the Government from requiring a licensee to share his frequency with others and to conduct himself as a proxy or fiduciary with obligations to present those views and voices which are representative of his community and which would otherwise, by necessity, be barred from the airwaves."[182] Justice Scalia, meanwhile, was a sharp critic of the fairness doctrine, believing it exacted too high a cost in terms of First Amendment values.[183]

Justice Black also believed in a level playing field in elections. He joined a dissent from denial of certiorari in a case involving the "equal time" requirement of the Federal Communications Act of 1934 in a presidential election. "The statute," Justice Goldberg wrote in dissent, "reflects a deep congressional conviction and policy that in our democratic society all qualified candidates should be given equally free access to broadcasting facilities, regardless of office or financial means, if any candidate is granted free time."[184] Justices Scalia and Thomas, by contrast, voted against two laws requiring a level playing field in federal and state elections.

In *Davis v. Federal Election Commission* (2006),[185] the Supreme Court struck down the so-called Millionaire's Amendment of the BCRA, which required that if congressional candidates planned to spend more than $350,000 of their own money, an opponent without such financial means would be eligible to receive three times the normal contribution caps, as well as coordinated contributions and expenditures from the national political party without any limitation. In an opinion by Justice Alito, which was joined by Scalia and Thomas, the court held that the asymmetrical contribution limit violates the First Amendment because "it imposes an unprecedented penalty on any candidate who robustly" spends personal funds for campaign speech. The court also rejected the government's intention to "level electoral opportunities for candidates of different personal wealth" as not being a compelling state interest.[186] Similarly, Justices Scalia and Thomas joined the court's decision that struck down an Arizona citizens' initiative requiring "matching funds" for publicly funded candidates if expenditures by privately financed candidates exceeded initial state allotments. "Under that provision," Chief Justice Roberts wrote for the court, "'the vigorous exercise of the right to use personal funds to finance campaign speech' leads to 'advantages for opponents in the competitive context of electoral politics.'"[187]

Justice Black would not have joined either of those decisions. As noted earlier, he supported a campaign expenditure limit when he ran for the Senate. "The people," he said in his opening campaign speech, "should frown upon huge campaign expenditures." "If the time has come when public office goes to the highest bidder," he added, "I lift my voice in vain. I could not compete with millionaire opponents on an advertising or money-spending campaign. I would not, if I could."[188] Nor would Black have agreed with the Roberts Court's decision in *McCutcheon v. Federal Election Commission* (2014),[189] which struck down the aggregate campaign contribution limits under the BCRA. During the oral argument in that case, Justice Scalia quipped, "I don't think $3.5 million [the supposed maximum amount an individual could contribute to candidate and noncandidate committees] is a heck of a lot of money."[190] Justice Black would have been aghast at that statement.

ESTABLISHMENT CLAUSE

Justice Black championed Thomas Jefferson's "high wall" theory and defended a strict neutralist perspective. In fact, Black insisted that the wall of separation "must be kept high and impregnable."[191] By contrast, Justices Scalia and Thomas have supported an accommodationist interpretation of the establishment clause and have sharply criticized the strict neutralist perspective. In speeches, Scalia disputed the idea that government must be neutral between religion and irreligion.[192] "God has been very good to us," he said in one speech. "That we won the Revolution was extraordinary; the Battle of Midway was extraordinary." "One of the reasons God has been good to us," he explained, "is that we have done Him honor." "Unlike the other countries of the world," Scalia observed, "that do not even invoke his Name, we do Him honor—in presidential addresses, in thanksgiving proclamations, and in many other ways." "There is nothing wrong with that," Scalia concluded, "and do not let anybody tell you that there is anything wrong with that."[193]

Justice Thomas has also been a sharp critic of the strict neutralist perspective. In a 2020 case he argued that a broad interpretation of the establishment clause impinges on religious freedom because the Supreme Court has held that the government's "antiestablishment" interest is compelling. "The modern view," Thomas wrote, "which presumes that States must remain both completely separate from and virtually silent on matters of religion to comply with the Establishment Clause, is fundamentally incorrect."[194] Interestingly, Thomas criticized Justice Black's strict neutralist perspective and suggested that it was motivated by an anti-Catholic bias. "Justice Black," observed Thomas, "well known for his role in formulating the Court's modern Establishment Clause jurisprudence, once described Catholic petitioners as 'powerful sectarian religious propagandists' 'looking toward complete domination and supremacy' of their 'preferences and prejudices.'"[195]

Religious Instruction Policy

Due to their fundamentally different approaches to the establishment clause, the three originalists would have disagreed about virtually every church-state controversy in which they participated.[196] Justice Black wrote the majority opinion in *McCollum v. Board of Education* (1948),[197] which struck down an Illinois school board policy that allowed clergy and rabbis to teach religion in public schools during school hours. For the court, Black observed that the policy violated government neutrality and the "high wall" theory because the state provided "an invaluable aid" by allowing students to participate in "religious classes through use of the State's compulsory public school machinery."[198] Four years later, Black filed a sharply worded dissent in *Zorach v. Clauson*

(1952),[199] in which the court upheld a program that allowed children to go off school grounds for religious training during the school day. Black disagreed with the court's analysis because he could find no meaningful distinction with *McCollum*. In his view, the state's compulsory education law was still being used to benefit religious instruction during school hours.

By contrast, Justice Scalia was a strong supporter of released-time programs for religious instruction. In fact, as pointed out in chapter 1, he was the beneficiary of the program upheld in *Zorach*. In speeches, he often cited New York's released-time program as a useful example of government accommodation of religion. It was "a good deal," he said. "Everyone else had to stay in school. You would take your time getting there [to religious classes]. You kicked cans along the gutters and what not."[200] He also quoted Justice Douglas's language from *Zorach* nearly verbatim: "We are a religious people whose institutions presuppose a Supreme Being. . . . When the state encourages religious instruction or cooperates with religious authorities by adjusting the schedule of public events to sectarian needs, it follows the best of our traditions."[201]

Government Aid to Religion

Justice Black firmly believed that *no* tax dollars could be used to support religious practices and institutions. In *Everson*, he reviewed the historical events leading up to the adoption of the establishment clause, placing special emphasis on the political struggle in Virginia. In December 1784 Patrick Henry proposed a bill to allow the use of state funds to support "teachers of the Christian religion." In response, James Madison wrote his famous "Memorial and Remonstrance against Religious Assessments" in June 1785. For Black, Madison "eloquently argued that a true religion did not need the support of law; that no person, either believer or nonbeliever, should be taxed to support a religious institution of any kind; that the best interest of a society required that the minds of men always be wholly free; and that cruel persecutions were the inevitable result of government-established religions."[202]

In *Board of Education of Central School District No. 1 v. Allen* (1968),[203] Black applied his understanding of Madison's "Memorial and Remonstrance" to a New York law that required local public authorities to lend secular textbooks free of charge to all students in grades seven through twelve, including those attending private religious schools. In an acerbic dissent, Black called the New York law "a flat, flagrant, open violation" of the establishment clause.

He acknowledged that the law did not "yet formally adopt or establish a state religion," but he believed it took "a great stride in that direction." One of the principal concerns of the nation's founders, Black contended, was use of the government's taxing power to compel obedience to a religious doctrine. "To authorize a State to tax its residents for such church purposes," he maintained, "is to put the State squarely in the religious activities of certain religious groups that happen to be strong enough politically to write their own religious preferences and prejudices into the laws." Black concluded his dissent by arguing that taxpayer funds "cannot constitutionally be used to support religious schools, buy their school books, erect their buildings, pay their teachers, or pay any other of their maintenance expenses, even to the extent of one penny."[204]

Justices Scalia and Thomas, by contrast, have supported the use of tax dollars to accommodate religion, including school vouchers.[205] In one case, Justice Thomas challenged Black's reading of Madison's "Memorial and Remonstrance." In *Rosenberger v. Rector and Visitors of the University of Virginia* (1995),[206] the Supreme Court ruled that the use of student activity fees to help fund a publication by a Christian student organization did not violate the establishment clause. Thomas wrote a concurring opinion in which he examined the original meaning of the establishment clause. According to Thomas, Madison's "Memorial and Remonstrance" did not oppose the use of taxpayer money to support religion generally. Rather, what Madison objected to was that the proposed state tax would have benefited only the Christian religion. As long as taxpayer money is used generally and does not prefer one religion over another, Thomas concluded that a state can use its taxing power to accommodate religion.

Prayer in School

Engel v. Vitale (1962)[207]—the school prayer decision—was authored by Justice Black. New York's Board of Regents recommended that all local school districts begin each school day with the following nondenominational prayer: "Almighty God, we acknowledge our dependence upon Thee, and we beg Thy blessings upon us, our parents, our teachers and our Country." In 1958 Union Free School District No. 9, located in Nassau County, adopted the recommendation and instructed teachers how to recite the prayer each day. Even though participation was voluntary, the parents of ten students challenged the daily exercise as contrary to their religious beliefs and a violation of the establishment clause.

In a 6–1 decision, the Supreme Court struck down prayers in public schools. "The history of governmentally established religion," wrote Black for the court, "both in England and in this country, showed that whenever government had allied itself with one particular form of religion, the inevitable result had been that it had incurred the hatred, disrespect and even contempt of those who held contrary beliefs."[208] For Black, the fact that the prayers were nondenominational and voluntary made no constitutional difference. The establishment clause, he claimed, "does not depend upon any showing of direct governmental compulsion and is violated by the enactment of laws which establish an official religion whether those laws operate directly to coerce nonobserving individuals or not."[209]

Justices Scalia's and Thomas's broad accommodationist view of religion would have placed them in dissent in *Engel*. In *Lee v. Weisman* (1992),[210] Justice Scalia (joined by Thomas) dissented when the court held that nondenominational prayers recited at graduation ceremonies violated the establishment clause. For the majority, Justice Kennedy relied on his "coercion test," which prohibits states from placing students in the "dilemma of participating [in the graduation prayer], with all that implies, or protesting."[211] While acknowledging that graduation ceremonies are, in a formal sense, "voluntary," Kennedy reasoned that the school's sponsorship of the exercises pressured students to participate.

In a passionate dissent, Scalia described the majority's analysis as "psychology practiced by amateurs." "Today's opinion," he wrote, "shows more forcefully than volumes of argumentation why our Nation's protection, that fortress which is our Constitution, cannot possibly rest upon the changeable philosophical predilections of the Justices of this Court, but must have deep foundations in the historic practices of our people."[212] Scalia pointed out that prayers have been a part of public school graduations since 1868 and that "nonsectarian prayer to God at public celebrations" has taken place since the time of the founding. He also took issue with the argument that students would feel pressure to participate. Students, he maintained, were not being coerced into taking part in the invocation or the benediction and had several options at their disposal: they could stand and participate in the religious exercises, they could stand in respectful silence while others participated in the exercises, or they could express their dissent by remaining seated. Even if it were true that someone might feel coerced into participating in the graduation prayer, Scalia maintained that showing respect for the religion of others is part of the civic responsibility of every individual:

> I may add, moreover, that maintaining respect for the religious observances of others is a fundamental civic virtue that government (including the public schools) can and should cultivate—so that even if it were the case that the displaying of such respect might be mistaken for taking part in prayer, I would deny that the dissenter's interest in avoiding *even the false appearance of participation* constitutionally trumps the government's interest in fostering respect for religion generally.[213]

Even though Justice Scalia distinguished graduation prayers from school prayers,[214] it is easy to see why he and Justice Thomas, as an original matter, would have dissented in *Engel*. Both justices have claimed that the only coercion prohibited by the establishment clause is "actual legal coercion."[215] Since New York's Board of Regents allowed students to remain silent or to be excused during the daily nondenominational prayer, Scalia and Thomas would have concluded that the students were not being coerced into participating. Justice Black, however, did not accept the school district's argument that the students were not being coerced. "When the power, prestige and financial support of government is placed behind a particular religious belief," wrote Black, "the indirect coercive pressure upon religious minorities to conform to the prevailing officially approved religion is plain."[216]

RELIGIOUS FREEDOM

In interpreting the free exercise clause, there were significant differences among the three justices. Justice Black regarded religion as a fundamental right and believed that government could not coerce individuals into believing in religion. "We repeat and again reaffirm," Black wrote for the court in *Torcaso v. Watkins* (1961), "that neither a State nor the Federal Government can constitutionally force a person 'to profess a belief or disbelief in any religion.'"[217] Black also joined the majority opinion in *Sherbert v. Verner* (1963),[218] where the court, using strict scrutiny, allowed a religious exemption to a state's unemployment compensation law.

Justice Scalia, by contrast, wrote the Supreme Court's decision in *Employment Division, Department of Human Resources of Oregon v. Smith* (1990),[219] which held that strict scrutiny does not apply to neutral, generally applicable laws that only incidentally impact religion. In that case, the court rejected two Native Americans' request for a religious exemption from a state criminal law banning the use of peyote. The free exercise clause, wrote Scalia for the court, "does not relieve an individual of the obligation to comply with a 'valid and neutral law of general applicability.'" Citing *Reynolds v. United States* (1879),[220] in which the court upheld a federal law criminalizing polygamy, Scalia argued that allowing exemptions from state criminal laws would "make the professed doctrines of religious belief superior to the law of the land, and in effect to permit every citizen to become a law unto himself."[221]

Justice Black would not have agreed with Scalia's analysis in *Smith* for several reasons—although he might have agreed with the result.[222] For one, Scalia expressed skepticism about expanding *Sherbert*'s strict scrutiny analysis. "Even if we were inclined to breathe into *Sherbert* some life beyond the unemployment compensation field," wrote Scalia, "we would not apply it to require exemptions from a generally applicable criminal law."[223] Justice Black, by contrast, interpreted the free exercise clause expansively. "The broad meaning given the [First] Amendment by these earlier cases," Black wrote in *Everson*, "has been accepted by the Court in its decision concerning an individual's religious freedom."[224] Black also would have disagreed with Scalia's analysis that strict scrutiny should not apply to neutral, generally applicable laws that only incidentally burden religion. As Justice O'Connor pointed out in her concurring opinion in *Smith*, "There is nothing talismanic about neutral laws of general applicability or general criminal prohibitions, for laws neutral toward religion can coerce a person to violate his religious conscience or intrude upon his religious duties just as effectively as laws aimed at religion."[225]

In addition, Justice Black would have strongly disagreed with Scalia's treatment of religious minorities in *Smith*. Scalia claimed that any society that allowed religious exemptions from generally applicable criminal laws "would be courting anarchy" and that this "danger increases in direct proportion to the society's diversity of religious beliefs, and its determination to coerce or suppress none of them."[226] Scalia acknowledged that the political process "will place at a relative disadvantage those religious practices that are not widely engaged in," but he concluded that this was an "unavoidable consequence of democratic government" and "must be preferred to a system in which each conscience is a law unto itself or in which judges weigh the social importance of all laws against the centrality of all religious beliefs."[227]

By contrast, Justice Black's opinions expressed deep concern for religious minorities, dissenters, and nonbelievers. In *Everson*, Black recalled the unfortunate history of religious persecution in colonial America, which the religious clauses had been designed to eliminate. In speaking about religious freedom in particular, Black stated that the government "cannot exclude individual Catholics, Lutherans, Mohammedans, Baptists, Jews, Methodists, Non-believers, Presbyterians, or the members of any other faith, *because of their faith, or lack of it*, from receiving the benefits of public welfare legislation."[228] "Certainly our democratic form of government," Black wrote in another case, "functioning under the historic Bill of Rights, has a high responsibility to accommodate itself to the religious views of minorities, however unpopular and unorthodox those views may be."[229]

Finally, Justice Black would have been deeply troubled by Justice Scalia's backhanded criticism of *Barnette*. In *Smith*, Scalia favorably quoted language from Justice Frankfurter's opinion in *Minersville School District v. Gobitis* (1940) to support the premise that religious convictions do not relieve individuals from the obligation to follow general laws of applicability.[230] He then countered famous language from Justice Jackson's opinion in *Barnette*, which overturned *Gobitis*. "The very purpose of a Bill of Rights," Jackson wrote in *Barnette*, "was to withdraw certain subjects from the vicissitudes of political controversy, to place them beyond the reach of majorities and officials and to establish them as legal principles to be applied by the courts."[231] In an unmistakable rejoinder, Scalia noted that the "values that are protected against government interference through enshrinement in the Bill of Rights are not thereby banished from the political process."[232] As examined in the next chapter, Justice Thomas has also disagreed with Scalia's decision in *Smith*.

SECOND AMENDMENT

Justice Black's interpretation of the Second Amendment differed fundamentally from that of Justices Scalia and Thomas. Black joined the unanimous decision in *United States v. Miller* (1939),[233] which upheld a firearms conviction under the National Firearms Act of 1934. Jack Miller and Frank Layton were charged with not registering a double-barrel twelve-gauge shotgun less than eighteen inches long and then transporting it by means of interstate commerce. Justice James McReynolds, writing for the court, observed that the original purpose of the Second Amendment was to allow citizens to form militias to counteract a large standing army, an entity that was "strongly disfavored" at the time. He then gave the following explanation of why the firearm in question was subject to prosecution under federal law: "In the absence of any evidence tending to show that possession or use of a 'shotgun having a barrel of less than eighteen inches in length' at this time has some reasonable relationship to the preservation or efficiency of a well regulated militia, we cannot say that the Second Amendment guarantees the right to keep and bear such an instrument." "Certainly," McReynolds continued, "it is not within judicial notice that this weapon is any part of the ordinary military equipment or that its use could contribute to the common defense."[234]

Justice Black signed on to that opinion, and twenty-one years later he reaffirmed the *Miller* interpretation of the Second Amendment. In a lecture at New York University School of Law, Black described how each of the guarantees of the Bill of Rights provides *absolute* protection against governmental regulation. When he got to the Second Amendment, he cited its exact language and remarked: "Although the Supreme Court had held this Amendment to include only arms necessary to a well-regulated militia, as so construed, its prohibition is absolute."[235] Justice Black also joined a unanimous court in *Burton v. Sills* (1969),[236] which held that a challenge to a state gun-control law did not present a substantial federal question. In that case, the New Jersey Supreme Court unequivocally (and unanimously) rejected the plaintiffs' claim that the Second Amendment protects an individual's right to bear arms. In short, Black did not believe the Second Amendment confers a personal right to possess and carry arms, other than as part of a state militia.

Justices Scalia and Thomas have advanced a very different interpretation of the Second Amendment. In fact, they led a constitutional revolution that resulted in a reinterpretation of the Second Amendment as protecting an individual's right to own and bear arms for self-defense. Justice Thomas spearheaded the legal movement by suggesting in a concurring opinion in *Printz v. United States* (1997)[237] that the Second Amendment might confer a personal right to bear arms. In that case, the Supreme Court struck down a provision of the Brady bill that required local officials to conduct background checks before individuals could purchase guns. In an opinion by Justice Scalia, the court ruled that such a mandate violated principles of federalism and the

Tenth Amendment. Justice Thomas wrote separately and observed that the court had not had "recent occasion" to examine the substantive right guaranteed by the Second Amendment. "If, however, the Second Amendment is read to confer a *personal* right to 'keep and bear arms,'" he noted, "a colorable argument exists that the Federal Government's regulatory scheme, at least as it pertains to the purely intrastate sale or possession of firearms, runs afoul of that Amendment's protections."[238]

Justice Thomas's dictum did have its intended consequence. In a 2001 case the Fifth Circuit became the first federal appellate court in US history to hold that the Second Amendment protects an individual's right to keep and bear arms. In reaching its conclusion, the majority cited Justice Thomas's concurring opinion in *Printz.*[239] Then, six years later, the DC Court of Appeals held that the Second Amendment confers a personal right to keep and bear arms apart from participation in a state militia.[240] The Ninth Circuit, meanwhile, had ruled the opposite: that the Second Amendment does not confer a personal right to bear arms.[241] To resolve the conflict, the Supreme Court agreed to hear the government's appeal in *District of Columbia v. Heller* (2008).[242]

Justice Scalia authored the court's opinion in *Heller*, which was joined by Thomas. As pointed out in chapter 3, Scalia decoupled the two clauses of the Second Amendment and placed primacy on the operative clause.[243] For Scalia, the phrase "the right of the people" was an unambiguous reference "to individual rights, not 'collective' rights."[244] Even though Scalia acknowledged that the primary purpose of the prefatory clause was to assuage Anti-Federalist concerns about the federal government disarming state militias, he insisted that a prefatory clause "does not limit or expand the scope of the operative clause."[245] Scalia also dismissed *Miller* for not providing a thorough analysis of the history of the Second Amendment, and "the mighty rock upon which the dissent rests its case."[246] In response to Justice Stevens's claim in dissent that "hundreds of judges" have interpreted *Miller* as not protecting a right to possess guns for purely private, civilian purposes, Scalia retorted: "they overread *Miller*." He also stated that "their erroneous reliance upon an uncontested and virtually unreasoned case cannot nullify the reliance of millions of Americans (as our historical analysis has shown) upon the true meaning of the right to keep and bear arms."[247]

FOURTH AMENDMENT

All three originalists defended similar interpretations of the Fourth Amendment, but there were some differences. Justice Black had a very broad interpretation of the search-incident-to-arrest exception. In *Chimel v. California* (1969), he dissented when the court disallowed a forty-five-minute search of an entire three-bedroom house, "including the attic, garage, and a small workshop," based on the search-incident-to-arrest exception.[248] As pointed out in chapter 2, *Chimel* was no aberration. In earlier cases, Black voted to allow full-blown searches of apartments and business establishments as searches incident to arrest.[249]

Justices Scalia and Thomas have drawn a sharp line when it comes to searches of people's homes. "A man's home is his castle," these two justices have argued.[250] In *Florida v. Jardines* (2013), Scalia (joined by Thomas) noted that the "very core" of the Fourth Amendment is "the right of a man to retreat into his home and there be free from unreasonable governmental intrusion."[251] In a 2021 case Justice Thomas wrote the court's decision limiting the "community caretaking" exception to cars on public highways. "What is reasonable for vehicles is different from what is reasonable for homes," Thomas wrote.[252] On this basis, it is hard to imagine Justices Scalia and Thomas approving a full-blown search of a home without a search warrant.[253]

The three originalists also came to different conclusions in cases applying the search-incident-to-arrest exception to automobiles. In *Coolidge v. New Hampshire* (1971),[254] the Supreme Court rejected several different exceptions to the Fourth Amendment, including the search-incident-to-arrest exception, when the police seized a car after the suspect had been arrested and removed from the home. Applying the pre-*Chimel* rule that police can search an area in the possession or under the control of the person arrested, Justice Stewart held for the court that even a contemporaneous search of the car would have been unlawful because Coolidge had been arrested in his home.[255] He also declined to expand the exception to cover a search of the vehicle two days later at the police station.[256] Justice Black dissented. In his view, there was probable cause to believe that the car had been used in the commission of a murder and that it contained evidence of the crime. "The test of reasonableness," Black wrote, "cannot be governed by such arbitrary rules." "On the facts of this case," he added, "it is my opinion that the seizure of petitioner's automobile was incident to his arrest and was reasonable under the terms of the Fourth Amendment."[257]

Meanwhile, in *Arizona v. Gant* (2009),[258] Justices Scalia and Thomas joined a decision holding that the police cannot conduct a *contemporaneous* search of a vehicle when a suspect has been arrested and placed securely in the back of a police car if there is no additional evidentiary basis for the search. In that case, Rodney Gant was arrested for driving with a suspended license, handcuffed, and locked in a patrol car before police officers searched his car and found cocaine in a jacket pocket in the backseat. In an opinion by Justice Stevens, the court held that police cannot search a vehicle after the arrestee has been secured and cannot access the interior of the vehicle unless it is reasonable to believe that evidence related to the offense leading to the arrest might be found in the vehicle. Moreover, Scalia wrote separately (not joined by Thomas) to argue that the court should overturn *New York v. Belton* (1981),[259] which he interpreted to mean "that arresting officers may always search an arrestee's vehicle in order to protect themselves from hidden weapons."[260] In dissent, Justice Alito defended *Belton* and argued that police should be able to conduct a warrantless search of the passenger compartment of an automobile incident to the lawful arrest of an occupant, regardless of whether the arrestee is handcuffed.[261] Justice Black likely would have supported Alito's opinion in *Gant.*

The three originalists also held different positions regarding modern technology and Fourth Amendment rights. Justice Scalia (joined by Thomas) authored the Supreme Court's decision in *Kyllo v. United States* (2001),[262] which held that use of a thermal imaging device to detect heat emanating from the roof of a house constituted a search. Justice Black, by contrast, joined the court's decision in *Goldman v. United States* (1942),[263] which held that use of a detectaphone by government agents to listen to conversations taking place in an adjoining office did not violate the Fourth Amendment. Two decades later, Black did join the court's decision in *Silverman v. United States* (1961),[264] which held that the use of "spike mike" violated the common-law trespass doctrine under the Fourth Amendment. However, that case is distinguishable from *Kyllo* because there was an actual physical intrusion into a person's home.

Warrantless Blood Tests

Another interesting area of disagreement involves the constitutionality of performing warrantless blood tests on suspected drunk drivers. Justice Black dissented in *Schmerber v. California* (1966),[265] which upheld a warrantless blood test based on the totality of the circumstances, even though the suspect refused to give his consent. Reflecting both his deferential approach to the Fourth Amendment and his expansive interpretation of the Fifth Amendment, Black argued that Schmerber's Fifth Amendment rights had been violated. Black could not understand how a nonconsensual blood test could be any less of a Fifth Amendment violation than the act of compelling an individual to produce personal papers in court.[266] In his view, evidence obtained from blood tests is ultimately communicative in nature because the results will be introduced at trial.

Justice Scalia also believed that warrantless, nonconsensual blood draws are unconstitutional. However, he based his opinion on the Fourth Amendment. In *Missouri v. McNeely* (2013),[267] the Supreme Court held that the natural metabolization of alcohol in the bloodstream does not constitute a per se exigent circumstance. In an opinion by Justice Sotomayor that was joined by Scalia, the court distinguished *Schmerber* on the grounds that there were additional "special facts" in *Schmerber* that justified the blood draw.[268] In McNeely's case, there were no other factors that necessitated a warrantless search. Justice Thomas filed a solo dissent in *McNeely*. He took the position that the body's natural metabolization of alcohol is an exigent circumstance justifying warrantless blood draws in all cases. "Each passing minute eliminates probative evidence of the crime," Thomas wrote. "A rule," he contended, "that requires officers (and ultimately courts) to balance transportation delays, hospital availability, and access to magistrates is not a workable rule for cases where natural processes inevitably destroy evidence with every passing minute."[269]

Administrative Searches

When it came to administrative searches, Justice Black was a constitutional purist. In a 1959 case, he dissented when the Supreme Court held that warrants were not required in civil cases because government inspections of a person's home touch only "the periphery" of Fourth Amendment interests.[270] That decision was subsequently overturned by two consolidated cases decided in 1967, one involving the inspection of an apartment and the other involving the inspection of a locked commercial warehouse. In an opinion by Justice White, which Black joined, the court rejected the distinction between criminal and civil cases, since even the latter types of inspections involve significant intrusions on privacy and can result in criminal punishment for noncompliance.[271]

Meanwhile, Justice Scalia wrote a vigorous dissent, joined by Thomas, in a case involving a warrantless search of a hotel registry. In *City of Los Angeles v. Patel* (2015),[272] hotel operators objected to a city ordinance that required them to make their registries available to the police on demand without a precompliance review by a neutral magistrate. The Supreme Court struck down the ordinance, relying on the two decisions handed down in 1967. Justice Sotomayor held that "a hotel owner who refuses to give an officer access to his or her registry can be arrested on the spot." And, she added, "the Court has held that business owners cannot reasonably be put to this kind of choice."[273] In dissent, Scalia argued that, because hotels are known to be places where crime and sex trafficking take place, no warrant is required. "The Court reaches its wrongheaded conclusion," he wrote, "not simply by misapplying our precedent, but by mistaking our precedent for the Fourth Amendment itself." "Rather than bother with the text of that Amendment," he continued, "the Court relies exclusively on our administrative-search cases." "But the Constitution predates 1967," he concluded, "and it remains the supreme law of the land today."[274]

FIFTH AMENDMENT

Another glaring difference among the three originalists involves their interpretation of several aspects of the Fifth Amendment.

Self-Incrimination Clause

During his time as a prosecuting attorney in Birmingham, Black adopted a policy of never trying a case based on a confession alone.[275] His investigation of police practices in Bessemer uncovered numerous instances of police beatings and torture to obtain confessions. As a Supreme Court justice, Black had one of the broadest (if not *the* broadest) interpretations of the self-incrimination clause in Supreme Court history. As pointed out in chapter 2, he wrote several important opinions foreshadowing the court's decision in *Miranda v. Arizona* (1966),[276] which ruled that in-custody interrogations are inherently coercive. He also wrote the court's opinion three years later in *Orozco v. Texas* (1969),[277] which expanded *Miranda* warnings to in-home interrogations.

In stark contrast, three decades after *Miranda*, Justices Scalia and Thomas called for it to be overturned. Scalia wrote a scathing dissent in *Dickerson v.*

United States (2000),[278] joined by Thomas, which argued that the Fifth Amendment does not prohibit voluntary confessions. "There is a world of difference," Scalia maintained, "between compelling a suspect to incriminate himself and preventing him from foolishly doing so of his own accord."[279] Scalia described *Miranda* as a "preposterous" decision, but he thought the court's current decision was even worse. "Today's judgment converts *Miranda* from a milestone of judicial overreaching into the very Cheops' Pyramid (or perhaps the Sphinx would be a better analogue) of judicial arrogance," he wrote. "In imposing its Court-made code upon the States," Scalia said, "the original opinion at least *asserted* that it was demanded by the Constitution." "Today's decision," he maintained, "does not pretend that it is—and yet *still* asserts the right to impose it against the will of the people's representatives in Congress."[280]

Failure to Testify

In addition to their differences over *Miranda*, the three originalists disagreed about whether prosecutors or judges can comment on a defendant's failure to take the stand. Justice Black joined the Supreme Court's decision in *Griffin v. California* (1965),[281] which held that the Fifth Amendment prohibits commentary on a defendant's failure to testify. "Comment on the refusal to testify is a remnant of the 'inquisitorial system of criminal justice,'" Justice Douglas wrote for the court. "It is a penalty imposed by courts for exercising a constitutional privilege," because "it cuts down the privilege by making its assertion costly."[282]

In contrast, Justice Thomas (joined by Scalia) argued that prosecutors and judges are *not* prevented from commenting on a defendant's failure to testify. "*Griffin*," Thomas wrote in a 2013 case, "is impossible to square with the text of the Fifth Amendment, which provides that '[n]o person . . . shall be compelled in any criminal case to be a witness against himself.'" "A defendant is not 'compelled . . . to be a witness against himself,'" he added, "simply because a jury has been told that it may draw an inference from his silence."[283] In addition, Justices Scalia and Thomas supported a number of exceptions to *Miranda* that Black would not have supported.[284]

Dual Sovereignty Doctrine

Justices Black and Thomas (and probably Scalia) also came to different conclusions about the dual sovereignty doctrine. According to this doctrine, which dates back to the mid-1800s, a defendant can be charged in both state and federal courts for the same offense because the two jurisdictions are regarded as separate sovereigns. In *Abbate v. United States* (1959),[285] Justice Brennan wrote the court's opinion supporting the dual sovereignty doctrine, and he cited Chief Justice Taft's opinion from a 1922 case. "We have [in the United States] two sovereignties," Taft wrote, "deriving power from different sources, capable of dealing with the same subject-matter within the same territory." "Each government," he added, "in determining what shall be an offense against its peace and dignity is exercising its own sovereignty, not that of the other."[286]

Justice Black strongly disagreed with that interpretation of the Fifth Amendment. In two dissenting opinions authored in 1959, he argued that the dual sovereignty doctrine violates the double jeopardy provision. "The legal logic used to prove one thing to be two is too subtle for me to grasp," Black wrote in *Abbate.* "I believe the Bill of Rights' safeguard against double jeopardy was intended to establish a broad national policy against federal courts trying or punishing a man a second time after acquittal or conviction in any court," he concluded.[287]

Justice Thomas, after initially hinting that he might reject the dual sovereignty doctrine,[288] made his peace with it in *Gamble v. United States* (2019).[289] Terance Gamble was pulled over in Alabama because of a damaged headlight, and during the stop it was discovered that he had a loaded handgun. Gamble's possession of the gun violated state law because he was a felon, having been previously convicted of armed robbery. Gamble pleaded guilty in state court but was then charged under federal law for the same offense. He claimed that the two prosecutions violated the double jeopardy clause and requested that the court abandon the dual sovereignty doctrine.

In an opinion by Justice Alito, the Supreme Court (7–2) refused to do so. The dual sovereignty doctrine, Alito reasoned, follows from the text of the double jeopardy clause itself, which prohibits being "twice put in jeopardy" for "the same offence." The court, he added, has "long held that a crime under one sovereign's laws is not 'the same offence' as a crime under the laws of another sovereign."[290] Justice Thomas wrote a short concurring opinion in which he stated that "the historical record does not bear out my initial skepticism of the dual-sovereignty doctrine."[291] Justice Scalia did not participate in *Gamble,* but it is unlikely he would have voted to overturn the doctrine based on its extensive use historically. Interestingly, one of the court's newest originalists, Neil Gorsuch, dissented in *Gamble,* arguing that the separate sovereigns doctrine "finds no support in the text of the Constitution, its original public meaning, structure, or history."[292]

SIXTH AMENDMENT

One of Justice Black's most significant legacies was his expansive interpretation of the Sixth Amendment's right "to have the assistance of counsel." He wrote the opinion in *Johnson v. Zerbst* (1938),[293] which ruled that indigent defendants charged with a felony have the right to government-supported counsel in federal cases. He also wrote the Supreme Court's decision in *Gideon v. Wainwright* (1963),[294] which expanded *Zerbst* and required the same right to counsel in all state cases. Justice Black's opinions in this area reflected his Jeffersonian instincts and desire for equal justice under the law. "The Sixth Amendment," he observed in *Zerbst*, "stands as a constant admonition that if the constitutional safeguards it provides be lost, justice will not 'still be done.'" "It embodies a realistic recognition of the obvious truth," he added, "that the average defendant does not have the professional legal skills to protect himself when brought before a tribunal with power to take his life or liberty, wherein the prosecution is presented by experienced and learned counsel."[295]

In stark contrast, Justices Scalia and Thomas have argued that the Sixth Amendment does not require the government to provide counsel to the poor. "The Sixth Amendment," Scalia wrote in one case, "as originally understood and ratified meant only that a defendant had a right to employ counsel, or to use volunteered services of counsel."[296] Scalia acknowledged that the court has expanded that right—providing publicly funded counsel for the poor and requiring that the assistance of counsel be "effective"—but he narrowly interpreted those rights during his tenure.[297] Meanwhile, Justice Thomas argued in a 2019 case that *Zerbst* and *Gideon* had been wrongly decided. According to Thomas, those two decisions were inconsistent with the original meaning of the Sixth Amendment and should not be expanded any further. "The right to counsel," Thomas wrote, "is not an assurance of an error-free trial or even a reliable result." "It ensures fairness in a single respect," he maintained. It allows "the accused to employ the services of an attorney."[298] In a footnote, Thomas observed that the 2018 federal budget for defense counsel had ballooned to more than $1 billion. "Nothing in the text or original meaning of the Sixth Amendment," he contended, "requires that this financial burden be placed on the state and federal governments."[299] Although Thomas did not call for *Zerbst* and *Gideon* to be overturned, he contended that "the Court should hesitate before further extending our precedents and imposing additional costs on the taxpayers and the Judiciary."[300]

Other Equal Justice Claims

Justices Scalia and Thomas took issue with two other "equal justice" cases supported by Justice Black. In *Griffin v. Illinois* (1956),[301] Black wrote the decision requiring the state to pay the cost of transcripts for those who cannot afford them during appeals. Even though the US Constitution does not guarantee a right of appeal, Black reasoned that once a state affords such a right, it may not discriminate against a person on account of income. "Such a denial," he wrote, "is a misfit in a country dedicated to affording equal justice to all and special privilege to none in the administration of its criminal law."[302] Then, in *Douglas v. California* (1963),[303] decided the same day as *Gideon*, Black joined the decision authored by Justice Douglas, holding that the Sixth Amendment's right to counsel must be provided to defendants in appeals as a matter of right.

By contrast, Justice Thomas, joined by Scalia, has sharply criticized both *Griffin* and *Douglas*. In *M.L.B. v. S.L.J.* (1996),[304] the Supreme Court ruled that the state must pay the costs of transcripts ($2,352.36) in an appellate case involving a mother whose parental rights had been terminated. In dissent, Thomas argued that there is no such right under the Fourteenth Amendment. He also used the occasion to criticize *Griffin* and *Douglas*. "If this case squarely presented the question," Thomas wrote, "I would be inclined to vote to overrule *Griffin* and its progeny."[305]

Right to a Speedy Trial

The Sixth Amendment guarantees "a speedy . . . trial" in criminal cases, but the meaning of "speedy" has been the subject of controversy. The Supreme Court has said that it is "necessarily relative" and "depends upon the circumstances."[306] Justice Black joined the court's 1967 decision that incorporated the right to a speedy trial to the states.[307] He also joined two cases in which the court defined the major concerns underlying that right. In *United States v. Ewell* (1966),[308] the court ruled that the guarantee has three objectives: (1) to prevent undue and oppressive pretrial incarceration, (2) to minimize anxiety and concern accompanying public accusation, and (3) to limit the possibility that long delays will impair the accused's ability to defend himself.[309] In fact, in *Barker v. Wingo* (1972),[310] decided one year after Black retired from the court, the justices said the third factor was the most important.

In *Doggett v. United States* (1992),[311] the Rehnquist Court was confronted with an unusual case. Marc Doggett was indicted for dealing and trafficking cocaine, but he fled to Colombia and returned to the United States two years later. The federal government did not pursue Doggett until six years after his return, which meant that he was not arrested until eight years after his indictment. During this time, Doggett reportedly redeemed himself. He got married, earned a college degree, and found a steady job as a computer operations manager. The Supreme Court, in an opinion by Justice Souter, ruled that Doggett's Sixth Amendment right to a speedy trial had been violated. Souter refuted the government's argument that the defendant had to show actual prejudice when bringing a speedy trial claim. "We generally have to recognize," Souter wrote, "that excessive delay presumptively compromises the reliability of a trial in ways that neither party can prove or, for that matter, identify."[312]

Justice Thomas (joined by Scalia) dissented. He argued that although the court has traditionally considered all three of the *Ewell* factors, the third factor—impairment of the accused's ability to defend himself—is not an essential element of the Sixth Amendment right. For Thomas, the basic purpose of the speedy trial clause is to protect against prolonged incarceration. Since Doggett was not arrested and may have been "blissfully unaware of the indictment all the while," Thomas argued that the Sixth Amendment was not violated. "Even though a defendant may be prejudiced by a pretrial delay, and even though the government may be unable to provide a valid justification for that delay," Thomas reasoned, "the Clause does not come into play unless the delay impairs the defendant's liberty."[313] It is safe to say that Justice Black would not have agreed with Thomas's dissent in *Doggett.*

EIGHTH AMENDMENT

None of the three originalists believed that the Constitution barred the imposition of the death penalty. As Birmingham's county prosecutor, Justice Black sought the death penalty in many cases, not just those involving murder. Justices Scalia and Thomas have also been strong supporters of the death penalty.

In a 2015 case Justice Thomas, joined by Scalia, remarked that he had not seen a capital case that did not merit the death penalty.[314] However, Black was much more scrupulous than Scalia and Thomas in ensuring that procedural protections were afforded in death penalty cases. In one capital case, Black observed: "where the denial of the constitutional right to assistance of counsel is asserted, its peculiar sacredness demands that we scrupulously review the record."[315] In another death penalty case, he wrote the court's decision holding that a confession to a state-employed psychiatrist was coercive. "For an hour and a half or more," Black wrote, "the techniques of a highly trained psychiatrist were used to break petitioner's will in order to get him to say he had murdered his parents."[316] Black extensively reviewed the record himself and requested that the tape recording of the confession be sent to the court. Black's insistence that the government respect basic procedural rights was also evident in other capital punishment cases.[317]

By contrast, Justices Scalia and Thomas have not been receptive to claims of procedural error in death penalty cases. In one capital case, Scalia filed a vigorous dissent (joined by Thomas) when the court held that "abandonment" of the defendant by two pro bono attorneys violated the Sixth Amendment. "Our precedents," Scalia wrote, "allow a State to stand on its rights and enforce a habeas petitioner's procedural default even when counsel is to blame." "Because a faithful application of those precedents," he added, "leads to the conclusion that [the defendant] has not demonstrated cause to excuse his procedural default; and because the reasoning by which the Court justifies the opposite conclusion invites future evisceration of the principle that defendants are responsible for the mistakes of their attorneys; I respectfully dissent."[318]

In a 2009 case, Scalia (again joined by Thomas) rejected an "actual innocence" claim in a death penalty case.[319] The petitioner's claim "is a sure loser," Scalia wrote. "This Court has *never* held that the Constitution forbids the execution of a convicted defendant who has had a full and fair trial but is later able to convince a habeas court that he is 'actually' innocent."[320] By contrast, Justice Black dissented in a 1953 decision when the court vacated stays of execution for Julius and Ethel Rosenberg. "I cannot believe," wrote Black, "that if the sentence of a citizen to death is plainly illegal, this Court would allow that citizen to be executed on the grounds that his lawyers had 'waived' plain error."[321] He also criticized his colleagues for acting with unseemly haste. When substantial legal questions are raised, Black contended, and "the life or death of citizens is involved," the court should not overturn a stay of execution.

"Judicial haste is peculiarly out of place where the death penalty has been imposed," wrote Black.[322]

Prison Conditions

In several opinions, Justice Thomas (joined by Scalia) argued that the Eighth Amendment does not apply to prison conditions, including beatings, sexual assault, and mistreatment. In his view, "punishments" under the Eighth Amendment "has always meant a 'fine, penalty, or confinement inflicted upon a person by the authority of the law and the judgment and sentence of a court, for some crime or offense committed by him.'"[323] Justice Black was not on the Supreme Court when the Eighth Amendment was applied to prison settings, but there is every reason to believe that he would have disagreed with Thomas's narrow interpretation of that amendment. Except for the Fourth Amendment, Black defended liberal constructions of the rights of the accused, and he joined the court's decision in *Trop v. Dulles* (1958),[324] which ruled that the cruel and unusual punishments clause extends to the deprivation of citizenship rights. In cases, Black favorably quoted Justice Bradley's opinion in *Boyd v. United States* (1886) that "a close and literal construction [of constitutional provisions for the security of person and property] deprives them of their efficacy, and leads to gradual depreciation of the right, as if it consisted more in sound than in substance." "It is the duty of courts," Bradley warned, "to be watchful for the constitutional rights of the citizen, and against any stealthy encroachments thereon."[325] In addition, Black often sided with the "weak" and "helpless" against what he called "tyrannical governments" that resort to "dictatorial criminal procedure and punishment."[326] After his investigation of prison conditions in Bessemer, Black sharply criticized the torturous practices of law enforcement and their "cruel and inhumane treatment to defenseless, weak, and unprotected prisoners."[327] It is for these reasons that Justice Black would have interpreted the Eighth Amendment to apply to prison conditions and treatment. He also would have strongly disagreed with Justice Scalia's claim that the Eighth Amendment does not apply to torture—although he might have relied on a different constitutional provision.[328]

PROPERTY RIGHTS

Justice Black supported the constitutional double standard when it came to property rights and civil rights, particularly during the early part of his judicial tenure. "When we balance the Constitutional rights of owners of property against those of the people to enjoy freedom of press and religion," Black wrote in one case, "we remain mindful of the fact that the latter occupy a preferred position."[329] By contrast, Justices Scalia and Thomas have criticized the constitutional double standard. At a 1984 conference sponsored by the Cato Institute, then-judge Scalia argued that the idea of differentiating civil rights from economic rights was "pernicious." "It leads to the conclusion," he said, "that economic rights and liberties are qualitatively distinct from, and fundamentally inferior to, other noble human values called civil rights, about which we should be more generous."[330] Similarly, in pre–Supreme Court speeches, Justice Thomas refuted the idea that economic rights are somehow inferior to civil rights. "After all," he said, "aren't free speech and work both means to an even higher end?"[331]

Lochner

The three originalists were all sharp critics of the *Lochner* era—albeit for different reasons. Black disagreed with *Lochner* both philosophically and judicially. In terms of the former, the Supreme Court was striking down progressive laws during that time that he fully supported, such as a minimum wage, maximum work hours, and child labor regulations. In terms of the latter, Justice Black strongly disagreed that the due process clause can be read to support a substantive "liberty of contract" right. Thus, he argued that the *Lochner* era was the worst form of judicial activism in Supreme Court history.

Justices Scalia and Thomas, meanwhile, have restricted their criticism of *Lochner* to the judicial function. Scalia described *Lochner* as "the moment of truth" for conservatives, and he worried that if the court actively protected economic and property rights under the due process clause, it would lead to other claims of unenumerated rights, such as the right to an abortion, the right to die, or a right of sexual preference.[332] Similarly, in pre–Supreme Court speeches, Justice Thomas criticized libertarian scholars who were eager for the court to strike down laws and regulations concerning economic and business activity. "Do such people really think such a powerful court would stop at striking down only those laws?" Thomas asked. "That defies reality."[333]

Takings Clause

Despite their shared concerns about *Lochner*, the three originalists had different interpretations of other constitutional provisions protecting property rights, particularly the takings clause. Justice Black supported a deferential approach in eminent domain cases. In *United States v. Causby* (1946),[334] he criticized the court for imposing "relatively absolute constitutional barriers" on Congress by its interpretation of the takings clause. "The concept of taking property as used in the Constitution," Black wrote in dissent, "has heretofore never been given so sweeping a meaning." "I am not willing," he added, "nor do I think the Constitution and the decisions authorize me, to extend that phrase [private property be taken] so as to guarantee an absolute constitutional right to relief not subject to legislative change."[335] As Black saw it, courts should defer to public officials and local planning commissions that have more expertise in the area.

Justices Scalia and Thomas, by constrast, have defended a robust interpretation of the takings clause. Both of them have written or joined opinions that expanded the guarantee to cover regulatory takings—although they acknowledged that the original intention of the takings clause was to protect against the physical confiscation of property. Scalia wrote the Supreme Court's decision in *Nollan v. California Coastal Commission* (1987),[336] which rejected a state commission's decision to require a public easement in front of an owner's beachfront property as a condition of obtaining a building permit. He also wrote the court's decision five years later, joined by Thomas, which ruled that the deprivation of all economic use of property constitutes a taking.[337] Both Scalia and Thomas then joined the court's decision in *Dolan v. City of Tigard* (1994),[338] which imposed a higher burden of proof in regulatory takings cases. Justice Black, by contrast, rejected a higher level of scrutiny in such cases. "The solution of the problems precipitated by these technological advances and new ways of living," wrote Black, "cannot come about through the application of rigid constitutional restraints formulated and enforced by the courts."[339]

Public Use

Justice Black joined the court's decision providing a broad interpretation of what constitutes "public use" in takings cases. In *Berman v. Parker* (1954),[340] the court upheld the District of Columbia Redevelopment Act of 1945, which allowed the acquisition of real property "injurious to the public health, safety, morals, and welfare." The act created a Redevelopment Land Agency, which was authorized to acquire real property by eminent domain for the "redevelopment of blighted territory." The appellant, who owned a department store in the redevelopment area, objected that the taking of his property did not constitute a "public use." The Supreme Court unanimously rejected that argument. In an opinion by Justice Douglas, the court described the scope of the police power very broadly. "An attempt to define its reach or trace its outer limits," wrote Douglas, "is fruitless, for each case must turn on its own facts." "Subject to specific constitutional limitations," he added, "when the legislature has spoken, the public interest has been declared in terms well-nigh conclusive." Consistent with this view, Douglas stated that courts should not second-guess the decisions of Congress and its authorized agencies. "The role of the judiciary in determining whether that power is being exercised for a public purpose is an extremely narrow one," he wrote. "The rights of these property owners are satisfied," Douglas concluded, "when they receive that just compensation which the Fifth Amendment exacts as the price of the taking."[341]

By contrast, Justices Scalia and Thomas have defended a narrow interpretation of "public use." In *Kelo v. City of New London* (2005),[342] the Supreme Court upheld a city's economic redevelopment plan designed to counteract a "distressed" economy marked by high unemployment and a large drop in population. Unlike the facts in *Berman*, the city of New London authorized a private corporation to purchase property or to acquire property by exercising eminent domain. Relying on long-established precedents (including *Berman*), the court expansively interpreted the police power and determined that "public use" should include "public purpose." "Those who govern the City," Justice Stevens wrote for the court, "were not confronted with the need to remove blight in the Fort Trumbull area, but their determination that the area was sufficiently distressed to justify a program of economic rejuvenation is entitled to our deference."[343]

Justices Scalia and Thomas joined a dissent authored by Justice O'Connor, who argued that "public use" should not always be equated with the police power. "Any property," O'Connor wrote, "may now be taken for the benefit of another private party." "The beneficiaries," she added, "are likely to be those citizens with disproportionate influence and power in the political process, including large corporations and development firms."[344] In a separate dissent, Justice Thomas agreed that eminent domain should not be equated with the police power, but he went a step further and argued that the government can "take property only if it actually uses or gives the public a legal right to use the property."[345] He thus called for the overturning of *Berman* and of another precedent authored by Justice O'Connor.[346]

Even though Justice Black was more supportive of property rights during the latter part of his tenure[347]—and probably would have been sympathetic to Suzette Kelo's loss of her home—he likely would have supported the court's decision in *Kelo.* "What adjustments may have to be made," Black wrote in *Causby,* "only the future can reveal." "It seems certain," he added, "that courts do not possess the techniques or the personnel to consider and act upon the complex combinations of factors entering into the problems."[348] Black also would not have supported Thomas's call for the court to reconsider *Berman.*

EQUAL PROTECTION

Justice Black joined the unanimous opinion in *Brown v. Board of Education* (1954).[349] During the conference in that case, he noted that "segregation *of itself* violates the Constitution." He also stated that segregation is premised on "the belief that Negroes are inferior," and "I do not need books to say that."[350] Years later, when asked whether there were any grounds that would have caused him to reach a different result in *Brown,* Black's unequivocal response was no. In a letter to professor Sydney Ulmer, who asked Black about his position during the first conference in the case, Black wrote, "if you are saying that under any circumstances I would have voted to continue to hold that segregation was constitutional then your statement is not correct."[351]

Justice Thomas's view is basically the same as Black's. "I think segregation is bad, I think it's wrong, it's immoral. I'd fight against it with every breath in my body," Thomas said in a 1987 interview.[352] Nonetheless, Thomas has strongly criticized the *Brown* court's reliance on psychological studies. "The evil of segregation was that black students had inferior facilities," Thomas told his colleagues during their conference in *Missouri v. Jenkins* (1995), "not that they were denied the chance to go to school with white students."[353]

In contrast, *Brown* represents a major challenge for a positivist-originalist like Justice Scalia.[354] When asked how he would have voted in *Brown*, Scalia always claimed he would have joined the decision, but there is little evidence of this. In a footnote in one case, Scalia maintained that the language of the Thirteenth and Fourteenth Amendments, taken together, prohibits racial segregation.[355] However, it is hard to see how a judge following Scalia's originalist philosophy could have sided with the petitioners in *Brown*. The language of the equal protection clause is not self-defining, and Scalia consistently argued that judges must follow tradition when constitutional language is uncertain.[356] In his article defending originalism "as the lesser of two evils," Scalia described the role of the judge as "sometimes better suited to the historian than the lawyer." It requires, in his words, "immersing oneself in the political and intellectual atmosphere of the time—somehow placing out of mind knowledge that we have which an earlier age did not, and putting on beliefs, attitudes, philosophies, *prejudices* and loyalties that are not those of our day."[357] How could a judge following that particular methodology come to a favorable ruling in *Brown*?

As Alexander Bickel convincingly demonstrated, the original intent of the Fourteenth Amendment was *not* to outlaw segregation in public schools.[358] In fact, by 1954, when *Brown* was decided, the District of Columbia and twenty-one states either permitted or required segregation in public schools.[359] Scalia seemed to admit that his originalist methodology did not support *Brown*. "We originalists refer to [the issue of segregation] as waving the bloody red shirt of *Brown v. Board of Education*." He then proceeded to claim that he "would have been with the majority in *Brown*, because I think I would have joined Harlan's dissent in *Plessy*." But, Scalia continued, "that is the less important answer." "I will stipulate that you can do some good things . . . with the living Constitution. A stopped clock is right twice a day."[360] For similar reasons, a strong case can be made that Justice Scalia's originalist approach would have placed him in a dissenting role in *Loving v. Virginia* (1967)[361]—a decision that Justice Black joined. In that case, the Supreme Court struck down Virginia's antimiscegenation law as a violation of the equal protection clause.[362]

Integration

Justice Black was a strong supporter of the Supreme Court's post-*Brown* decisions requiring school districts to take affirmative steps to dismantle historically segregated schools. He joined the court's decision in *Green v. County School Board of New Kent County* (1968),[363] which ruled that "freedom of choice" plans were not an adequate remedy to effectuate a unitary school system. Black also joined the court's decision in *Swann v. Charlotte-Mecklenburg Board of Education* (1971),[364] where the justices unanimously held that busing was an appropriate remedy to achieve racial integration in formerly de jure segregated school districts.

By contrast, Justices Scalia and Thomas have been staunch critics of both *Green* and *Swann*. In a separate concurrence in *Freeman v. Pitts* (1992),[365] Scalia argued that *Green* created an "insurmountable burden" on school districts by requiring them to prove that any sort of racial imbalances in their schools were not the result of discrimination.[366] Prior to his appointment to the Supreme Court, Thomas criticized *Green* for ushering in the idea that "*Brown* not only ended segregation but required school integration." In the aftermath of *Green*, Thomas explained, there has been "a disastrous series of cases requiring busing and other policies that were irrelevant to parents' concern for a decent education."[367] In a 2007 case Justices Scalia and Thomas joined a decision that struck down two *voluntary* desegregation plans as a violation of the Fourteenth Amendment's equal protection clause.[368] Based on his small *d* democratic views and the votes he cast in *Green* and *Swann*, it is highly unlikely that Justice Black would have supported that decision.

Reapportionment

Justice Black was an early and avid supporter of the concept of "one person, one vote." In *Colegrove v. Green* (1946),[369] he dissented when the Supreme Court rejected a challenge to malapportioned congressional districts in Illinois. "While the Constitution contains no express provision requiring that congressional election districts established by the States must contain approximately equal populations," Black wrote, "the constitutionally guaranteed right to vote, and the right to have one's vote counted clearly imply the policy that state election systems, no matter what their form, should be designed to give approximately equal weight to each vote cast."[370] Black then joined the court's decision in *Baker v. Carr* (1962),[371] which essentially overturned *Colegrove.* Two years later, he wrote the court's decision in *Wesberry v. Sanders* (1964),[372] which held that congressional districts must be drawn on the basis of one person, one vote, and he joined the court's decision four months later holding that the same principle must be applied to both houses of state legislatures.[373]

Prior to his appointment to the federal judiciary, then-professor Scalia took issue with the fact that "state legislatures [cannot] be structured like the federal Congress, with one house selected on a basis that is not proportional to population."[374] Then, in a 2012 interview, Scalia acknowledged that, as an original matter, he would not have supported the one person, one vote cases. NPR's Nina Totenberg asked Scalia about his view of stare decisis, and he admitted that he would abide by certain decisions he did not agree with. "One person, one vote," Totenberg asked, "you wouldn't have reached that decision?" "Certainly not," Scalia replied.[375]

For his part, Justice Thomas has challenged the constitutional foundation of the one person, one vote principle. As early as 2001, Thomas signaled that the Supreme Court has not provided adequate guidance on what the relevant population is: "total population" or "citizen voting age population."[376] Fifteen years later, the court was faced with that precise question. In *Evenwel v. Abbott* (2016),[377] a group of citizens challenged the way Texas drew its legislative districts. Like every other state in the country, Texas based the size of its legislative districts on total population. The appellants challenged this uniform method of districting on the grounds that it produced unequal districts when measured by voter-eligible population. The court unanimously rejected the appellants' equal protection challenge.

Justice Ginsburg, writing for the court, cited substantial evidence to support Texas's use of total population in drawing its districts, including the views of James Madison and Alexander Hamilton, the debates surrounding the adoption of section 2 of the Fourteenth Amendment, judicial precedent, the methods courts have previously used to apportion districts, and the uniform practice of all fifty states. "The rule appellants urge has no mooring in the Equal Protection Clause," concluded Ginsburg. "Adopting voter-eligible apportionment as constitutional command would upset a well-functioning approach to districting that all 50 States and countless local jurisdictions have followed for decades, even centuries."[378]

Justice Thomas concurred—although his opinion sounded more like a dissent. After reviewing the court's reapportionment decisions, Thomas concluded that there is no clear consensus on what population a state has to use to satisfy the one person, one vote principle. For this reason, he argued that decisions about the drawing of legislative districts should be left to the states. The states, he wrote, can apportion "their own districts to equalize total population, to equalize eligible voters, or to promote any other principle consistent with a republican form of government."[379] Because the state of Texas drew its districts based on total population, Thomas concluded there is no constitutional violation. He did not stop there, however. Throughout his opinion, Thomas questioned the constitutional basis of the principle of one person, one vote. "In my view," Thomas wrote, "the majority has failed to provide a sound basis for the one-person, one-vote principle because no such basis exists."[380] Thomas argued that the framers were concerned about tyranny of the majority. "As a result," he contended, "many viewed antidemocratic checks as indispensable to republican government." "Included among the antidemocratic checks," he pointed out, "were legislatures that deviated from perfect equality of representation."[381] Because Thomas did not believe the Constitution contained "a single, comprehensive theory of representation," he argued that the Supreme Court had been wrong back in the 1960s to impose the one person, one vote concept on the American people. "The Court's attempt to impose its political theory upon the States has produced a morass of problems," Thomas wrote. "These problems are antithetical to the values that the Framers embraced in the Constitution," and they "confirm that the Court has been wrong to entangle itself with the political process."[382]

As an original matter, it is safe to assume that Justices Scalia and Thomas would have dissented in *Baker v. Carr* (1962)[383]—the decision that Chief Justice Warren described as the most important case handed down during his tenure.[384] Even though Justices Scalia and Thomas did not support the principle of one person, one vote, they relied on it in *Bush v. Gore* (2000),[385] where the Supreme Court stopped a hand recount of votes in the state of Florida in the 2000 presidential election.

Racial Gerrymandering

In *Wright v. Rockefeller* (1964),[386] Justice Black wrote the 7–2 decision that rejected a challenge to the gerrymandering of four congressional districts in Manhattan, finding that there was insufficient proof that race was the sole motivating factor in drawing the districts. The petitioners were African Americans who objected to blacks being packed into one district. Instead, they believed they had the right to compete for representatives in all four districts. However, leaders of the Democratic Party, including prominent black elected officials such as representative Adam Clayton Powell Jr. (D-NY), liked the system of packing because it made it more likely that a black or Puerto Rican candidate would be elected. Justice Black deferred to the three-judge panel in the lower court, which found that the appellants failed to prove a prima facie case of racial motivation. "It may be true, as Judge Feinberg thought, that there was evidence which could have supported inferences that racial considerations might have moved the state legislature, but, even if so, we agree that there also was evidence to support his finding that the contrary inference was 'equally, or more, persuasive.'"[387] "Undoubtedly some of these voters," Black wrote, "as shown by this lawsuit, would prefer a more even distribution of minority groups among the four congressional districts, but others, like the intervenors in this case, would argue strenuously that the kind of districts for which appellants contended would be undesirable and, because of race or place of origin, would themselves be unconstitutional."[388]

Justices Scalia and Thomas have been sharp critics of racial gerrymandering. In contrast to their views about political gerrymandering,[389] they have defended strict scrutiny in such cases.[390] In *Holder v. Hall* (1994),[391] Thomas criticized *Wright* for starting the process of "political apartheid" in the United States. Justice Thomas praised Justice Douglas's dissent in that case, which predicted that racial gerrymandering would result in "antagonisms that relate to race or to religion rather than to political issues." Douglas also stated that "communities [will] seek not the best representative but the best racial or religious partisan."[392] In Thomas's view, "racial gerrymandering offends the Constitution whether the motivation is malicious or benign." "It is not a defense," he added, "that the legislature merely may have drawn the district based on the stereotype that blacks are reliable Democratic voters."[393] "Despite Justice Douglas' warning sounded 30 years ago," Thomas wrote in *Holder*, "our voting rights decisions are rapidly progressing towards a system that is indistinguishable in principle from a scheme under which members of different racial groups are divided into separate electoral registers and allocated a proportion of political power on the basis of race."[394]

Despite all being originalists, Justices Black, Scalia, and Thomas interpreted the Constitution in fundamentally different ways. They defended vastly different views of legal standing. Justice Black supported citizen lawsuits and the Supreme Court's decision in *Flast*, while Justices Scalia and Thomas have not. In traditional disputes about the separation of powers, Justice Black defended a narrow conception of executive power, while Justices Scalia and Thomas have been strong defenders of Alexander Hamilton's broad definition of presidential power. These different perspectives would have placed the three justices on opposite sides in *Humphrey's Executor v. United States, Johnson v. Eisentrager, Boumediene v. Bush, Morrison v. Olson, United States v. Morrison, Printz v. United States*, and *Cheney v. United States District Court.*

On the issue of federalism, Justice Black regarded Congress's commerce power as plenary. After initially defending a political process approach, Justice Scalia gravitated toward a "middle ground" Madisonian perspective. Justice Thomas, meanwhile, has defended a strict constructionist interpretation of Congress's enumerated powers. These different perspectives would have placed the three originalists (especially Black and Thomas) on opposite sides in numerous federalism cases, including *Hammer v. Dagenhart, United States v. Darby Lumber Co., Wickard v. Filburn, Perez v. United States, United States v. Lopez, United States v. Morrison, Printz v. United States*, and *National Federation of Independent Business v. Sebelius.*

Justice Black argued that the legislative history of the Thirty-Ninth Congress supported total incorporation of the Bill of Rights to the states; Justice Scalia argued that *no* incorporation was supported by the text of the Fourteenth Amendment; and Justice Thomas has defended a selective incorporation process, but only under the privileges or immunities clause. Despite all three originalists supporting robust interpretations of political speech, there were important differences in how they interpreted the First Amendment. Based on their deferential approach to executive power, Justices Scalia and Thomas would not have supported Justice Black's absolutist defense of free speech during the Red Scare. Nor would they have joined his concurring opinion in the Pentagon Papers Case. For his part, Justice Black would not have joined the Supreme Court's decision in *Holder v. Humanitarian Law Project*, which upheld a federal ban on providing "material support" to foreign terrorist groups. Justice Black would not have joined Scalia's dissent in *Rutan v. Republican Party of Illinois*, where he argued that public employees can be hired or fired based on their political views. Nor would he have joined Justice Scalia's dissent (joined by Thomas) in *Agency for International Development*, where he argued that state and federal officials have to swear allegiance to the Constitution.

Justice Black extended his absolutist approach to the First Amendment to cover obscenity and libel, whereas Justices Scalia and Thomas have allowed government regulation in those areas. Most importantly, Scalia and Thomas have argued that *New York Times v. Sullivan* is inconsistent with the original meaning of the Constitution. At the same time, Justices Scalia and Thomas have been more libertarian than Justice Black in certain areas of First Amendment law. Black did not believe flag burning is protected under the First Amendment, but Scalia did. Black did not believe commercial speech is within the purview of the First Amendment, while both Scalia and Thomas (especially the latter) have argued that it is. Justice Black likely would have joined the Roberts Court's decision in *Citizens United*, but he would not have supported Scalia's and Thomas's call for strict scrutiny in campaign contribution cases, nor would he have supported their votes to strike down legislative efforts to equalize candidates' expenditures in state and federal elections.

In interpreting the religion clauses, Justice Black constitutionalized Jefferson's "high wall" theory and defended a strict neutralist perspective. Justices Scalia and Thomas have sharply criticized that perspective. In one speech, Scalia stated that the claim that government has to be neutral between religion and irreligion is "a lie."[395] The three justices also maintained very different interpretations of the free exercise clause. Justice Black regarded religion as a fundamental right, while Justice Scalia wrote the court's decision in *Employment Division, Department of Human Resources of Oregon v. Smith*, which carved out a major exception to the court's use of strict scrutiny in such cases. As discussed in the next chapter, Justice Thomas does not support *Smith* either.

With regard to the Second Amendment, Justice Black joined the unanimous decision in *United States v. Miller*, which connected the right to keep and bear arms to participation in state militias. Justices Scalia and Thomas, however, ushered in a new understanding of the Second Amendment as guaranteeing an individual right to own guns for self-defense. In interpreting the Fourth Amendment, the three originalists came to different conclusions in certain areas. For example, they had different interpretations of the search-incident-to-arrest exception, the constitutionality of warrantless blood tests of suspected drunk drivers, and the applicability of the Fourth Amendment to administrative searches. There were dramatic differences in other areas of criminal procedure as well, including whether *Miranda* is consistent with the self-incrimination clause, whether the government has to provide counsel to those who cannot afford an attorney, whether the dual sovereignty doctrine is consistent with the double jeopardy clause, and the purpose and scope of the speedy trial provision. Justice Black also would have been more scrupulous than Justices Scalia and Thomas in ensuring procedural protections in capital punishment cases.

All three originalists rejected *Lochner*—albeit for different reasons. At the same time, they had different interpretations of the scope of the takings clause. Justice Black was very deferential in takings cases, while Justices Scalia and Thomas have defended a robust judicial role in such cases. Justice Black also did not support Justice Thomas's narrow construction of a "public use" under the takings clause.

The three originalists interpreted the equal protection clause in fundamentally different ways. Justice Black viewed segregation as a per se violation of the equal protection clause. Similarly, Justice Thomas called *Brown* a "landmark" decision, but he criticized the court for relying on psychological studies to support integration efforts. By contrast, Justice Scalia's methodological approach to originalism (text and tradition) would have had him dissenting in *Brown*—a fact he essentially admitted. The three originalists also differed over the Supreme Court's role in remedying segregation. Justice Black joined all the major decisions calling for school districts to take affirmative steps to rectify segregation, including mandatory busing. But Justices Scalia and Thomas, meanwhile, have been sharp critics of *Green* and *Swann*.

The three originalists also maintained markedly different views of the judicial role in reapportionment cases. Black was a champion of the concept of "one person, one vote," while Scalia and Thomas have sharply criticized it. In fact, according to Thomas, the court's "single, correct answer" to the issue of reapportionment has created "a morass of problems."

In summary, although there are important areas of agreement among the three originalists, their differences are profound and go to the very heart of the US constitutional system. One of the major claims of originalists is that their interpretative philosophy limits judicial discretion, but when one looks at the originalist opinions of Justices Black, Scalia, and Thomas, that assertion does not hold up in practice.

6. Scalia v. Thomas

Antonin Scalia and Clarence Thomas served together on the Supreme Court for nearly twenty-five years. Despite voting the same way in 90.9 percent of cases, there were important fault lines in their respective approaches to originalism. In fact, if only nonunanimous cases are considered, the level of agreement between Scalia and Thomas drops to 83 percent.[1] During his first years on the Supreme Court, some commentators pejoratively called Thomas a "clone"[2] or a "Pavlovian puppet"[3] of Scalia's, but that was not the case. In fact, some legal scholars claim that Thomas is "the more intellectually serious of the two" and that his jurisprudence "has a greater chance of making an enduring contribution to constitutional law."[4] What cannot be denied is that Thomas is more of a constitutional purist. "He [Thomas] does not believe in *stare decisis*, period," Scalia observed in an interview with Ken Foskett. "If a constitutional line of authority is wrong, he would say let's get it right. I wouldn't do that."[5] "I'm an originalist," Scalia remarked on another occasion, "but I'm not a nut."[6]

This chapter examines the originalist philosophies of Justices Scalia and Thomas across a wide array of constitutional areas, including separation of powers, the scope of executive power, administrative law (including the nondelegation doctrine and *Chevron* deference), federalism, free speech (including anonymous speech and the rights of minors), religious freedom, criminal procedure, property rights, natural law, the privileges or immunities clause, and equal protection.

EXECUTIVE POWER

Justices Scalia and Thomas can both be considered strong executivists. They have each supported Alexander Hamilton's broad interpretation of executive power under Article II and the "sole organ" theory in foreign affairs. This does not mean, however, that the two justices reached the same conclusion in every case involving executive power. One case in which their analysis varied dramatically was *Hamdi v. Rumsfeld* (2004).[7] Yaser Esam Hamdi, a US citizen, was captured in Afghanistan by the Northern Alliance, a coalition of military groups opposed to the Taliban government. Hamdi was turned over to the US government, which initially detained and interrogated him in Afghanistan before sending him to the US naval base at Guantanamo Bay, Cuba. After it was discovered that Hamdi was a US citizen, he was transferred to a navy brig in Norfolk, Virginia, and then to another one located in Charleston, South Carolina.

Relying on the commander-in-chief clause of Article II and the Authorization for Use of Military Force (AUMF), passed by Congress one week after the 9/11 attacks, the Bush administration claimed that Hamdi was an "enemy combatant" and could be detained "indefinitely" during the "war on terror. The government's evidence of Hamdi's enemy combatant status consisted of several interrogations by military personnel, as well as the so-called Mobbs declaration, an affidavit compiled by Michael Mobbs, a special adviser to the undersecretary of defense for policy. According to this declaration, Hamdi had trained with the Taliban before 9/11, remained with his Taliban unit after the 9/11 attacks, and surrendered his Kalashnikov assault rifle to the Northern Alliance after being captured. Hamdi's father filed a petition for habeas corpus on behalf of his son, claiming that he was not an enemy combatant but rather was a relief worker who had arrived in Afghanistan only two months before the 9/11 attacks.

In *Hamdi*, a plurality of the Supreme Court held that the AUMF allowed the Bush administration to indefinitely detain a US citizen during the war on terror. Justice O'Connor, author of the plurality opinion, reasoned that the capture and detention of enemy combatants are incidents of war and that the AUMF authorized the president "to use all necessary and appropriate force" in the war on terrorism. In reaching that conclusion, the plurality relied on the court's decision in *Ex parte Quirin* (1942)[8]—the Nazi saboteur case—where the justices upheld the detention of eight enemy combatants (one of whom was a US citizen) and their subsequent trial by military commission during World War II. Although siding with the administration with respect to the lawfulness of Hamdi's detention, the plurality ruled against its assertion that the evidence gleaned from Hamdi's interrogations and the Mobbs declaration was sufficient to hold him indefinitely. Balancing the weighty concern of national security against Hamdi's substantial interest in not being deprived of his liberty, the plurality ruled that some meaningful due process had to be afforded. At the same time, the plurality observed that when the nation is at war, normal criminal procedural rights are not required. For example, the government could use hearsay evidence, its evidence could be presumed valid (i.e., the defendant would have the burden of rebutting his enemy combatant classification), and military officers (not Article III judges or juries) could be the "neutral" decision makers.

Justice Scalia filed a dissenting opinion. He claimed that under US law and tradition, Hamdi had to be released unless criminal charges were brought against him or Congress suspended the writ of habeas corpus. Scalia began his opinion by underscoring the significance of the Fifth Amendment's due process clause and Article I, section 9's writ of habeas corpus as crucial safeguards against unlawful detention. He maintained that throughout US history, American citizens who have been accused of waging war against the United States were treated as traitors and subject to criminal process, unless Congress suspended the writ of habeas corpus. If Congress did not suspend the writ and the courts were still open, Scalia argued that the suspected traitor had to be either criminally charged or released. Scalia also criticized the government's reliance on *Quirin*. Reminiscent of remarks made by Justice Frankfurter, who participated in that decision, Scalia described *Quirin* as "not the Court's finest hour."[9] The *Quirin* court, Scalia maintained, unfaithfully interpreted the court's opinion in *Ex parte Milligan* (1866),[10] which held that during wartime, and absent a suspension of habeas corpus, there is "no exception to the right to trial by jury for citizens who could be called 'belligerents' or 'prisoners of war.'"[11] For Scalia, *Milligan* applied in this case, and anything to the contrary in *Quirin* should not be given precedential weight. Since no one had argued that the AUMF suspended the writ of habeas corpus, and since no criminal charges had been brought against Hamdi, Scalia argued that he must be released or turned over to law enforcement to be charged criminally.

Justice Thomas also dissented in *Hamdi*, but he came to a very different conclusion than Scalia. Thomas argued that the executive branch's determination that Hamdi was an enemy combatant should receive *complete* deference from the courts. Beginning with first principles, Thomas argued that the security of the nation is the primary responsibility of the federal government and, in particular, the president. Relying on Hamilton's theory of an energetic executive, Thomas observed that the nation speaks with one voice in times of national crisis and that the executive branch is specially designed to handle sensitive matters of foreign affairs and national security. Thomas cited Justice Jackson's opinion for the court in *Chicago & Southern Air Lines, Inc. v. Waterman S.S. Corp.* (1948), where he observed, "the very nature of executive decisions as to foreign policy is political, not judicial," and "the Judiciary has neither aptitude, facilities nor responsibility" for inquiring into those decisions.[12]

As for the case at hand, Thomas strongly suggested that the president has the inherent authority to indefinitely detain enemy combatants under Article II, but (like the plurality) he argued that the AUMF gave the president the statutory authority to detain enemy combatants during the war on terror. Thomas took issue with the plurality, however, for not deferring to the president's judgment that Hamdi was an enemy combatant. Thomas maintained that "a good-faith executive determination" that a detainee is an enemy combatant is sufficient, although he admitted that, in a particular case, that determination could turn out to be "mistaken."[13] On this basis, Thomas argued that the plurality's additional due process requirements of access to counsel and a factual basis for the enemy combatant designation were not necessary and could, in fact, be detrimental to national security.

Interestingly, Thomas also gave several reasons why he disagreed with Justice Scalia's dissent. While he agreed that *Milligan* supported Scalia's opinion, Thomas said that case was distinguishable from Hamdi's because "the [*Milligan*] Court referred frequently and pervasively to the criminal nature of the proceedings," whereas *Hamdi* involved only the detention of an enemy combatant during wartime. Unlike Scalia, Thomas also contended that "*Quirin* overruled *Milligan* to the extent those cases are inconsistent."[14] Ironically, Thomas cited a decision written by then-judge Scalia when he served on the DC Court of Appeals to support the contention that the federal courts lacked the information and expertise to determine whether Hamdi was actually an enemy combatant:

> In Old Testament days, when judges ruled the people of Israel and led them into battle, a court professing the belief that it could order a halt to a military operation in foreign lands might not have been a startling phenomenon. But in modern times, and in a country where such governmental functions have been committed to elected delegates of the people, such an assertion of jurisdiction is extraordinary. The court's decision today reflects a willingness to extend judicial power into areas where we do not know, and have no way finding out, what serious harm we may be doing.[15]

Recognition Power

Justices Scalia and Thomas also came to different conclusions in an important case involving the political status of Jerusalem. In 1948 the US government formally recognized Israel as a sovereign country, but it took no position on whether Israel had sovereign authority over Jerusalem. Instead, the State Department instructed its employees to record "Jerusalem," not "Jerusalem, Israel," as the place of birth on passports of US citizens born in Jerusalem. In 2002, however, Congress passed the Foreign Relations Authorization Act (FRAA), section 214 of which mandates that the State Department, upon the request of a US citizen born in Jerusalem, record the place of birth as "Israel." Menachem Binyamin Zivotofsky was born to two US citizens living in Jerusalem, and his mother requested that the place of birth on his passport be listed as "Jerusalem, Israel"—a request that was denied by the State Department.

In *Zivotofsky v. Kerry* (2015),[16] the Supreme Court, in an opinion by Justice Kennedy, struck down section 214. Relying on the reception clause (Article II, section 3) and the president's authority to enter into treaties and to make appointments of "Ambassadors" and "other public Ministers and Consuls," Kennedy determined that the president has the authority to recognize foreign nations and governments. For Kennedy, the bigger question was whether that authority is exclusive, and he concluded that it is. For support, he cited the "sole organ" theory of the presidency, Hamilton's case for a unitary executive in Federalist No. 70, texts and treatises on international law dating back to the founding, judicial precedent, and historical practices beginning with the Washington administration. "If Congress could command the President to state a recognition position inconsistent with his own," Kennedy wrote, "Congress could override the President's recognition determination."[17]

Justice Thomas concurred with the majority, but he arrived at his decision in a very different way. In fact, Thomas criticized the court's "distortion of the President's recognition power." Like the dissenters, he did not believe the case was about recognition at all. Instead, Thomas based his opinion on the president's residual authority under Article II's vesting clause. Thomas cited historical practices dating back to the king of England that regarded the regulation of passports as "controlled by the body exercising executive power."[18] He could find no constitutional authority giving Congress the power to regulate passports, and he rejected arguments by Zivotofsky and congressional amici that Congress had plenary or implied authority to enact section 214. He also rejected congressional authority pursuant to three enumerated powers: "to regulate Commerce with foreign Nations" (Article I, section 8, clause 3), "to establish an [*sic*] uniform Rule of Naturalization" (Article I, section 8, clause 4), and "to make Laws which shall be necessary and proper for carrying into Execution the foregoing Powers" (Article I, section 8, clause 18). None of these enumerated powers, Thomas contended, authorizes Congress to regulate passports under the FRAA. Thus, he concluded that section 214 was unconstitutional "insofar as it directs the President, contrary to his wishes, to list 'Israel' as the place of birth of Jerusalem-born citizens on their passports."[19]

Justice Scalia dissented. He conceded that the president has the authority to recognize foreign governments, but he was much less certain that such authority is exclusive, which contradicted testimony he gave back in 1975 when he unequivocally stated that it was.[20] Scalia observed that eleven of the powers granted to Congress under Article I, section 8 deal with foreign affairs. In contrast to Justice Thomas, he found specific authority for section 214 under Congress's authority to "establish an [*sic*] uniform Rule of Naturalization" and to "make all Laws which shall be necessary and proper for carrying into Execution the foregoing Powers." Instead of basing his dissent on constitutional grounds, however, Scalia interpreted the FRAA as not implicating the president's recognition power at all. According to Scalia, "a state must perform an act that unequivocally manifests" an intention to extend recognition, and Congress did not do that in this case. All Congress did, he maintained, was to allow Americans born in Jerusalem to request that "Israel" be listed on their passports or their birth records. Making such a designation, he contended, "does not encumber the Republic with any international obligations."[21] Scalia acknowledged that listing "Israel" on passports and birth certificates might have symbolic significance in terms of international diplomacy, but, in his view, "it makes no difference as a matter of constitutional law."[22]

Interestingly, Scalia also took strong exception to Justice Thomas's concurrence. He disputed what he called his colleague's "stingy interpretation" of Congress's enumerated powers. For example, Scalia noted that Congress has the authority to regulate foreign commerce and that "passports facilitate the transportation of passengers." He also observed that "passports issued to citizens, like birth reports, 'have the same force and effect as proof of United States citizenship as certificates of naturalization,'" which supports congressional authority to regulate passports under its naturalization power.[23] Scalia also challenged Thomas's defense of presidential "primacy" over passports and cited historical examples of Congress passing laws in that area. "History and precedent," wrote Scalia, "refute any suggestion that the Constitution disables Congress from regulating the President's issuance and formulation of passports."[24] In dramatic fashion, Scalia then described Thomas's broad "assertion" of presidential "residual powers," coupled with his "parsimonious" interpretation of Congress's enumerated powers (including its necessary and proper authority), as resulting in "a presidency more reminiscent of George III than George Washington."[25] In contrast to Scalia and Thomas, Justice Black argued that the regulation of passports was the exclusive province of Congress.[26]

Line-Item Veto

In addition to their differences in *Hamdi* and *Zivotofsky*, Justices Scalia and Thomas were on opposite sides of the Supreme Court's decision in *Clinton v. City of New York* (1998).[27] In 1996 Congress passed the Line Item Veto Act, which authorized the president to "cancel in whole" three kinds of provisions already signed into law: "(1) any dollar amount of discretionary budget authority; (2) any item of new direct spending; or (3) any limited tax benefit."[28] The president could exercise such authority only after determining that it would reduce the federal budget deficit, not impair essential government functions, and not harm the national interest.

To exercise this cancellation authority, the president had to transmit a special message to Congress within five calendar days after enactment of the provision in question. Cancellation took effect upon Congress's receipt of this special message, and the act provided a process by which Congress could "disapprove" of the president's cancellation. According to the act, the cancellation of an item of new direct spending or a limited tax benefit prevented that item from having "legal force or effect." Prior to the act being challenged, President Clinton exercised his line-item veto authority on eighty-two separate occasions.

In an opinion by Justice Stevens, the Supreme Court held that the cancellation authority granted to the president violated the presentment clause (Article I, section 7). According to Stevens, the authority conferred under the act differed from the process outlined in the presentment clause in two fundamental ways. First, under the presentment clause, the president must return a bill *before* it becomes a law, whereas a cancellation under the Line Item Veto Act occurs *after* the bill becomes law. Second, when the president returns a bill under the presentment clause, he is required to submit the entire bill; conversely, under the Line Item Veto Act, the president sends a special message to Congress notifying it only of the canceled provision.[29] Although Stevens admitted that the Constitution is silent on the specific question of whether the president can repeal or amend only parts of duly enacted statutes, he maintained that "constitutional silence on this profoundly important issue" was "equivalent to an express prohibition."[30]

Justice Thomas joined the court's decision but did not author a separate opinion. However, in a subsequent speech, he explained his thinking. "While certain innovations, such as the legislative veto or the line-item veto, might improve the operation of government," Thomas remarked, "they are not permitted by the separation of powers because they would undermine the abilities of the branches to control one another, and thereby obviate the need for government actions to undergo careful thought, scrutiny, and consensus."[31] Justice Scalia, by contrast, dissented in *City of New York.* Despite the title of the act, Scalia maintained that the Line Item Veto Act did not actually give the president line-item veto authority. In his view, when the president exercises his cancellation authority, the laws do not change; they stay exactly the same. Because the laws involved in this case had been passed in compliance with the presentment clause, Scalia saw no constitutional problem. He also argued that the discretion given to the president did not violate the nondelegation doctrine, which he considered the more challenging issue. According to Scalia, the authority conferred by the Line Item Veto Act did not dramatically differ from the president's authority under ordinary spending laws. "Insofar as the degree of political, 'law-making' power conferred upon the Executive is concerned," wrote Scalia, "there is not a dime's worth of difference between Congress's authorizing the President to *cancel* a spending item, and Congress's authorizing money to be spent on a particular item at the President's discretion."[32]

Scalia's opinion in *Clinton v. City of New York* stands in sharp contrast to his strenuous criticism of the legislative veto dating back to the 1970s. As assistant attorney general under the Ford administration, Scalia argued before Congress on numerous occasions that the legislative veto violates the presentment clause because congressional resolutions that defeat executive policy circumvent the president's role in the lawmaking process.[33] Although Scalia's contrasting views of the legislative veto and the line-item veto are irreconcilable as a matter of constitutional interpretation, they can be reconciled if one takes into account his Hamiltonian political philosophy. For the Hamiltonian Scalia, legislative vetoes violate the presentment clause because they attempt to negate previously conferred authority on the executive branch; in contrast, the Line Item Veto Act was simply an effort by Congress to confer discretionary tax and spending authority on the president that did not conflict with Article I's requirements for the passage of laws or a broad interpretation of the nondelegation doctrine.

Nondelegation Doctrine

The nondelegation doctrine prohibits core legislative power from being transferred to the executive branch. In 1928 the Supreme Court ruled that Congress did not run afoul of the nondelegation doctrine if it laid down "an intelligible principle to which the person or body authorized to [exercise the delegated authority] is directed to conform."[34] However, the court has not been particularly emphatic in enforcing the doctrine. In the history of the Supreme Court, only two federal laws have been struck down as violations of the nondelegation doctrine,[35] leading some judges and constitutional scholars to wonder whether the doctrine has become "moribund."[36]

Prior to his appointment to the Supreme Court, then-professor Scalia suggested that it might be worth "hewing from the ice" the nondelegation doctrine, "even with all of its Frankenstein-like warts, knobs, and (concededly) dangers."[37] However, he provided two cautionary tales for why the judiciary should not do so. First, he argued that a revitalization of the nondelegation doctrine would conflict with long-standing precedent. Second, he emphasized the difficulties of establishing a judicial standard for determining when a delegation of power becomes too excessive. Without such a clear standard, Scalia worried that it would amount to "an invitation to judicial policy making in the guise of constitutional law." During his confirmation hearings, Scalia reiterated that "it is very difficult for the courts to say how much delegation is too much," and "in most cases, the courts are just going to have to leave that constitutional issue to be resolved by the Congress." "Congress," he reminded the senators, "has a constitutional obligation to follow the Constitution as well."[38]

As a judge, Scalia never strayed from his basic position that it is too difficult to develop a judicial standard in nondelegation cases. In contrast to the formalistic approach he used in other matters related to the separation of powers, Scalia did not support a strict interpretation of the nondelegation doctrine. As he put it in one case, "the doctrine of unconstitutional delegation" is "preeminently *not* a doctrine of technicalities."[39] In *Synar v. United States* (1986),[40] Scalia wrote the decision for the three-judge panel of the DC District Court, which struck down the removal provision of the Balanced Budget and Emergency Deficit Act. Even though it was not necessary for the court's decision, Scalia weighed in on whether the act violated the doctrine of unconstitutional delegation by conferring broad authority on the comptroller general to make budget recommendations to the president. Scalia observed that the act assumes "the continuation of current law in the case of revenues and spending authority" and defines such terms as "real economic growth," "budget outlays," "budget authority," and "deficit." Moreover, Scalia contended that "the required assumptions and definitions are given additional meaning by reference to years of administrative and congressional experience in making similar economic projections and calculations under the Congressional Budget Act of 1974." For these reasons, Scalia held for the three-judge panel that the act did not violate the nondelegation doctrine. Though he admitted that the congressional authority conferred on the comptroller general involved "a good deal of judgment," he insisted that Congress made the "hard political choices."[41]

As a Supreme Court justice, Scalia continued to reject unconstitutional delegation claims. In *Whitman v. American Trucking Associations* (2001),[42] the court upheld the Clean Air Act's conferral of broad authority on the administrator of the Environmental Protection Agency (EPA) to set national ambient air quality standards. In his opinion for the court, Scalia observed that "the scope of discretion [under the act] is in fact well within the outer limits of our nondelegation precedents." He also distinguished the two cases in which the court had found unconstitutional delegation, observing that in those cases Congress had provided virtually no guidance to constrain the policymaking discretion conferred on the executive branch. Scalia then cited many Supreme Court precedents in which broad delegations of power had been challenged but upheld. On this basis, he concluded, "we have 'almost never felt qualified to second-guess Congress regarding the permissible degree of policy judgment that can be left to those executing or applying the law.'"[43]

On the one occasion Scalia did find a violation of the nondelegation doctrine, he had a very specific reason. In *Mistretta v. United States* (1989),[44] the Supreme Court upheld the Sentencing Reform Act of 1984, which created the US Sentencing Commission as an independent body located within the judicial branch. Scalia filed a solo dissent. Like the majority, Scalia maintained that Congress *did* provide an intelligible principle for the commission to develop sentencing guidelines. Nonetheless, he concluded that the law violated the nondelegation doctrine because the commission was placed in the judiciary, where its decisions were not subject to the control of the executive branch.[45] Fully cognizant of the politics of nondelegation cases, Scalia noted that when Congress confers legislative authority, it usually benefits the executive branch. "The need for delegation," he wrote, "would have to be important enough to induce Congress to aggrandize its primary competitor for political power, and the recipient of the policymaking authority, while not Congress itself, would at least be politically accountable."[46]

Other than *Mistretta*-type cases, Scalia viewed the delegation of lawmaking authority to the executive branch as basically a nonjusticiable political question. "While the doctrine of unconstitutional delegation is unquestionably a fundamental element of our constitutional system," Scalia wrote in *Mistretta*, "it is not an element readily enforceable by the courts." "Once it is conceded," he continued, "that no statute can be entirely precise, and that some judgments, even some judgments involving policy considerations, must be left to the officers executing the law and to the judges applying it, the debate over unconstitutional delegation becomes a debate not over a point of principle but over a question of degree."[47]

In congressional testimony in 2011, Scalia reaffirmed his basic position regarding the nondelegation doctrine. When asked by senator Mike Lee (R-UT) if the courts should provide a stricter check on delegations of power to the executive branch, Scalia said that any conferral of authority on a public entity not subject to executive control would violate the nondelegation doctrine. However, if the authority was vested in an administrative agency under the control of the executive branch, Scalia thought the courts should not get involved because there was no principled standard to apply in such cases. "Is it up to the courts to decide where the line is drawn between giving enough authority to the chief executive and too much authority? It is simply a nonjusticiable question, and I, for one, would not let the courts apply the doctrine of unconstitutional delegation where the delegation is to the executive."[48]

Justice Thomas, meanwhile, is a sharp critic of the nondelegation doctrine. Prior to Thomas's appointment to the Supreme Court, only Justice Rehnquist seriously questioned the lenient standard used in nondelegation cases, but he did not continue to do so.[49] From 1991 to 2019 Justice Thomas was the *only* Supreme Court justice to raise any serious concerns about unconstitutional delegations of legislative power. For example, in *Whitman*, Thomas agreed with Scalia's analysis that, based on court precedent, the EPA could establish national ambient air quality standards. The "directive to the [EPA] is no less an 'intelligible principle' than a host of other directives that we have approved," Thomas wrote. In contrast to the majority, however, Thomas raised concerns about the intelligible principle itself. "I believe," he wrote, "that there are cases in which the principle is intelligible and yet the significance of the delegated decision is simply too great for the decision to be called anything other than 'legislative.'" Although the parties to the case did not ask the court to reconsider its precedents on the subject, Thomas observed that he would be willing to reconsider in a future case "whether our delegation jurisprudence has strayed too far from our Founders' understanding of separation of powers."[50]

That opportunity came in *Department of Transportation v. Association of American Railroads* (2015),[51] when the Supreme Court narrowly held that Amtrak is a governmental entity for purposes of determining the "metrics and standards" under the Passenger Rail Investment and Improvement Act (PRIIA). In an opinion by Justice Kennedy, which was joined by Scalia, the court ruled that Amtrak "was created by the government, is controlled by the government, and operates for the government's benefit."[52] In a long concurring opinion, Justice Thomas agreed with the majority that Amtrak is a governmental entity and that the court of appeals should have the first opportunity to tackle the legal issues raised in the case. However, he wanted to give more guidance to that court. Beginning with first principles, Thomas argued that the only institution that can formulate rules for private conduct is Congress. Because the PRIIA attempted to transfer that authority to Amtrak, Thomas argued that it constituted an unconstitutional delegation of authority and violated Article I of the Constitution, which confers "all legislative" powers on Congress. Thomas criticized the court for "largely abdicat[ing]" its judicial responsibility to enforce the boundary between the legislative and executive branches of government. "Although the Court may never have intended the boundless standard the 'intelligible principle' test has become," Thomas wrote, "it is evident that it does not adequately reinforce the Constitution's allocation of legislative power." Accordingly, he called for a "return to the original understanding of the federal legislative power," which would "require that the Federal Government create generally applicable rules of private conduct only through the constitutionally prescribed legislative process." The harm of the court's malleable and deferential test, Thomas maintained, is that "we have overseen and sanctioned the growth of an administrative system that concentrates the power to make laws and the power to enforce them in the hands of a vast and unaccountable administrative apparatus that finds no comfortable home in our constitutional structure."[53] Thomas concluded that it was imperative for the Supreme Court to fulfill its constitutional obligation and predicted that failure to do so will result in the loss of individual liberty that the Constitution protects.

In 2017 Neil Gorsuch was appointed to the Supreme Court, filling the vacancy left by the death of Justice Scalia. He soon made it apparent that, like Thomas, he was willing to reexamine the court's nondelegation jurisprudence. In *Gundy v. United States* (2019),[54] the court upheld the delegation of power to the attorney general to apply the requirements of the Sex Offender Registration and Notification Act (SORNA) to offenders convicted before its enactment. Herman Gundy, who was convicted of a sex crime in 2006 (pre-SORNA), argued that the discretion granted to the attorney general violated the nondelegation doctrine. In a 5–3 decision, the Supreme Court ruled against him. Justice Kagan, writing for the court, called the question an "easy" one and held that the delegation authority granted under SORNA was well within the scope of previous delegations upheld by the court. She also argued that acceptance of Gundy's position would mean that "most of Government is unconstitutional—dependent as Congress is on the need to give discretion to executive officials to implement its programs."[55]

Justice Gorsuch filed a vigorous dissent that was joined by Justice Thomas and Chief Justice Roberts. He argued that the intelligible principle is not rooted in the original meaning of the Constitution and does not provide "sufficiently definite and precise" standards to determine whether Congress's guidance has been followed. He thus called for the court to reexamine the intelligible principle. "If the separation of powers means anything," Gorsuch wrote, "it must mean that Congress cannot give the executive branch a blank check to write a code of conduct governing private conduct for a half-million people."[56]

In 2020 President Trump appointed judge Amy Coney Barrett—a self-described originalist and former law clerk to Justice Scalia—to the Supreme Court. Depending on what the conservative justices want to do, they are well poised to reexamine the intelligible principle. Justice Alito concurred in *Gundy* but also indicated that he would be willing to reconsider the court's jurisprudence in a future case. Justice Kavanaugh, appointed to the Supreme Court in 2018, did not participate in *Gundy*. However, in a subsequent case, Kavanaugh praised Gorsuch's opinion and expressed a willingness to reconsider the court's nondelegation doctrine, particularly in cases in which Congress has delegated authority to an agency both to decide a major policy question and to regulate and enforce it.[57] In this area of constitutional law, Scalia's absence (and Hamiltonian instincts) could very well make a difference. During his time on the court, Justice Black either joined or wrote several opinions that supported a broad interpretation of the nondelegation doctrine.[58]

Chevron *Deference*

In *Chevron U.S.A. Inc. v. Natural Resources Defense Council* (1984),[59] the Supreme Court devised a two-pronged test to determine the proper scope of judicial review of agency constructions of law. According to *Chevron*'s first prong, a reviewing court must determine whether Congress has "directly spoken" on the underlying issue being regulated. If so, the court "must give effect to the unambiguously expressed intent of Congress." But "if the statute is silent or ambiguous with respect to the specific issue," *Chevron*'s second prong requires a reviewing court to respect the agency's construction of the statute if it is reasonable or permissible.[60] As a former administrative law professor, Justice Scalia was a tremendous defender of *Chevron*, referring to it as the most important decision in the area of administrative law since *Vermont Yankee* (1978).[61]

In a 1989 speech at Duke University, Scalia discussed several possible rationales for *Chevron* deference. Interestingly, he rejected a defense of *Chevron* based on separation of powers principles. Instead, Scalia's support of *Chevron* was based on practical realities and the presumed or actual intent of Congress. "Congress," Scalia remarked, "now knows that the ambiguities it creates, whether intentionally or unintentionally, will be resolved, within the bounds of permissible interpretations, not by the courts but by a particular agency, whose policy biases will ordinarily be known."[62] In fact, Scalia defended "an across-the-board presumption" of deference rather than the "statute-by-statute" evaluation that preceded *Chevron*. During his time on the Supreme Court, Scalia strongly defended *Chevron*. In *INS v. Cardoza-Fonseca* (1987),[63] he criticized the majority opinion authored by Justice Stevens—who wrote *Chevron*!—for misapplying the two-part test and suggesting that the court could substitute its own judgment for that of the agency whenever it was able to determine the proper interpretation of a statute. Scalia maintained that such an "approach would make deference a doctrine of desperation, authorizing courts to defer only if they would otherwise be unable to construe the enactment at issue." "This," according to Scalia, "is not an interpretation but an evisceration of *Chevron*."[64]

Justice Scalia also defended expansive interpretations of *Chevron* deference. In *United States v. Mead Corp.* (2001),[65] the Supreme Court devised a new test for judicial review of agency interpretations of law. Instead of giving deference to informal agency constructions of law such as policy statements, opinion letters, manuals, enforcement guidelines, and court briefs, the court held that judicial deference applies only to notice-and-comment rule making and formal adjudications—that is, agency decisions that have the "force of law."[66] Dissenting alone, Scalia argued that the court's adaptation of *Chevron* deference contradicted precedent and was wrong in principle. He argued that both formal and *informal* agency decisions should receive deference from the courts. In addition to referring to the court's reasoning as "quite absurd" and "mak[ing] no sense," Scalia described the new test as "irresponsible." *Mead*, Scalia claimed, will result in "an avulsive change in judicial review of federal administrative action," and he predicted that "its consequences will be enormous, and almost uniformly bad."[67]

Scalia also wrote the court's decision in *City of Arlington v. Federal Communications Commission* (2013),[68] which expanded *Chevron* deference to include the scope of an agency's regulatory authority. Referring to the "now-canonical" two-part test of *Chevron*, Scalia could find no reason why courts should not defer to agency interpretations of their own jurisdiction. "The false dichotomy between 'jurisdictional' and 'nonjurisdictional' agency interpretations," wrote Scalia, "may be no more than a bogeyman, but it is dangerous all the same." "Like the Hound of the Baskervilles," he continued, "it is conjured by those with greater quarry in sight." "Make no mistake," Scalia warned, "the ultimate target here is *Chevron* itself."[69] In response to Chief Justice Roberts's dissent, which raised concerns about the growth of agency power, Scalia acknowledged that agencies make rules and conduct adjudications. "These activities," he observed, "take 'legislative' and 'judicial' forms, but they are exercises of—indeed, under our constitutional structure they *must be* exercises of—the 'executive Power.'"[70]

Justice Scalia did reconsider one aspect of *Chevron* deference toward the end of his judicial tenure. Beginning with a 2011 case, Scalia said it might be time to reconsider *Auer* deference. In *Auer v. Robbins* (1997),[71] a decision Scalia authored himself, the Supreme Court ruled unanimously that *Chevron* deference should apply to an agency's reinterpretation of its own rules and regulatory schemes. At the time, Scalia believed this was a logical corollary to *Chevron* deference. Following that decision, Scalia applied *Auer* deference in other cases, most notably in a dissenting opinion in *Gonzales v. Oregon* (2006),[72] where the court ruled that the attorney general had overstepped his authority in attempting to prohibit doctors from prescribing federally regulated drugs for use in physician-assisted suicide. At the same time, Scalia became frustrated with agencies enacting "vague rules" that then gave them "the power, in future adjudications, to do what [they] please."[73] He ultimately regarded this as a separation of powers issue—that is, the power to make rules (a legislative function) had been combined with the power to interpret rules (a judicial function). He also believed it was a way to get around the Administrative Procedure Act's notice and comment requirement. In a 2013 case, Scalia declared: "Enough is enough."[74] Then, in a 2015 case, he voted to abandon *Auer* altogether. "The agency," Scalia wrote, "is free to interpret its own regulations with or without notice and comment; but courts will decide—with no deference to the agency—whether that interpretation is correct."[75]

However, Justice Scalia's concerns about *Auer* deference did not mean that he changed his mind about *Chevron* deference in general. The same year he called for *Auer* deference to be reconsidered, he wrote the court's decision expanding *Chevron* deference to include questions about an agency's jurisdiction. During his last full term on the Supreme Court, when he called for *Auer* to be overturned, he wrote the decision in *Michigan v. EPA* (2015),[76] where the court ruled that the EPA's interpretation of the Clean Air Act was unreasonable based on the two-pronged *Chevron* approach. Importantly, that decision was handed down three and a half months *after* Scalia called for the overturning of *Auer.*[77] And, of course, one cannot overlook the politics of *Chevron* deference. If one accepts the reality of the modern administrative state, which Justice Scalia certainly did,[78] then *Chevron* deference was an important way to ensure a policymaking role for the executive branch. "If Congress is to delegate broadly, as modern times are thought to demand," Scalia wrote in 1989, "it seems to me desirable that the delegee be able to suit its actions to the times, and that continuing political accountability be assured, through direct political pressures upon the Executive and through the indirect political pressure of congressional oversight." "All this is lost," he added, "if 'new' or 'changing' agency interpretations are somehow suspect."[79] Scalia would have preferred Republican administrations to be the ones making the necessary policy adjustments,[80] but he was willing to live with some results he disagreed with.[81] At the end of the day, Scalia believed the executive branch (as opposed to the courts) should be making those policy decisions based on "new information or even new social attitudes impressed upon it through the political process."[82]

Meanwhile, Justice Thomas has called for a reexamination of *Chevron* deference entirely. In a 1991 speech at Creighton University, then-judge Thomas suggested that the courts should defer to administrative agencies only if there is a clear delegation of power. "Without finding such a delegation from Congress," he stated, "one wonders whose intent the agency is really interpreting."[83]

Interestingly, Thomas referred to Scalia's speech at Duke University and called his defense of *Chevron* "circular" because "whenever there is ambiguity, delegation of authority to the agency might be assumed."[84] During the twenty-five years Scalia and Thomas served together on the Supreme Court, they agreed in a number of *Chevron* cases,[85] but they did not agree in all of them. For example, Thomas did not join Scalia's dissent in *Mead*, where the court limited *Chevron* deference to formal rule making and adjudication. In a 2005 case, Scalia agreed with the court that disparate impact suits could be pursued under the Age Discrimination in Employment Act (ADEA); however, his analysis differed from the plurality's because he relied exclusively on *Chevron*. Calling this "an absolutely classic case for deference to agency interpretation," Scalia cited an Equal Employment Opportunity Commission (EEOC) regulation that interpreted the ADEA to allow disparate impact claims. By contrast, Justice Thomas joined Justice O'Connor's concurring opinion, which argued that disparate impact suits were not cognizable under the ADEA.[86]

That same year, the two justices were on the opposite sides in a case asking whether *Chevron* deference should apply when a court has already provided an interpretation of a statute. In *National Cable & Telecommunications Association v. Brand X Internet Services* (2005),[87] Thomas, writing for the court, ruled that an earlier court interpretation trumped *Chevron* deference only when its construction followed from the unambiguous terms of the statute and left no room for agency discretion. Justice Scalia filed a vigorous dissent, arguing that *Chevron* deference should not apply in such cases because it would "make judicial decisions subject to reversal by executive officers."[88]

Nonetheless, the fundamental difference between these two justices involved *Chevron* itself. In *Michigan v. EPA*, Scalia authored the court's decision holding that *Chevron* deference did not apply because the EPA refused to consider the cost of regulating power plant emissions under the Clean Air Act. Thomas wrote a separate concurrence in which he criticized *Chevron* itself. According to Thomas, *Chevron* violated separation of powers principles and conflicted with the federal judiciary's authority to exercise judicial review. Written just a few months after his criticism of the intelligible principle in nondelegation cases,[89] Thomas reasoned that the court's ongoing use of *Chevron* deference provided little protection against the growth of the administrative state. "As in other areas of our jurisprudence concerning administrative agencies," Thomas wrote, "we seem to be straying further and further from the Constitution without so much as pausing to ask why." "We should stop to consider that document," he added, "before blithely giving the force of law to any other agency 'interpretations' of federal statutes."[90]

Thomas continued his attack on *Chevron* deference in *Baldwin v. United States* (2020), where he wrote a dissent from denial of certiorari asking the Court to reconsider his own opinion in *Brand X*.[91] "*Brand X*," Thomas wrote, "gives agencies the power to effectively overrule judicial precedents" and therefore should be revisited. More important, Thomas asked his colleagues to reexamine *Chevron* itself. "My skepticism of *Brand X*," wrote Thomas, "begins at its foundation—*Chevron* deference." "In 1984," he noted, "a bare quorum of six Justices decided *Chevron*," and that decision "rests on the fiction that silent or ambiguous statutes are an implicit delegation from Congress to agencies." "*Chevron* is in serious tension with the Constitution, the [Administrative Procedure Act], and over 100 years of judicial decisions," Thomas concluded.[92]

Once again, Scalia's absence could lead to significant changes in another important area of administrative law—this time involving *Chevron* deference. In *Kisor v. Wilkie* (2019), the Supreme Court came one vote shy of overturning *Auer* deference, and Justice Gorsuch wrote a concurring opinion (joined by Justices Thomas, Alito, and Kavanaugh) calling for *Auer* to be overturned.[93] As an appeals court judge, Gorsuch authored a scathing critique of *Chevron*, calling it inconsistent with the Administrative Procedure Act and separation of powers. "None of this is to suggest that *Chevron* is 'the very definition of tyranny,'" wrote Gorsuch. "But on any account it certainly seems to have added prodigious new powers to an already titanic administrative state."[94] It will be interesting to see whether Thomas and Gorsuch can convince some of their conservative colleagues to take a second look at *Chevron* itself.

FEDERALISM

In the area of federalism, there were important differences in the originalist philosophies of Justices Scalia and Thomas, but they were muted because the two justices often voted the same way. Both justices provided critical votes in the so-called federalism revolution of the mid-1990s. During that period, a five-justice conservative bloc on the Rehnquist Court limited Congress's authority to regulate commerce and expanded state sovereign immunity under the Eleventh Amendment.[95] Justices Scalia and Thomas also shared the same view of the court's "negative" commerce clause jurisprudence, although Thomas wanted to go a step further and abandon the doctrine altogether.[96] Besides these important areas of agreement, there were fundamental differences in how these two justices viewed federal-state relations.

Justice Thomas has defended a strict constructionist interpretation of congressional powers, arguing that the original meaning of "commerce" was the "buying," "selling," and "transportation" of goods, but not how they were produced.[97] Justice Scalia flatly rejected such an approach. Textualism, Scalia observed, is not the same thing as strict constructionism, which he called "a degraded form of textualism that brings the whole philosophy into disrepute." "I am not a strict constructionist," he added, "and no one ought to be—though better that, I suppose, than a nontextualist."[98] For this reason, Scalia never joined any of Thomas's opinions that called on the court to reexamine the "substantial effects" test.

These two different interpretations of interstate commerce came to a head in *Gonzales v. Raich* (2005).[99] In that case, the Supreme Court considered whether the Controlled Substances Act of 1970 (CSA), which regulates the manufacture, importation, possession, use, and distribution of illicit drugs, applied to the use of homegrown marijuana for medicinal purposes. In 1996 California passed the Compassionate Use Act, which legalized the use of marijuana by "seriously ill" residents. Diane Monson had been prescribed medicinal marijuana under the state law, but federal agents seized and destroyed six of her marijuana plants. Monson, joined by Angel Raich,[100] sought a declaratory judgment that applying the CSA to locally cultivated and prescribed marijuana exceeded Congress's commerce authority.

In a 6–3 decision, the Supreme Court held that the CSA could be applied to locally grown marijuana. In an opinion by Justice Stevens, the court placed considerable reliance on *Wickard v. Filburn* (1942),[101] in which the justices upheld a fine imposed on a small farmer for exceeding his wheat quota under the Agricultural Adjustment Act of 1938.[102] Justice Jackson, for the court, devised the cumulative effect test. Even if economic incentives did not compel a farmer to introduce his wheat into the free market, Jackson reasoned, the use of homegrown wheat reduced the demand for that product in the market. And although the loss of one farmer's demand for wheat might not be considered substantial, Jackson maintained that the cumulative effect of other farmers doing the same thing could substantially affect the market price of wheat.

Applying *Wickard*'s analysis to the facts in *Raich*, Justice Stevens argued that an exemption for marijuana grown and used locally for medical purposes could substantially affect the supply of and demand for marijuana in the illegal drug market. "The likelihood that all [marijuana] production will promptly terminate when patients recover or will precisely match the patients' medical needs during their convalescence seems remote," observed Stevens. And the high demand for marijuana in the interstate market, despite vigorous law enforcement efforts to ban such drug transactions entirely, will lead "no small number of unscrupulous people [to] make use of the California exemption to serve their own ends whenever it is feasible to do so."[103]

Demonstrating his Hamiltonian instincts, Justice Scalia joined the court's decision but wrote a separate opinion. Wanting to take a "more nuanced" approach, Scalia argued that Congress could regulate intrastate noneconomic activities that do not substantially affect interstate commerce if they are part of a comprehensive effort by Congress to regulate interstate commerce. In reaching this conclusion, Scalia relied on the necessary and proper clause, which gives Congress the necessary and proper authority to execute its laws.[104] The CSA, according to Scalia, was a comprehensive effort to "extinguish" the interstate commerce of controlled substances, including the mere possession of drugs, and Congress had the necessary and proper authority to enforce that goal. Scalia also agreed with the court that homegrown marijuana "is never more than an instant from the interstate market." "Not only is it impossible to distinguish 'controlled substances manufactured and distributed intrastate' from 'controlled substances manufactured and distributed interstate,'" Scalia maintained, "but it hardly makes sense to speak in such terms." "Drugs like marijuana are fungible commodities," he wrote.[105] Scalia also distinguished recent decisions in which the court restricted the scope of Congress's commerce authority.[106] In those cases, he reasoned, efforts to regulate noneconomic intrastate activity were *not* part of a comprehensive plan to regulate interstate commerce.

Justice Thomas dissented. He disputed the conclusion that homegrown marijuana had anything to do with interstate commerce. "If the activity is purely intrastate," Thomas wrote, "then it may not be regulated under the Commerce Clause. And if the regulation of the intrastate activity is purely incidental, then it may not be regulated under the Necessary and Proper Clause." Thomas viewed the Compassionate Use Act as part of the state's authority to regulate the health and welfare of its citizens. "The majority prevents States like California," he wrote, "from devising drug policies that they have concluded provide much-needed respite to the seriously ill." "It does so," he added, "without any serious inquiry into the necessity for federal regulation or the propriety of 'displac[ing] state regulation in areas of traditional state concern.'" Thomas also took the opportunity to criticize once again the substantial effects test. Congress did not provide sufficient evidence to support its regulation, Thomas contended. "If Congress can regulate this [sort of activity] under the Commerce Clause," he wrote, "it can regulate virtually anything—and the Federal Government is no longer one of limited and enumerated powers."[107]

In addition to the commerce clause, Justices Scalia and Thomas held different interpretations of the general welfare clause,[108] the Indian commerce clause,[109] and (as just suggested) the necessary and proper clause.[110]

Tenth Amendment

Justice Thomas views the Tenth Amendment as an important source of authority for the states. In several cases, he claimed the Tenth Amendment reflects the fundamental principle that "the States can exercise all powers that the Constitution does not withhold from them."[111] By contrast, Justice Scalia viewed the Tenth Amendment as a constitutional redundancy.[112] "The Tenth Amendment does not mean anything," Scalia said in 1996. "What limits the national government's powers are the enumerated powers."[113] One case that illustrates these important differences is *Printz v. United States* (1997).[114] In that case, the Supreme Court ruled that the Brady Handgun Violence Prevention Act of 1993 (the so-called Brady bill) violated basic principles of federalism. Under the act's interim provisions, local law enforcement officials were required to conduct a background check within five days of a request to purchase a gun to determine whether the potential purchaser was among a class of individuals prohibited from buying a gun. In a 5–4 decision, the court struck down the law because the *means* chosen by Congress constituted an unlawful attempt to "conscript" state officials into administering or enforcing a federal regulatory program.

Justice Scalia authored the court's decision and made essentially a structural argument. He argued that the law conflicted with various constitutional provisions, including Article IV, section 3, which prohibits "any involuntary reduction or combination of a State's territory"; Article III, section 2, which contains the judicial power provision; Article IV, section 2, which contains the privileges or immunities clause; Article V, which explains the process for amending the Constitution; and Article IV, section 4, which contains the guarantee clause.[115] These provisions, according to Scalia, confirm the federal nature of the US Constitution. He also noted that the enumeration of powers in the Constitution suggests (at least implicitly) that the states have "a residuary and inviolable sovereignty."[116] Last (and undoubtedly by design), Scalia addressed the Tenth Amendment. "Residual state sovereignty," he wrote, "was also implicit, of course, in the Constitution's conferral upon Congress of not all governmental powers, but only discrete, enumerated ones, which implication was rendered express by the Tenth Amendment's assertion that 'the powers not delegated to the United States by the Constitution, nor prohibited by it to the States, are reserved to the States respectively, or to the people.'" Interestingly, Scalia even admitted—albeit in an ambiguous way—that the Tenth Amendment does not pose an affirmative limit on congressional authority.[117]

The short shrift given to the Tenth Amendment did not go unnoticed by Scalia's more ardent states' rights colleagues. Justice O'Connor wrote a short concurring opinion in which she argued that the Brady bill violated the Tenth Amendment "to the extent it forces States and local law enforcement officers to perform background checks on prospective handgun owners and to accept Brady Forms from firearms dealers."[118] Justice Thomas also wrote a separate opinion. "The Court today properly holds," he wrote, "that the Brady Bill violates the Tenth Amendment in that it compels state law enforcement officers to 'administer or enforce a federal regulatory program.'" In contrast to Scalia, however, Thomas stressed that Congress's authority to regulate commerce is more limited. "The Tenth Amendment affirms," wrote Thomas, "the undeniable notion that under our Constitution, the Federal Government is one of enumerated, hence limited, powers." Thomas described the activity regulated by the Brady bill as "wholly *intra*state, point-of-sale transactions," which lay outside Congress's authority to regulate interstate commerce. He thus urged his colleagues to "return to an interpretation better rooted in the Clause's original understanding" by reexamining the "substantial effects" test.[119]

Preemption

In contrast to Tenth Amendment cases, where the central question is whether Congress has the *constitutional* authority to regulate a particular activity, preemption asks whether Congress intended (either expressly or implicitly) to regulate an area of traditional state concern. In other words, preemption cases are matters of *statutory* interpretation. If a state law conflicts with federal law, the Supreme Court has held that it must yield under the supremacy clause. Justice Scalia was a strong supporter of federal preemption, particularly in cases involving product liability. During his tenure, he had one of the highest voting percentages among his colleagues (both liberal and conservative) in support of federal preemption.[120] Justice Thomas, by contrast, has one of the lowest voting percentages among his conservative colleagues.[121]

One area that illustrates the two justices' different perspectives involves the Supreme Court's "obstacle" preemption jurisprudence. According to this doctrine, even in the absence of a direct conflict between federal and state law, a state law can be regarded as an obstacle to the accomplishment of a federal objective. This implied preemption doctrine requires courts to discern Congress's objectives or purposes in passing a statute. In several cases, Thomas has argued that he will no longer follow the obstacle preemption doctrine because it gives the court too much discretion to determine the objectives of federal law.

Passive Restraints

In *Geier v. American Honda Motor Company* (2000),[122] the Supreme Court ruled that the 1984 version of Federal Motor Vehicle Safety Standard 208 (FMVSS 208), as promulgated by the Department of Transportation (DOT), *impliedly* preempted state common-law suits against car manufacturers for failing to install airbags as passive-restraint devices. The National Traffic and Motor Vehicle Safety Act of 1966 (NTMVSA) was intended to "reduce traffic accidents and deaths and injuries to persons resulting from traffic accidents."[123] It delegated the power to create federal motor vehicle safety standards to the DOT. Specifically, Congress authorized the DOT to provide "minimum" safety standards for all automobiles sold in the United States.[124] In July 1984, then–secretary of transportation Elizabeth Dole adopted a gradual phase-in of passive restraints (FMVSS 208). Under this plan, vehicle manufacturers were required to equip a minimum of 10 percent of their new passenger cars with passive restraints by 1987. That percentage would grow in three stages until September 1989, when 100 percent of all new cars had to be equipped with such devices.[125]

In 1992 Alexis Geier was seriously injured when the 1987 Honda Accord she was driving collided with a tree. The car was equipped with manual shoulder and lap belts, which Geier had buckled at the time of the accident. However, the car was not equipped with airbags or other passive restraints.

American Honda Motor Company (Honda) had complied with the DOT's minimum standard—that is, 10 percent of its vehicles manufactured in 1987 were equipped with passive restraints—but Geier and her parents brought suit under District of Columbia tort law, alleging that Honda was negligent in not equipping her car with a driver's-side airbag.

In an opinion by Justice Breyer that Justice Scalia joined, the Supreme Court held that Geier's common-law action was preempted by the NTMVSA and FMVSS 208. According to Breyer, although the NTMVSA did not expressly preempt common-law actions, it (along with FMVSS 208) impliedly did. "No–air bag" lawsuits, Breyer reasoned, would frustrate the overall purpose of FMVSS 208 by penalizing automobile manufacturers for not doing something they were not required to do. What made the court's ruling particularly noteworthy is that the NTMVSA contained a saving clause explicitly exempting common-law actions from the act's preemption provision.

Justice Thomas joined Justice Stevens's dissent, which accused the majority of judicial legislation. In other cases in which the court found that common-law actions were superseded by broad preemptive language, Stevens argued that the statute did not include a saving clause. The saving clause here explicitly exempted common-law liability from the scope of the preemption provision. As a result, he argued, the text of the statute itself established that the NTMVSA did not intend to expressly preempt common-law tort claims. Justice Stevens also criticized the court's implied preemption analysis. For support of its "obstacle" preemption argument, Honda relied on various forms of administrative intent, such as the DOT's litigation strategy involving FMVSS 208, the history of passive-restraint regulation generally, and the DOT's commentary on the final version of the federal safety standard. Justice Stevens argued that these sources were not sufficient to overcome the presumption against preemption when a statute contains a saving clause. In contrast to cases involving federal laws or administrative regulations, where the court has previously applied conflict obstacle analysis, administrative intent is not subject to the formal rules and procedures of the democratic process, Stevens maintained. On this basis, he (along with Thomas) rejected the court's reliance on conflict obstacle preemption analysis.

Failure to Warn

Justices Scalia and Thomas were also on opposite sides in a 2009 case involving the court's obstacle preemption jurisprudence. Diana Levine's left arm had to be amputated because Phenergan, a drug manufactured by Wyeth, had allegedly been administered negligently, causing gangrene. Her injury resulted from an intravenous (IV)-push injection of Phenergan, which she received to treat migraine headaches. Even though the drug's labeling warned of the danger of gangrene and amputation following inadvertent intra-arterial injection, Levine alleged that the labeling was defective because it failed to instruct clinicians to use the safer IV-drip method of administration. Wyeth countered that Levine's failure-to-warn claims were preempted by federal law. In particular, Wyeth argued that requiring it to comply with a state law mandating a stronger warning about IV-push administration would obstruct the purposes and objectives of federal drug labeling regulations, since it would interfere with "Congress's purpose to entrust an expert agency to make drug labeling decisions that strike a balance between competing objectives."[126] A Vermont jury found that Wyeth had failed to provide adequate warning of the risk and awarded Levine damages in the amount of $7.4 million. In *Wyeth v. Levine* (2009),[127] the Supreme Court upheld the award. In an opinion by Justice Stevens, the court distinguished its earlier decision in *Geier*. In that case, the DOT had conducted formal rule making and then adopted a plan to phase in various passive-restraint devices. But here, Stevens pointed out, there was no specific agency regulation bearing the force of law. He also discounted the Food and Drug Administration's (FDA's) "newfound opinion" expressed in 2006 "that state law 'frustrated the agency's implementation of its statutory mandate,'" because that opinion was inconsistent with earlier views expressed by the FDA.[128]

Justice Thomas wrote a separate concurring opinion in which he observed that he had "become increasingly skeptical of this Court's 'purposes and objectives' pre-emption jurisprudence."[129] Discussing *Hines v. Davidowitz* (1941),[130] a decision authored by Justice Black that originated the doctrine,[131] Thomas remarked that "the Court looked far beyond the relevant federal statutory text and instead embarked on its own freeranging speculation about what the purposes of the federal law must have been."[132] Thomas took particular exception to the court's decision in *Geier*. The decision "to apply 'purposes and objectives' pre-emption based on agency comments, regulatory history, and agency litigating positions was especially flawed," he wrote, "given that it conflicted with the plain statutory text of the saving clause within the Safety Act."[133] For this reason, Thomas concluded that he would "no longer assent to a doctrine that pre-empts state laws merely because they 'stan[d] as an obstacle to the accomplishment and execution of the full purposes and objectives' of federal law . . . as perceived by this Court."[134] In stark contrast, Scalia joined Justice Alito's dissent in *Wyeth*, which argued that Levine's common-law action was preempted because Wyeth had complied with the required warning labels. "Neither the [Federal Food, Drug, and Cosmetic Act] nor its implementing regulations," Alito wrote, "suggest that juries may second-guess the FDA's labeling decisions."[135]

Voting Rights

Justices Scalia and Thomas also reached different outcomes in a preemption case involving voting rights. In 2004 Arizonans passed a constitutional initiative requiring county recorders to reject any voter registration application that was not accompanied by satisfactory evidence of US citizenship. This state law was challenged under the National Voter Registration Act of 1993 (NVRA), which requires states to "accept and use" a uniform federal form to register voters for federal elections. The federal form required applicants to attest, under penalty of perjury, that they are citizens, but it did not require concrete evidence of citizenship.

In *Arizona v. The Inter Tribal Council of Arizona* (2013),[136] the Roberts Court held that the state law was preempted by the federal law. In an opinion by Justice Scalia, the court held that because Arizona could reject an application that did not include proof of citizenship, it conflicted with federal policy. Scalia also disagreed with the state's argument that the presumption against preemption should apply in this case. Unlike other cases that have followed this doctrine, Scalia argued that the elections clause (Article I, section 4) contains its own preemption provision. Congress, he argued, has the authority "to make or alter" state election regulations.[137] "Because the power the Elections Clause confers is none other than the power to pre-empt," wrote Scalia, "the reasonable assumption is that the statutory text accurately communicates the scope of Congress's pre-emptive intent." Scalia also regarded the federalism concerns as "somewhat weaker" in cases involving the elections clause. "Unlike the States' 'historic police powers,'" he wrote, "the States' role in regulating congressional elections—while weighty and worthy of respect—has always existed subject to the express qualification that it 'terminates according to federal law.'"[138]

Justice Thomas dissented. He argued that a reasonable interpretation of the federal "accept and use" requirement is that a state has to use the federal form as part of its voter registration process, but it does not preclude a state from requiring additional information "to ensure that voters meet the qualifications it has constitutional authority to establish."[139] More fundamentally, Thomas maintained that the case raises serious constitutional issues because it implicates the states' "exclusive" authority to establish qualifications for voters in federal elections under the voter qualifications clause (Article I, section 2, clause 1).[140] Thomas interpreted Congress's authority under the elections clause (to make or alter "the Times, Places and Manner of holding Elections for Senators and Representatives") as much narrower in scope than the states' authority to establish qualifications for voters in federal elections. In fact, he questioned Supreme Court precedents (as well as the majority's conclusion) that Congress has *any* constitutional authority to regulate voter qualifications, including registration requirements. Because the states possess exclusive authority to set voter qualifications, Thomas argued that they must be able to verify that those requirements have been satisfied. Since Arizona did not challenge the constitutionality of the NVRA, Thomas simply rejected the court's holding that the "accept and use" provision requires states to register anyone who completes and submits the form. "It matters not," Thomas wrote, "whether the United States has specified one way in which *it* believes Arizona might be able to verify citizenship." "Arizona," he argued, "has the independent constitutional authority to verify citizenship in the way it deems necessary." "By requiring Arizona to register people who have not demonstrated to Arizona's satisfaction that they meet its citizenship qualification for voting," Thomas added, "the NVRA, as interpreted by the Court, would exceed Congress' powers under Article I, §4, and violate Article I, §2."[141]

FREE SPEECH

During their time together on the Supreme Court, Justices Scalia and Thomas defended a robust view of political speech, particularly as it relates to the regulation of offensive speech. Justice Scalia wrote the court's decision in *R.A.V. v. City of St. Paul* (1992),[142] which held that a city's ban on symbols that cause "anger, alarm or resentment in others on the basis of race, color, creed, religion or gender" violated the First Amendment. In that case, Scalia used a novel "underinclusive" argument and criticized the city for trying to regulate only certain types of fighting words. "St. Paul," he argued, "has no authority to license one side of a debate to fight freestyle, while requiring the other to follow Marquis of Queensberry Rules."[143] Similarly, Justice Thomas has been critical of political correctness, or what he refers to as the "herd mentality."[144] In a 1993 speech he criticized what he called the "New Intolerance." "In the name of fostering tolerance, sensitivity, or a sense of community," the new intolerance provides justification "to intimidate and silence those who dare to question popular political, social, or economic fads."[145] In addition to laws relating to hate speech, Scalia and Thomas sought to apply strict scrutiny to the regulation of protests at abortion clinics.[146]

Obscenity

Despite their agreement in several areas of First Amendment law,[147] Justices Scalia and Thomas reached different conclusions in other areas. One broad area of disagreement was whether the pandering of pornography could be banned, even if the material in question was not regarded as obscene. Relying on *Ginzburg v. United States* (1966),[148] Scalia argued that "sexually-oriented" businesses could be banned altogether. "Our jurisprudence supports," Scalia wrote in a 1990 case, "the proposition that even though a particular work of pornography is not obscene under *Miller* [*v. California* (1973)], a merchant who concentrates upon the sale of such works is engaged in the business of obscenity, which may be entirely prohibited and hence (a fortiori) licensed as required here."[149] Interestingly, Justice Thomas did not join any opinion in which Scalia made that argument,[150] perhaps because it conflicted with his own view that the advertisement of lawful commercial material should receive the court's highest level of scrutiny under the First Amendment. It should be noted that Justice Black dissented in *Ginzburg*.[151]

In two other obscenity cases, Scalia and Thomas arrived at different conclusions. In *Ashcroft v. Free Speech Coalition* (2002),[152] the Supreme Court struck down two provisions of the Child Pornography Prevention Act of 1996, one of which banned the possession and distribution of "any visual depiction" that "is, or appears to be, of a minor engaging in sexually explicit conduct." In an opinion by Justice Kennedy, the court ruled that the provision violated the First Amendment because the prohibited depictions could be of youthful-looking adults or computer-generated images of children. On this basis, Kennedy found the law to be overly broad because it could be interpreted to ban literary or artistic works such as *Romeo and Juliet*, *Traffic*, or *American Beauty*.

Justice Thomas filed an opinion concurring in the judgment. He raised concerns that the government might be unable to prosecute cases involving child pornography using real children because the defendant could argue that the images were computer generated. Thomas thought an affirmative defense might be a good way to narrowly tailor the law. Nonetheless, because he did not want to prejudge whether that was the only way to narrowly construe the law, he supported the court's holding. Meanwhile, Justice Scalia joined the dissenting opinions authored by Justices O'Connor and Rehnquist, both of whom argued that the provision should be construed to cover its basic aims without completely overturning it.

Two years later, Justice Thomas joined the court's decision in *Ashcroft v. American Civil Liberties Union* (2004),[153] which struck down the Child Online Protection Act of 1998. That law attempted to protect minors from exposure to sexually explicit materials over the internet by banning the posting, for "commercial purposes," of material "harmful to minors." In another opinion by Justice Kennedy, the court applied strict scrutiny and ruled that Congress had not used the least restrictive means of limiting minors' access of such materials, including by encouraging the use of blocking or filtering technology. Justice Scalia dissented and was the only justice to argue that strict scrutiny should *not* apply to the subject matter covered by the law. Based on these decisions, a strong case can be made that Scalia was more deferential to governmental regulation of obscenity than Justice Thomas.

Anonymous Speech

Justices Scalia and Thomas also reached different conclusions about whether anonymous speech is protected under the First Amendment. Margaret McIntyre was fined $100 under an Ohio election law for distributing leaflets in opposition to a proposed school tax levy. Some of the leaflets were unsigned, but they contained nothing that was false, misleading, or libelous. McIntyre had been warned that the unsigned leaflets violated state law, but she went ahead and distributed them anyway. In *McIntyre v. Ohio Elections Commission* (1995),[154] the Supreme Court upheld a citizen's right to engage in anonymous campaign speech. Relying extensively on Justice Black's opinion in *Talley v. California* (1960),[155] Justice Stevens, writing for the court, observed that "anonymous pamphlets, leaflets, brochures and even books have played an important role in the progress of mankind."[156] Under the Constitution,

Stevens wrote, "anonymous pamphleteering" has had "an honorable tradition of advocacy and of dissent," and it has served as "a shield from the tyranny of the majority." One of the fundamental purposes of the First Amendment, he wrote, is "to protect unpopular individuals from retaliation—and their ideas from suppression—at the hand of an intolerant society."[157]

Justice Thomas concurred in the court's judgment—although he did not cite Justice Black's opinion in *Talley*.[158] Thomas acknowledged that anonymous speech had not been discussed during debates over the Bill of Rights but argued that "Founding-era Americans opposed attempts to require that anonymous authors reveal their identities."[159] He pointed out that anonymous speech had a long history in the United States, dating back to the famous 1735 trial of John Peter Zenger. He also placed great reliance on the near-universal use of anonymous writing during the Constitution's ratification process, citing the *Federalist Papers* as the classic example.[160] Thomas also found support in the enormous public backlash over Federalists' attempts to require newspapers to reveal the names of Anti-Federalists during the ratification period. Although acknowledging that common practice at the time of the founding does not necessarily mean that the First Amendment was intended to protect anonymous speech, Thomas found the historical record sufficiently compelling to outlaw Ohio's ban on anonymous campaign literature.

Justice Scalia dissented. While he conceded that the original meaning of the First Amendment was unclear on the question of whether anonymous campaign speech is a protected constitutional right, Scalia based his decision on tradition and the forty-nine state laws that currently banned anonymous electioneering speech. Scalia disputed the notion that the frequent use of anonymous speech in the past established a constitutional "right-to-speak-incognito" in campaigns and elections, given that almost every state banned the practice. "A government practice that has become general throughout the United States, and particularly one that has the validation of long, accepted usage, bears a strong presumption of constitutionality," wrote Scalia.[161]

Disclosure Laws

Justices Scalia and Thomas also disagreed over whether the First Amendment protects anonymous campaign advertisements. In *Citizens United v. Federal Election Commission* (2010),[162] the Supreme Court struck down the federal ban on electioneering ads by corporations under the Bipartisan Campaign Reform

Act of 2002 (BCRA). Justice Thomas agreed with the court's judgment, but he filed a short solo dissent arguing that the BCRA's disclaimer and disclosure requirements were unconstitutional as well. "I cannot endorse a view of the First Amendment," wrote Thomas, "that subjects citizens of this Nation to death threats, ruined careers, damaged or defaced property, or pre-emptive and threatening warning letters as the price for engaging in core political speech."[163] Justice Scalia also joined the court's decision in *Citizens United*, but he did not sign on to Thomas's separate dissent. In fact, in a 2013 interview, Scalia said he did not have "a whole lot of toleration" for those who argue that disclosure requirements in elections inhibit freedom of speech. "Oh, the poor dears," he said, "toughen up." "I think a democracy requires a certain amount of what you might call moral courage on behalf of its people," Scalia observed.[164]

In a decision handed down just five months after *Citizens United*, Justice Thomas expanded his defense of anonymous speech to cover state referenda. In 2009 a group called Protect Marriage Washington collected enough signatures to get a referendum on the ballot allowing citizens to vote on a state law that would expand the rights of same-sex domestic partners. Proponents of the state law requested copies of the petition to identify supporters, and two organizations expressed a willingness to publish their names and addresses on the internet. Alarmed by this prospect, the petition's sponsor and other signers filed suit, contending that the disclosure of such personal information constituted an abridgment of freedom of speech under the First Amendment. In *Doe v. Reed* (2010),[165] the Supreme Court held that the disclosure of names and addresses on referendum petitions generally does not violate the First Amendment. In an opinion by Chief Justice Roberts, the court applied intermediate scrutiny and found that public disclosure of referendum petitions is substantially related to the important state interest of preserving the integrity of the electoral process. However, the court noted that the petitioners could prevail under the First Amendment if they showed a "reasonable probability" that the compelled disclosure of personal information would subject them to threats and harassment from either government officials or private parties.

Justice Scalia filed a concurring opinion. He questioned whether the signing of a petition is even covered by the First Amendment. When voters sign referendum petitions, Scalia argued, they act as legislators, and the lawmaking power has traditionally not been subject to First Amendment protections. Accordingly, Scalia disagreed with the court's use of intermediate scrutiny in this case. "There are laws against threats and intimidation," Scalia wrote, "and harsh criticism, short of unlawful action, is a price our people have traditionally been willing to pay for self-governance." "Requiring people to stand up in public for their political acts fosters civic courage," Scalia observed, "without which democracy is doomed." "For my part, I do not look forward to a society which, thanks to the Supreme Court, campaigns anonymously (*McIntyre*) and even exercises the direct democracy of initiative and referendum hidden from public scrutiny and protected from the accountability of criticism." "This does not resemble the Home of the Brave," he concluded.[166]

Justice Thomas filed a solo dissent. In contrast to the majority, Thomas argued that strict scrutiny should apply in this case. He claimed that the act of signing a petition amounts to "political association," which is protected by the First Amendment. A core ingredient of this First Amendment right, he said, is "privacy in one's association." Applying this heightened level of scrutiny, Thomas questioned whether the state's interest of protecting the integrity and reliability of its referendum process was "compelling," but he was sure that the "on-demand" disclosure of petition signers was not narrowly tailored to serve that interest. On this basis, he argued that Washington's decision to subject all referendum petitions to public disclosure was unconstitutional. "Compelling disclosure of signed referendum and initiative petitions under the Washington Public Records Act," Thomas wrote, "severely burdens [political speech and association] and chills citizen participation in the referendum process."[167] In a 2021 case, Thomas argued that strict scrutiny should also apply to reporting and disclosure requirements related to donations made to charitable organizations.[168]

Minors

The free speech rights of minors was another area of disagreement between Scalia and Thomas. In *Tinker v. Des Moines Independent Community School District* (1969),[169] the Warren Court struck down a policy prohibiting students from wearing black armbands in school to protest the Vietnam War. In an opinion by Justice Fortas, the court observed that students do not "shed their constitutional right to freedom of speech or expression at the schoolhouse gate."[170] Justice Black filed a vigorous dissent in that case, arguing that school administrators must have substantial disciplinary authority to foster an effective learning environment. "If the time has come," wrote Black, "when pupils of state-supported schools, kindergartens, grammar schools, or high schools can defy and flout orders of school officials to keep their minds on their own schoolwork, it is the beginning of new revolutionary era of permissiveness in this country fostered by the judiciary."[171]

In a 2007 case, Justice Thomas endorsed Black's analysis.[172] In *Morse v. Frederick* (2007),[173] a teenager was disciplined for displaying a banner during a school-sponsored event that read: "BONG HITS 4 JESUS." In upholding the school officials' actions, the court limited *Tinker*'s rationale to speech related to political concerns. Chief Justice Roberts, the author of the court's opinion, acknowledged that the banner unfurled by Frederick could have several different messages, including both political and religious, but the court deferred to the principal's judgment that the banner promoted the use of illegal drugs. Justice Scalia joined the court's decision.

In a solo concurring opinion, Justice Thomas argued that the court should have overturned *Tinker*. He maintained that *Tinker* "effected a sea change in students' speech rights" that was not supported by the Constitution. Under the common law, Thomas argued, school officials had the authority to discipline students pursuant to the doctrine of in loco parentis.[174] Citing Justice Black's dissent in *Tinker*, Thomas wrote, "To elevate [Frederick's] impertinence to the status of constitutional protection would be farcical and would indeed be to 'surrender control of the American public school system to public school students.'"[175] In a 2021 case, Thomas argued (in solo dissent) that public schools should be able to punish a student's *off-campus* speech that negatively impacts the learning environment.[176]

The different views of Justices Scalia and Thomas were also prominently displayed in *Brown v. Entertainment Merchants Association* (2011).[177] In that case, the Supreme Court examined a California law banning the sale or rental of "violent video games" to minors under the age of eighteen. In an opinion by Scalia, the court (7–2) struck down the law. "Minors," Scalia wrote, "are entitled to a significant measure of First Amendment protection, and only in relatively narrow and well-defined circumstances may government bar public dissemination of protected materials to them."[178] In Scalia's view, California was attempting to carve out another content-based exception to the First Amendment. Following the court's decision one year earlier in *United States v. Stevens* (2010),[179] which struck down a federal ban on commercial depictions of animal cruelty, Scalia refused to find an exception for violent speech. In fact, the court applied its highest level of scrutiny—strict scrutiny—and found that California did not demonstrate a compelling state interest. Justice

Scalia disputed psychological studies that attempt to draw a causal link between violent video games and harm to minors. He also argued that the law was both underinclusive, because it did not include "booksellers, cartoonists, and movie producers," and overinclusive, because many parents do not believe video games are harmful to their children. Scalia admitted that he and his colleagues might not allow their own children to play violent video games, but the content of such videos was fully protected by the First Amendment and was not readily distinguishable from the sort of violence described in literature such as Grimm's fairy tales.

Justice Thomas dissented. He noted that the California law did not prohibit parents or guardians from buying or renting violent video games for their minor children; thus, the sole issue was whether minors have the constitutional right to access speech without going through a parent or guardian. Based on his reading of "the original public understanding of the First Amendment," Thomas answered that question in the negative. As far back as Puritan New England, Thomas observed, parents had the absolute authority to regulate the upbringing and education of their children—a fact that did not substantially change when the Constitution was adopted in 1788. "Jefferson's rigorous management of his charges was not uncommon," wrote Thomas, and "children were expected to be dutiful and obedient."[180] He cited other areas of the law where either parents had to give consent for a minor child to undertake certain obligations (e.g., work, join the military, get married) or minors were prohibited from undertaking certain functions because of their age (e.g., voting, serving on juries, being a witness in a criminal case). All this evidence, he contended, led to the conclusion that the founding generation did not believe in "a right to speak to minors without going through the minors' parents or guardians." "All that [California's] law does," Thomas concluded, "is prohibit the direct sale or rental of a violent video game to a minor by someone other than the minor's parent, grandparent, aunt, uncle, or legal guardian." "Because such speech does not fall within 'the freedom of speech' as originally understood," he said, "California's law does not ordinarily implicate the First Amendment and is not facially unconstitutional."[181]

Hate Speech

In *Virginia v. Black* (2003),[182] the Supreme Court struck down Virginia's 1952 law that criminalized burning a cross on public or private property. In 1968 the law was amended to include the following provision: "Any such burning of a cross shall be prima facie evidence of an intent to intimidate a person or group of persons." A plurality of the court struck down the statute on facial grounds because the prima facie provision assumed that all cross burnings are intended to intimidate. However, the plurality remanded the case to the lower court to determine whether that provision was severable from the rest of the statute.

Justice Scalia wrote a separate opinion. He agreed that a state could prohibit cross burning carried out with the intention to intimidate, but he disagreed with the plurality's judgment that the statute had to be struck down on facial grounds due to the prima facie provision. For Scalia, the prima facie language merely created a presumption that a cross burning was done with the intention to intimidate, so the defendant had a right to rebut that presumption. Nonetheless, he agreed with the plurality that the case should be remanded to the Virginia Supreme Court to provide an authoritative construction of the provision. Like the plurality, he also voted to reverse the conviction of one of the defendants who had burned a cross as part of a Ku Klux Klan rally in southwestern Virginia. In that case, the jury had been instructed that "the burning of a cross, *by itself*, is sufficient evidence from which you may infer the required intent."[183]

Justice Thomas was the only justice to uphold all three convictions in the case. He argued that burning a cross falls completely outside the First Amendment because it involves more conduct than expression. Thomas recounted the history of violence and terrorism associated with cross burnings in the United States. "The perception that a burning cross is a threat and a precursor of worse things to come is not limited to blacks," wrote Thomas. "Because the modern Klan expanded the list of its enemies beyond blacks and 'radicals,' to include Catholics, Jews, most immigrants, and labor unions, a burning cross is now widely viewed as a signal of impending terror and lawlessness."[184] Thomas also pointed out the irony of the court's decision. "It strains credulity," wrote Thomas, "to suggest that a state legislature that adopted a litany of segregationist laws self-contradictorily intended to squelch the segregationist message." "Even for segregationists, violent and terroristic conduct, the Siamese twin of cross burning, was intolerable," he concluded.[185]

Confederate Flag

Justices Scalia and Thomas came to different conclusions in a case involving the display of the Confederate flag on specialty license plates. The Texas

Department of Motor Vehicles Board denied a request by the Texas Division of the Sons of Confederate Veterans to use its design of the Confederate flag on specialty license plates. The board based its decision on public comments indicating that many people found the design offensive. In a 5–4 decision authored by Justice Breyer, the Supreme Court ruled that license plates are government property, and the government has the discretion to select the messages it endorses.[186] Thomas joined the four liberal justices in that case. By contrast, Justice Scalia joined Justice Alito's dissent, which argued that messages on license plates are private speech and the government was discriminating on the basis of viewpoint.

Threats over the Internet

Justice Thomas was the only dissenter in a case involving a federal conviction for the transmission of threats over the internet. Anthony Douglas Elonis posted several "threatening" messages on Facebook directed at coworkers, his ex-wife, local police, a kindergarten class, and an FBI agent, and he was charged under a federal law criminalizing the transmission in interstate commerce of "any communication containing any threat . . . to injure the person of another." The jury was instructed that a true threat is one "wherein a reasonable person would foresee that the statement would be interpreted" as a threat, but it did not require the defendant to understand the message to be a threat. Chief Justice Roberts, writing for the court, held that the "general rule" is that a guilty mind is "a necessary element in the indictment and proof of every crime," and the objective reasonable person standard (borrowed from tort law) was not sufficient to convict a person of a crime.[187] Justice Scalia joined the court's decision, but Justice Thomas dissented. He argued that court precedent required only that the defendant knowingly and willingly transmitted a statement that a reasonable observer would understand to be a threat.

Commercial Speech

Since 1980, the Supreme Court has applied the *Central Hudson* test, a form of intermediate scrutiny, to laws regulating commercial speech.[188] In *44 Liquormart, Inc. v. Rhode Island* (1996),[189] the court struck down two Rhode Island laws that imposed a blanket ban on the advertisement of liquor prices. Justice Stevens, writing for the court, relied on the *Central Hudson* test, but Justice Thomas filed a separate concurrence in which he argued that lawful commercial speech should be treated no differently than political speech.[190] In other words, Thomas argued that the court should apply strict scrutiny in such cases. Justice Scalia also filed a concurring opinion in *44 Liquormart*, but he stopped short of endorsing Thomas's strict scrutiny analysis. Instead, Scalia based his opinion on tradition and prior case law. "It would also be paternalism for us," Scalia wrote, "to prevent the people of the States from enacting laws that we consider paternalistic, unless we have good reason to believe the Constitution itself forbids them."[191] One year later, Scalia again declined to join part of Thomas's dissent in which he expressed disagreement with "the use of the *Central Hudson* balancing test and the discounted weight given to commercial speech generally."[192]

Political Parties

Justice Scalia wrote the Supreme Court's decision in *California Democratic Party v. Jones* (2000),[193] which struck down California's "blanket" primary system as an encroachment on a political party's ability to recruit and select candidates who represent the party's ideologies and preferences.[194] Subsequently, the Ninth Circuit Court of Appeals struck down Washington State's blanket primary system based on the Supreme Court's decision in *Jones.*[195] In 2004 the citizens of Washington, through the initiative process, changed the state's primary system to allow candidates to self-identify their "party preference" on the ballot. Under this system, the top two vote getters in the primary (even if they self-identified as members of the same political party) would compete in the general election. The Washington State Republican Party (as well as other state political parties) objected that the new system violated their associational rights by usurping their right to nominate their own candidates and by forcing them to associate with candidates they did not endorse.[196]

In a 7–2 decision, the Supreme Court rejected a facial challenge to the law.[197] In an opinion by Justice Thomas, the court held that concerns about voter confusion were premature, since there was a possibility that ballots could be printed to reduce voter confusion and the impression that the parties endorsed particular candidates. As one example, Thomas noted that the "ballot could include prominent disclaimers explaining that party preference reflects only the self-designation of the candidate and not an official endorsement by the party." Another possibility was that "the ballots might note preference in the form of a candidate statement that emphasizes the candidate's personal determination rather than the party's acceptance of the candidate, such as 'my party preference is the Republican Party.'"[198]

Justice Scalia filed a vigorous dissent, which was joined only by Justice Kennedy. Scalia argued that Washington's primary system was indistinguishable from the blanket primary overturned in *Jones* and therefore should be struck down on its face. "When the state-printed ballot for the general election causes a party to be associated with candidates who may not fully (if at all) represent its views," wrote Scalia, "it undermines" the effectiveness of political parties.[199] Scalia also rejected a "wait and see" approach to determine whether ballots could be printed in a way that avoided voter confusion. "We have here a system," Scalia concluded, "which, like the one it replaced, does not merely refuse to assist, but positively impairs, the legitimate role of political parties." "I dissent from the Court's conclusion that the Constitution permits this sabotage," he wrote.[200]

RELIGIOUS FREEDOM

Religious freedom was another major area of difference between Justices Scalia and Thomas. Scalia wrote the Supreme Court's decision in *Employment Division, Department of Human Resources of Oregon v. Smith* (1990),[201] which held that neutral, generally applicable laws that only incidentally impact religious practices do not have to satisfy strict scrutiny. Justice Thomas did not challenge that particular ruling for thirty years. However, in *Fulton v. City of Philadelphia* (2021),[202] he joined two opinions that called for *Smith* to be overturned. In the principal dissent, Justice Alito argued in a lengthy opinion that *Smith* conflicted with court precedent, the original public meaning of the free exercise clause, and had proven to be unworkable in practice.[203] In a shorter dissent, Justice Gorsuch expressed frustration with the court's "studious indecision about *Smith* when the costs are so many."[204] Both Alito and Gorsuch (joined by Thomas) argued that strict scrutiny should apply to laws that substantially burden religious practices, irrespective of whether they are neutral or target religion.

FOURTH AMENDMENT

By and large, Justices Scalia and Thomas shared similar interpretations of the Fourth Amendment. They have both claimed that its "touchstone" is "reasonableness." They have also supported several important exceptions to the Fourth Amendment, criticized the exclusionary rule, and claimed the Fourth Amendment does not apply to electronic surveillance. Despite these important areas of agreement, they came to some notably different conclusions in Fourth Amendment cases.

Anonymous Tips

In *Navarette v. California* (2014),[205] Justice Thomas wrote the 5–4 decision holding that a police officer had reasonable suspicion to pull over a motorist based on an anonymous tip. On the afternoon of August 23, 2008, the Mendocino County unit of the California Highway Patrol received a call from a dispatcher in a neighboring county that a "Silver Ford 150 pickup" with license plate number "8-David-9425" had run a motorist off the road and had last been seen five minutes ago. Two police officers responded to the radio broadcast of the information. After trailing the pickup for approximately five minutes, one of the officers pulled the vehicle over, and the second officer arrived shortly thereafter. When the two officers checked the driver's identification, they smelled marijuana and then discovered thirty pounds of marijuana in the truck bed.

For the majority, Justice Thomas reasoned that, based on the totality of the circumstances, the officers had reasonable suspicion to stop the truck. Although anonymous tips generally do not rise to the level of reasonable suspicion, Thomas believed that in this case there were sufficient indicia of reliability. The anonymous caller, he noted, was the motorist who had been run off the road, and she provided specific information about the vehicle and an accurate timeline of events. Thomas also placed some reliance on the fact that the anonymous caller used the 911 emergency system, which can trace phone calls and therefore provide some protection against false reports. Additionally, Thomas noted that in this case there was an ongoing safety concern—possible drunk driving—which provided further reason to pull over the pickup. "Under the totality of the circumstances," he concluded, "we find the indicia of reliability in this case sufficient to provide the officer with reasonable suspicion that the driver of the reported vehicle had run another vehicle off the road."[206]

In dissent, Justice Scalia argued that uncorroborated anonymous tips do not provide reasonable suspicion. He questioned the veracity of a tipster who does not provide her name. He also found that the factual record was not sufficiently noteworthy or specific to make this tip more reliable than any other anonymous tip. Furthermore, Scalia argued that the average anonymous 911 caller is not aware that the call is being traced and he pointed out that a single instance of erratic driving does not give rise to suspicion of intoxication. In fact, since the police officer who followed the pickup for five minutes did not witness any additional evidence of drunk driving, Scalia claimed, he should not have stopped the truck. Scalia also worried about the precedent established by this case. "So long as the caller identifies where the car is," he reasoned, "anonymous claims of a single instance of possibly careless or reckless driving, called in to 911, will support a traffic stop." In typical dramatic fashion, Scalia described the court's decision as serving up "a freedom-destroying cocktail of two parts patent falsity: (1) that anonymous 911 reports of traffic violations are reliable so long as they correctly identify a car and its location, and (2) that a single instance of careless or reckless driving necessarily supports a reasonable suspicion of drunkenness."[207]

Drug-Sniffing Dogs during Traffic Stops

Justices Scalia and Thomas were also on opposite sides in *Rodriguez v. United States* (2015).[208] In an earlier decision, *Illinois v. Caballes* (2005),[209] the Supreme Court ruled that the use of drug-sniffing dogs during lawful traffic stops is permissible because the practice reveals "no information other than the location of a substance that no individual has a right to possess." Importantly, the length of the stop in *Caballes* was no longer than ten minutes. In the 2015 case, a police officer pulled Dennys Rodriguez over for driving on a highway shoulder. After checking the driver's licenses of Rodriguez and his passenger, the police officer issued a warning ticket, but he also asked Rodriguez for permission to walk his narcotics dog around the vehicle. Rodriguez refused. The two men were then asked to get out of the car to await the arrival of a second police officer. Seven or eight minutes after the officer issued the warning ticket (a twenty-nine-minute stop altogether), the dog positively identified methamphetamine in the car.

In an opinion by Justice Ginsburg, the Supreme Court held that "a traffic stop 'can become unlawful if it is prolonged beyond the time reasonably required to complete th[e] mission' of issuing a warning ticket."[210] However, the court remanded the case to the lower court to determine whether there was reasonable suspicion to detain the motorist. Justice Scalia joined the court's 6–3 decision, but Justice Thomas dissented. "The ultimate touchstone of the Fourth Amendment," wrote Thomas, "is 'reasonableness.'"[211] Because the officer had probable cause to pull over the vehicle, Thomas thought it was reasonable to have the dog sniff the car. Thomas also took issue with the majority for placing so much emphasis on the length of the stop, which was not dramatically different from that of other stops. The Fourth Amendment, he said, "does not turn upon such trivialities," which would require courts to consider the characteristics of the officer conducting the stop. "If the driver is stopped by a particularly efficient officer," Thomas reasoned, "then he will be entitled to be released from the traffic stop after a shorter period of time than a less efficient officer."[212] He also criticized the majority for imposing a bright-line test between "traffic-based inquiries" and those inquiries directed at criminal wrongdoing. In his view, this type of restriction on police practices was inconsistent with the court's decision in *Caballes* and was irreconcilable with the common practice of warrant checks.

Finally, Thomas took the majority to task for not recognizing the distinction between stops based on probable cause and those based on reasonable suspicion. In the former cases, he pointed out, police have considerably more leeway. The officer can arrest the driver without a warrant, search the driver incident to arrest, and search the vehicle "if it is reasonable to believe evidence relevant to the crime of arrest might be found there."[213] Although the lower court did not reach this issue, Thomas also said the officer had reasonable suspicion to detain Rodriguez because of various suspicious circumstances that came to light during the investigatory stop.

Strip Searches

Justices Scalia and Thomas were on opposite sides of a dramatic case involving the strip search of a thirteen-year-old middle school student. In October 2003 Savana Redding was strip-searched based on the suspicion that she was distributing prescription and over-the-counter drugs in school. In *Safford Unified School District v. Redding* (2009),[214] the court ruled (8–1) that even though school authorities had reasonable suspicion to search Redding's backpack and outer clothing, a strip search was "excessively intrusive in light of the age and sex of the student and the nature of the infraction."[215] Justice Scalia joined the court's decision, but Justice Thomas filed a solo dissent. Based on court precedents, he argued that the strip search was "reasonable" under the circumstances. Since the court acknowledged that the search of Savana's backpack and outer clothing was supported by reasonable suspicion, Thomas contended that the assistant principal was fully justified in believing that Savana was carrying the drugs in her bra or underpants. The reasonableness of a search's scope, Thomas observed, depends on whether it is limited to an area capable of concealing the object of the search. "It was eminently reasonable to conclude," he wrote, "that the backpack was empty because Redding was secreting the pills in a place she thought no one would look."[216]

More broadly, Thomas questioned the courts' role in supervising the administration of public schools. Consistent with his concurring opinion in *Frederick*, Thomas relied on the common-law doctrine of in loco parentis, whereby parents delegate authority to school administrators and teachers to maintain order and discipline in public schools. Thomas claimed that the court's decision put school officials in an "impossible spot." "Had the suspected infraction involved a street drug," Thomas wrote, "the majority implies that it would have approved the scope of the search." But "judges," he insisted, "are not qualified to second-guess the best manner for maintaining quiet and order in the school environment." He thus called on the court to abandon any sort of oversight of public schools, leaving it to school officials and teachers to administer their affairs. "I cannot join this regrettable decision," Thomas concluded.[217]

Warrantless Blood and DNA Tests

Justices Scalia and Thomas also reached different results in *Missouri v. McNeely* (2013),[218] where the Supreme Court ruled (8–1) that the natural metabolization of alcohol in the bloodstream does not constitute a per se exigency to conduct warrantless blood tests on suspected drunk drivers. "Because the body's natural metabolization of alcohol inevitably destroys evidence of the crime," Thomas wrote in solo dissent, "it constitutes an exigent circumstance."[219]

The two justices also disagreed about whether DNA tests could be performed during the booking process of arrestees charged with serious crimes. Alonzo King was arrested in 2009 and charged with first- and second-degree assault for menacing a group of people with a shotgun. Booking personnel conducted a DNA test on King, which involved the application of a cotton swab to the inside of his cheeks. The test results matched the DNA obtained from a rape victim back in 2003. King was charged with that crime and eventually sentenced to life in prison without the possibility of parole.

In *Maryland v. King* (2013),[220] the Supreme Court ruled that routine DNA testing of arrestees charged with serious crimes does not violate the Fourth Amendment. According to Justice Kennedy, who authored the 5–4 decision, DNA testing, like fingerprinting and photographing, serves the legitimate government interest of processing and identifying persons who are taken into police custody. Justice Thomas joined that decision, but Justice Scalia wrote a sharply worded dissent. DNA tests of arrestees, Scalia argued, violates the Fourth Amendment's "categorical" rule against "searching a person for evidence of a crime when there is no basis for believing the person is guilty of the crime or is in possession of incriminating evidence." Scalia took issue with the court's comparison of DNA tests to fingerprints or photographs. "The Court's assertion that DNA is being taken, not to solve crimes, but to *identify* those in the State's custody, taxes the credulity of the credulous," he wrote.[221] Scalia analogized the search conducted in this case to "general warrants" (or writs of assistance), which were particularly disfavored at the time of the founding. "I doubt," Scalia wrote, "that the proud men who wrote the charter of our liberties would have been so eager to open their mouths for royal inspection."[222]

Summers *Rule*

In *Michigan v. Summers* (1981),[223] the Supreme Court held that occupants of a dwelling can be detained without probable cause in the immediate vicinity of their premises during the execution of a search warrant. The court recognized three important law enforcement interests that justified this exception to the Fourth Amendment: preventing flight, ensuring officer safety, and facilitating completion of the search.[224] The Rehnquist and Roberts Courts heard several cases involving the *Summers* rule, most of which found Justices Scalia and Thomas on the same side.[225] But that was not the case in *Bailey v. United States* (2013).[226]

In *Bailey*, Long Island police officers obtained a search warrant for the defendant's apartment after a confidential source reported that he had observed a gun in the apartment during a drug purchase. Two police officers were conducting surveillance in an unmarked car outside the residence when two men, later identified as Chunon Bailey and Bryant Middleton, got in a car parked in the driveway and drove off. The officers followed the car for approximately a mile before pulling it over. During a pat-down search, the police found no weapons on Bailey, but they did discover a ring of keys. They then escorted the two men back to the apartment, where the search team had already found a gun and illicit drugs. After arresting the two men, police discovered that one of Bailey's keys unlocked the door to the apartment. The issue was whether the detention of Bailey a mile away from the apartment was consistent with the rule in *Summers.*

In a 6–3 decision, the Supreme Court held that it was not. Justice Kennedy, writing for the court, held that detention a mile away from the home did not fall under any of the rationales established in *Summers.* "Limiting the rule in *Summers* to the area in which an occupant poses a real threat to the safe and efficient execution of a search warrant," Kennedy wrote, "ensures that the scope of the detention incident to a search is confined to its underlying justification."[227] Justice Scalia wrote a short concurring opinion and argued that *Summers* established a categorical rule. "The question in this case," he wrote, "is whether *Summers* applies at all." *Summers* applies, he insisted, "only to seizures of 'occupants'—that is, persons within 'the immediate vicinity of the premises to be searched.'" Since Bailey was seized a mile away, Scalia determined that "*Summers* cannot sanction Bailey's detention." "It really is that simple," he concluded.[228] By contrast, Justice Thomas joined the dissent authored by Justice Breyer, who argued that, under the circumstances of this case, it was reasonable to detain the suspects a mile away from the apartment.

CONFRONTATION CLAUSE

Justice Scalia wrote the Supreme Court's decision (joined by Thomas) in *Crawford v. Washington* (2004),[229] which held that the confrontation clause forbids the admission of out-of-court testimonial statements not subject to cross-examination in criminal cases. However, the two justices disagreed over what constitutes "testimonial" statements for purposes of applying *Crawford.* In several cases, Thomas has maintained that testimonial evidence subject to the strictures of the confrontation clause must be made in a "formalized" fashion, such as extrajudicial statements contained in affidavits, depositions, prior testimony, or confessions; otherwise, in his view, they are admissible.[230] Scalia, by contrast, did not require such "solemnity" when it came to testimonial statements.

This divergence of opinion was revealed in *Michigan v. Bryant* (2011).[231] In that case, Detroit police officers were responding to a shooting and found the victim, Anthony Covington, lying on the ground next to his car in a gas station parking lot. Covington had been mortally wounded and "spoke with difficulty." The police officers asked Covington "what had happened, who shot him, and where the shooting had occurred."[232] Covington identified the defendant, Richard Bryant, as the person who shot him and said the shooting had taken place on the back porch of Bryant's home. In an opinion by Justice Sotomayor, the Supreme Court ruled that the "primary purpose" of the interrogation was to allow the police to assist in an ongoing emergency, so *Crawford* did not apply. In a concurring opinion, Justice Thomas maintained his view that out-of-court statements had to be "formalized" to be protected by the Sixth Amendment. "As the majority notes," Thomas wrote, the victim "interacted with the police under highly informal circumstances, while he bled from a fatal gunshot wound." "The police questioning," he added, "was not 'a formalized dialogue,' did not result in 'formalized testimonial materials' such as a deposition or affidavit, and bore no 'indicia of solemnity.'"[233]

Justice Scalia wrote an incredulous dissent in which he accused the majority of "a gross distortion of the facts" and "a gross distortion of the law." He argued that the primary purpose of the police questioning in this case was *not* to determine Covington's medical needs but to investigate a crime. "None of the officers asked Covington how he was doing," Scalia wrote, "attempted more than superficially to assess the severity of his wounds, or attempted to administer first aid." Instead, they asked about "the address where a shooting took place," "the name of the shooter," and "the shooter's height and weight." "The Court's distorted view," wrote Scalia, "creates an expansive exception to the Confrontation Clause for violent crimes." How long can an ongoing emergency last? he asked. In this case, he speculated that it could have lasted until the police were able to secure the scene of the shooting, which might have been "two-and-a-half hours later."[234] Unlike Thomas, Scalia would have excluded Covington's statements as "testimonial" under the confrontation clause.

RIGHT TO A JURY TRIAL

Justices Scalia and Thomas played major roles in providing a more robust interpretation of the Sixth Amendment's right to a jury trial. In *Apprendi v.*

New Jersey (2000),[235] the Supreme Court held that any fact that increases the penalty for a state crime beyond the prescribed statutory maximum—not including a prior conviction—had to be submitted to a jury and proved beyond a reasonable doubt. In that case, Charles C. Apprendi was sentenced to twelve years in prison under a New Jersey statute that increased the maximum term of imprisonment from ten years to twenty years if the trial judge found by a preponderance of the evidence that the defendant had committed the crime with racial bias. In subsequent cases, Justices Scalia and Thomas either wrote or joined decisions applying the *Apprendi* principle in capital cases and to state and federal sentencing guidelines.[236] But they did not agree in all these cases.

In *Harris v. United States* (2002),[237] the Supreme Court ruled that judicial fact-finding that increases a mandatory *minimum* sentence for a crime does not violate the Sixth Amendment. In that case, William Joseph Harris's minimum sentence was increased from five years to seven years when the judge concluded by a preponderance of the evidence that he had brandished a gun during a drug trafficking crime. Justice Scalia joined that decision, but Justice Thomas filed a vigorous dissent. "It is true," Thomas wrote, "that *Apprendi* concerned a fact that increased the penalty for a crime beyond the prescribed statutory maximum, but the principles upon which it relied apply with equal force to those facts that expose the defendant to a higher mandatory minimum." "When a fact exposes a defendant to greater punishment than what is otherwise legally prescribed," Thomas reasoned, "that fact is 'by definition [an] "element" of a separate legal offense.'"[238]

Justice Thomas got the final word on this subject. In *Alleyne v. United States* (2013),[239] he wrote the 5–4 decision overturning *Harris* by holding that any fact that increases the penalty for a crime must be submitted to the jury and proved beyond a reasonable doubt. Not unlike Harris, Allen Ryan Alleyne's sentence was increased from five years to seven years when a district court judge determined that he had brandished a gun during a robbery. The jury did not make that specific finding—although the jurors noted on the verdict form that Alleyne had "used or carried a firearm during and in relation to a crime of violence."[240] "*Apprendi*'s definition of 'elements,'" Thomas wrote for the court, "necessarily includes not only facts that increase the ceiling, but also those that increase the floor," both of which "alter the prescribed range of sentences to which a defendant is exposed and do so in a manner that aggravates the punishment."[241] Justice Scalia joined Chief Justice Roberts's dissent in *Alleyne*.

EXCESSIVE FINES

Although Justices Scalia and Thomas consistently voted together in Eighth Amendment cases, they were on opposite sides in a case examining the original meaning of the excessive fines clause.[242] On June 9, 1994, Hosep Bajakajian, his wife, and two daughters were waiting to board a plane at Los Angeles International Airport, with the ultimate destination of Cyprus. The US Customs Service initiated a search by a dog, which discovered approximately $230,000 in cash concealed in their checked luggage. After discovering the hidden currency, a customs inspector stopped the defendant and his family and informed them that federal law required them to report all money in both their personal possession and their baggage that exceeded $10,000. Bajakajian told the customs inspector that he had $8,000 and his wife had $7,000, but they had no additional money to report. In fact, customs inspectors discovered a total of $357,144 in US currency in their baggage, a wallet, and a purse. Federal law provides that a person convicted of willfully violating the $10,000 reporting requirement shall forfeit to the government "any property . . . involved in such offense."

The federal district court found that the entire $357,144 was "involved in" the offense and therefore subject to forfeiture to the government. However, it reduced the forfeiture amount to $15,000 because forfeiture of the entire amount would have been grossly disproportionate to the offense in question. That ruling was affirmed by the Ninth Circuit Court of Appeals. In *United States v. Bajakajian* (1998),[243] the Supreme Court agreed. In an opinion by Justice Thomas, the court acknowledged that it "has had little occasion to interpret, and has never actually applied, the Excessive Fines Clause." In criminal cases, Thomas said, the "touchstone" principle of the excessive fines clause was "proportionality." Although the text and history of the clause "provide little guidance as to how disproportional a punitive forfeiture must be to the gravity of an offense," Thomas concluded that a forfeiture of the entire amount ($357,144) in this case would be grossly disproportionate to the offense. Thomas noted that the money was not connected to any other crime and was allegedly intended to repay a lawful debt. He characterized Bajakajian's crime as a relatively "minor" reporting offense. "Whatever his other vices," Thomas wrote, "respondent does not fit into the class of persons for whom the statute was principally designed." "He is not a money launderer, a drug trafficker, or a tax evader," he concluded.[244]

Justice Kennedy wrote a passionate dissent, joined by Scalia, which characterized the court's holding as a "disturbing" and "disrespectful" violation of separation of powers. In particular, Kennedy disagreed with the description of Bajakajian's offense as "minor." Congress, Kennedy maintained, determined that the failure to report large amounts of money leaving the country is a serious crime because it is not always apparent what the "smuggled" money is intended for. "The drug trade, money laundering, and tax evasion all depend in part on smuggled and unreported cash," wrote Kennedy. He also took issue with the court's conclusion that Bajakajian's penalty should be $15,000. "Money launderers," he said, "will rejoice to know they face forfeiture of less than 5% of the money transported, provided they hire accomplished liars to carry their money for them." "Five percent," he continued, "is not much of a deterrent or punishment; it is comparable to the fee one might pay for a mortgage lender or broker."[245] Because of the severity of the offense, Kennedy argued that Congress's legislative judgment should be respected and that full forfeiture of the concealed money was appropriate.

EMINENT DOMAIN

Justices Scalia and Thomas defended expansive interpretations of the takings clause, but they did not agree in all eminent domain cases. The two justices joined Justice O'Connor's opinion in *Eastern Enterprises v. Apfel* (1998),[246] which held that a federal law requiring a company to make retroactive payments of medical benefits to former coal-mining employees constituted a taking. Thomas filed a separate concurrence in which he argued that the retroactive payments also likely violated the ex post facto clause, which historically had been interpreted to apply only to criminal penalties.[247] Justice Scalia did not join Thomas's separate opinion in that case.

Moreover, Justices Scalia and Thomas viewed the "public use" requirement differently. Both justices dissented in *Kelo v. City of New London* (2005),[248] where the court upheld a local government's authority to use its eminent domain power for "economic development." In a separate dissent, Justice Thomas argued that "the government may take property only if it actually uses or gives the public a legal right to use the property." He also called for the overturning of two court precedents.[249] Once again, Justice Scalia did not join Thomas's dissent.

NATURAL LAW

Justice Scalia was a legal positivist who drew a sharp distinction between law and morality. Law, in his view, did not have to comport with justice in order to require individuals to follow it.[250] In a 1996 speech delivered at Gregorian University in Rome, Scalia argued that it would be improper for judges to rely on natural law. "The whole theory of democracy," Scalia maintained, "is that the majority rules." "You protect minorities," he added, "only because the majority determines that there are certain minorities or certain minority positions that deserve protection." When asked specifically about the Declaration of Independence and what role it played in interpreting the Constitution, Scalia said it had none. "Well, unfortunately, or to my mind fortunately," Scalia remarked, "the Supreme Court of the United States, no federal court to my knowledge, in 220 years has ever decided a case on the basis of the Declaration of Independence." "It is not part of our law," he added. "It expresses the underlying sentiment which gave rise to the creation of this Constitution. But it is the Constitution that is the document that governs us."[251]

In stark contrast, Justice Thomas's originalist jurisprudence is fundamentally rooted in natural law. In pre–Supreme Court speeches, Thomas argued that the Declaration of Independence, particularly its assertion that "all men are created equal," is the foundation of the US Constitution.[252] In fact, he maintained that the Constitution would be incomprehensible without reliance on the Declaration of Independence. Quoting Abraham Lincoln, Thomas argued that the declaration's principle of inherent equality was "a standard maxim for free society, which should be familiar to all, and revered by all; constantly looked to, constantly labored for, and even though never perfectly attained, constantly approximated, and thereby constantly spreading and deepening its influence, and augmenting the happiness and value of life to all people of all colors everywhere."[253] Thus, in direct opposition to Scalia, Thomas argued that "the jurisprudence of original intention" can be understood only "as the fulfillment of the ideals of the Declaration of Independence."[254] These two vastly different interpretations of natural law manifested themselves in particular areas of constitutional law.

PRIVILEGES OR IMMUNITIES CLAUSE

Even though Justices Scalia and Thomas both rejected substantive due process rights, they came to different conclusions in cases involving other unenumerated rights. In *Saentz v. Roe* (1999),[255] for example, the Supreme Court struck down California's dual-track system for welfare benefits. During the first twelve months of residency in California, the amount of welfare a family could receive was limited to the amount received from their prior state of residence. In an opinion by Justice Stevens, the court ruled that California's dual-track system violated the right to travel under the Fourteenth Amendment's privileges or immunities clause. Somewhat surprisingly, Justice Scalia joined that decision. Justice Thomas, meanwhile, dissented and argued that the claimed right was not "fundamental" under the privileges or immunities clause and that newly arrived residents did not have the same right to welfare benefits as longtime residents.

In *Troxel v. Granville* (2000),[256] the two justices came to different conclusions about parental rights. In that case, the Supreme Court struck down a state law that interpreted visitation rights liberally. The state of Washington allowed "any person" to obtain visitation rights if they could demonstrate to a court that it was in "the best interest of the child." Tommie Granville challenged a visitation decree that granted her ex-boyfriend's parents additional visitation rights with her two daughters. Granville claimed the decree violated parents' fundamental right to rear their children as they see fit under the liberty provision of the due process clause.

In an opinion by Justice O'Connor, the Supreme Court agreed. "The liberty interest at issue in this case," O'Connor wrote, "is perhaps the oldest of the fundamental liberty interests recognized by this Court." Since no one alleged that Granville was an unfit parent, O'Connor reasoned that "the visitation order . . . was an unconstitutional infringement on Granville's fundamental right to make decisions concerning the care, custody, and control of her two daughters."[257] In a short concurrence, Justice Thomas agreed with the court's reliance on *Pierce v. Society of Sisters* (1925),[258] which recognized parents' fundamental right to direct the upbringing of their children. However, he questioned the court's substantive due process analysis.[259] In a footnote, Thomas suggested that parental rights were more soundly lodged under the privileges or immunities clause.[260] Unlike the majority, he also argued that strict scrutiny should be applied to laws infringing on parental rights.

Justice Scalia dissented. Even though he viewed parental rights as "fundamental," Scalia argued that the court had no business finding such a right under the due process clause. "A right of parents to direct the upbringing of their children is among the 'unalienable Rights' with which the Declaration of Independence proclaims 'all Men . . . are endowed by their Creator,'" Scalia wrote. It is also "among the 'other [rights] retained by the people' which the Ninth Amendment says the Constitution's enumeration of rights 'shall not be construed to deny or disparage." But, he concluded, judges have no authority to rely on the Declaration of Independence as a source of constitutional interpretation because it "is not a legal prescription conferring powers upon the courts." Scalia also contended that "the Constitution's refusal to 'deny or disparage' other rights" under the Ninth Amendment "is far removed from affirming any one of them, and even farther removed from authorizing judges to identify what they might be, and to enforce the judges' list against laws duly enacted by the people."[261]

INCORPORATION

Justices Scalia and Thomas defended very different interpretations of the incorporation doctrine, which became apparent in *McDonald v. City of Chicago* (2010).[262] That case challenged two local ordinances that effectively banned residents from owning and keeping guns in their homes. A plurality of the Supreme Court, relying on the due process clause, held that the Second Amendment is "fundamental to *our* scheme of ordered liberty and system of justice" and therefore must be incorporated to apply against the states. "Despite my misgivings about substantive due process as an original matter," Scalia wrote in a separate concurrence, "I have acquiesced in the Court's incorporation of certain guarantees in the Bill of Rights 'because it is both long established and narrowly limited.'"[263] Interestingly, during the oral argument in *McDonald*, Scalia chastised the petitioners' counsel for relying so heavily on the privileges or immunities clause instead of the due process clause. "Why are you asking us to overrule 150, 140 years of prior law—when you can reach your result under substantive due [process]," asked Scalia, "unless you're bucking for a place on some law school faculty." "What you argue is the darling of the professoriate," he added, "but it's also contrary to 140 years of our jurisprudence."[264]

Scalia's sharp questioning of counsel did not deter Justice Thomas from arguing in a long and extensively researched concurring opinion that the only legitimate way to incorporate the individual right to bear arms was through the Fourteenth Amendment's privileges or immunities clause. In a fifty-three-page opinion, Thomas referred to the privileges or immunities provision as the more "straightforward path" of incorporation and "one that is more faithful to the Fourteenth Amendment's text and history." "I cannot accept a theory of constitutional interpretation [i.e., substantive due process] that rests on such tenuous footing," he wrote. "I believe the original meaning of the [privileges or immunities clause] offers a superior alternative, and that a return to that meaning would allow this Court to enforce the rights the Fourteenth Amendment is designed to protect with greater clarity and predictability than the substantive due process framework has so far managed."[265]

EQUAL PROTECTION

Justices Scalia and Thomas invariably took the same position in equal protection cases. Both justices defended a narrow scope of the equal protection clause. Justice Scalia argued that, as an original matter, the equal protection clause does not apply to gender cases,[266] and he filed a strenuous solo dissent in *United States v. Virginia* (1996),[267] which prohibited state-funded universities from discriminating on the basis of sex. Justice Thomas did not participate in the Virginia Military Institute case, but he criticized the analysis of that decision in a subsequent case.[268] Justices Scalia and Thomas did not believe the equal protection clause protects gays and lesbians from attempts to eliminate antidiscrimination laws;[269] nor did they believe the Constitution prevents states from defining marriage as a union between one man and one woman.[270] But there were some differences between the two justices in this area.

AFFIRMATIVE ACTION

Justices Scalia and Thomas were vociferous critics of affirmative action, but they based their opposition on different sources of law. Justice Scalia relied exclusively on the text of the equal protection clause. In *Adarand Constructors v. Pena* (1995),[271] the Supreme Court first applied strict scrutiny to a federal affirmative action program. In a short concurring opinion, Scalia observed that "the concept of racial entitlement" underlying the federal program was incompatible with the Constitution's focus on individual rights.[272] In contrast, Justice Thomas based his objection to affirmative action on natural law. He argued that the federal government's affirmative action program violated the principle of equality embedded in the Declaration of Independence. "There can be no doubt," he wrote, "that the paternalism that appears to lie at the heart of this [affirmative action] program is at war with the principle of inherent equality that underlies and infuses our Constitution," and he then cited the Declaration of Independence.[273] Scalia did not join Thomas's concurring opinion in *Adarand*, nor did he join other affirmative action opinions by Justice Thomas where he cited the Declaration of Independence.[274]

Justices Scalia and Thomas arrived at their positions regarding affirmative action based on different life experiences and perspectives. Scalia was a first-generation Italian American. In a 1979 article he observed that his father had never seen a black man before immigrating to the United States, and he pointed out that many white ethnic immigrants ("Italians, Jews, Irish, Poles") faced their own forms of discrimination. On this basis, Scalia claimed there should be no debtor or creditor race in the United States.[275] "In the eyes of government," Scalia wrote in *Adarand*, "we are just one race here. It is American."[276] Scalia underscored his primary concern with affirmative action during the oral argument in *Grutter v. Bollinger* (2003). When the attorney for the University of Michigan stated that affirmative action did not generate racial hostility if the gap in qualifications between whites and minorities was small, Scalia caustically remarked: "The people you want to talk to are the high school seniors who have seen people visibly less qualified than they are get into prestigious institutions where they are rejected. If you think that is not creating resentment, you are wrong."[277]

By contrast, when Justice Thomas discusses affirmative action, he often speaks of it as one of its beneficiaries. At Yale Law School, Thomas felt he was never viewed as an equal by his white classmates and professors. It was the "monkey on my back," he said. He also blamed affirmative action for his inability to immediately get a job after graduating from Yale. "I'd learned the hard way," Thomas wrote in his 2007 memoir, "that a law degree from Yale meant one thing for white graduates and another for blacks, no matter how much anyone denied it."[278] For this reason, Thomas tends to emphasize that affirmative action "demeans" its recipients. "When the less fortunate do accomplish something," Thomas said in a 1996 speech, "they are often denied the sense of achievement which is so very important for strengthening and empowering the human spirit." Instead, "they owe all of their achievements to the 'anointed' in society," he noted, "who supposedly changed the circumstances—not to their own efforts." "Long hours, hard work, discipline, and sacrifice are all irrelevant," he concluded.[279]

There were many interpretative differences between Justices Scalia and Thomas. They reached different results regarding habeas corpus rights for US citizens classified as "enemy combatants"; they held different views about Congress's authority to regulate the passports of US citizens born in Jerusalem; and they were on opposite sides in the case challenging the president's line-item veto authority. Another major area of disagreement involved the administrative state. Justice Scalia regarded the nondelegation doctrine as a nonjusticiable political question, while Justice Thomas has urged his colleagues to reexamine the "intelligible principle" test used in such cases. The two justices also took different positions regarding the two-step *Chevron* test. On the twenty-fifth anniversary of *Chevron*, Scalia called it a "watershed" decision and criticized his colleagues for not applying *Chevron* deference across the board to include informal agency decisions. Thomas, by contrast, has called for a reexamination of *Chevron* because, in his view, *Chevron* conflicts with the Administrative Procedure Act and separation of powers, and provides an insufficient check on the growth of the administrative state.

There were major interpretative differences between Scalia and Thomas in the area of federalism. Scalia began his judicial career by defending the political process approach to federal-state relations but then shifted to a more nuanced middle-ground approach. Nonetheless, he never deviated from his view that the Tenth Amendment is not an affirmative limit on federal power. Thomas, by contrast, believes the Tenth Amendment *is* an affirmative limit on federal power. These fundamentally different perspectives were on full display in *Gonzales v. Raich*, where Scalia defended a robust view of federal power (both the commerce clause and the necessary and proper clause) to argue that the Controlled Substances Act could be applied to the use of homegrown marijuana for medicinal purposes. Justice Thomas argued in dissent that there was no connection between locally grown marijuana and interstate commerce, and he called the Compassionate Use Act a classic example of the use of the police power under the Tenth Amendment.

Justices Scalia and Thomas interpreted federal preemption quite differently, particularly when it came to the court's "obstacle" preemption doctrine. During his tenure on the Supreme Court, Scalia supported federal preemption in numerous cases and believed it was one constructive means of using federal power to limit state court theories of liability.[280] Justice Thomas has been more reluctant to rule in favor of preemption, particularly when a federal statute contains a saving clause exempting actions for common-law damages. These two justices also reached dramatically different conclusions over the federal government's authority to regulate voting requirements.

In the area of the First Amendment, Justices Scalia and Thomas disagreed in several obscenity cases. They also defended dramatically different interpretations of anonymous speech and the free speech rights of minors. In *Virginia v. Black*, Justice Thomas argued that cross burning is completely unprotected by the First Amendment, while Justice Scalia found that it could be protected if it lacked the intention to intimidate.[281] The two justices were on opposites sides of cases involving whether the Confederate flag could be placed on license plates and whether *mens rea* was required for the federal crime of sending "threatening" messages over the internet. They also supported different levels of scrutiny in commercial speech cases.

For most of his judicial tenure, Justice Thomas did not challenge Scalia's 1990 opinion in *Employment Division, Department of Human Resources of Oregon v. Smith*, which held that the free exercise clause is not violated by neutral, generally applicable laws that only incidentally impact religion. That changed in 2021 when Thomas joined two dissenting opinions in *Fulton v. City of Philadelphia* that called for the overturning of *Smith*. Those two dissents argued that the government has to satisfy strict scrutiny if a law substantially burdens religion, irrespective of whether it is neutral and generally applicable.

Justices Scalia and Thomas were on opposite sides in several areas of Fourth Amendment law, including whether anonymous tips are sufficient to allow police officers to stop motorists for careless or reckless driving; the length of time drug-sniffing dogs should be permitted to investigate vehicles pulled over for traffic violations; whether nonconsensual blood draws of suspected drunk drivers can be required as a per se exigent circumstance; whether children can be strip-searched in public schools for suspected possession of prescription drugs; and whether police can conduct DNA tests during the booking process of arrestees charged with serious crimes. The two justices also came to different conclusions about what constitutes "testimonial" statements under the confrontation clause; they disagreed over whether the *Apprendi* rule applies to fact-finding by judges that increases mandatory minimum sentences; and they arrived at opposite conclusions in an important excessive fines case. In the area of property rights, both justices pushed for a more robust judicial role in regulatory takings cases, but they interpreted the scope of "public use" differently.

Justices Scalia and Thomas also had markedly different interpretations of the Fourteenth Amendment's privileges or immunities clause. Scalia ridiculed that clause as "the darling of the professoriate" that runs "contrary to 140 years of our jurisprudence."[282] Thomas, meanwhile, firmly believes the privileges or immunities clause is an important source of fundamental rights in the United States. Justices Scalia and Thomas also maintained very different perspectives on whether judges can rely on natural law in making decisions. Scalia was a legal positivist who believed a law did not have to be just for it to command obedience. Meanwhile, Thomas believes the Constitution can be understood only on the basis of its natural law foundation. These different perspectives were most apparent in affirmative action cases, but they also surfaced in an important case involving parental rights. Based on their different interpretations of natural law, a strong case can be made that, had Justices Scalia and Thomas served together on earlier courts, their different approaches would have placed them on opposite sides of historically significant cases, including *Dred Scott v. Sandford* (1857),[283] *Buck v. Bell* (1927),[284] *Brown v. Board of Education* (1954),[285] and *Loving v. Virginia* (1967).[286]

Conclusion

This book has examined originalism in operation rather than as a theoretical proposition. The three originalists studied here—Hugo Black, Antonin Scalia, and Clarence Thomas—have all defended originalism in a dogmatic and systematic manner. In their view, originalism is the *only* defensible approach to constitutional interpretation. Justices Black, Scalia, and Thomas have argued that the Constitution is a social compact that requires all public officials, including federal judges, to follow basic rules. For judges to strike down democratically enacted laws as inconsistent with the Constitution, their mandate must be clear. If text and history do not support a particular constitutional right, the three originalists have maintained that it does not exist and can be created only through the formal amendment process prescribed under Article V of the Constitution.

Justices Black, Scalia, and Thomas have made two practical arguments to back up their theoretical approach. On the one hand, they have argued that reliance on text and history is the best way to protect individual rights. If judges adhere to the original meaning of the Constitution, they will have the fortitude to defend rights that may become unpopular. There is no better example than Justice Black's strenuous defense of freedom of speech and association during the Red Scare. "In calmer times, when present pressures, passions and fears subside," Black wrote in *Dennis v. United States* (1951), "this or some later Court will restore the First Amendment liberties to the high preferred place where they belong in a free society."[1] Justices Scalia and Thomas have also taken unpopular positions in the defense of individual rights. They both interpreted the confrontation clause to prohibit out-of-court "testimony" by witnesses unavailable for cross-examination. In *Crawford v. Washington* (2004), Scalia wrote the Supreme Court's decision overturning an earlier precedent allowing the admission of out-of-court statements if they bore sufficient "indicia of reliability." Such a "malleable standard," he wrote, "often fails to protect against paradigmatic confrontation violations."[2] Both Scalia and Thomas also voted to overturn state and federal sentencing guidelines that permitted judges to increase sentences based on a preponderance of the evidence.[3] That sort of judicial authority, they maintained, was a patent violation of the defendant's right to a jury trial under the Sixth Amendment.

On the other hand, the three originalists have defended originalism as the best way to curb judicial discretion. Judges are not infallible creatures and, like other human beings, are subject to the seductive influences of power. During a period when the Supreme Court was being asked to resolve a whole host of social and economic issues under the due process clause, Justice Black cautioned against a return to the *Lochner* era. "What has occurred may occur again," he said. "I would much prefer," he added, "to put my faith in the people and their elected representatives to choose the proper policies for our government to follow, leaving to the courts questions of constitutional interpretation and enforcement."[4] Similarly, Justice Scalia defended originalism because it "establishes a historical criterion that is conceptually quite separate from the preferences of the judge himself." The "main danger in judicial interpretation of the Constitution," he wrote, "is that the judges will mistake their own predilections for the law."[5] In a 1996 speech Justice Thomas also defended originalism as the best way to satisfy the ideal of "impartiality" in judging. "The popular idea that Justices and judges somehow 'make' the law," he argued, "or represent the interests of certain constituencies (or help the Constitution 'evolve') is a dangerous idea that is at war with the very concept of impartial judging and the rule of law."[6] By using the tools of originalism (text and history), judges will be able to avoid policy decisions that are better left to the political branches of government.

THE LIMITS OF CONSTRAINT

A major theme of this book is that originalism promises more than it can deliver. There are numerous examples of Justices Black, Scalia, and Thomas reaching different conclusions when interpreting the same constitutional provision, demonstrating that originalism does not completely constrain judicial behavior. This, of course, does not mean that the search for original meaning is unimportant or illegitimate. The text of the Constitution and its historical meaning are the essential starting places for any honest interpretation of that document. But the defenders of originalism have made their case too strongly. Justice Scalia liked to say that the Constitution provides clear and fixed answers to many legal issues, but is that really true? Some constitutional provisions have a precise meaning, but many others contain abstract concepts. For example, what constitutes a law "abridging the freedom of speech" or an "unreasonable" search and seizure? Similarly, what is "cruel and unusual punishment" or the meaning of "liberty" or "equal protection"? Justice Felix Frankfurter referred to the open-ended language of the Constitution as "Delphic provisions" whose content must be supplied (however cautiously) over time.[7] Added to this are the structural provisions of the Constitution—separation of powers and federalism—that are not explicitly mentioned in the text. "Experience has instructed us," James Madison wrote in Federalist No. 37, "that no skill in the science of government has yet been able to discriminate and define, with sufficient certainty, its three great provinces—legislative, executive, and judiciary; or even the privileges and powers of the different legislative branches." "Questions daily occur," he added, "which prove the obscurity which reigns in these subjects, and which puzzle the greatest adepts in political science."[8]

Many federal judges and legal commentators have acknowledged the ambiguous nature of constitutional language. In interpreting the word "necessary" in the necessary and proper clause, chief justice John Marshall admitted that "such is the character of human language, that no word conveys to the human mind, in all situations, one single definite idea; and nothing is more common than to use words in a figurative sense." "The word 'necessary' is of this description," he wrote. "It admits of all degrees of comparison; and is often connected with other words, which increase or diminish the impression the mind receives of the urgency it imports."[9] In his *Commentaries on the Constitution*, Joseph Story recognized "the imperfection of all human language," where words "acquire different shades of meaning, each of which is equally appropriate and equally legitimate; each of which recedes in a wider or narrower degree from the others, according to circumstances; and each of which receives from its general use some indefiniteness and obscurity as to its exact boundary and extent."[10] For this reason, Story warned against an excessively narrow focus on particular words because "a constitution of government does not, and cannot, from its nature, depend in any great degree upon mere verbal criticism, or upon the import of single words." "Such criticism," he added, "may not be wholly without use; it may sometimes illustrate or unfold the appropriate sense; but unless it stands well with the context and subject-matter, it must yield to the latter."[11]

Throughout US history, judges and commentators have acknowledged the ambiguous nature of constitutional text. In an early contracts clause case, justice William Johnson lamented "that words of less equivocal signification, had not been adopted" in Article I, section 10. He then explained that he rested his opinion not on the text of the contracts clause but "on a general principle, on the reason and nature of things: a principle which will impose laws even on the deity."[12] In a 1918 decision Oliver Wendell Holmes Jr. observed that "a word is not a crystal, transparent and unchanged; it is the skin of a living thought and may vary greatly in color and content according to the circumstances and time in which it is used."[13] Even the so-called godfather of originalism, Robert Bork, recognized the ambiguous nature of constitutional language.[14] "The text of the Constitution," Bork wrote in a 1968 article, "as anyone experienced in words might expect, is least precise where it is most important." "History can be of considerable help," he added, "but it tells us much too little about the specific intentions of the men who framed, adopted, and ratified the great clauses."[15]

"LAW OFFICE" HISTORY

Just as importantly, the three originalists have not escaped criticism for practicing "law office" history—that is, the "selection of data favorable to the position being advanced without regard to or concern for contradictory data or proper evaluation of the relevance of the data proffered."[16] For example, Justice Black's interpretation of the incorporation doctrine received extensive criticism. Charles Fairman argued that when the Thirty-Ninth Congress proposed the Fourteenth Amendment, it did not intend for the Bill of Rights to be incorporated to apply against the states—and he was not alone.[17] Without question, a few leading members of Congress, such as representative John A. Bingham (R-OH) and senator Jacob M. Howard (R-MI), supported incorporation of the Bill of Rights to the states, but did they represent the views of two-thirds of both houses of Congress and three-fourths of the state legislatures that ratified the Fourteenth Amendment? Even if we concede that Justice Black's total incorporation theory won out in the court of public opinion and that his colleagues have moved substantially in that direction, it seems fair to ask whether his reading of the debates on the Fourteenth Amendment was selective or even accurate. Was Black channeling the views of his hero Thomas Jefferson or James Madison?[18] After all, Black called Congressman Bingham "the [James] Madison of the first section of the Fourteenth Amendment."[19]

Justice Black's interpretation of the First Amendment also received some criticism. Leonard Levy, a Pulitzer Prize–winning legal historian, argued that the prevailing view at the time of the founding was that the First Amendment did not prevent the government from banning criminal sedition. Instead, according to Levy, most of the founding generation accepted Blackstone's common-law doctrine of no prior restraints.[20] Black's absolutist position regarding libel and obscenity was also subjected to scrutiny. Many scholars argued that, under the common law, states had the authority to regulate those particular areas.[21] Other scholars argued that Black's opinion in *Everson*, which incorporated the establishment clause to apply to the states, selectively relied on the views of Jefferson and Madison in Virginia.[22] Black's robust interpretations of the Fifth and Sixth Amendments received criticism as well. Levy contended that Black's votes in *Ullmann v. United States* (1956),[23] *Griffin v. California* (1965),[24] and *Miranda v. Arizona* (1966)[25] lacked historical support.[26] Meanwhile, William Beaney argued that the prevailing view of the Sixth Amendment at the time of the founding was that "the right to counsel meant the right to retain counsel of one's own choice and at one's own expense."[27] Finally, Justice Black's views of "one person, one vote" did not go unchallenged. Justice Harlan filed a sharp dissent in *Wesberry v. Sanders* (1964),[28] where he argued that the one person, one vote concept was not required by the text of the Constitution, nor was it supported by the delegates at the Philadelphia Convention. Along the same lines, historian Alfred Kelly claimed that Justice Black "mangled constitutional history" by quoting from the debates about the Connecticut Compromise, which had "nothing to do with the question of representation within the states."[29]

Justice Scalia has been charged with some "law office" history of his own. His opinion for the court in *District of Columbia v. Heller* (2008)[30] has been described as "faux originalism" and "evidence of the ability of well-staffed courts to produce snow jobs."[31] In examining the original public meaning of the Second Amendment, Scalia decoupled the preamble from the operative clause, thereby minimizing the central purpose behind the amendment: to protect state militias from being disarmed by Congress. Under the newly ratified Constitution, Congress had the authority "to provide for organizing, arming, and disciplining" the militia (Article I, section 8, clause 16), which raised concerns that the federal government could eliminate state militias by not funding them. Thus, the Second Amendment was essentially a federalism principle that protected the states from a tyrannical federal government that could now raise an army.[32] It is for this reason that chief justice Warren Burger contended that the Second Amendment "must be read as though the word 'because' was the opening word of the guarantee," since the purpose of the provision was to maintain state militias against a large standing army.[33] Likewise, Robert Bork did not interpret the Second Amendment as protecting an individual's right to bear arms. "I'm not an expert on the second amendment," Bork said in 1989, "but its intent was to guarantee the right of states to form militia, not for individuals to bear arms." In a follow-up question, Bork was asked whether his statement applied to all gun control. "Probably," he replied. "It doesn't mean it's a great idea. It's probably constitutional."[34]

Not only did Justice Scalia downplay the central purpose behind the Second Amendment but his textual analysis of several critical words has been criticized. For example, Scalia broke up the phrase "to keep and bear Arms" and turned it into two verbs: "to keep" and "to bear." After consulting founding-era dictionaries, Scalia concluded that the words encompassed "an individual right unconnected with militia service."[35] However, as Justice Stevens pointed out in dissent, the phrase "to keep and bear Arms" had a distinct meaning at the founding: "to possess arms if needed for military purposes and to use them in conjunction with military activities."[36]

Justice Scalia was also quite cavalier about the drafting history of the Second Amendment. James Madison's first draft placed great weight on two proposed amendments from his home state of Virginia. It read: "The right of the people to keep and bear arms shall not be infringed; a well armed, and well regulated militia being the best security of a free country." Note that Madison's proposal makes no mention of a nonmilitary use or possession of weapons (such as for self-defense or hunting); rather, it concentrates on the necessity of state militias.[37] Madison then included the following clause: "but no person religiously scrupulous of bearing arms, shall be compelled to render military service in person."[38] Although the Senate ultimately removed this clause, it is instructive that Madison's draft of the Second Amendment included an exemption for conscientious objectors.

Justice Scalia's analysis of contemporary "analogous arms-bearing rights" in state constitutions has also been found wanting. Paul Finkelman points out that Scalia privileged two states that protected an individual right to bear arms (Pennsylvania and Vermont) and downplayed two states that clearly connected the right to bear arms to service in the state militia (North Carolina and Massachusetts). Scalia also cited Thomas Jefferson's proposal for the Virginia Declaration of Rights of 1776, which described the right as a personal one,[39] but he did not acknowledge that Virginia rejected Jefferson's proposal and instead adopted one by George Mason that strongly resembled the language of the Second Amendment.[40]

Finally, and perhaps most importantly, Scalia did not discuss judicial precedents until the end of his textual and historical analysis. He then criticized *United States v. Miller* (1939), a unanimous opinion, for the deficiency of its decisional process and for not providing a thorough analysis of the history of the Second Amendment. However, since *Miller* was decided, *every* federal court, including the Supreme Court,[41] had followed the *Miller* court's interpretation of the Second Amendment: the right to bear arms had to be connected to the state militia.[42] Even if the Second Amendment could be regarded as ambiguous, many scholars have argued that the court should have given more respect to prior decisions and the different needs of rural and urban communities.[43] It is possible that by the time the Fourteenth Amendment was ratified, the Second Amendment was understood to protect an individual right to own guns for personal use, but Justice Scalia was interpreting the Second Amendment at the time of the founding. Perhaps his selective use of the historical record was motivated by an enthusiasm for guns and a desire to convince more Americans that guns are not just for criminals but can be used for self-defense and recreational purposes.[44]

Legal standing is another major area in which Justice Scalia engaged in some law office history. Nothing in Article III requires the three-part test the Supreme Court uses to determine whether the parties have legal standing. Chief Justice Warren described standing as "one of 'the most amorphous [concepts] in the entire domain of public law.'"[45] Yet Justice Scalia insisted on a rigid interpretation of the court's standing doctrine. From his days as an appeals court judge, Scalia argued that Congress cannot convert a generalized grievance into a personal injury.[46] He also argued that the court's standing doctrine trumps congressional efforts to create "citizen lawsuits."[47] In other areas of law, Scalia played the role of gatekeeper. He narrowly interpreted the "commonality requirement" under the Federal Rules of Civil Procedure to make it harder to bring class-action lawsuits against corporations.[48] He wrote two important opinions under the Federal Arbitration Act that strictly enforced class arbitration waivers in contracts.[49] He also narrowly interpreted implied causes of action by injured parties under both federal statutes and the Constitution.[50] Finally, Scalia expanded federal common law to create a government contractor defense that immunizes corporations from liability when they make defective products for the government.[51] As Edward Purcell has pointed out, Scalia "sought to restrict the power of the federal courts, [and] deny their authority to provide remedies for those injured by violations of federal law," while at the same time, he "relieve[d] business and government of liability from many of their wrongdoings."[52]

Justice Thomas can also be criticized for practicing some law office history of his own. Even though his dissenting opinion in *U.S. Term Limits, Inc. v. Thornton* (1995)[53] was extensively researched and analyzed, he was very selective about the authorities he relied on. Justice Thomas cited Thomas Jefferson as a supporter of state-imposed term limits on Congress,[54] but he did not sufficiently acknowledge that Jefferson himself had mixed views on the subject. Jefferson expressed *some* support for the idea that the states could impose terms limits on Congress,[55] but he also admitted that "on so recent a change of view caution requires us not to be too confident, and that we admit this to be one of the doubtful questions on which honest men may differ with the purest motives; and the more readily, as we find we have differed from ourselves on it."[56] Nor did Justice Thomas mention the views of James Madison and Alexander Hamilton, both of whom interpreted the qualifications clauses as fixed and unalterable.[57] In fact, during the state ratification debates in New York, Hamilton referred to rotation in office as a "feeble principle" that may in time prove "fatal to the prosperity of our country."[58] Thomas acknowledged that Joseph Story believed that the states could *not* impose term limits on members of Congress,[59] but he dismissed that view as "more nationalist than the Constitution warrants." "Justice Story," Thomas wrote, "was a brilliant and accomplished man," but "he was not a member of the Founding generation, and his *Commentaries on the Constitution* were written a half century after the framing." On this basis, Thomas concluded that Story's view did not represent "the original understanding of the Constitution" but rather "his own understanding."[60]

Justice Thomas has also played fast and loose with history to support his strict constructionist interpretation of federal power. For instance, he argued that the Supreme Court's "substantial effects" test was an "innovation" of the 1930s. To bolster this view, he argued that Chief Justice Marshall's opinion in *Gibbons v. Ogden* (1824) did not support the substantial effects test but "took great pains to make clear that Congress could *not* regulate commerce 'which is completely internal, which is carried on between man and man in a State, or between different parts of the same State, and which does not extend to or affect other States.'" On this basis, Thomas concluded that Marshall did not believe that "whenever an activity affects interstate commerce, it necessarily follows that Congress can regulate such activities."[61]

However, there is language in Marshall's opinion that *does* support the substantial effects test. "Commerce among the States," Marshall wrote, "cannot stop at the external boundary line of each State, but may be introduced into the interior." He noted that "the genius and character of the whole government" are that its laws apply not only to foreign commerce but also "to those internal concerns which affect the States generally."[62] It is true that Congress did not extensively regulate the domestic affairs of states until the twentieth century, but Chief Justice Marshall was not a defender of a formalistic interpretation of federal-state relations. In fact, he said that Congress's commerce power was "complete in itself, may be exercised to its utmost extent, and acknowledges no limitations, other than are prescribed in the constitution."[63] Marshall was also an early proponent of the political process approach to federalism. In *Gibbons*, he said the sole restraint on Congress's exercise of its commerce authority was the political process itself, and in *McCulloch v. Maryland* (1819), he supported the Federalist view that the Tenth Amendment did not constitute a substantive limit on federal power.[64] Citing *Gibbons*, Justice Jackson remarked that "Chief Justice Marshall described the federal commerce power with a breadth never yet exceeded."[65]

Justice Thomas also challenged Justice Black's understanding of James Madison's "Memorial and Remonstrance against Religious Assessments." In Thomas's view, Madison did not oppose the use of tax dollars to support religion generally; instead, he objected only if taxes were used to support one religious sect or denomination.[66] Thomas acknowledged, however, that there were other interpretations of "Memorial and Remonstrance." "Even if more extreme notions of the separation of church and state can be attributed to Madison," Thomas wrote, "many of them clearly stem from 'arguments reflecting the concepts of natural law, natural rights, and the social contract between government and a civil society,' rather than the principle of nonestablishment in the Constitution." "In any event," he added, "the views of one man do not establish the original understanding of the First Amendment."[67]

Both Justice Scalia and Justice Thomas can be criticized for *not* employing an originalist methodology in certain areas of the law. Scalia's opinion in *Employment Division, Department of Human Resources of Oregon v. Smith* (1990)[68] did not utilize an originalist approach in interpreting the free exercise clause, and it has been sharply criticized on both textualist and historical grounds.[69] In a concurring opinion in *Fulton v. City of Philadelphia* (2021), Justice Alito, joined by Thomas, said "*Smith* . . . paid shockingly little attention to the text of the Free Exercise Clause." He added, "This strange treatment of the constitutional text cannot be justified—and is especially surprising since it clashes so sharply with the way in which *Smith*'s author, Justice Scalia, generally treated the text of the Constitution (and, indeed, with his entire theory of legal interpretation)."[70]

It might have been too late in the day, but neither Justice Scalia nor Justice Thomas examined whether corporations are "persons" under the Fourteenth Amendment. As pointed out in chapter 5, Justice Black did. In one interview, Scalia defended the Supreme Court's decision in *Citizens United* by claiming that "Thomas Jefferson would have said the more speech, the better."[71] But Jefferson was deeply concerned about the corrupting influences of corporations in a democracy and consistently cited "restrictions on monopolies" as one of his preferred guarantees in a bill of rights.[72] Nor did Scalia and Thomas defend their expansive interpretation of the takings clause on originalist grounds—even though they both acknowledged, as a historical matter, that the clause probably applied only to physical appropriations.[73] In addition, neither Scalia nor Thomas supported their strenuous criticism of affirmative action based on an originalist interpretation of the Fourteenth Amendment. As several scholars have pointed out, there were contemporary federal efforts to redress historical discrimination (e.g., the Freedmen's Bureau Acts) when the Fourteenth Amendment was adopted.[74]

Finally, the two justices' expansive interpretation of the Eleventh Amendment does not square with a textualist approach to the Constitution. The Eleventh Amendment provides: "The Judicial power of the United States shall not be construed to extend to any suit in law or equity, commenced or prosecuted against any of the United States by Citizens of another State, or by Citizens or Subjects of any Foreign State." By its express language, the Eleventh Amendment bars federal suits in diversity cases, but it does not prohibit suits against states "arising under" the Constitution, federal statutes, or treaties—that is, federal question jurisdiction. In fact, as professor Ralph Rossum points out, the drafters of the Eleventh Amendment rejected a proposal that would have expanded state sovereign immunity to include federal questions.[75] However, in *Hans v. Louisiana* (1890),[76] the court broadly interpreted the Eleventh Amendment to embody a general principle of state sovereign immunity that barred federal question jurisdiction in a suit brought by an individual against his own state. Despite claiming to be textualists, Scalia and Thomas wrote or joined several opinions that interpreted *Hans* expansively. In a 1989 case, Scalia rejected the invitation to overturn *Hans*—although he admitted it was a "close" question. After examining the court's precedents in the area, Scalia concluded that *Hans* should be upheld based on its longevity and "mere venerability."[77] During their tenure together on the Supreme Court, Justices Scalia and Thomas joined decisions that struck down "seven federal laws on the grounds that they violate[d] the 'presupposition' of the Eleventh Amendment that the states enjoy state sovereign immunity and cannot be sued without their consent."[78] Moreover, the two justices' acceptance (and indeed, expansion) of *Hans* stands in sharp contrast to their ardent opposition to the court's negative commerce clause jurisprudence—the origins of which precede *Hans* by two decades.[79]

ORIGINALISM AS AN ISM

It is important to recognize that originalism is not ideologically neutral. During the oral argument in a 2013 case, Justice Scalia expressed skepticism that, based on its original meaning, the Fourteenth Amendment forbids states to prohibit gay marriage. "I'm curious," he asked attorney Ted Olson, "when did it become unconstitutional to exclude homosexual couples from marriage? 1791? 1868, when the Fourteenth Amendment was adopted?" "It seems to me," he added, "you ought to be able to tell me when. Otherwise, I don't know how to decide the case."[80] Scalia's stock answer to those who argued for the inclusion of an unenumerated right in the Constitution was that they had to pass a constitutional amendment. However, it is exceedingly difficult to pass a constitutional amendment in the United States, which is why only seventeen amendments have been adopted since 1791.[81] In short, originalism places a premium on stability and a heavy burden on the expansion of constitutional rights.

Moreover, a strong argument can be made that the three originalists adopted their respective interpretative approaches for specific reasons. For Justice Black, the main reason was to put the "nail in the coffin" of the *Lochner* era. In a 1966 conversation with John Frank, Black said that "the biggest concern of his intellectual life was that substantive due process might return in some form of natural law." From his earliest days as a US senator, Black viewed the *Lochner* era as "the grossest abuse of constitutional government by judges."[82]

Justice Scalia also likely adopted his originalist approach for a specific reason: to defeat *Roe v. Wade* (1973) and other substantive due process claims. In *Webster v. Reproductive Health Services* (1989), Scalia expressed frustration that the court did not explicitly overturn *Roe v. Wade.* It is not "statesmanlike," wrote Scalia, "needlessly to prolong this Court's self-awarded sovereignty over a field where it has little proper business since the answers to most of the cruel questions posed are political and not juridical."[83] Interestingly, Scalia always cited abortion, the right to die, gay rights, and capital punishment as areas where originalism provides clear answers.[84] Similarly, a good case can be made that Justice Thomas had a specific reason for choosing his originalist approach. Before his appointment to the Supreme Court, Thomas criticized the positivist-originalist approach of Chief Justice Taney in *Dred Scott v. Sandford* (1857). Thomas not only denounced Taney's conclusion that African Americans were not included in the Declaration of Independence ("all men are created equal") but also argued that natural law provides solutions to other constitutional issues. For example, in a 1987 address Thomas praised an article by Lewis E. Lehrman, a Heritage Foundation trustee, that relied on the Declaration of Independence to repudiate a woman's right to choose.[85] "May it be reasonably supposed," Lehrman argued, "that an expressly stipulated right to life, as set forth in the Declaration and the Constitution, is to be set aside in favor of the conjured right to abortion in *Roe v. Wade,* a spurious right born exclusively of judicial supremacy with not a single trace of lawful authority, implicit or explicit, in the actual text or history of the Constitution itself?"[86]

THE FEDERALIST SOCIETY

Today's conservative originalists are using the legal system in a more systematic way to effectuate legal change—a development Justice Black would not have approved of. In a 1985 address to the American Bar Association, attorney general Edwin Meese announced that the Reagan administration would interpret the Constitution based on its "original intent" in all federal cases in which the administration filed a brief or joined as amicus. "We will pursue our agenda within the context of our written Constitution of limited yet energetic powers," Meese stated.[87] During Meese's tenure, two Justice Department manuals were published with the express aim of educating government attorneys about an originalist approach that they could use in litigation.[88]

In 1982 the Federalist Society for Law and Public Policy was founded to counteract the perceived liberal hegemony in law schools. Three law students—Steven Calabresi (Yale), Lee Liberman (Otis) (Chicago), and David McIntosh (Chicago)—set up student organizations at their respective law schools to provide a safe place where conservatives could meet to discuss and debate law and public policy. What began as a small group of disaffected and marginalized law students has turned out to be one of the most powerful conservative legal organizations in the world. The Federalist Society serves as an important network that connects its members to public-interest firms, government employment (particularly at the Justice Department), and judicial appointments. There was a running joke during the Reagan administration that all a person had to do to become a federal judge was to serve as a faculty adviser for the organization.

During their tenure together on the Supreme Court, both Antonin Scalia and Clarence Thomas maintained close connections to the Federalist Society, particularly Scalia. As Steven Teles points out, Scalia was "perhaps the most important elite sponsor of the [Federalist] Society in its early years."[89] As a law professor, Scalia agreed to serve as the first faculty adviser for the student chapter established at the University of Chicago, and after he became a federal judge, he maintained close ties with the organization. Many of his law clerks were Federalist Society members, including two of its founding members.[90] Scalia gave numerous speeches at regional and national Federalist Society meetings, including the keynote addresses at the National Lawyers Conventions in 1988, 2006, 2008, and 2014. He also delivered the Barbara K. Olson Memorial Lecture in 2004, was interviewed by Jan Crawford at the 2010 national convention, and occasionally cotaught a ten-hour course on separation of powers for Federalist Society members.[91] Upon his death, Eugene Meyer, the longtime president of the organization, announced that the annual National Lawyers Convention would be named in Scalia's honor. The impact Scalia had on the development of the Federalist Society was underscored by Leonard Leo, executive vice president, who observed, "If it weren't for Justice Scalia's encouragement and moral support, I'm not sure this organization would be anywhere near where it is today."[92]

Even though the Federalist Society professes *not* to get directly involved in public policy (i.e., it does not lobby members of Congress or file cases as amici), it can hardly be described as politically neutral. Its mission statement defines its founding principles as "the state exists to preserve freedom, . . .

the separation of governmental powers is central to our Constitution, and . . . [it] is emphatically the province and duty of the judiciary to say what the law is, not what it should be." It aims to bring conservatives and libertarians together "both to promote an awareness of these principles and to further their application through its activities."[93] In fact, in the mid-1990s, largely due to the defeat of Robert Bork's Supreme Court nomination, the Federalist Society pivoted in a more political direction. It established fifteen practice groups modeled after the American Bar Association's sections, and although it swears off direct involvement with public policy, the Federalist Society has a Pro Bono Center that connects members with conservative public-interest groups. The networking provided by the Federalist Society has clearly paid off. As noted by Amanda Hollis-Brusky, the Federalist Society provided the "intellectual capital" to bring about a rightward shift in the Supreme Court's jurisprudence in the areas of gun rights, federalism, and corporate speech.[94]

BAND OF BROTHERS

A humorous story dates back to Scalia's first term on the Supreme Court, when he attended the celebration for Justice Brennan's eightieth birthday. Brennan's law clerks gathered all their boss's important opinions and set them on a table. Not missing a beat, Scalia looked at the opinions and quipped, "So little time, so much to overrule!" Brennan reportedly "roared with laughter."[95] During his thirty years on the bench, Scalia strenuously pushed to limit or overturn many Warren and Burger Court precedents, but he probably did not accomplish everything he wanted to do.

Justice Thomas, however, is taking up the mantle. Many conservatives regard Thomas as the more principled originalist, and he has now been joined by two other originalists: Neil Gorsuch and Amy Coney Barrett.[96] During the Trump administration, Thomas reportedly served as a major pipeline for appointments to federal judgeships.[97] To his credit, Justice Thomas has exercised more restraint than Scalia when it comes to personal criticism of his colleagues, but his originalist views are arguably more drastic than Scalia's, particularly with regard to the scope of federal power and the administrative state. In fact, Scalia referred to Thomas as a "blood thirsty" originalist.[98] Justice Thomas is not concerned about court precedent and, as a constitutional purist, wants to get things right. If the Roberts Court reexamines the administrative state, it will not be because Justice Scalia wanted the court to do so, but because Justice Thomas has insisted that it does so.

At the end of the day, both Scalia and Thomas are "cause" originalists. After Bork's death, Scalia credited his good friend with being "the intellectual point-man for the movement to curb the pretentions of the Warren Court and return the meaning of the Constitution to what it said." Bork's "views were not," Scalia admitted, "much different from my own."[99] When Scalia died, Thomas described their relationship as "a band of brothers." They came from vastly different backgrounds, Thomas observed at the 2016 National Lawyers Convention, but they agreed on the same basic interpretative philosophy. He then urged the audience to join the fight and reclaim the form of government the framers intended. "Whether we win or lose," Thomas remarked, "we are in this battle together."[100]

What must be remembered, however, is that no single approach to constitutional interpretation can claim with absolute certainty to be the "correct" one. The founders did not require, nor did they intend, future generations to be governed by their specific intentions. Their use of broad language was both necessary and purposeful. "It is a constitution we are expounding," Chief Justice Marshall wrote, one that "is intended to endure for ages to come, and, consequently, to be adapted to the various crises of human affairs."[101] Justice Scalia often claimed that originalism was orthodoxy until the Warren Court,[102] but there are many examples of a living Constitution that predated Chief Justice Warren's tenure. In 1920 Justice Holmes wrote:

> When we are dealing with words that also are a constituent act, like the Constitution of the United States, we must realize that they have called into life a being the development of which could not have been foreseen completely by the most gifted of its begetters. It was enough for them to realize or to hope that they had created an organism; it has taken a century and has cost their successors much sweat and blood to prove that they created a nation. The case before us must be considered in the light of our whole experience and not merely in that of what was said a hundred years ago.[103]

For much of US history, judges have relied on various sources of law to interpret the US Constitution. To be sure, text and history have always been the primary focus, but judges have used other sources too. For example, the justices in *Brown v. Board of Education* were clearly concerned about the moral question of segregation, not simply its historical practice. Under a common-law approach, words, context, effects, and the spirit of the law all matter in interpreting legal documents—an interpretative approach defended by none other than William Blackstone.[104] Such a view does not make judges unconstrained actors. They must cite the reasons for their decisions in written opinions. Ultimately, their legitimacy is based on public opinion and the persuasive authority of their legal opinions, which includes the sources of law they rely on. Judges should not make decisions that run counter to the precise language of the Constitution, but as Justice Frankfurter remarked, "the meaning of phrases like 'due process of law,' and of simple terms like 'liberty' and 'property,' is not revealed within the Constitution; their meaning is derived from without."[105] A common-law approach to interpreting the US Constitution has been utilized since the time of the founding, and it is a wholly legitimate way of doing so.

Notes

INTRODUCTION

1. See, e.g., Antonin Scalia, "Originalism: The Lesser Evil," *University of Cincinnati Law Review* 57 (1989): 849–865; Antonin Scalia, *A Matter of Interpretation: Federal Courts and the Law*, ed. Amy Gutmann (Princeton, NJ: Princeton University Press, 1997); Antonin Scalia and Bryan A. Garner, *Reading Law: The Interpretation of Legal Texts* (St. Paul, MN: Thomson/West, 2012); Antonin Scalia, *Scalia Speaks: Reflections on Law, Faith, and Life Well Lived*, ed. Christopher J. Scalia and Edward Whelan (New York: Crown Forum, 2017).

2. Hugo L. Black, *A Constitutional Faith* (New York: Alfred A. Knopf, 1968), 66 (describing the Constitution as his "legal bible").

3. *Griswold v. Connecticut*, 381 U.S. 479, 510 (1965) (Black, J., dissenting).

4. Clarence Thomas, "Judging," *Kansas Law Review* 45 (1996): 1.

5. *U.S. Term Limits Inc. v. Thornton*, 514 U.S. 779, 845 (1995) (Thomas, J., dissenting).

6. See *United States v. Lopez*, 514 U.S. 549, 584 (1995) (Thomas, J., concurring); *United States v. Morrison*, 529 U.S. 598, 627 (2000) (Thomas, J., concurring).

7. See, e.g., *Elk Grove Unified School District v. Newdow*, 542 U.S. 1, 45, 50–51 (2004) (Thomas, J., concurring in the judgment).

8. *Whitman v. American Trucking Associations*, 531 U.S. 457 (2001) (Thomas, J., concurring); *Department of Transportation v. Association of American Railroads*, 575 U.S. 43 (2015) (Thomas, J., concurring).

9. *Saentz v. Roe*, 526 U.S. 489, 521 (1999) (Thomas, J., dissenting); *McDonald v. Chicago*, 561 U.S. 742, 805 (2010) (Thomas, J., concurring in part and concurring in the judgment).

10. Ralph A. Rossum, *Understanding Clarence Thomas: The Jurisprudence of Constitutional Restoration* (Lawrence: University Press of Kansas, 2014), 129.

11. Randy Barnett, "Scalia's Infidelity: A Critique of 'Faint-Hearted' Originalism," *University of Cincinnati Law Review* 75 (2006): 7, 13.

12. Interestingly, there are now two other originalists on the Supreme Court: Neil Gorsuch (2017) and Amy Coney Barrett (2020). Early signs indicate that Gorsuch shares some of the libertarian views of Justice Thomas. See, e.g., *Gundy v. United States*, 139 S. Ct. 2116 (2019) (Gorsuch, J., with whom Thomas, J., joined, dissenting) (questioning the court's "intelligible principle" in nondelegation cases); and *Gutierrez-Brizuela v. Lynch*, 834 F.3d 1142, 1149 (2016) (Gorsuch, J., concurring) (criticizing *Chevron* deference and stating that "maybe the time has come to face the behemoth").

13. Black's historical analysis of the incorporation doctrine drew sharp criticism from many commentators, including contemporary originalists. See, e.g., Charles Fairman, "Does the Fourteenth Amendment Incorporate the Bill of Rights?" *Stanford Law Review* 2, 1 (1949): 5–139; Raoul Berger, *Government by Judiciary: The Transformation of*

the Fourteenth Amendment (Cambridge, MA: Harvard University Press, 1977), 134–156. Other legal scholars who were not originalists themselves have criticized Black's historical analysis in certain areas of the law. See, e.g., Leonard W. Levy, *Original Intent and the Framers' Constitution* (New York: Macmillan, 1988), 269 ("few Justices in the history of the Supreme Court have contributed so much to the Court's effectiveness as a constitutional convention as Justice Black, especially in his First and Fifth Amendment opinions"); Alexander M. Bickel, "Mr. Justice Black: The Unobvious Meaning of Plain Words," *New Republic*, March 14, 1960, 13–15.

14. See, e.g., Berger, *Government by Judiciary*, 200–201n27 (claiming that although Black was correct in not viewing the due process clause as a "blank check" for altering the meaning of the Constitution, he did not always follow the logic of this view); Christopher Wolfe, review of Gerald Dunne's *Hugo Black and the Judicial Revolution*, in *The Alternative: An American Spectator* (October 1977): 31–33 ("The notable thing about Black's own interpretation is the extent to which he does not follow the words of the Constitution").

15. For the most part, Justice Black's writings are not included in the extensive literature surrounding debates over modern originalism. See, e.g., *Original Meaning Jurisprudence: A Sourcebook* (Washington, DC: Office of Legal Policy, US Department of Justice, 1987); *Guidelines on Constitutional Litigation* (Washington, DC: Office of Legal Policy, US Department of Justice, 1988); Steven G. Calabresi, *Originalism: A Quarter-Century of Debate* (Washington, DC: Regnery, 2007); Scalia and Garner, *Reading Law* (citing one edited volume of Black's opinions). Many legal scholars date the origins of modern originalism to 1971, when Robert Bork authored an important article titled "Neutral Principles and Some First Amendment Problems," *Indiana Law Journal* 47, 1 (1971): 1–35. In fact, Steven Calabresi, cofounder of the Federalist Society, credits Judge Bork as being the "intellectual godfather" of originalism. See Calabresi, *Originalism*, 14. The one important exception to Black's omission from the abundant literature on originalism was a 1986 speech delivered by attorney general Edwin Meese at St. Louis Law School. See *Major Policy Statements of the Attorney General: Edwin Meese III, 1985–1988* (Washington, DC: Government Printing Office, 1989), 31–37. In that speech, Meese was quite complimentary of Justice Black's originalist methodology, although he did express disagreement with Black's "absolutist" view of incorporation. More recently, Akhil Amar, a self-described progressive originalist, has recognized the important accomplishments of Black's originalist approach. See Akhil Reed Amar, "Rethinking Originalism," *Slate*, September 21, 2005; Akhil Reed Amar, "Hugo Black and the Hall of Fame," *Alabama Law Review* 53 (2002): 1221.

16. See Lee Epstein, Jeffrey A. Segal, Harold J. Spaeth, and Thomas G. Walker, *The Supreme Court Compendium: Data, Decisions, and Developments*, 6th ed. (Washington, DC: Congressional Quarterly, 2015), 620, 623. However, if one looks at only nonunanimous cases, the level of agreement drops to 83 percent. I am grateful to Lee Epstein for providing this statistic from the Supreme Court database. See Thomas G. Walker, Nancy Staudt, Scott Hendrickson, and Jason Roberts, "The U.S. Supreme Court Justices Database," http://epstein.wustl.edu/research/justicesdata.html.

17. *Clinton v. City of New York*, 524 U.S. 417, 469 (1998).

18. Antonin Scalia, "Remarks by the Honorable Antonin Scalia for the 25th Anniversary of *Chevron v. NRDC*," *Administrative Law Review* 66, 2 (2014): 243; *United States v. Mead Corp.*, 533 U.S. 218 (2001) (Scalia, J., dissenting).

19. In *Auer v. Robbins*, 519 U.S. 452 (1997), a decision Scalia authored himself, the court unanimously ruled that *Chevron* deference should apply to an agency's reinterpretation of its own rules and regulatory schemes. Scalia later had second thoughts about that particular decision.

20. Antonin Scalia, "Judicial Deference to Administrative Interpretations of Law," *Duke Law Journal* (1989): 521.

21. Scalia based the Justice Department's legal opinion on several factors: the historical understanding and practices since George Washington's administration, the assumption that the president's papers were his personal property when Congress passed the Presidential Libraries Act of 1955, and the absence of any modern statutory language that stated anything to the contrary. See 43 Op. Atty. Gen. 1 (1974).

22. "Executive Privilege—Secrecy in Government," Hearings before the Subcommittee on Intergovernmental Relations of the Committee on Government Operations, US Senate, 94th Cong., 1st sess., 1975, 72.

23. Clarence Thomas, graduation speech, Thomas G. Pullen School, June 1996, http://justicethomas.blogspot.com/2007/09/graduation-speech-thomas-g-pullen.html.

24. Clarence Thomas, *My Grandfather's Son: A Memoir* (New York: HarperCollins, 2007), 79.

25. *Grutter v. Bollinger*, 539 U.S. 306, 349 (2003) (Thomas, J., concurring in part and dissenting in part).

26. Thomas Jefferson to James Madison, December 20, 1787, in *The Papers of Thomas Jefferson*, ed. Julian P. Boyd (Princeton, NJ: Princeton University Press, 1955), vol. 12, 442.

27. Jefferson to Madison, 440.

28. Roger K. Newman, *Hugo Black: A Biography*, 2nd ed. (New York: Fordham University Press, 1997), 67.

29. Daniel J. Meador, "Hugo Black and Thomas Jefferson," *Virginia Quarterly Review* 79, 3 (Summer 2003): 464.

30. "The voice of the people," Hamilton proclaimed, "has been said to be the voice of God; and however generally this maxim has been quoted and believed, it is not true in fact. The people are turbulent and changing; they seldom judge or determine right." Alexander Hamilton, "Constitutional Convention Speech on a Plan of Government" (Robert Yates's version), June 18, 1787, in *The Papers of Alexander Hamilton*, ed. Harold C. Syrett (New York: Columbia University Press, 1962), vol. 4, 200.

31. Hamilton, "Constitutional Convention Speech" (James Madison's version), in *Papers of Alexander Hamilton*, 4:193.

32. Hamilton, "Constitutional Convention Speech," 200.

33. The conference was sponsored by the Federalist Society and held at Yale Law School on April 23–25, 1982—only four months prior to Scalia's appointment to the DC Court of Appeals. See generally "A Symposia on Federalism," *Harvard Journal of Law and Public Policy* 6 (1982): 1–147.

34. Antonin Scalia, "The Two Faces of Federalism," *Harvard Journal of Law and Public Policy* 6 (1982): 19.

35. "Nomination of Judge Antonin Scalia," Hearings before the Committee on the Judiciary, US Senate, 99th Cong., 2nd sess., August 5–6, 1986, 99–100.

36. Betsey Blaney, "Scalia, Breyer Bandy about How to Decide Cases," Associated Press, November 12, 2010, http://archive.boston.com/news/nation/articles/2010/11/12/scalia_breyer_bandy_about_how_to_decide_cases/.

37. *New York Times v. Sullivan*, 376 U.S. 254 (1964).

38. Prior to his appointment to the Supreme Court, Thomas expressed appreciation for Jefferson's authorship of the Declaration of Independence: "We join all Americans in revering and cherishing the memory of Thomas Jefferson." Speech by Clarence Thomas, University of Virginia, Charlottesville, October 19, 1983, Mark Paoletta Files, no. 45512-004, George H. W. Bush Presidential Library, College Station, TX. Thomas also praised the political philosophy of Alexander Hamilton, particularly as it related to executive power and the free-market system: "Perhaps the most important Founding Father for refuting [Charles] Beard's economic interpretation of the Constitution and its latest adherents is Alexander Hamilton." Clarence Thomas, speech before American Bar Association, San Francisco, August 11, 1987, Paoletta Files, no. 45514-002. See also Clarence Thomas, "Hamilton's Constitutional Vision," letter to the editor, *Washington Times*, September 2, 1987, A10. More recently, Thomas's appreciation of Hamilton seems to have reduced. In a 2021 address, he described his political views as "closer to the Anti-Federalists" and raised concerns about the expansive interpretations of federal power, including Chief Justice Marshall's opinion in *McCulloch v. Maryland* (1819). He then jokingly said, "I didn't go watch *Hamilton*, I can tell you that." Clarence Thomas, 2021 Tocqueville Lecture, University of Notre Dame, September 16, 2021. https://constudies.nd.edu/events-news/events/2021/09/16/2021/tocqueville-lecture-justice-clarence-thomas/.

39. Clarence Thomas, "The Higher Law Background of the Privileges or Immunities Clause of the Fourteenth Amendment," *Harvard Journal of Law and Public Policy* 12, 1 (Winter 1989): 63, 65 ("Abraham Lincoln's argument for the anti-slavery cause was powerful because he understood the Constitution in light of the Declaration of Independence").

40. Thomas, *My Grandfather's Son*, 2, 28.

41. Clarence Thomas, speech before Pacific Research Institute, San Francisco, August 10, 1987, Paoletta Files, no. 45511-005.

42. Clarence Thomas, "Personal Responsibility," *Regent University Law Review* 12 (1999–2000): 323.

43. Bill Kauffman, "Clarence Thomas," *Reason* (November 1987): 29–33.

44. During his confirmation hearings, Thomas contended that he was interested in natural law "purely in the context of political theory" and that it would be inappropriate for a judge to rely on it when deciding cases. See "Nomination of Judge Clarence Thomas to Be Associate Justice of the Supreme Court of the United States," Hearings before the Committee on the Judiciary, US Senate, 102nd Cong., 1st sess. (September 12, 1991), pt. 1, 112.

45. Thomas, "Higher Law Background of Privileges or Immunities Clause," 65.

46. Thomas, speech before Pacific Research Institute.

47. *Lawrence v. Texas,* 539 U.S. 558, 605–606 (2003) (Thomas, J., dissenting).

48. Thomas, speech before Pacific Research Institute; Clarence Thomas, speech at Cato Institute, April 23, 1987, Paoletta Files, no. 45514-001.

49. James B. Staab, "The Tenth Amendment and Justice Scalia's 'Split Personality,'" *Journal of Law and Politics* 16, 2 (Spring 2000): 231–379.

50. *Brown v. Board of Education of Topeka,* 347 U.S. 483 (1954).

51. Clarence Thomas, speech delivered to Black Law Students Association Conference, Yale Law School, April 7, 1984, Paoletta Files, no. 45510-005.

52. *Hamdi v. Rumsfeld,* 542 U.S. 507 (2004) (Scalia, J., dissenting) (Thomas, J., dissenting).

53. *Gonzales v. Raich,* 545 U.S. 1 (2005) (Scalia, J., concurring) (Thomas, J., dissenting).

54. *Zivotofsky v. Kerry,* 576 U.S. 1059 (2015) (Thomas, J., concurring in part and dissenting in part) (Scalia, J., dissenting).

55. *Employment Division, Department of Human Resources of Oregon v. Smith,* 494 U.S. 872 (1990).

56. *Fulton v. City of Philadelphia,* 141 S. Ct. 1868 (2021) (Alito, J., concurring in the judgment) (Gorsuch, J., concurring in the judgment).

57. The Fifth Amendment's grand jury provision states, "No person shall be held to answer for a capital, or otherwise infamous crime, unless on presentment or indictment of a Grand Jury." The Fifth Amendment's double jeopardy provision protects individuals from being "twice put in jeopardy of life or limb" for the same offense. The due process clauses of the Fifth and Fourteenth Amendments guarantee that no person shall be deprived of "life, liberty or property, without due process of law."

58. *Fay v. New York,* 332 U.S. 261, 282 (1947).

59. J. Harvie Wilkinson III, *Cosmic Constitutional Theory: Why Americans Are Losing Their Inalienable Right to Self-Governance* (New York: Oxford University Press, 2012).

1. BIOGRAPHICAL SKETCHES

1. Oliver Wendell Holmes Jr., *The Common Law* (Boston: Little, Brown, 1881), 1.

2. Benjamin N. Cardozo, *The Nature of the Judicial Process* (New Haven, CT: Yale University Press, 1921), 13.

3. Roger K. Newman, *Hugo Black: A Biography,* 2nd ed. (New York: Fordham University Press, 1997), 3–4; Steve Suitts, *Hugo Black of Alabama: How His Roots and Early Career Shaped the Great Champion of the Constitution* (Montgomery, AL: NewSouth Books, 2005), 42.

4. Newman, *Hugo Black,* 16.

5. After completing a summer internship with his brother, Hugo discovered that "he could not escape a physical reaction to the blood, smells, and crude nature of the healing arts." Suitts, *Hugo Black of Alabama,* 97.

6. *Lochner v. New York*, 198 U.S. 45 (1905).

7. Suitts, *Hugo Black of Alabama*, 101. See also Hugo L. Black, "Reminiscences," *Alabama Law Review* 18 (1965): 3, 10.

8. Black paid $1,500 for the collection. Suitts, *Hugo Black of Alabama*, 104; Daniel M. Berman, "The Political Philosophy of Hugo L. Black" (diss., Rutgers University, 1957), 4–5.

9. Suitts, *Hugo Black of Alabama*, 10; Virginia Van der Veer Hamilton, *Hugo Black: The Alabama Years* (Baton Rouge: Louisiana State University Press, 1972), 77.

10. Black later referred to the convict lease system as "revengeful hells." He was also instrumental in ending the inhumane practice in Alabama, which was the last state to do so in 1928. Suitts, *Hugo Black of Alabama*, 371, 386; Newman, *Hugo Black*, 65.

11. Suitts, *Hugo Black of Alabama*, 130–132. Birmingham had a debt of $500,000, and the new police court position was intended to save the city about $12,000.

12. See Suitts, *Hugo Black of Alabama*, 132, 141; Newman, *Hugo Black*, 30.

13. Suitts, *Hugo Black of Alabama*, 137. See also John P. Frank, *Mr. Justice Black: The Man and His Opinions* (New York: Alfred A. Knopf, 1949), 18–19.

14. "Black a Champion of the Under Dog," *New York Times*, August 15, 1937, 2. See also Gene L. Mason, "Hugo Black and the United States Senate" (MA thesis, University of Kansas, 1964), 199–200.

15. Hamilton, *Hugo Black*, 45.

16. Suitts, *Hugo Black of Alabama*, 148. When the case was retried, Black received a jury award of $3,500.

17. As a Supreme Court justice, Black raised concerns about this practice and defended a broad interpretation of the Seventh Amendment's jury provision. See, e.g., *Stewart v. Southern Railway Co.*, 315 U.S. 283 (1942).

18. Suitts, *Hugo Black of Alabama*, 149.

19. Newman, *Hugo Black*, 34, 54, 61.

20. Heflin was the brother of US senator J. Thomas Heflin. The other two candidates were Zebulon T. Rudolph, who had the support of Birmingham's establishment, and F. D. McArthur, who had the backing of organized labor. Newman, 36–37.

21. Hamilton, *Hugo Black*, 57.

22. Newman, *Hugo Black*, 36.

23. Hamilton, *Hugo Black*, 57.

24. Newman, *Hugo Black*, 38.

25. Suitts, *Hugo Black of Alabama*, 108.

26. Newman, *Hugo Black*, 39.

27. Newman, 38.

28. Suitts, *Hugo Black of Alabama*, 222. Black also attempted to convict fifteen men of rape and seven men of carnal knowledge of girls under the age of twelve, but the all-male juries rendered convictions in only five of the former cases and three of the latter.

29. Suitts, 187.

30. Hamilton, *Hugo Black*, 60.

31. Suitts, *Hugo Black of Alabama*, 217.

32. When Hugo was fourteen, his father died from cirrhosis of the liver, making Hugo an early and fervent prohibitionist. His older brother Pelham also lost his life in an alcohol-related accident at age sixteen. Suitts, 94.

33. Hamilton, *Hugo Black*, 62.

34. *State ex rel. Black v. Delaye*, 68 So. 993 (1915).

35. Black joined the unanimous decision in *Valentine v. Chrestensen*, 316 U.S. 52 (1942), which held that "the Constitution imposes no restraint on government as respects purely commercial advertising."

36. Hamilton, *Hugo Black*, 66.

37. Suitts, *Hugo Black of Alabama*, 200–208.

38. Hamilton, *Hugo Black*, 66.

39. *Hemmelweit v. State ex rel. Dedge*, 75 So. 961 (1917).

40. See, e.g., Jacob W. Landynski, "In Search of Justice Black's Fourth Amendment," *Fordham Law Review* 45 (1976–1977): 453–496.

41. Suitts, *Hugo Black of Alabama*, 169.

42. "Bessemer Police Are Excoriated in Partial Report by Grand Jury," *Birmingham Age-Herald*, September 18, 1915.

43. The grand jury report was passed on to a special investigative committee of Bessemer residents, which vindicated the findings in the report. The committee recommended the resignation of the mayor, two aldermen, and five police officers. Unfortunately, none of the public officials resigned, and several of the officers were later reinstated, including Maddox. See Frank, *Mr. Justice Black*, 29; Suitts, *Hugo Black of Alabama*, 178.

44. Hugo Black Jr., *My Father: A Remembrance* (New York: Random House, 1975), 28–29.

45. In 1915 the Alabama legislature passed a court reform law that gave the circuit solicitor, not the county solicitor, the authority to appoint assistants. Suitts, *Hugo Black of Alabama*, 167, 221.

46. Suitts, 221.

47. Black initially adopted William Jennings Bryan's neutrality position. As his son, Hugo Jr., points out, Black was a pacifist at heart who "hated wars." Black, *My Father*, 32. He was later a strong critic of the Korean and Vietnam Wars.

48. Suitts, *Hugo Black of Alabama*, 239.

49. Black was "flat broke" because of the extensive amount of public service he had done and the hospital bills he had to pay after contracting the flu in the epidemic of 1918. Suitts, 240.

50. One client, John Brown, was a black convict who had been "severely burned and charred" in a major mining accident. However, because he was serving a life sentence, the Alabama Supreme Court ruled that Brown was "civilly dead." Another client, Henry Lewis, was permanently crippled when a mine's roof collapsed. Black received a $4,000 judgment for Lewis. See Suitts, 370–371, 377–378.

51. Between 1923 and 1925 Black earned approximately $47,000 per year. Newman, *Hugo Black*, 54–70.

52. Illinois did not segregate the races in the coach section of its trains.

53. Suitts, *Hugo Black of Alabama*, 270–271. It should be noted that the Miniard case appears to be an aberration. Black never used the word "nigger" in any case while he was the solicitor for Jefferson County. Suitts, 287–288.

54. Black requested $2,999 because if he asked for $3,000, the case could have been transferred to federal court, which he always tried to avoid. Black won a jury award of $2,999, but the Alabama Supreme Court reversed that decision twice. However, in 1923 Black's third try resulted in a jury award for Mrs. Miniard. Suitts, 244, 284; Newman, *Hugo Black*, 57–58.

55. Suitts, *Hugo Black of Alabama*, 342.

56. Suitts, 352.

57. Suitts, 359. See also Newman, *Hugo Black*, 71–88.

58. Howard Ball, *Hugo L. Black: Cold Steel Warrior* (New York: Oxford University Press, 1996), 63–64.

59. Black described immigration as "a serious American problem" and stated that he opposed any further immigration "until we can educate and Americanize those already here." "The melting-pot idea," he said, "is dangerous to our national heritage." Hugo Black, "Opening Speech of the Hon. Hugo L. Black, March 20, 1926," Ashland, AL, Hugo L. Black Papers, Library of Congress, Manuscript Division, box 105.

60. Black, "Opening Speech." See also Hamilton, *Hugo Black*, 123–126.

61. Black, "Opening Speech."

62. Hamilton, *Hugo Black*, 134. See also Suitts, *Hugo Black of Alabama*, 482–525.

63. Hamilton, *Hugo Black*, 138–139.

64. "I believe," Black told his Senate colleagues, "that for the manufacture of fertilizer under a chemical process, which . . . is constantly changing, a private company that is in the business would more likely benefit the farmers than would the Agricultural Department of the Government." But Black was willing to compromise on how Muscle Shoals would be managed because, more than anything, he wanted farmers from his home state to get inexpensive fertilizer. "I am anxious and ready and willing to meet with Members of this body on any common ground where we can stand and pass any law that will reduce the price of fertilizer, either by Government operation or private operation." *Congressional Record* (hereafter *CR*), vol. 69, pt. 4, 70th Cong., 1st sess., March 6, 1928, 4189–4190.

65. President Coolidge pocket-vetoed the bill, but Senator Norris's public ownership concept eventually won the day when the Tennessee Valley Authority was created by the Roosevelt administration in 1933.

66. *CR*, vol. 69, pt. 4, 70th Cong., 1st sess., March 13, 1928, 4634.

67. *CR*, vol. 75, pt. 4, 72nd Cong., 1st sess., February 8, 1932, 3516–3517.

68. According to his proposed bill, goods would be banned from interstate or foreign commerce if employees worked more than five days per week or six hours per day.

69. Hugo Black to Elizabeth Brandeis, July 22, 1955, Black Papers, box 58.

70. Hamilton, *Hugo Black*, 218.

71. Under this act, trade or industrial associations representing labor and management were to draft codes of fair competition subject to alteration by and approval of the president.

72. *CR*, vol. 77, pt. 6, 73rd Cong., 1st sess., June 8, 1933, 5284.

73. *Panama Refining Company v. Ryan*, 293 U.S. 388 (1935); *Schechter Poultry Corporation v. United States*, 295 U.S. 495 (1935).

74. Hugo Black to Demps A. Oden, February 14, 1935, Black Papers, box 211.

75. See Hamilton, *Hugo Black*, 214–234; Newman, *Hugo Black*, 161–166; Frank, *Mr. Justice Black*, 65–74.

76. See William A. Gregory and Rennard Strickland, "Hugo Black's Congressional Investigation of Lobbying and the Public Utilities Holding Company Act: A Historical View of the Power of Trusts, New Deal Politics, and Regulatory Propaganda," *Oklahoma Law Review* 29 (1976): 543–576.

77. The lawsuit claimed that the broad searches were a fishing expedition and violated the Fourth Amendment. Newman, *Hugo Black*, 185–188.

78. *CR*, vol. 80, pt. 3, 74th Cong., 2nd sess. March 9, 1936, 3436.

79. William E. Leuchtenburg, "A Klansman Joins the Court: The Appointment of Hugo L. Black," *University of Chicago Law Review* 41, 1 (Fall 1973): 1–31.

80. Newman, *Hugo Black*, 220–246.

81. The six-part series ran September 13–18, 1937. The first story was titled "Justice Black Revealed as a Ku Klux Klansman" and included a copy of what it called "Klansman Black's (Temporary) Resignation." In fact, Black was inducted into the Robert E. Lee Klan No. 1 (Birmingham) on September 11, 1923, and resigned his membership on July 9, 1925. See Newman, *Hugo Black*, 247–263.

82. When Black ran for the Senate, the *New York Times* reported that he had the support of the Klan, which suggests that it was common knowledge that he had at least some connection to the Klan. "Klan Support Two in Alabama Primary," *New York Times*, August 9, 1926, 4. In response to a 1968 article about his Supreme Court appointment, Black took the opportunity to explain his own understanding of FDR's knowledge of his Klan affiliation. "When I went up to lunch with [President Roosevelt]," Black recalled, he "told me that there was no reason for my worrying about my having been a member of the Ku Klux Klan. . . . He never in any way, by word or attitude, indicated any doubt about my having been in the Klan nor did he indicate any criticism of me for having been a member of that organization. The rumors and statements to the contrary are wrong." Ball, *Hugo L. Black*, 98–99 (citing Hugo Black, note to the file, May 1968, Black Papers, box 31). The 1968 article was authored by Virginia Van der Veer Hamilton, "Hugo Black and the K.K.K.," *American Heritage* 19, 3 (April 1968): 61–64, 108–111. See also Martin Carcasson and James Arnt Aune, "Klansman on the Court: Justice Hugo Black's 1937 Radio Address to the Nation," *Quarterly Journal of Speech* 89, 2 (May 2003): 156.

83. Carcasson and Aune, "Klansman on the Court," 156.

84. See Hugo L. Black, "I Did Join the Klan," radio address, October 1, 1937, *Vital Speeches* 4, 1 (October 15, 1937): 20–21. Black's speech had the desired effect. Prior to the speech, 59 percent of the public believed he should resign; after the speech, 56 percent thought he should stay on the court. See Frank, *Mr. Justice Black*, 106. Many liberal members of the press, however, were critical of Black for not disavowing the KKK more forcefully.

85. Newman, *Hugo Black*, 97–100.

86. "Justice Black, Champion of Civil Liberties for 34 Years on Court, Dies at Age 85," *New York Times*, September 26, 1971, 76. See also Suitts, *Hugo Black of Alabama*, 409–414. One should not overlook the ideological compatibility between Black and the Klan: populism, nativism, Christianity, and Prohibition. However, Black did not share its anti-Catholic, anti-Jewish, and white supremacist views, and he never supported any sort of violent behavior.

87. Black described the Klan he joined as a mostly law-abiding organization, but he acknowledged the existence of some extremist elements. He also reportedly spoke out against any sort of lawless action. Suitts, *Hugo Black of Alabama*, 415–416, 432–433.

88. *Brown v. Board of Education of Topeka*, 347 U.S. 483 (1954).

89. In 1970, one year before his death, Black returned to Alabama, accompanied by Chief Justice Burger, to give an address before the Birmingham Bar Association. See Suitts, *Hugo Black of Alabama*, 13–23.

90. Catherine was born in New York City, and her family subsequently moved to Trenton. Joan Biskupic, *American Original: The Life and Constitution of Supreme Court Justice Antonin Scalia* (New York: Sarah Crichton Books, 2009), 366n2.

91. Biskupic, 13.

92. Antonin Scalia, "The Limits of the Law," *New Jersey Law Journal* 119 (1987): 4. Scalia said that his father always had a book in his hand (French, Spanish, or Italian) and that the elder Scalia corrected his judicial opinions when he was on the DC Court of Appeals. "Q & A with Justice Antonin Scalia," Brian Lamb interview, C-SPAN, May 2, 2008.

93. Margaret Talbot, "Supreme Confidence," *New Yorker*, March 28, 2005, 43.

94. In the early years, Catherine had plenty of help from aunts and uncles, since Nino was the only child of his generation on either side of the family. All this attention led Scalia to confess years later that he was "spoiled rotten." "Justice Scalia on the Record," Leslie Stahl interview, *60 Minutes*, April 27, 2008, http://www.cbsnews.com/videos/antonin-scalia-the-60-minutes-interview/.

95. "Q & A with Scalia."

96. In 1985 Scalia's DC Court of Appeals clerks had this saying inscribed on a plaque that they then presented to their boss as a gift. Ruth Marcus and Susan Schmidt, "Scalia Tenacious after Staking out a Position," *Washington Post*, June 22, 1986, A16.

97. Kannon K. Shanmugam, "Justice Scalia: A Personal Remembrance," *Journal of Supreme Court History* 41, 3 (2016): 252, 255.

98. George Kannar, "The Constitutional Catechism of Antonin Scalia," *Yale Law Journal* 99 (1990): 1297–1357.

99. S. Eugene Scalia, *Carducci: His Critics and His Translators in England and America, 1881–1932* (1937), 90, 95.

100. Antonin Scalia, address before the Attorney General's Conference on Economic Liberties, Washington, DC, June 14, 1986, in *Original Meaning Jurisprudence: A Sourcebook, Appendix C* (Washington, DC: Office of Legal Policy, US Department of Justice, 1987), 3.

101. Marcus and Schmidt, "Scalia Tenacious," A1. Vincent Panaro later served as a state assemblyman and Mercy County prosecutor.

102. Antonin Scalia, "Supreme Court Justice Perspective," a conversation with students from Thomas Jefferson High School, Fairfax County, VA, Supreme Court Building, C-SPAN, April 9, 2008. See also Bruce Allen Murphy, *Scalia: A Court of One* (New York: Simon & Schuster, 2014), 30.

103. Murphy, *Scalia*, 12–13.

104. Antonin Scalia, "Constitutional Interpretation," Julius J. Oppenheimer Lecture, University of Central Missouri, March 4, 2008.

105. Biskupic, *American Original*, 21.

106. Antonin Scalia, *Scalia Speaks: Reflections on Law, Faith, and Life Well Lived*, ed. Christopher J. Scalia and Edward Whelan (New York: Crown Forum, 2017), 312–313.

107. Murphy, *Scalia*, 16–17.

108. Scalia, "Supreme Court Justice Perspective."

109. Scalia, *Scalia Speaks*, 63.

110. Marcus and Schmidt, "Scalia Tenacious," A16.

111. Biskupic, *American Original*, 22.

112. Antonin Scalia, "Economic Affairs as Human Affairs," *Cato Journal* 4, 3 (Winter 1985): 703.

113. Irvin Molotsky, "Judge with Tenacity and Charm: Antonin Scalia," *New York Times*, June 18, 1986, A31.

114. After Scalia died, his successor, Neil Gorsuch, was asked if he would be willing to keep the trophy in his office, and Gorsuch graciously agreed. "Neil Gorsuch Has an Elk Named Leroy as a Supreme Court Office Mate," *Denver Post*, October 6, 2017.

115. Scalia, *Scalia Speaks*, 63.

116. Murphy, *Scalia*, 22.

117. Murphy, 25–27.

118. Samuel Alito, "A Tribute to Justice Scalia," *Yale Law Journal* 126 (2017): 1605.

119. Antonin Gregory Scalia, "Cohonguroton Address," June 9, 1957, *Georgetown College Journal* 86, 1 (Autumn 1957): 12–14, Booth Family Center for Special Collections, Lauinger Library, Georgetown University. See also Biskupic, *American Original*, 25–26; Murphy, *Scalia*, 28–29.

120. Richard A. Brisbin Jr., *Justice Antonin Scalia and the Conservative Revival* (Baltimore: Johns Hopkins University Press, 1997), 15.

121. The casebook for this course was published posthumously. See Henry M. Hart Jr. and Albert M. Sacks, *The Legal Process: Basic Problems in the Making and Application of Law*, ed. William N. Eskridge Jr. and Philip P. Frickey (Westbury, NY: Foundation Press, 1994).

122. See, e.g., Brisbin, *Justice Antonin Scalia and the Conservative Revival*; Peter B. Edelman, "Justice Scalia's Jurisprudence and the Good Society: Shades of Felix Frankfurter and the Harvard Hit Parade of the 1950s," *Cardozo Law Review* 12 (1991): 1799–1815.

123. Interestingly, during Scalia's second year at Harvard, Herbert Wechsler gave a famous lecture that reflected this aspect of the legal process school. Herbert Wechsler,

"Toward Neutral Principles of Constitutional Law," *Harvard Law Review* 73 (1959): 1–35. Although Wechsler agreed with the court's decision in *Brown v. Board of Education,* he criticized the justices for relying on psychological studies that he believed might later change.

124. See Antonin Scalia, *A Matter of Interpretation: Federal Courts and the Law,* ed. Amy Gutmann (Princeton, NJ: Princeton University Press, 1997); Robert H. Bork, "Neutral Principles and Some First Amendment Problems," *Indiana Law Journal* 47, 1 (1971): 1–35.

125. See, e.g., *Planned Parenthood of Southeastern Pennsylvania v. Casey,* 505 U.S. 833 (1992) (Scalia, J., concurring in the judgment in part and dissenting in part); *Board of County Commissioners v. Umberhr,* 518 U.S. 668 (1996) (Scalia, J., dissenting); *O'Hare Truck Service Inc. v. City of Northlake,* 518 U.S. 712 (1996) (Scalia, J., dissenting); *Roper v. Simmons,* 543 U.S. 551 (2005) (Scalia, J., dissenting); *Obergefell v. Hodges,* 576 U.S. 644 (2015). Scalia was equally critical of "hard look" scrutiny in administrative law cases and the use of legislative history in statutory cases, both of which were supported by legal process theorists.

126. Antonin Scalia, "The Rule of Law as a Law of Rules," *University of Chicago Law Review* 56 (1989): 1179; Antonin Scalia, "Morality, Pragmatism, and the Legal Order," *Harvard Journal of Law and Public Policy* 9 (1986): 125.

127. Marcus and Schmidt, "Scalia Tenacious," A16.

128. "Justice Scalia on the Record," Stahl interview, *60 Minutes,* April 27, 2008.

129. Scalia often complimented Maureen for being the primary caretaker of their nine children and a great cook.

130. Remarks at the swearing-in ceremony for William H. Rehnquist as chief justice and Antonin Scalia as associate justice of the Supreme Court of the United States, September 26, 1986, https://www.reaganlibrary.gov/research/speeches/092686a.

131. Pope John Paul II, *The Gospel of Life* [*Evangelium Vitae*] (New York: Random House, 1995), 100.

132. Antonin Scalia, "God's Justice and Ours," *First Things: A Monthly Journal of Religion and Public Life* 123 (May 2002): 18–19 (quoting Romans 13:1–5).

133. Stephen J. Adler, "Live Wire on the DC Circuit, *American Lawyer,* March 1985, 86.

134. Paul Marcotte, "New Kid on the Block: Scalia Seen as a Charming Conservative with Ability to Effect Compromises," *American Bar Association Journal* 72 (1986): 20.

135. Robert L. Jackson and Ronald J. Ostrow, "He Has His Own Style of Conservatism; Scalia's Independent Past Suggests Future Surprises," *Los Angeles Times,* July 6, 1986, 1.

136. Adler, "Live Wire on the DC Circuit," 89.

137. Adler, 89. See also Honorable Charles S. Gubser, "Appointment of Antonin Scalia to Be Chairman of the Administrative Conference of the United States," *CR,* October 14, 1972, 36547.

138. Antonin Scalia, "Don't Go Near the Water," *Federal Communications Bar Journal* (1972): 111–120.

139. *Telecommunications Research & Action Center v. FCC,* 801 F.2d 501 (D.C. Cir.

1986); *Telecommunications Research & Action Center v. FCC*, 806 F.2d 1115 (1986) (petition for rehearing en banc denied).

140. See, e.g., "To Establish an Independent Consumer Protection Agency," Joint Hearings before the Subcommittee on Reorganization, Research, and International Organizations of the Committee on Government Operations and the Subcommittee on Consumers of the Committee on Commerce, US Senate, 93rd Cong., 1st sess., April 5, 1973, 578 ("On the basic issue of desirability of a consumer advocate, if you will, I am not an unrestricted enthusiast of the concept").

141. "Chairman's Foreword," in *1973–74 Report, Administrative Conference of the United States, September 1974* (Washington, DC: Government Printing Office, 1974), 1.

142. In *Immigration and Naturalization Service v. Chadha*, 462 U.S. 919 (1983), the Supreme Court struck down the legislative veto as a violation of the presentment clause and the separation of powers.

143. See, e.g., Antonin Scalia, "The Legislative Veto: A False Remedy for System Overload," *Regulation* 3, 6 (1979): 19–26.

144. "Newsmen's Privilege," Hearings before the Subcommittee on Courts, Civil Liberties, and the Administration of Justice of the Committee on the Judiciary, House of Representatives, 94th Cong., 1st sess., April 23, 1975, 2–36.

145. "1976 Bicentennial Institute—Oversight and Review of Agency Decisionmaking," *Administrative Law Review* 28, 4 (1976): 695.

146. "An Imperial Judiciary: Fact or Myth? A Roundtable Sponsored by the American Enterprise Institute for Public Policy Research," Washington, DC, 1979.

147. Antonin Scalia, "The Freedom of Information Act Has No Clothes," *Regulation* 6, 2 (March–April 1982): 15–19.

148. Antonin Scalia, "Rulemaking as Politics," *Administrative Law Review* 34, 3 (1982): v–xi.

149. *Chevron U.S.A., Inc. v. Natural Resources Defense Council, Inc.*, 467 U.S. 837 (1984).

150. See, e.g., *Synar v. United States*, 626 F. Supp. 1374 (D. D.C. 1986) (holding that the Balanced Budget and Emergency Deficit Control Act of 1985 violated the separation of powers).

151. *Center for Auto Safety v. N.H.T.S.A*, 793 F.2d 1322 (D.C. Cir. 1986) (Scalia, J., dissenting); *In re Center for Auto Safety*, 793 F.2d 1346 (D.C. Cir. 1986) (Scalia, J., dissenting) (arguing that consumer organizations had no standing to challenge a National Highway Traffic Safety Administration rule reducing fuel economy standards for light trucks).

152. *Ramirez de Arellano v. Weinberger*, 745 F.2d 1500 (D.C. Cir. 1984) (Scalia, J., dissenting) (arguing that the federal courts had no jurisdiction over a case challenging the establishment of a military base in Honduras); *Sanchez-Espinoza v. Reagan*, 770 F.2d. 202 (D.C. Cir. 1985) (Scalia, J.) (dismissing a suit challenging the Reagan administration's financial and military support of the Contra rebels in Nicaragua).

153. *Halperin v. Kissinger*, 807 F.2d 180 (D.C. Cir. 1986); *Smith v. Nixon*, 807 F.2d 197 (D.C. Cir. 1986); *Ellsberg v. Mitchell*, 807 F.2d 204 (D.C. Cir. 1986).

154. *Molerio v. F.B.I.*, 749 F.2d 815 (D.C. Cir. 1984) (Scalia, J.) (when "the whole object

of the suit and of the discovery is to establish a fact that is a state secret, we are of the view that it suffices for the cabinet secretary to determine on personal consideration that disclosure of that fact would impair national security, whereupon compliance with the discovery request is excused in gross, without the necessity of examining individual documents").

155. *Center for Auto Safety v. Peck*, 751 F.2d 1336 (D.C. Cir. 1985) (rejecting "hard look" scrutiny of new automobile safety standards for bumpers during the Reagan administration).

156. *Synar*, 626 F. Supp. 1374.

157. W. John Moore, "Tugging to the Right," *National Journal*, October 20, 1990, 1215.

158. Molotsky, "Judge with Tenacity and Charm," A31.

159. See David G. Savage, *Turning Right: The Making of the Rehnquist Supreme Court* (New York: John Wiley & Sons, 1993), 17–18.

160. Speech by Ronald Reagan at the investiture of chief justice William H. Rehnquist and associate justice Antonin Scalia, September 26, 1986, in Steven G. Calabresi, *Originalism: A Quarter Century of Debate* (Washington, DC: Regnery, 2007), 95–97.

161. Clarence Thomas, *My Grandfather's Son: A Memoir* (New York: HarperCollins, 2007), 4–5.

162. C. Thomas, 6.

163. Andrew Peyton Thomas, *Clarence Thomas: A Biography* (San Francisco: Encounter Books, 2001), 63.

164. Clarence Thomas, "The Second Annual William French Smith Memorial Lecture: A Conversation with Justice Clarence Thomas," *Pepperdine Law Review* 37 (December 2009): 12.

165. C. Thomas, *My Grandfather's Son*, 2.

166. A. P. Thomas, *Clarence Thomas*, 70; R. T. Edwards, "Mutual Admiration: Nuns Who Taught U.S. Supreme Court Nominee Remember Him with Fondness, as He Does Them," *Catholic Standard* 4, 27 (July 4, 1991): 16.

167. A. P. Thomas, *Clarence Thomas*, 71.

168. Clarence Thomas, "Remembering the Island of Hope," *St. Croix Review* 19, 6 (December 1986): 12.

169. Ken Foskett, *Judging Thomas: The Life and Times of Clarence Thomas* (New York: HarperCollins, 2004), 66.

170. A. P. Thomas, *Clarence Thomas*, 85.

171. A. P. Thomas, 85–86.

172. A. P. Thomas, 89. The other black student, Richard Chisolm, did not return after Thomas's first year.

173. A. P. Thomas, *Clarence Thomas*, 84, 89.

174. Clarence Thomas, speech at Cato Institute, April 23, 1987, Mark Paoletta Files, no. 45514-001, George H. W. Bush Presidential Library and Museum, College Station, TX.

175. Thomas, speech at Cato Institute, 5.

176. A. P. Thomas, *Clarence Thomas*, 88.

177. A. P. Thomas, 95–101.

178. C. Thomas, *My Grandfather's Son*, 40.

179. C. Thomas, 43.

180. C. Thomas, 45–46.

181. Foskett, *Judging Thomas*, 96; C. Thomas, *My Grandfather's Son*, 50.

182. See Corey Robin, *The Enigma of Clarence Thomas* (New York: Metropolitan Books, 2019) (arguing that Thomas's conservative black nationalist beliefs are a major influence on his jurisprudence).

183. Foskett, *Judging Thomas*, 97.

184. The earlier protest involved a recruitment visit by General Electric, which was a major manufacturer of weapons used in the Vietnam War and was reportedly conducting business in South Africa, which then had a system of apartheid.

185. C. Thomas, *My Grandfather's Son*, 57–58.

186. Kevin Cullen, "Court Nominee as an Activist at Holy Cross," *Boston Globe*, July 23, 1991, 10. See also A. P. Thomas, *Clarence Thomas*, 127.

187. C. Thomas, *My Grandfather's Son*, 59.

188. A. P. Thomas, *Clarence Thomas*, 117.

189. Cullen, "Court Nominee as an Activist," 10.

190. At the time, less than 2 percent of the population was black. See A. P. Thomas, *Clarence Thomas*, 114.

191. Thomas came in as a sophomore, and the institution admitted nineteen students in the freshmen class. Diane Brady, *Fraternity* (New York: Spiegel & Grau, 2012), 3. See also "Historical Timeline of Holy Cross: 1950–1989," https://www.holycross.edu/175th-anniversary/historical-timeline-holy-cross/1950-1989.

192. C. Thomas, *My Grandfather's Son*, 54.

193. Thomas ranked in the top 7 percent of his class. In recognition of his academic achievement, he was selected for membership in Alpha Sigma Nu, which is the Jesuit equivalent of Phi Beta Kappa. See Cullen, "Court Nominee as an Activist," 10.

194. A. P. Thomas, *Clarence Thomas*, 119.

195. C. Thomas, *My Grandfather's Son*, 74, 98.

196. Juan Williams, "Black Conservatives, Center Stage," *Washington Post*, December 16, 1980, A21.

197. C. Thomas, *My Grandfather's Son*, 75, 99–100.

198. Danforth promised Clarence "more work for less money than anyone else in the country," and he kept his word. C. Thomas, 94.

199. *State v. Torrence*, 519 S.W.2d 360 (Mo. App. 1975).

200. C. Thomas, *My Grandfather's Son*, 94–95.

201. Foskett, *Judging Thomas*, 147.

202. Williams, "Black Conservatives, Center Stage."

203. C. Thomas, *My Grandfather's Son*, 138.

204. Clarence Thomas, speech at Clark College, August 23, 1983, Paoletta Files, no. 45510-006.

205. A. P. Thomas, *Clarence Thomas*, 202–203. In fact, as a Supreme Court justice, Thomas became a sharp critic of the Voting Rights Act's preclearance requirement and

joined the court's decision striking down section 4 of that act. However, Thomas wanted to strike down section 5 as well. See *Shelby County v. Holder*, 570 U.S. 529 (2013) (Thomas, J., concurring).

206. *Bob Jones University v. United States*, 461 U.S. 574 (1983).

207. In an 8–1 decision, the Supreme Court upheld the IRS's authority to deny tax-exempt status to Bob Jones.

208. C. Thomas, *My Grandfather's Son*, 146–147.

209. Thomas claimed that working at the EEOC would "irreparably harm" his career. See Williams, "Black Conservatives, Center Stage." In one interview, Thomas said he was "insulted" when he was offered the civil rights post at the Department of Education and the chairmanship of the EEOC. Interview with Bill Kauffman, "Clarence Thomas," *Reason*, November 1987, 33.

210. At the end of his tenure, Thomas also oversaw the EEOC's relocation to a new building.

211. Clarence Thomas, "Transition from Policymaker to Judge—A Matter of Deference," *Creighton Law Review* 26 (1993): 241–253; Clarence Thomas, "Affirmative Action Goals and Timetables: Too Tough? Not Tough Enough!" *Yale Law and Policy Review* 5 (1987): 402–411. Statistically, during Thomas's tenure the EEOC filed the highest average number of lawsuits per year and had the highest litigation rate. However, there was also an increase in the backlog of cases and a decline in the number of investigations based on broad-scale employment data. See Maurice E. R. Munroe, "The EEOC: Pattern and Practice Imperfect," *Yale Law and Policy Review* 13 (1995): 266–270.

212. Thomas did not personally support goals and timetables, but he believed Supreme Court precedent allowed them. In addition, as chair of a five-member bipartisan commission, he felt obligated to represent the views of the other commissioners.

213. C. Thomas, *My Grandfather's Son*, 176–178.

214. Foskett, *Judging Thomas*, 189.

215. C. Thomas, *My Grandfather's Son*, 180–182; Laura Blumenfeld, "The Nominee's Soul Mate," *Washington Post*, September 10, 1991, F01.

216. C. Thomas, *My Grandfather's Son*, 182. In fact, when the Supreme Court decided *National Federation of Independent Business v. Sebèlius* (2012), which challenged the individual mandate of the Patient Protection and Affordable Care Act (ACA), Thomas was asked to recuse himself because Ginni had recently served as president and CEO of Liberty Organization, a conservative Tea Party group that was opposed to the "tyranny" of the Obama administration. In particular, the organization argued that the ACA was an unconstitutional infringement on individual freedom. See Michael O'Brien, "Democrats: Justice Thomas Should Recuse Himself in Healthcare Reform Case," *Hill*, February 9, 2011, https://thehill.com/blogs/blog-briefing-room/news/142969-democrats-justice-thomas-should-recuse-himself-in-healthcare-reform-case; David G. Savage, "Justice's Wife Plans to Leave Political Spotlight," *Seattle Times*, November 15, 2010; Jeffrey Toobin, "Partners: Will Clarence and Virginia Thomas Succeed in Killing Obama's Healthcare Plan?" *New Yorker*, August 29, 2001. See also Jane Mayer, "Ginni Thomas's Crusades," *New Yorker*, January 31, 2022, vol. 97, issue 47, 16–23.

217. In late 1999 the couple purchased their motor home, which they use to travel across the United States in the summer. These excursions give them an opportunity to get out of the Washington Beltway—or what Justice Thomas calls the rarefied world of DC politics—and commune with ordinary people in RV parks and Walmart parking lots.

218. He was confirmed on March 6, 1990.

219. *United States v. Poston*, 902 F.2d 90 (D.C. Circ. 1990); *United States v. Rogers*, 918 F.2d 207 (D.C. Cir. 1990).

220. *United States v. Halliman*, 923 F.2d 873 (D.C. Cir. 1991).

221. This speech was delivered as the annual TePoel Lecture at Creighton University School of Law on February 14, 1991, and was subsequently published in the *Creighton Law Review*. During his remarks, Thomas said: "To the extent that this determination or assumption is invalid [i.e., that the agency has been delegated authority], deference to the agency's exercise of discretion would appear to be without basis and thus improper." Thomas, "Transition from Policymaker to Judge," 251.

222. *Metro Broadcasting, Inc. v. FCC*, 497 U.S. 547 (1990).

223. *Lamprecht v. FCC*, 958 F.2d 382 (D.C. Cir. 1992).

224. President Bush nominates Clarence Thomas, C-SPAN, https://www.c-span.org/video/?c4536760/president-bush-nominates-clarence-thomas.

225. The NAACP opposed Thomas's nomination because of his views on affirmative action, while the National Organization for Women was concerned about Thomas potentially voting to overturn *Roe v. Wade*, 410 U.S. 113 (1973).

226. "Nomination of Judge Clarence Thomas to Be Associate Justice of the Supreme Court of the United States," Hearings before the Committee on the Judiciary, US Senate, 102nd Cong., 1st sess. (September 10–16, 1991), pt. 1, 112, 116, 222.

227. Hill recalled that at the Department of Education, Thomas had "spoke[n] about acts that he had seen in pornographic films involving such matters as women having sex with animals, and films showing group sex or rape scenes." He also allegedly spoke "graphically of his own sexual prowess" and "of the pleasures he had given to women with oral sex." "Nomination of Judge Clarence Thomas," pt. 4, 37, 45. Hill claimed that there were similar issues at the EEOC. She recounted one incident when "Thomas was drinking a Coke in his office" and "got up from the table at which we were working, went over to his desk to get the Coke, looked at the can and asked, 'Who has put pubic hair on my Coke?'" "Nomination of Judge Clarence Thomas," pt. 4, 38, 45.

228. "Nomination of Judge Clarence Thomas," pt. 4, 39, 46. See also Anita Hill, *Speaking Truth to Power* (New York: Anchor Books, 1997), 78–79, 81.

229. "Nomination of Judge Clarence Thomas," pt. 4, 157–158.

230. "The Supreme Court is not worth it," Thomas testified. "No job is worth it. I am not here for that. I am here for my name, my family, my life and my integrity." "Nomination of Judge Clarence Thomas," pt. 4, 157.

231. In 1881 Stanley Matthews was confirmed to the Supreme Court by a vote of 24–23. In 2018 Brett Kavanaugh, who had been accused of sexual assault by Dr. Christine Blasey Ford, was confirmed by a vote of 50–48.

2. HUGO BLACK'S ORIGINALISM: JEFFERSONIAN

1. Hugo Black to Alexander Meiklejohn, August 28, 1962, Hugo Black Papers, Library of Congress, box 42.

2. Justice Frankfurter inscribed a 1939 book he bought for Black as follows: "For Hugo L. Black, a true apostle of Jefferson." Daniel J. Meador, "Hugo Black and Thomas Jefferson," *Virginia Quarterly Review* 79, 3 (Summer 2003): 467.

3. Thomas Jefferson, "Manufactures," Query XIX, in *Notes on the State of Virginia*, ed. William Peden (Chapel Hill: University of North Carolina Press, 1955), 164–165.

4. Roger K. Newman, *Hugo Black: A Biography*, 2nd ed. (New York: Fordham University Press, 1997), 67.

5. Meador, "Hugo Black and Thomas Jefferson," 464; "Opening Speech of the Hon. Hugo L. Black, March 20, 1926," Ashland, AL, Black Papers, box 105, 1.

6. Daniel J. Meador, *Mr. Justice Black and His Books* (Charlottesville: University Press of Virginia, 1974), 3.

7. Thomas Jefferson, *Memoir, Correspondence, and Miscellanies from the Papers of Thomas Jefferson*, ed. Thomas Jefferson Randolph (Charlottesville, VA: F. Carr, 1829).

8. *Congressional Record* (hereafter *CR*), vol. 80, pt. 3, 74th Cong., 2nd sess., March 9, 1936, 3436. See also Newman, *Hugo Black*, 143.

9. *CR*, vol. 75, pt. 4, 72nd Cong., 1st sess., February 8, 1932, 3516.

10. *CR*, vol. 70, pt. 3, 70th Cong., 2nd sess., January 31, 1929, 2519.

11. *CR*, vol. 71, pt. 4, 71st Cong., 1st sess., October 11, 1929, 4469.

12. *CR*, vol. 80, pt. 4, 74th Cong., 2nd sess., March 20, 1936, 4103.

13. *CR*, vol. 79, pt. 6, 74th Cong., 1st sess., April 29, 1935, 6533.

14. Claude Bowers, *Jefferson and Hamilton: The Struggle for Democracy in America* (Boston: Houghton Mifflin, 1925).

15. *CR*, vol. 75, pt. 4, 72nd Cong., 1st sess., February 8, 1932, 3524.

16. *CR*, vol. 71, pt. 2, 71st Cong., 1st sess., May 15, 1929, 1334–1335.

17. *CR*, vol. 75, pt. 4, 72nd Cong., 1st sess., February 8, 1932, 3517.

18. Fireside Chat 9: On "Court-Packing," March 9, 1937, https://millercenter.org/the-presidency/presidential-speeches/march-9-1937-fireside-chat-9-court-packing.

19. Hugo L. Black, "Reorganization of Federal Judiciary," address delivered in New York City, March 24, 1937, in *CR*, vol. 81, pt. 9 (appendix), 75th Cong., 1st sess., March 25, 1937, 638.

20. Hugo L. Black, radio address, February 23, 1937, in *CR*, vol. 81, pt. 9 (appendix), 75th Cong., 1st sess., March 25, 1937, 306–307.

21. Hugo L. Black, address to Southern Conference on Human Welfare, Birmingham, AL, November 23, 1938, Black Papers, box 478.

22. Hugo L. Black, commencement address at Swarthmore College, June 6, 1955, Black Papers, box 481. The themes of this speech were strikingly similar to those raised by FDR in a 1925 book review. See Franklin D. Roosevelt, "Is There a Jefferson on the Horizon?" *New York Evening World*, December 3, 1925.

23. See, e.g., *Konigsberg v. State Bar of California*, 366 U.S. 36, 78 (1961) (Black, J., dissenting).

24. Joseph Wershba, "The Great Dissenter Marks 25 Years on Supreme Court," *New York Post*, June 27, 1962, 46.

25. Meador, *Black and His Books*, 17 (quoting Anthony Lewis, "The Authentic Voice," *New York Times*, October 5, 1970, 43).

26. See, e.g., Leonard Levy, *Jefferson & Civil Liberties: The Darker Side* (Cambridge MA: Belknap Press, 1963).

27. See, e.g., *Smith v. California*, 361 U.S. 147, 159, n. 2 (1959) (Black, J., concurring):

> Thomas Jefferson's views of the breadth of the First Amendment's prohibition against abridgment of speech and press by the Federal Government are illustrated by the following statement he made in 1798: "[The First Amendment] thereby guard[s] in the same sentence, and under the same words, the freedom of religion, of speech, and of the press; insomuch, that whatever violates either, throws down the sanctuary which covers the others, and that libels, falsehood, and defamation, equally with heresy and false religion, are withheld from the cognizance of federal tribunals."

28. Hugo Lafayette Black, *A Constitutional Faith* (New York: Alfred A. Knopf, 1968), 45.

29. *Milk Wagon Drivers Union of Chicago, Local 753 v. Meadowmoor Dairies*, 312 U.S. 287, 301 (1941) (Black, J., dissenting) (describing the First Amendment as "the foundation upon which [the US] governmental structure rests and without which it could not continue to endure as conceived and planned").

30. "Justice Black and the First Amendment 'Absolutes': A Public Interview," *New York University Law Review* 37 (1962): 549–563, 558.

31. See, e.g., *Dennis v. United States*, 341 U.S. 494, 579 (1951) (Black, J., dissenting); *Yates v. United States*, 354 U.S. 298, 339 (1957) (Black, J., dissenting); *Barenblatt v. United States*, 360 U.S. 109, 134 (1959) (Black, J., dissenting); *Communist Party of the United States v. Subversive Activities Control Board*, 367 U.S. 1, 137 (1961) (Black, J., dissenting); *Scales v. United States*, 367 U.S. 203, 259 (1961) (Black, J., dissenting).

32. *Communist Party of the United States*, 367 U.S. at 137.

33. *Communist Party of the United States*, 367 U.S. at 147–148 (Black, J., dissenting): "The only remedy for communism, or advocacy of the violent overthrow of government, was 'the same remedy that is applied to the danger that comes from any other erroneous talk—education and contrary argument. If that remedy is not sufficient, the only meaning of free speech must be that the revolutionary ideas will be allowed to prevail,'" citing *Gitlow v. New York*, 268 U.S. 652, 673 (1925) (Holmes, J., dissenting) ("If in the long run the beliefs expressed in proletarian dictatorship are destined to be accepted by the dominant forces of the community, the only meaning of free speech is that they should be given their chance and have their way").

34. *Communist Party of the United States*, 367 U.S. at 169.

35. Memo from Hugo Black to John Marshall Harlan, December 10, 1969, John

Marshall Harlan Papers, box 484, Public Policy Papers, Department of Rare Books and Collections, Princeton University Library.

36. *Ginzburg v. United States*, 383 U.S. 463, 481 (1966) (Black, J., dissenting).

37. *Smith v. California*, 361 U.S. 147, 159–160 (1959) (Black, J., concurring).

38. See *Milk Wagon Drivers Union of Chicago*, 312 U.S. at 302 n. 4 (1941) (Black, J., dissenting) (quoting Jefferson's letter to Edward Carrington, January 16, 1787, in *The Papers of Thomas Jefferson*, ed. Julian P. Boyd [Princeton, NJ: Princeton University Press, 1955], 11:48–50).

39. *Bridges v. California*, 314 U.S. 252 (1941).

40. Anthony Lewis, "Justice Black and the First Amendment," in *Justice Hugo Black and Modern America*, ed. Tony Freyer (Tuscaloosa: University of Alabama Press, 1990), 241.

41. Lewis, 265.

42. *New York Times v. United States*, 403 U.S. 713 (1971).

43. *New York Times*, 403 U.S. at 715, 717.

44. *New York Times*, 403 U.S. at 717.

45. Newman, *Hugo Black*, 619.

46. *Time, Inc. v. Hill*, 385 U.S. 374, 400 n. 2 (1967) (Black, J., concurring) (quoting from Jefferson, *Works* [Ford ed., 1904], 8:464–465).

47. *New York Times v. Sullivan*, 376 U.S. 254 (1964) (Black, J., concurring) (stating that the Sedition Act "came to an ignominious end and by common consent has generally been treated as having been a wholly unjustifiable and much to be regretted violation of the First Amendment"). See also *Beauharnais v. Illinois*, 343 U.S. 250, 267 (1952) (Black, J., dissenting); *Garrison v. Louisiana*, 379 U.S. 64, 79 (1964) (Black, J., concurring) ("under our Constitution there is absolutely no place in this country for the old, discredited English Star Chamber law of seditious criminal libel").

48. *Sullivan*, 376 U.S. 254.

49. *Sullivan*, 376 U.S. at 293.

50. *Curtis Publishing Co. v. Butts*, 388 U.S. 130, 171 (1967) (concurring in part and dissenting in part). See also *Rosenblatt v. Baer*, 383 U.S. 75, 95 (1966) (Black, J., concurring); *Time*, 385 U.S. at 398 (Black, J., concurring); *Ginzburg v. Goldwater*, 396 U.S. 1049 (1970) (Black, J., dissenting from the denial of certiorari).

51. See, e.g., *Rosenbloom v. Metromedia*, 403 U.S. 29, 57 (1971) (Black, J., concurring in the judgment).

52. Thomas Jefferson, "To the Danbury Baptist Association," January 1, 1802, in *The Papers of Thomas Jefferson*, ed. Barbara P. Oberg (Princeton, NJ: Princeton University Press, 2009), 36:258.

53. *Everson v. Board of Education of the Township of Ewing*, 330 U.S. 1 (1947).

54. Justice Black cited *Reynolds v. United States*, 98 U.S. 145, 164 (1879), where the court approvingly quoted Jefferson's letter to the Danbury Baptist Association. *Everson*, 330 U.S. at 16.

55. In *Everson*, the court upheld a local school board program that reimbursed parents for the transportation costs of sending children to schools outside the district, some

of which were private religious schools. The dissenters claimed that Black did not follow the strict neutrality principle he announced in the case. See, e.g., *Everson*, 330 U.S. at 18 (Jackson, J., dissenting) ("In fact, the undertones of the opinion, advocating complete and uncompromising separation of Church and State, seem utterly discordant with its conclusion yielding support to their commingling in educational matters").

56. *Everson*, 330 U.S. at 18.

57. *Everson*, 330 U.S. at 15.

58. *Engel v. Vitale*, 370 U.S. 421 (1962).

59. *Engel*, 370 U.S. at 425.

60. *School District of Abington Township v. Schempp*, 374 U.S. 203 (1963).

61. *Lemon v. Kurtzman*, 403 U.S. 602 (1971).

62. According to this test, (1) a law must have a secular legislative purpose, (2) its principal or primary effect must be one that neither advances nor inhibits religion, and (3) the statute must not foster an excessive entanglement with religion. *Lemon*, 403 U.S. at 612–613.

63. In *Everson*, Black quoted from Jefferson's Statute for Religious Liberty: "That no man shall be compelled to frequent or support any religious worship, place, or ministry whatsoever, nor shall be enforced, restrained, molested or burthened in his body or goods, nor shall otherwise suffer on account of his religious opinions or belief." *Everson*, 330 U.S. at 13.

64. *Everson*, 330 U.S. at 15.

65. *Minersville School District v. Gobitis*, 310 U.S. 586 (1940).

66. *Jones v. City of Opelika*, 316 U.S. 584, 624 (1942).

67. *Jones*, 316 U.S. at 624 (Black, J., dissenting).

68. *West Virginia State Board of Education v. Barnette*, 319 U.S. 624 (1943).

69. *Barnette*, 319 U.S. at 644 (Black, J., concurring).

70. *Cantwell v. Connecticut*, 310 U.S. 296 (1940).

71. *Torcaso v. Watkins*, 367 U.S. 488 (1961).

72. *Sherbert v. Verner*, 374 U.S. 398 (1963).

73. *United States v. Ballard*, 322 U.S. 78 (1944).

74. *Welsh v. United States*, 398 U.S. 333 (1970).

75. *Welsh*, 398 U.S. at 344.

76. *CR*, vol. 73, 71st Cong., special sess., July 9, 1930, 41.

77. *CR*, 39.

78. *Korematsu v. United States*, 323 U.S. 214 (1944).

79. *Youngstown Sheet & Tube Co. v. Sawyer*, 343 U.S. 579 (1952).

80. *Youngstown*, 343 U.S. at 587.

81. *Youngstown*, 343 U.S. at 587. Black's strict interpretation of Article II caused several of his colleagues to write separate opinions. In a concurring opinion, Justice Frankfurter wrote: "Although the considerations relevant to the legal enforcement of the principle of separation of powers seem to me more complicated and flexible than may appear from what Mr. Justice Black has written, I join his opinion because I thoroughly agree with the application of the principle to the circumstances of this case." *Youngstown*, 343 U.S.

at 589 (Frankfurter, J., concurring). Justice Jackson developed his now famous three-part test for measuring presidential power. *Youngstown*, 343 U.S. at 635–640 (Jackson, J., concurring). In dissent, Chief Justice Vinson rejected the majority's "messenger-boy" conception of presidential power. *Youngstown*, 343 U.S. at 708–709.

82. *Duncan v. Kahanamoku*, 327 U.S. 304 (1946).

83. *Johnson v. Eisentrager*, 339 U.S. 763 (1950).

84. *Zemel v. Rusk*, 381 U.S. 1 (1965).

85. *Zemel*, 381 U.S. at 14.

86. Black based that authority on Article I's vesting clause, which states that "all legislative Powers herein granted shall be vested in a Congress of the United States."

87. *Zemel*, 381 U.S. at 20 (Black, J., dissenting).

88. *Zemel*, 381 U.S. at 21.

89. Black's complete rejection of substantive due process left considerable discretion for states to regulate social and economic policy within their borders. He was also deferential to the legislative process in equal protection cases unless there was clear evidence of state-sponsored racial discrimination. As pointed out in chapter 5, he was a sharp critic of the Supreme Court's dormant commerce decisions. Black also viewed the preclearance requirements of section 5 of the Voting Rights Act as an affront to states' rights, and he wrote the important "Our Federalism" decision, holding that federal courts should not stay or enjoin pending state court proceedings except under special circumstances. See *South Carolina v. Katzenbach*, 383 U.S. 301 (1966) (Black, J., dissenting); *Allen v. State Board of Elections*, 393 U.S. 544, 595–596 (1969) (Black, J., dissenting); *Younger v. Harris*, 401 U.S. 37 (1971). Finally, Black wrote the opinion in *Oregon v. Mitchell*, 400 U.S. 112 (1970), which held that although Congress can reduce the minimum voting age requirements in federal elections, it cannot do so in state and local elections.

90. Jefferson, by contrast, was a principled defender of states' rights who believed that the Tenth Amendment was "the foundation of the Constitution." See Opinion against the Constitutionality of a National Bank, February 15, 1791, in *The Writings of Thomas Jefferson*, ed. Andrew A. Lipscomb and Albert Ellery Bergh (Washington, DC: Thomas Jefferson Memorial Association, 1903–1904): 3:146.

91. *CR*, vol. 77, 73rd Cong., 1st sess., April 3, 1933, 1122: "Congress, as has been so held in numerous cases which I have read, has police power with reference to the subjects which have been entrusted to its care; and it has entrusted to its care the sole, exclusive, and plenary power over interstate commerce."

92. *CR*, 1120–1121 (claiming that the federal government's new role was supported by "both the Hamiltonian idea and the Jeffersonian idea"). One way that Black justified this reading of Jefferson was by relying on the Declaration of Independence. For example, when he was a senator, Black defended the new Social Security program and cited the following language from the Declaration of Independence: "it is the right of the people . . . to institute . . . Government, laying its foundation on such principles and organizing its powers in such form as *to them* shall seem most likely to effect their safety and happiness." Hugo Black, "Social Security," December 15, 1934, *Vital Speeches* 1, 8 (January 14, 1935): 249–251.

93. See, e.g., Roosevelt, "Is There a Jefferson on the Horizon?"; Charles A. Beard, *The Supreme Court and the Constitution* (New York: Macmillan, 1912); Bowers, *Jefferson and Hamilton*; Herbert Croly, *The Promise of American Life* (New York: Macmillan, 1909).

94. *CR*, vol. 77, 73rd Cong., 1st sess., April 3, 1933, 1123.

95. *United States v. Darby Lumber Co.*, 312 U.S. 100 (1941).

96. *Darby*, 312 U.S. at 124.

97. *Wickard v. Filburn*, 317 U.S. 111 (1942).

98. *United States v. South-Eastern Underwriters Association*, 322 U.S. 533 (1944) (Black, J.).

99. *South-Eastern Underwriters*, 322 U.S. at 552–553.

100. *Heart of Atlanta Motel v. United States*, 379 U.S. 241, 271 (1964), and *Katzenbach v. McClung*, 379 U.S. 294 (1964) (Black, J., concurring), quoting *Gibbons v. Ogden*, 22 U.S. 1, 196 (1824): Congress's commerce power is "plenary, 'complete in itself, may be exercised to its utmost extent, and acknowledges no limitations, other than are prescribed in the constitution.'"

101. *Adamson v. California*, 332 U.S. 46 (1947).

102. *Adamson*, 332 U.S. at 71–72 (Black, J., dissenting).

103. Black arguably could not rely on his idol Thomas Jefferson for his total incorporation theory. Jefferson was a strong defender of states' rights and believed that the Bill of Rights was not intended to apply against state power. In a letter to Abigail Adams in which he elaborated on the reasons why he regarded the Alien and Sedition Acts as unlawful, Jefferson conceded that although the federal government did not have power to regulate libel and slander, the states did. Thomas Jefferson to Abigail Adams, September 11, 1804, in *The Papers of Thomas Jefferson*, ed. James P. McClure (Princeton, NJ: Princeton University Press, 2019), 44: 379–381. However, Black could have maintained that an updated Jefferson would have accepted total incorporation of the Bill of Rights after adoption of the Fourteenth Amendment. After all, it was Jefferson who spearheaded the movement for a Bill of Rights in the first place. Jefferson to James Madison, December 20, 1787, in Boyd, *Papers of Thomas Jefferson*, 12:438–443. In a 1932 Senate speech, Black stated: "Every word spoken by that great exponent of Democracy, Thomas Jefferson, tended toward the point of not subtracting from the rights of the people but giving them the maximum liberty that could be given consistent with orderly government." *CR*, vol. 75, pt. 4, 72nd Cong., 1st sess., February 8, 1932, 3516.

104. The only guarantees that have not been incorporated to apply to the states are the Third Amendment's restriction on the quartering of soldiers in a person's home in times of peace, the Fifth Amendment's right to an indictment by a grand jury, and the Seventh Amendment's right to a jury trial in civil cases.

105. Hugo L. Black, "The Bill of Rights," *New York University Law Review* 35 (1960): 865, 873. See also Jacob W. Landynski, "In Search of Justice Black's Fourth Amendment," *Fordham Law Review* 45 (1976–1977): 453–496.

106. In interpreting the Fourth Amendment, Justice Black distinguished the reasonableness clause from the warrant clause.

107. *Coolidge v. New Hampshire*, 403 U.S. 443, 509 (1971) (Black, J., concurring and dissenting).

108. *Coolidge*, 403 U.S. at 509–510.

109. *Chimel v. California*, 395 U.S. 752 (1969).

110. Interestingly, the lower courts ruled that the arrest warrant was invalid but that the officers had acted in good faith and had probable cause to arrest Chimel; therefore, the Supreme Court operated under the assumption that the arrest was valid under the Constitution.

111. *Chimel*, 395 U.S. at 754.

112. *Chimel*, 395 U.S. at 780 (White, J., with whom Black, J., joined, dissenting).

113. See, e.g., *Harris v. United States*, 331 U.S. 145 (1947) (Vinson, C.J., with whom Black, J., joined) (upholding search of a four-room apartment, including a desk drawer); *Trupiano v. United States*, 334 U.S. 699 (1948) (Vinson, C.J., with whom Black, J., joined, dissenting) (arguing that a search of a distillery incident to arrest was permissible). But see *United States v. Rabinowitz*, 339 U.S. 56, 67 (1950) (Black, J., dissenting) (disagreeing with the court's decision to overturn *Trupiano* because "it aggravates existing uncertainty"). In *Rabinowitz*, the court (5–3) upheld a search incident to arrest of a one-room business office, including the desk, safe, and file cabinets.

114. *Coolidge*, 403 U.S. 443.

115. *Coolidge*, 403 U.S. at 504.

116. *Terry v. Ohio*, 392 U.S. 1 (1968).

117. Justice Brennan advised Chief Justice Warren to switch the court's analysis from probable cause to reasonable suspicion and then to rest the decision entirely on the reasonableness clause, which Warren did. Memo from Brennan to Warren, "The 'Stop and Frisk' Cases," March 14, 1968, William J. Brennan Papers, Library of Congress, pt. I, 168.

118. *Terry*, 392 U.S. at 24.

119. Draft concurrence by justice Hugo Black in *Terry v. Ohio*, February 19, 1968, Black Papers, box 402, 1–2, 5.

120. *Peters v. New York*, 392 U.S. 40 (1968).

121. *Sibron v. New York*, 392 U.S. 40 (1968).

122. *Sibron*, 392 U.S. at 79 (Black, J., concurring in No. 74 and dissenting in No. 63) (emphasis added).

123. *Sibron*, 392 U.S. at 80.

124. *Sibron*, 392 U.S. at 82.

125. *Berger v. New York*, 388 U.S. 41 (1967) (Black, J., dissenting); *Katz v. United States*, 389 U.S. 347 (1967) (Black, J., dissenting); *Alderman v. United States*, 394 U.S. 165 (1969) (Black, J., dissenting).

126. *Katz*, 389 U.S. 347.

127. *Katz*, 389 U.S. at 365 (Black, J., dissenting).

128. *Katz*, 389 U.S. at 373.

129. *Wolf v. Colorado*, 338 U.S. 25 (1949).

130. *Wolf*, 338 U.S. at 39–40 (Black, J., concurring).

131. *Mapp v. Ohio*, 367 U.S. 643 (1961).

132. *Mapp*, 367 U.S. at 662 (Black, J., concurring). In fact, in *Linkletter v. Walker*, 381

U.S. 618 (1965), Justice Black argued in dissent that the exclusionary rule should apply retroactively to all prisoners whose Fourth Amendment rights were violated.

133. *Bumper v. North Carolina*, 391 U.S. 543 (1968).

134. *Bumper*, 391 U.S. at 550.

135. *Bumper*, 391 U.S. at 560 (Black, J., dissenting).

136. *Coolidge*, 403 U.S. at 493–510.

137. *Miranda v. Arizona*, 384 U.S. 436 (1966).

138. *Chambers v. Florida*, 309 U.S. 227 (1940).

139. *Chambers*, 309 U.S. at 236.

140. *Ashcraft v. Tennessee*, 322 U.S. 143 (1944).

141. *Ashcraft*, 322 U.S. at 154.

142. *Escobedo v. Illinois*, 378 U.S. 478 (1964).

143. *Orozco v. Texas*, 394 U.S. 324 (1969).

144. *Schmerber v. California*, 384 U.S. 757 (1966) (Black, J., dissenting).

145. *Ullmann v. United States*, 350 U.S. 422 (1956) (Douglas, J., with whom Black, J., concurs, dissenting).

146. *Johnson v. Zerbst*, 304 U.S. 458 (1938).

147. *Johnson*, 304 U.S. at 465.

148. *Betts v. Brady*, 316 U.S. 455 (1942).

149. *Betts*, 316 U.S. at 476.

150. *Gideon v. Wainwright*, 372 U.S. 335 (1963).

151. *Gideon*, 372 U.S. at 344.

152. *Douglas v. California*, 372 U.S. 353 (1963).

153. *Boddie v. Connecticut*, 401 U.S. 371 (1971).

154. *Meltzer v. C. Buck LeCraw & Co.*, 402 U.S. 954 (1971).

155. *Meltzer*, 402 U.S. at 955–956 (Black, J., dissenting from the denial of certiorari).

156. Steve Suitts, *Hugo Black of Alabama: How His Roots and Early Career Shaped the Great Champion of the Constitution* (Montgomery, AL: NewSouth Books, 2005), 222.

157. *Boykin v. Alabama*, 395 U.S. 238 (1969).

158. Memo from Hugo Black to John Marshall Harlan, May 28, 1969, John Marshall Harlan Papers, box 484, Seeley G. Mudd Manuscript Library, Princeton University.

159. *McGautha v. California*, 402 U.S. 183 (1971).

160. *Furman v. Georgia*, 408 U.S. 238 (1972).

161. *Furman*, 408 U.S. at 226 (Black, J., concurring).

162. *CR*, vol. 77, 73rd Cong., 1st sess., April 3, 1933, 1115.

163. Memo from chief justice Charles Evans Hughes to Hugo Black in *Avery v. Alabama*, December 29, 1939, Black Papers, box 258.

164. *Indiana ex rel. Anderson v. Brand*, 303 U.S. 95 (1938).

165. *Indiana ex rel. Anderson*, 303 U.S. at 117.

166. *Wood v. Lovett*, 313 U.S. 362 (1941).

167. *Lovett*, 313 U.S. at 368–369.

168. *Lovett*, 313 U.S. at 374 (Black, J., dissenting).

169. *Lovett*, 313 U.S. at 373.

170. *Lovett*, 313 U.S. at 381.

171. *Lovett*, 313 U.S. at 382 (quoting *Home Building & Loan Association v. Blaisdell*, 290 U.S. at 428 [1934]). Interestingly, Chief Justice Hughes joined the majority opinion in *Lovett*.

172. *Lovett*, 313 U.S. at 383.

173. *City of El Paso v. Simmons*, 379 U.S. 497 (1965).

174. *Simmons*, 379 U.S. at 532 (Black, J., dissenting).

175. He also argued that the state violated the takings clause by taking private property for public use without just compensation.

176. *Simmons*, 379 U.S. at 522.

177. *Fletcher v. Peck*, 10 U.S. 87 (1810).

178. *Simmons*, 379 U.S. at 522.

179. Black, "Bill of Rights," 865.

180. See *Bell v. Maryland*, 378 U.S. 226, 343 (1964) (Black, J., dissenting). Black did not believe the Fourteenth Amendment, standing alone, could "interfere with a storekeeper's right to choose his customers or with a property owner's right to choose his social and business associates, so long as he does not run counter to valid state or federal regulation." Black subsequently voted with the unanimous court to uphold Title II of the Civil Rights Act of 1964, which was enacted shortly after the court's decision in *Bell*. See *Heart of Atlanta Motel*, 379 U.S. 241; *Katzenbach*, 379 U.S. 294.

181. *Amalgamated Food Employees Union Local 590 v. Logan Valley Plaza*, 391 U.S. 308 (1968) (Black, J., dissenting).

182. It is not entirely clear how much of a shift Black actually made in the area of property rights. On Justice White's draft opinion in *Simmons*, Black penciled "I do not agree" when White cited Chief Justice Hughes's language from *Blaisdell* stating that the contracts clause is not an absolute. Black Papers, box 382. At the same time, Black did not back away from his dissent in *Lovett*, where he also quoted Hughes's language from *Blaisdell*. *Simmons*, 379 U.S. at 527 n. 17.

183. *Simmons*, 379 U.S. at 532.

184. *United States v. Causby*, 328 U.S. 256 (1946).

185. The aircraft passed over their property at eighty-three feet, frightening the Causbys and interfering with their sleep. Moreover, they lost their chicken business because six to ten chickens died each day due to the low-flying aircraft.

186. *Causby*, 328 U.S. at 274 (Black, J., dissenting).

187. *Berman v. Parker*, 348 U.S. 26 (1954).

188. Black, *Constitutional Faith*, 31–33.

189. The era is named after a leading case of the period, *Lochner v. New York*, 198 U.S. 45 (1905), in which the court struck down a state's maximum hour law for bakers.

190. Black, radio address, February 23, 1937, 307.

191. Black, "Reorganization of Federal Judiciary," 638–639.

192. *Lincoln Federal Labor Union v. Northwestern Iron Metal Company*, 335 U.S. 525 (1949).

193. *Lincoln Federal Labor Union*, 335 U.S. at 537.

194. *Ferguson v. Skrupa*, 372 U.S. 726 (1963).

195. *Ferguson*, 372 U.S. at 730–732. Justice Black's opinion was reminiscent of Justice Holmes's dissent in *Lochner*. "The Fourteenth Amendment," Holmes wrote, "does not enact Mr. Herbert Spencer's Social Statics." *Lochner*, 198 U.S. at 75 (Holmes, J., dissenting).

196. *Griswold v. Connecticut*, 381 U.S. 479 (1965).

197. Justices Harlan and White lodged the right of privacy in the liberty provision of the Fourteenth Amendment, and Justice Arthur Goldberg (joined by Brennan and Warren) relied on the Ninth Amendment.

198. *Griswold*, 381 U.S. at 511 (Black, J., dissenting).

199. *Griswold*, 381 U.S. at 522.

200. *United States v. Vuitch*, 402 U.S. 62 (1971).

201. See Justice Brennan's conference notes in *United States v. Vuitch*, Brennan Papers, pt. I, 228.

202. Harry A. Blackmun Papers, Library of Congress, Manuscript Division, No. 84—*United States v. Vuitch*, box 123.

203. *Sniadach v. Family Finance Corp.*, 395 U.S. 337 (1969).

204. *Sniadach*, 397 U.S. at 345.

205. *Goldberg v. Kelly*, 397 U.S. 254 (1970).

206. *Goldberg*, 397 U.S. at 277.

207. *In re Winship*, 397 U.S. 358 (1970).

208. *In re Winship*, 397 U.S. at 385.

209. *Smith v. Allwright*, 321 U.S. 649 (1944).

210. *Marsh v. Alabama*, 326 U.S. 501 (1946).

211. *Marsh*, 326 U.S. at 506.

212. *Shelley v. Kraemer*, 334 U.S. 1 (1948).

213. In 1961 Black joined a decision in which the court ruled that a privately owned coffee shop that denied service to African Americans violated the equal protection clause because the building in which it operated was owned by an agency of the state. *Burton v. Wilmington Parking Authority*, 365 U.S. 715 (1961).

214. *Evans v. Newton*, 382 U.S. 296 (1966).

215. *Evans v. Abney*, 396 U.S. 435 (1970).

216. Black also wrote the court's decision in *Palmer v. Thompson*, 403 U.S. 217 (1971), which allowed the city of Jackson, Mississippi, to close its public swimming pools after federal courts ruled that its operation of segregated pools violated the equal protection clause. For the 5–4 court, Black argued that judges should not second-guess the motivations of the city council, which had purportedly closed the pools for financial reasons. According to Black, the impact of the decision was facially neutral—that is, it affected all citizens equally.

217. *Bell*, 378 U.S. 226.

218. *Heart of Atlanta Motel*, 379 U.S. at 278 (Black, J., concurring).

219. *Jones v. Alfred H. Mayer Co.*, 392 U.S. 409 (1968).

220. *Hunter v. Erickson*, 393 U.S. 385 (1969).

221. See also *Reitman v. Mulkey*, 387 U.S. 369 (1967) (Harlan, J., with whom Black, J., joined, dissenting) (arguing that a California constitutional initiative that gave homeowners full discretion to decline to rent or sell their property to anyone they wished did not violate the Constitution); *James v. Valtierra*, 402 U.S. 137 (1971) (Black, J.) (upholding California's referendum that any additional public housing in local communities must be approved by the voters). Black distinguished *Valtierra* from *Hunter* on the grounds that the latter case involved racial discrimination, whereas the former involved the allocation of financial resources to subsidize low-cost public housing.

222. *Harper v. Virginia Board of Elections*, 383 U.S. 663 (1966).

223. *Harper*, 383 U.S. at 666.

224. *Harper*, 383 U.S. at 675 (Black, J., dissenting).

225. Del Dickson, ed., *The Supreme Court in Conference (1940–1985): The Private Discussions behind Nearly 300 Supreme Court Decisions* (New York: Oxford University Press, 2001), 648–649.

226. Dickson, 638–639.

227. *Brown v. Board of Education of Topeka*, 347 U.S. 483 (1954).

228. Dickson, *Supreme Court in Conference*, 648. See also Richard Kluger, *Simple Justice: The History of* Brown v. Board of Education *and Black America's Struggle for Equality* (New York: Vintage Books, 1975), 593.

229. *Brown v. Board of Education II*, 349 U.S. 294 (1955) (holding that schools must desegregate "with all deliberate speed"). Black expressed frustration with the "all deliberate speed" language because, in his view, it was too vague. "There has been entirely too much deliberation and not enough speed," Black wrote a decade later. *Griffin v. County School Board of Prince Edward County*, 377 U.S. 218, 229 (1964). In a 1969 case, Black urged his colleagues to abandon the ineffectual language altogether, observing that the phrase "has turned out to be a soft euphemism for delay." *Alexander v. Holmes County Board of Education*, 396 U.S. 1218 (1969) (Black, J., sitting as circuit justice).

230. *Cooper v. Aaron*, 358 U.S. 1 (1958).

231. The school board asked for the delay to allow the political unrest to subside.

232. *Griffin*, 377 U.S. 218.

233. *Griffin*, 377 U.S. at 231.

234. *Green v. County School Board of New Kent County*, 391 U.S. 430 (1968).

235. *Swann v. Charlotte-Mecklenburg Board of Education*, 402 U.S. 1 (1971).

236. *Swann*, 402 U.S. at 30.

237. Black Papers, box 432.

238. *Colegrove v. Green*, 328 U.S. 549 (1946).

239. Those two justices were Stanley Reed and Harold Burton.

240. *Colegrove*, 328 U.S. at 569 (Black, J., dissenting).

241. See, e.g., *Cook v. Fortson*, 329 U.S. 675 (1946); *Colegrove v. Barrett*, 330 U.S. 804 (1947); *South v. Peters*, 339 U.S. 276 (1950); *Remmey v. Smith*, 342 U.S. 916 (1952); *Cox v. Peters*, 342 U.S. 936 (1952); *Anderson v. Jordan*, 343 U.S. 912 (1952); *Hartsfield v. Sloan*, 357 U.S. 916 (1958).

242. *Baker v. Carr*, 369 U.S. 186 (1962).

243. *Wesberry v. Sanders*, 376 U.S. 1 (1964).

244. That provision states: "Members [of the House shall be] chosen every second Year by the People of the several States."

245. *Reynolds v. Sims*, 377 U.S. 533 (1964).

246. Tinsley E. Yarbrough, "Justice Black and Equal Protection," *Southwestern University Law Review* 9 (1977): 899, 912.

247. Justice Black did not immediately adopt an originalist approach to the Constitution, but by the time he authored his dissent in *Adamson v. California*, 332 U.S. 46 (1947), it was in full bloom.

248. Black, *Constitutional Faith*, 66.

249. Black, "Bill of Rights," 881.

250. *New York Times*, 403 U.S. at 714–715 (Black, J., concurring).

251. Jefferson to Madison, December 20, 1787, in Boyd, *Papers of Thomas Jefferson*, 12:440.

252. Newman, *Hugo Black*, 44.

253. *Boykin v. Alabama*, 395 U.S. 238 (1969) (Harlan, J., with whom Black, J., joined, dissenting); *Rudolph v. Alabama*, 375 U.S. 889 (1963) (Goldberg, J., with whom Douglas, J., and Brennan, J., joined, dissenting from denial).

254. John P. Frank, "Justice Black and the New Deal," *Arizona Law Review* 9 (1967): 26, 35.

255. *Harper*, 383 U.S. at 678 n. 7 (1966) (Black, J., dissenting).

256. *Griswold*, 381 U.S. at 509 (Black, J., dissenting).

257. *Harper*, 383 U.S. at 675 (Black, J., dissenting).

258. Hugo L. Black, foreword to *Confronting Justice: The Edmond Cahn Reader* (Boston: Little, Brown, 1966), xii.

259. Black, *Constitutional Faith*, 21.

3. ANTONIN SCALIA'S ORIGINALISM: HAMILTONIAN

1. *Tome v. United States*, 513 U.S. 150, 168 (1995) (Scalia, J., concurring in part and concurring in the judgment).

2. James Madison, Alexander Hamilton, and John Jay, *The Federalist Papers*, ed. Isaac Kramnick (New York: Penguin Books, 1987), No. 15, 150.

3. *Federalist Papers*, No. 76, 431 ("The supposition of universal venality in human nature is little less an error in political reasoning than the supposition of universal rectitude").

4. *Federalist Papers*, No. 72, 414.

5. *The Papers of Alexander Hamilton* (hereafter *PAH*), 27 vols., ed. Harold C. Syrett (New York: Columbia University Press, 1962), 5:95.

6. Antonin Scalia, "The Two Faces of Federalism," *Harvard Journal of Law and Public Policy* 6 (1982): 19, 22.

7. See, e.g., Address to the American Bar Association, July 9, 1985, in *Major Policy*

Statements of the Attorney General, Edwin Meese III, 1985–1988 (Washington, DC: Government Printing Office, 1989), 7.

8. Final Version of an Opinion on the Constitutionality of an Act to Establish a Bank, February 23, 1791, *PAH,* 8:111.

9. Antonin Scalia, "Use of Legislative History: Judicial Abdication to Fictitious Legislative Intent," speech delivered to various law schools in 1985–1986, on file with the author.

10. Antonin Scalia, address before the Attorney General's Conference on Economic Liberties, Washington, DC, June 14, 1986, in *Original Meaning Jurisprudence: A Sourcebook, Appendix C* (Washington, DC: Office of Legal Policy, US Department of Justice, 1987), 3.

11. Antonin Scalia and Stephen G. Breyer, "A Conversation on the Constitution: Judicial Interpretation," Annenberg Foundation Trust at Sunnylands, http://www.annenbergclassroom.org/page/a-conversation-on-the-constitution-judicial-interpretation.

12. *Plaut v. Spendthrift Farm,* 514 U.S. 211, 219–220 (1995) (citing Edward S. Corwin, *The Doctrine of Judicial Review* [Princeton, NJ: Princeton University Press, 1914], 37).

13. *Williams-Yulee v. State Bar of Florida,* 575 U.S. 433 (2015).

14. *Williams-Yulee,* 575 U.S. at 472–473.

15. Remarks by Justice Antonin Scalia to Dr. Henry J. Abraham's class from the University of Virginia, Supreme Court Building, Washington, DC, December 2, 1996.

16. Antonin Scalia, address delivered at Thomas Aquinas College, Santa Paula, CA, January 24, 1997, on file with the author.

17. Calvin Massey, "Legally Speaking: A Conversation with Antonin Scalia," Hastings College of Law, September 26, 2010, https://www.youtube.com/watch?v=KvttIukZEtM.

18. "To Preserve Elite Federal Courts," *L.A. Times Daily Journal,* February 20, 1987, 4. Interestingly, Justice Black was a strong defender of an independent judiciary during his time on the Supreme Court, but when he was in the Senate he supported the direct election of federal judges. *Congressional Record,* vol. 79, pt. 6, 74th Cong., 1st sess., April 29, 1935, 6529.

19. See, e.g., *Lujan v. Defenders of Wildlife,* 504 U.S. 555, 577 (1992).

20. See *Wal-Mart Stores v. Dukes,* 564 U.S. 338 (2011); *AT&T Mobility LLC v. Concepcion,* 563 U.S. 333 (2011); *American Express Company v. Italian Colors Restaurant,* 570 U.S. 228 (2013).

21. See, e.g., *Austin v. Michigan Chamber of Commerce,* 494 U.S. 652 (1990) (Scalia, J., dissenting); *Citizens United v. Federal Election Commission,* 558 U.S. 310 (2010).

22. Constitutional Convention Speech on a Plan of Government, *PAH,* 4:200.

23. *New York Times v. Sullivan,* 376 U.S. 254 (1964).

24. *Ollman v. Evans,* 750 F.2d 970 (D.C. Cir. 1984) (Scalia, J., dissenting).

25. Betsey Blaney, "Scalia, Breyer Bandy about How to Decide Cases," Associated Press, November 12, 2010, http://archive.boston.com/news/nation/articles/2010/11/12/scalia_breyer_bandy_about_how_to_decide_cases/.

26. Ian Millhiser, "Scalia Jumps on the Anti–Seventeenth Amendment Bandwagon,"

Think Progress, November 15, 2010, https://archive.thinkprogress.org/scalia-jumps-on-the-anti-seventeenth-amendment-bandwagon-f7c4776e5ad6/.

27. Antonin Scalia, "Reflections on the Constitution," address at Kennedy Political Union at American University, C-SPAN, November 17, 1988.

28. In 2006 I wrote a book on Justice Scalia titled *The Political Thought of Justice Antonin Scalia: A Hamiltonian on the Supreme Court* (Lanham, MD: Rowman & Littlefield, 2006). When Justice Scalia visited the University of Central Missouri, where I teach, in 2008, he graciously inscribed the book as follows: "To Jim Staab—For writing a fine book that probably is, in basic thrust if not in each detail, right on." He also acknowledged an indebtedness to Hamiltonian political principles in a lecture he gave in my Public Law and Judicial Process course.

29. "1976 Bicentennial Institute—Oversight and Review of Agency Decisionmaking," *Administrative Law Review* 28, 4 (1976): 569–742, 693.

30. See, e.g., *Plaut*, 514 U.S. at 221 (approvingly citing Madison's remark from Federalist No. 48 that, in republican government, the legislature "is everywhere extending the sphere of its activity, and drawing all power into its impetuous vortex").

31. Jennifer Senior, "In Conversation: Antonin Scalia," *New York Magazine*, October 6, 2013.

32. Staab, *Political Thought of Justice Antonin Scalia*, 35–45.

33. *Synar v. United States*, 626 F. Supp. 1374 (D. D.C. 1986).

34. *Synar*, 626 F. Supp. at 1401.

35. *Mistretta v. United States*, 488 U.S. 361 (1989).

36. The US Sentencing Commission consolidated the power previously exercised by the sentencing judge and the Parole Commission, an executive branch agency.

37. *Mistretta*, 488 U.S. at 420–421.

38. *Morrison v. Olson*, 487 U.S. 654 (1988).

39. Under the law, independent counsels were appointed by a special division of judges consisting of a panel of three circuit court judges who served two-year terms and were appointed by the chief justice of the United States.

40. Independent counsels could be removed only by the attorney general for cause.

41. *Morrison*, 487 U.S. at 699 (Scalia, J., dissenting).

42. *Morrison*, 487 U.S. at 702–703.

43. *Morrison*, 487 U.S. at 732–733.

44. See Antonin Scalia, "Originalism: The Lesser Evil," *University of Cincinnati Law Review* 57 (1989): 849–865.

45. Staab, *Political Thought of Justice Antonin Scalia*, 89–136.

46. The sole organ theory is often credited to John Marshall, who said, "The President is the sole organ of the nation in its external relations, and its sole representative with foreign nations." *Annals*, 6th Cong., col. 613. However, Hamilton concluded his "Pacificus" essays—authored seven years earlier—by observing that the president is the "constitutional organ of intercourse between the UStates & foreign Nations—whenever he speaks to them, it is in that capacity; it is in the name and on behalf of the UStates." *PAH*, 15:135.

47. "Congressional Oversight of Executive Agreements—1975," Hearings before the Subcommittee on Separation of Powers of the Committee on the Judiciary, US Senate, 94th Cong., 1st sess., 303.

48. *Ramirez de Arellano v. Weinberger*, 745 F.2d 1500 (D.C. Cir. 1984). The Reagan administration sought to establish the center on a private cattle ranch to train soldiers from El Salvador.

49. *Ramirez de Arellano*, 734 F.2d at 1562.

50. *Sanchez-Espinoza v. Reagan*, 770 F.2d 202 (D.C. Cir. 1985).

51. *Sanchez-Espinoza*, 770 F.2d at 205. The government's support of the Contras was also challenged by twelve members of the House who claimed that such support violated Congress's authority to declare war (Article I, section 8, clause 11), the War Powers Resolution of 1973, and the Boland Amendment, which prohibited financial assistance "to any group or individual, not part of the country's armed forces, for the purpose of overthrowing the Government of Nicaragua." Scalia ruled against the congressional petitioners on two separate grounds. First, following precedent established by the DC Court of Appeals, he determined that the constitutional issues surrounding the war powers raised a nonjusticiable political question. Second, he dismissed the congressional parties' suit because the Boland Amendment had expired in 1983. *Sanchez-Espinoza*, 770 F.2d at 210.

52. *Rasul v. Bush*, 542 U.S. 466 (2004).

53. *Hamdan v. Rumsfeld*, 548 U.S. 557 (2006).

54. *Hamdan*, 548 U.S. at 677.

55. *Boumediene v. Bush*, 553 U.S. 723 (2008).

56. *Boumediene*, 553 U.S. at 769.

57. *Boumediene*, 553 U.S. at 827–828 (Scalia, J., dissenting).

58. James B. Staab, "The Tenth Amendment and Justice Scalia's 'Split Personality,'" *Journal of Law and Politics* 16, 2 (2000): 231–379.

59. James Madison is often given credit as the originator of the political process approach to federalism disputes, but that accolade should really go to Alexander Hamilton. "The question . . . of the division of powers between the general and state governments, is a question of convenience," wrote Hamilton. "It becomes a prudential enquiry, what powers are proper to be reserved to the latter; and this immediately involves another enquiry into the proper objects of the two governments." Remarks at New York Ratifying Convention, June 27, 1788, *PAH*, 5:97. For an extended discussion of how Hamilton and Madison differed over the issue of federalism, see Staab, "Tenth Amendment and Justice Scalia's 'Split Personality.'"

60. "Nomination of Judge Antonin Scalia to Be Associate Justice of the Supreme Court," Hearings before the Committee on the Judiciary, US Senate, 99th Cong., 1st sess., August 5–6, 1986, 81.

61. *Printz v. United States*, 521 U.S. 898 (1997).

62. *Printz*, 521 U.S. at 915, n. 9.

63. Madison defended neither a strict interpretation of the Constitution, nor an overly broad interpretation, but a "true & fair" construction. James Madison to M. L. Hurlbert, May 1830, and Madison to John G. Jackson, December 27, 1821, in *The Writings*

of James Madison, vol. 9, ed. Gaillard Hunt (New York: G. P. Putnam's Sons, 1910), 74, 371–372. For a discussion of why Scalia could have moved toward a middle-ground Madisonian approach, see Staab, *Political Thought of Justice Antonin Scalia*, 293–294.

64. *United States v. Lopez*, 514 U.S. 549 (1995) (striking down the Gun-Free School Zones Act of 1990); *Printz*, 521 U.S. 898 (striking down the interim provisions of the Brady Handgun Violence Prevention Act of 1993); *United States v. Morrison*, 529 U.S. 598 (2000) (striking down a provision of the Violence against Women Act of 1994).

65. *Seminole Tribe of Florida v. Florida*, 517 U.S. 44 (1996) (striking down the Indian Gaming Regulatory Act of 1988); *Kimel v. Florida Board of Regents*, 528 U.S. 62 (2000) (denying state employees' claims brought under the Age Discrimination in Employment Act of 1967); *Board of Trustees of the University of Alabama v. Garrett*, 531 U.S. 356 (2001) (disallowing federal suits based on the Americans with Disabilities Act of 1990).

66. James B. Staab, "Conservative Activism on the Rehnquist Court: Federal Preemption Is No Longer a Liberal Issue," *Roger Williams University Law Review* 9, 1 (2003): 129–186.

67. Antonin Scalia, "Constitutional Interpretation," Julius J. Oppenheimer Lecture, University of Central Missouri, March 4, 2008.

68. See, e.g., *United States v. Windsor*, 570 U.S. 744 (2013) (Scalia, J., dissenting) (arguing that, under the Defense of Marriage Act of 1996, the federal government has the authority to deny benefits to same-sex couples).

69. *Gonzales v. Raich*, 545 U.S. 1 (2005).

70. *Gonzalez*, 545 U.S. at 35–36 (Scalia, J., concurring).

71. *Wickard v. Filburn*, 317 U.S. 111 (1942).

72. *Gonzalez*, 545 U.S. at 37 n. 2.

73. *National Federation of Independent Business v. Sebelius*, 567 U.S. 519 (2012).

74. *Sebelius*, 567 U.S. at 656 (Scalia, J., Kennedy, J., Thomas, J., Alito, J., dissenting).

75. See, e.g., *Tyler Pipe Industries, Inc. v. Washington State Department of Revenue*, 483 U.S. 232 (1987) (Scalia, J., concurring in part and dissenting in part) (arguing that the court's negative commerce clause jurisprudence did not have textual support and amounted to "a sort of intellectual adverse possession").

76. *Printz*, 521 U.S. 898 (Scalia, J.).

77. *Missouri v. Holland*, 252 U.S. 416 (1920).

78. *Bond v. United States*, 572 U.S. 844 (2014) (Scalia, J., concurring in the judgment) (finding that the Chemical Weapons Convention Implementation Act cannot be interpreted to apply to local crimes). See also *Medellín v. Texas*, 552 U.S. 491 (2008) (Roberts, C.J., with whom Scalia, J., joined) (ruling that the Optional Protocol Concerning the Compulsory Settlement of Disputes to the Vienna Convention does not provide for direct enforcement of International Court of Justice rulings and that the president cannot unilaterally execute a non-self-executing treaty by giving it domestic effect).

79. Antonin Scalia, *A Matter of Interpretation: Federal Courts and the Law*, ed. Amy Gutmann (Princeton, NJ: Princeton University Press, 1997), 135.

80. Scalia, 138–139.

81. *Texas v. Johnson*, 491 U.S. 397 (1989).

82. *McIntyre v. Ohio Elections Commission*, 514 U.S. 334, 378 (1995) (Scalia J., dissenting) (quoting *Texas v. Johnson*, 491 U.S. at 414).

83. *R.A.V. v. City of St. Paul*, 505 U.S. 377 (1992).

84. *R.A.V.*, 505 U.S. at 391–392.

85. *Brown v. Entertainment Merchants Association*, 564 U.S. 786 (2011).

86. *United States v. Stevens*, 559 U.S. 460 (2010).

87. *Snyder v. Phelps*, 562 U.S. 443 (2011).

88. *Hill v. Colorado*, 530 U.S. 703 (2000).

89. *Austin v. Michigan Chamber of Commerce*, 494 U.S. 652 (1990).

90. These special advantages cited by the court included limited liability, perpetual life, and favorable treatment of the accumulation and distribution of assets.

91. *Austin*, 494 U.S. at 679–680, 684 (Scalia, J., dissenting).

92. *McConnell v. FEC*, 540 U.S. 93 (2003).

93. *McConnell*, 540 U.S. at 248 (Scalia, J., concurring in part and dissenting in part).

94. *FEC v. Wisconsin Right to Life*, 551 U.S. 449 (2007) (Scalia, J., concurring in part and concurring in the judgment).

95. *Citizens United*, 558 U.S. 310.

96. *R.A.V.*, 505 U.S. at 387. See also *McDonald v. City of Chicago*, 561 U.S. 742 (2010) (Scalia, J., concurring) ("No fundamental right—not even the First Amendment—is absolute").

97. See, e.g., Antonin Scalia, *Scalia Speaks: Reflections on Law, Faith, and Life Well Lived*, ed. Christopher J. Scalia and Edward Whelan (New York: Crown Forum, 2017), 201–212.

98. See *Miller v. California*, 413 U.S. 15 (1973).

99. *Pope v. Illinois*, 481 U.S. 497, 504 (1987) (Scalia, J., concurring).

100. In addition to his view that nude dancing is not constitutionally protected speech, *Barnes v. Glen Theatre*, 501 U.S. 560 (1991) (Scalia, J., concurring in the judgment), Scalia dissented in two cases in which the court struck down the federal government's efforts to regulate child pornography. See *Ashcroft v. Free Speech Coalition*, 535 U.S. 234 (2002) (Scalia, J., dissenting); *Ashcroft v. American Civil Liberties Union*, 542 U.S. 656 (2004) (Scalia, J., dissenting). He also maintained that municipalities can regulate "sexually oriented businesses." In fact, if the business's primary purpose is "the sordid business of pandering [sex]," he thought it lay outside the protection of the First Amendment altogether. See *FW/PBS, Inc. v. Dallas*, 493 U.S. 215 (1990) (Scalia, J., concurring in part and dissenting in part).

101. *Rust v. Sullivan*, 500 U.S. 173 (1991).

102. *National Endowment for the Arts v. Finley*, 524 U.S. 569 (1998) (Scalia, J., concurring in the judgment).

103. *Rumsfeld v. Forum for Academic and Institutional Rights*, 547 U.S. 47 (2006) (upholding the Solomon Amendment).

104. *Agency for International Development v. Alliance for Open Society International*, 570 U.S. 205 (2013).

105. *Agency for International Development*, 570 U.S. at 221 (Scalia, J., dissenting).

106. *Rutan v. Republican Party of Illinois*, 497 U.S. 62 (1990).

107. *Rutan*, 497 U.S. at 95 (Scalia, J., dissenting).

108. *Board of County Commissioners v. Umbehr*, 518 U.S. 668 (1996) (Scalia, J., dissenting); *O'Hare Truck Service Inc. v. City of Northlake*, 518 U.S. 712 (1996) (Scalia, J., dissenting).

109. *Rankin v. McPherson*, 483 U.S. 378 (1987).

110. *Rankin*, 483 U.S. at 396–401 (Scalia, J., dissenting). Justice Scalia once told Floyd Abrams and Nadine Strossen, two principled defenders of the First Amendment, "I'm really not bad on the First Amendment." David Lat, "Justice Scalia, Originalism, Free Speech and the First Amendment," *Above the Law*, November 22, 2016. But that statement requires some qualification. Outside the realm of political speech, Scalia allowed for a substantial amount of regulation of speech.

111. Scalia, "Constitutional Interpretation."

112. Antonin Scalia, "On Realism and the Religion Clauses," address delivered at Archbishop Rummel High School, Metairie, LA, January 2, 2016, https://www.americanrhetoric.com/speeches/antoninscaliarealismreligionconstitution.htm.

113. *McCreary County v. ACLU*, 545 U.S. 844, 893 n. 3 (2005) (Scalia, J., dissenting).

114. *Board of Education of Kiryas Joel Village v. Grumet*, 512 U.S. 687, 751 (1994) (Scalia J., dissenting).

115. Scalia, "On Realism and the Religion Clauses."

116. *Zelman v. Simmons-Harris*, 536 U.S. 639 (2002).

117. *Board of Education of the Westside Community Schools v. Mergens*, 496 U.S. 226 (1990); *Lamb's Chapel v. Center Moriches Union Free School District*, 508 U.S. 384 (1993) (Scalia, J., concurring in the judgment).

118. *Rosenberger v. The Rector and Visitors of the University of Virginia*, 515 U.S. 819 (1995).

119. *Lee v. Weisman*, 505 U.S. 577 (1992) (Scalia, J., dissenting).

120. *Santa Fe Independent School District v. Doe*, 530 U.S. 290 (2000) (Scalia, J., dissenting).

121. Scalia did not participate in the Pledge of Allegiance case. See *Elk Grove Unified School District v. Newdow*, 542 U.S. 1 (2004). However, he did express his views on the subject. See Gina Holland, "Scalia Withdraws from Pledge of Allegiance Decision," *Kansas City Star*, October 20, 2003, A4.

122. *Edwards v. Aguillard*, 482 U.S. 578 (1987) (Scalia, J., dissenting).

123. *County of Allegheny v. American Civil Liberties Union, Greater Pittsburgh Chapter*, 492 U.S. 573 (1989) (concurring in the judgment in part and dissenting in part).

124. *McCreary County*, 545 U.S. 844 (Scalia, J., dissenting); *Van Orden v. Perry*, 545 U.S. 677 (2005) (Scalia, J., concurring).

125. *Town of Greece v. Galloway*, 572 U.S. 565 (2014).

126. *Lemon v. Kurtzman*, 403 U.S. 602 (1971).

127. *Lamb's Chapel*, 508 U.S. at 398 (Scalia, J., concurring in the judgment).

128. *Tangipahoa Parish Board of Education v. Freiler*, 530 U.S. 1251 (2000) (Scalia, J., dissenting from the denial of certiorari) (arguing that the court should grant certiorari in the case to "inter the *Lemon* test once [and] for all").

129. *Lee*, 505 U.S. 577.

130. *Lee*, 505 U.S. at 632, 636 (Scalia, J., dissenting).

131. *Employment Division, Department of Human Resources of Oregon v. Smith*, 494 U.S. 872 (1990).

132. Justice Scalia made an exception for hybrid cases in which other constitutional rights were at issue. See, e.g., *Wisconsin v. Yoder*, 406 U.S. 205 (1972) (invalidating a compulsory education law as applied to the Amish on grounds of both free exercise of religion and parental rights).

133. According to Scalia's analysis, the court still had to apply strict scrutiny when state and local governments targeted or discriminated against particular religious practices. A dramatic example of this occurred in *Church of Lukumi Babalu Aye v. Hialeah*, 508 U.S. 520 (1993), where a unanimous court struck down city ordinances that banned animal sacrifices during religious ceremonies.

134. *City of Boerne v. Flores*, 521 U.S. 507 (1997).

135. *Flores*, 521 U.S. at 544 (Scalia, J., concurring).

136. *Sherbert v. Verner*, 374 U.S. 398 (1963).

137. Scalia, "On Realism and the Religion Clauses."

138. Oral argument in *Holt v. Hobbs*, No. 13-6827, October 7, 2014, https://www.supremecourt.gov/oral_arguments/argument_transcripts/13-6827_8758.pdf. Unlike the Religious Freedom Restoration Act, the Religious Land Use and Institutionalized Persons Act requires strict scrutiny only in cases involving land use and prisoner rights.

139. *Cutter v. Wilkinson*, 544 U.S. 709 (2005).

140. *Holt v. Hobbs*, 574 U.S. 352 (2015).

141. *Gonzales v. O Centro Espirita Beneficente União do Vegetal*, 546 U.S. 418 (2006).

142. *Burwell v. Hobby Lobby Stores*, 573 U.S. 682 (2014).

143. *Christian Legal Society v. Martinez*, 561 U.S. 661 (2010).

144. *Locke v. Davey*, 540 U.S. 712 (2004).

145. *District of Columbia v. Heller*, 554 U.S. 570 (2008).

146. Those other examples were the First, Fourth, and Ninth Amendments.

147. Article I, section 8, clause 16 of the Constitution grants Congress the power "to provide for organizing, arming, and disciplining, the Militia, and for governing such Part of them as may be employed in the Service of the United States, reserving to the States respectively, the Appointment of the Officers, and the Authority of training the Militia according to the discipline prescribed by Congress."

148. *Heller*, 554 U.S. at 599.

149. *Heller*, 554 U.S. at 636.

150. *United States v. Emerson*, 270 F.3d 203 (2001).

151. *Friedman v. City of Highland Park*, 136 S. Ct. 447 (2015) (Thomas, J., dissenting from the denial of certiorari).

152. Interview with Nina Totenberg, Smithsonian Associates Interview, Lisner Auditorium, George Washington University, Washington, DC, February 12, 2013, 2013 WLNR 10286459.

153. David M. Dorsen, *The Unexpected Scalia: A Conservative Justice's Liberal Opinions* (Cambridge: Cambridge University Press, 2017).

154. *Arizona v. Hicks*, 480 U.S. 321, 325 (1987).

155. *National Treasury Employees Union v. Von Raab*, 489 U.S. 656 (1989) (Scalia, J., dissenting).

156. *County of Riverside v. McLaughlin*, 500 U.S. 44 (1991) (Scalia, J., dissenting).

157. *Kyllo v. United States*, 533 U.S. 27 (2001).

158. *Florida v. Jardines*, 569 U.S. 1 (2013).

159. *United States v. Jones*, 565 U.S. 400 (2012).

160. *Coy v. Iowa*, 487 U.S. 1012 (1988).

161. *Maryland v. Craig*, 497 U.S. 836 (1990).

162. *Craig*, 497 U.S. at 860–861 (Scalia, J., dissenting).

163. *Crawford v. Washington*, 541 U.S. 36 (2004).

164. *Ohio v. Roberts*, 448 U.S. 56 (1980).

165. *Crawford*, 541 U.S. at 53–54. Scalia cited the use of ex parte testimony in the trial of Sir Walter Raleigh (1603) as a notorious example of a practice the confrontation clause was designed to correct.

166. *Crawford*, 541 U.S. at 68–69. Scalia did acknowledge two hearsay exceptions recognized at the time of the nation's founding that could apply to testimonial statements: dying declarations and forfeiture by wrongdoing (i.e., when the defendant prevents the witness from testifying).

167. *Davis v. Washington*, 547 U.S. 813 (2006).

168. *Giles v. California*, 554 U.S. 353 (2008).

169. *Melendez-Diaz v. Massachusetts*, 557 U.S. 305 (2009).

170. *Michigan v. Bryant*, 562 U.S. 344 (2011).

171. *Bryant*, 562 U.S. at 379 (Scalia, J., dissenting).

172. *Ohio v. Clark*, 576 U.S. 237 (2015).

173. *Clark*, 576 U.S. at 252–253 (Scalia, J., concurring in the judgment).

174. Scalia, "Constitutional Interpretation."

175. It should be noted that the right to a jury trial in criminal cases is also guaranteed by Article III, section 3.

176. *Almendares-Torres v. United States*, 523 U.S. 224 (1998) (Scalia, J., dissenting); *Monge v. California*, 524 U.S. 721 (1998) (Scalia, J., dissenting).

177. *Blakely v. Washington*, 542 U.S. 296 (2004).

178. *Apprendi v. New Jersey*, 530 U.S. 446 (2000).

179. *Blakely*, 542 U.S. at 306.

180. *United States v. Booker*, 543 U.S. 220 (2005) (Scalia, J., dissenting in part).

181. Scalia, "Constitutional Interpretation." See also Jerry de Jaager, "Justice Scalia Comes Home to the Law School," Record Online, Spring 2012, http://www.law.uchicago.edu/alumni/magazine/spring12/scalia.

182. Data from Harold J. Spaeth, Lee Epstein, Andrew D. Martin, Jeffrey A. Segal, Theodore J. Ruger, and Sara C. Benesh, 2016 Supreme Court database, http://Supremecourtdatabase.org.

183. *California v. Acevedo*, 500 U.S. 565, 581 (1991) (Scalia, J., concurring).

184. *City of Los Angeles v. Patel*, 576 U.S. 409, 430–431 (2015) (Scalia, J., dissenting).

185. See *Minnesota v. Dickerson*, 508 U.S. 366, 380–382 (1993) (Scalia, J., concurring). See also *Maryland v. Buie*, 494 U.S. 325 (1990); *Illinois v. Wardlow*, 528 U.S. 119 (2000); *United States v. Arvizu*, 534 U.S. 266 (2002); *Arizona v. United States*, 567 U.S.387 (2012).

186. See, e.g., *Kentucky v. King*, 563 U.S. 452 (2011); *United States v. Drayton*, 536 U.S. 194 (2002); *Georgia v. Randolph*, 547 U.S. 103 (2006) (Scalia, J., dissenting); *Fernandez v. California*, 571 U.S. 292 (2014) (Scalia, J., concurring).

187. *Vernonia School District 47J v. Acton*, 515 U.S. 646 (1995).

188. *Board of Education of Independent School District No. 92 of Pottawatomie County v. Earls*, 536 U.S. 822 (2002).

189. *Ferguson v. City of Charleston*, 532 U.S. 67 (2001) (Scalia, J., dissenting).

190. *Patel*, 576 U.S. 409 (Scalia, J., dissenting).

191. *Florence v. Board of Chosen Freeholders of the County of Burlington*, 566 U.S. 318 (2012).

192. *California v. Hodari D.*, 499 U.S. 621, 626 (1991).

193. *Scott v. Harris*, 550 U.S. 372 (2007).

194. *Safford United School District #1 v. Redding*, 557 U.S. 364 (2009).

195. *New York v. Belton*, 453 U.S. 454 (1981).

196. *Arizona v. Gant*, 556 U.S. 332 (2009) (Scalia, J., concurring).

197. *Maryland v. King*, 569 U.S. 435 (2013) (Scalia, J., dissenting).

198. *Missouri v. McNeely*, 569 U.S. 141 (2013).

199. *Minnesota v. Carter*, 525 U.S. 83 (1998).

200. *Katz v. United States*, 389 U.S. 347 (1967).

201. *Carter*, 525 U.S. at 97 (Scalia, J., concurring).

202. *Carter*, 525 U.S. at 111 n. 3 (Ginsburg, J., dissenting). In speeches, Scalia speculated about whether *Katz* was hurting the war on terror. The federal government, he said in 2008, can no longer wiretap international phone calls "to find out what the bad guys are doing." Scalia, "Constitutional Interpretation."

203. Scalia, "Constitutional Interpretation" (referring to the exclusionary rule as "water under the bridge").

204. *Mapp v. Ohio*, 367 U.S. 643 (1961).

205. *Hudson v. Michigan*, 547 U.S. 586 (2006).

206. *Hudson*, 547 U.S. at 595.

207. *Arizona v. Evans*, 514 U.S. 1 (1995).

208. *Herring v. United States*, 555 U.S. 135 (2009).

209. *Miranda v. Arizona*, 384 U.S. 436 (1966).

210. The four basic warnings are: (1) the right to remain silent, (2) that anything said can and will be used against the individual, (3) the right to have counsel present during the interrogation, and (4) if the individual cannot afford counsel, one will be appointed for him or her.

211. *Dickerson v. United States*, 530 U.S. 428 (2000).

212. *Dickerson*, 530 U.S. at 443.

213. *Dickerson*, 530 U.S. at 465 (Scalia, J., dissenting).

214. See, e.g., *Minnick v. Mississippi*, 498 U.S. 146 (1990) (Scalia, J., dissenting);

Missouri v. Seibert, 542 U.S. 600 (2004); *Maryland v. Shatzer*, 559 U.S. 98 (2010); *Berghuis v. Thompkins*, 560 U.S. 370 (2010); *J.D.B v. North Carolina*, 564 U.S. 261 (2011); *Howes v. Fields*, 565 U.S. 499 (2012); *Salinas v. Texas*, 570 U.S. 178 (2013).

215. *Padilla v. Kentucky*, 559 U.S. 356 (2010).

216. *Padilla*, 559 U.S. at 389 (Scalia J., dissenting).

217. *Gideon v. Wainwright*, 372 U.S. 335 (1963); *Strickland v. Washington*, 466 U.S. 668 (1984).

218. *Padilla*, 559 U.S. at 388.

219. *Lafler v. Cooper*, 566 U.S. 156 (2012) (Scalia, J., dissenting); *Missouri v. Frye*, 566 U.S. 134 (2012) (Scalia, J., dissenting).

220. *Cooper*, 566 U.S. at 170.

221. *Frye*, 566 U.S. at 155 (Scalia, J., dissenting).

222. *Turner v. Rogers*, 564 U.S. 431 (2011) (Thomas, J., with whom Scalia, J., joined, dissenting).

223. *Indiana v. Edwards*, 554 U.S. 164, 185 (2008) (Scalia, J., dissenting).

224. *Maples v. Thomas*, 565 U.S. 266 (2012).

225. *Trop v. Dulles*, 356 U.S. 86, 101 (1958).

226. Scalia argued that judicial reliance on foreign law was irrelevant to American traditions and was too prone to manipulation by judges—that is, there was a selective bias as to when foreign law was consulted and which countries were referenced. See "Foreign Courts and U.S. Constitutional Law," debate between Antonin Scalia and Stephen Breyer, American University, C-SPAN, January 13, 2005; *Roper v. Simmons*, 543 U.S. 551 (2005) (Scalia, J., dissenting).

227. See, e.g., *Schad v. Arizona*, 501 U.S. 624, 650 (1991) (Scalia, J., concurring in part and concurring in the judgment).

228. *Harmelin v. Michigan*, 501 U.S. 957 (1991). Chief Justice Rehnquist was the only other justice who joined that part of Scalia's opinion. Justice Thomas has since adopted the same interpretation.

229. *Ewing v. California*, 528 U.S. 11 (2003) (concurring in the judgment); *Graham v. Florida*, 560 U.S. 48 (2010) (Thomas, J., with whom Scalia, J., joined, dissenting).

230. *Montgomery v. Louisiana*, 136 S. Ct. 718 (2016) (Scalia, J., dissenting).

231. *Miller v. Alabama*, 567 U.S. 460 (2012).

232. In *Callins v. Collins*, 510 U.S. 1141 (1994), Scalia criticized Justice Blackmun's view that the death penalty "as currently administered" violates the Eighth Amendment: "If the people conclude," reasoned Scalia, "that . . . brutal deaths may be deterred by capital punishment; indeed, if they merely conclude that justice requires such brutal deaths to be avenged by capital punishment; the creation of false, untextual and unhistorical contradictions within 'the Court's Eighth Amendment jurisprudence' should not prevent them." *Callins*, 510 U.S. at 1143 (Scalia, J., concurring in the denial of certiorari). In *Baze v. Rees*, 553 U.S. 35 (2008), Scalia criticized Justice Stevens's conclusion that "the imposition of the death penalty represents the pointless and needless extinction of life with only marginal contributions to any discernible social or public purposes." *Baze*, 553 U.S. at 86 (Stevens, J., concurring in the judgment). "Of all Justice Stevens' criticisms of the death

penalty," wrote Scalia in a concurring opinion, "the hardest to take is his bemoaning of 'the enormous costs that death penalty litigation imposes on society,' including the 'burden on the courts and the lack of finality for victims' families.'" "Those costs," he added, "those burdens, and that lack of finality are in large measure the creation of Justice Stevens and other Justices opposed to the death penalty, who have 'encumber[ed it] . . . with unwarranted restrictions neither contained in the text of the Constitution nor reflected in two centuries of practice under it.'" *Baze*, 553 U.S. at 92 (Scalia, J., concurring in the judgment). And in *Glossip v. Gross*, 576 U.S. 863 (2015), Scalia challenged Justice Breyer's claim that it is "highly likely" that the death penalty violates the Eighth Amendment. "By arrogating to himself the power to overturn [the will of the people]," Scalia wrote, "Justice Breyer does not just reject the death penalty, he rejects the Enlightenment." *Glossip*, 576 U.S. at 899 (Scalia, J., concurring).

233. *Walton v. Arizona*, 497 U.S. 639, 656–674 (1990) (Scalia, J., concurring in part and concurring in the judgment) (arguing for reversal of the *Woodson-Lockett* line of cases).

234. *McCleskey v. Zant*, 499 U.S. 467 (1991).

235. *Booth v. Maryland*, 482 U.S. 496 (1987) (Scalia, J., dissenting); *South Carolina v. Gathers*, 490 U.S. 805 (1989) (Scalia, J., dissenting); *Payne v. Tennessee*, 501 U.S. 808 (1991).

236. *McCleskey v. Kemp*, 481 U.S. 279 (1987).

237. Memorandum to Conference, re: No. 84-6811—*McCleskey v. Kemp*, January 6, 1987, Thurgood Marshall Papers, Library of Congress, box 425, folder 7.

238. *In re Davis*, 557 U.S. 952 (2009) (Scalia, J., dissenting).

239. *Atkins v. Virginia*, 536 U.S. 304 (2002) (Scalia, J., dissenting).

240. *Roper*, 543 U.S. 551 (Scalia, J., dissenting). See also *Thompson v. Oklahoma*, 487 U.S. 815 (1988) (Scalia, J., dissenting).

241. *Roper*, 543 U.S. at 608.

242. *Kennedy v. Louisiana*, 554 U.S. 407 (2008).

243. See, e.g., *Hudson v. McMillian*, 503 U.S. 1 (1992) (Thomas, J., dissenting, with whom Scalia joined).

244. *Brown v. Plata*, 563 U.S. 493 (2011).

245. *Brown*, 563 U.S. at 550 (Scalia, J., dissenting).

246. See, e.g., Bernard H. Siegan, *Economic Liberties and the Constitution* (Chicago: University of Chicago Press, 1980); Stephen Macedo, *The New Right v. the Constitution* (Washington, DC: Cato Institute, 1986).

247. Antonin Scalia, "Economic Affairs as Human Affairs," *Cato Journal* 4, 3 (Winter 1985): 706.

248. See, e.g., *BMW of North America v. Gore*, 517 U.S. 559 (1996) (Scalia, J., dissenting); *State Farm Mutual Automobile Insurance Co. v. Campbell*, 538 U.S. 408 (2003) (Scalia, J., dissenting).

249. *BMW of North America*, 517 U.S. at 598.

250. *Nollan v. California Coastal Commission*, 483 U.S. 825 (1987).

251. *Pennell v. City of San Jose*, 485 U.S. 1 (1988) (Scalia, J., concurring in part and dissenting in part).

252. *Lucas v. South Carolina Coastal Council*, 505 U.S. 1003 (1992).

253. *Lucas*, 505 U.S. at 1019.

254. *Lucas*, 505 U.S. at 1028 n. 15: "Justice Blackmun is correct that early constitutional theorists did not believe the Takings Clause embraced regulations of property at all, but even he does not suggest (explicitly, at least) that we renounce the Court's contrary conclusion in [*Pennsylvania Coal Co.*] v *Mahon* [1922]."

255. *Dolan v. City of Tigard*, 512 U.S. 374 (1994). See also *Koontz v. St. Johns River Water Management District*, 570 U.S. 595 (2013).

256. *Kelo v. City of New London*, 545 U.S. 469 (2005).

257. *Stop the Beach Renourishment v. Florida Department of Environmental Protection*, 560 U.S. 702 (2010).

258. *Horne v. Department of Agriculture*, 576 U.S. 351 (2015).

259. Scalia, *Matter of Interpretation*, 24.

260. *Lawrence v. Texas*, 539 U.S. 558, 592 (2003) (Scalia, J., dissenting).

261. Black told his former law clerk John Frank: "I don't know of any law I've thought worse than that one in a long time. I'd have loved to declare [the ban on the use and advocacy of contraceptives] unconstitutional. But I can't do it without saying that Justices can hold anything unconstitutional that they don't like. I'm just not going to decide that way." John P. Frank, "The Shelf Life of Justice Hugo L. Black: The Fairfield Lecture," *Wisconsin Law Review* (1997): 1, 8–9.

262. Scalia, "Constitutional Interpretation."

263. *Roe v. Wade*, 410 U.S. 113 (1973).

264. *Webster v. Reproductive Health Services*, 492 U.S. 490, 537 (1989) (Scalia, J., concurring in part and concurring in the judgment).

265. *Planned Parenthood of Southeastern Pennsylvania v. Casey*, 505 U.S. 833 (1992).

266. *Planned Parenthood of Southeastern Pennsylvania*, 505 U.S. at 996, 1002 (Scalia, J., concurring in the judgment in part and dissenting in part).

267. *Cruzan v. Director, Missouri Department of Health*, 497 U.S. 261 (1990).

268. *Cruzan*, 497 U.S. at 293 (Scalia, J., concurring).

269. *Cruzan*, 497 U.S. at 296.

270. *Cruzan*, 497 U.S. at 293. Scalia's comment here is reminiscent of a famous remark by William F. Buckley Jr., the conservative founder of the *National Review*. Buckley once said "he would rather be governed by the first two thousand people in the phone book than by the members of the Harvard faculty." Michael M. Uhlmann, "Justice Scalia and His Critics," *Perspectives on Political Science* 28, 1 (Winter 1999): 31.

271. *Lawrence v. Texas*, 539 U.S. 558 (2003).

272. *Lawrence*, 539 U.S. at 590, 602 (Scalia, J., dissenting).

273. *Michael H. v. Gerald D.*, 491 U.S. 110 (1989).

274. *Troxel v. Granville*, 530 U.S. 57 (2000).

275. *Troxel*, 530 U.S. at 91–92 (Scalia, J., dissenting).

276. The father finally beat his son so severely that he suffered permanent brain damage and was rendered profoundly impaired. See *DeShaney v. Winnebago County Department of Social Services*, 489 U.S. 189 (1989).

277. *Town of Castle Rock v. Gonzales*, 545 U.S. 748 (2005).

278. *NASA v. Nelson*, 562 U.S. 134, 161 (2011) (Scalia, J., concurring in the judgment).

279. *McDonald v. City of Chicago*, 561 U.S. 742 (2010).

280. See Scalia, *Matter of Interpretation*, 136–137n13 ("properly understood," the Second Amendment "is no limitation upon arms control by the states").

281. *Green v. County School Board of New Kent County*, 391 U.S. 430 (1968).

282. *Freeman v. Pitts*, 503 U.S. 467 (1992).

283. *Freeman*, 503 U.S. at 503–507 (Scalia, J., concurring).

284. *Freeman*, 503 U.S. at 500.

285. *United States v. Fordice*, 505 U.S. 717 (1991) (Scalia, J., concurring in the judgment in part and dissenting in part).

286. *Parents Involved in Community Schools v. Seattle School District No. 1*; *Meredith v. Jefferson County Board of Education*, 551 U.S. 701 (2007).

287. Calvin Massey, "Legally Speaking."

288. Nina Totenberg, "Interviewing Scalia: Verbal Wrestling Match with a Master," NPR, July 25, 2012.

289. *United States v. Virginia*, 518 U.S. 515 (1996).

290. *US v. Virginia*, 518 U.S. at 539–540.

291. *US v. Virginia*, 518 U.S. at 566, 569 (Scalia, J., dissenting).

292. During an interview, Professor Massey asked Scalia: "In 1868, when the 39th Congress was debating and ultimately proposing the 14th Amendment, I don't think anybody would have thought that equal protection applied to sex discrimination, or certainly not to sexual orientation. So does that mean that we've gone off in error by applying the 14th Amendment to both?" Scalia responded: "Yes, yes. Sorry, to tell you that." Massey, "Legally Speaking."

293. *Romer v. Evans*, 517 U.S. 620 (1996).

294. *Romer*, 517 U.S. at 632.

295. *Romer*, 517 U.S. at 636 (Scalia, J., dissenting).

296. *Romer*, 517 U.S. at 636.

297. *Obergefell v. Hodges*, 576 U.S. 644 (2015).

298. *Obergefell*, 576 U.S. at 672.

299. Scalia described Justice Kennedy's opinion as "couched in a style that is as pretentious as its content is egotistical." He added, "If, even as the price to be paid for a fifth vote, I ever join an opinion for the Court that began: 'The Constitution promises liberty to all within its reach, a liberty that includes certain specific rights that allow persons, within a lawful realm, to define and express their identity,' I would hide my head in a bag." "The Supreme Court of the United States," he concluded, "has descended from the disciplined legal reasoning of John Marshall and Joseph Story to the mystical aphorisms of the fortune cookie." *Obergefell*, 576 U.S. at 719 n. 22 (Scalia, J., dissenting). See also Richard L. Hasen, "The Most Sarcastic Justice," *Green Bag* 2, 18 (2015): 215.

300. *Obergefell*, 576 U.S. at 713–714 (Scalia, J., dissenting).

301. Antonin Scalia, "The Disease as Cure: 'In Order to Get beyond Racism, We Must First Take Account of Race,'" *Washington University Law Quarterly* (1979): 147–157.

302. Scalia, "The Disease as Cure," 153.

303. Scalia, 155.

304. *Fisher v. University of Texas*, 136 S. Ct. 2198 (2016).

305. Oral argument in *Fisher v. University of Texas*, No. 14-981, December 9, 2015, 67–68. In an opinion by Justice Kennedy handed down just four months after Scalia's death, the court (4–3) upheld the University of Texas's affirmative action program. *Fisher*, 136 S. Ct. 2198.

306. *City of Richmond v. J. A. Croson Co.*, 488 U.S. 469 (1989).

307. *J. A. Croson*, 488 U.S. at 524 (Scalia, J., concurring in the judgment).

308. *Adarand Constructors, Inc. v. Pena*, 515 U.S. 200 (1995).

309. *Adarand*, 515 U.S. at 239 (Scalia, J., concurring in part and concurring in the judgment).

310. *Grutter v. Bollinger*, 539 U.S. 306 (2003).

311. *Grutter*, 539 U.S. at 347 (Scalia, J., concurring in part and dissenting in part).

312. *Grutter*, 539 U.S. at 349.

313. *Johnson v. Transportation Agency*, 480 U.S. 616 (1987).

314. *Johnson*, 480 U.S. at 677.

315. See Richard C. Reuben, "Scalia: The Bill of Rights 'an Afterthought,'" *Los Angeles Daily Journal*, 1992, B1, 20.

316. See also Antonin Scalia, "Forward: The Importance of Structure in Constitutional Interpretation," *Notre Dame Law Review* 83 (2008): 1417 ("It is a mistake to think that the Bill of Rights is the defining, or even the most important, feature of American Democracy").

317. It should be noted that Scalia did not always side with the executive branch in disputes involving the separation of powers. In *Hamdi v. Rumsfeld*, 542 U.S. 507 (2004), he argued in dissent that the Bush administration could not indefinitely detain a US citizen labeled an enemy combatant. In *National Labor Relations Board v. Noel Canning*, 573 U.S. 513 (2014), Scalia argued in a concurring opinion that the recess appointments clause applies only to intersessions and not to vacancies that occur during the session. And in *Zivotofsky v. Kerry*, 576 U.S. 1 (2015), Scalia wrote a concurring opinion that questioned whether the president has the exclusive authority to recognize foreign governments.

318. "Nomination of Judge Antonin Scalia," 99–100.

319. The First Amendment states: "Congress shall make no law . . . abridging *the* freedom of speech." See Scalia, *Scalia Speaks*, 202–204.

320. In *The Federalist*, both Hamilton and Madison addressed Anti-Federalist concerns about a new standing arming and the possibility that Congress might not support state militias. Under the proposed constitution, Congress had the authority to organize, arm, and discipline state militias. Hamilton argued that there were political checks against a large standing army (i.e., elections and the requirement of making appropriations every two years). *Federalist Papers*, No. 26, 199–200. Both he and Madison emphasized that the states still had the authority to appoint the officers for state militias and to train the militias according to the discipline prescribed by Congress. *Federalist Papers*, No. 29, 211; No. 46, 301–302. Hamilton favored "a select corps" of "well-trained

militia ready to take the field whenever the defense of the State shall require it," which he believed would make a standing army less necessary. *Federalist Papers*, No. 29, 210. Meanwhile, Madison thought all able-bodied men should participate in the militia. "It may well be doubted," he wrote, "whether a militia thus circumstanced could ever be conquered by such a proportion of regular troops." *Federalist Papers*, No. 46, 301. In none of their essays did Hamilton or Madison ever suggest that there was an individual right to bear arms. Scalia often quoted from Federalist No. 46, claiming that Madison "spoke contemptuously of the countries of Europe, which 'are afraid to trust their people with arms.'" Scalia, *Scalia Speaks*, 63. But Madison was referring primarily to issues of federalism and gun ownership related to participation in the state militia. Following that particular statement, Madison wrote: "But were the people to possess the additional advantages of local governments chosen by themselves, who could collect the national will and direct the national force, and of officers appointed out of the militia, by these governments, and attached both to them and to the militia, it may be affirmed with the greatest assurance that the throne of every tyranny in Europe would be speedily overturned in spite of the legions which surround it." *Federalist Papers*, No. 46, 301–302. Further evidence that Hamilton and Madison did not support an individual-rights interpretation of the Second Amendment is that they both supported a conscientious objector exemption for service in the state militias. Madison's initial proposal for the Second Amendment included such a provision. See *Annals of Congress*, vol. 1, 1st Cong., 1st sess., June 8, 1789, 451. During New York's ratifying convention, Hamilton supported a religious exemption from service in state militias, although he did "not wish to encourage this idea." *PAH*, 5:181.

321. *Obergefell*, 576 U.S. at 715 (Scalia, J., dissenting).

4. CLARENCE THOMAS'S ORIGINALISM: NATURAL LAW LIBERTARIAN

1. Clarence Thomas, speech to the National Bar Association, Memphis, TN, July 28, 1998, https://teachingamericanhistory.org/document/speech-to-the-national-bar-association/.

2. Clarence Thomas, "Victims and Heroes in the 'Benevolent State,'" *Harvard Journal of Law and Public Policy* 19, 3 (Spring 1996): 671.

3. Clarence Thomas, "Freedom: A Responsibility, Not a Right," Kormendy Lecture, *Ohio Northern University Law Review* 21 (1994): 10.

4. Clarence Thomas, *My Grandfather's Son: A Memoir* (New York: HarperCollins, 2007), 125–126.

5. Thomas Sowell, *Race and Economics* (New York: David McKay, 1975), 238.

6. Bill Kauffman, "Clarence Thomas," *Reason*, November 1987, 30.

7. David G. Savage, "Clarence Thomas Is His Own Man," *Los Angeles Times*, July 3, 2011.

8. Clarence Thomas, "Speech before the Kiwanis Club," Washington, DC, January

14, 1987, Mark Paoletta Files, no. 45513-008, George H. W. Bush Presidential Library and Museum, College Station, TX.

9. R. T. Edwards, "Mutual Admiration," *Catholic Standard* 41, 27 (July 4, 1991): 16.

10. Harry V. Jaffa, *Crisis of the House Divided: An Interpretation of the Issues in the Lincoln-Douglas Debates* (New York: Doubleday, 1959), 22.

11. Andrew Peyton Thomas, *Clarence Thomas: A Biography* (San Francisco: Encounter Books, 2001), 307–308. See, e.g., Clarence Thomas, "The Higher Law Background of the Privileges or Immunities Clause of the Fourteenth Amendment," *Harvard Journal of Law and Public Policy* 12, 1 (Winter 1989): 63–70; Clarence Thomas, Remarks at Claremont McKenna College, Claremont, CA, November 16, 1987, Paoletta Files, no. 45514-002.

12. Clarence Thomas, "The Modern Civil Rights Movement: Can a Regime of Individual Rights and the Rule of Law Survive," remarks delivered at Tocqueville Forum, Wake Forest University, April 28, 1988, Paoletta Files, no. 45511-005.

13. Thomas Jefferson, "Opinion against the Constitutionality of the National Bank," February 15, 1791, in *The Writings of Thomas Jefferson*, vol. 3, ed. Andrew A. Lipscomb and Albert Ellery Bergh (Washington, DC: Thomas Jefferson Memorial Association, 1904), 147.

14. *Hammer v. Dagenhart*, 247 U.S. 251 (1918).

15. Jefferson, "Opinion against the Constitutionality of the National Bank," 146.

16. *United States v. Lopez*, 514 U.S. 549 (1995).

17. *Lopez*, 514 U.S. at 587 (Thomas, J., concurring).

18. *Lopez*, 514 U.S. at 584.

19. *Lopez*, 514 U.S. at 601–602.

20. *United States v. Morrison*, 529 U.S. 598 (2000).

21. *Morrison*, 529 U.S. at 627 (Thomas, J., concurring).

22. *Gonzales v. Raich*, 545 U.S. 1 (2005).

23. *Gonzales*, 545 U.S. at 74 (Thomas, J., dissenting).

24. *National Federation of Independent Business v. Sebelius*, 567 U.S. 519 (2012).

25. *Sebelius*, 567 U.S. at 708 (Thomas, J., dissenting).

26. *Cedar Rapids Community School District v. Garret F.*, 526 U.S. 66 (1999) (Thomas, J., dissenting); *Sebelius*, 567 U.S. 519 (Thomas, J., coauthor of joint dissent).

27. *Sabri v. United States*, 541 U.S. 600 (2004) (concurring in the judgment); *United States v. Comstock*, 560 U.S. 126 (2010) (Thomas, J., dissenting); *United States v. Kebodeaux*, 570 U.S. 387 (2013) (Thomas, J., dissenting).

28. *United States v. Lara*, 541 U.S. 193 (2004) (Thomas, J., concurring in the judgment); *Adoptive Couple v. Baby Girl*, 570 U.S. 637 (2013) (Thomas, J., concurring); *United States v. Bryant*, 136 S. Ct. 1954 (2016) (Thomas, J., concurring).

29. *Camps Newfound/Owatonna v. Town of Harrison*, 520 U.S. 564 (1997).

30. *Camps Newfound/Owatonna*, 520 U.S. at 609–640 (Thomas, J., dissenting). See also *United Haulers Association v. Oneida-Herkimer Solid Waste Management Authority*, 550 U.S. 330 (2007) (Thomas, J., concurring in the judgment) (equating the court's negative commerce clause jurisprudence to the *Lochner* era); *Comptroller of the Treasury of Maryland v. Wynne*, 575 U.S. 542 (2015) (Thomas, J., dissenting).

31. *Seminole Tribe of Florida v. Florida*, 517 U.S. 44 (1996) (striking down Indian Gaming Regulatory Act of 1988); *Kimel v. Florida Board of Regents*, 528 U.S. 62 (2000) (denying state employees' claims brought under the Age Discrimination in Employment Act of 1967); *Board of Trustees of the University of Alabama v. Garrett*, 531 U.S. 356 (2001) (disallowing federal suits based on the Americans with Disabilities Act of 1990).

32. See, e.g., *Wyeth v. Levine*, 555 U.S. 555 (2009) (Thomas, J. concurring in the judgment). See also *Williamson v. Mazda Motor of American, Inc.*, 562 U.S. 323 (2011) (Thomas, J., concurring in the judgment); *Kansas v. Garcia*, 140 S. Ct. 791 (2020) (Thomas, J., concurring).

33. *U.S. Term Limits, Inc. v. Thornton*, 514 U.S. 779 (1995).

34. *Thornton*, 514 U.S. at 846 (Thomas, J., dissenting).

35. *Thornton*, 514 U.S. at 846.

36. *Thornton*, 514 U.S. at 848.

37. *Thornton*, 514 U.S. at 845.

38. *Chiafalo v. Washington*, 140 S. Ct. 2416 (2020).

39. That provision states: "Each State shall appoint, in such Manner as the Legislature thereof may direct, a Number of Electors, equal to the whole Number of Senators and Representatives to which the State may be entitled in the Congress: but no Senator or Representative, or Person holding an Office of Trust or Profit under the United States, shall be appointed an Elector."

40. *Chiafalo*, 140 S. Ct. at 2326.

41. *Chiafalo*, 140 S. Ct. at 2333 (Thomas, J., concurring in the judgment).

42. *Hamdi v. Rumsfeld*, 542 U.S. 507, 580–581 (2004) (Thomas, J., dissenting) (quoting Federalist No. 70). See also *Trump v. Vance*, 140 S. Ct. 2412 (2020) (Thomas, J., dissenting).

43. *Humphrey's Executor v. United States*, 295 U.S. 602 (1935).

44. *Seila Law LLC v. Consumer Financial Protection Bureau*, 140 S. Ct. 2183 (2020) (Thomas, J., concurring in part and dissenting in part).

45. *Rasul v. Bush*, 542 U.S. 466 (2004) (Scalia, J., with whom Thomas, J., joined, dissenting).

46. *Hamdi*, 542 U.S. 507 (Thomas, J., dissenting).

47. *Hamdan v. Rumsfeld*, 548 U.S. 557 (2006).

48. *Hamdan*, 548 U.S. at 719 (Thomas, J., dissenting).

49. *Boumediene v. Bush*, 553 U.S. 723 (2008).

50. *Zivotofsky v. Kerry*, 576 U.S. 1059 (2015).

51. *Zivotofsky*, 576 U.S. 1059 (Thomas, J., concurring). Interestingly, Justice Black took the exact opposite view. In *Zemel v. Rusk*, 381 U.S. 1 (1965), he argued in a dissenting opinion that the president was "completely devoid" of authority to regulate the issuance of passports for travel abroad to Cuba. *Zemel*, 381 U.S. at 22 (Black, J., dissenting).

52. The countries impacted by the travel restrictions were Chad, Iran, Iraq, Libya, North Korea, Syria, Venezuela, and Yemen. After a fifty-day review period, the Trump administration lifted the restrictions on Iraq.

53. *Trump v. Hawaii*, 138 S. Ct. 2392 (2018).

54. *Trump*, 138 S. Ct. at 2424 (Thomas, J., concurring).

55. *Department of Homeland Security v. Regents of the University California*, 140 S. Ct. 1891 (2020).

56. *Regents of the University of California*, 140 S. Ct. at 1926 (Thomas, J., concurring in the judgment in part and dissenting in part).

57. *Trump v. Vance*, 140 S. Ct. 2412 (2020).

58. *United States v. Burr*, 25 F. Cas. 30 (No. 14,692d) (CC Va. 1807).

59. Roberts also rejected the argument that the state court must satisfy a heightened standard of need before a subpoena can be issued against a sitting president.

60. *Vance*, 140 S. Ct. at 2438 (Thomas, J., dissenting).

61. *Trump v. Mazars USA, LLP*, 140 S. Ct. 2019 (2020).

62. *Mazars*, 140 S. Ct. at 2034.

63. *McGrain v. Daugherty*, 273 U.S. 135 (1927).

64. *Mazars*, 140 S. Ct. at 2045 (Thomas, J., dissenting).

65. *Mazars*, 140 S. Ct. at 2047. In a footnote, Thomas said he expressed no view on whether there are limits on the impeachment power that would prevent the House from subpoenaing the documents at issue here. Justice Black would not have agreed with Thomas's opinion in *Mazars*. See Hugo L. Black, "Inside a Senate Investigation," *Harper's Monthly Magazine*, February 1936, 275 (describing congressional investigations as "among the most useful and fruitful functions of the national legislature").

66. Clarence Thomas, "The New Intolerance," speech delivered at Mercer University, May 1993, https://www.americanrhetoric.com/speeches/clarencethomasthenewintolerance.htm.

67. *RAV v. City of St. Paul*, 505 U.S. 377 (1992).

68. *United States v. Stevens*, 559 U.S. 460 (2010).

69. *Snyder v. Phelps*, 562 U.S. 443 (2011).

70. See, e.g., *Hill v. Colorado*, 530 U.S. 703 (2000) (Scalia, J., with whom Thomas, J., joined, dissenting).

71. *Virginia v. Black*, 538 U.S. 343 (2003).

72. It should be noted that the plurality suggested that if the Virginia legislature removed the "prima facie" language, the statute would survive First Amendment analysis.

73. *Black*, 538 U.S. at 352, 356.

74. *Black*, 538 U.S. at 391 (Thomas, J., dissenting).

75. Oral argument in *Virginia v. Black*, December 11, 2002, No. 01-1107. See also *Capitol Square Review and Advisory Board v. Pinette*, 515 U.S. 753 (1995) (Thomas, J., concurring) ("The cross is associated with the Klan not because of religious worship, but because of the Klan's practice of cross-burning").

76. *Elonis v. United States*, 135 S. Ct. 2001, 2016 (2015) (Alito, J., concurring in part and dissenting in part).

77. The law made it unlawful to transmit in interstate commerce "any communication containing any threat . . . to injure the person of another."

78. *Elonis*, 135 S. Ct. 2001.

79. *Rosen v. United States*, 161 U.S. 29 (1896).

80. *Elonis*, 135 S. Ct. at 2028 (Thomas, J., dissenting).

81. Commercial speech was distinguished from political speech because it was deemed to be more hardy (i.e., the profit motive makes it difficult to suppress commercial speech) and more objective (e.g., the price of a bar of soap compared to a person's political opinion).

82. *Central Hudson Gas & Electric Corp. v. Public Service Commission of New York*, 447 U.S. 557 (1980).

83. *44 Liquormart v. Rhode Island*, 517 U.S. 484 (1996).

84. *44 Liquormart*, 517 U.S. at 518 (Thomas, J., concurring).

85. *Lorillard Tobacco Co. v. Reilly*, 533 U.S. 525, 572 (2001) (Thomas, J., concurring in part and concurring in the judgment). See also *Glickman v. Wileman Brothers & Elliot, Inc.*, 521 U.S. 457, 504 (1997) (Thomas, J., dissenting).

86. *Buckley v. Valeo*, 424 U.S. 1 (1976).

87. *Colorado Republican Federal Campaign Committee v. Federal Election Commission*, 518 U.S. 604 (1996) (Thomas, J., concurring in the judgment and dissenting in part).

88. *Nixon v. Shrink Missouri Government PAC*, 528 U.S. 377, 416 (2000) (Thomas, J., dissenting).

89. See, e.g., *McIntyre v. Ohio Elections Commission*, 514 U.S. 334 (1995) (Thomas, J., concurring).

90. *Citizens United v. Federal Election Commission*, 558 U.S. 310 (2010) (Thomas, J., concurring in part and dissenting in part).

91. Thomas, *My Grandfather's Son*, 12 (describing how his grandfather controlled every aspect of his life).

92. *Morse v. Frederick*, 551 U.S. 393 (2007) (Thomas, J., concurring); *Brown v. Entertainment Merchants Association*, 564 U.S. 786 (2011) (Thomas, J., dissenting); *Mahanoy Area School District v. B.L.*, 141 S. Ct. 2038 (2021) (Thomas, J., dissenting).

93. The *Miller* test derives from the court's decision in *Miller v. California*, 413 U.S. 15 (1973). Thomas applied the *Miller* test in his opinion for the court in *Ashcroft v. ACLU*, 535 U.S. 564 (2002) (upholding the Child Online Protection Act). But see *Ashcroft v. American Civil Liberties Union*, 542 U.S. 656 (2004) (where he joined the court's decision that the Child Online Protection Act did not use the least restrictive means of regulating the dissemination of obscene materials to minors over the internet); *Ashcroft v. Free Speech Coalition*, 535 U.S. 234 (2002) (Thomas, J., concurring in the judgment) (joining the court's decision that the Child Pornography Prevention Act of 1996 was overbroad—although leaving open the possibility that the government could regulate virtual child pornography if it becomes impossible to prove that certain pornographic images are of real children).

94. *City of Erie v. Pap's A. M. TDBA "Kandyland,"* 529 U.S. 277 (2000) (Scalia, J., with whom Thomas, J., joined, concurring in the judgment).

95. See, e.g., *National Endowment for the Arts v. Finley*, 524 U.S. 569 (1998) (Scalia, J., with whom Thomas, J., joined, concurring in the judgment).

96. See., e.g., *Garcetti v. Ceballos*, 547 U.S. 410 (2006) (Kennedy, J., with whom Thomas, J., joined) (the Constitution does not insulate the communications of public employees from employer discipline).

97. *Board of County Commissioners v. Umbehr*, 518 U.S. 668 (1996) (Scalia, J., dissenting); *O'Hare Truck Service Inc. v. City of Northlake*, 518 U.S. 712 (1996) (Scalia, J., with whom Thomas, J., joined, dissenting).

98. *New York Times v. Sullivan*, 376 U.S. 254 (1964).

99. *McKee v. Cosby*, 139 S. Ct. 675 (2019) (Thomas, J., concurring in the denial of certiorari). See also *Berisha v. Lawson*, 141 S. Ct. 2424 (2021) (Thomas, J., dissenting from the denial of certiorari).

100. *United States v. Alvarez*, 567 U.S. 709 (2012).

101. See, e.g., Akhil Reed Amar, "Some Notes on the Establishment Clause," *Roger Williams University Law Review* 2 (1996): 1–14; Vincent Phillip Muñoz, "The Original Meaning of the Establishment Clause and the Impossibility of Its Incorporation," *Journal of Constitutional Law* 8, 4 (2006): 585–639.

102. See, e.g., *Elk Grove Unified School District v. Newdow*, 542 U.S. 1, 45, 50–51 (2004) (Thomas, J., concurring in the judgment) ("I would welcome the opportunity to consider more fully the difficult questions whether and how the Establishment Clause applies against the States").

103. *Town of Greece v. Galloway*, 572 U.S. 565, 605 (2014) (Thomas, J., concurring in the judgment).

104. *Newdow*, 542 U.S. at 51 (Thomas, J., concurring in the judgment).

105. *Galloway*, 572 U.S. at 608.

106. *Newdow*, 542 U.S. at 49 (Thomas, J., concurring in the judgment).

107. *Zelman v. Simmons-Harris*, 536 U.S. 639 (2002).

108. *Zelman*, 536 U.S. at 676 (Thomas, J., concurring) (quoting "The Blessings of Liberty and Education," address delivered in Manassas, VA, September 3, 1894, in *The Frederick Douglass Papers*, ed. J. Blassingame and J. McKivigan [New Haven, CT: Yale University Press, 1992], 5:623).

109. *Rosenberger v. Rector and Visitors of the University of Virginia*, 515 U.S. 819 (1995) (Thomas, J., concurring)

110. *Mitchell v. Helms*, 530 U.S. 793 (2000).

111. *Van Orden v. Perry*, 545 U.S. 677 (2005) (Thomas, J., concurring).

112. *McCreary County v. American Civil Liberties Union of Kentucky*, 545 U.S. 844 (2005) (Scalia, J., dissenting, with whom Thomas, J., joined).

113. *Galloway*, 572 U.S. 565 (Thomas, J., concurring in the judgment).

114. See, e.g., *Rosenberger*, 515 U.S. 819 (Thomas, J., concurring).

115. See, e.g., *Tangipahoa Parish Board of Education v. Freiler*, 530 U.S. 1251 (2000) (Scalia, J., with whom Thomas, J., joined, dissenting from the denial of certiorari) (urging the court "to inter *Lemon* once [and] for all").

116. *American Legion v. American Humanist Association*, 139 S. Ct. 2067, 2097–2098 (2019) (Thomas, J., concurring in the judgment, quoting *McCreary County*, 545 U.S. at 900 [Scalia, J., dissenting]).

117. *Utah Highway Patrol Association v. American Atheists, Inc.*, 565 U.S. 994 (2011) (Thomas, J., dissenting from the denial of certiorari).

118. *Lee v. Weisman*, 505 U.S. 577 (1992).

119. *Newdow*, 542 U.S. at 49 (Thomas, J., concurring in the judgment).

120. *Employment Division, Department of Human Resources of Oregon v. Smith*, 494 U.S. 872 (1990).

121. "Nomination of Judge Clarence Thomas to Be Associate Justice of the Supreme Court of the United States," Hearings before the Committee on the Judiciary, US Senate, 102nd Cong., 1st sess., September 10–16, 1991, pt. I, 136: "I think [*Smith*] is an important departure from prior approaches and it is one that anyone who approaches these cases should be concerned about or at least watchful for."

122. *City of Boerne v. Flores*, 521 U.S. 507 (1997).

123. By contrast, Justice O'Connor dissented in that case. As in *Smith*, O'Connor challenged Justice Scalia's interpretation of the free exercise clause, particularly his claim that strict scrutiny is not necessary when laws are neutral and generally applicable. Significantly, Justice Thomas did not join O'Connor's dissent.

124. *Fulton v. City of Philadelphia*, 141 S. Ct. 1868 (2021) (Alito, J., concurring in the judgment) (Gorsuch, J., concurring in the judgment).

125. *Fulton*, 141 S. Ct. at 1888.

126. *Church of the Lukumi Babalu Aye v. City of Hialeah*, 508 U.S. 520 (1993).

127. *Gonzales v. O Centro Espirita Beneficente União do Vegetal*, 546 U.S. 418 (2006).

128. *Cutter v. Wilkinson*, 544 U.S. 709 (2005) (rejecting a facial challenge to the RLUIPA); *Holt v. Hobbs*, 135 S. Ct. 853 (2015) (striking down a state prison ban on short beards).

129. *Cutter*, 544 U.S. 709.

130. The RLUIPA prohibits both the state and federal governments from imposing "a substantial burden on the religious exercise of a person residing in or confined to an institution," unless the burden furthers "a compelling state interest."

131. *Sossamon v. Texas*, 563 U.S. 277 (2011).

132. *Espinoza v. Montana Department of Revenue*, 140 S. Ct. 2246, 2263 (2020) (Thomas, J., concurring).

133. *Locke v. Davey*, 540 U.S. 712 (2004).

134. *Trinity Lutheran Church of Columbia v. Comer*, 137 S. Ct. 2012, 2025 (2017) (Thomas, J., concurring in part).

135. *Espinoza*, 140 S. Ct. 2246.

136. *Espinoza*, 140 S. Ct. at 2265, 2267.

137. *Hosanna-Tabor Evangelical Lutheran Church and School v. Equal Employment Opportunity Commission*, 565 U.S. 171 (2012).

138. *Hosanna-Tabor*, 565 U.S. at 196 (Thomas, J., concurring).

139. *Our Lady of Guadalupe School v. Morrissey-Berru*, 140 S. Ct. 2049 (2020).

140. *Our Lady of Guadalupe School*, 140 S. Ct. at 2070.

141. *Christian Legal Society Chapter of the University of California v. Martinez*, 561 U.S. 661 (2010) (Alito, J., dissenting, with whom Thomas, J., joined).

142. *Masterpiece Cakeshop v. Colorado Civil Rights Commission*, 138 S. Ct. 1719 (2018).

143. *Fulton*, 141 S. Ct. 1868.

144. *Burwell v. Hobby Lobby*, 573 U.S. 682 (2014).

145. *Zubik v. Burwell*, 136 S. Ct. 1557 (2016).

146. Little Sisters of the Poor and other nonprofits argued that the self-certification process made them complicit in the government's contraceptive program.

147. *Little Sisters of the Poor Saints Peter & Paul Home v. Pennsylvania*, 140 S. Ct. 2367 (2020).

148. Thomas, "Freedom: A Responsibility," 9.

149. Clarence Thomas, "'Rights Revolution' Excesses Weaken Fight against Crime," *Human Events*, June 10, 1994, 12.

150. "Nomination of Judge Clarence Thomas," pt. I, 260.

151. Lee Epstein, Jeffrey A. Segal, Harold J. Spaeth, and Thomas G. Walker, *The Supreme Court Compendium: Data, Decisions, and Developments*, 6th ed. (Washington, DC: Congressional Quarterly, 2015), 569–572.

152. See, e.g., *Brumfield v. Cain*, 576 U.S. 305, 325–326 (2015) (Thomas, J., dissenting) (describing the victim, police officer Betty Smothers, as a single mom and a fourteen-year veteran of the Baton Rouge police department who was working a second job when she was murdered).

153. *Kyllo v. United States*, 533 U.S. 27 (2001).

154. *United States v. Jones*, 565 U.S. 400 (2012).

155. *Florida v. Jardines*, 569 U.S. 1 (2013).

156. *Ohio v. Roberts*, 448 U.S. 56 (1980) (allowing the admission of hearsay evidence if it bears adequate "indicia of reliability").

157. *White v. Illinois*, 502 U.S. 346 (1992) (Thomas, J., concurring).

158. *Crawford v. Washington*, 541 U.S. 36 (2004).

159. *Apprendi v. New Jersey*, 530 U.S. 446 (2000).

160. *Blakely v. Washington*, 542 U.S. 296 (2004); *United States v. Booker*, 543 U.S. 220 (2005) (Thomas, J., dissenting in part).

161. *Kimbrough v. United States*, 552 U.S. 85 (2007) (Thomas, J., dissenting).

162. *Alleyne v. United States*, 570 U.S. 99 (2013).

163. *Groh v. Ramirez*, 540 U.S. 551 (2004).

164. *Groh*, 540 U.S. at 572 (Thomas, J., with whom Scalia, J., joined, dissenting).

165. In a 2018 case Justice Thomas wrote the court's decision that the arrest of twenty-one individuals at "a raucous, late-night party" was supported by probable cause. Thomas rejected a civil suit brought by sixteen of those individuals on the grounds of false arrest. *District of Columbia v. Wesby*, 138 S. Ct. 577 (2018).

166. *Minnesota v. Dickerson*, 508 U.S. 366 (1993); *Illinois v. Wardlow*, 528 U.S. 119 (2000); *Arizona v. Johnson*, 555 U.S. 323 (2009); *Arizona v. United States*, 567 U.S. 387 (2012).

167. *Navarette v. California*, 572 U.S. 393 (2014).

168. *Kansas v. Glover*, 140 S. Ct. 1183 (2020).

169. *Georgia v. Randolph*, 547 U.S. 103 (2006).

170. *Randolph*, 547 U.S. at 146 (Thomas, J., dissenting). See also *Fernandez v. California*,

571 U.S. 292 (2014) (Thomas, J., concurring) (arguing that a warrantless search is reasonable if police obtain voluntary consent of a person authorized to give it); *United States v. Drayton*, 536 U.S. 194 (2002) (officers need not personally advise passengers of their right to refuse to consent to a search on a bus).

171. *Kentucky v. King*, 563 U.S. 452 (2011).

172. *Missouri v. McNeely*, 569 U.S. 141 (2013).

173. *McNeely*, 569 U.S. at 180–181 (Thomas, J., dissenting).

174. *Birchfield v. North Dakota*, 136 S. Ct. 2160 (2016).

175. *Birchfield*, 136 S. Ct. at 2196–2197 (Thomas, J., concurring in the judgment in part and dissenting in part). See also *Mitchell v. Wisconsin*, 139 S. Ct. 2525 (2019) (Thomas, J., concurring in the judgment).

176. *Board of Education of Independent School District No. 92 of Pottawatomie City v. Earls*, 536 U.S. 822 (2002).

177. *Safford Unified School District v. Redding*, 557 U.S. 364 (2009) (Thomas, J., concurring in the judgment in part and dissenting in part).

178. *Maryland v. King*, 569 U.S. 435 (2013).

179. *City of Los Angeles v. Patel*, 576 U.S. 409 (2015) (Scalia, J., with whom Thomas, J., joined, dissenting).

180. *Carpenter v. United States*, 138 S. Ct. 2206 (2018) (Thomas, J., dissenting). According to this two-part test: (1) an individual must exhibit an actual (subjective) expectation of privacy, and (2) the expectation must be one that society is prepared to recognize as reasonable. *Katz v. United States*, 389 U.S. 347, 361 (1967) (Harlan, J., concurring).

181. See, e.g., *Pennsylvania Board of Probation and Parole v. Scott*, 524 U.S. 357 (1998) (refusing to apply the exclusionary rule to parole revocation hearings); *Hudson v. Michigan*, 547 U.S. 586 (2006) (declining to apply the rule in "knock and announce" cases).

182. See, e.g., *Arizona v. Evans*, 514 U.S. 1 (1995) (the exclusionary rule does not apply to the arresting officer's good-faith belief that a warrant was still outstanding due to an error committed by an employee in the clerk's office); *Herring v. United States*, 555 U.S. 135 (2009) (refusing to apply the exclusionary rule when a similar error was committed by an employee in the sheriff's office).

183. *Utah v. Strieff*, 136 S. Ct. 2056 (2016).

184. *Collins v. Virginia*, 138 S. Ct. 1663 (2018).

185. *Collins*, 138 S. Ct. at 1677 (Thomas, J., concurring).

186. *Mapp v. Ohio*, 367 U.S. 643 (1961).

187. *Dickerson v. United States*, 530 U.S. 428 (2000).

188. *United States v. Patane*, 542 U.S. 630 (2004).

189. *Salinas v. Texas*, 570 U.S. 178, 192–193 (2013) (Thomas, J., concurring in the judgment).

190. *Missouri v. Seibert*, 542 U.S. 600 (2004) (O'Connor, J., with whom Rehnquist, C.J., Scalia, J., and Thomas J., joined, dissenting).

191. *J.D.B. v. North Carolina*, 564 U.S. 261 (2011) (Alito, J., with whom Roberts, C.J., Scalia, J., and Thomas, J., joined, dissenting).

192. *Berghuis v. Thompkins*, 560 U.S. 370 (2010).

193. *Howes v. Fields*, 565 U.S. 499 (2012).

194. *Garza v. Idaho*, 139 S. Ct. 738 (2019).

195. *Johnson v. Zerbst*, 304 U.S. 458 (1938).

196. *Gideon v. Wainwright*, 372 U.S. 335 (1963).

197. *Garza*, 139 S. Ct. at 757–758, 759 (Thomas, J., dissenting).

198. *Turner v. Rogers*, 564 U.S. 431 (2011) (Thomas, J., dissenting).

199. *Missouri v. Frye*, 566 U.S. 134 (2012) (Scalia, J., with whom Thomas, J., joined, dissenting); *Lafler v. Cooper*, 566 U.S. 156 (2012) (Scalia, J., with whom Thomas, J., joined, dissenting).

200. *Maples v. Thomas*, 565 U.S. 266 (2012) (Scalia, J., with whom Thomas, J., joined, dissenting).

201. *McCoy v. Louisiana*, 138 S. Ct. 1500 (2018) (Alito, J., with whom Thomas, J., joined, dissenting).

202. *Ewing v. California*, 528 U.S. 11 (2003) (Thomas, J., concurring in the judgment).

203. *Graham v. Florida*, 560 U.S. 48 (2010).

204. *Graham*, 560 U.S. at 123–124 (Thomas, J., dissenting).

205. *Atkins v. Virginia*, 536 U.S. 304 (2002); *Roper v. Simmons*, 543 U.S. 551 (2005).

206. *Kennedy v. Louisiana*, 554 U.S. 407 (2008).

207. *In re Davis*, 557 U.S. 952 (2009).

208. *Baze v. Rees*, 553 U.S. 35 (2008).

209. *Baze*, 553 U.S. at 95 (Thomas, J., concurring in the judgment).

210. *Baze*, 553 U.S. at 94.

211. *Glossip v. Gross*, 576 U.S. 863 (2015) (Thomas, J., concurring). See also *Ramirez v. Collier*, 2022 U.S. Lexis 1670, 87 (Thomas, J., dissenting) (the court "grants equitable relief for a demonstrably abusive and insincere claim filed by a prisoner with an established history of seeking unjustified delay, harming the State and Ramirez's victims in the process").

212. *Batson v. Kentucky*, 476 U.S. 79 (1986).

213. *Georgia v. McCollum*, 505 U.S. 42 (1992) (Thomas, J., concurring) (extending *Batson* to peremptory challenges exercised by criminal defendants). See also *Miller-El v. Dretke*, 545 U.S. 231 (2005) (Thomas, J., dissenting); *Snyder v. Louisiana*, 552 U.S. 472 (2008) (Thomas, J., dissenting).

214. *Foster v. Chatman*, 136 S. Ct. 1737 (2016).

215. *Flowers v. Mississippi*, 139 S. Ct. 2228 (2019).

216. *Hudson v. McMillian*, 503 U.S. 1, 4 (1992).

217. *Hudson*, 503 U.S. 1.

218. *Hudson*, 503 U.S. at 18 (Thomas, J., dissenting).

219. *Estelle v. Gamble*, 429 U.S. 97 (1976).

220. *Helling v. McKinney*, 509 U.S. 25, 42 (1993) (Thomas, J., dissenting) ("Were the issue squarely presented, therefore, I might vote to overrule *Estelle*").

221. *Hudson*, 503 U.S. at 28.

222. *Helling*, 509 U.S. 25; *Farmer v. Brennan*, 511 U.S. 825 (1994) (Thomas, J., concurring in the judgment).

223. *Brown v. Plata*, 563 U.S. 493 (2011) (Scalia, J., with whom Thomas, J., joined, dissenting).

224. Clarence Thomas, "Speech before the American Bar Association," San Francisco, August 11, 1987, Paoletta Files, no. 45514-002.

225. Clarence Thomas, "Speech before the Pacific Research Institute," San Francisco, August 10, 1987, Paoletta Files, no. 45511-005.

226. Thomas, "Speech before the Pacific Research Institute," 9.

227. Thomas, "Speech before the American Bar Association," 7–8.

228. Thomas, "Speech before the Pacific Research Institute," 16.

229. See, e.g., *Parents Involved in Community Schools v. Seattle School District No. 1*, 551 U.S. 701, 767 n. 15 (2007) (Thomas, J., concurring) ("The Fourteenth Amendment does not enact the dissent's newly minted understanding of liberty," citing *Lochner v. New York*, 198 U.S. 45 [1905]); *TXO Production Corp. v. Alliance Resources Corp.*, 509 U.S. 443, 470 (1993) (Scalia, J., with whom Thomas, J., joined, concurring in the judgment) ("I do not accept the proposition that [the Fourteenth Amendment] is the secret repository of all sorts of other, unenumerated, substantive rights—however fashionable that proposition may have been [even as to the economic rights of the sort involved here] at the time of [the] *Lochner* era"); *Planned Parenthood of Southeastern Pennsylvania v. Casey*, 505 U.S. 833, 961–962 (1992) (Rehnquist, J., with whom Thomas, J., joined, dissenting) (arguing that *Lochner* was overturned not because the economic theory supporting it had fallen into disfavor, but because "the Constitution does not speak of freedom of contract").

230. *United Haulers Association v. Oneida-Herkimer Solid Waste Management Authority*, 550 U.S. 330, 355 (2007) (Thomas, J., concurring).

231. See, e.g., *BMW of North America v. Gore*, 517 U.S. 559 (1996) (Scalia, J., with whom Thomas, J., joined, dissenting); *State Farm Mutual Automobile Insurance Co. v. Campbell*, 538 U.S. 408 (2003) (Thomas, J., dissenting).

232. *Lucas v. South Carolina Coastal Council*, 505 U.S. 1003 (1992).

233. *Dolan v. City of Tigard*, 512 U.S. 374 (1994). See also *Koontz v. St. Johns River Water Management District*, 570 U.S. 595 (2013).

234. *Parking Association of Georgia v. City of Atlanta*, 515 U.S. 1116 (1995) (Thomas, J., dissenting from the denial of certiorari).

235. *Tahoe-Sierra Preservation Council v. Tahoe Regional Planning Agency*, 535 U.S. 302 (2002).

236. *Eastern Enterprises v. Apfel*, 524 U.S. 498 (1998).

237. *Eastern Enterprises*, 524 U.S. at 538–539 (Thomas, J., concurring). See *Calder v. Bull*, 3 U.S. 386 (1798) (holding that the ex post facto clause applied only to criminal penalties).

238. *Horne v. Department of Agriculture*, 135 S. Ct. 2419 (2015).

239. *Murr v. Wisconsin*, 137 S. Ct. 1933, 1957 (2017) (Thomas, J., dissenting).

240. *Cedar Point Nursery v. Hassid*, 141 S. Ct. 2063 (2021).

241. *Kelo v. City of New London*, 545 U.S. 469 (2005).

242. *Kelo*, 545 U.S. at 483.

243. *Kelo*, 545 U.S. at 521 (Thomas, J., dissenting).

244. *Berman v. Parker*, 348 U.S. 26 (1954).

245. *Hawaii Housing Authority v. Midkiff*, 467 U.S. 229 (1984).

246. Thomas noted that "over 97 percent of the individuals forcibly removed from their homes [in Washington, DC] by the slum-clearance project upheld by this Court in *Berman* were black." *Kelo*, 545 U.S. at 522.

247. *Kelo*, 545 U.S. at 522.

248. Under Louisiana law, a person acquitted by reason of insanity could be kept in a mental institution if he or she was deemed "dangerous."

249. *Foucha v. Louisiana*, 504 U.S. 71 (1992) (Thomas, J., dissenting).

250. *City of Chicago v. Morales*, 527 U.S. 41, 114–115 (1999) (Thomas, J., dissenting).

251. *Griswold v. Connecticut*, 381 U.S. 479 (1965).

252. Thomas argued that Justice Harlan had the better position in the case. See, e.g., "Nomination of Judge Clarence Thomas," pt. I, 127, 255.

253. *Lawrence v. Texas*, 539 U.S. 558 (2003).

254. *Lawrence*, 539 U.S. at 605–606 (Thomas, J., dissenting).

255. *Roe v. Wade*, 410 U.S. 113 (1973).

256. "Nomination of Judge Clarence Thomas," pt. I, 222–223; *Planned Parenthood of Southeastern Pennsylvania v. Casey*, 505 U.S. 833 (Scalia, J., with whom Thomas, J., joined, concurring in the judgment in part and dissenting in part).

257. *Stenberg v. Carhart*, 530 U.S. 914 (2000).

258. *Stenberg*, 530 U.S. at 980 (Thomas, J., dissenting).

259. *Gonzalez v. Carhart*, 550 U.S. 124 (2007).

260. *Gonzalez*, 550 U.S. at 169 (Thomas, J., concurring).

261. *Whole Woman's Health v. Hellerstedt*, 136 S. Ct. 2292 (2016) (Thomas, J., dissenting).

262. *June Medical Services LLC v. Russo*, 140 S. Ct. 2103 (2020) (Thomas, J., dissenting). In December 2021 the Roberts Court heard oral arguments in *Dobbs v. Jackson Women's Health Organization*, No. 19-1392, involving a Mississippi law that bans abortion after fifteen weeks' gestational age. Because the law runs counter to the holdings in *Roe* and *Casey*—that is, that a woman has a fundamental right to an abortion until the point of fetal viability (twenty-four weeks)—this case is an opportunity for a more conservative court to dramatically limit or overturn *Roe*.

263. *Box v. Planned Parenthood of Ind. & Ky., Inc.*, 139 S. Ct. 1780 (2019).

264. *Box*, 139 S. Ct. at 1783, 1790 (Thomas, J., concurring).

265. *Washington v. Glucksberg*, 521 U.S. 702 (1997).

266. *Gonzalez v. Oregon*, 546 U.S. 243 (2006).

267. *Gonzales v. Raich*, 545 U.S. 1 (2005).

268. *Gonzalez v. Oregon*, 546 U.S. at 299–302 (Thomas, J., dissenting).

269. *Obergefell v. Hodges*, 576 U.S. 644 (2015).

270. *Loving v. Virginia*, 388 U.S. 1 (1967) (striking down laws prohibiting interracial marriages).

271. *Obergefell*, 576 U.S. at 728 (Thomas, J., dissenting).

272. *Obergefell*, 576 U.S. at 735–736.

273. *Troxel v. Granville*, 530 U.S. 57 (2000).

274. The Troxels were the parents of Brad Troxel, who was the father of Isabelle and Natalie. Brad Troxel and Tommie Granville separated in June 1991, and Brad later committed suicide.

275. *Pierce v. Society of Sisters*, 268 U.S. 510 (1925).

276. *Troxel*, 530 U.S. at 80 (Thomas, J., concurring in the judgment) (citing *Pierce*, 268 U.S. 510).

277. *Troxel*, 530 U.S. at 80 n. 1.

278. *Troxel*, 530 U.S. at 80.

279. *Saentz v. Roe*, 526 U.S. 489 (1999).

280. *Corfield v. Coryell*, 6 Fed. Cas. 546 (C.C.E.D. Penn. 1825).

281. *Saentz*, 526 U.S. at 527 (Thomas, J., dissenting).

282. *Saentz*, 526 U.S. at 527–528.

283. *McDonald v. City of Chicago*, 561 U.S. 742 (2010).

284. *District of Columbia v. Heller*, 554 U.S. 570 (2008).

285. *McDonald*, 561 U.S. at 768, 778.

286. *McDonald*, 561 U.S. at 806 (Thomas, J., concurring in part and concurring in the judgment).

287. *The Butchers' Benevolent Association of New Orleans v. The Crescent City Live-Stock Landing and Slaughter-House Co.*, 83 U.S. 36 (1873) (known as the *Slaughter-House Cases*).

288. *Slaughter-House Cases*, 83 U.S. at 74. The *Slaughter-House* court distinguished national from state citizenship by relying on a literal reading of the privileges or immunities clause: "No State shall make or enforce any law which shall abridge the privileges or immunities of *citizens of the United States*" (emphasis added). Justice Miller, writing for the court, placed great weight on the "citizens of the United States" language to conclude that the provision protected only the rights of *federal* citizenship, not those of *state* citizenship.

289. *McDonald*, 561 U.S. at 838, 852–853.

290. See *United States v. Cruikshank*, 92 U.S. 542 (1876); *Presser v. Illinois*, 116 U.S. 252 (1886); *Miller v. Texas*, 153 U.S. 535 (1894).

291. See *McDonald*, 561 U.S. at 851 n. 20 ("I note, however, that I see no reason to assume that the constitutionally enumerated rights protected by the Privileges or Immunities Clause should consist of all the rights recognized in the Bill of Rights and no others"). In addition to the right to pursue a lawful trade, an interesting question is whether Thomas would now consider parental rights a privilege of state and national citizenship. If he believes there is a right of marital privacy in the Constitution, he might prefer to locate that specific right under the privileges or immunities clause. He has also suggested that regulatory takings might be better analyzed under the privileges or immunities clause. See *Murr v. Wisconsin*, 137 S. Ct. 1933, 1957 (2017) (Thomas, J., dissenting).

292. See *Timbs v. Indiana*, 139 S. Ct. 682 (2019) (Thomas, J., concurring in the

judgment) (arguing that the Eighth Amendment's excessive fines clause should be applied to the states under the privileges or immunities clause); *Ramos v. Louisiana*, 140 S. Ct. 1390 (2020) (Thomas, J., concurring in the judgment) (arguing that unanimous verdicts are required as part of the right to a jury and are made applicable to the states under the privileges or immunities clause).

293. Clarence Thomas, "Black Americans & the Constitution," in *The New Federalist Papers* (Lanham, MD: University Press of America, 1988), 308.

294. *Dred Scott v. Sandford*, 60 U.S. 393 (1857).

295. *Plessy v. Ferguson*, 163 U.S. 537 (1896).

296. In pre–Supreme Court speeches, Thomas referred to justice John Marshall Harlan's "great dissent" in *Plessy* as a classic example of natural law. Although Harlan did not cite the Declaration of Independence, Thomas claimed that his interpretation of the Thirteenth and Fourteenth Amendments was fundamentally based on natural law. "Harlan kept alive," Thomas maintained, "the higher law background of the Constitution, which was present at the Founding and reaffirmed in the Civil War." Thomas, "Modern Civil Rights Movement," 14. See also Clarence Thomas, "The Virtue of Defeat: *Plessy v. Ferguson* in Retrospect," *Journal of Supreme Court History* 2 (1997): 15–24.

297. *Brown v. Board of Education of Topeka*, 347 U.S. 483 (1954).

298. Clarence Thomas, "Speech Delivered to Black Law Students Association Conference," Yale Law School, New Haven, CT, April 7, 1984, Paoletta Files, no. 45510-005.

299. *Brown*, 347 U.S. at 494.

300. Kauffman, "Clarence Thomas," 32. See also *Missouri v. Jenkins*, 515 U.S. 70, 121 (1995) (Thomas, J., concurring):

> Segregation was not unconstitutional because it might have caused psychological feelings of inferiority. Public school systems that separated blacks and provided them with superior educational resources—making blacks "feel" superior to whites sent to lesser schools—would violate the Fourteenth Amendment, whether or not the white students felt stigmatized, just as do systems in which the positions of the races are reversed. Psychological injury or benefit is irrelevant to the question whether state actors have engaged in intentional discrimination—the critical inquiry for *ascertaining* violations of the Equal Protection Clause.

301. *Jenkins*, 515 U.S. at 114.

302. *Parents Involved in Community Schools v. Seattle School District No. 1*; *Meredith v. Jefferson County Board of Education*, 551 U.S. 701, 761 (2007) (Thomas, J., concurring).

303. Those compelling state interests were (1) an interest in setting right the consequences of prior conditions of segregation, (2) an educational element, and (3) a democratic element. *Parents Involved in Community Schools*, 551 U.S. at 838–845 (Breyer, J., dissenting).

304. *Parents Involved in Community Schools*, 551 U.S. at 772–782.

305. *Adarand Constructors, Inc. v. Pena*, 515 U.S. 200 (1995).

306. The court overturned *Metro Broadcasting, Inc. v. FCC*, 497 U.S. 547 (1990), where the justices applied intermediate scrutiny to a federal affirmative action program.

307. *Adarand*, 515 U.S. at 240 (Thomas, J., concurring in part and concurring in the judgment).

308. *Grutter v. Bollinger*, 539 U.S. 306 (2003).

309. *Grutter*, 539 U.S. at 353 (Thomas, J., concurring in part and dissenting in part). See, e.g., *Johnson v. California*, 543 U.S. 499 (2005) (Thomas, J., dissenting) (arguing that a racial segregation policy in prisons was constitutional and not subject to strict scrutiny).

310. *Grutter*, 539 U.S. at 364.

311. *Grutter*, 539 U.S. at 371.

312. *Fisher v. University of Texas at Austin*, 570 U.S. 297 (2013).

313. *Fisher v. University of Texas at Austin*, 136 S. Ct. 2198 (2016).

314. *Fisher*, 136 S. Ct. at 2215 (Thomas, J., dissenting) (quoting *Grutter*, 539 U.S. at 353).

315. *Fisher*, 136 S. Ct. at 2215. Justice Thomas might get his wish. The Roberts Court will be hearing two cases during its 2022–2023 term where it is considering whether to overturn *Grutter*. See *Students for Fair Admissions, Inc. v. President & Fellows of Harvard College*, 980 F.3d 157 (2020); *Students for Fair Admissions, Inc. v. University of North Carolina*, 2019 U.S. Dist. Lexis 169181.

316. Thomas, "Speech before the American Bar Association" (criticizing economic redistribution programs, starting with FDR's New Deal, as a form of despotism).

317. Thomas, *My Grandfather's Son*, 188.

318. *Adarand*, 515 U.S. at 240 (Thomas, J., concurring in part and concurring in the judgment).

5. BLACK V. SCALIA AND THOMAS

1. *Southern Pacific v. Arizona ex. rel. Sullivan*, 325 U.S. 761, 788 (1945) (Black, J., dissenting). As noted in chapters 3 and 4, Justices Scalia and Thomas have also criticized the court's negative commerce clause jurisprudence. In fact, Thomas has called for its complete abandonment. See, e.g., *Tyler Pipe Industries, Inc. v. Washington State Department of Revenue*, 483 U.S. 232, 265 (1987) (Scalia, J., concurring in part and dissenting in part); *Camps Newfound/Owatonna v. Town of Harrison*, 520 U.S. 564 (1997) (Thomas, J., with whom Scalia, J., joined, dissenting); *United Haulers Association v. Oneida-Herkimer Solid Waste Management Authority*, 550 U.S. 330 (2007) (Thomas, J., concurring in the judgment).

2. See, e.g., *Coolidge v. New Hampshire*, 403 U.S. 443 (1971) (Black, J., concurring and dissenting); *California v. Acevedo*, 500 U.S. 565 (1991) (Scalia, J., concurring in the judgment); *Groh v. Ramirez*, 540 U.S. 551 (2004) (Thomas, J., with whom Scalia, J., joined, dissenting).

3. It should be recalled that Justice Black thought there was probable cause to stop and frisk Terry and the two other suspects in *Terry v. Ohio*, 392 U.S. 1 (1968).

4. Justice Black dissented in *Bivens v. Six Unknown Named Agents of Federal Bureau of Narcotics*, 403 U.S. 388 (1971), where the court recognized a private cause of action against

government officials for violations of Fourth Amendment rights. Justice Scalia called *Bivens* "the relic of the heady days in which this Court assumed common-law powers to create causes of action." *Correctional Services Corp. v. Malesko*, 534 U.S. 61, 75 (2001) (Scalia, J., concurring). Justice Thomas has also written or joined opinions calling for a narrow interpretation of *Bivens*. *Wilkie v. Robbins*, 551 U.S. 537 (2007) (Thomas, J., with whom Scalia, J., joined, concurring). In fact, in a 2020 case Thomas contended that it was "time . . . to consider discarding the *Bivens* doctrine altogether." *Hernández v. Mesa*, 140 S. Ct. 735, 750 (2020) (Thomas, J., concurring). During its 2021–2022 term, the Roberts Court is hearing a case, *Boule v. Egbert*, 998 F.3d 370 (2021), where it is reconsidering its decision in *Bivens*.

5. A former county prosecutor, Justice Black thought peremptory strikes were an essential trial strategy and did not believe the Constitution placed any restrictions on their use. In *Swain v. Alabama*, 380 U.S. 202 (1965), he rejected a claim of systematic racial discrimination, even though no African American had served on a petit jury in Talladega County, Alabama, in over a decade. In a letter to Justice White, author of the court's decision, Black maintained that systematic claims of racial discrimination would open the door to numerous challenges and jeopardize the peremptory strike system itself. Hugo Black to Justice Byron White, February 17, 1965, Hugo Black Papers, Library of Congress, box 384. During their tenure together, Justices Scalia and Thomas were sharp critics of *Batson v. Kentucky*, 476 U.S. 79 (1986), the case that partly overturned *Swain* by allowing race-based challenges to peremptory strikes in specific cases. Scalia and Thomas rejected *Batson* challenges in virtually every case they heard. See, e.g., *Holland v. Illinois*, 493 U.S. 474 (1990) (Scalia, J.); *Miller-El v. Dretke*, 545 U.S. 231 (2005) (Thomas, J., with whom Scalia, J., joined, dissenting); *Snyder v. Louisiana*, 552 U.S. 472 (2008) (Thomas, J., with whom Scalia, J., joined, dissenting); *Foster v. Chatman*, 136 S. Ct. 1737 (2016) (Thomas, J., dissenting); *Flowers v. Mississippi*, 139 S. Ct. 2228 (2019) (Thomas, J., dissenting). They also dissented in the case in which the court extended *Batson* to challenges based on gender. *J.E.B. v. Alabama*, 511 U.S. 127 (1994) (Scalia, J., with whom Thomas, J., joined, dissenting).

6. According to this doctrine, restrictions on the democratic process can be justified if the law in question has a discriminatory impact on minorities. See *Hunter v. Erickson*, 393 U.S. 385 (1969) (Black, J., dissenting); *Schuette v. Coalition to Defend Affirmative Action, Integration and Immigrant Rights and Fight for Equality by Any Means Necessary (BAMN)*, 572 U.S. 291 (2014) (Scalia, J., with whom Thomas, J., joined, concurring in the judgment).

7. *Harper v. Virginia Board of Elections*, 383 U.S. 663 (1966).

8. Justice Black dissented in *Harper*. In *Crawford v. Marion County Election Board*, 553 U.S. 181, 208 (2008), Scalia wrote a concurrence, joined by Thomas, which argued that generally applicable, nondiscriminatory voting regulations should not be subject to strict scrutiny. In a footnote, Scalia cast doubt on the court's use of strict scrutiny in *Harper*.

9. In one case, Hugo Black joined the court's opinion denying legal standing to a taxpayer who claimed injury because five Bible verses were being read in public schools. *Doremus v. Board of Education of the Borough of Hawthorne*, 342 U.S. 429 (1952). By contrast, Justice Douglas dissented in that case.

10. Antonin Scalia, "The Doctrine of Standing as an Essential Element of the Separation of Powers," *Suffolk University Law Review* 17 (1983): 881–899.

11. Scalia, 897.

12. *Named Individual Members of the San Antonio Conservation Society v. Texas Highway Department*, 400 U.S. 968–969 (1970) (Black, J., dissenting from the denial of certiorari).

13. *Named Individual Members*, 400 U.S. at 971–972.

14. *Citizens to Preserve Overton Park v. Volpe*, 401 U.S. 402, 421–422 (1971) (Black, J., concurring).

15. *Lujan v. Defenders of Wildlife*, 504 U.S. 555 (1992).

16. *Lujan*, 504 U.S. at 564.

17. *Lujan*, 504 U.S. at 577 (quoting US Constitution, Article II, section 3).

18. *Flast v. Cohen*, 392 U.S. 83 (1968).

19. *Hein v. Freedom from Religion Foundation*, 551 U.S. 587 (2007).

20. *Hein*, 551 U.S. at 618 (Scalia, J., with whom Thomas, J., joined, concurring in the judgment).

21. See, e.g., *Arizona Christian School Tuition Organization v. Winn*, 563 U.S. 125, 146–147 (2011) (Scalia, J., with whom Thomas, J., joined, concurring) ("I would repudiate that misguided decision and enforce the Constitution"); *United States v. Windsor*, 570 U.S. 744, 785 (2013) (Scalia, J., with whom Thomas, J., joined, dissenting) ("We have been living with the chaos created by that power-grabbing decision ever since").

22. "London Naval Treaty," in *Congressional Record* (hereafter *CR*), vol. 73, 71st Cong., special sess., July 9, 1930, 39, 41, 43.

23. In one separation of powers case, Scalia quoted James Madison's famous description that "the legislative department is everywhere extending the sphere of its activity, and drawing all power into its impetuous vortex." See *Plaut v. Spendthrift Farm, Inc.*, 514 U.S. 211, 221–222 (1995) (citing Federalist No. 48).

24. "Executive Privilege—Secrecy in Government," Hearings before the Subcommittee on Intergovernmental Relations of the Committee on Government Operations," US Senate, 94th Cong., 1st sess., 1975, 94.

25. In one speech, Thomas related how his agency had been "virtually shut down by a willful committee staffer, who has succeeded in getting a Senate committee to subpoena volumes of EEOC records." Clarence Thomas, "The Higher Law and the Privileges or Immunities Clause," Seventh Annual Symposium sponsored by the Federalist Society, University of Virginia, Charlottesville, March 5, 1988, Mark Paoletta Files, no. 45510-005, George H. W. Bush Presidential Library, College Station, TX. See also Clarence Thomas, "Congress, the Bureaucracy, and the Enforcement of Civil Rights," paper presented at the annual meeting of the American Political Science Association, Chicago, September 3, 1987, Paoletta Files, no. 45510-005.

26. Thomas, "Congress, the Bureaucracy, and the Enforcement of Civil Rights," 13. See also "Remarks of Clarence Thomas, Chairman of the EEOC," Gordon Public Policy Center, Brandeis University, April 8, 1988, Paoletta Files, no. 45510-005.

27. *Ramirez de Arellano v. Weinberger*, 745 F.2d. 1500, 1562 (D.C. Cir. 1984) (Scalia, J.,

dissenting) (arguing that the president must "speak and act with a single voice"); *Hamdi v. Rumsfeld*, 542 U.S. 507, 581 (2004) (Thomas, J., dissenting) ("John Marshall explained that 'the President is the sole organ of the nation in its external relations, and its sole representative with foreign nations'").

28. *Humphrey's Executor v. United States*, 295 U.S. 602 (1935).

29. *Synar v. United States*, 626 F. Supp. 1374, 1398 (D. D.C. 1986).

30. *Seila Law LLC v. Consumer Financial Protection Bureau*, 140 S. Ct. 2183, 2216, 2218–2219 (2020) (Thomas, J., concurring in part and dissenting in part).

31. *Wiener v. United States*, 357 U.S. 349 (1958).

32. Alexander Hamilton, "Pacificus No. 1," June 29, 1793, in *The Papers of Alexander Hamilton*, ed. Harold C. Syrett (New York: Columbia University Press, 1969), 15:39.

33. "London Naval Treaty," 44.

34. *Youngstown Sheet & Tube Co. v. Sawyer*, 343 U.S. 579 (1952).

35. *Youngstown*, 343 U.S. at 587.

36. Antonin Scalia, "Originalism: The Lesser Evil," *University of Cincinnati Law Review* 57 (1989): 849–865.

37. *Zivotofsky v. Kerry*, 576 U.S. 1, 34–35 (2015) (Thomas, J., concurring in the judgment in part and dissenting in part). This semantic difference is sometimes referred to as "Morris's joker," and it is the same argument Hamilton made in defending the Washington administration's neutrality proclamation. See Hamilton, "Pacificus No. 1," 39.

38. *Johnson v. Eisentrager*, 339 U.S. 763 (1950).

39. *Eisentrager*, 339 U.S. at 768.

40. *Eisentrager*, 339 U.S. at 779.

41. *Eisentrager*, 339 U.S. at 795 (Black, J., dissenting).

42. *Eisentrager*, 339 U.S. at 795.

43. *Rasul v. Bush*, 542 U.S. 466 (2004).

44. *Rasul*, 542 U.S. at 499 (Scalia, J., with whom Thomas, J., joined, dissenting).

45. *Boumediene v. Bush*, 553 U.S. 723 (2008).

46. *Boumediene*, 553 U.S. at 842, 850 (Scalia, J., with whom Thomas, J., joined, dissenting).

47. *Morrison v. Olson*, 487 U.S. 654 (1988).

48. The special division was a panel of three circuit court judges who served two-year terms and were appointed by the chief justice of the United States.

49. *Morrison*, 487 U.S. at 695.

50. *Morrison*, 487 U.S. at 693–694 (quoting *United States v. Nixon*, 418 U.S. 683, 707 [1974]).

51. *Morrison*, 487 U.S. at 705 (Scalia, J., dissenting).

52. *Morrison*, 487 U.S. at 706, 726.

53. *Bowsher v. Synar*, 478 U.S. 714 (1986) (striking down the removal provision of the Balanced Budget and Emergency Deficit Control Act because Congress reserved the power to remove the comptroller general to itself).

54. Clarence Thomas, "How to Talk about Civil Rights: Keep It Principled and Positive," keynote address celebrating the formation of the Pacific Research Institute's

Civil Rights Task Force, Vista Hotel, San Francisco, August 4, 1988, Paoletta Files, no. 45511-005.

55. Executive privilege is "the right of the president and important executive branch officials to withhold information from Congress, the courts, and, ultimately, the public." Mark J. Rozell, *Executive Privilege: The Dilemma of Secrecy and Democratic Accountability* (Baltimore: Johns Hopkins University Press, 1994), xi.

56. During his time in the Senate, Black criticized the fact that the Constitutional Convention was conducted in secret and argued that the Senate's executive sessions should be open to the public. See *CR*, vol. 70, pt. 3, 70th Cong., 2nd sess., January 31, 1929, 2518–2519.

57. *CR*, vol. 73, 71st Cong., special sess., July 9, 1930, 27, 38.

58. "Senators to Assert Right to Navy Data," *New York Times*, June 11, 1930, 1.

59. *CR*, vol. 73, 71st Cong., special sess., 38.

60. "Executive Privilege—Secrecy in Government," 86.

61. *Cheney v. United States District Court*, 542 U.S. 367 (2004).

62. One of persons rumored to be involved in the group's deliberations was Kenneth Lay, the former CEO of Enron.

63. *United States v. Nixon*, 418 U.S. 683 (1974).

64. Scalia almost certainly would have authored an opinion, but he was asked to recuse himself because of a duck-hunting trip he took with Vice President Cheney, a named party, three weeks after the court granted certiorari in the case. See James B. Staab, *The Political Thought of Justice Antonin Scalia: A Hamiltonian on the Supreme Court* (Lanham, MD: Rowman & Littlefield, 2006), 113–120, 315–317.

65. The Federal Advisory Committee Act of 1972 imposed a variety of public disclosure obligations on groups that advise officers and agencies in the executive branch. Exempted from the act's requirements "is any committee that is composed wholly of full-time, or permanent part-time, officers or employees of the Federal Government." 5 U.S.C. App. Section 3(2).

66. Thomas pointed out that the district court left open the possibility that the government might prevail on summary judgment, because the de facto member doctrine might not apply to the NEPDG.

67. Roger K. Newman, *Hugo Black: A Biography* (New York: Fordham University Press, 1997), 157.

68. *Gibbons v. Ogden*, 22 U.S. 1 (1824).

69. *CR*, vol. 77, pt. 1, 73rd Cong., 1st sess., April 3, 1933, 1120 (quoting *Gibbons*, 22 U.S. at 194, 196).

70. *Garcia v. San Antonio Metropolitan Transit Authority*, 469 U.S. 527 (1985).

71. "Nomination of Judge Antonin Scalia to Be Associate Justice of the Supreme Court," Hearings before the Committee on the Judiciary, US Senate, 99th Cong., 1st sess., August 5–6, 1986, 82.

72. *Printz v. United States*, 521 U.S. 898, 915 n. 9 (1997).

73. *U.S. Term Limits, Inc. v. Thornton*, 514 U.S. 779 (1995).

74. *Thornton*, 514 U.S. at 845, 846, 848 (Thomas, J., dissenting).

75. First and foremost, Black joined the Supreme Court's decision in *Powell v.*

McCormack, 395 U.S. 486 (1969), which held that an attempt by the House to "exclude" a duly elected member violated the qualifications clauses. Chief Justice Warren held for the court that the qualifications clauses were "fixed" and "unalterable." *Powell* did not explicitly resolve whether the states could impose term limits on members of Congress, but Black would have agreed with the *Thornton* majority that there was substantial evidence demonstrating that they could not. Moreover, Black interpreted "We the People" to be all the people residing in the United States, not just the people residing in individual states. In his opinion for the court in *Wesberry v. Sanders*, 376 U.S. 1 (1964), Black described how the framers moved away from a confederal system under the Articles of Confederation and established a wholly new form of government based on the consent of the people. Black would have agreed with the *Thornton* court's statement that "the framers envisioned a uniform national system, rejecting the notion that the Nation was a collection of States, and instead creating a direct link between the National Government and the people of the United States." *Thornton*, 514 U.S. at 803. Finally, Black was very protective of the prerogatives of Congress. Justice Thomas's interpretation of the Tenth Amendment would have given the states wide latitude to add qualifications to the ones already mentioned in the Constitution. Although people might not object to a ban on ex-felons serving in Congress, what about other requirements, such as district residency, property ownership, religion, mandatory retirement, or more restrictive term limits? Nothing in Thomas's opinion would prevent any of these additional qualifications from being enacted at the state level. Justice Black, like the majority in *Thornton*, would have been deeply concerned that state-imposed term limits could negatively impact Congress as a national institution.

76. *United States v. Lopez*, 514 U.S. 549 (1995).

77. *Lopez*, 514 U.S. at 585, 587 (Thomas, J., concurring).

78. *Hammer v. Dagenhart*, 247 U.S. 251 (1918).

79. *Hammer*, 247 U.S. at 271–272.

80. *CR*, vol. 77, pt. 1, 73rd Cong., 1st sess., April 3, 1933, 1122.

81. Scalia likely would have concluded that Congress could regulate child labor if it wanted to. He did not believe in a formalistic interpretation of federal-state relations, and he never deviated from the view that the Tenth Amendment does not impose an affirmative limit on national power. In describing the Tenth Amendment, Scalia often paraphrased language from *United States v. Darby*, 312 U.S. 100 (1941), which overturned *Hammer*. "The [Tenth] amendment," Justice Stone wrote for the unanimous Court, "states but a truism that all is retained which has not been surrendered." *Darby*, 312 U.S. at 124.

82. *Darby*, 312 U.S. 100.

83. *Wickard v. Filburn*, 317 U.S. 111 (1942).

84. John P. Frank, "The Shelf Life of Justice Hugo L. Black: The Fairfield Lecture," *Wisconsin Law Review* (1997): 1, 10.

85. See, e.g., Antonin Scalia and Bryan A. Garner, *Reading Law: The Interpretation of Legal Texts* (St. Paul, MN: Thomson/West, 2012), 406. At the same time, he relied on *Wickard* in *Gonzales v. Raich*, 545 U.S. 1 (2005) (Scalia, J., concurring in the judgment).

86. Interview with Nina Totenberg, Smithsonian Associates Interview, Lisner Auditorium, George Washington University, Washington, DC, February 12, 2013, 2013 WLNR 10286459.

87. *Perez v. United States*, 402 U.S. 146 (1971).

88. *Perez*, 402 U.S. at 154.

89. *National Federation of Independent Business v. Sebelius*, 567 U.S. 519, 657 (2012) (Scalia, J., Kennedy, J., Thomas, J., Alito, J., dissenting).

90. *CR*, vol. 81, pt. 5, 75th Cong., 1st sess., 5517.

91. Newman, *Hugo Black*, 225.

92. *Sebelius*, 567 U.S. 519.

93. *Sebelius*, 567 U.S. at 648 (Scalia, J., Kennedy, J., Thomas, J., Alito, J., dissenting).

94. Hugo Lafayette Black, *A Constitutional Faith* (New York: Alfred A. Knopf, 1968), 34. See also *Adamson v. California*, 332 U.S. 46 (1947) (Black, J., dissenting).

95. Antonin Scalia, *A Matter of Interpretation: Federal Courts and the Law*, ed. Amy Gutmann (Princeton, NJ: Princeton University Press, 1997), 142: "If the *text* of the Fourteenth Amendment said that 'the Bill of Rights, which has hitherto been a restriction only upon the federal government, shall henceforth be a restriction also upon the states,' there might be room for an argument. . . . But it does not say that."

96. *McDonald v. City of Chicago*, 561 U.S. 742, 851 n. 20 (2010) (Thomas, J., concurring in part and concurring in the judgment).

97. Frank, "Shelf Life of Justice Hugo L. Black," 10.

98. Steve Suitts, *Hugo Black of Alabama: How His Roots and Early Career Shaped the Great Champion of the Constitution* (Montgomery, AL: NewSouth Books, 2005), 144–149.

99. See, e.g., *Stewart v. Southern Railway Co.*, 315 U.S. 283 (1942) (Black, J., dissenting) ("Because it must rely on the written page rather than living words, an appellate court can never fully appreciate the effect of testimony heard by a jury of local citizens"). See also *Warner v. Kewanee Machinery & Conveyor Co.*, 398 U.S. 906 (1970) (Black, J., dissenting from the denial of certiorari); *Rodicker v. Illinois Central Railroad Co.*, 400 U.S. 1012 (1971) (Black, J., dissenting from the denial of certiorari); *Eilers v. Hercules, Inc.*, 403 U.S. 937 (1971) (Black, J., dissenting from the denial of certiorari.).

100. *Warner*, 398 U.S. 906.

101. See, e.g., *BMW of North America v. Gore*, 517 U.S. 559 (1996) (Scalia, J., with whom Thomas, J., joined, dissenting).

102. It should be noted that, unlike Black, Scalia and Thomas have never claimed that the First Amendment absolutely protects free speech.

103. *Milk Wagon Drivers Union of Chicago, Local 753 v. Meadowmoor Dairies*, 312 U.S. 287, 302 (1941) (Black, J., dissenting).

104. *Milk Wagon Drivers Union*, 312 U.S. at 303 n. 4. Black did not provide a citation for this quote, but it can be found in Thomas Jefferson's letter to Edward Carrington, January 16, 1787, in *The Papers of Thomas Jefferson*, ed. Julian P. Boyd (Princeton, NJ: Princeton University Press, 1955), 11:49.

105. William Safire, "Free Speech v. Scalia," *New York Times*, April 29, 1985, A17.

106. Antonin Scalia, "The Freedom of Information Act Has No Clothes," *Regulation* 6, 2 (March–April 1982): 15–19.

107. Clarence Thomas, *My Grandfather's Son: A Memoir* (New York: HarperCollins, 2007), 268–269.

108. See, e.g., *Clapper v. Amnesty International USA*, 568 U.S. 398 (2013) (Alito, J., with whom Scalia, J., and Thomas, J., joined) (denying standing to parties challenging the 2008 amendments to the Foreign Intelligence Surveillance Act, which no longer required the government to identify a specific target and facility "at which its surveillance would be directed, thus permitting surveillance on a programmatic, not necessarily individualized, basis"). In one case, Scalia suggested that he would have used strict scrutiny in cases in which individuals spread "a political philosophy hostile to the Constitution." *Brown v. Entertainment Merchants Association*, 564 U.S. 786, 801 n. 8 (citing *Noto v. United States*, 367 U.S. 290 [1961]). However, it is highly unlikely he would have done so during the height of the Red Scare. Scalia's originalist interpretation of the First Amendment—that is, that it protects the then extant rights of Englishmen—would not have put him at the forefront of the court's more stringent tests used in free speech cases. In fact, he was generally critical of higher levels of scrutiny because they "put a thumb on the scale." Interview with Calvin Massey, "Legally Speaking: A Conversation with Antonin Scalia," Hastings College of Law, September 26, 2010, https://www.youtube.com/watch?v=KvttIukZEtM. Moreover, when he served on the DC Court of Appeals, Scalia wrote opinions broadly interpreting the "state secrets" privilege and qualified immunity for government officials. See, e.g., *Molerio v. FBI*, 749 F.2d 815 (D.C. Cir. 1984); *Halperin v. Kissinger*, 807 F.2d 180 (D.C. Cir. 1986); *Smith v. Nixon*, 807 F.2d 197 (D.C. Cir. 1986); *Ellsberg v. Mitchell*, 807 F.2d 204 (D.C. Cir. 1986). In a 1986 case, Scalia wrote an opinion that upheld the Justice Department's classification of three Canadian films as "political propaganda" under the Foreign Agents Registration Act. See *Block v. Meese*, 793 F.2d 1303 (1986). Justice Thomas has also defended a deferential approach to state secrets. See *United States v. Zubaydah*, 142 S. Ct. 959 (2022) (Thomas, J., concurring in part and concurring in the judgment).

109. *New York Times v. United States*, 403 U.S. 713 (1971).

110. *New York Times*, 403 U.S. at 715 (Black, J., concurring). At a minimum, Scalia and Thomas would have wanted more time to consider the government's national security argument. By contrast, Black was willing to lift the injunction on the *New York Times* without the benefit of oral argument or briefing. Howard Ball, *Hugo L. Black: Cold Steel Warrior* (New York: Oxford University Press, 1996), 197.

111. *Holder v. Humanitarian Law Project*, 561 U.S. 1 (2010).

112. The material support ban was initially adopted under the Antiterrorism and Effective Death Penalty Act of 1996 but has been amended several times since then.

113. The Kurdistan Workers' Party in Turkey and the Liberation Tigers of Tamil Eelam in Sri Lanka were among thirty foreign terrorist organizations identified by the State Department.

114. The *O'Brien* test was established in *United States v. O'Brien*, 391 U.S. 367 (1968),

where the court rejected a First Amendment challenge to the burning of a draft card and applied "intermediate" scrutiny to a generally applicable content-neutral regulation.

115. *Humanitarian Law Project*, 561 U.S. at 31.

116. *Humanitarian Law Project*, 561 U.S. at 35.

117. *Brandenburg v. Ohio*, 395 U.S. 444 (1969).

118. In a short concurring opinion, Black argued that the "'clear and present danger' doctrine should have no place in the interpretation of the First Amendment." *Brandenburg*, 395 U.S. at 449–450.

119. David Cole, "The First Amendment's Borders: The Place of *Holder v. Humanitarian Law Project* in First Amendment Doctrine," *Harvard Law and Policy Review* 6 (2012): 147, 149.

120. *Humanitarian Law Project*, 561 U.S. at 56 (Breyer, J., dissenting). Justice Breyer also noted that the court's decision conflicted with a decision handed down during Justice Black's tenure. In *Scales v. United States*, 367 U.S. 203 (1961), the court held that a person could not be convicted under the Smith Act unless he had knowledge of the group's illegal advocacy and a specific intent to bring about the violent overthrow of the government. Justice Black dissented in *Scales* on the grounds that the federal government had no authority to ban membership in the Communist Party. See also *De Jonge v. Oregon*, 299 U.S. 353 (1937) ("Peaceable assembly for lawful discussion cannot be made a crime").

121. Interestingly, a good case can be made that the Supreme Court should have remanded the case to the lower courts, since the government did not argue that the material support ban had to survive strict scrutiny.

122. *United Public Workers of America v. Mitchell*, 330 U.S. 75 (1947).

123. *United Public Workers*, 330 U.S. at 101.

124. *United Public Workers*, 330 U.S. at 106, 114 (Black, J., dissenting).

125. *Rutan v. Republican Party of Illinois*, 497 U.S. 62 (1990).

126. See *Elrod v. Burns*, 427 U.S. 347 (1976); *Branti v. Finkel*, 445 U.S. 507 (1980).

127. *Rutan*, 497 U.S. at 79.

128. Scalia argued that the court's decisions in *Elrod* and *Branti* should be overturned.

129. *Board of County Commissioners v. Umbehr*, 518 U.S. 668 (1996) (Scalia, J., dissenting); *O'Hare Truck Service Inc. v. City of Northlake*, 518 U.S. 712 (1996) (Scalia, J., dissenting).

130. See, e.g., *Rust v. Sullivan*, 500 U.S. 173 (1991) (upholding a ban on the use of federal money for counseling abortion as a method of family planning); *National Endowment for the Arts v. Finley*, 524 U.S. 569 (1998) (Scalia, J., concurring in the judgment) (upholding congressionally imposed decency standards in the funding of the arts); *Rumsfeld v. Forum for Academic and Institutional Rights*, 547 U.S. 47 (2006) (upholding the Solomon Amendment, which tied federal funding for higher education to providing equal access to military recruiters).

131. Antonin Scalia, *Scalia Speaks: Reflections on Law, Faith, and Life Well Lived*, ed. Christopher J. Scalia and Edward Whelan (New York: Crown Forum, 2017), 206.

132. *Agency for International Development v. Alliance for Open Society International*, 570 U.S. 205 (2013).

133. The full name of the law was the United States Leadership against HIV/AIDs, Tuberculosis, and Malaria Act of 2003.

134. *Agency for International Development*, 570 U.S. at 220.

135. *Agency for International Development*, 570 U.S. at 220 (citing *West Virginia Board of Education v. Barnette*, 319 U.S. 624, 642 [1943]).

136. *Agency for International Development*, 570 U.S. at 221, 222 (Scalia, J., with whom Thomas, J., joined, dissenting).

137. *Agency for International Development*, 570 U.S. at 227.

138. *Agency for International Development v. Alliance for Open Society International*, 140 S. Ct. 2082, 2090 (2020) (Thomas, J., concurring).

139. *Speiser v. Randall*, 357 U.S. 513, 532 (1958) (Black, J., concurring).

140. *Adler v. Board of Education*, 342 U.S. 485, 497 (1952) (Black, J., dissenting).

141. "Justice Black and the Bill of Rights," CBS News Special, December 3, 1968, *Southwestern University Law Review* 9 (1977): 945.

142. *Kingsley International Pictures Corp. v. Regents of the University of the State of New York*, 360 U.S. 684, 690 (1959) (Black, J., concurring).

143. *United States v. Thirty-Seven (37) Photographs*, 402 U.S. 363, 380 (1971) (Black, J., dissenting).

144. Scalia, *Scalia Speaks*, 204.

145. *Barnes v. Glen Theatre*, 501 U.S. 560, 575 (1991) (Scalia, J., concurring in the judgment).

146. *New York Times v. Sullivan*, 376 U.S. 254 (1964).

147. *Rosenblatt v. Baer*, 383 U.S. 75, 95 (1966) (Black, J., concurring and dissenting). See also *Time v. Hill*, 385 U.S. 374, 398 (1967) (Black, J., concurring); *Curtis Publishing Co. v. Butts*, 388 U.S. 130, 170 (1967) (Black, J., concurring in part and dissenting in part).

148. *Ginzburg v. Goldwater*, 396 U.S. 1049 (1970) (Black, J., dissenting from the denial of certiorari) ("The public has an unqualified right to have the character and fitness of anyone who aspires to the Presidency held up to the closest scrutiny").

149. *Ollman v. Evans*, 750 F.2d 970 (D.C. Cir. 1984).

150. *Ollman*, 750 F.2d at 1039 (Scalia, J., dissenting). See also Scalia, *Scalia Speaks*, 204.

151. *McKee v. Cosby*,139 S. Ct. 675 (2019).

152. *McKee*, 139 S. Ct. at 679 (Thomas, J., concurring in the denial of certiorari).

153. *McKee*, 139 S. Ct. at 682. See also *Berisha v. Lawson*, 141 S. Ct. 2424 (2021) (Thomas, J., dissenting from the denial of certiorari).

154. In a 1955 commencement address, Black remarked, "There was thus written into the Constitution the often expressed idea of [Thomas] Jefferson that the Government should have power to punish acts alone, not language, not words, not ideas, not beliefs—only overt acts." Hugo Black, commencement address at Swarthmore College, June 6, 1955, Black Papers, box 481.

155. *Street v. New York*, 394 U.S. 567, 610 (1969) (Black, J., dissenting) ("It passes my belief that anything in the Federal Constitution bars a State from making the deliberate burning of the American flag an offense").

156. *Texas v. Johnson*, 491 U.S. 397 (1989). See also *United States v. Eichman*, 496 U.S. 310 (1990) (striking down the federal Flag Protection Act of 1989).

157. *Valentine v. Chrestensen*, 316 U.S. 52 (1942).

158. *44 Liquormart v. Rhode Island*, 517 U.S. 484 (1996) (Scalia, J., concurring in part and concurring in the judgment).

159. *44 Liquormart*, 517 U.S. 484 (Thomas, J., concurring in part and concurring in the judgment).

160. *Austin v. Michigan Chamber of Commerce*, 494 U.S. 652 (1990).

161. *McConnell v. Federal Election Commission*, 540 U.S. 93 (2003) (Scalia, J., concurring in part and dissenting in part) (Thomas, J., concurring in part and dissenting in part).

162. *Citizens United v. Federal Election Commission*, 558 U.S. 310 (2010).

163. *CR*, vol. 79, pt. 2, 74th Cong., 1st sess., February 7, 1935, 1663.

164. *Connecticut General Life Insurance Co. v. Johnson*, 303 U.S. 77 (1938) (Black, J., dissenting).

165. *Wheeling Steel Corp. v. Glander*, 337 U.S. 562 (1949).

166. *United States v. Congress of Industrial Organizations*, 335 U.S. 106 (1948).

167. *Congress of Industrial Organizations*, 335 U.S. at 155 (Rutledge, J., with whom Black, J., joined, dissenting).

168. *United States v. International Union United Automobile, Aircraft and Agricultural Implement Workers of America (UAW-CIO)*, 352 U.S. 567 (1957).

169. *UAW-CIO*, 352 U.S. at 598 (Douglas, J., with whom Black, J., joined, dissenting).

170. *Mills v. Alabama*, 384 U.S. 214 (1966).

171. *UAW-CIO*, 352 U.S. at 597.

172. *Buckley v. Valeo*, 424 U.S. 1, 20–21 (1976).

173. *Buckley*, 424 U.S. at 21.

174. "Klan Supports Two in Alabama Primary," *New York Times*, August 9, 1926, 4.

175. "Klan Supports Two in Alabama Primary." The $10,000 must have been a state limit because the Supreme Court had previously ruled against congressional authority to regulate primaries under the Federal Corrupt Practices Act. See *Newberry v. United States*, 256 U.S. 232 (1921).

176. "Opening Speech of the Hon. Hugo L. Black," Ashland, AL, March 20, 1926, Black Papers, box 105, 3.

177. *United States v. International Union United Automobile*, 352 U.S. at 598 n. 2 (Douglas, J., with whom Black, J., joined, dissenting).

178. *Colorado Republican Federal Campaign Committee v. Federal Election Commission*, 518 U.S. 604 (1996) (Thomas, J., concurring in the judgment and dissenting in part); *Nixon v. Shrink Missouri Government PAC*, 528 U.S. 377 (2000) (Thomas, J., with whom Scalia, J., joined, dissenting); *Randall v. Sorrell*, 548 U.S. 230 (2006) (Thomas, J., with whom Scalia, J., joined, concurring in the judgment); *McCutcheon v. Federal Election Commission*, 572 U.S. 185 (2014) (Thomas, J., concurring in the judgment).

179. *Colorado Republican Federal Campaign Committee*, 518 U.S. at 636.

180. *Colorado Republican Federal Campaign Committee*, 518 U.S. at 639.

181. *Red Lion Broadcasting v. Federal Election Commission*, 395 U.S. 367 (1969).

182. *Red Lion Broadcasting*, 395 U.S. at 389.

183. Antonin Scalia, "Don't Go Near the Water," *Federal Communications Bar Journal* (1972): 111, 117 ("Perfect licensee reasonableness is not worth the price of day-to-day government involvement in journalistic decisions"). Justice Thomas has also criticized the fairness doctrine based on changes in the availability of broadcast media. See *Federal Communications Commission v. Fox Television Stations*, 556 U.S. 502 (2009) (Thomas, J., concurring).

184. *Goldwater v. Federal Communications Commission*, 379 U.S. 893 (1964) (Goldberg, J., with whom Black, J., joined, dissenting from the denial of certiorari).

185. *Davis v. Federal Election Commission*, 554 U.S. 724 (2006).

186. *Davis*, 554 U.S. at 739, 741.

187. *Arizona Free Enterprise Club's Freedom Club PAC v. Bennett*, 564 U.S. 721, 736 (2011).

188. "Opening Speech of the Hon. Hugo L. Black."

189. *McCutcheon v. Federal Election Commission*, 572 U.S. 185 (2014).

190. Oral argument, *McCutcheon v. Federal Election Commission*, No. 12-536, October 8, 2013, 45.

191. *Everson v. Board of Education of the Township of Ewing*, 330 U.S. 1, 18 (1947).

192. Antonin Scalia, "Constitutional Interpretation," University of Central Missouri, March 4, 2008.

193. See Antonin Scalia, "On Realism and the Religion Clauses," address delivered at Archbishop Rummel High School, Metairie, LA, January 2, 2016, https://www.americanrhetoric.com/speeches/antoninscaliarealismreligionconstitution.htm.

194. *Espinoza v. Montana Department of Revenue*, 140 S. Ct. 2246, 2264 (Thomas, J., concurring).

195. *Espinoza*, 140 S. Ct. at 2266 (quoting *Board of Education of Central School District No. 1 v. Allen*, 392 U.S. 236, 251 [1968]).

196. Ironically, the three originalists would have reached the same result in *Everson*, but Scalia and Thomas would not have agreed with Black's "high wall" theory.

197. *McCollum v. Board of Education*, 333 U.S. 203 (1948).

198. *McCollum*, 333 U.S. at 212.

199. *Zorach v. Clauson*, 343 U.S. 306 (1952).

200. Scalia, "Constitutional Interpretation."

201. *Zorach*, 343 U.S. at 313–314.

202. *Everson*, 330 U.S. at 11–13. Black also mentioned Thomas Jefferson's Bill for Religious Freedom of 1786.

203. *Board of Education of Central School District No. 1*, 392 U.S. 236.

204. *Board of Education of Central School District No. 1*, 392 U.S. at 250, 251, 253–254 (Black, J., dissenting).

205. *Zelman v. Simmons-Harris*, 536 U.S. 639 (2002) (Rehnquist, C.J., with whom Scalia, J., joined) (Thomas, J., concurring) (upholding school vouchers against an establishment clause challenge). See also *Mitchell v. Helms*, 530 U.S. 793 (2000) (Thomas,

J., with whom Scalia, J., joined) (rejecting a challenge to a federal program that gave educational materials and equipment, including computers, to religious elementary and secondary schools).

206. *Rosenberger v. Rector and Visitors of the University of Virginia*, 515 U.S. 819 (1995).

207. *Engel v. Vitale*, 370 U.S. 421 (1962).

208. *Engel*, 370 U.S. at 431.

209. *Engel*, 370 U.S. at 430.

210. *Lee v. Weisman*, 505 U.S. 577 (1992).

211. *Lee*, 505 U.S. at 593.

212. *Lee*, 505 U.S. at 632, 636 (Scalia, J., dissenting).

213. *Lee*, 505 U.S. at 628 (emphasis in the original).

214. Scalia pointed out that school prayers were distinguishable from graduation prayers because the states have compulsory education laws and "the classroom is inherently an instructional setting" where prayers could interfere "with the liberty of parents to direct the religious upbringing of their children." At the same time, his lack of support for those decisions was noticeable. "But whatever the merit of those cases," wrote Scalia, "they do not support, much less compel, the Court's psycho-journey." He observed, "The question whether the opt-out procedure in *Engel* sufficed to dispel the coercion resulting from the mandatory attendance requirement is quite different from the question whether forbidden coercion exists in an environment *utterly devoid of legal compulsion.*" *Lee*, 505 U.S. at 643–644.

215. *Lee*, 505 U.S. at 642 (Scalia, J., dissenting) ("I see no warrant for expanding the concept of coercion beyond acts backed by threat of penalty—a brand of coercion that, happily, is readily discernible to those of us who have made a career of reading the disciples of Blackstone rather than of Freud"); *Elk Grove Unified School District v. Newdow*, 542 U.S. 1, 49 (2004) (Thomas, J., concurring in the judgment) (providing two examples of actual legal coercion: when individuals are required to attend church or they have to pay tithes to generate church revenue); *Town of Greece v. Galloway*, 572 U.S. 565 (2015) (Thomas, J., with whom Scalia, J., joined in part, concurring).

216. *Engel*, 370 U.S. at 431.

217. *Torcaso v. Watkins*, 367 U.S. 488, 495 (1961) (striking down a state religious oath requirement for public office).

218. *Sherbert v. Verner*, 374 U.S. 398 (1963).

219. *Employment Division, Department of Human Resources of Oregon v. Smith*, 494 U.S. 872 (1990).

220. *Reynolds v. United States*, 98 U.S. 145 (1879).

221. *Smith*, 494 U.S. at 879.

222. An argument could be made that Justice Black (like Justice O'Connor, who concurred in *Smith*) would have sided with the state of Oregon. Black always made a distinction between belief and conduct, and he supported the court's decision in *Reynolds*. See Black, *Constitutional Faith*, 53–56. However, unlike Scalia, he would not have supported restricting the use of strict scrutiny in religious freedom cases.

223. *Smith*, 494 U.S. at 884. Scalia did acknowledge that there were "hybrid" cases, involving religious freedom and other fundamental rights, where strict scrutiny would be required.

224. *Everson*, 330 U.S. at 15.

225. *Smith*, 494 U.S. at 901 (O'Connor, J., concurring in the judgment).

226. *Smith*, 494 U.S. at 888.

227. *Smith*, 494 U.S. at 890.

228. *Everson*, 330 U.S. at 16.

229. *Jones v. City of Opelika*, 316 U.S. at 624 (1942).

230. Scalia quoted Justice Frankfurter for the following proposition: "Conscientious scruples have not, in the course of the long struggle for religious toleration, relieved the individual from obedience to a general law not aimed at the promotion or restriction of religious beliefs. The mere possession of religious convictions which contradict the relevant concerns of a political society does not relieve the citizen from the discharge of political responsibilities." *Smith*, 494 U.S. at 879 (quoting *Minersville School District v. Gobitis*, 310 U.S. 586, 594–595 [1940]). It is interesting that Scalia placed so much reliance on *Gobitis*, which was overturned three years later in *Barnette*.

231. *Barnette*, 319 U.S. at 638.

232. *Smith*, 494 U.S. at 890.

233. *United States v. Miller*, 307 U.S. 174 (1939).

234. *Miller*, 307 U.S. at 178–179.

235. Hugo Black, "The Bill of Rights," *New York University Law Review* 35 (1960): 865, 873.

236. *Burton v. Sills*, 394 U.S. 812 (1969).

237. *Printz*, 521 U.S. 898 (1997).

238. *Printz*, 521 U.S. at 936–939 (Thomas, J., concurring).

239. *United States v. Emerson*, 270 F.3d 203, n. 19 (2001).

240. *Parker v. District of Columbia*, 478 F.3d 370 (D.C. Cir. 2007).

241. *Silveira v. Lockyer*, 312 F.3d 1052 (9th Cir. 2002).

242. *District of Columbia v. Heller*, 554 U.S. 570 (2008).

243. The operative clause states: "the right of the people to keep and bear Arms, shall not be infringed."

244. *Heller*, 554 U.S. at 579.

245. *Heller*, 554 U.S. at 578. The prefatory clause states: "A well-regulated Militia, being necessary to the security of a free state."

246. *Heller*, 554 U.S. at 624.

247. *Heller*, 554 U.S. at 624 n. 25.

248. *Chimel v. California*, 395 U.S. 752 (1969) (White, J., with whom Black, J., joined, dissenting).

249. See, e.g., *Harris v. United States*, 331 U.S. 145 (1947) (Vinson, C.J., with whom Black, J., joined) (upholding search of a four-room apartment, including a desk drawer); *Trupiano v. United States*, 334 U.S. 699 (1948) (Vinson, C.J., with whom Black, J., joined, dissenting) (arguing that a search of a distillery incident to arrest was permissible).

250. *Minnesota v. Carter*, 525 U.S. 83, 94 (1998) (Scalia, J., with whom Thomas, J., joined, concurring).

251. *Florida v. Jardines*, 569 U.S. 1, 6 (2013) (Scalia, J., with whom Thomas, J., joined) (quoting *Silverman v. United States*, 365 U.S. 505, 511 [1961]).

252. *Caniglia v. Strom*, 141 S. Ct. 1596, 1600 (2021).

253. In fact, Scalia and Thomas joined the court's decision in *Riley v. California*, 573 U.S. 373 (2014), which relied on *Chimel* in holding that a search incident to arrest of a cell phone violated the Fourth Amendment.

254. *Coolidge v. New Hampshire*, 403 U.S 443 (1971).

255. Coolidge was tried for a murder that took place in 1964, which is why the court applied the broader pre-*Chimel* rule.

256. The vehicle was searched two more times a year later.

257. *Coolidge*, 403 U.S. at 503–504 (Black, J., concurring and dissenting).

258. *Arizona v. Gant*, 556 U.S. 332 (2009).

259. *New York v. Belton*, 453 U.S. 454 (1981).

260. *Gant*, 556 U.S. at 351 (Scalia, J., concurring).

261. *Gant*, 556 U.S. at 362–363 (Alito, J., dissenting).

262. *Kyllo v. United States*, 533 U.S. 27 (2001) (Scalia, J., with whom Thomas, J., joined).

263. *Goldman v. United States*, 316 U.S. 129 (1942).

264. *Silverman v. United States*, 365 U.S. 505 (1961).

265. *Schmerber v. Cailfornia*, 384 U.S. 757 (1966).

266. *Boyd v. United States*, 116 U.S. 616 (1886).

267. *Missouri v. McNeely*, 569 U.S. 141 (2013).

268. In *Schmerber*, the suspect and his companion were injured in a car crash and taken to a hospital for treatment. Because the accused had to be brought to the hospital and the police officer had to investigate the scene of the accident, the court ruled that evidence could be lost based on the natural dissipation of alcohol in the bloodstream.

269. *McNeely*, 569 U.S. at 177, 182 (Thomas, J., dissenting). See also *Birchfield v. North Dakota*, 136 S. Ct. 2160 (2016) (Thomas, J., concurring in the judgment in part and dissenting in part); *Mitchell v. Wisconsin*, 139 S. Ct. 2525 (2019) (Thomas, J., concurring in the judgment).

270. *Frank v. Maryland*, 359 U.S. 360 (1959).

271. *Camara v. Municipal Court of the City and County of San Francisco*, 387 U.S. 523 (1967); *See v. City of Seattle*, 387 U.S. 541 (1967). The court stated, however, that the probable cause determination might be different in civil cases.

272. *City of Los Angeles v. Patel*, 576 U.S. 409 (2015).

273. *Patel*, 576 U.S. at 421. Sotomayor pointed out that the hotel operator could consent to the search or there could be exigent circumstances allowing police to search a hotel registry in particular cases. However, she held that hotel operators could not be compelled to turn over their registries without a warrant in all instances.

274. *Patel*, 576 U.S. at 440 (Scalia, J., dissenting).

275. Hugo Black Jr., *My Father: A Remembrance* (New York: Random House, 1975), 28–29.

276. *Miranda v. Arizona*, 384 U.S. 436 (1966). See, e.g., *Chambers v. Florida*, 309 U.S. 227 (1940); *Ashcraft v. Tennessee*, 322 U.S. 143 (1944).

277. *Orozco v. Texas*, 394 U.S. 324 (1969).

278. *Dickerson v. United States*, 530 *U.S.* 428 (2000).

279. *Dickerson*, 530 U.S. at 449 (Scalia, J., dissenting).

280. *Dickerson*, 530 U.S. at 465. Black and Scalia also disagreed over whether the admission of an unlawful confession constituted "harmless error." Black wrote the decision in which the court ruled that admission of evidence in violation of the Fifth Amendment's self-incrimination clause was not harmless error. See *Chapman v. California*, 386 U.S. 18 (1967). Scalia joined an opinion finding that it was. See *Arizona v. Fulminante*, 499 U.S. 279 (1991).

281. *Griffin v. California*, 380 U.S. 609 (1965).

282. *Griffin*, 380 U.S. at 614.

283. *Salinas v. Texas*, 570 U.S. 178, 192–193 (2013) (Thomas, J., with whom Scalia, J., joined, concurring in the judgment). See also *Mitchell v. United States*, 526 U.S. 314, 341, 343 (1999) (Thomas, J., dissenting) (claiming that "*Griffin* constitutionalizes a policy choice" that "lacks foundation in the Constitution's text, history, or logic").

284. *Missouri v. Seibert*, 542 U.S. 600 (2004) (O'Connor, J., with whom Rehnquist, C.J., Scalia, J., and Thomas J., joined, dissenting) (arguing that a two-stage interrogation technique—question first and warn later—did not violate the Fifth Amendment); *Berghuis v. Thompkins*, 560 U.S. 370 (2010) (ruling that a criminal suspect must invoke the right to remain silent "unambiguously" before the police are prevented from questioning); *Howes v. Fields*, 565 U.S. 499 (2012) (holding that an inmate was not in custody for *Miranda* purposes when he was questioned in a prison conference room about alleged preincarceration criminal activity).

285. *Abbate v. United States*, 359 U.S. 187 (1959).

286. *Abbate*, 359 U.S. at 194 (citing *United States v. Lanza*, 260 U.S. 377, 382 [1922]).

287. *Abbate*, 359 U.S. at 202, 203 (Black, J., dissenting). See also *Bartkus v. Illinois*, 359 U.S. 121 (1959).

288. *Commonwealth of Puerto Rico v. Sanchez Valle*, 136 S. Ct. 1863 (2016) (Ginsburg, J., with whom Thomas, J., joined, concurring) ("The [dual sovereignty doctrine] warrants attention in a future case in which a defendant faces successive prosecutions by parts of the whole USA").

289. *Gamble v. United States*, 139 S. Ct. 1960 (2019).

290. *Gamble*, 139 S. Ct. at 1964.

291. *Gamble*, 139 S. Ct. at 1980 (Thomas, J., concurring).

292. *Gamble*, 139 S. Ct. at 1196 (Gorsuch, J., dissenting).

293. *Johnson v. Zerbst*, 304 U.S. 458 (1938).

294. *Gideon v. Wainwright*, 372 U.S. 335 (1963).

295. *Zerbst*, 304 U.S. at 462–463.

296. *Padilla v. Kentucky*, 559 U.S. 356, 389 (2010) (Scalia, J., with whom Thomas, J., joined, dissenting).

297. See, e.g., *Missouri v. Frye*, 566 U.S. 134 (2012) (Scalia, J., with whom Thomas, J., joined, dissenting); *Lafler v. Cooper*, 566 U.S. 156 (2012) (Scalia, J., with whom Thomas, J., joined, dissenting) (the right to counsel does not apply during the plea-bargaining stage of a case).

298. *Garza v. Idaho*, 139 S. Ct. 738, 759 (2019) (Thomas, J., dissenting).

299. *Garza*, 139 S. Ct. at 759 n. 5.

300. *Garza*, 139 S. Ct. at 759.

301. *Griffin v. Illinois*, 351 U.S. 12 (1956).

302. *Griffin*, 351 U.S. at 19.

303. *Douglas v. California*, 372 U.S. 353 (1963).

304. *M.L.B. v. S.L.J.*, 519 U.S. 102 (1996).

305. *M.L.B.*, 519 U.S. at 139. Thomas favorably quoted from Justice Clark's dissent in *Douglas*, where he said the court's "fetish for indigency" has placed "an intolerable burden on the State's judicial machinery." *M.L.B.*, 519 U.S. at 134 (quoting *Griffin*, 372 U.S. at 359 [Clark, J., dissenting]). He also quoted Justice Harlan's dissent, which argued that the equal protection clause "does not impose on the States 'an affirmative duty to lift the handicaps flowing from differences in economic circumstances.'" *M.L.B.*, 519 U.S. at 134–135 (quoting *Griffin*, 372 U.S. at 362 [Harlan, J., dissenting]).

306. *United States v. Ewell*, 383 U.S. 116 (1966).

307. *Klopfer v. North Carolina*, 386 U.S. 213 (1967).

308. *Ewell*, 383 U.S. 116.

309. *Ewell*, 383 U.S. at 120. See also *Smith v. Hooey*, 393 U.S. 374 (1969).

310. *Barker v. Wingo*, 407 US. 514 (1972).

311. *Doggett v. United States*, 505 U.S. 647 (1992).

312. *Doggett*, 505 U.S. at 655.

313. *Doggett*, 505 U.S. at 661 (Thomas, J., dissenting).

314. *Glossip v. Gross*, 135 S. Ct. 2726, 2752 (2015) (Thomas, J., with whom Scalia, J., joined, concurring).

315. *Avery v. Alabama*, 308 U.S. 444, 447 (1940).

316. *Leyra v. Denno*, 347 U.S. 556, 559 (1954).

317. *Rosenberg v. United States*, 346 U.S. 273 (1953) (Black, J., dissenting); *Stein v. New York*, 346 U.S. 156 (1953) (Black, J., dissenting); *Jackson v. Denno*, 378 U.S. 368 (1964) (Black, J., dissenting).

318. *Maples v. Thomas*, 565 U.S. 266 (2012) (Scalia, J., with whom Thomas, J., joined, dissenting).

319. *In re Davis*, 557 U.S. 952 (2009) (Scalia, J., with whom Thomas, J., joined, dissenting).

320. *In re Davis*, 557 U.S. at 955. In a 2018 capital case, Thomas joined a dissent arguing that an attorney's admission of guilt over a client's objection did not violate the Sixth Amendment. See *McCoy v. Louisiana*, 138 S. Ct. 1500 (2018) (Alito, J., with whom Thomas, J., joined, dissenting).

321. *Rosenberg*, 346 U.S. at 299–300 (Black, J., dissenting).

322. *Rosenberg*, 346 U.S. at 298–299.

323. *Helling v. McKinney*, 509 U.S. 25, 38 (1993) (Thomas, J., dissenting) (quoting *Black's Law Dictionary* [6th ed., 1990], 1234). See also *Hudson v. McMillian*, 503 U.S. 1 (1992) (Thomas, J., dissenting); *Farmer v. Brennan*, 511 U.S. 825 (1994).

324. *Trop v. Dulles*, 356 U.S. 86 (1958) (Black, J., concurring).

325. See, e.g., *Schmerber v. California*, 384 U.S. 757, 776–777 (1966) (Black, J., dissenting) (quoting *Boyd v. United States*, 116 U.S. 616, 635 [1886]).

326. *Chambers v. Florida*, 309 U.S. 227, 236 (1940).

327. Suitts, *Hugo Black of Alabama*, 177.

328. In a 2008 interview, Scalia maintained that the George W. Bush administration's controversial torture policies (including waterboarding) were not banned by the Eighth Amendment because that amendment addressed "punishments," not interrogation practices. Interview with Leslie Stahl, *60 Minutes*, CBS News, April 27, 2008, https://www.cbsnews.com/news/justice-scalia-on-the-record/. "It might be a bad thing to do," Scalia observed elsewhere, "but not everything that is bad is unconstitutional." See Scalia, "Constitutional Interpretation." Justice Black would have found that the Bush administration's "enhanced" interrogation techniques violated the Constitution, but he likely would have relied on the Fifth Amendment's self-incrimination clause.

329. *Marsh v. Alabama*, 326 U.S. 501, 509 (1946). See also *Morey v. Doud*, 354 U.S. 457, 471 (1957) (Black, J., dissenting): "I think state regulation should be viewed quite differently where it touches or involves freedom of speech, press, religion, petition, assembly, or other specific safeguards of the Bill of Rights. It is the duty of this Court to be alert to see that these constitutionally preferred rights are not abridged."

330. Antonin Scalia, "Economic Affairs as Human Affairs," *Cato Journal* 4, 3 (Winter 1985): 703–704.

331. Clarence Thomas, speech before Pacific Research Institute, San Francisco, August 10, 1987, Paoletta Files, no. 45511-005.

332. Scalia, "Economic Affairs as Human Affairs," 703, 707.

333. Clarence Thomas, speech at Cato Institute, April 23, 1987, Paoletta Files, no. 45514-001.

334. *United States v. Causby*, 328 U.S. 256 (1946).

335. *Causby*, 328 U.S. at 271 (Black, J., dissenting).

336. *Nollan v. California Coastal Commission*, 483 U.S. 825 (1987).

337. *Lucas v. South Carolina Coastal Council*, 505 U.S. 1003 (1992).

338. *Dolan v. City of Tigard*, 512 U.S. 374 (1994).

339. *Causby*, 328 U.S. at 274–275.

340. *Berman v. Parker*, 348 U.S. 26 (1954).

341. *Berman*, 348 U.S. at 32, 36.

342. *Kelo v. City of New London*, 545 U.S. 469 (2005).

343. *Kelo*, 545 U.S. at 483.

344. *Kelo*, 545 U.S. at 505 (O'Connor, J., dissenting).

345. *Kelo*, 545 U.S. at 521 (Thomas, J., dissenting).

346. *Hawaii Housing Authority v. Midkiff*, 467 U.S. 229 (1984) (upholding Hawaii's Land Reform Act, which authorized the transfer of fee titles from lessors to lessees in order to reduce the concentration of landownership from the state's feudal land-tenure system).

347. See, e.g., *City of El Paso v. Simmons*, 379 U.S. 497 (1965) (Black, J., dissenting) (arguing that a five-year limitation on foreclosures violated the contracts clause); *Bell v. Maryland*, 378 U.S. 226 (1964) (Black, J., dissenting) (contending that a sit-in violated property rights); *Amalgamated Food Employees Union Local 590 v. Logan Valley Plaza*, 391 U.S. 308 (1968) (Black, J., dissenting) (arguing that union organizers did not have a right to picket in front of a supermarket in a private mall).

348. *Causby*, 328 U.S. at 274–275.

349. *Brown v. Board of Education of Topeka*, 347 U.S. 483 (1954).

350. Del Dickson, ed., *The Supreme Court in Conference (1940–1985): The Private Discussions behind Nearly 300 Supreme Court Decisions* (New York: Oxford University Press, 2001), 648.

351. Hugo Black to Sydney Ulmer, September 8, 1970, Black Papers, box 53. See also Richard Kluger, *Simple Justice: The History of* Brown v. Board of Education *and Black America's Struggle for Equality* (New York: Vintage Books, 1975), 594–595.

352. Bill Kauffman, "Clarence Thomas," *Reason*, November 1987, 32.

353. See Jeffrey Rosen, "Moving On," *New Yorker*, April 29, 1996.

354. Many defenders of originalism concede that if their theory cannot support *Brown*, the theory "is seriously discredited." See, e.g., Michael W. McConnell, "Originalism and the Desegregation Decisions," *Virginia Law Review* 81 (1995): 947, 952.

355. *Rutan*, 497 U.S. at 95 n. 1 (Scalia, J., dissenting). See also Scalia and Garner, *Reading Law*, 87–88 (making the same argument).

356. Ronald Turner, "A Critique of Justice Antonin Scalia's Originalist Defense of *Brown v. Board of Education*," *UCLA Law Review Discourse* 62 (2014): 170.

357. Scalia, "Originalism: The Lesser Evil," 856–857 (emphasis added).

358. Alexander M. Bickel, "The Original Understanding of the Segregation Decision," *Harvard Law Review* 69, 1 (1955): 1–65.

359. Dickson, *Supreme Court in Conference*, 646 n. 35.

360. Scalia, "Constitutional Interpretation."

361. *Loving v. Virginia*, 388 U.S. 1 (1967).

362. There is virtually no evidence that the framers of the Fourteenth Amendment intended to prohibit bans against interracial marriage. See, e.g., Bickel, "Original Understanding of the Segregation Decision," 7, 58; Michael J. Klarman, "Brown, Originalism, and Constitutional Theory: A Response to Professor McConnell," *Virginia Law Review* 81 (1995): 1881, 1919–1920. But see Steven G. Calabresi and Andrea Matthews, "Originalism and *Loving v. Virginia*," *Brigham Young University Law Review* (2012): 1393 (arguing that the court's decision in *Loving* could be justified based on the original public meaning of the equal protection clause).

363. *Green v. County School Board of New Kent County*, 391 U.S. 430 (1968).

364. *Swann v. Charlotte-Mecklenburg Board of Education*, 402 U.S. 1 (1971).

365. *Freeman v. Pitts*, 503 U.S. 467 (1992).

366. *Freeman*, 503 U.S. at 503 (Scalia, J., concurring).

367. Clarence Thomas, "Civil Rights as a Principle versus Civil Rights as an Interest," in *Assessing the Reagan Years*, ed. David Boaz (Washington, DC: Cato Institute, 1988), 393. In one case, Thomas acknowledged that *Green* was perhaps an understandable response to the resistance of *Brown*, but he then remarked, "such extraordinary remedial measures" should have been "temporary and used only to overcome the widespread resistance to the dictates of the Constitution." "The judicial overreaching we see before us today," he added, "perhaps is the price we now pay for our approval of such extraordinary remedies in the past." *Missouri v. Jenkins*, 515 U.S. 70, 125 (1995) (Thomas, J., concurring).

368. *Parents Involved in Community Schools v. Seattle School District No. 1*; *Meredith v. Jefferson County Board of Education*, 551 U.S. 701 (2007).

369. *Colegrove v. Green*, 328 U.S. 549 (1946).

370. *Colegrove*, 328 U.S. at 570 (Black, J., dissenting).

371. *Baker v. Carr*, 369 U.S. 186 (1962).

372. *Wesberry v. Sanders*, 376 U.S. 1 (1964).

373. *Reynolds v. Sims*, 377 U.S. 533 (1964).

374. Antonin Scalia, "The Judges Are Coming," *Panhandle*, Spring 1980, reprinted in *CR* 126 (July 21, 1980): 18920, 18921.

375. Nina Totenberg, "Interviewing Scalia: Verbal Wrestling Match with a Master," NPR, July 25, 2012.

376. *Chen v. City of Houston*, 532 U.S. 1046 (2001) (Thomas, J., dissenting from the denial of certiorari).

377. *Evenwel v. Abbott*, 136 S. Ct. 1120 (2016).

378. *Evenwel*, 136 S. Ct. at 1132.

379. *Evenwel*, 136 S. Ct. at 1133 (Thomas, J., concurring).

380. *Evenwel*, 136 S. Ct. at 1133.

381. *Evenwel*, 136 S. Ct. at 1138.

382. *Evenwel*, 136 S. Ct. at 1140.

383. *Baker v. Carr*, 369 U.S. 186 (1962).

384. "If we had had [*Baker*] shortly after the Fourteenth Amendment was adopted," Warren stated, "most of these problems that are confronting us today, particularly the racial problems, would have been solved by the political process where they should have [been] decided, rather than through the courts acting only under the bare bones of the Constitution." See David M. O'Brien, *Constitutional Law and Politics: Struggles for Power and Government Accountability*, vol. 1, 10th ed. (New York: W. W. Norton, 2017), 807.

385. *Bush v. Gore*, 531 U.S. 98 (2000).

386. *Wright v. Rockefeller*, 376 U.S. 52 (1964).

387. *Wright*, 376 U.S. at 56–57.

388. *Wright*, 376 U.S. at 57–58

389. *Vieth v. Jubelirer*, 541 U.S. 267 (2004) (Scalia, J., with whom Thomas, J., joined) (concluding for a plurality of the court that partisan gerrymandering is a nonjusticiable

political question); *Rucho v. Common Cause*, 139 S. Ct. 2484 (2019) (Roberts, C.J., with whom Thomas, J., joined) (holding that partisan gerrymandering is a nonjusticiable political question).

390. See, e.g., *Shaw v. Reno*, 509 U.S. 630 (1993).

391. *Holder v. Hall*, 512 U.S. 874 (1994).

392. *Holder*, 512 U.S. at 907 (Thomas, J., with whom Scalia, J., joined, concurring in the judgment) (quoting *Wright*, 376 U.S. at 67 [Douglas, J., dissenting]).

393. *Hunt v. Cromartie*, 532 U.S. 234, 266–267 (2001) (Thomas, J., with whom Scalia, J., joined, dissenting).

394. *Holder*, 512 U.S. at 906.

395. Scalia, "Constitutional Interpretation."

6. SCALIA V. THOMAS

1. I am grateful to Lee Epstein for providing this statistic from the Supreme Court database. See Thomas G. Walker, Nancy Staudt, Scott Hendrickson, and Jason Roberts, "The U.S. Supreme Court Justices Database," January 17, 2021, http://epstein.wustl.edu/research/justicesdata.html.

2. Carl Rowan, "Thomas Is Far from 'Home,'" *Chicago Sun Times*, July 4, 1993, 41.

3. Vincent T. Bugliosi, "None Dare Call It Treason," *Nation*, January 3, 2001.

4. Jeffrey Toobin, "Annals of Law: Partners—Will Clarence and Virginia Thomas Succeed in Killing Obama's Health-Care Plan?" *New Yorker*, August 29, 2011 (quoting professor Sanford Levinson from the University of Texas School of Law); Mark Tushnet, *A Court Divided: The Rehnquist Court and the Future of Constitutional Law* (New York: W. W. Norton, 2005), 72.

5. Ken Foskett, *Judging Thomas: The Life and Times of Clarence Thomas* (New York: HarperCollins, 2004), 281–282.

6. Jeffrey Toobin, "Clarence Thomas Has His Own Constitution," *New Yorker*, June 30, 2016.

7. *Hamdi v. Rumsfeld*, 542 U.S. 507 (2004).

8. *Ex parte Quirin*, 317 U.S. 1 (1942).

9. *Hamdi*, 542 U.S. at 569 (Scalia, J., dissenting). Years after the decision, Frankfurter described *Quirin* as "not a happy precedent." David J. Danelski, "The Saboteur's Case," *Journal of Supreme Court History* 1 (1996): 61–82, 80.

10. *Ex parte Milligan*, 71 U.S. 2 (1866).

11. *Hamdi*, 542 U.S. at 571.

12. *Hamdi*, 542 U.S. at 582–583 (Thomas, J., dissenting) (quoting *Chicago & Southern Air Lines, Inc. v. Waterman S.S. Corp.*, 333 U.S. 103, 111 [1948]).

13. *Hamdi*, 542 U.S. at 589–590.

14. *Hamdi*, 542 U.S. at 592–593.

15. *Hamdi*, 542 U.S. at 586 (Thomas, J., dissenting) (quoting *Ramirez de Arellano v. Weinberger*, 745 F.2d 1500, 1550–1551 [D.C. Cir. 1984]).

58. Black disapproved of Congress conferring unfettered discretion to the executive branch in particular areas of the law. One of the most difficult votes he cast in the Senate was against the National Industrial Recovery Act because, in his view, it gave too much authority to trade associations and private industry to determine codes of regulation. *Congressional Record*, vol. 77, pt. 6, 73rd Cong., 1st sess., June 8, 1933, 5284. Justice Black also raised concerns about broad delegations of power in the area of foreign affairs. See, e.g., *Zemel*, 381 U.S. at 22 (Black, J., dissenting) ("I do not think the authors of the Constitution, who gave 'All' legislative power to Congress, intended . . . for a citizen of this country to be told that he cannot get a passport because Congress has given unlimited discretion to an executive official (or viewed practically, to his subordinates) to decide when and where he may go"). Nor did Black support broad delegations of power that conflicted with constitutional rights, particularly the First Amendment. See, e.g., *Peters v. Hobby*, 349 U.S. 331, 350 (1955) (Black, J., concurring) (arguing that the relevant executive "order and others associated with it" were unconstitutional because they "look more like legislation to me than properly authorized regulations to carry out a clear and explicit command of Congress"). At the same time, Justice Black was considerably more deferential to delegations of authority in the area of social and economic policy. See, e.g., *Yakus v. United States*, 321 U.S. 414 (1944) (Stone, C.J., with whom Black, J., joined) (upholding the price administrator's broad authority to set maximum prices for the meat industry pursuant to the Emergency Price Control Act); *American Power & Light Co. v. Securities & Exchange Commission*, 329 U.S. 90 (1946) (Murphy, J., with whom Black, J., joined) (rejecting a challenge to the Securities and Exchange Commission's order to dismantle American Power and Light's pyramid structure for, among other things, unfairly and inequitably distributing voting power among security holders under the Public Utility Holding Company Act); *Lichter v. United States*, 334 U.S. 742 (1948) (Burton, J., with whom Black, J., joined) (upholding the delegation of authority to recapture "excessive profits" under the wartime Renegotiation Act); *Arizona v. California*, 373 U.S. 546 (1963) (Black, J.) (rejecting a challenge to the secretary of the interior's authority to apportion and distribute water under the Boulder Canyon Project Act). "Congress can undoubtedly reduce or enlarge the Secretary's power if it wishes," Black wrote in *Arizona v. California*. "Unless and until it does," he added, "we leave in the hands of the Secretary, where Congress placed it, full power to control, manage, and operate the Government's Colorado River works and to make contracts for the sale and delivery of water on such terms as are not prohibited by the Project Act." 373 U.S. at 594.

59. *Chevron U.S.A. Inc. v. Natural Resources Defense Council*, 467 U.S. 837 (1984).

60. *Chevron*, 467 U.S. at 842–843.

61. Antonin Scalia, "Judicial Deference to Administrative Interpretations of Law," *Duke Law Journal* (1989): 511–521. See also Antonin Scalia, "Remarks by the Honorable Antonin Scalia for the 25th Anniversary of *Chevron v. NRDC*," *Administrative Law Review* 66, 2 (2014): 243 (describing *Chevron* as "a watershed decision"). In *Vermont Yankee Nuclear Power Corp. v. Natural Resources Defense Council*, 435 U.S. 519 (1978), the court held that, except in "extremely rare" circumstances, judges cannot force agencies to utilize rule-making procedures (so-called hybrid rule-making) beyond those prescribed in

the Administrative Procedure Act or other statutes. Scalia was a big supporter of that decision. See Antonin Scalia, "*Vermont Yankee*: The APA, the D.C. Circuit, and the Supreme Court," *Supreme Court Review* (1978): 345–409.

62. Scalia, "Judicial Deference to Administrative Interpretations of Law," 517.

63. *INS v. Cardoza-Fonseca*, 480 U.S. 421 (1987).

64. *Cardoza-Fonseca*, 480 U.S. at 454 (Scalia, J., concurring in the judgment).

65. *United States v. Mead Corp.*, 533 U.S. 218 (2001).

66. According to this new test, "Administrative implementation of a particular statutory provision qualifies for *Chevron* deference when it appears that Congress delegated authority to the agency generally to make rules carrying the force of law, and that the agency interpretation claiming deference was promulgated in the exercise of that authority." *Mead*, 533 U.S. at 226–227.

67. *Mead*, 533 U.S. at 239, 261 (Scalia, J., dissenting). See also Scalia, "Remarks for the 25th Anniversary of *Chevron*," 244 ("I believe I can safely say that my predictions about the harmful effects of *Mead* were if anything not pessimistic enough").

68. *City of Arlington v. Federal Communications Commission*, 569 U.S. 290 (2013).

69. *City of Arlington*, 569 U.S. at 304.

70. *City of Arlington*, 569 U.S. at 304 n. 4. Chief Justice Roberts, who was joined by Justices Kennedy and Alito, issued a vigorous dissent arguing that courts should make an initial determination about whether Congress has given the agency the authority to exercise discretion. "We do not leave it to the agency," the chief justice wrote, "to decide when it is in charge." *City of Arlington*, 569 U.S. at 327 (Roberts, C.J., dissenting).

71. *Auer v. Robbins*, 519 U.S. 452 (1997).

72. *Gonzales v. Oregon*, 546 U.S. 243 (2006).

73. *Talk America v. Michigan Bell Telephone Co.*, 564 US. 50, 69 (2011) (Scalia, J., concurring).

74. *Decker v. Northwest Environmental Defense Center*, 568 U.S. 597, 616 (2013) (Scalia, J., concurring in part and dissenting in part).

75. *Perez v. Mortgage Bankers Association*, 575 U.S. 92, 112 (2015) (Scalia, J., concurring in the judgment).

76. *Michigan v. EPA*, 135 S. Ct. 2699 (2015).

77. In his last opinion involving *Chevron* deference, Scalia used the two-step approach—although he decided deference was not warranted in the case. See *Federal Energy Regulatory Commission v. Electric Power Supply Association*, 136 S. Ct. 760 (2016) (Scalia, J., dissenting).

78. Scalia, "Judicial Deference to Administrative Interpretations of Law," 521: "I tend to think, however, that in the long run *Chevron* will endure and be given its full scope—not so much because it represents a rule that is easier to follow and thus easier to predict (though that is true enough), but because it more accurately reflects the reality of government, and thus more adequately serves its need."

79. Scalia, 518.

80. It appears that, during the Obama administration, Scalia was less willing to give the executive branch deference under *Chevron*.

81. See, e.g., *Smith v. City of Jackson*, 544 U.S. 228 (2005) (Scalia, J., concurring in part and concurring in the judgment) (applying *Chevron* deference to the EEOC's interpretation that disparate impact claims can be brought under the Age Discrimination in Employment Act).

82. Scalia, "Judicial Deference to Administrative Interpretations of Law," 519.

83. Clarence Thomas, "Transition from Policymaker to Judge—A Matter of Deference," *Creighton Law Review* 26 (1993): 241, 251. When he was chairman of the EEOC, Thomas complained that his own agency misinterpreted Title VII of the Civil Rights Act of 1964. According to Thomas, the provision banned employment discrimination on the basis of race and therefore did not allow affirmative action.

84. Thomas, 251.

85. Somewhat surprisingly, Thomas joined Scalia's opinion in *City of Arlington*, 569 U.S. 290, which extended *Chevron* deference to an agency's interpretation of its own jurisdiction. Like Scalia, Thomas called for the overturning of *Auer* deference in several cases. See *Perez v. Mortgage Bankers Association*, 135 S. Ct. 1199 (2015) (Thomas, J., concurring); *Kisor v. Wilkie*, 139 S. Ct. 2400 (2019) (Gorsuch, J., with whom Thomas, J., joined, concurring in the judgment).

86. *Smith*, 544 U.S. 228.

87. *National Cable & Telecommunications Association v. Brand X Internet Services*, 545 U.S. 967 (2005).

88. *Brand X Internet Services*, 545 U.S. at 1016 (Scalia, J., dissenting).

89. *Association of American Railroads*, 575 U.S. 43 (Thomas, J., concurring in the judgment).

90. *Michigan*, 135 S. Ct. at 2713–2714 (Thomas, J., concurring).

91. *Baldwin v. United States*, 140 S. Ct. 690 (2020) (Thomas, J., dissenting from the denial of certiorari).

92. *Baldwin*, 140 S. Ct. at 695, 691.

93. *Kisor*, 139 S. Ct. 2400 (2019) (Gorsuch, J., concurring in the judgment).

94. *Gutierrez-Brizuela v. Lynch*, 834 F.3d 1142, 1155 (2016) (Gorsuch, J., concurring).

95. See, e.g., *United States v. Lopez*, 514 U.S. 549 (1995); *Seminole Tribe of Florida v. Florida*, 517 U.S. 44 (1996).

96. Based on stare decisis, Scalia said he would enforce the court's negative commerce clause jurisprudence in two areas: "(1) against a state law that facially discriminates against interstate commerce, and (2) against a state law that is indistinguishable from a type of law previously held unconstitutional by this Court." *West Lynn Creamery, Inc. v. Healy*, 512 U.S. 186, 210 (1994) (Scalia, J., concurring in the judgment). Meanwhile, Justice Thomas has sought to jettison the doctrine altogether. See *United Haulers Association, Inc. v. Oneida-Herkimer Solid Waste Management Authority*, 550 U.S. 330 (2007) (Thomas, J., concurring in the judgment).

97. *Lopez*, 514 U.S. at 585, 587 (Thomas, J., concurring).

98. Antonin Scalia, *A Matter of Interpretation: Federal Courts and the Law*, ed. Amy Gutmann (Princeton, NJ: Princeton University Press, 1996), 23.

99. *Gonzales v. Raich*, 545 U.S. 1 (2005).

100. Raich, the named party in the case, suffered from an inoperable brain tumor and other life-threatening medical conditions. She argued that marijuana was the only effective form of pain relief that did not cause intolerable side effects.

101. *Wickard v. Filburn*, 317 U.S. 111 (1942).

102. Instead of growing his allotted 11.1 acres of wheat, Roscoe Filburn sowed 23 acres and was fined for the overage. Filburn contested the fine on the grounds that the nearly 12 acres of extra wheat did not affect interstate commerce, since it was intended entirely for use on his farm.

103. *Raich*, 545 U.S. at 32.

104. *Raich*, 545 U.S. at 34–35 (Scalia, J., concurring in the judgment) ("The authority to enact laws necessary and proper for the regulation of interstate commerce is not limited to laws governing intrastate activities that substantially affect interstate commerce. Where necessary to make a regulation of interstate commerce effective, Congress may regulate even those intrastate activities that do not themselves substantially affect interstate commerce").

105. *Raich*, 545 U.S. at 40.

106. *Lopez*, 514 U.S. 549; *United States v. Morrison*, 529 U.S. 598 (2000).

107. *Raich*, 545 U.S. at 71, 74, 57–58 (Thomas, J., dissenting).

108. See, e.g., *Cedar Rapids Community School District v. Garret F.*, 526 U.S. 66, 84 (1999) (Thomas, J., dissenting) ("It follows that we must interpret Spending Clause legislation narrowly, in order to avoid saddling the States with obligations that they did not anticipate").

109. See, e.g., *United States v. Lara*, 541 U.S. 193, 215 (2004) (Thomas, J., concurring) ("I cannot agree with the Court . . . that the Constitution grants to Congress plenary power to calibrate the 'metes and bounds of tribal sovereignty'"); *Adoptive Couple v. Baby Girl*, 570 U.S. 637 (2013) (Thomas, J., concurring) ("Congress' assertion of 'plenary power' over Indian affairs is also inconsistent with the history of the Indian Commerce Clause").

110. Traditionally, the necessary and proper clause was not seen as a limit on Congress's enumerated powers, but both Scalia and Thomas argued that the exercise of such authority must be not only necessary but "proper." See *Printz v. United States*, 521 U.S. 898, 923–924 (1997). However, Scalia did not go as far as Thomas. In *Raich*, Scalia gave an expansive interpretation of the necessary and proper clause, and he did not join two of Thomas's dissents that narrowly interpreted the necessary and proper clause. See *United States v. Comstock*, 560 U.S. 126 (2010) (Thomas, J., dissenting); *United States v. Kebodeaux*, 570 U.S. 387 (2013) (Thomas, J., dissenting).

111. See, e.g., *U.S. Terms Limits, Inc. v. Thornton*, 514 U.S. 779, 848 (1995) (Thomas, J., dissenting). Interestingly, Scalia joined Thomas's dissent in *Thornton.* As I have argued elsewhere, however, Scalia's vote in that case can be explained on various practical grounds. See James B. Staab, *The Political Thought of Justice Antonin Scalia: A Hamiltonian on the Supreme Court* (Lanham, MD: Rowman & Littlefield, 2006), 271–282.

112. Antonin Scalia, "Constitutional Interpretation," Julius J. Oppenheimer Lecture, University of Central Missouri, March 4, 2008.

113. Remarks by Justice Scalia to Dr. Henry J. Abraham's constitutional law class from the University of Virginia, Supreme Court Building, Washington DC, December 2, 1996.

114. *Printz*, 521 U.S. 898.

115. *Printz*, 521 U.S. at 919.

116. *Printz*, 521 U.S. at 919 (quoting Federalist No. 39).

117. In a footnote, Scalia claimed that the dissent's necessary and proper clause argument "falsely presumes that the Tenth Amendment is the exclusive textual source of protection for principles of federalism." "Our system of dual sovereignty," he wrote, "is reflected in numerous constitutional provisions . . . and not only those, like the Tenth Amendment, that speak to the point explicitly." *Printz*, 521 U.S. at 924 n. 13. Scalia also argued that "what destroys the dissent's Necessary and Proper Clause argument . . . is not the Tenth Amendment but the Necessary and Proper Clause itself." *Printz*, 521 U.S. at 923.

118. *Printz*, 521 U.S. at 935–936 (O'Connor, J., concurring).

119. *Printz*, 521 U.S. at 936, 937 (Thomas, J., concurring.

120. James B. Staab, "Conservative Activism on the Rehnquist Court: Federal Preemption Is No Longer a Liberal Issue," *Roger Williams University Law Review* (2003): 129–186. See, e.g., *Cipollone v. Liggett Group, Inc.*, 505 U.S. 504 (1992) (Scalia, J., concurring in part and dissenting in part) (arguing for federal preemption of failure-to-warn claims under the Federal Labeling and Advertising Act of 1965 and all common-law actions under the Public Health Cigarette Smoking Act of 1969); *Riegel v. Medtronic, Inc.*, 552 U.S. 312 (2008) (Scalia, J.) (holding that state tort claims were preempted by the Medical Device Amendments of 1976); *Bruesewitz v. Wyeth LLC*, 562 U.S. 223 (2011) (Scalia, J.) (ruling that the Vaccine Act of 1986 preempted design-defect claims against manufacturers).

121. This is not to say that Justice Thomas has not supported federal preemption. See *Pliva, Inc. v. Mensing*, 564 U.S. 604 (2011) (Thomas, J.) (holding that federal law preempted state failure-to-warn actions because there was a direct conflict between federal and state law); *Mutual Pharmaceutical Company, Inc. v. Bartlett*, 570 U.S. 472 (2013) (state law design defect claims that turn on the adequacy of a drug's warning were preempted by federal law). Thomas's main concern has been the court's "obstacle" preemption jurisprudence—although he has criticized its "physical impossibility" preemption jurisprudence as well. See *Wyeth v. Levine*, 555 U.S. 555 (2009) (Thomas, J., concurring in the judgment); *Merck Sharp v. Dohme Corp. v. Albrecht*, 139 S. Ct. 1668 (2019) (Thomas, J., concurring).

122. *Geier v. American Honda Motor Company*, 529 U.S. 861 (2000).

123. 15 U.S.C. section 1381.

124. 15 U.S.C. section 1391(2) (defining "safety standard" as a "minimum standard for motor vehicle performance, or motor vehicle equipment performance").

125. 49 *Fed. Reg.* 28962 (1984).

126. *Wyeth*, 555 U.S. at 573 (2009).

127. *Wyeth*, 555 U.S. 555.

128. *Wyeth*, 555 U.S. at 580.

129. *Wyeth*, 555 U.S. at 583 (Thomas, J., concurring in the judgment).

130. *Hines v. Davidowitz*, 312 U.S. 52 (1941).

131. *Hines* held that Pennsylvania's alien registration system was superseded by the Alien Registration Act because it was an "obstacle to the accomplishment" of the act's goals.

132. *Wyeth*, 555 U.S. at 595.

133. *Wyeth*, 555 U.S. at 598–599.

134. *Wyeth*, 555 U.S. at 604. See also *Williamson v. Mazda Motor of American, Inc.*, 562 U.S. 323 (2011) (Thomas, J., concurring in the judgment); *Kansas v. Garcia*, 140 S. Ct. 791 (2020) (Thomas, J., joined by Gorsuch, J., concurring).

135. *Wyeth*, 555 U.S. at 608 (Alito, J., with whom Roberts, C.J., and Scalia, J., joined, dissenting).

136. *Arizona v. The Inter Tribal Council of Arizona*, 570 U.S. 1 (2013).

137. The elections clause (Article I, section 4, clause 1) states: "The Times, Places and Manner of holding Elections for Senators and Representatives, shall be prescribed in each State by the Legislature thereof; but the Congress may at any time make or alter such Regulation, except as to the places of chusing [*sic*] Senators."

138. *Inter Tribal Council of Arizona*, 570 U.S. at 14–15.

139. *Inter Tribal Council of Arizona*, 570 U.S. at 23 (Thomas, J., dissenting).

140. According to that provision, "the Electors in each State shall have the Qualifications requisite for Electors of the most numerous Branch of the State Legislature" in elections for the US House of Representatives.

141. *Inter Tribal Council of Arizona*, 570 U.S. at 36–37.

142. *R.A.V. v. City of St. Paul*, 505 U.S. 377 (1992).

143. *R.A.V.*, 505 U.S. at 392. Scalia's novel approach to the First Amendment led two of his colleagues to file sharply worded concurring opinions. Justice White maintained that Scalia's underinclusive analysis was not argued by any of the parties and would encourage hate speech. *R.A.V.*, 505 U.S. at 402 (White, J., concurring in the judgment). Justice Blackmun expressed "fear that the Court has been distracted from its proper mission by the temptation to decide the issue over 'politically correct speech' and 'cultural diversity,' neither of which is presented here." *R.A.V.*, 505 U.S. at 415–416 (Blackmun, J., concurring in the judgment).

144. Clarence Thomas, *My Grandfather's Son: A Memoir* (New York: HarperCollins, 2007), 74, 98.

145. Clarence Thomas, "The New Intolerance," speech delivered at Mercer University, May 1993.

146. *Hill v. Colorado*, 530 U.S. 703 (2000) (Scalia, J., with whom Thomas, J., joined, dissenting) (arguing that an eight-foot buffer zone around health care facilities was content based and therefore subject to strict scrutiny).

147. As pointed out in previous chapters, Scalia and Thomas have been vociferous critics of *New York Times v. Sullivan*, 376 U.S. 254 (1964). See, e.g., *Ollman v. Evans*, 750 F.2d 970 (D.C. Cir. 1984) (Scalia, J., dissenting); *McKee v. Cosby*, 139 S. Ct. 675 (2019)

(Thomas, J., concurring in the denial of certiorari). They have also supported the government's ability to place conditions on the speech it subsidizes and restrictions on the free speech rights of public employees. See, e.g., *National Endowment for the Arts v. Finley*, 524 U.S. 569 (1998) (Scalia, J., with whom Thomas, J., joined, concurring in the judgment); *Garcetti v. Ceballos*, 547 U.S. 410 (2006) (Kennedy, J., with whom Scalia, J., and Thomas, J., joined) (the Constitution does not insulate the communications of public employees from employer discipline).

148. *Ginzburg v. United States*, 383 U.S. 463 (1966).

149. *FW/PBS, Inc. v. Dallas*, 493 U.S. 215, 256 (1990) (Scalia, J., concurring in part and dissenting in part).

150. See, e.g., *United States v. Playboy Entertainment Group*, 529 U.S. 803 (2000) (Scalia, J., dissenting); *City of Los Angeles v. Alameda Books*, 535 U.S. 425 (2002) (Scalia, J., concurring); *Ashcroft v. American Civil Liberties Union*, 542 U.S. 656 (2004) (Scalia, J., dissenting). But see *United States v. Williams*, 553 U.S. 285 (2008) (Scalia, J.) (upholding a federal ban on pandering or solicitation of child pornography).

151. "I find it difficult to see," Black wrote in that case, "how talk about sex can be placed under the kind of censorship the Court here approves without subjecting our society to more dangers than we can anticipate at the moment." *Ginzburg*, 383 U.S. at 482 (Black, J., dissenting).

152. *Ashcroft v. Free Speech Coalition*, 535 U.S. 234 (2002).

153. *Ashcroft v. ACLU*, 542 U.S. 656 (2004).

154. *McIntyre v. Ohio Elections Commission*, 514 U.S. 334 (1995).

155. *Talley v. California*, 362 U.S. 60 (1960). In that case, Black wrote the court's decision striking down a city ordinance that banned handbills not containing the name and address of their creator and distributor.

156. *McIntyre*, 514 U.S. at 341 (citing *Talley*, 362 U.S. at 64).

157. *McIntyre*, 514 U.S. at 357.

158. One reason might be that Justice Black relied so extensively on preconstitutional cases from England.

159. *McIntyre*, 514 U.S. at 361 (Thomas, J., concurring in the judgment).

160. Thomas also cited the famous postratification debate between Alexander Hamilton ("Pacificus") and James Madison ("Helvidius") over the scope of executive power. *McIntyre*, 514 U.S. at 369.

161. *McIntyre*, 514 U.S. at 375 (Scalia, J., dissenting).

162. *Citizens United v. Federal Election Commission*, 558 U.S. 310 (2010).

163. *Citizens United*, 558 U.S. at 485 (Thomas, J., concurring in part and dissenting in part).

164. Interview with Nina Totenberg, Smithsonian Associates Interview, Lisner Auditorium, George Washington University, Washington, DC, February 12, 2013, 2013 WLNR 10286459.

165. *Doe v. Reed*, 561 U.S. 186 (2010).

166. *Doe*, 561 U.S. at 228 (Scalia, J., concurring in the judgment).

167. *Doe*, 561 U.S. at 228–229 (Thomas, J., dissenting).

168. *Americans for Prosperity Foundation v. Bonta*, 141 S. Ct. 2373 (2021) (Thomas, J., concurring in the judgment).

169. *Tinker v. Des Moines Independent Community School District*, 393 U.S. 503 (1969).

170. *Tinker*, 393 U.S. at 506.

171. *Tinker*, 393 U.S. at 518 (Black, J., dissenting).

172. Black's and Thomas's narrow view of the rights of minors is probably attributable to their own parenting styles and childhood experiences. Hugo Black was regarded as a strict disciplinarian by his son, Hugo Jr., and Clarence Thomas certainly lived under the roof of one. See Hugo Black Jr., *My Father: A Remembrance* (New York: Random House, 1975), viii (describing how his father's harsh criticism hurt him emotionally); Thomas, *My Grandfather's Son*, 12 (describing how his grandfather controlled every aspect of his life).

173. *Morse v. Frederick*, 551 U.S. 393 (2007).

174. According to this doctrine, parental authority is delegated to school officials when children are at school, including the power to enforce rules and maintain order.

175. *Frederick*, 551 U.S. at 421 (citing *Tinker*, 393 U.S. at 526 [Black, J., dissenting]).

176. *Mahanoy Area School District v. B.L.*, 141 S. Ct. 2038 (2021) (Thomas, J., dissenting).

177. *Brown v. Entertainment Merchants Association*, 564 U.S. 786 (2011).

178. *Brown*, 564 U.S. at 794 (quoting *Erznoznik v. Jacksonville*, 422 U.S. 205, 212–213 [1975]).

179. *United States v. Stevens*, 559 U.S. 460 (2010).

180. *Brown*, 564 U.S. at 829–830 (Thomas, J., dissenting).

181. *Brown*, 564 U.S. at 839.

182. *Virginia v. Black*, 538 U.S. 343 (2003).

183. *Black*, 538 U.S. at 379–380 (Scalia, J., concurring in part, concurring in the judgment in part, and dissenting in part) (emphasis added).

184. *Black*, 538 U.S. at 391 (Thomas, J., dissenting).

185. *Black*, 538 U.S. at 394. See also *Dawson v. Delaware*, 503 U.S. 159 (1992) (Thomas, J., dissenting) (arguing that a defendant's membership in the Aryan Brotherhood prison gang could be used to rebut his claim of "good" character during the sentencing phase of a capital punishment case).

186. *Walker v. Texas Division, Sons of Confederate Veterans*, 576 U.S. 200 (2015).

187. *Elonis v. United States*, 135 S. Ct. 2001, 2009 (2015).

188. The test comes from the Supreme Court's decision in *Central Hudson Gas & Electric Corp. v. Public Service Commission of New York*, 447 U.S. 557 (1980).

189. *44 Liquormart, Inc. v. Rhode Island*, 517 U.S. 484 (1996).

190. *44 Liquormart*, 517 U.S. at 518 (Thomas, J., concurring).

191. *44 Liquormart*, 517 U.S. at 517 (Scalia, J., concurring in part and concurring in the judgment).

192. *Glickman v. Wileman Brothers & Elliot, Inc.*, 521 U.S. 457, 504 (1997) (Thomas, J., dissenting). See also *Lorillard Tobacco Co. v. Reilly*, 533 U.S. 525, 572 (2001) (Thomas, J.,

concurring in part and concurring in the judgment) (calling for the court to use strict scrutiny "whether or not the speech in question may be characterized as 'commercial'").

193. *California Democratic Party v. Jones*, 530 U.S. 567 (2000).

194. A blanket primary allowed any person who was entitled to vote, including individuals who were not registered members of any party, to vote for any candidate of any party for a given office.

195. *Democratic Party of Washington v. Reed*, 343 F. 3d 1198 (9th Cir. 2003).

196. More specifically, these parties claimed that the party-preference designation on the ballot created a risk that primary winners would be perceived as the parties' nominees, which produced an impression of association between candidates and political parties—even if the party did not endorse a particular candidate.

197. *Washington State Grange v. Washington State Republican Party*, 552 U.S. 442 (2008).

198. *Washington State Grange*, 552 U.S. at 456.

199. *Washington State Grange*, 552 U.S. at 462 (Scalia, J., dissenting).

200. *Washington State Grange*, 552 U.S. at 471.

201. *Employment Division, Department of Human Resources of Oregon v. Smith*, 494 U.S. 872 (1990).

202. *Fulton v. City of Philadelphia*, 141 S. Ct. 1868 (2021).

203. *Fulton*, 141 S. Ct. at 1883–1926 (Alito, J., with whom Thomas, J., joined, concurring in the judgment).

204. *Fulton*, 141 S. Ct. at 1926–1931 (Gorsuch, J., with whom Thomas, J., joined, concurring in the judgment).

205. *Navarette v. California*, 572 U.S. 393 (2014).

206. *Navarette*, 572 U.S. at 404.

207. *Navarette*, 572 U.S. at 405, 413 (Scalia, J., dissenting).

208. *Rodriguez v. United States*, 575 U.S. 348 (2015).

209. *Illinois v. Caballes*, 543 U.S. 405 (2005).

210. *Rodriguez*, 575 U.S. at 354–355 (quoting *Caballes*, 543 U.S. at 407).

211. *Rodriguez*, 575 U.S. at 359 (Thomas, J., dissenting).

212. *Rodriguez*, 575 U.S. at 361.

213. *Rodriguez*, 575 U.S. at 365–366.

214. *Safford Unified School District v. Redding*, 557 U.S. 364 (2009).

215. *Redding*, 557 U.S. at 375–377.

216. *Redding*, 557 U.S. at 389–390 (Thomas, J., concurring in the judgment in part and dissenting in part).

217. *Redding*, 557 U.S. at 392–393, 403.

218. *Missouri v. McNeely*, 569 U.S. 141 (2013).

219. *McNeely*, 569 U.S. at 176 (Thomas, J., dissenting).

220. *Maryland v. King*, 569 U.S. 435 (2013).

221. *King*, 569 U.S. at 466 (Scalia, J., dissenting).

222. *King*, 569 U.S. at 482.

223. *Michigan v. Summers*, 452 U.S. 692 (1981).

224. *Summers*, 452 U.S. at 702–703.

225. *Muehler v. Mena*, 544 U.S. 93 (2005) (upholding a two- to three-hour detention in handcuffs); *L.A. County v. Rettele*, 550 U.S. 609 (2007) (upholding the deputies' order for the residents to get out of bed and remain unclothed until the deputies determined that the suspects were not present).

226. *Bailey v. United States*, 568 U.S. 186 (2013).

227. *Bailey*, 568 U.S. at 201.

228. *Bailey*, 568 U.S. at 203 (Scalia, J., concurring).

229. *Crawford v. Washington*, 541 U.S. 36 (2004) (Scalia, J., with whom Thomas, J., joined).

230. See, e.g., *White v. Illinois*, 502 U.S. 346 (1992) (Thomas, J., concurring in part and concurring in the judgment); *Davis v. Washington*, 547 U.S. 813 (2006) (Thomas, J., concurring in the judgment in part and dissenting in part).

231. *Michigan v. Bryant*, 562 U.S. 344 (2011).

232. *Bryant*, 562 U.S. at 349.

233. *Bryant*, 562 U.S. at 379 (Thomas, J., concurring in the judgment).

234. *Bryant*, 562 U.S. at 385, 388 (Scalia, J., dissenting).

235. *Apprendi v. New Jersey*, 530 U.S. 466 (2000).

236. *Ring v. Arizona*, 536 U.S. 584 (2002) (Scalia, J., with whom Thomas, J., joined, concurring); *Blakely v. Washington*, 542 U.S. 296 (2004) (Scalia, J., with whom Thomas, J., joined); *United States v. Booker*, 543 U.S. 220 (2005) (Scalia, J., dissenting in part) (Thomas, J., dissenting in part).

237. *Harris v. United States*, 536 U.S. 545 (2002).

238. *Harris*, 536 U.S. at 579 (Thomas, J., dissenting).

239. *Alleyne v. United States*, 570 U.S. 99 (2013).

240. *Alleyne*, 570 U.S. at 104.

241. *Alleyne*, 570 U.S. at 108.

242. The Eighth Amendment provides: "Excessive bail shall not be required, nor excessive fines imposed, nor cruel and unusual punishments inflicted."

243. *United States v. Bajakajian*, 542 U.S. 321 (1998).

244. *Bajakajian*, 542 U.S. at 327, 335, 338.

245. *Bajakajian*, 542 U.S. at 351, 354 (Kennedy, J., dissenting).

246. *Eastern Enterprises v. Apfel*, 524 U.S. 498 (1998).

247. *Apfel*, 524 U.S. at 538–539 (Thomas, J., concurring). See *Calder v. Bull*, 3 U.S. 386 (1798) (holding that the ex post facto clause applies only to criminal penalties).

248. *Kelo v. City of New London*, 545 U.S. 469 (2005).

249. *Kelo*, 545 U.S. at 521 (Thomas, J., dissenting) (calling for *Berman v. Parker*, 348 U.S. 26 [1954] and *Hawaii Housing Authority v. Midkiff*, 467 U.S. 229 [1984] to be reconsidered).

250. See, e.g., Antonin Scalia, "Of Democracy, Morality and the Majority," *Origins: CNS Documentary Service* 26, 6 (June 26, 1996): 81–90; Antonin Scalia, "Morality, Pragmatism, and the Legal Order," *Harvard Journal of Law and Public Policy* 9 (1986): 123–127; Antonin Scalia, "The Limits of the Law," *New Jersey Law Journal* 119 (1987): 4–5, 22–23;

Antonin Scalia, "God's Justice and Ours," *First Things: A Monthly Journal of Religion and Public Life* 123 (May 2002): 17–21.

251. Scalia, "Of Democracy, Morality and the Majority," 88–89.

252. See, e.g., Clarence Thomas, "Toward a 'Plain Reading' of the Constitution—The Declaration of Independence in Constitutional Interpretation," *Howard Law Journal* (1987): 691–703; Clarence Thomas, "The Higher Law Background of the Privileges or Immunities Clause of the Fourteenth Amendment," *Harvard Journal of Law and Public Policy* 12, 1 (Winter 1989): 63–70.

253. See Thomas, "Toward a 'Plain Reading' of the Constitution," 692 (quoting Lincoln's speech at Springfield, IL, June 26, 1857).

254. Thomas, "Toward a 'Plain Reading' of the Constitution," 693.

255. *Saentz v. Roe*, 526 U.S. 489 (1999).

256. *Troxel v. Granville*, 530 U.S. 57 (2000).

257. *Troxel*, 530 U.S. at 65, 72,

258. *Pierce v. Society of Sisters*, 268 U.S. 510 (1925).

259. *Troxel*, 530 U.S. at 80 (Thomas, J., concurring in the judgment) (citing *Pierce*, 268 U.S. 510).

260. *Troxel*, 530 U.S. at 80 n. 1 ("This case does not involve a challenge based upon the Privileges and Immunities Clause and thus does not present an opportunity to reevaluate the meaning of that Clause").

261. *Troxel*, 530 U.S. at 91–93 (Scalia, J., dissenting).

262. *McDonald v. City of Chicago*, 561 U.S. 742 (2010).

263. *McDonald*, 561 U.S. at 791 (Scalia, J., concurring). Scalia's vote in *McDonald* contradicted his earlier expressed view that, "properly understood," the Second Amendment "is no limitation upon arms control by the states." See Scalia, *Matter of Interpretation*, 136–137 n. 13.

264. Oral argument in *McDonald v. City of Chicago*, No. 08-1521, March 2, 2010, 7.

265. *McDonald*, 561 U.S. at 805–806, 812 (Thomas, J., concurring in part and concurring in the judgment).

266. Calvin Massey, "Legally Speaking: A Conversation with Antonin Scalia," University of Hastings College of Law, September 26, 2010 (referring to sex discrimination cases as "a modern invention").

267. *United States v. Virginia*, 518 U.S. 515 (1996).

268. See *Grutter v. Bollinger*, 539 U.S. 306, 366 (2003) (Thomas, J., concurring in part and dissenting in part): "In [*United States v.*] *Virginia*, a majority of this Court, without a word about academic freedom, accepted the all-male Virginia Military Institute's (VMI) representation that some changes in its 'adversative' method of education would be required with the admission of women . . . , but did not defer to VMI's judgment that these changes would be too great."

269. *Romer v. Evans*, 517 U.S. 620 (1996) (Scalia, J., with whom Thomas, J., joined, dissenting).

270. *Obergefell v. Hodges*, 576 U.S. 644 (2015) (Scalia, J., dissenting) (Thomas, J., dissenting).

271. *Adarand Constructors v. Pena*, 515 U.S. 200 (1995).

272. *Adarand*, 515 U.S. at 239 (Scalia, J., concurring in part and concurring in the judgment).

273. *Adarand*, 515 U.S. at 240 (Thomas, J., concurring in part and concurring in the judgment).

274. See also *Grutter*, 539 U.S. at 347, 349 (Thomas, J., with whom Scalia, J., joined, dissenting, except for the last paragraph, where Thomas cited the Declaration of Independence).

275. Antonin Scalia, "The Disease as Cure: 'In Order to Get beyond Racism We Must First Take Account of Race,'" *Washington University Law Quarterly* (1979): 147–157.

276. *Adarand*, 515 U.S. at 239.

277. Oral argument in *Grutter v. Bollinger*, No. 02-241, Washington DC, April 1, 2003.

278. Thomas, *My Grandfather's Son*, 99.

279. Clarence Thomas, "Victims and Heroes in the 'Benevolent State,'" *Harvard Journal of Law and Public Policy* 19, 3 (Spring 1996): 679.

280. Antonin Scalia, "The Two Faces of Federalism," *Harvard Journal of Law and Public Policy* 6 (1982): 19.

281. It should be noted that Justice Black also believed that cross burnings were protected under the First Amendment. See *Brandenburg v. Ohio*, 395 U.S. 444 (1969) (Black, J., concurring).

282. Oral argument in *McDonald*, 7.

283. *Dred Scott v. Sandford*, 60 U.S. (19 How.) 393 (1857). Prior to his appointment, Justice Thomas was a fierce critic of *Dred Scott* and based his criticism on natural law principles. See, e.g., Thomas, "Toward a 'Plain Reading' of the Constitution," 692 (a primary task for defenders of constitutional government is "to challenge the *Dred Scott* decision"); Thomas, "Higher Law Background," 64 (criticizing Taney's opinion in *Dred Scott* as "the greatest violation of the [Declaration of Independence's] fundamental principle of equality, one of the higher law principles informing the Constitution"). Justice Scalia was also a critic of *Dred Scott*, but he challenged the decision on different grounds. For Scalia, the major problem with *Dred Scott* was its reliance on substantive due process. See *Planned Parenthood of Southeastern Pennsylvania v. Casey*, 505 U.S. 833 (1992) (Scalia, J., dissenting) (comparing the court's attempt to resolve the divisive issue of abortion to Chief Justice Taney's attempt to resolve the slavery issue before the Civil War). Toward the end of his opinion, Taney argued that, under the Fifth Amendment, slave owners who travel to federal territories have property rights in their slaves, which Congress could not interfere with under Article IV, section 3. What Scalia failed to mention, however, was that Taney's opinion utilized a thoroughly (albeit controversial) originalist approach in determining that Dred Scott was not a US citizen. See, e.g., Christopher L. Eisgruber, "*Dred* Again: Originalism's Forgotten Past," *Constitutional Commentary* 10 (1993): 37–65, 46 (describing Taney's opinion as "a riot of originalism"). In addition to arguing that the Declaration of Independence did not include African Americans in its famous statement that "all men are created equal," Taney cited many other originalist sources, including the state of public opinion at the time of the founding, constitutional text (the

importation clause and the fugitive slave clause), contemporary practices, scholarly and executive branch opinions, and court precedents. As for Dred Scott's claim that he was a free man because he had lived in the free state of Illinois, Taney relied on the Missouri Supreme Court's opinion that Dred Scott was still a slave. *Scott v. Emerson*, 15 Mo. 576 (1852). For additional support, Taney cited his recent opinion for the court in *Strader v. Graham*, 51 U.S. (10 How.) 82 (1851), which held that the status of three Kentucky slaves, who had traveled to the free state of Ohio and later escaped to Canada, was governed by Kentucky law. In a 2008 speech, Scalia acknowledged other deficiencies in Chief Justice Taney's opinion, including his interpretation of the Declaration of Independence (which went against Scalia's claim that judges should not rely on the declaration to interpret the Constitution), his failure to acknowledge that five of the original thirteen states treated blacks as citizens, and his crabbed view of Congress's authority to regulate slavery in federal territories. Scalia, *Scalia Speaks*, 358–369. However, for a positivist-originalist like Scalia, the most challenging issue in *Dred Scott* was the threshold jurisdictional issue involving the diversity of citizenship. Some constitutional scholars have pointed out that "Taney's constitutional claims were well within the mainstream of antebellum constitutional thought," and "the judicial denial of black citizenship reflected beliefs held by the overwhelming majority of antebellum American jurists." Mark A. Graber, "Desperately Ducking Slavery: *Dred Scott* and Contemporary Constitutional Theory," *Constitutional Commentary* 14 (1997): 271, 280–281. A judge following Scalia's methodological approach might not have joined the court's decision in *Dred Scott*, but it is a debatable point. See, e.g., Harry V. Jaffa, *Storm over the Constitution* (Lanham, MD: Lexington Books, 1999) (criticizing Scalia's democratic theory of the Constitution and the idea that the Declaration of Independence is not part of US law, particularly with regard to the court's decision in *Dred Scott*).

284. *Buck v. Bell*, 274 U.S. 200 (1927) (upholding Virginia's sterilization law for the feebleminded). A good case can be made that Justice Thomas would have relied on the privileges or immunities clause to hold that a state cannot sterilize a person against her will. In one abortion case, he controversially connected birth control and the later abortion movement to eugenics and criticized the court's decision in *Buck v. Bell*. See *Box v. Planned Parenthood*, 139 S. Ct. 1780 (2019) (Thomas, J., concurring). There was no similar argument for a positivist-originalist like Justice Scalia. Scalia rejected substantive due process claims across the board and argued that if the text did not clearly protect the right, the court had to defer to the majoritarian process.

285. *Brown v. Board of Education*, 347 U.S. 483 (1954).

286. *Loving v. Virginia*, 388 U.S. 1 (1967).

CONCLUSION

1. *Dennis v. United States*, 341 U.S. 494, 581 (1951) (Black, J., dissenting).

2. *Crawford v. Washington*, 541 U.S. 36, 60 (2004) (overturning *Ohio v. Roberts*, 448 U.S. 56 [1980]).

3. See, e.g., *Apprendi v. New Jersey*, 530 U.S. 446 (2000); *Blakely v. Washington*, 542 U.S. 296 (2004) (Scalia, J.); *United States v. Booker*, 543 U.S. 220 (2005) (Thomas, J., dissenting in part).

4. Hugo LaFayette Black, *A Constitutional Faith* (New York: Alfred A. Knopf, 1968), 11.

5. Antonin Scalia, "Originalism: The Lesser Evil," *Cincinnati Law Review* 57 (1989): 849, 863–864.

6. Clarence Thomas, "Judging," *Kansas Law Review* 45 (1996): 1, 2.

7. Felix Frankfurter, "John Marshall and the Judicial Function," *Harvard Law Review* 69 (1955): 217, 231.

8. *The Federalist Papers*, ed. Isaac Kramnick (New York: Penguin Books, 1987), 244.

9. *McCulloch v. Maryland*, 17 U.S. 316, 414 (1819).

10. Joseph Story, *Commentaries on the Constitution of the United States*, vol. 1 (Boston: Little, Brown, 1905), 345.

11. Story, 348.

12. *Fletcher v. Peck*, 10 U.S. 87, 143–144 (1810) (Johnson, J., concurring).

13. *Towne v. Eisner*, 245 U.S. 418, 425 (1918).

14. Steven G. Calabresi, *Originalism: A Quarter-Century of Debate* (Washington, DC: Regnery, 2007), 14.

15. Robert Bork, "The Supreme Court Needs a New Philosophy," *Fortune*, December 1968, 141.

16. Alfred H. Kelly, "Clio and the Court: An Illicit Love Affair," *Supreme Court Review* (1965): 119, 122 n. 13.

17. Charles Fairman, "Does the Fourteenth Amendment Incorporate the Bill of Rights," *Stanford Law Review* 2, 1 (1949): 5–139. See also Felix Frankfurter, "Memorandum on 'Incorporation' of the Bill of Rights into the Due Process Clause of the Fourteenth Amendment," *Harvard Law Review* 78 (1965): 746–783; Raoul Berger, *Government by Judiciary: The Transformation of the Fourteenth Amendment* (Cambridge, MA: Harvard University Press, 1977), 134–165.

18. Although Thomas Jefferson was a strong defender of states' rights, he argued that "a bill of rights is what the people are entitled to against every government on earth, general or particular, & what no just government should refuse or rest on inference." Thomas Jefferson to James Madison, December 20, 1787, in *The Papers of Thomas Jefferson*, vol. 12 (Princeton, NJ: Princeton University Press, 1955), 440. Meanwhile, one of Madison's proposed amendments to the Constitution, which he regarded as "the most valuable," provided: "No state shall violate the equal rights of conscience, or the freedom of the press, or the trial by jury in criminal cases." *The Papers of James Madison*, vol. 12 (Charlottesville: University Press of Virginia, 1979), 202, 344.

19. *Adamson v. California*, 332 U.S. 46, 74 (1947) (Black, J., dissenting).

20. Leonard W. Levy, *Legacy of Suppression: Freedom of Speech and Press in Early American History* (Cambridge, MA: Belknap Press of Harvard University Press, 1964). Levy also criticized the libertarian views of Thomas Jefferson, arguing that he was less than consistent in the area of civil liberties. Leonard W. Levy, *Jefferson & Civil Liberties: The Darker Side* (Cambridge, MA: Belknap Press of Harvard University Press, 1963).

21. See, e.g., Walter Berns, *The First Amendment and the Future of American Democracy* (New York: Basic Books, 1976); Louis L. Jaffe, "The Court Debated—Another View," *New York Times*, June 5, 1960.

22. Vincent Phillip Muñoz, "The Original Meaning of the Establishment Clause and the Impossibility of Its Incorporation," *Journal of Constitutional Law* 8, 4 (2006): 585–639, 605 (noting that Black emphasized the "Virginia Understanding" of church-state relations, which "effectively privatized religion").

23. *Ullmann v. United States*, 350 U.S. 422 (1956) (Douglas, J., with whom Black, J., joined, dissenting) (arguing that immunity from prosecution violates the Fifth Amendment).

24. *Griffin v. California*, 380 U.S. 609 (1965) (Douglas, J., with whom Black, J., joined) (ruling that the prosecutor's comment about the defendant's failure to take the stand violated the Fifth Amendment).

25. *Miranda v. Arizona*, 384 U.S. 436 (1966) (Warren, C.J., with whom Black, J., joined) (ruling that the self-incrimination clause applies to in-custody interrogations).

26. Leonard Levy, *Constitutional Opinions: Aspects of the Bill of Rights* (New York: Oxford University Press, 1986), 193–209.

27. William M. Beaney, *The Right to Counsel in American Courts* (Ann Arbor: University of Michigan Press, 1955), 21.

28. *Wesberry v. Sanders*, 376 U.S. 1, 20–50 (1964) (Harlan, J., dissenting).

29. Kelly, "Clio and the Court," 135. See also Berger, *Government by Judiciary*, 69–98; Robert H. Bork, *The Tempting of America: The Political Seduction of the Law* (New York: Free Press, 1990), 84–90.

30. *District of Columbia v. Heller*, 554 U.S. 570 (2008).

31. Richard A. Posner, "In Defense of Looseness: The Supreme Court and Gun Control," *New Republic*, August 27, 2008. See also Paul Finkelman, "The Living Constitution and the Second Amendment: Poor History, False Originalism, and a Very Confused Court," *Cardozo Law Review* 37 (2015): 623, 626 (describing Scalia's opinion as "a deeply conservative 'living Constitution' jurisprudence, masquerading (rather poorly) as an original intent jurisprudence"); Saul Cornell, "Originalism on Trial: The Use and Abuse of History in *District of Columbia v. Heller*," *Ohio State Law Journal* 69 (2008): 626; Patrick J. Charles, *The Second Amendment: The Intent and Its Interpretation by the States and the Supreme Court* (Jefferson, NC: McFarland, 2009).

32. On this reading, individuals could own and train with firearms, but for the express purpose of assisting with the state militia when called into action.

33. Warren E. Burger, "The Right to Bear Arms," *Parade Magazine*, January 14, 1990, 4. In a 1991 interview, Chief Justice Burger remarked, "[The Second Amendment] has been the subject of one of the greatest pieces of fraud, I repeat the word 'fraud,' on the American public by special interest groups that I have ever seen in my lifetime." *MacNeil/Lehrer NewsHour*, December 16, 1991, https://www.youtube.com/watch?app=desktop&v=Eya_k4P-iEo.

34. Claudia Luther, "Lectures at UCI with Rose Bird: Bork Says State Gun Law Constitutional," *Los Angeles Times*, March 15, 1989.

35. *Heller*, 554 U.S. at 582.

36. *Heller*, 554 U.S. at 646 (Stevens, J., dissenting).

37. New York and North Carolina sent similar proposals to Congress connecting the right to keep and bear arms to the militia. New Hampshire sent a proposal that would have protected the use and possession of weapons more broadly—although it expressed concerns about a large standing army. Maryland, Pennsylvania, and Massachusetts did not send formal amendments to Congress, but each of those states published minority reports in pamphlet form. The minority reports from Pennsylvania and Massachusetts proposed a more personal right to bear arms, but they were authored by individuals who opposed the Constitution.

38. *Heller*, 554 U.S. at 659–660 (Stevens, J., dissenting) (quoting Neil H. Cogan, ed., *The Complete Bill of Rights* [New York: Oxford University Press, 1997], 169).

39. Jefferson's proposal stated: "No freeman shall ever be debarred the use of arms [within his own lands or tenements]." *Heller*, 554 U.S. at 602 (quoting *The Papers of Thomas Jefferson*, vol. 1, ed. J. Boyd [1950], 344).

40. Finkelman, "Living Constitution and the Second Amendment," 640–649; *Heller*, 554 U.S. at 659. The Virginia Declaration of Rights (1776) provided: "That a well-regulated Militia, composed of the body of the people, trained to arms, is the proper, natural, and safe defence of a free State; that Standing Armies, in time of peace, should be avoided, as dangerous to liberty; and that, in all cases, the military should be under strict subordination to, and governed by, the civil power." *Heller*, 554 U.S. at 641 n. 5.

41. In *Lewis v. United States*, 445 U.S. 55 (1980), the Supreme Court upheld the conviction of a felon who received a firearm in violation of federal law. In a footnote, the court observed: "These legislative restrictions on the use of firearms are neither based upon constitutionally suspect criteria, nor do they trench upon any constitutionally protected liberties. See *United States* v. *Miller*, 307 U.S. 174, 178 (1939) (the Second Amendment guarantees no right to keep and bear a firearm that does not have 'some reasonable relationship to the preservation or efficiency of a well regulated militia')." *Lewis*, 445 U.S. at 65 n. 8

42. The Fifth Circuit was the first federal court to take a contrary view in *United States v. Emerson*, 270 F.3d 203 (5th Cir. 2001).

43. See, e.g., J. Harvie Wilkinson III, "Of Guns, Abortions, and the Unraveling of the Rule of Law," *Virginia Law Review* 95 (2009): 253–323. In his dissenting opinion in *Heller*, Justice Breyer also discussed the different concerns about gun violence in urban versus rural communities.

44. Antonin Scalia, *Scalia Speaks: Reflections on Law, Faith, and Life Well Lived*, ed. Christopher J. Scalia and Edward Whelan (New York: Crown Forum, 2017), 63.

45. *Flast v. Cohen*, 392 US. 83, 99 (1968).

46. Antonin Scalia, "The Doctrine of Standing as an Essential Element of the Separation of Powers," *Suffolk University Law Review* 17 (1983): 881.

47. *Lujan v. Defenders of Wildlife*, 504 U.S. 555 (1992).

48. *Wal-Mart Stores, Inc. v. Dukes*, 564 U.S. 338 (2011).

49. *AT&T Mobility LLC v. Conception*, 563 U.S. 333 (2011); *American Express Co. v. Italian Colors Restaurant*, 570 U.S. 228 (2013).

50. *United States v. Stanley*, 483 U.S. 669 (1987) (Scalia, J.); *Thompson v. Thompson*, 484 U.S. 174 (1988) (Scalia, J., concurring in the judgment); *Correctional Services Corp. v. Malesko*, 534 U.S. 61, 75 (2001) (Scalia, J., concurring) (arguing for a narrow interpretation of *Bivens*-type cases).

51. *Boyle v. United Technologies Corp.*, 487 U.S. 500 (1988). In that case, the Supreme Court overturned a $725,000 jury award to the family of Lieutenant David Boyle who was killed when his military helicopter crashed off the coast of Virginia Beach. Justice Black would have strongly disagreed with Scalia's opinion for the court in *Boyle.* He joined the court's decision in *Erie Railroad Co. v. Tompkins*, 304 U.S. 64 (1938), which largely abandoned federal common law. In a 1942 speech Black called *Erie* a "landmark" opinion. Reflecting his Jeffersonian values, Black claimed that *Erie* represented "one of the great victories of state sovereignty" because it "extends democracy further into law by returning the task of law fashioning to the largest possible group in the society, the group which is closest to the people." Hugo L. Black, address to the Missouri Bar annual banquet, *Journal of Missouri Bar* 64 (January–February 2008): 27. A good case can be made that Justice Thomas would not have agreed with Scalia's opinion in *Boyle* either.

52. Edward A. Purcell, Jr., *Antonin Scalia and American Constitutionalism: The Historical Significance of a Judicial Icon* (New York: Oxford University Press, 2020), 223–224.

53. *U.S. Term Limits, Inc. v. Thornton*, 514 U.S. 779 (1995).

54. *Thornton*, 514 U.S. at 873–874 n. 14.

55. In a letter responding to a request for his opinion on whether the states could add to the qualifications for members of Congress, Jefferson wrote:

> Had the Constitution been silent, nobody can doubt but that the right to prescribe all the qualifications and disqualifications of those they would send to represent them, would have belonged to the State. So also the Constitution might have prescribed the whole, and excluded all others. It seems to have preferred the middle way. It has exercised the power in part, by declaring some disqualifications. . . . But it does not declare, itself, that the member shall not be a lunatic, a pauper, a convict of treason, of murder, of felony, or other infamous crime, or a non-resident of his district; nor does it prohibit to the State the power of declaring these, or any other disqualifications which its particular circumstances may call for; and these may be different in different States. Of course, then, by the tenth amendment, the power is reserved to the State.

Thomas Jefferson to Joseph C. Cabell, January 31, 1814, in *The Writings of Thomas Jefferson*, vol. 14, ed. Albert Ellery Bergh (Washington, DC: Thomas Jefferson Memorial Association, 1907), 82–83.

56. Jefferson to Cabell, 82–83.

57. In Federalist No. 52, Madison wrote that, under the "reasonable limitations" established in the Constitution, "the door of this part of the federal government is open to merit of every description, whether native or adoptive, whether young or old, and

without regard to poverty or wealth, or to any particular profession of religious faith." In Federalist No. 60, Hamilton wrote, "The qualifications of the persons who may choose or be chosen, as has been remarked upon other occasions, are defined and fixed in the Constitution, and are unalterable by the legislature." *Federalist Papers*, 323, 360. See also James B. Staab, *The Political Thought of Justice Antonin Scalia: A Hamiltonian on the Supreme Court* (Lanham, MD: Rowman & Littlefield, 2006), 271–282.

58. *The Debates in the Several State Conventions on the Adoption of the Federal Constitution*, 2nd ed., vol. 1, ed. Jonathan Elliot (Philadelphia: J. B. Lippincott, 1836), 320–321.

59. Story, *Commentaries on the Constitution of the United States*, vol. 1, sections 623–628, 460–463.

60. *Thornton*, 514 U.S. at 856.

61. *United States v. Lopez*, 514 U.S. 549, 594 (1995) (Thomas, J. concurring) (quoting *Gibbons v. Ogden*, 22 U.S. 1, 194 [1824]).

62. *Gibbons*, 22 U.S. at 194–195.

63. *Gibbons*, 22 U.S. at 196.

64. *McCulloch*, 17 U.S. at 406 (Marshall, C.J.):

> Even the 10th amendment, which was framed for the purpose of quieting the excessive jealousies which had been excited, omits the word "expressly," and declares only, that the powers "not delegated to the United States, nor prohibited to the states, are reserved to the states or to the people"; thus leaving the question, whether the particular power which may become the subject of contest, has been delegated to the one government, or prohibited to the other, to depend on a fair construction of the whole instrument.

65. *Wickard v. Filburn*, 317 U.S. 111, 120 (1942).

66. *Rosenberger v. Rector and Visitors of the University of Virginia*, 515 U.S. 819, 854–858 (1995) (Thomas, J., concurring).

67. *Rosenberger*, 515 U.S. at 856.

68. *Employment Division, Department of Human Resources of Oregon v. Smith*, 494 U.S. 872 (1990).

69. See, e.g., Michael W. McConnell, "Free Exercise Revisionism and the *Smith* Decision," *University of Chicago Law Review* 57 (1990): 1009.

70. *Fulton v. City of Philadelphia*, 141 S. Ct. 1868, 1894 (2021).

71. Interview with Antonin Scalia, *Piers Morgan Tonight*, CNN, July 18, 2012, https://www.youtube.com/watch?v=it7sN2jqpNs.

72. See, e.g., Thomas Jefferson to James Madison, December 20, 1787, in *Papers of Thomas Jefferson*, 12:440.

73. *Lucas v. South Carolina Coastal Council*, 505 U.S. 1003, 1028 n. 15 (1992) (Scalia, J.); *Murr v. Wisconsin*, 137 S. Ct. 1933, 1957 (2017) (Thomas, J., dissenting).

74. See, e.g., Eric Schnapper, "Affirmative Action and the Legislative History of the Fourteenth Amendment," *Virginia Law Review* 71 (1985): 753; Jed Rubenfeld, "Affirmative Action," *Yale Law Journal* 107 (1997): 427; Stephen A. Siegel, "The Federal Government's

Power to Enact Color-Conscious Laws: An Originalist Inquiry," *Northwestern University Law Review* 92 (1998): 477.

75. Ralph A. Rossum, *Antonin Scalia's Jurisprudence: Text and Tradition* (Lawrence: University Press of Kansas, 2006), 109.

76. *Hans v. Louisiana*, 134 U.S. 1 (1890).

77. *Pennsylvania v. Union Gas Co.*, 491 U.S. 1, 34 (1989) (Scalia, J., concurring in part and dissenting in part).

78. Rossum, *Antonin Scalia's Jurisprudence*, 113; Ralph A. Rossum, *Understanding Clarence Thomas: The Jurisprudence of Constitutional Restoration* (Lawrence: University Press of Kansas, 2014), 86–94. See also James B. Staab, "Conservative Activism on the Rehnquist Court: Federal Preemption Is No Longer a Liberal Issue," *Roger Williams University Law Review* 9, 1 (2003): 129, 134–140.

79. Purcell, *Antonin Scalia and American Constitutionalism*, 121.

80. Oral argument in *Hollingsworth v. Perry*, No. 12-144 (2013), 38, 41.

81. Article V of the Constitution requires supermajorities both to propose and to ratify constitutional amendments.

82. John P. Frank, "The Shelf Life of Justice Hugo L. Black: The Fairfield Lecture," *Wisconsin Law Review* (1997): 8. It should be remembered that Justice Black's adoption of an originalist approach was not immediate. In his first year on the Supreme Court, Black joined Justice Cardozo's opinion in *Palko v. Connecticut*, 302 U.S. 319 (1937), which adopted a selective approach to incorporation. Black told Frank that his vote in *Palko* was "the biggest mistake of his judicial career," and he later spent an entire summer researching the Fourteenth Amendment, which would form the basis of his dissent in *Adamson v. California*, 332 U.S. 46 (1947). Frank, "Shelf Life," 4.

83. *Webster v. Reproductive Health Services*, 492 U.S. 490, 532 (1989) (Scalia, J., concurring in part and concurring in the judgment).

84. Antonin Scalia and Bryan Garner, *Reading Law: The Interpretation of Legal Texts* (St. Paul, MN: Thomson/West, 2012), 401–402; interview with Nina Totenberg, Smithsonian Associates Interview, Lisner Auditorium, George Washington University, Washington, DC, February 12, 2013, 2013 WLNR 10286459; Scalia, *Scalia Speaks*, 229.

85. Clarence Thomas, "Why Black Americans Should Look to Conservative Policies," *Heritage Lectures* 119 (June 18, 1987): 1, 8 (describing Lehrman's article as "a splendid example of applying natural law").

86. Lewis E. Lehrman, "The Declaration of Independence and the Right to Life," *American Spectator*, April 1987, 21–23. Justices Scalia and Thomas might get their wish. During its 2021–2022 term, the Roberts Court is hearing a major challenge to *Roe* and *Casey*. See *Jackson Women's Health Organization v. Dobbs*, 945 F.3d. 265 (2019) (striking down Mississippi's ban on abortions after fifteen weeks' gestation as a substantial obstacle to a woman's right to have an abortion before fetal viability). During the oral argument, a majority of the justices seemed prepared to allow for abortion restrictions pre-viability and perhaps even overturn *Roe* and *Casey*. See oral argument in *Dobbs v. Jackson Women's Health Organization*, December 1, 2021, No. 19-1392.

87. Speech by attorney general Edwin Meese III before the American Bar Association, July 9, 1985, in Calabresi, *Originalism*, 54.

88. *Original Meaning Jurisprudence: A Sourcebook* (Washington, DC: Office of Legal Policy, US Department of Justice, 1987); *Guidelines on Constitutional Litigation* (Washington, DC: Office of Legal Policy, US Department of Justice, 1988).

89. Steven M. Teles, "*The Rise of the Conservative Legal Movement: The Battle for Control of the Law* (Princeton, NJ: Princeton University Press, 2008), 141.

90. Those two founding members were Lee Liberman (Otis) (1986–1987) and Steven Calabresi (1987–1988), both of whom continue to play major roles in the organization.

91. Scalia was the featured guest at the Fifteenth Annual Faculty Conference, and he wrote the foreword for the book celebrating the twenty-fifth anniversary of the Federalist Society. See Calabresi, *Originalism*.

92. Leonard Leo, introduction of Scalia, National Lawyers Convention, November 22, 2008, http://www.fed-soc.org/multimedia/detail/address-by-justice-antonin-scalia-audiovideo.

93. Federalist Society Mission Statement, http://www.fed-soc.org/aboutus/.

94. Amanda Hollis-Brusky, *Ideas with Consequences: The Federalist Society and the Conservative Counterrevolution* (New York: Oxford University Press, 2015).

95. Lee Liberman Otis, "Antonin Scalia—A Justice in Full," *National Review*, February 21, 2016.

96. "Celebrating Justice Thomas's 25 Years on the Supreme Court," *National Review* Symposium, July 1, 2016 (see especially Randy Barnett's comments); Mark Paoletta, "For 29 Years, Justice Clarence Thomas Has Been the North Star for Originalism on the Supreme Court," *Daily Signal*, October 23, 2020. See also Myron Magnet, *Clarence Thomas and the Lost Constitution* (New York: Encounter Books, 2019).

97. Jeffrey Toobin, "The Conservative Pipeline to the Supreme Court," *New Yorker*, April 17, 2017.

98. "Created Equal: Clarence Thomas in His Own Words," PBS, May 18, 2020 (comment by Ginni Thomas).

99. Antonin Scalia, "In Memoriam: Robert Bork," *Harvard Journal of Law and Public Policy* 36 (2013): 1233.

100. Clarence Thomas, keynote address at National Lawyers Convention annual dinner, Washington, DC, November 17, 2016, http://www.fed-soc.org/multimedia/detail/keynote-address-by-justice-clarence-thomas-event-audiovideo.

101. *McCulloch*, 17 U.S. at 407, 415.

102. See, e.g., Scalia and Garner, *Reading Law*, 405.

103. *Missouri v. Holland*, 252 U.S. 416, 433 (1920). See also *Home Building & Loan Association v. Blaisdell*, 290 U.S. 398, 442–443 (1934) (Hughes, C.J.) ("If by the statement that what the Constitution meant at the time of its adoption it means today, it is intended to say that the great clauses of the Constitution must be confined to the interpretation which the framers, with the conditions and outlook of their time, would have placed upon them, the statement carries its own refutation"). "Just what our forefathers did envision," Justice Jackson wrote in the Steel Seizure Case, "or would have envisioned

had they foreseen modern conditions, must be divined from materials almost as enigmatic as the dreams Joseph was called upon to interpret for Pharaoh." "A century and a half of partisan debate and scholarly speculation," he added, "yields no net result but only supplies more or less apt quotations from respected sources on each side of any question. They largely cancel each other." *Youngstown Sheet & Tube Co. v. Sawyer*, 343 U.S. 579, 634–635 (1952) (Jackson, J., concurring).

104. William Blackstone acknowledged that when the language of a law was "dubious," other factors—context, subject matter, effects, and the spirit or reason of the law—could be evaluated by the judge. Indeed, unlike modern positivist-originalists, Blackstone spoke rather favorably about the spirit or reason of the law. "The most universal and effectual way of discovering the true meaning of a law, when the words are dubious," explained Blackstone, "is by considering the *reason* and *spirit* of it; or the cause which moved the legislator to enact it. For when this reason ceases, the law itself ought likewise to cease with it." *Blackstone's Commentaries*, vol. 1, ed. St. George Tucker (New York: Augustus M. Kelley, 1969), 61.

105. Archibald MacLeish and E. F. Prichard Jr., eds., *Law and Politics: Occasional Papers of Felix Frankfurter 1913–1938* (New York: Harcourt, Brace, 1939), 13.

Selected Bibliography

WORKS ON ORIGINALISM

Amar, Akhil Reed. *America's Constitution: A Biography.* New York: Random House, 2005.

———. "Rethinking Originalism." *Slate,* September 21, 2005.

Balkin, Jack M. *Living Originalism.* Cambridge, MA: Belknap Press of Harvard University Press, 2011.

Barnett, Randy E. *Restoring the Lost Constitution: The Presumption of Liberty.* Princeton, NJ: Princeton University Press, 2004.

Bennett, Robert W., and Lawrence B. Solum. *Constitutional Originalism: A Debate.* Ithaca, NY: Cornell University Press, 2011.

Berger, Raoul. *Government by Judiciary: The Transformation of the Fourteenth Amendment.* Cambridge, MA: Harvard University Press, 1977.

Berns, Walter. *Taking the Constitution Seriously.* Lanham, MD: Madison Books, 1987.

Bork, Robert H. "Neutral Principles and Some First Amendment Problems." *Indiana Law Journal* 47, 1 (1971): 1–35.

———. "The Supreme Court Needs a New Philosophy." *Fortune,* December 1968, 139–141, 166–178.

———. *The Tempting of America: The Political Seduction of the Law.* New York: Free Press, 1990.

Calabresi, Steven G. *Originalism: A Quarter-Century of Debate.* Washington, DC: Regnery, 2007.

Gorsuch, Neil M. *A Republic, If You Can Keep It.* New York: Crown Forum, 2019.

Hollis-Brusky, Amanda. *Ideas with Consequences: The Federalist Society and the Conservative Counterrevolution.* New York: Oxford University Press, 2015.

Huscroft, Grant, and Bradley W. Miller, eds. *The Challenge of Originalism: Theories of Constitutional Interpretation.* New York: Cambridge University Press, 2011.

Jaffa, Harry V. *Original Intent and the Framers of the Constitution.* Washington, DC: Regnery Gateway, 1994.

———. *Storm over the Constitution.* Lanham, MD: Lexington Books, 1999.

Kelly, Alfred H. "Clio and the Court: An Illicit Love Affair." *Supreme Court Review* (1965): 119–158.

Levy, Leonard W. *Original Intent and the Framers' Constitution.* New York: Macmillan, 1988.

Macedo, Stephen. *The New Right v. the Constitution.* Washington, DC: Cato Institute, 1986.

Meese, Edwin. "Toward a Jurisprudence of Original Intent." *Benchmark* 2 (1986): 1–10.

O'Neill, Johnathan. *Originalism in American Law and Politics: A Constitutional History.* Baltimore: Johns Hopkins University Press, 2005.

Posner, Richard A. *Overcoming Law.* Cambridge, MA: Harvard University Press, 1995.

Powell, H. Jefferson. "The Original Understanding of Original Intent." *Harvard Law Review* 98 (1985): 885–948.
Rakove, Jack N. *Original Meanings: Politics and Ideas in the Making of the Constitution.* New York: Alfred A. Knopf, 1996.
Rehnquist, William H. "The Notion of a Living Constitution." *Texas Law Review* 54 (1976): 693–706.
Siegan, Bernard H. *Economic Liberties and the Constitution.* Chicago: University of Chicago Press, 1980.
Teles, Steven M. *The Rise of the Conservative Legal Movement: The Battle for Control of the Law.* Princeton, NJ: Princeton University Press, 2008.
Wechsler, Herbert. "Toward Neutral Principles of Constitutional Law." *Harvard Law Review* 73 (1959): 1–35.
Whittington, Keith E. *Constitutional Interpretation: Textual Meaning, Original Intent, and Judicial Review.* Lawrence: University Press of Kansas, 1999.
Wilkinson, J. Harvie, III. *Cosmic Constitutional Theory: Why Americans Are Losing Their Inalienable Right to Self-Governance.* New York: Oxford University Press, 2012.

PUBLICATIONS, SPEECHES, AND INTERVIEWS BY THE THREE ORIGINALISTS

The works are listed in chronological order.

Hugo L. Black

"Muscle Shoals." *Congressional Record* (hereafter *CR*), vol. 69, pt. 4, 70th Cong., 1st sess., March 6 and 13, 1928, 4179–4635.
"Open Executive Sessions." *CR*, vol. 70, pt. 3, 70th Cong., 2nd sess., January 31, 1929, 2514–2519.
"Reapportionment." *CR*, vol. 71, pt. 2, 71st Cong., 1st sess., May 15, 1929, 1321–1336.
"Censorship." *CR*, vol. 71, pt. 4, 71st Cong., 1st sess., October 11, 1929, 4445–4471.
"London Naval Treaty." *CR*, vol. 73, 71st Cong., special sess., July 9, 1930, 1–61.
"Relief of Unemployment." *CR*, vol. 75, pt. 4, 72nd Cong., 1st sess., February 8, 1932, 3516–3525.
"Federal Emergency Relief Board." *CR*, vol. 75, pt. 4, 72nd Cong., 1st sess., February 16, 1932, 4042–4052.
"5-Day Week and 6-Hour Day." *CR*, vol. 77, pt. 1, 73rd Cong., 1st sess., April 3, 1933, 1113–1129.
"National Industrial Recovery Act." *CR*, vol. 77, pt. 6, 73rd Cong., 1st sess., June 8, 1933, 5278–5290.
"Social Security." December 15, 1934. *Vital Speeches* 1, 8 (January 14, 1935): 249–251.
"System of Health Insurance." *CR*, vol. 79, pt. 1, 74th Cong., 1st sess., January 7, 1935, 142.
"The 30-Hour Week." *Vital Speeches* 3, 22 (February 5, 1935): 681–684.

"Farm Credit Act of 1935." *CR*, vol. 79, pt. 2, 74th Cong., 1st sess., February 7, 1935, 1638–1671.
"Farmer." *Vital Speeches* 3, 22 (March 9, 1935): 684–686.
"Regulation of Lobbying." *CR*, vol. 79, pt. 5, 74th Cong. 1st sess., April 4, 1935, 4983.
"Prevention of Lynching." *CR*, vol. 79, pt. 6, 74th Cong., 1st sess., April 29, 1935, 6520–6547.
"Regulation of Public-Utility Holding Companies." *CR*, vol. 79, 74th Cong., 1st sess., June 4, 1935, 8606–8636.
"Lobby Investigation." *Vital Speeches* 1, 24 (August 8, 1935): 762–765.
"Inside a Senate Investigation." *Harper's Monthly Magazine*, February 1936, 275–286.
"Inspection and Alleged Seizure of Telegrams." *CR*, vol. 80, pts. 3 and 4, 74th Cong., 2nd sess., March 9 and 20, 1936, 3432–3437, 4095–4105.
"Reorganization of the Federal Judiciary." Radio address, February 23, 1937. *Vital Speeches* 3, 22 (September 1, 1937): 675–677.
"Federal Aid to Education." *CR*, vol. 81, pt. 9 (appendix), 75th Cong., 1st sess., March 22, 1937, 593–594.
"Reorganization of the Federal Judiciary." Address delivered in New York City, March 24, 1937. *CR*, vol. 81, pt. 9 (appendix), 75th Cong., 1st sess., March 25, 1937, 636–639.
"Hours and Wages." *Vital Speeches* 3, 22 (June 7, 1937): 686–689.
"Investigation Relative to a National Public-Health Policy." *CR*, vol. 81, pt. 5, 75th Cong., 1st sess., June 10, 1937, 5517.
"I Did Join the Klan." Radio address, October 1, 1937. *Vital Speeches* 4, 1 (October 15, 1937): 20–21.
"The Bill of Rights." *New York University Law Review* 35 (1960): 865–881.
"Justice Black and the First Amendment 'Absolutes': A Public Interview." *New York University Law Review* 37 (1962): 549–563.
"Reminiscences." *Alabama Law Review* 18 (1965): 3–11.
Foreword to *Confronting Justice: The Edmond Cahn Reader*. Boston: Little, Brown, 1966.
"There Is a South of Union and Freedom." *Georgia Law Review* 2 (1967): 10–15.
Interview with *New York Times*, 1967. Published posthumously in "Justice Black, Champion of Civil Liberties for 34 Years on Court, Dies at Age 85." *New York Times*, September 26, 1971.
A Constitutional Faith. New York: Alfred A. Knopf, 1968.
"Justice Black and the Bill of Rights." CBS News television interview, December 3, 1968. *Southwestern University Law Review* 9 (1977): 937–951.

Antonin Scalia

"Don't Go Near the Water." *Federal Communications Bar Journal* (1972): 111–120.
"*Vermont Yankee*: The APA, the D.C. Circuit Court, and the Supreme Court." *Supreme Court Review* (1978): 345–409.
"The Disease as Cure." *Washington University Law Quarterly* (1979): 147–157.
"The Legislative Veto: A False Remedy for System Overload." *Regulation* 3, 6 (1979): 19–26.
"The Judges Are Coming." *Congressional Record* 126 (July 21, 1980): 18920–18922.

"A Note on the Benzene Case." *Regulation* 4, 4 (July–August 1980): 25–28.

"Regulatory Reform—The Game Has Changed." *Regulation* 5, 1 (1981): 13–15.

"Rulemaking as Politics." *Administrative Law Review* 34, 3 (1982): v–xi.

"Reagulation—The First Year: Regulatory Review and Management." *Regulation* 6, 1 (February 1982): 19–21.

"The Freedom of Information Act Has No Clothes." *Regulation* 6, 2 (March–April 1982): 14–19.

"The Two Faces of Federalism." *Harvard Journal of Law and Public Policy* 6 (1982): 19–22.

"The Doctrine of Standing as an Essential Element of the Separation of Powers." *Suffolk University Law Review* 17 (1983): 881–899.

"Historical Anomalies in Administrative Law." *Supreme Court Historical Society Yearbook* (1985): 103–111.

"Economic Affairs as Human Affairs." *Cato Journal* 4, 3 (Winter 1985): 703–709.

"Use of Legislative History: Judicial Abdication to Fictitious Legislative Intent." Speech delivered to various law schools in 1985–1986 (on file with the author).

"Morality, Pragmatism and the Legal Order." *Harvard Journal of Law and Public Policy* 9 (1986): 123–127.

"The Role of the Judiciary in Deregulation." *Antitrust Law Journal* 55 (1986): 191–198.

Address before the Attorney General's Conference on Economic Liberties, Washington, DC, June 14, 1986. In *Original Meaning Jurisprudence: A Sourcebook, Appendix C* (Washington, DC: Office of Legal Policy, US Department of Justice, 1987).

"The Limits of the Law." *New Jersey Law Journal* 119 (1987): 4–5, 22–23.

"A House with Many Mansions: Categories of Speech under the First Amendment." In *The Constitution, the Law, and Freedom of Expression 1787–1987*, ed. James Breyer Stewart. Carbondale: Southern Illinois University Press, 1987.

"Responsibilities of Federal Regulatory Agencies under Environmental Laws." *Houston Law Review* 24 (1987): 97–109.

Remarks at panel discussion, "Separation of Powers in the Constitution," Washington, DC. C-SPAN, November 15, 1988.

"Reflections on the Constitution." Address at Kennedy Political Union at American University. C-SPAN, November 17, 1988.

"The Rule of Law as a Law of Rules." *University of Chicago Law Review* 56 (1989): 1175–1188.

"Originalism: The Lesser Evil." *University of Cincinnati Law Review* 57 (1989): 849–865.

"The Courts and the Press." Francis Boyer Lecture on Public Policy, American Enterprise Institute for Public Policy Research, Washington, DC, 1989.

"Is There an Unwritten Constitution?" *Harvard Journal of Law and Public Policy* 12 (1989): 1–2.

"Judicial Deference to Administrative Interpretations of Law." *Duke Law Journal* (1989): 511–521.

"Assorted Canards of Contemporary Legal Analysis." *Case Western Reserve Law Review* 40 (1989–1990): 581–597.

"The Dissenting Opinion." *Journal of Supreme Court History* (1994): 33–44.

"Of Democracy, Morality and the Majority." *Origins: CNS Documentary* 26, 6 (June 26, 1996): 81–90.

A Matter of Interpretation: Federal Courts and the Law. Edited by Amy Gutmann. Princeton, NJ: Princeton University Press, 1997.

"God's Justice and Ours." *First Things: A Monthly Journal of Religion and Public Life* 123 (May 2002): 17–21.

Remarks at Fribourg University, Geneva, Switzerland, March 8, 2006. http://www.bafweb.com/2006/03/09/antonin-scalia-a-fribourg/.

"Constitutional Interpretation." Julius J. Oppenheimer Lecture, University of Central Missouri, March 4, 2008 (video recording on file with the author).

Interview with Leslie Stahl. *60 Minutes*, CBS News, April 27, 2008. https://www.cbsnews.com/news/justice-scalia-on-the-record/.

"Forward: The Importance of Structure in Constitutional Interpretation," *Notre Dame Law Review* 83 (2008): 1417–1420.

"Methodology of Originalism." Twelfth Annual Henry J. Abraham Distinguished Lecture, University of Virginia School of Law, April 16, 2010.

Interview with Calvin Massey. "Legally Speaking: A Conversation with Antonin Scalia." Hastings College of Law, September 26, 2010. https://www.youtube.com/watch?v=KvttIukZEtM.

Interview with Piers Morgan. *Piers Morgan Tonight*, CNN, July 18, 2012. https://www.youtube.com/watch?v=it7sN2jqpNs.

Interview with Chris Wallace. *Fox News Sunday*, July 29, 2012. https://video.foxnews.com/v/1760716797001#sp=show-clips.

Scalia, Antonin, and Bryan A. Garner. *Reading Law: The Interpretation of Legal Texts*. St. Paul, MN: Thomson/West, 2012.

"In Memoriam: Robert Bork." *Harvard Journal of Law and Public Policy* 36 (2013): 1233–1234.

Interview with Nina Totenberg. Smithsonian Associates Interview, Lisner Auditorium, George Washington University, Washington, DC, February 12, 2013. 2013 WLNR 10286459.

Interview with Jennifer Senior. "In Conversation: Antonin Scalia." *New York Magazine*, October 6, 2013. http://nymag.com/news/features/antonin-scalia-2013-10/.

"Remarks by the Honorable Antonin Scalia for the 25th Anniversary of *Chevron v. NRDC*." *Administrative Law Review* 66, 2 (2014): 243–251.

Scalia Speaks: Reflections on Law, Faith, and Life Well Lived. Edited by Christopher J. Scalia and Edward Whelan. New York: Crown Forum, 2017.

On Faith: Lessons from an American Believer. Edited by Christopher J. Scalia and Edward Whelan. New York: Crown Forum, 2019.

The Essential Scalia: On the Constitution, the Courts, and the Rule of Law. Edited by Jeffrey S. Sutton and Edward Whelan. New York: Crown Forum, 2020.

Clarence Thomas

"Current Litigation Trends and Goals at the EEOC." *Labor Law Journal* 34 (April 1983): 208–214.
Interview with William Raspberry. "Are the Problems of Blacks Too Big for Government to Solve?" *Washington Post*, July 17, 1983.
Speech at Clark College, August 23, 1983. Mark Paoletta Files, no. 45512-006, George H. W. Bush Presidential Library, College Station, TX (hereafter Paoletta Files).
Speech at University of Virginia, Charlottesville, October 19, 1983. Paoletta Files, no. 45512-004.
"Discrimination and Its Effects." *Integrated Education* 21 (January–December 1983): 204–207.
"20 Years after the Passage of the Civil Rights Act." Speech for civil rights celebration, Atlanta, July 2, 1984. Paoletta Files, no. 45510-005.
"The Equal Employment Opportunity Commission: Reflections on a New Philosophy." *Stetson Law Review* 15 (1985): 29–36.
Remarks at symposium, "Black America under the Reagan Administration." *Policy Review* (Fall 1985): 27–41.
"Remembering the Island of Hope." *St. Croix Review* 19, 6 (December 1986): 7–13.
Speech at Cato Institute, April 23, 1987. Paoletta Files, no. 45514-001.
"Toward a 'Plain Reading' of the Constitution—The Declaration of Independence." *Howard Law Journal* (1987): 691–703.
"Why Black Americans Should Look to Conservative Policies." *Heritage Lectures* 119 (June 18, 1987): 1–9.
Speech before Pacific Research Institute, San Francisco, August 10, 1987. Paoletta Files, no. 45511-005.
Speech before American Bar Association, San Francisco, August 11, 1987. Paoletta Files, no. 45514-002.
"Hamilton's Constitutional Vision." Letter to the editor, *Washington Times*, September 2, 1987.
"Congress, the Bureaucracy, and the Enforcement of Civil Rights." Paper presented at the annual meeting of the American Political Science Association, Chicago, September 3, 1987. Paoletta Files, no. 45511-005.
"Affirmative Action Goals and Timetables: Too Tough? Not Tough Enough!" *Yale Law and Policy Review* 5 (1987): 402–411.
Remarks at Claremont McKenna College, Claremont, CA, November 16, 1987. Paoletta Files, no. 45514-002.
Interview with Bill Kauffman. "Clarence Thomas." *Reason*, November 1987, 29–33.
Remarks at panel discussion, "Affirmative Action: Cure or Contradiction." *Center Magazine* 20, 6 (November–December 1987): 20–28.
"The Modern Civil Rights Movement: Can a Regime of Individual Rights and the Rule of Law Survive." Remarks delivered at Tocqueville Forum, Wake Forest University, April 28, 1988. Paoletta Files, no. 45511-005.

"How to Talk about Civil Rights: Keep It Principled and Positive." Keynote address celebrating formation of the Pacific Research Institute's Civil Rights Task Force, Vista Hotel, San Francisco, August 4, 1988. Paoletta Files, no. 45511-005.

"Thomas Sowell and the Heritage of Lincoln: Ethnicity and Individual Freedom." *Lincoln Review* 8, 2 (Winter 1988): 7–19.

"Black Americans & the Constitution." In *The New Federalist Papers*. Lanham, MD: University Press of America, 1988.

"Civil Rights as a Principle versus Civil Rights as an Interest." In *Assessing the Reagan Years*, ed. David Boaz. Washington, DC: Cato Institute, 1988.

"The Higher Law Background of the Privileges or Immunities Clause of the Fourteenth Amendment." *Harvard Journal of Law and Public Policy* 12, 1 (Winter 1989): 63–68.

"Transition from Policymaker to Judge—A Matter of Deference." *Creighton Law Review* 26 (1993): 241–253.

"The New Intolerance." Speech delivered at Mercer University, May 1993. https://www.americanrhetoric.com/speeches/clarencethomasthenewintolerance.htm.

"'Rights Revolution' Excesses Weaken Fight against Crime." *Human Events*, June 10, 1994, 12–13.

"Freedom: A Responsibility, Not a Right." Kormendy Lecture. *Ohio Northern University Law Review* 21 (1994): 5–12.

"Victims and Heroes in the 'Benevolent State.'" *Harvard Journal of Law and Public Policy* 19, 3 (Spring 1996): 671–683.

"Judging." *Kansas Law Review* 45 (1996): 1–8.

"The Virtue of Defeat: *Plessy v. Ferguson* in Retrospect." *Journal of Supreme Court History* 2 (1997): 15–24.

"Personal Responsibility." *Regent University Law Review* 12 (1999–2000): 317–327.

"Why Federalism Matters." Dwight D. Opperman Lecture, September 24, 1999. *Drake Law Review* 48 (2000): 231–238.

My Grandfather's Son: A Memoir. New York: HarperCollins, 2007.

"The Second Annual William French Smith Memorial Lecture: A Conversation with Justice Clarence Thomas." *Pepperdine Law Review* 37 (December 2009): 7–32.

Joseph Story Lecture, Heritage Foundation, October 26, 2016. https://www.heritage.org/courts/event/the-joseph-story-distinguished-lecture-justice-clarence-thomas.

Keynote address at National Lawyers Convention annual dinner, Washington, DC, November 17, 2016. http://www.fed-soc.org/multimedia/detail/keynote-address-by-justice-clarence -thomas-event-audiovideo.

"A Tribute to Justice Antonin Scalia." *Yale Law Journal* 126 (2017): 1600–1604.

"Created Equal: Clarence Thomas in His Own Words." PBS, May 18, 2020.

SCHOLARSHIP ON THE THREE ORIGINALISTS

Hugo L. Black

Amar, Akhil Reed. "Hugo Black and the Hall of Fame." *Alabama Law Review* 53 (2002): 1221–1248.

Ball, Howard. *Hugo L. Black: Cold Steel Warrior.* New York: Oxford University Press, 1996.

———. "Hugo L. Black: A Twentieth Century Jeffersonian." *Southwestern University Law Review* 9 (1977): 1049–1068.

Berman, Daniel M. "The Political Philosophy of Hugo L. Black." Diss., Rutgers University, 1957.

Bickel, Alexander M. "Mr. Justice Black: The Unobvious Meaning of Plain Words." *New Republic*, March 14, 1960.

Black, Hugo, Jr. *My Father: A Remembrance.* New York: Random House, 1975.

Dillard, Irving, ed. *One Man's Stand for Freedom: Mr. Justice Black and the Bill of Rights.* New York: Alfred A. Knopf, 1963.

Dunne, Gerald T. *Hugo Black and the Judicial Revolution.* New York: Simon & Schuster, 1977.

Durr, Clifford J. "Hugo L. Black: A Personal Appraisal." *Georgia Law Review* 6, 1 (1971): 1–16.

Fairman, Charles. "Does the Fourteenth Amendment Incorporate the Bill of Rights?" *Stanford Law Review* 2, 1 (1949): 5–139.

Frank, John P. "Justice Black and the New Deal." *Arizona Law Review* 9 (1967): 26–58.

———. *Mr. Justice Black: The Man and His Opinions.* New York: Alfred A. Knopf, 1949.

———. "The Shelf Life of Justice Hugo L. Black: The Fairfield Lecture." *Wisconsin Law Review* (1997): 1–30.

Freyer, Tony, ed. *Justice Hugo Black and Modern America.* Tuscaloosa: University of Alabama Press, 1990.

Hamilton, Virginia Van der Veer. *Hugo Black: The Alabama Years.* Baton Rouge: Louisiana State University Press, 1972.

———. "Hugo Black and the K.K.K." *American Heritage* 19, 3 (April 1968): 61–64, 108–111.

Harlan, John M. "Mr. Justice Black—Remarks of a Colleague." *Harvard Law Review* 81, 1 (1967): 1–3.

Howard, A. E. Dick. "Mr. Justice Black: The Negro Protest Movement and the Rule of Law." *Virginia Law Review* 53, 5 (June 1967): 1030–1090.

Kluger, Richard. *Simple Justice: The History of* Brown v. Board of Education *and Black America's Struggle for Equality.* New York: Vintage Books, 1975.

Landynski, Jacob W. "In Search of Justice Black's Fourth Amendment." *Fordham Law Review* 45 (1976–1977): 453–496.

Leuchtenburg, William E. "A Klansman Joins the Court: The Appointment of Hugo L. Black." *University of Chicago Law Review* 41, 1 (Fall 1973): 1–31.

Levy, Leonard W. *Legacy of Suppression: Freedom of Speech and Press in Early American History.* Cambridge, MA: Belknap Press of Harvard University Press, 1964.

Lewis, Anthony. *Gideon's Trumpet.* New York: Vintage Books, 1964.
Magee, James J. *Mr. Justice Black: Absolutist on the Court.* Charlottesville: University Press of Virginia, 1980.
Mason, Gene L. "Hugo Black and the United States Senate." MA thesis, University of Kansas, 1964.
Meador, Daniel J. "Hugo Black and Thomas Jefferson." *Virginia Quarterly Review* 79, 3 (Summer 2003): 459–468..
———. *Mr. Justice Black and His Books.* Charlottesville, VA: University Press of Virginia, 1974
Mendelson, Wallace. *Justices Black and Frankfurter: Conflict in the Court.* Chicago: University of Chicago Press, 1966.
Newman, Roger K. *Hugo Black: A Biography.* 2nd ed. New York: Fordham University Press, 1997.
Silverstein, Mark. *Constitutional Faiths: Felix Frankfurter, Hugo Black, and the Process of Judicial Decision Making.* Ithaca, NY: Cornell University Press, 1984.
Suitts, Steve. *Hugo Black of Alabama: How His Roots and Early Career Shaped the Great Champion of the Constitution.* Montgomery, AL: NewSouth Books, 2005.
Yarbrough, Tinsley E. "Justice Black and Equal Protection." *Southwestern University Law Review* 9 (1977): 899–935.
———. *Mr. Justice Black and His Critics.* Durham, NC: Duke University Press, 1988.
———. "Mr. Justice Black and Legal Positivism." *Virginia Law Review* 57 (1971): 375–407.

Antonin Scalia

Barnett, Randy. "Scalia's Infidelity: A Critique of 'Faint-Hearted' Originalism." *University of Cincinnati Law Review* 75 (2006): 7–24.
Bernick, Evan. "Why Scalia Was Wrong about Chevron." Federalist Society blog, March 23, 2017.
Biskupic, Joan. *American Original: The Life and Constitution of Supreme Court Justice Antonin Scalia.* New York: Sarah Crichton Books, 2009.
Bogus, Carl T. "Fresh Looks: The History and Politics of Second Amendment Scholarship: A Primer." *Chicago-Kent Law Review* 76 (2000): 3–25.
Brisbin, Richard A., Jr. *Justice Antonin Scalia and the Conservative Revival.* Baltimore: Johns Hopkins University Press, 1997.
Cornell, Saul. "Originalism on Trial: The Use and Abuse of History in *District of Columbia v. Heller.*" *Ohio State Law Journal* 69 (2008): 625–640.
Dorsen, David M. *The Unexpected Scalia: A Conservative Justice's Liberal Opinions.* Cambridge: Cambridge University Press, 2017.
Finkelman, Paul. "The Living Constitution and the Second Amendment: Poor History, False Originalism, and a Very Confused Court." *Cardozo Law Review* 37 (2015): 623–662.
Garner, Bryan A. *Nino and Me: My Unusual Friendship with Justice Antonin Scalia.* New York: Threshold Editions, 2018.

Hasen, Richard L. *The Justice of Contradictions: Antonin Scalia and the Politics of Disruption.* New Haven, CT: Yale University Press, 2018.

Kannar, George. "The Constitutional Catechism of Antonin Scalia." *Yale Law Journal* 99 (1990): 1297–1357.

McConnell, Michael W. "Free Exercise Revisionism and the *Smith* Decision." *University of Chicago Law Review* 57 (1990): 1109–1153.

Murphy, Bruce Allen. *Scalia: A Court of One.* New York: Simon & Schuster, 2014.

Pilon, Roger. "Justice Scalia's Originalism: Original or Post–New Deal?" *Cato Supreme Court Review* (2016): vii–xxxii.

Posner, Richard A. "In Defense of Looseness: The Supreme Court and Gun Control." *New Republic*, August 27, 2008.

Pryor, William H., Jr., John S. Baker, Ron DeSantis, Roger Pilon, Luther Strange, and Jonathan Turley. "Justice Scalia on Federalism and Separation of Powers." *Regent University Law Review* 30 (2017): 57–103.

Purcell, Edward A., Jr. *Antonin Scalia and American Constitutionalism: The Historical Significance of a Judicial Icon.* New York: Oxford University Press, 2020.

Rossum, Ralph A. *Antonin Scalia's Jurisprudence: Text and Tradition.* Lawrence: University Press of Kansas, 2006.

Schultz, David A., and Christopher E. Smith. *The Jurisprudential Vision of Justice Antonin Scalia.* Lanham, MD: Rowman & Littlefield, 1996.

Shanmugam, Kannon K. "Justice Scalia: A Personal Remembrance." *Journal of Supreme Court History* 41, 3 (2016): 252–256.

Staab, James B. "Conservative Activism on the Rehnquist Court: Federal Preemption Is No Longer a Liberal Issue." *Roger Williams University Law Review* 9, 1 (2003): 129–185.

———. *The Political Thought of Justice Antonin Scalia: A Hamiltonian on the Supreme Court.* Lanham, MD: Rowman & Littlefield, 2006.

———. "The Tenth Amendment and Justice Scalia's 'Split Personality.'" *Journal of Law and Politics* 16, 2 (2000): 231–379.

———. "Was Antonin Scalia a 'Great' Supreme Court Justice?" In *The Conservative Revolution of Antonin Scalia*, ed. David A. Schultz and Howard Schweber. Lanham, MD: Lexington Books, 2018.

Sunstein, Cass R. "What's Standing after *Lujan?* Of Citizen Suits, 'Injuries,' and Article III." *Michigan Law Review* 91 (1992): 163–236.

Talbot, Margaret. "Supreme Confidence." *New Yorker*, March 28, 2005.

Totenberg, Nina. "Even Scalia's Dissenting Opinions Get Major Scrutiny." *All Things Considered*, NPR, July 16, 2012.

———. "Interviewing Scalia: Verbal Wrestling Match with a Master." NPR, July 25, 2012.

Turner, Ronald. "A Critique of Justice Antonin Scalia's Originalist Defense of *Brown v. Board of Education.*" *UCLA Law Review Discourse* 62 (2014): 170–184.

Uhlmann, Michael M. "Justice Scalia and His Critics." *Perspectives on Political Science* 28, 1 (Winter 1999): 29–31.

Wilkinson, J. Harvie, III. "Of Guns, Abortions, and the Unraveling of the Rule of Law." *Virginia Law Review* 95 (2009): 253–323.

Clarence Thomas

Barnett, Randy, Josh Blackman, Richard A. Epstein, Orrin G. Hatch, Mario Loyola, Carrie Severino, Ed Whelan, and John Yoo. "Celebrating Justice Thomas's 25 Years on the Supreme Court." *National Review* Symposium, July 1, 2016.

Dean, Nathan W. "The Primacy of the Individual in the Political Philosophy and Civil Rights Jurisprudence of Justice Clarence Thomas." *George Mason University Civil Rights Journal* 14 (2004): 27–73.

Foskett, Ken. *Judging Thomas: The Life and Times of Clarence Thomas.* New York: Harper Collins, 2004.

Garnett, Nicole Stelle. "'But for the Grace of God There Go I': Justice Thomas and the Little Guy." *NYU Journal of Law and Liberty* 4 (2009): 626–647.

Gerber, Scott. *First Principles: The Jurisprudence of Clarence Thomas.* New York: New York University Press, 1999.

Hakim, Danny and Jo Becker. "The Long Crusade of Clarence and Ginni Thomas." *The New York Times Magazine.* February 22, 2022.

Hill, Anita. *Speaking Truth to Power.* New York: Anchor Books, 1997.

Kennedy, Kirk A. "Reaffirming the Natural Law Jurisprudence of Justice Clarence Thomas." *Regent University Law Review* 9 (1997): 33–87.

"Law Symposium: Justice Thomas's Thirty-Year Legacy on the Court." Co-hosted by the Heritage Foundation and the C. Boyden Gray Center for the Study of the Administrative State, October 21, 2021, Heritage Foundation, Washington, DC.

Lichtman, Steven B. "Black Like Me: The Free Speech Jurisprudence of Clarence Thomas." *Penn State Law Review* 114 (2009): 415–468.

Lin, Elbert. "At the Front of the Train: Justice Thomas Reexamines the Administrative State." *Yale Law Journal Forum* 127 (2017): 182–195.

Maggs, Gregory E. "Which Original Meaning of the Constitution Matters to Justice Thomas?" *NYU Journal of Law and Liberty* 4 (2009): 494–516.

Magnet, Myron. *Clarence Thomas and the Lost Constitution.* New York: Encounter Books, 2019.

Masugi, Ken. "Natural Right and Oversight: The Use and Abuse of 'Natural Law' in the Clarence Thomas Hearings." *Political Communication* 9 (1992): 231–250.

Morrison, Toni, ed. *Race-ing Justice, En-gendering Power: Essays on Anita Hill, Clarence Thomas, and the Construction of Social Reality.* New York: Pantheon Books, 1992.

Muñoz, Vincent Phillip. "The Original Meaning of the Establishment Clause and the Impossibility of Its Incorporation." *Journal of Constitutional Law* 8, 4 (2006): 585–639.

Munroe, Maurice E. R. "The EEOC: Pattern and Practice Imperfect." *Yale Law and Policy Review* 13 (1995): 266–270.

Onwuachi-Willig, Angela. "Just Another Brother on the SCT? What Justice Clarence Thomas Teaches Us about the Influence of Racial Identity." *Iowa Law Review* 90 (2005): 931–1009.

———. "Using the Master's 'Tool' to Dismantle His House: Why Justice Clarence Thomas Makes the Case for Affirmative Action." *Arizona Law Review* 47 (2005): 113–165.

Paoletta, Mark. "For 29 Years, Justice Clarence Thomas Has Been the North Star for Originalism on the Supreme Court." *Daily Signal*, October 23, 2020.

Robin, Corey. *The Enigma of Clarence Thomas.* New York: Metropolitan Books, 2019.

Rosen, Jeffrey. "Moving On." *New Yorker*, April 29, 1996.

Rossum, Ralph A. *Understanding Clarence Thomas: The Jurisprudence of Constitutional Restoration.* Lawrence: University Press of Kansas, 2014.

Savage, David G. "Clarence Thomas Is His Own Man." *Los Angeles Times*, July 3, 2011.

Sharkey, Catherine M. "Against Freewheeling, Extratextual Obstacle Preemption: Is Justice Clarence Thomas the Lone Principled Federalist?" *NYU Journal of Law and Liberty* 5 (2010): 63–114.

Smith, Stephen F. "Clarence X? The Black Nationalist behind Justice Thomas's Constitutionalism." *NYU Journal of Law and Liberty* 4 (2009): 583–625.

Strange, Lee J. "The Most Faithful Originalist? Justice Thomas, Justice Scalia, and the Future of Originalism." *University of Detroit Mercy Law Review* 88 (2011): 873–882.

Thomas, Andrew Peyton. *Clarence Thomas: A Biography.* San Francisco: Encounter Books, 2001.

Toobin, Jeffrey. "Clarence Thomas Has His Own Constitution." *New Yorker*, June 30, 2016.

———. "The Conservative Pipeline to the Supreme Court." *New Yorker*, April 17, 2017.

Tushnet, Mark. "Clarence Thomas's Black Nationalism." *Howard Law Journal* 47 (2004): 323– 339.

Weiner, Hannah L. "The Next 'Great Dissenter'? How Clarence Thomas Is Using the Words and Principles of John Marshall Harlan to Craft a New Era of Civil Rights." *Duke Law Journal* 58 (2008): 130–176.

Williams, Juan. "Black Conservatives, Center Stage." *Washington Post*, December 16, 1980.

———. "A Question of Fairness." *Atlantic Monthly*, February 1987.

Case Index

Subject Index